COLLECTED WORKS OF ERASMUS

VOLUME 18

THE CORRESPONDENCE OF
ERASMUS

LETTERS 2472 TO 2634

April 1531–March 1532

translated by Charles Fantazzi

annotated by James M. Estes

University of Toronto Press

Toronto / Buffalo / London

The research and publication costs of the
Collected Works of Erasmus are supported by
University of Toronto Press

ISBN 978-1-4875-0199-0

Printed on acid-free, 100% post-consumer recycled paper
with vegetable-based inks.

Library and Archives Canada Cataloguing in Publication

Erasmus, Desiderius, –1536
[Works. English]
Collected works of Erasmus.

Includes bibliographical references and indexes.
Contents: v. 18. The correspondence of Erasmus,
letters 2472 to 2634, April 1531–March 1532.
ISBN 978-1-4875-0199-0 (v. 18: hardcover)

I. Title.

PA8500 1974   199'.492   C740-06326X

University of Toronto Press acknowledges the financial assistance
to its publishing program of the Canada Council for the Arts
and the Ontario Arts Council, an agency of the Government of Ontario.

 **Canada Council Conseil des Arts
for the Arts du Canada**

 ONTARIO ARTS COUNCIL
CONSEIL DES ARTS DE L'ONTARIO
an Ontario government agency
un organisme du gouvernement de l'Ontario

Funded by the   Financé par le
Government   gouvernement
of Canada   du Canada 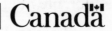 Canada

Collected Works of Erasmus

The aim of the Collected Works of Erasmus
is to make available an accurate, readable English text
of Erasmus' correspondence and his
other principal writings. The edition is planned
and directed by an Editorial Board, an Executive Committee,
and an Advisory Committee.

Contents

Illustrations

Preface

This volume comprises Erasmus' correspondence for the twelve-month period 1 April 1531–30 March 1532. The most persistent theme in the letters is the fear, to which Erasmus had long been prey, that the religious strife in Germany and Switzerland would eventually lead to armed conflict. 'Eventually' now seemed to mean 'very soon.' The Diet of Augsburg (June–November 1530), which had begun in the hope of a negotiated settlement of the religious divisions in Germany, had ended with the Protestant princes and cities convinced that the emperor and his Catholic allies intended to make war on them because of their religion. By the end of the year they had formed the League of Schmalkalden, an alliance aimed at mounting armed resistance to any such attack. As it happened, however, the emperor had on his agenda matters more urgent than the suppression of his heretical subjects in the Holy Roman Empire. Foremost among these was the Turkish threat on the eastern frontiers of the Empire and in the Mediterranean. It was clear that the Turks, who had come close to taking Vienna in the autumn of 1529, were going to renew their attack (which they ultimately did in April 1532), and there were many rumours of a Turkish fleet being assembled in a Mediterranean port. This being the case, Emperor Charles and his brother King Ferdinand were willing, as became clear in the spring of 1532, to enter into a truce with the Lutheran estates that granted them temporary religious concessions – in effect, the free practice of their religion where it was currently established – in return for their financial and military support against the Turks. The truce, the so-called Religious Peace of Nürnberg (25 July 1532), cleared the way for the Protestant estates to vote aid against the Turks at the diet that was meeting in Regensburg. It was to be the first of several such temporary settlements that would postpone until 1546–7 the religious war that Erasmus had feared. None of this, however, could be foreseen during the months covered by this volume, and the fear that things might well take a turn for the worse pervades the correspondence.[1]

* * * * *

1 On the fear of war, see especially Epp 2472, 2479, 2522:29–31.

In April 1531 Erasmus was about to enter his third year of residence
in Freiburg im Breisgau, where he had been generously and hospitably received in April 1529 but which he had never really come to like.[2] It was
more provincial than Basel, the cost of living was high, the plague visited
from time to time.[3] Above all, it seemed too close to likely scenes of conflict
should a religious war break out.[4] Erasmus' first thoughts of moving further
away had yielded to advice from friends to await the outcome of the Diet
of Augsburg.[5] He now claimed to have been advised to await the outcome
of the diet that had been summoned to meet at Speyer in September 1531.[6]
When that diet was postponed until January 1532 in Regensburg (and did
not in fact convene until April), the same wait-and-see attitude prevailed. But
the prospects for peace did not seem bright. A long-feared religious war in
nearby Switzerland broke out in October 1531, with dramatic consequences
for the Swiss Confederation: the catastrophic defeat of Zürich and the death
of Huldrych Zwingli at the battle of Kappel (11 October), and the establishment of religious parity between the Catholic and Protestant cantons in the
ensuing Peace of Kappel (24 November). On the other hand, none of the allies that either side had in the Empire – all of them, including King Ferdinand
and his brother the emperor, too preoccupied with the Turkish threat to trouble themselves with Switzerland – had been willing to become involved, so
the conflict had remained local as well as brief. In the Empire itself, however,
the fear of armed conflict between the emperor and the Protestant princes
remained. No one knew for sure what the emperor's intentions were.[7] What
would be the outcome of the diet?[8] Erasmus feared that the emperor, in his
piety, was too inclined to do exactly what the pope wanted, that is, attempt
to crush the Reformation by force, thus making war more likely.[9] He expected no greater degree of enlightenment from the emperor's opponents. This
led him, on the one hand, to publish his *Precatio ad Dominum Iesum pro pace
ecclesiae* (March 1532),[10] and, on the other hand, to announce to friends that

* * * * *

2 Ep 2514:3–12 with n1
3 Epp 2472:13–15 with nn4–5, 2479:5–9, 2514:18–22, 2517:33–7
4 Ep 2514:13–16
5 Ep 2534:15–18 with n2
6 Ep 2534:18–20 with n3
7 Epp 2516:12–32, 2517:26–7
8 Epp 2527:67–70, 2593:18–20
9 Ep 2472:33–5 with n9
10 Ep 2618

he was 'tired of Germany' and needed to move to a more agreeable and safer place.[11] But, as ever, the old question 'Where?' eluded clear answer.

For all its limitations, Freiburg offered Erasmus the same advantages that Basel had offered until the triumph there of the Reformation: secure exercise of the Catholic faith, good friends (including other exiles from Basel), and freedom from the pressures for partisanship and servility that membership in a princely court, or even proximity to one, would have involved. It also had the advantage of being close enough to Basel for ease of communication with the Froben press and with his friends there, above all Bonifacius Amerbach, his most frequent correspondent by far (thirty letters in this volume). But what if Freiburg should in fact prove unsafe, where could Erasmus find a 'nest'? The list of places where he knew he would be welcome was long.[12] Anton Fugger, for example, never tired of inviting Erasmus to settle in Augsburg at his expense.[13] But if the point was to get further away from the religious conflicts causing turmoil in Germany, that was hardly the place to go.[14] Erasmus was given to musing that Italy, where several young friends of his were studying, would be a fine place to be, if only the journey there were not so long and dangerous.[15] More tempting, perhaps, was the prospect of returning to Brabant, where many old friends entertained the hope that he would 'come home' and where the regent, Mary of Austria, would reward his presence with the resumption of his long-unpaid imperial pension.[16] On the other hand, his dislike of princely courts, the never-forgotten and still lively hostility of the Louvain theologians, and his feeling that the country was too much subject to the 'tyranny of villainous monks' and their harsh edicts against heresy, made Erasmus shy away from choosing that course.[17] He seems to have given the most serious thought to moving to Besançon, then part of Hapsburg Burgundy (but safely distant from the imperial court and inquisitorial theologians), which had been one of the options considered in 1529 before he chose Freiburg. He broached the subject with the city fathers and arranged for Emperor Charles to write them a letter urging them to accommodate him should circumstances compel him to seek refuge

* * * * *

11 Epp 2485:10, 2566:189
12 Epp 2479:49–52 with nn10–11, 2514:34–5 with n6
13 Epp 2525, 2561:15–17
14 Ep 2479:49–52
15 See Epp 2105:20–2, 2328:55–7, 2481:49–51. There were even rumours in Padua that Erasmus was going to settle there; see Ep 2594:50–1.
16 Ep 2511:34–5 with n17
17 Epp 2485:10–19, 2613:21–36, 49–58, 2620:25–9

there.[18] Meanwhile, in the midst of all this fretting about where to move, Erasmus spent the summer of 1531 purchasing and occupying a new house in Freiburg.

The acquisition of a new house was the latest episode in the saga of Erasmus' living arrangements in Freiburg. When he moved to that city in 1529, he was given the use, rent-free, of the house 'Zum Walfisch,' which belonged to Jakob Villinger (d August 1529), former chief treasurer to Emperor Maximilian. As it turned out, however, the terms of Erasmus' use of the house were unclear, and there was another resident, Ottmar Nachtgall, preacher at the cathedral, who claimed legal title to be there. In January 1530, after an unsuccessful attempt to secure exclusive use of the house in return for payment of a suitable rent, Erasmus learned that Villinger's heirs wanted to reclaim the house for themselves and that he would consequently have to move. Not until mid-March 1531, however, did he finally receive notice to vacate the house by 24 June of that year, which was rather short notice.[19] With the help of influential friends, he managed to secure permission to remain in the house until 29 September.[20] By June he was already negotiating the purchase of an expensive new house; by mid-July the deal had been closed; and by the end of September the required repairs and renovations, including the installation of a fireplace, were sufficiently advanced that Erasmus was able to move in on schedule.[21] At the news of this complicated and expensive change of domicile, Erasmus' friend Maarten Lips admonished him to cease once and for all talking about how tired he was of Germany and how much he wanted to move away.[22] Erasmus, on the other hand, insisted that the acquisition of the new house would not detain him in Freiburg if circumstances should dictate his move elsewhere.[23] As it turned out, circumstances would permit him to remain in Freiburg until his return to Basel in the final months of his life.

Meanwhile, in the midst of all this domestic turmoil, Erasmus' Catholic and Evangelical critics continued to exasperate him, as old controversies either persisted or, in some cases, were re-opened. Taking the Catholic critics in more or less ascending order of importance, one comes first to Eustachius van

* * * * *

18 Epp 2514, 2553
19 Ep 2497 introduction
20 Epp 2503:19–22, 2505:11–38
21 Epp 2506 n1, 2517 n11
22 Ep 2566:189–92
23 Epp 2517:35–7, 2530:19–22, 2534:43–4, 2578:21–2

der Rivieren, Dominican, and dean of the faculty of theology at Louvain, long known for his stentorian denunciations of Erasmus and other humanist scholars. He had recently published at Antwerp his *Apologia pro pietate in Erasmi Roterod. Enchiridion canonem quintum* (c January 1531). Erasmus deemed the work too childish to warrant a response, but he did arrange for the publication by Froben of a satirical poem in which Erasmus' admirer, the Portuguese Dominican André de Resende, who had lived in the Dominican house at Louvain while studying at the Collegium Trilingue, made Rivieren the butt of his ridicule.[24] More seriously, Erasmus took umbrage at the acceptance by his long-time patron, Erard de la Marck, bishop of Liège, of the dedication of Rivieren's book. Erasmus refused to take seriously Bishop Erard's protestations of his innocence and good will, and relations between them, which had always been a bit stormy, now ceased.[25]

A rather more substantial critic than Rivieren was the Italian scholar and future Vatican librarian Agostino Steuco. In March 1531 Erasmus had written a long letter to Steuco (Ep 2465) full of hectoring criticism of the latter's *Recognitio Veteris Testamenti ad Hebraicam veritatem* (1529), which contained not only questionable views concerning the authority of the received Vulgate text of the Old Testament but also covert criticism of Erasmus as the source of the Lutheran heresy. In July 1531, Steuco responded at similar length with a letter (Ep 2513) in which he managed to score some points against Erasmus but, on the whole, defended himself with rather bad arguments. When Erasmus made the dispute public by publishing his letter to Steuco in the *Epistolae floridae* (September 1531), Steuco responded by publishing both letters at the end of his commentary on Psalms 18 and 138 (1533), and there the matter rested, with neither party having gained much glory in the exchange.[26]

At roughly the same time that Rivieren's volume was published at Antwerp, Alberto Pio's final work against Erasmus, *Tres et viginti libri in locos lucubrationum Erasmi,* was published at Paris, two months after Pio's death on 7 January 1531. Erasmus quickly persuaded himself that its publication was the work not of Pio alone but rather of a conspiracy of old adversaries who shared Pio's view of him as the source of the Lutheran heresy and used Pio as their mouthpiece. Identified as the chief conspirators were Girolamo Aleandro, Erasmus' old foe but Pio's friend from their

* * * * *

24 Ep 2500 nn3–4
25 Ep 2590 n6
26 Ep 2513 introduction

time together at the Vatican, and Noël Béda, syndic of the faculty of theology at Paris and Erasmus' most relentless critic in France, whose influence Erasmus had also imagined to be behind the publication at Paris of Pio's first book against him in 1529. Even though Pio was now dead, Erasmus responded to his book with the vituperative *Apologia adversus rhapsodias Alberti Pii* (June 1531). Not content with that, he delivered the final insult by including in a new edition of the *Colloquies* (September 1531) the colloquy *Exequiae seraphicae* 'The Seraphic Funeral,' in which Pio's burial in the habit of a Franciscan was lampooned.[27]

Béda's silence since the publication in 1529 of his *Adversus clandestinos Lutheranos* had lulled Erasmus into thinking that his controversy with the Paris syndic was behind him.[28] Now, however, Erasmus saw the publication of Pio's *Tres et viginti libri* as proof that Béda had 'recovered his confidence' and was once again actively working against him.[29] Confirmation came with the long-delayed publication in July 1531 of the *Determinatio facultatis theologiae in schola Parisiensi super quam plurimis assertionibus D. Erasmi Roterodami*, a compendium of errors found in Erasmus' works that the faculty, under Béda's leadership, had condemned in 1526 and 1527. Once again, moreover, Erasmus believed Béda to be in league with Aleandro. Indeed, he persuaded himself that both Aleandro, who had not visited Paris for many years, and Johann Eck, who had recently accused Erasmus of heretical views but who (as far as we know) never set foot in France, had been at Paris and encouraged the theologians to publish their censures. Although Erasmus felt that he had long since dealt adequately with most of the theologians' accusations, he responded 'with the utmost moderation' in his *Declarationes ad censuras Lutetiae vulgatas sub nomine facultatis theologiae Parisiensis* (April 1532; augmented edition September 1532). It was the final instalment in his long controversy with Béda and his colleagues.[30] The publication of the Paris censure also moved Erasmus to publish (February 1532) a long-contemplated rebuttal of the attacks on his view of marriage by Béda's close ally, Josse Clichtove: *Dilutio eorum quae Iodocus Clithoveus scripsit adversus declamationem Des. Erasmi suasoriam matrimonii*, a work that attracted little attention.[31]

* * * * *

27 Epp 2486:35–9 with nn9–11, 2505:50–5 with n13, 2508:12–13 with n7, 2513:681–93, 2522:68–83, 2565:9–18, 2572:7–15, 2600 n9, 2623 n5
28 Epp 2371:5–6, 2375:84–5
29 Ep 2486:38–9
30 Epp 2552 n10, 2587:3–13, 2600:10–19, 2620:30–2, 2623 n5
31 Ep 2604 n12

Meanwhile both Béda and Aleandro were, it seemed to Erasmus, fomenting still further mischief against him, this time in the form of a belated contribution to the now almost dormant controversy over Erasmus' *Ciceronianus*.[32] In September 1531 there appeared at Paris an *Oratio pro M. Tullio Cicerone contra Des. Erasmum Roterodamum*, in which the author, the then unknown Julius Caesar Scaliger, accused Erasmus of slandering Cicero and attacking the Christian religion. It had taken Scaliger two years to find a publisher for the book, doing so finally with the help of Noël Béda. Erasmus instantly jumped to the conclusion that 'Julius Caesar Scaliger' was a pseudonym and that the real author was Girolamo Aleandro, whose supposedly unmistakable style he detected in the work. Despite his indignation at this 'raving mad' collection of 'mad lies' and 'scurrilous abuse,' Erasmus chose not to publish a reply, in large measure because he deemed Aleandro, who enjoyed the confidence of the pope and was the current papal legate at the imperial court, too dangerous an enemy to attack directly.[33]

While his Catholic critics enraged him with their accusation that he was the source of the Lutheran heresy, Erasmus' former friends among the 'false evangelicals' embarrassed him by claiming him as the source of their unacceptable views. By the time the first letters in this volume were written, Erasmus' public controversy with Martin Bucer, Gerard Geldenhouwer, and the other Strasbourg preachers had come to a conclusion with the publication in August 1530 of his *Epistola ad fratres Inferioris Germaniae*.[34] But grounds for complaint against the Strasbourgers continued to accumulate. In August 1531 the radical Spiritualist Sebastian Franck published at Strasbourg his *Chronica, Zeytbuch vnd Geschychtbybell*, in which Erasmus is quoted approvingly and by name in passages harshly critical of the imperial house of Hapsburg and elsewhere in passages advocating the view that princes have no right to put heretics to death. For good measure he is also hailed as one of the great and unjustly persecuted heretics of Christendom. Informed of the existence of the book by Bernhard von Cles, chancellor to King Ferdinand, Erasmus was understandably alarmed by what seemed to be an attempt to discredit him in the eyes of his princely patrons and protectors by associating him

* * * * *

32 For the origins and early history of the controversy, see Ep 1948 introduction.
33 Epp 2564 n2, 2565:24–6 with n12, 2577, 2578:31–4, 2579:34–7, 2581:1–13, 2587:12–15, 2600:17–21, 2613:43–9, 2615:521–8, 2620:32–4, 2632 n18, 2633:33–8. It is noteworthy that in the letters cited Erasmus avoids mentioning Aleandro by name except in letters to trusted friends that were not included in any editions of his correspondence during his lifetime.
34 See CWE 17 xv.

with heresy and sedition. Blaming publication of the book on Martin Bucer, Erasmus wrote a letter of complaint to the city fathers, who, after investigation, banned the book and expelled Franck from the city. Meanwhile, in a letter to Erasmus now lost, Bucer not only denied his responsibility for the publication of Franck's book but also reviewed the entire history of Erasmus' relations with the Evangelical reformers, all of whom had started out as his disciples. In so doing, he reiterated their conviction that the logic of Erasmus' own position dictated that he should be in the Evangelical camp. In response, Erasmus wrote the longest letter in this volume (Ep 2615), in which, while apologizing for his mistake concerning the publication of Franck's work, he presented an unsympathetic, unyielding, point-by-point response to Bucer that emphasized his doctrinal differences with the Evangelical reformers and his low opinion of their moral character. Erasmus, however, never published the letter (it was first published by Allen), and there is no evidence that he ever sent it or that Bucer ever saw it. Be that as it may, it is an important document that deserves to be numbered among Erasmus' apologias against the 'false evangelicals.'

Given his preoccupation with the practical problems of moving house and with controversies old and new, and given also his advancing age and fragile health, it is not surprising that Erasmus' contributions to pure scholarship in the twelve months covered by this volume were, by his standards, meagre. Rather reluctantly, he produced the *Epistolae floridae*, as a favour to the publisher Johann Herwagen, whose first independent publication in Basel it was.[35] Rather more willingly, or at least with less complaint, he also produced an edition of the comedies of Terence,[36] a substantial commentary on Psalm 38,[37] and a translation of St Basil the Great's homily *De laudibus ieiunii*.[38]

Erasmus' financial affairs, which did not loom large in the correspondence of the months covered in CWE 17, once again figure prominently in the sixteen letters between him and his friend Erasmus Schets that are included in this volume. The Antwerp banker had been responsible for the collection and remittance of the income from Erasmus' livings in England and the Netherlands since 1525. The letters between them are testimony to Erasmus' impatience with people who owed him money, his frequent inability to understand the details of his own finances, and his quickness to assume that

* * * * *

35 Ep 2518
36 Ep 2584
37 Ep 2608
38 Ep 2617

people he had trusted were cheating him. But the letters are also testimony
to Schets' infinite patience, care, and rectitude in the efforts that guaranteed
Erasmus' financial security, and for that Erasmus was duly grateful.[39]

Of the 163 letters in this volume, 85 were written by Erasmus and 77
were addressed to him. One was written by a third party at Erasmus' request. These surviving letters include more than 100 references to letters that
are no longer extant. Since some of these references are to an unspecified
number of letters, no exact total of letters known to have been written during the period covered by this volume can be determined, but 285 would be
a cautious estimate. Of the surviving letters, 38 were published by Erasmus
himself. Of these, 17 appeared in the *Epistolae floridae* of 1531, and 15 appeared in the *Epistolae palaeonaeoi* of 1532. Another 6 were prefaces to works
or editions by Erasmus. The remaining letters were published by a variety
of scholars in the period from 1531 to 2017. Fifty of them were first published
by Allen. One is published for the first time in this volume (see below). To
allow the reader to discover the sequence in which the letters became known,
the introduction to each letter cites the place where it was first published and
identifies the manuscript source if one exists. Allen's text and his numbering
of the letters have been followed. One letter unknown to Allen and never before published, Ep 2563A, has been added, and the Latin original is included
in an appendix to the volume. Another letter, published by Allen as Ep 2509,
has been redated to 1534 and will appear in CWE 20 as Ep 2917A.

All of Erasmus' correspondents and all of the contemporaries of
Erasmus who are mentioned in the letters are referred to by the version of
their name that is used in CEBR. Wherever biographical information is supplied in the notes without the citation of a source, the reader is tacitly referred
to the appropriate article in CEBR and to the literature there cited. The index to
this volume contains references to the persons, places, and works mentioned
in the volume, following the plan for the Correspondence series in CWE. When
that series of volumes is completed, the reader will also be supplied with an
index of topics, as well as of classical, scriptural, and patristic references.

As with all the other volumes in this series, the basis for translation and
the starting point for annotation is the edition of the *Erasmi epistolae* that was
founded by P.S. Allen. This is, however, the third of the volumes in the CWE
Correspondence series to be based on volumes 9–11 of Allen's edition, which
were completed after his death (1938) by his widow, Helen Mary Allen, and
H.W. Garrod, who had been his collaborators on earlier volumes. At the time

* * * * *

39 See especially Epp 2487–8, 2494, 2511–12, 2527, 2530, 2558, 2620.

of his death Allen had, with few exceptions, collected and provisionally arranged all the letters for vols 9–11, but had done the notes for only 27 of them. The remaining work of annotation had to be done by Mrs Allen and Garrod. In many cases, therefore, 'Allen' is used in the notes as shorthand for 'the Allen editors.' Where their work has needed to be corrected, updated, or expanded – far more often in their case than in that of Allen himself – I was able to rely on the advice and assistance of distinguished colleagues here in Toronto and elsewhere. The great majority of the classical and patristic references that were not provided by Allen were supplied by the translator, Charles Fantazzi. Timothy J. Wengert and Amy Nelson Burnett read the entire manuscript and made suggestions that led to important corrections and additions to the notes. In addition, Frank Collins, James Farge, Mark Crane, Hartwig Mayer, Daniel Sheerin, Mark Vessey, Robert Sider, Bruce W. Frier, Silvana Seidel-Menchi, and Erika Rummel responded generously to requests for help with difficult matters of history, bibliography, or translation. The notes on coinage were contributed by Lawrin Armstrong. Mary Baldwin once again earned her reputation as copyeditor without peer.

As ever, two libraries were of special importance in the preparation of this volume: that of the Centre for Reformation and Renaissance Studies at Victoria College in the University of Toronto, and that of the Pontifical Institute of Mediaeval Studies on the campus of St Michael's College in the University of Toronto. To Natalie Oeltjen, Assistant to the Director of the Centre for Reformation and Renaissance Studies, and to William Edwards, reference librarian of the Pontifical Institute, I am indebted for a degree of support and assistance that amounts to special treatment.

JME

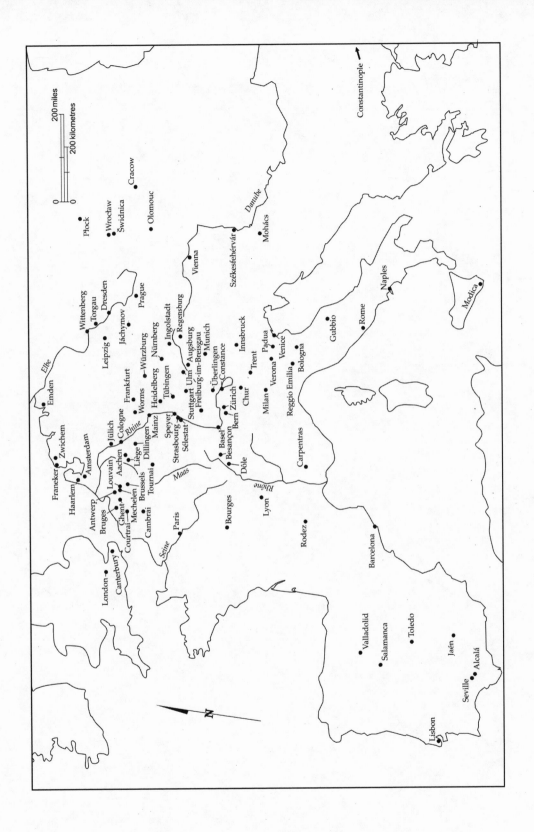

200 miles

200 kilometres

Constantinople

Cracow

Wrocław
Świdnica

Olomouc

Płock

Danube

Mohács

Vienna

Székesfehérvár

Wittenberg
Torgau
Dresden

Jáchymov

Prague

Leipzig

Würzburg

Nürnberg

Ingolstadt

Regensburg

Augsburg

Munich

Naples

Modica

Elbe

Emden

Frankfurt

Worms

Heidelberg

Mainz

Tübingen

Stuttgart Ulm

Freiburg-im-Breisgau

Überlingen

Constance

Innsbruck

Trent

Padua

Verona

Venice

Bologna

Gubbio

Rome

Franeker

Zwichem

Amsterdam

Jülich

Cologne

Rhine

Haarlem

Aachen

Liège

Dillingen

Speyer

Strasbourg

Sélestat

Basel

Bern

Zürich

Chur

Milan

Reggio Emilia

Antwerp

Louvain

Ghent

Brussels

Mechelen

Tournai

Courtrai

Cambrai

Bruges

Maas

Besançon

Dôle

Carpentras

London

Canterbury

Paris

Bourges

Seine

Lyon

Rhône

Rodez

Barcelona

Valladolid

Salamanca

Toledo

Jaén

Alcalá

Seville

Lisbon

N

THE CORRESPONDENCE OF ERASMUS

LETTERS 2472 TO 2634

2472 / To Antoine d'Albon   Freiburg, 1 April 1531

For Antoine d'Albon, abbot of the Benedictine house at Saint-Martin-de-l'Île-Barbe, a short distance north of Lyon, see Ep 2410 introduction. The letter was first published in the *Epistolae floridae*. It is possible that, like Epp 2433 and 2466, this letter and Epp 2468, 2473, and 2479 were carried by Ottmar Nachtgall; cf Epp 2477 n3, and cf 2565 n16. It appears that this is Erasmus' polite refusal of an invitation to settle in Île-Barbe (see lines 8–9, 70–1).

ERASMUS OF ROTTERDAM TO ANTOINE D'ALBON, ABBOT, GREETING
If bodies could cross over mountains and valleys as easily as souls fly through the air, Île-Barbe, in my view more worthy to be called the Blessed Isle, would have had Erasmus as its guest long ago. But besides the length of the jour-ney, a lengthy letter of Maillard deterred me,[1] in which he wove a long tale   5
about the tumult certain hooded individuals have stirred up against him in his absence because he was said to have sought a meeting with Erasmus. What would they do if I had gone to live there and they would see that we were joined together by a close friendship? I really take pity on such people. If such is the behaviour of those who by their title and their habit profess   10
perfect piety,[2] what is to be expected from those whom they call men of the world? But I answered Maillard more copiously on this subject.[3]

There were enough troubles here even without adding others. The plague has been tormenting us for a long time and is unwilling to end.[4] The cost of living increases from day to day.[5] Only God knows what will follow. I   15
am totally averse to prognostications, and yet it is inconvenient for this frail little body to change its nest, especially since at this point it is safe. They say that the Turks are getting three armies ready, of which one will make an at-tack on Austria against Ferdinand, another will attack Poland, which it has long been threatening, and a third will be sent against Naples,[6] from there to   20
seek benediction from the sovereign pontiff. This is a harsh state of affairs, but less grave, I think, than if all of Germany and surrounding regions were

* * * * *

2472
1 Ep 2424
2 Franciscan Observants; see Epp 2424:28–9, 2466:31–6.
3 Ep 2466
4 See Epp 2426 n3, 2443:463–5, 2450:12–13, 2479:5, 2517:35–7, 2533:127–9, 2542:16–18.
5 See Ep 2403 n13.
6 The attack on Ferdinand was launched in April 1532. There were no attacks on Poland or Naples.

engaged in mutual slaughter. You will say that this is a severe malady that
cannot be cured by ordinary remedies. Yes, but I hate remedies that are worse
than the disease. If it comes to armed conflict, the brunt of the disaster will be   25
borne by the innocent, and under pretext of defending religion the world will
be filled with pillaging. Spain nurtures many clandestine Jews,[7] Germany
harbours many of them, who are both inclined by nature and accustomed by
war to looting. All this rabble will spill first into Germany, then into the rest
of the world. They do not know how to put down their arms once they have   30
been given them. Already more than once they have proved this by their
example, in Rome and Vienna.[8]

The world never had a more powerful emperor than it has now. In his
piety and religious respect for the see of Rome it seems that he will do anything the bishop of Rome prescribes.[9] We must congratulate the human race   35
if nothing will come to the mind of the vicar of Christ except what is worthy
of Christ. In the eyes of many, however, it seems to be an unfavourable omen
that Florence was treated so inclemently by Clement.[10] Just as children do
not have a right to take vengeance on their parents even if they have been

* * * * *

7 Ie *conversos*, the descendants of Jews forcibly converted in the period 1391–
   1492, widely suspected and frequently accused of secret adherence to Jewish
   belief and practice
8 Cf the similar passage in Ep 2479:17–25. Erasmus' concern is the tendency of
   mercenary armies, even those supposedly engaged in the defence of religion, to
   engage in the looting and pillaging of friend and foe alike, and he dreads what
   will happen to Germany should such armies be sent there in consequence of
   the religious conflict. As examples he cites the sack of Rome by the emperor's
   rebellious troops in 1527, and the siege of Vienna in 1529, during which the
   city suffered at least as much from the depredations of its defenders as it did
   from bombardment by the Turks (see Ep 2313:19–26). The idea that 'clandestine
   Jews' from Spain, present also in large numbers in Germany, were a significant
   presence in such armies and were particularly inclined to looting and pillage,
   appears to be original to Erasmus. As the Gerlo editors observe in their note,
   the assertion stands in surprising contrast to the charge of cringing cowardice
   that was normally levelled against Jews.
9 Ie follow a policy of harsh repression of religious dissent and thus increase the
   likelihood of religious war (cf Ep 2366:20–2 with n7, 2479:40–1), a fear that was
   reinforced by the unhappy outcome of the Diet of Augsburg (Ep 2403 nn10–11).
10 The siege of Florence (24 October 1529–10 August 1530) by imperial troops ended with the decisive defeat of the Florentine forces and the restoration to power
   of the pope's relatives, the Medici family, who had been expelled in 1527. The
   revenge of the victors was merciless and brutal. See Pastor 10 chapter 3; cf also
   Ep 2366 n11.

treated unjustly, so to many pagans it did not seem right to take up the sword   40
against one's country no matter how much it deserved it. Themistocles and
Aristides, though exiled because of envy, nevertheless came conspicuously
to the aid of their country.[11] A Spartan king, undeservedly exiled, endured
his banishment without even uttering a complaint about his native country.[12] Coriolanus suppressed a most justified resentment in deference to the   45
authority of his mother.[13] And yet I fear that we, who are driven headlong
by the desire for revenge, will suffer the fate of the horse who, while he took
vengeance on a stag, received a rider on its back and a bit in its mouth.[14] 'One
omen is best, to fight for one's country,' says Hector in Homer.[15] But in the
present state of affairs it seems to me that 'one omen is best, that all appease   50
the divinity.' But this, which is a matter of prime importance, is neglected
above all. For whence come so many evils in the Christian world, governed
by such excellent princes, if not from God, who is angered by our crimes?
When did your France ever receive a graver blow? It has the good fortune
that serenity has followed immediately after that storm.[16] Who ever saw Italy   55
more afflicted?[17] It will take many years, I fear, before she recovers the former

* * * * *

11 Themistocles (524–459 BC), the general who in 480 commanded the Greek forces
   in several decisive battles in the Persian War, was nonetheless ostracized and
   went to live first in Argos, then in Corcyra and Epirus, and then in Asia Minor.
   Aristides, a fifth-century BC Athenian politician, was ostracized in 483 but returned to lead a hoplite contingent against the Persians at the battle of Salamis
   in 480.
12 Probably a reference to Lycurgus of Sparta, who according to legend rose to
   power when his brother the king died but was then forced into exile. After
   many travels he returned to Sparta and reformed the laws and constitution of
   the Spartan state.
13 Marcius Coriolanus was a Roman general who participated in the capture of
   the city of Corioli (whence his name) from the Volscians. Charged with tyrannical conduct, he went into exile and became the leader of the Volscians against
   Rome. After capturing several towns in Latium, he led his forces to the gates of
   Rome, but turned back in deference to his mother, Veturia.
14 This is Aesop's fable of the horse, the stag, and the man (*Aesopica* 269).
15 *Iliad* 12.242
16 The most recent calamity to befall France was the decisive defeat of its armies
   in Italy by imperial forces in the summer of 1529. This led in August 1529 to the
   'Ladies Peace' of Cambrai, which lasted until 1536; see Ep 2207 n5.
17 By the wars between France and Spain (the Hapsburg-Valois wars), which were
   fought primarily in the Italian peninsula in the years 1494–1559, with only brief
   interludes of peace, including that described in the preceding note

vigour in which we saw her. What is now more turbulent than Germany?[18] What is more pitiful if what seems to hang over her should come to pass? To drink less, that there be less luxury in banquets and dress, that the clergy have a wider tonsure on their heads, that they let their habit fall to their heels, 60 that they sleep alone – it is easy for men to prescribe all these things; only God has the power to cleanse the source of all good actions, and with sincere and complete confidence. Hearkening to our prayers, he will give the leaders of the church a mind that will subordinate all the advantages of the world to the glory of Christ. He will give to princes a discernment that rises above 65 wealth and glory and vengeance and all human cupidity; he will give them heavenly wisdom that prevails over all earthly malice; he will give priests and monks a true contempt for the world and a love of the Scriptures; he will give magistrates and the people fear of him.

I shall put an end to my philosophizing by testifying to you that I shall 70 be no less in your debt for the things you offer me than if I had used them. I hope that your piety, together with all those dear to you, will enjoy the best of health.

At Freiburg im Breisgau, 1 April 1531

2473 / To Pierre de Mornieu   Freiburg, 2 April 1531

For Pierre Mornieu, abbot of the Cistercian house of Saint-Sulpice near Chambéry in Savoy, see Ep 1777 introduction. First published in the *Epistolae floridae*, this letter responds to one now lost inviting Erasmus to settle in Savoy. It was probably carried by Ottmar Nachtgall; see Ep 2472 introduction.

ERASMUS OF ROTTERDAM TO PIERRE DE MORNIEU,
ABBOT OF SAINT-SULPICE, GREETING
If only the present situation, just as it impels me to change dwellings for various reasons, would also provide a convenient route for me to such an amiable host. But both the length of the journey and its inconvenience deter me, and 5 this frail little body of mine has now ceased to be adaptable to the undertaking

* * * * *

18 Ever since 1526, tension between Catholic and Protestant princes and cities in Germany had been increasing, with both sides making preparations for possible armed conflict. In 1530, the Protestant princes left the Diet of Augsburg convinced that the emperor and the Catholic princes intended to make war on them, and by February 1531 had established the League of Schmalkalden for their mutual defence against attack. War did not come until 1546–7, but by that time the fear of it had pervaded German politics for more than twenty years.

of any journey, no matter how intense the desire. But I acknowledge the fate of the tortoise that carries its own house; the home I carry around impedes its guest, even threatening collapse with each passing day.

With various arguments you commend your Savoy to me, even though it is not altogether unknown to me. For once, en route to Italy from Paris via Lyon, I saw a good part of that region. I stopped in Turin for a while and was enormously pleased by the kindness of the people.[1] But among all the advantages of the region that you enumerate nothing tempts me as much as your sincere and friendly character. I hope that if Germany begins to be torn apart by internal warfare your region will remain at peace. Although I hear that there was some kind of controversy between you and the people of Bern,[2] I think it has been put to rest. Further on you relate the sad fate of Roland, nephew of Charlemagne, who died of thirst in Spain. 'But the most pitiful thing is to die of hunger and meet one's fate,' said Homer,[3] since I see that you gladly speak Greek. But doctors think that it is much more agonizing to die of thirst. But for Roland, Spain obviously meant privation. That is what Paul calls it.[4] The mention of Castor and Pollux amused me.

According to Horace, 'Castor delights in horses, and the one born of the same egg [Pollux] in boxing.'[5] I confess that I was once captivated by a passion for riding and the raising of horses cost me a good sum of money, but I have long ceased to be a Castor. I don't know if you are still playing the part of Pollux, for I knew you were once a robust pugilist, as you yourself told me when we used to exchange stories familiarly among ourselves in Basel. But as the same Horace says, the friendship of the two brothers split apart because of unlike pursuits.[6] As for us, the common love for literature will join us more closely than the same birth joined Castor and Pollux, provided I can stealthily make my way there. If it is not possible physically, at least my

* * * * *

2473
1 Erasmus took his doctorate in theology during a brief visit to Turin in September 1506; see Ep 200 introduction.
2 Cf Ep 2410:48–50.
3 *Odyssey* 13.342, cited in Greek
4 This is a play on the Greek words σπανία 'privation' and Σπανία, the word for Spain used by Paul at Rom 15:24, 28.
5 Horace *Satires* 2.1.26
6 Erasmus here switches abruptly to another myth about twin brothers, that of Amphion and Zethus, as related by Horace (*Epistles* 1.18.41–4). They were the sons of Zeus by Antiope, one a great singer and musician, the other a hunter and herdsman. They had a falling out that dissolved their brotherly feelings for a time. Since Zethus disliked the sound of the lyre, Amphion ceased to play it.

spirit will often fly to you. I must live with only few people if I wish to live, so
precarious is my health. At any rate, among your illiterate colleagues, as you   35
call them, I can babble a few words; here I am completely silent: I can neither
understand anyone nor can I be understood by anyone. I have no affinity for
the court. What you mean by a thoroughly French court I do not understand;
you mean kind and affable, I think, but our Germans interpret it otherwise.

Still, putting jokes aside, I am most grateful for the offer you make of   40
yourself and all that you possess without exception. But by the law of gratitude you are indebted to me, although I am even more indebted to you. I
will not be a great burden to your fortunes. For a fate commensurate with
my character has fallen to me, intermediate between rich and poor. I published this winter six books of *Apophthegmata* and a Commentary on Psalm   45
33.[7] I wrote a preface to an edition of the Greek text of Aristotle, much more
emended than previously, which anyone can now purchase at a low price.
I wrote a preface to an edition of Livy,[8] which included an additional five
books never published until now, besides innumerable letters. Such was the
production of my garden during the winter months; what would it not pro-   50
duce in the summer? But the life of one's mental faculties, once it is over,
never returns. The rest when we meet, if the condition of the times and health
permit. Farewell.

Given at Freiburg im Breisgau, 2 April 1531

2474 / From Bonifacius Amerbach   Basel, 3 April 1531

First published by Allen, this letter (= AK Ep 1521) is a response to Epp 2462,
2467. The basis of Allen's text was an autograph in the Öffentliche Bibliothek of
the University of Basel that is 'carefully written and with no corrections, folded
as a letter, but not addressed and apparently not sent' (MS C VIa 54 60). There
are also two rough drafts and two beginnings of the letter (MS C VIa 54 13 verso),
but Allen found no important variants in them.

Cordial greetings. Your letter, illustrious Erasmus, written 25 March,[1] I received the day before yesterday when I returned home. I am extremely dis-

* * * * *

7 See Epp 2431 (*Apophthegmata*), 2428 (*Enarratio psalmi 33*).
8 Epp 2432 (Aristotle), 2435 (Livy)

2474
1 Ep 2462

tressed by what you write about Nachtgall and Eck.[2] But in your wisdom
you will, as is your wont, pay no heed to such injuries. The reputation of
your name among the best of men is too great for its brightness to be dimmed   5
by that kind of rabble. Envy, a famous writer said, seeks out the exalted and
passes over the lowly.[3] This week or at the latest at Easter I will visit you.
Would that I could comply with your wishes in actual fact as I earnestly desire to do. Keep well, illustrious Erasmus.

In haste at Basel, the day after Palm Sunday 1531   10

We will talk about Alciati when we meet. For at this very moment I
received your letter together with his, as you sent them,[4] through the letter
carrier.

Sincerely, your Bonifacius

2475 / From Christoph Freisleben   Augsburg, 3 April 1531

First published as Ep 91 in Enthoven, the manuscript of this letter is in the
Rehdiger Collection of the University Library at Wrocław (ms Rehd 254 66).

Christoph Freisleben of Linz, Upper Austria (documented 1517–after 1551)
enrolled at the University of Vienna in 1517 and afterwards became a school-
teacher in Wels (near Linz). From 1521 until c 1528 he had a scantily documented career as an adherent of the Reformation, first as a Lutheran and then as an
Anabaptist. In late 1527 he was in Esslingen, and in 1528 his pamphlet *Vom
warhafftigen Tauff Joannis, Christi und der Aposteln* was printed at Strasbourg. In
1530, however, having recently returned to the Catholic fold, he was appointed
teacher at the chapter school of St Moritz in Augsburg. In 1537, following the
introduction of the Reformation at Augsburg, he left the city and may have
been a schoolmaster for a time in Ingolstadt. After studying law at Bourges
(1544–5), he went to Vienna, where he was appointed syndic of the university
and procurator-in-ordinary to the government of the city, as well as syndic and
ordinary to the bishop. Among his publications were a collection of 172 of his
own sermons and a German translation of sermons by Gregory of Nazianzus
and Gregory of Nyssa.

If Erasmus wrote a reply to this awkwardly obsequious message of self-
introduction, it has not survived.

* * * * *

2 See Ep 2462:1–21 (Ottmar Nachtgall), 22–3 (Johann Eck).
3 Cf Plutarch *De invidio et odio* 6.
4 Erasmus' letter is Ep 2467; the letter of Alciati that Erasmus sent with it (Ep
   2467:2–3) is not extant.

Greetings. If I had not made the acquaintance of Polyphemus at dinner,[1] a man whom you, dearest Erasmus, know inside and out, as they say,[2] one who is frank and open to serve the interests of many people, and therefore not unworthy of his name[3] – I met him once, I say, at the home of the venerable Doctor Wolfgang Kress, preacher at the Dominican church in Augsburg,[4] and   5 again at the home of the eminent Doctor Wolfgang Rem, father of Wolfgang Andreas Rem, principal of the college of St Moritz (both of them not un-known to you, if I am not mistaken),[5] and if I had not, with his encourage-ment, seized the long-desired opportunity of writing to you, I would never have dared even to greet you by name, still less to address this kind of letter,   10 barbarous and practically worthless, to you.

But aided not so much by Polyphemus as by some divine power, I write to you, more out of audacity than any pretence of knowledge, and if through them I obtain anything from your generosity, I shall acknowledge that it is owed to them rather than to this letter. I beseech you therefore, most kind   15 sir, that you and those like you who are attacked in all quarters of the world will not refuse to inscribe an obscure and insignificant person like me in the album of your friends. You are not concerned, I think, with personal appear-ance, as long as one's character and morals are sufficiently unsullied and worthy of your acceptance, and I should wish that mine are of such a kind,   20 and that they have been so described to you that they will meet with your complete approval.

Therefore, do not refuse to hear me. Let me say that hitherto I have been involved persistently for ten years with almost every sect that has sprung up, to the point of defending some of them passionately. But even if, like   25 the Phrygians, I have learned wisdom too late,[6] nevertheless the Lord, my strength and my refuge, in the end rescued me, to whom be dominion and power forever. Amen. But so that you will not remain unaware of one reason among many why I deserted the heresies, a very strong one in my estima-tion, I relate the following: I saw and observed in many of the members of   30 the sects and in those who present themselves to be supporters of them such

* * * * *

2475
1 For Erasmus' wayward servant Felix Rex, nicknamed Polyphemus, who was currently in Augsburg, see Epp 2130 introduction, 2334 n1.
2 *Adagia* I ix 89, citing Persius *Satires* 3.30
3 The literal meaning of Polyphemus is 'One who talks a lot.'
4 Presumably a reference to the Dominikanerkirche St Magdalena, which was attached to the house of the Dominicans in Augsburg
5 For the two Rems see Epp 2269 n2, 2419 introduction.
6 *Adagia* I i 28

discord, inconstancy, and prejudice under the guise of the pristine gospel
that it compelled me to come to my senses again and return to the unity
of the church. This seems to cause great displeasure now to the majority of
those with whom I then associated, who sometimes accuse me of defection   35
and inconstancy, and at other times, when I advise them to repent, abandon
these extraneous entities, and return to the universal church, ask me what is
this organization that I call the Catholic church, or who are their rulers and
bishops, what gifts allow them to exert power, with what authority and what
testimonies of the Scriptures do they act, and how do they act, and lastly   40
what do I think of the primitive church and that which derives from it, and
how do the papists (that is what they call them) distinguish or categorize
that one dove of Christ?[7] I have answered that Christ is neither so treacher-
ous nor so protean that he did not remain with us for a thousand years, as
he promised, or that he slipped away from us at times, or changed his mind,   45
or revealed himself anew during these past ten years. But they do not deny
that he existed in spirit; they deny that there have been true ministers of the
Spirit. Truly, what a monstrous and mutilated church would that be?

What I would earnestly like to know, most learned sir, is what you think
one should respond to these criticisms. Although I too have resolved, as is   50
just, to make known to them the reason for my faith, nevertheless a word or
two coming from you would be no small counsel and consolation. I would
by no means extort this from you with such audacity unless you could do it
in virtue of your dignity, or better said, unless in view of your humanity you
could not be unwilling to help anyone, so far is it from you not to be willing   55
to render me this pious service.

But that you may be aware of the remaining circumstances of my life,
I have recently begun to give classes at the College of St Moritz, in which
I strive to be of help not so much by my own diligence, of whatever value
that may be, but by using the little works in various genres you dedicat-   60
ed to teaching. Here too I would have questions to ask of you that pertain
to scholastic matters, like orthography, in which I see there is much varied
opinion among men of learning. I would wish that, just as in the case of
many other grammatical points where habitual practices have resulted in
improper usage, so rules regarding orthography should be observed and   65
written. For example, there are those who pronounce and write *adprehendo*
for *apprehendo*, and some write *interpres* and *otio*, while others write *ocio* and
interpraes with 'c' and a diphthong, etc. These are not such slight matters that
they are not important to grammar, and it would be more in accordance with

* * * * *

7 On the church as Christ's dove, cf Ep 2037:285.

grammatical procedure if they were pointed out rather than that they be sim-   70
ply condemned as trivial errors.

In addition I have, for the benefit of Christianity, translated in recent
days certain apologetic arguments from your letter that you sent to the brethren of Friesland,[8] truly worthy of being known and of practical use to many.
Things pertaining to your relation with the people of Strasbourg and others I   75
purposely left out. Hence there is hope that you will not be averse to lending
your service to the commonwealth and also to the church,[9] and that when
occasion arises it will be assisted according to the advice of Paul.[10] I hope also
that you will not be annoyed that I have written you with more impudence
than prudence or learning, and that, should you write back some day, you   80
will not find fault with my audacity. But if you think well of it, I shall take
care to write other letters that perhaps will be more worthy of your reading.

Farewell, and may you preside for a very long time over letters and the
lettered. Again and again farewell.

Given at Augsburg, 3 April 1531   85
Christopher Freisleben, pedagogue

May this be delivered to the most learned Master Desiderius Erasmus
of Rotterdam of Freiburg im Breisgau, indefatigable restorer of literary learning. At Freiburg im Breisgau

2476 / To Anton Fugger   Freiburg, 4 April 1531

This letter was first published in the *Epistolae floridae*. For Anton Fugger, head of
the great Augsburg banking house, see Ep 2145 introduction.

ERASMUS OF ROTTERDAM TO ANTON FUGGER, GREETING
When I reflect upon your extraordinary friendship, distinguished sir; when
I consider the accumulated benefits you have bestowed on me, though I am

* * * * *

8 Incorrectly identified by Allen as the *Epistola contra pseudevangelicos* (March 1530).
   Freisleben is referring to the *Epistola ad fratres Inferioris Germaniae* (September
   1530), which was addressed to the brethren of Lower Germany 'and East
   Friesland'; see CWE 78 265. Freisleben's translation was never published.
9 The Latin is *in rem publicam, eanque divinam* 'the commonwealth and the divine
   commonwealth.'
10 The Latin of this passage is vague. The meaning seems to be that the publication of Freisleben's translation of passages from Erasmus' *Epistola ad fratres
   Inferioris Germaniae* would be a service to commonwealth and church, and the
   'advice of Paul' is perhaps that found in 1 Thess 5:27: 'I charge you before the
   Lord that this letter be read to all the brethren.'

in no way deserving of them; lastly, when I reflect that you with your great
riches invite me to share in your fortunes: on the one hand I seem to myself 5
to be extremely fortunate that such a patron and friend has been allotted to
me by divine agency, and on the other I am overcome by a feeling of shame
and am tormented in spirit when, examining all my resources, I find nothing I can do that is equal in worth.[1] Did I say equal? Something, at least, by
which I can indicate the eager willingness of one who is gratefully indebted. 10
In the same way, I renounced a long-standing friendship with our mutual
friend, Johann Koler, if he did not in good faith provide me an opportunity to
proclaim how much I esteem your loving heart, adorned with so many gifts
of benevolence.[2] Great riches usually produce arrogance and pride in the
possessor. But in the ranks of those with meagre income whom can we find 15
of equal affability, civility, and modesty? Wealth usually incites thirst of itself,
like a kind of dropsy. You on the contrary, on whom benign divinity pours it
out in excess, seem to possess it for others rather than for yourself, as a true
master of riches, over whom they have no right but serve you at your discretion. Beatus Rhenanus, a man of eminent learning, in a letter to Dr Philipp 20
Puchaimer, so described your home,[3] which Polyphemus praised to me with
little use of rhetoric,[4] that I would not have seen more if I had seen it in its entirety. But of how much felicity does the iniquity of these times deprive me?
May some propitious deity ward off civil war from Germany. But wherever
the Fates want Erasmus to be, be assured that in that place there will be an 25
ardent devotee of Fugger and of the Fugger name.

For that flagon of wine you sent me by another courier, I expressed my
thanks through the one who brought it. But since he too delivered the flagon
to me no fuller than Polyphemus had sent it, and on that account my servant

* * * * *

2476
1 In 1529 Fugger had offered Erasmus generous financial support if he would
make Augsburg his permanent place of residence, an offer for which Erasmus
expressed genuine gratitude but politely declined (Ep 2145), as he would again
when the offer was repeated (Ep 2525). When Fugger sent him a gold cup
(Ep 2192:59–61), Erasmus responded by dedicating to him his translation of
Xenophon's *Hieron* (Ep 2273). Delighted at this mark of honour, Fugger assisted
Erasmus in his search for wine that was good for his health (see lines 27–32
below), and arranged for members of the extensive Fugger network to assist in
remitting money and forwarding mail (Ep 2403:16–25; Allen Ep 2701:18–19).
2 Koler was a canon of St Moritz at Augsburg (Ep 2195 introduction).
3 Puchaimer was physician to Albert of Brandenburg, cardinal-archbishop-
elector of Mainz. For Rhenanus' letter to him see BRE Ep 274; the description of
Fugger's home is on pages 393–4.
4 For Erasmus' wayward servant and messenger Polyphemus (Felix Rex), see Ep
2475 n1.

complained, it could happen that he suppressed my letter to you,[5] fearing that   30
it might betray him. I write this because I see that Koler is worried that the
wine that was sent later was not delivered.[6] The other vessels were full. If any
similar shipment is to be made, it would be necessary to put it in a reliable
container well smeared with pitch and add some purple dye, as if it were being sent to some other personage of great importance. When they hear that it is   35
for Erasmus, they conclude that it is abandoned booty without risk. Farewell.

Given at Freiburg, 4 April 1531

2477 / From Ottmar Nachtgall   [Freiburg], 4 April 1531

First published as Ep 150 in Förstemann / Günther, the autograph of this letter
was in the Burscher Collection of the University Library at Leipzig (Ep 1254
introduction). Allen took the reference to Quirinus Talesius in line 3 as evidence that Nachtgall was writing from Freiburg. Ep 2462, written at Freiburg
on 23 March 1531, was addressed in Quirinus' hand; and he was the bearer
(with Karel Uutenhove) of Ep 2487, sent from Freiburg on 18 April 1531 (see
Ep 2494:1–3). For Nachtgall, Erasmus' troublesome neighbour in Freiburg, see
Ep 2166 n3.

Cordial greetings. Being extremely occupied, I write to you at the spur of the
moment, most distinguished Master Erasmus; therefore in your kindness
please pardon the lack of polish. Yesterday it occurred to me, immediately
after our friend Quirinus left my house,[1] that I should ask him to inform you
that if you had any business to attend to in Besançon, Lyon, or on either bank   5
of the Rhône (for after the Easter holidays I shall set out for those shores,
God willing),[2] I shall see to it that you will not be without my loyalty and
diligence, for I am totally at your service. In return, you could do me a great
favour without any cost to yourself if in writing to your friends you would
recommend me to them in some small way;[3] likewise, if in exchange for Basel   10

* * * * *

5 Not extant
6 Koler's anxiety is expressed in Epp 2437:29–37 and 2438:25–34.

2477
1 Quirinus Talesius, Erasmus' servant and messenger
2 In 1531 Easter fell on 12 April.
3 To Ep 2466, carried by Nachtgall to Nicolas Maillard, Erasmus added a postscript
   (lines 258–61) with mild praise of Nachtgall. But there is no mention of him in
   Ep 2473, which he is also thought to have carried (see Ep 2472 introduction).

coins, or batzen, as they are called, you could send me twenty or twenty-five crowns for my trip.[4] Then I will go to Marseille to places that they say are sacred to the repentance of Mary Magdalene, where I shall do penance for my faults.[5] I hope that the Villinger house, which was rented to you, is to your liking, and I will send all the keys, all purchased with my money, but I do not ask anything for them. In the meantime it will be arranged that some of my belongings will be put in a trunk.[6] Farewell and love me in return, as one most devoted to you, or I shall be content if you place me in the lowest ranks of your friends.

    4 April 1531
    Ottmar Nachtgall
    To the most celebrated Master Desiderius Erasmus of Rotterdam, most dear patron and friend

2478 / To Bonifacius Amerbach   [Freiburg], 6 April [1531]

First published in the *Epistolae familiares*, the autograph is in the Öffentliche Bibliothek of the University of Basel (MS AN III 25 68). Allen established the year-date on the basis of the watermark on the paper, which corresponds to that of the paper Erasmus used in 1530–1, as well as on the reference to Luther's treatise in line 6, which clearly indicates 1531.

Greetings. The interview with this doctor was most pleasant. He seems to be a young man endowed with singular modesty and good judgment.[1] If you

* * * * *

4 In light of his itinerary, Nachtgall presumably means the French écu au soleil ('crown'), which was officially valued in 1531 at 76d groot Flemish, so that 25 crowns were equivalent to just under a year's wage (230 days) of an Antwerp master mason/carpenter at 9.05d per day (CWE 12 650 Table 3, 691 Table 13). Originally issued by Bern in 1492, the batzen was a silver coin worth 1/15 of a gulden or Rhenish florin. Many cities in Switzerland and southern Germany soon issued their own batzen, which were widely employed in exchanging high for lower-value currencies.

5 According to tradition, Mary Magdalene and her brother Lazarus travelled to Marseille and preached Christianity to the local population. Her shrine is at La Sainte-Baume, about thirty miles northeast of Marseille.

6 For the story of Erasmus, Nachtgall, and the Villinger house in Freiburg, see Ep 2462 introduction.

2478
1 Allen suggests 'possibly Sinapius'; see Ep 2461 introduction.

come, it will give me great pleasure,[2] provided that it does not cause any inconvenience to you. We are trying to move out of this place, if at all possible.[3]
But we will discuss all of this when we meet. If it is no trouble, I would like   5
to see the treatise of Luther on the keys, provided that he wrote it in Latin.[4]

Farewell. 6 April

The rest you know.

To the excellent doctor of laws Bonifacius Amerbach. In Basel

2479 / To Léonard de Gruyères   Freiburg, 6 April 1531

> This letter, probably one of those carried by Ottmar Nachtgall (see Ep 2472 intro-
> duction), was first published in the *Epistolae floridae*. For Léonard de Gruyères,
> official (ie chief judge) of the diocesan court at Besançon, see Epp 1534, 2139.

ERASMUS OF ROTTERDAM TO LÉONARD,
OFFICIAL OF THE ARCHBISHOP OF BESANÇON, GREETING
Today at last I savoured the wine that you had the kindness to send me;[1] I
hope it will be suitable both for my stomach and for the summer months,
which I fondly hope we can pass peacefully here, as we have done so far.   5
We have had enough calamities, and more than enough, without anything
else being added. We endured a plague that raged all winter,[2] we are suffering an enormous scarcity of everything,[3] and what is even more ominous, it
increases day by day, although the population has diminished significantly,
and last year's harvest was quite plentiful.   10

We have had for a long time now three ill-omened divinities: discord,
ravenous hunger, and plague, to which, if the battle cry is added, I fear that
we will see in all of Germany a pitiable spectacle to behold. I pray that this
augury of mine is groundless, but at any rate the preludes up to now are not
promising. And furthermore I fear that the position of priests, whose cause   15
seems to be at stake, will be in no better condition than it is now – let us hope
it will not be worse. Even supposing that the intention of princes is upright

* * * * *

2 Cf Ep 2474:7.
3 On Erasmus' search for a new house in Freiburg see Ep 2497.
4 Luther's treatise *Von den Schlüsseln* (On the Power of the Keys) was published
  in the autumn of 1530; there was no Latin edition. See WA 30/2 428–36.

2479
1 See Epp 2397:3–17, 2401A:15–25.
2 See Epp 2426 n3, 2443:463–5, 2450:12–13.
3 Cf Ep 2215 n10.

and straightforward, what dregs of mankind will flow into Germany under
the pretext of this war – Jews, who cannot be safe in Spain, accustomed to
pillage and plundering in all of Germany.[4] Add to this that all of this brood   20
are either drawn to the side of the sects or by nature are averse to religion.
Are we to think that the ploughing will turn out well with unwilling oxen?

But, you will say, their boldness will be held in check by the authority
of princes. Rome, evidently, is an example to us, and all of Italy, so pitifully
devastated. Vienna is an example, which suffered more from its defenders   25
than from the Turks, if what those who live there write is true.[5] But in what
war, no matter how fair, no matter how just, do we not hear such complaints?
A terrible disease must be cured by harsh remedies, you will say. But Seneca
does not approve remedies more grave than the disease.[6] And Crassus, at the
mercy of the doctors, after undergoing the amputation of one leg, forbade   30
the surgeon to proceed to the other since he thought the cure would be worse
than the malady.[7] But in the meantime what will become of good and pious
men who have no opportunity to move away from their cities, seeing that
they have a wife there, young children, aged parents, homes, property, debtors, and other ties. The greatest part of the calamity will fall on their heads.   35

What kind of a war, which will involve the greater part of the world,
will this be? What doctor will think that he must resort to cauterization or
amputation when the disease does not leave any part of the body intact?
We have two monarchs, by far the most powerful of all,[8] who love religion,
but they are young and all the more susceptible to deception the more hon-   40
est and high-minded they are. Charles seems to be ready to obey whatever
Clement VII prescribes.[9] Now if God will inspire him to prescribe nothing
that is unworthy of Christ, one can hope for a happy outcome of these tumults. But, but, but – I say no more. We need in the present circumstances
some owls who can see in the dark.   45

Finally, what will become of people like me? Partly because of my age,
partly because of my poor health, I have been changed from a mobile object
into a stationary one. That is what you usually say. I seem to be transformed
into the kind of living creature that is called fixed. If tumult should arise,

* * * * *

4 Cf Ep 2472:27–32 with nn7–8.
5 See Ep 2472 nn8, 10; cf 55–6 with n17.
6 Seneca *De tranquillitate animi* 9.3
7 This corresponds to no tale of any Crassus that we can identify.
8 Charles v and Francis i
9 See Ep 2472 n9.

what is left to me but to depart from this life with resignation? I am invited 50
to Augsburg both affectionately and on magnificent terms, but I do not want
to exchange one danger for another.[10] I am invited to Italy, to Savoy, and
to France,[11] but I am resolved not to leave the domain of the emperor by
whose favour I have subsisted until now, and I do not dare expose this little
body to a long journey. I can emigrate to your land with the authority of 55
the emperor and Ferdinand,[12] but I would not wish to be a burden to you,
for whom I have the highest regard, unless perhaps the situation becomes
more peaceful.[13]

I would have sent you some books, but there was no one here who
could transport the bundle. As soon, however, as Hieronymus Froben re- 60
turns from the Frankfurt fair, I will make sure the bundle is conveyed to you
from Basel. If you will advise me what good office I can perform to compensate in part for your services to me, I shall fulfil them most willingly. I speak
most sincerely, for I owe a good part of my life to you. Farewell.

Given at Freiburg im Breisgau, 6 April 1531

2480 / From Christoph von Stadion   Dillingen, 10 April 1531

This letter was first published as Ep 16 in Horawitz I. The autograph is in the
Württembergische Landesbibliothek Stuttgart (MS Hist Fol 47 folio 3). For
Christoph von Stadion, bishop of Augsburg, see Ep 2029 introduction.

Cordial greetings. I have nothing to write you, dearest friend, except that
King Ferdinand has betaken himself to Bohemia and Moravia with the

* * * * *

10 See Epp 2476 n1, 2525 n4.
11 For the most recent invitation to France see Ep 2472. For Savoy see Ep 2473. As
    for Italy, in 1529 Karel Uutenhove invited Erasmus to join him in Padua, where
    he had gone to study (Ep 2209:31–5). But it was just at this point (April 1531)
    that Uutenhove, on his way home to his native Ghent, paid Erasmus a visit at
    Freiburg (cf Ep 2483 n1). It is possible, however, that one or more of Erasmus'
    musings that Italy would be a good place to be (were it not too arduous a jour-
    ney for an old man) were his polite responses to invitations or encouragements
    from Italians to settle there; see Epp 2105:20–2, 2328:55–7, 2481:49–51. Cf Ep
    2594:50–1, where Viglius Zuichemus mentions rumours that Erasmus intend-
    ed to settle in Padua.
12 Besançon was in Franche-Comté, which at this time was one of the Burgundian
    territories under the rule of Charles v.
13 Ie the situation in Besançon, where there was dissension between the canons
    and the town magistrates; see Ep 2410:48–50.

intention of asking for help against the enemy of the Christian faith. But, as
I hear, they refuse to provide him with money. In the event that the Turks
invade them they offered twenty-five thousand warriors for the defence of   5
Moravia and Silesia.[1] It is said that the pope is besieging the city of Siena,
although there are those who maintain that this is a pretence and that under
this guise the pope intends to expel the duke of Ferrara. The duke, warned
of this, is beginning to make preparations for war, so that he will not be
caught unawares.[2]   10

Ferdinand and his allies claim that the Turks are rapidly advancing towards Germany, but the merchants vehemently proclaim the contrary, af-
firming that the Turks will by no means invade Germany this year. Which of
these views is closer to the truth we will shortly find out by experience, and
perhaps not without danger to ourselves.   15

A certain man of good faith told me that the Turks had indicated to the
envoys of Ferdinand that the pope, the French, Venetians, and some princes
of Germany had encouraged them to make an attack on Ferdinand himself
after the capture of the king.[3] The same man reported to the same envoys everything that had been discussed and decided at the Diet of Augsburg, just as   20
if he had been present at the diet, among other things the day and the month
Ferdinand was to be elected king of the Romans, indicating the princes who
had attempted to impede this election.[4] What good can come for Christianity
from such tales I do not quite understand.

The Lutherans among us are exerting every effort to abolish the mass,   25
and they will not cease, in my opinion, until they have achieved their purpose. The people of Augsburg removed the father-in-law of Anton Fugger

* * * * *

2480
1 The expected attack would come in April 1532.
2 Cf Ep 2491:16–19.
3 Following his defeat at the battle of Pavia on 24 February 1524 and his subsequent imprisonment by Charles v, which lasted until 17 March 1526, Francis i
  actively sought alliance with Sultan Suleiman the Magnificent, whose ambi-
  tions against the house of Hapsburg coincided with his own. Although Francis
  was chiefly interested in an Ottoman attack on Hapsburg interests in Italy and
  the Mediterranean, his overtures provided Suleiman with an additional in-
  centive for the incursions into Central Europe that began with the attack on
  Hungary in 1526 and continued beyond the unsuccessful siege of Vienna in
  1529. See Knecht 186–7, 214–15. These diplomatic efforts continued following
  the Peace of Cambrai in 1529; see Ep 2511 n22.
4 For the election and coronation of Ferdinand as king of the Romans, see Ep 2384
  n7.

from the city council this year, a pious and prudent man, for no other reason
than that he refuses to join the Lutherans.[5]

I wanted to let you know these things for no other reason than not to   30
have Polyphemus return to you without a letter from me.[6] I wish you every
blessing.

From Dillingen, 10 April 1531

Your friend, the bishop of Augsburg

To the excellent theologian Erasmus of Rotterdam, a friend dear to my   35
heart. At Freiburg

2481 / To Bernardo Boerio   Freiburg, 11 April 1531

This letter was first published in the *Epistolae floridae*. For Bernardo Boerio, who,
with his brother Giovanni, had been Erasmus' pupil in Italy in 1506, see Ep 2255
introduction.

ERASMUS OF ROTTERDAM TO MASTER BERNARDO BOERIO, GREETING
If you have any faith at all in my words, I wish you to be persuaded, my
dearest Bernardo, that although packets of letters are brought to me from every region of the world, for many months no letter has come to me more welcome than that which you sent me on 15 March,[1] so much so that, although   5
at that time I was near death as a result of gripping pains in the bowels,[2] on
reading your letter I came back to life, so pleasant was the recollection of our
former association. But much more enjoyable was my recognition that the
seed of learning, which in Bologna I sowed in the newly cultivated land of
youthful intelligence, had yielded such a splendid, ripe harvest. Otherwise I   10
was somewhat fearful that, as often occurs with the great majority of people,

* * * * *

5 Fugger's father-in-law was Johann Rehlinger, member of an old patrician family in Augsburg. In 1531 he and others were removed from the city council
  because of their opposition to he Lutheran party, but they were soon restored to
  office (Ep 2631:96–100). On the progress of evangelical reform in Augsburg see
  Ep 2430:11–19.
6 For Polyphemus (Felix Rex), see Ep 2475 n1.

2481
1 Written in answer to Ep 2255; not extant
2 This indicates that Boerio's letter arrived during the early stage of Erasmus'
  grave illness in 1530, which started sometime in March and turned worse on
  Easter Monday (18 April). See Ep 2331:2–12.

riches, the delights of Rome, public office, and your associates in this mundane occupation would distract your mind from the companionship of philology. I am happy that this concern arising from my affection for you proved to be pointless and through you has been completely removed from me. For the rare discernment in your letter, the perceptive ideas, not taken from the street, the graceful turns of phrase, and the choice of words give ample testimony that you frequent the gardens of the Muses.

What delighted me most of all was your marvellous devotion to me, which the whole letter exudes in every way. For that devotion, which such a great interval of time and place, such a long physical separation, and the disruption of familiar intercourse was not able to render even the slightest bit weaker but, as it appears, has made more intense, must be genuine and lively. Even concerning that matter of the signature, which caused you some misgivings, I have no regrets, dear Bernardo, since it moved you to express more vividly your great affection for me. If in a young man it cooled on several occasions, it would not have been anything unusual in human relations or anything rare or novel, as I have mentioned. I experienced all the more pleasure after I learned that your memory of me had not only not faded from your mind but was still reverent and sacrosanct, for that is what you write, and I believe you. For if you did not write sincerely, you would not write with such ardour.

Furthermore, that the name of Erasmus was for both of you like a wreath of ivy and won for you a great reputation for learning with everyone, would that it were as true as you have described it. I owe it to that Beetle not only that I left you too early but also that the pleasantness of our relationship was tempered with a good deal of bitterness,[3] so much so that if a sense of fidelity had not kept me at my post, may I cease to live if for an Attic talent I could have been prevailed upon to put up with this monster for another month's time.[4] I have often wondered how your father, a prudent man, could have been so governed by an adverse fate in this matter as to entrust his prospects of a bright future to a man who was barely suited to take care of pigs, or rather who was in need of someone to take care of him because of his mental deficiency. But this is the unhappy condition of human affairs.

I am glad that you liked Frans van der Dilft,[5] who suffered a fate very different from mine. There was nothing more fortunate than that talented

* * * * *

3 The Beetle (*Scarabaeus*) was the boys' tutor Clyfton (Ep 194:36n); cf Ep 2255 n3.
4 An Attic talent was the value of nine man-years of work.
5 Dilft had delivered Ep 2255 to the Boerio brothers at Genoa.

man; but when he moved to Basel in the flower of his youth he was lured away from his studies by certain debauchers, famous for having been corrupted, to lead a life of pleasure and luxury.[6] As for myself, many things drive me away from here, and many more invite me to Italy, but this frail little 50
body is not suited to any travels;[7] I do not care about terms and conditions; I have all that is necessary for my frugal existence. I need only a tranquil location, which is very difficult to find in this fatal tumult in human affairs, especially for Erasmus, weighed down by the heavy burden of a reputation that arouses envy, which he carries around with him, whether he likes it or 55
not, wherever he goes, even if he were to set out for Constantinople. And just as there is nowhere where I do not have those who wish me well, so there is nowhere where those of opposite sentiments are not present. But most of the time the perversity of the wicked has far more power than the favour of the good. I do not know how much light I provided for Germany; certainly 60
it poured out many mists and tempests upon me. I was delighted, however, by your comparison with the sun, which imparts its light in its revolution to all the regions of the earth, not because it is appropriate but because that is its nature. Indeed all this subject matter that you elaborated in various and clever analyses gave me great delight. 65

The rumour here – or rather not a rumour, but a public announcement – is that the Turks are going to invade Germany with all the forces of their kingdom, to decide the final outcome, whether Charles will be the sole ruler of the whole world, or the Turks.[8] The world can no longer support two suns. If this happens, I do not know whether you will be free from danger. 70

I was greatly astonished that there is no mention of your brother Giovanni Boerio in the whole letter. If he has met his fate, I am sorry, but if you are not getting along, I am even more sorry. You would do me a great favour if you remove this anxiety from my mind, and at the same time I would like to know what your excellent mother, Signora Giulia, is doing, 75
and what your cousin Vincenzo is doing.[9] I had heard that the military Order of St Peter, which Leo instituted, had been suppressed by Adrian VI. And yet your letter still has this title, from which I conjecture that the rumour was

* * * * *

6 This appears to be an expression of annoyance that Dilft was off seeking his fortunes as a courtier rather than pursuing scholarship; see Ep 2222 n15.
7 Cf Ep 2479 n11.
8 The anticipated Turkish attack would occur in April 1532, but without the decisive results predicted here.
9 Nothing is known of Signora Giulia or Vincenzo.

false.[10] Farewell, dearest Boerio, and if the Fates obstinately refuse a closer relationship, at least it will be possible to converse with one another through mutual correspondence. Whatever you send to Hieronymus Froben will be safely delivered to me. 80

At Freiburg im Breisgau, 11 April 1531

2482 / To Agostino Trivulzio   Freiburg, 12 April 1531

This letter, which was first published in the *Epistolae floridae*, is apparently Erasmus' answer to a letter, not extant, in which Agostino Cardinal Trivulzio (Ep 2405 n1) had replied graciously to Ep 2423. The surviving manuscript is an autograph rough draft in the Royal Library at Copenhagen (MS GKS 95 Fol, folio 232).

TO CARDINAL AGOSTINO TRIVULZIO, GREETING

Immortal God! how often audacious plans turn out more successfully than modest ones. Not long ago I was angry with our friend Germain because he had urged me on with his forceful letter to this audacious undertaking.[1] Now after having had such good success with it,[2] I think it is appropriate 5 that I render him profound thanks for his insistence, which contributed such great happiness to my present circumstances. For who would not consider himself fortunate if, even after long aspiring to it, he were to be accepted into the service of such a great and renowned prince? But these honorific words, coming from my humble station, are not in keeping with your exceptional 10 modesty; you accept me into your friendship, or rather you do not accept me, but rather consider yourself happy to have had the opportunity of being introduced into my friendship. Through this modesty, by which you lower yourself immoderately, you are more noble, in my opinion, than by virtue of your other qualities or distinctions, which Germain de Brie praised in his 15

* * * * *

10 The Order of St Peter was established by Leo X in 1520 and confirmed by Clement VII in 1526. Bernardo had evidently signed himself as a knight of St Peter.

2482
1 In Ep 2405:3–97 Brie had sung the praises of Trivulzio and urged Erasmus to initiate correspondence with him and seek his friendship and patronage, something that Erasmus here characterizes as 'an audacious undertaking.' Erasmus responded by addressing Ep 2423 to Trivulzio.
2 Ie having elicited a friendly reply to Ep 2324

eloquent letter. He praised them in his letter; you gave proof of them in your letter, written with such wisdom and affection.

To remedy the German fever I have devoted my loyal, vigorous, and constant energies up to the present moment, at a great expense to my fortunes and at great risk to my health and life. But for these well exerted efforts the most deplorable gratitude is given in return, and that by those very people for whom I do battle. That the opposing faction attacks me with all its instruments of war may be seen as giving me my just deserts as well as within their rights. But that I should be attacked in so many pamphlets dipped in poison by those for whose sake I expose myself to danger, I cannot cease to wonder. At Rome too there were not lacking those who tried to alienate the feelings of Clement to me by their pernicious accusations, yet they achieved nothing.[3] But if the supreme pontiff knew thoroughly the circumstances of this whole affair, he would not at all number Erasmus among the lowest of those he esteems worthy of his favour. For I do not seek to obtain mitres and riches. I would prefer that his authority serve to keep the barking of the evilminded at a distance.

Therefore let these be the first offerings of your friendly offices towards me, that through you the supreme pontiff will understand that Erasmus has occupied himself with the affairs of Christ with the greatest sincerity, and with equal constancy, and has exposed his life to so many dangers that if I were to aspire to a human recompense, I would refuse the offer of the papacy. I have made enemies of almost all men of learning, and those whom previously I dealt with as intimate friends and who were privy to all my secrets I now suffer as my most mortal enemies.[4] But none are better equipped to destroy a man than those who lived on familiar terms with him. For these people, although they have no knowledge of any wrongdoing, nevertheless have enough material to fabricate plausible calumnies. And for getting rid of those whom they perceive to be hostile to them they have accomplices possessed of every kind of malice.

As for the French king, just as I was earlier immensely grieved at his personal disaster,[5] so now I rejoice greatly at his tranquillity. I ask nothing

* * * * *

3 A clear reference to Girolamo Aleandro and Alberto Pio; see Epp 1553 n9, 1987 introduction.
4 Another reference to Aleandro. On his transformation from friend to enemy, see Ep 1553 n9.
5 Ie his catastrophic defeat at the battle of Pavia in February 1525, followed by a year in Madrid as the prisoner of Charles v

but to be dear to him, as he has frequently declared his good will towards me.[6] What your generosity promises, I accept with all my heart, and in turn I offer all the expressions of deference that a loyal and grateful client can and   50 should render to a patron deserving of the highest esteem.

May the Lord Jesus protect and prosper your reverend Lordship in all things.

Given at Freiburg im Breisgau, 12 April 1531

2483 / To Levinus Ammonius   Freiburg, 13 April 1531

This letter, first published in the *Epistolae floridae*, was carried by Karel Uutenhove, who was travelling in the company of Quirinus Talesius. Uutenhove and Quirinus, who also delivered Ep 2487 (Ep 2494:1–3), were presumably the carriers of Epp 2485–6 as well. Ammonius did not respond to this letter until 9 June 1533 (Ep 2817).

For Levinus Ammonius, Carthhusian of St Maartensbos, see Epp 1463, 2016.

ERASMUS OF ROTTERDAM TO LEVINUS AMMONIUS, CARTHUSIAN, GREETING

As the sight of our Karel returning from Italy brought me incredible pleasure,[1] so too I have no doubt that he will inspire great joy in all of you. It will be possible to learn from him not only in what state our affairs are, but also   5 about Rome, Venice, Bologna, and about Germany he will weave a long Iliad. For he returns like Ulysses, having suffered and learned much.[2]

Sometimes, dearest Ammonius, when I contemplate what kind of talents are repressed and buried in these ceremonies, the thought, a human one perhaps, enters my mind that the prisons of this kind of life were introduced   10 not without the instigation of Satan. What is the extinguishing of the spirit, if not this? But Paul forbids this to be done,[3] and Christ does not want the smoldering wick to be extinguished but rather that it be brought back to

* * * * *

6 See, for example, Ep 1375.

2483
1 Having lived with Erasmus at Basel from June 1528 through February 1529, Karel Uutenhove of Ghent (Ep 2001 n7) had spent two years in Italy completing his studies. Now on his way home to his native city, he was paying a visit to Erasmus in Freiburg. See also Ep 2485:1–2.
2 Homer *Odyssey* 1.3–4
3 1 Thess 5:19

life.⁴ On the other hand, when I consider your soul, so simply dependent on
the will of Christ and ready to suffer all the wrongs of this life, I cannot but   15
call you happy. There are various kinds of martyrdom, and I think that we
cannot rank among the least of them the life of one who in such discomforts
has constantly preserved his tranquillity of mind to the last breath. The rack
provides more painful torture, but briefer. And it usually happens that the
more gifted intellects are allotted weaker bodies. By the same token, what a   20
great inequity it is to compel such unequal natures to equal labours, just as
if you were to lead an ox and a lamb bound by the same yoke to plough the
field. Yet the lamb could serve some other use. And I don't know whether
the eating of fish, fasts, vigils, solitude, and other external practices are the
least part of these discomforts. But in a great many flocks there are lovers of   25
self, the headstrong, the hard to please, some not of sound mind, who create
rare tragedies out of the merest trifles and stir up contention out of matters
of no importance. And it usually happens that the more ignorant and stupid
a man is, the more highly regarded he is in this form of life, puffed up with
pride through his confidence in ceremonies, and unjust in his appraisal of   30
someone of a difference disposition. To bear these things patiently, to preserve peace and tranquillity of mind with such persons is, I think, the most
difficult of all.

    Recently I had to laugh about the complaint of someone in your order
who wrote that he endured dreadful torments because of the hatred of cer-   35
tain confrères. I expected some grave reason for this hatred. What do you
expect? The reason was that he had the first place on the left side of the choir,
an honour which many thought belonged to them. Perhaps in your community there are no such individuals; but if there are, seeing that you preserve
your sweetness of soul unimpaired, I am confident that you will not have   40
the lowest place among the blessed martyrs. The world for a long time has
produced abortions; when it will bring forth a live birth I do not know. So
far the indications are not promising. But Christ lives, directing the scenes
of human history by his secret counsel. Yet before that stage director adds
the dénouement to this play, I have to live out the drama of my life, since   45
this domicile of the soul is threatening collapse, not so much because of old
age and poor health as because of the weariness of the venomous intrigues
directed against me by both sides, one of which numbers cacolycs instead of

* * * * *

4 Matt 12:20

Catholics,[5] and the other dysangelicals instead of evangelicals.[6] I pray that
the Lord will refashion all of them to his glory.   50
     All of last summer was virtually sterile for me while I struggled with
severe pains in the bowels and later with an abscess.[7] In the winter months I
published six books of apophthegms and a little commentary on Psalm 33.[8]
My mind refused to have any enthusiasm for the work on preaching that was
often solicited from me.[9] May the Lord gladden your spirit, dearest friend   55
and brother in the Lord. You will learn the rest of the news from our mutual
friend Karel Uutenhove.
     At Freiburg im Breisgau, 13 April 1531

2484 / To Viglius Zuichemus   Freiburg, 14 April 1531

First published as Ep 16 in Horawitz 1, the autograph is in the University
Library at Leiden (Papanbroeck 2). For Viglius Zuichemus, at this time studying law with Andrea Alciati (Ep 1250) at Bourges, see Ep 2101.

Cordial greetings. Would that there were something, my Viglius, that I could
promise you from here worthy of your virtues! I wrote to Zasius, for we do
not communicate with each other in any other way. He did not respond even
with a grunt, which is not his custom. If anything should happen to him, I
think Bonifacius Amerbach will succeed him.[1] There is no teaching position   5
vacant here.
     I do not wish you to mention Kan from now on. He excuses himself by
letter and also accuses himself. He has now become a priest. I do not wish
that any trace of his former offence remain, now that he is another person.[2]

* * * * *

5 'Cacolycs' (*cacolycos*) is a play on the Greek words κακός 'bad' and λύκος 'wolf.'
  For a similar use of κακός to denigrate a 'cacolyc' opponent, see Ep 2263 n30.
6 Here the play is on the prefixes *dys-* 'bad,' and *ev* 'good.'
7 For Erasmus' illness in 1530 see Ep 2320 n1.
8 See Epp 2428 (*Enarratio psalmi 33*) and 2431 (*Apophthegmata*).
9 *Ecclesiastes*, not published until 1535

2484
1 Erasmus had written to Udalricus Zasius in support of Alciati's unsuccessful
  campaign to get Viglius appointed as Zasius' successor at Freiburg; see Epp
  2394:133–7, 2418:15–23, 2468:174–91. Bonifacius Amerbach did not succeed him.
2 On Erasmus' annoyance with Nicolaas Kan (Ep 1832), whom he suspected of
  having aligned himself with the reformers at Strasbourg and elsewhere, see Ep
  2356:1–34.

The honorific recommendation given to you by Alciati pleased me immense- 10
ly.[3] For my part I think it is a more outstanding achievement to be praised by
such a man than to be crowned with riches. A splendid destiny will not be
lacking to your native abilities. But everything has its time and, as Theocritus
said, 'Some things come in summer, some in winter.'[4]

> Farewell. 14 April 1531 15
> Freiburg im Breisgau.
> Erasmus of Rotterdam, in his own hand
> To the most distinguished young man Viglius of Friesland. At Bourges

2485 / To Omaar van Edingen   Freiburg, 16 April 1531

This letter was first published in the *Epistolae floridae*. Edingen (Ep 2060) was
clerk of the council of Flanders, kinsman of Karel Uutenhove (line 2), and
close friend of Levinus Ammonius (Ep 2483). When Erasmus left Basel in
1529, Edingen, who joined Ammonius and others in urging him to return to
the Netherlands, offered him spacious accommodation in or near his home in
Ghent (Flanders); see Ep 2197:98–126.

ERASMUS OF ROTTERDAM TO OMAAR VAN EDINGEN, GREETING
Our friend Karel Uutenhove gave me great pleasure on his return to us from
Italy.[1] Though he prevailed on me to write something to you, I have reason to
write rather sparingly, because you will be able to learn everything in greater
detail from him than from my letter, however prolix it may be. You will hear 5
him speaking with Italian or even Ciceronian eloquence.

Jealous Fate has taken from us a truly guileless spirit, Antonius Clava,
which makes you all the more dear to me, Omaar, because there are fewer
people like you there.[2]

For a long time now I have had enough of Germany, to the point of 10
vomiting. Those whom I should avoid I see, those whom I should seek out I
do not see. I often think of Flanders, but because of the beggar-tyrants I doubt

* * * * *

3 See Ep 2394:133–7.
4 *Idylls* 11.58

2485
1 See Ep 2483 n1.
2 Clava (Ep 175:13n) died in Ghent on 31 May 1529; see Ep 2260:44–53.

whether it would be safe.³ Mary, once queen of Hungary,⁴ who I hear has taken the place of Margaret,⁵ is favourably disposed towards me. But if she were to do things differently than is fervently desired by some (I shall not call them Catholics but rather hot-headed fanatics), they would say that it was I who had whispered something in her ear, even if I had advised against it. Nor would she be able to protect me against those who are armed with both papal and imperial authority.⁶ I should not wish your country to experience the situation that is said to exist in certain other countries, where tumult among the various sects leaves nothing in peace, or else where the Evangelicals have complete freedom while the others are forced to accept things they do not approve. To use force is certainly not in accordance with the gospel. I am distinctly afraid that as long as some are Lutherans, others are Zwinglians, others Anabaptists, we will, while fighting the Turks, become Turks ourselves.⁷ I hope this prediction is false. I pray for a tranquil life for you; I must fall in this gladiatorial arena, into which certain friends have pushed me despite my cries to the contrary.⁸ I confess that I am much indebted to you for your devotion to me and for your expressions of kindness, and even without these I could not help loving such an open and friendly spirit. For virtue bears within itself a most efficacious love potion. Karel will tell you the rest.

Farewell.

Freiburg, 16 April 1531

* * * * *

3 The 'beggar tyrants' (Greek in the text) were mendicant friars (Dominicans, Franciscans, Carmelites, and others). Erasmus regularly referred to mendicants as 'well-to-do beggars' (see CWE 39 468–98) and as 'potbellies' (*ventres*), ie men who 'under the pretext of religion' serve the cause of 'their own bellies' (see Ep 1980 n1). From the ranks of the mendicants had emerged many of Erasmus' most vehement theological critics, Franciscans (especially Frans Titelmans at Louvain) having recently become the most troublesome (see Ep 2275). Erasmus' recent letters include frequent references to the 'tyranny of the monks' in Brabant, 'who sometimes burn their sacrificial victims.' See Ep 2249:31–2 with n8.

4 See Ep 2100 introduction.

5 See Ep 2463 n3.

6 Ie officials in the Netherlands charged with enforcing the emperor's edicts against heresy, and in some cases claiming to exercise papal authority as well; see James D. Tracy *Holland under Habsburg Rule, 1506–1566: The Formation of a Body Politic* (Berkeley: University of California Press 1990) 152–60.

7 Ie Christians will make war on Christians

8 Erasmus was fond of the image of gladiatorial combat in describing his conflicts with theological adversaries; see Epp 1934 n1, 1943 n4.

2486 / To Nikolaus Winmann   Freiburg, 16 April 1531

First published in the *Epistolae floridae*, this is Erasmus' answer to Ep 2439.

ERASMUS OF ROTTERDAM TO NIKOLAUS WINMANN, GREETING
From your letter I seem to have perceived clearly a man of truly Christian
spirit, free of all pretence, and especially one who wishes me well. But I suspect that you are the one whom some friends of mine, in jest, kept from meeting me and afterwards granted access, instigating someone to dress up in   5
my habit and play the part of Erasmus. It was Konrad Brunner, if by chance
you know the name.[1] In general, I am not usually difficult in admitting those
who want to greet me, except that of late I have found that some come not
to greet me, but to make fun of me or to set a trap for me. For there are some
untrustworthy people who, hiding under the name of the gospel and defy-   10
ing all laws, human and divine, are persuaded that whatever pleases them
is holy. And among them some are so stupid that they think they are being
treated badly when they are receiving the most help. They remind me of
those flies that the Hebrew sage mentioned, which, dying in ointment, corrupt its sweetness;[2] and while Christ commands us to bless those who curse   15
us,[3] these people, against whom it is not worth fighting, never cease to attack
with reproaches the one who deserves well of them. I acknowledge my poverty, but nonetheless, after the example of the widow in the gospel, I bring
my two mites to the temple of the Lord.[4] He who alone looks into our hearts
will repay us.[5] There are many who bark from both sides, but I oppose to   20
them many learned and great men who befriend me wholeheartedly, any of
whom I value more than three hundred Vulturiuses or Bucephaluses.[6] Would
that these men so manage their affairs that with the approval of leading citizens the Christian world will be transformed into a better condition than it
has been in thus far. The first of those mentioned has so changed direction   25

* * * * *

2486
1 Erasmus is clearly mistaken in associating Winmann's visit (of uncertain date)
  to him in Basel with a trick played by Konrad Brunner on what must have been
  an earlier occasion; see Ep 2439 n4.
2 Eccl 10:1
3 Luke 6:28
4 Luke 21:2
5 Ps 7:9
6 Vulturius is Gerard Geldenhouwer (Ep 2238 n1); Bucephalus (the name of
  Alexander the Great's horse) is Erasmus' newly coined nickname for Martin
  Bucer (Ep 1901).

that he seems to me to have been inspired by an evil spirit. As for the book
of Bucephalus (for he was the author under the false title of 'preachers'),[7] I
have never read anything more stupid. He challenged me to speak, if I could,
against Oecolampadius, and against Capito,[8] as if I would lack things to say
if I permitted myself to play the fool and put into writing whatever is gener-   30
ally bandied about. He tells many such shamelessly false stories there that
even the Evangelicals themselves laugh.

I am aware that many people are, as you write, annoyed with me because of my two books, but I do not yet sense that others have been won over.
X, who I was previously convinced was a friend, rages furiously.[9] In Paris a   35
huge volume is being printed against me under the name of the prince of
Carpi, who died recently, but under his name certain Franciscans and theologians will pour out their venom.[10] Moreover, Béda has recovered his confidence and is totally engrossed in the affair.[11] These are the consolations of my
old age, which, however, I shall never admit is miserable as long as Christ   40
is propitious to me. You have a treasure which you did not dare to ask for,

* * * * *

7 The *Epistola apologetica*, written by Bucer but published in the name of all the
  Strasbourg preachers (Ep 2312 n2).
8 Johannes Oecolampadius (Ep 224:30n) was leader of the Reformation at Basel;
  Wolfgang Capito (Ep 459) was Bucer's fellow reformer in Strasbourg.
9 Presumably Girolamo Aleandro; cf Ep 2482 n4.
10 For the history of Erasmus' controversy with Alberto Pio, prince of Carpi, see
  Epp 1634 and 1987, and see also the introduction to CWE 84. Pio's final work
  against Erasmus, *Tres et viginti libri in locos lucubrationum Erasmi*, was published by Josse Bade at Paris on 9 March 1531, two months after Pio's death on
  7 January. Despite Pio's being dead, Erasmus responded with the vituperative
  Apologia adversus rhapsodias Alberti Pii (cf Ep 2505:50). Erasmus was convinced,
  correctly in the case of Girolamo Aleandro (Ep 2482 n4), that Pio had been in
  league with his other enemies, including the Franciscans; see Ep 2441:66–72.
11 For Noël Béda, syndic of the faculty of theology at Paris and Erasmus' most
  implacable foe in France, see Ep 2082 n56, and for the history of his controversy
  with Erasmus see the introduction to CWE 82. Erasmus suspected that Pio's first
  book against him had been published at Paris 'to please Béda and his like' (Ep
  2329:91–3), and he was now confident of Bèda's involvement in the publication of the second book. Béda's silence since the publication of his *Adversus
  clandestinos Lutheranos* in 1529 had deceived Erasmus into believing that the
  conflict with the Paris syndic and the faculty was behind him (Epp 2371:5–6,
  2375:84–5). The reference to Béda's having 'recovered his confidence' indicates
  that Erasmus had concluded otherwise even before Béda and his colleagues
  inaugurated the last phase of the conflict by publishing (July 1531) the formal
  censure of 175 propositions drawn from Erasmus' works that they had already
  prepared in 1527; see Ep 2552:20.

a letter of just about the right length, and that both an autograph and an original, together with erasures and mistakes. From now on Winmann will be inscribed in the catalogue of my friends. Farewell.

Freiburg im Breisgau, 16 April 1531   45

2487 / To Erasmus Schets   Freiburg, 18 April [1531]

> First published by Allen on the basis of the autograph in the British Library (MS Add 38512 folio 52), this is apparently Erasmus' answer to a letter no longer extant. Schets replied with Ep 2494, which confirms the year-date. For Schets, the Antwerp banker who managed the collection of Erasmus' income from his livings in England and the Netherlands, see Epp 1541, 1931.

Cordial greetings. I have to inform you that the letter which you say you sent here in the month of December was not delivered to me, and no letter from Jan de Hondt or from Barbier or from Molendino was brought to me.[1] Many conjectures lead me to suspect that this packet of letters was intercepted by the Evangelicals, for under that name villainous scoundrels are hidden. 5
Without doubt they are on the lookout for my letters.[2]

I received one letter from you in which you write that the pension for six months was delivered by Jan de Hondt.[3]

You should know that Barbier owes me a pension payment for six months that he purloined four years ago when he was in Rome.[4] He prom- 10
ised that he would pay it. And I suspect this is what he sent now.

But in addition to that, instalments for three semesters are owed, and on the next feast day of John the Baptist[5] four will be owed. The first was owed from the feast of St John of the year 1529 up to the feast of the Purification.[6]
The second from the feast of the Purification until the feast of St John 1530. 15
The third from the feast of John to the feast of the Purification of the year 1531. The fourth will be due on the next feast of John of the same year.

* * * * *

2487
1 Schets mentions no letter from De Hondt in Ep 2494, and no such letter exists. The letters from Pierre Barbier and Johannes de Molendino are Epp 2404, 2407. The delay in delivery is mentioned again in Epp 2488:3–6, 2490:8–10, 2494:4–5. Ep 2501:1–5 indicates that the letters reached Erasmus in June.
2 Cf Epp 2379:455–6, 2490:9–10, 2494:7–8.
3 Ep 2364
4 The incident referred to took place in the summer of 1524, ie more than six years earlier; see Ep 2404 n8.
5 24 June
6 2 February

I don't know whether the English trust Luis.[7] I recommended him several times and ordered that money be entrusted only to him. The archbishop is extremely old now, and there are very many in his household who think   20
that whatever is given to others is taken away from them.[8] They all protest vigorously against his wish to give money away.

I wrote recently via a certain Grynaeus, a learned man, trying, if possible, to redeem my English pensions. At Easter fifty pounds sterling were owed me. If in addition to paying that sum they would be willing to pay in   25
cash for the next three years, I will not ask anything more of them.[9] I expect an answer from Grynaeus, for he has a wife in Basel. Farewell.

Freiburg, 18 April

To the honourable gentleman Erasmus Schets. In Antwerp

2488 / To Erasmus Schets   Freiburg, 20 April 1531

First published by Allen on the basis of the autograph in the British Library (MS Add 38512 folio 54), this letter was written to accompany one (not extant) to Pierre Barbier, to whom Erasmus had earlier not felt well enough to write (line 2).

Cordial greetings. When my servant Quirinus was here,[1] I was so overwhelmed with cares and the state of my health that I didn't feel like writing.

* * * * *

7 Luis de Castro, Schet's agent in London; see Epp 2403 n4, 2413:7–14, 2494:14–16.
8 Born c 1456, William Warham, archbishop of Canterbury, to whom Erasmus owed his English livings, was in his mid-seventies. For Erasmus' worries about Warham's age and health see Epp 2459:43, 2488:6–8, 2490:5–6. Erasmus' fear that after Warham's death, which finally came in August 1532, his English pensions would cease, ultimately proved groundless. Warham's successor as archbishop of Canterbury, Thomas Cranmer, chose to continue payment (see Allen Epp 2815, 2879:30–5).
9 On 18 March 1531 Simon Grynaeus, professor Greek at Basel (Epp 1657, 2433), departed for England in the company of the Basel publisher Johann Bebel, armed with letters of introduction from Erasmus (Epp 2459–60), and entrusted with the task of attempting to secure the redemption of Erasmus' English pensions; see Epp 2488:8–9, 2494:16–18, 2496:18–22. By early June they were on their way home (Epp 2499:5–10, 2502:1–9), and by mid-July they had arrived (Ep 2512:6–7).

2488
1 Erasmus' servant-messenger Quirinus Talesius (Ep 1966) had just this month left Erasmus' service to return to the Netherlands, where in May 1532 he was appointed pensionary of his native town of Haarlem; see Ep 2389:12–23.

Now I am sending a letter to Pierre Barbier to find out by what right and by
what insolence they hold on to my money.[2] If they respond, be very careful
in entrusting the letter to anyone. If it reaches Hieronymus Froben, it will   5
be in safe hands.[3] I am aware that the archbishop of Canterbury was at the
point of death three times this year, and he is in his eighties.[4] If he dies, the
English will not care in the least. I am waiting for an answer from Bebel and
Simon, who I think were at your house.[5] It is my desire that you be in the best
of health, dearest Schets. For a long time I have been sick of Germany, but I   10
do not see a nest.[6]

    Freiburg, 20 April 1531
    Yours, Erasmus of Rotterdam
    To the illustrious Erasmus Schets, merchant. In Antwerp

2489 / From Bonifacius Amerbach   [Basel, April 1531]

This letter (= AK Ep 1525, where it is dated 'before 21 April 1531') was first
published by Allen. The autograph rough draft is in the Öffentliche Bibliothek
of the University of Basel (MS C VIa 54 11). Erasmus' reply is Ep 2490. Allen assigned the approximate date because the letter appears to have been written on
the receipt by Bonifacius of Alciati's letter to him of 12 March 1531 (AK Ep 1508).

Cordial greetings. I returned to Basel at the right moment, for on the next
day the bookseller from Lyon departed,[1] to whom I confided our letters to
Alciati,[2] and I do not doubt that with his usual integrity he will fulfil his
promise to deliver them. The previous letter,[3] which I sent off, you may be
sure, on the first of November, went astray through the perfidy of messengers,   5

* * * * *

2 'They' includes Molendino with Barbier; cf Ep 2487:3.
3 Ie if it is sent via Froben in Basel it will be forwarded safely to Erasmus in
    Freiburg
4 Warham was in his mid-seventies; see Ep 2487 n8.
5 See Ep 2487 n9.
6 Ie I do not see an alternative place where I can settle conveniently and safely

    2489
1 Michel Parmentier (see AK Ep 1524:9–10), bookseller and publisher at the Ecu
    de Bâle in Lyon, a major facility for the sale and distribution of Basel publi-
    cations in France. He frequently carried letters between scholars in Basel and
    those in France.
2 Erasmus' Ep 2468 and Bonifacius' AK Ep 1523
3 Not extant, probably written in response to Ep 2394

as Alciati complains to me in his last letter, delivered to me yesterday.[4] He claims that the letters of Erasmus are a treasure for him and earnestly asks me to obtain a copy of it, in which you, I am certain, in your kindness, will oblige him, provided that the original of the letter to him still exists.[5]

I would like to know more about the state of your health. I hope our   10
friend Episcopius will report that you are well.[6] Nothing could be more desirable to us than this news, nothing equally gratifying. Indeed, acts of thanksgiving for it would be owed. I offer you my meagre efforts, whatever their worth, dear Erasmus – extremely small, if you assess them carefully, but very great if you consider my devotion and love towards you. If you will   15
always make use of them, as I wish you to, you will do me a great kindness, for I consider it a great gift to have done you a good service. Farewell.

2490 / To Bonifacius Amerbach   Freiburg, 21 April 1531

This letter (= AK Ep 1526) was first published in the *Epistolae familiares*. Allen based his text on the autograph in the Öffentliche Bibliothek of the University of Basel (MS AN III 15 29).

Cordial greetings. I do not quite remember the letter recently sent to Alciati;[1] I will look into it, however. Today my slight fever lessened a bit, but I don't expect to get better unless this very disagreeable weather changes. My servant Mercury in Augsburg has not yet returned [2]

They write from England that the archbishop of Canterbury has been   5
repeatedly at the point of death. He is in his eighties. They owe me three hundred gold florins in arrears; for each year they owe me two hundred. If anything happens, the English won't give me a pittance.[3] The man in Tournai

* * * * *

4 AK Ep 1508:15–23
5 See Ep 2490:1–2.
6 Nicolaus Episcopius (Ep 2233A n4)

2490
1 Ie the letter, now lost, sent in November 1530 but not delivered. Through Bonifacius Alciati had requested a copy of it; see Ep 2489:4–9.
2 Doubtless Polyphemus (Felix Rex), for whose recent wanderings see Ep 2334 n1.
3 Archbishop Warham was in his seventies. Erasmus had long been worried that Warham's death would disrupt the payment of his English pensions; see Ep 2487 nn8–9.

responsible for the payment of my pension wrote to me via Schets, but the
Evangelicals intercepted the letter.⁴   10
    If the weather changes, perhaps I will set out for Neuenburg.⁵ There I
will make my will.⁶ You even send me thanks? How you never change! I consider you a unique friend, dear Bonifacius, a treasure compared to which a
man can have nothing more precious. Farewell. Abundant greetings to your
wife and Basilius.⁷   15
    Freiburg, 21 April 1531
    To the illustrious Master Bonifacius Amerbach. In Basel

2491 / From Erasmus Schets   Antwerp, 2 May 1531

This letter was first published by Allen, on the basis of the autograph in the
Öffentliche Bibliothek of the University of Basel (MS Scheti epistolae 25).

Cordial greetings. I wrote you a letter,¹ dear Erasmus, at the end of the
Frankfurt fair, which I asked to be given to Froben right away. I think you
will have received it. I have nothing to write at the moment except that I send
enclosed with this some letters for Karel Uutenhove, who I have learned is
with you. But I can hardly believe that he has stayed there until now. For he   5
is being summoned to hurry home; his mother has died. He will learn of it in
these letters, if he is still with you when they arrive.²

* * * * *

4 Ep 2404, from Pierre Barbier; see Ep 2487:1–6 with n1.
5 Neuenburg am Rhein, about halfway between Basel and Freiburg, was the
  home of Bonifacius' father-in-law Leonhard Fuchs, who was also burgomaster.
6 Erasmus made his first will in 1527 (CWE 12 538–50). In 1530 he decided to make
  a new one, procuring from King Ferdinand and Emperor Charles documents
  aimed at clearing away any legal impediments there might be to his doing so
  (Epp 2417–18). His original intention was that Udalricus Zasius should draw
  up the will (Ep 2320:12–13), but the reference here to making his will during a
  visit to Neuenburg indicates that the task was to be entrusted to someone else,
  perhaps Bonifacius himself. For reasons unknown, Erasmus did not carry out
  his intention at this time. Not until 1536, shortly before his death, did he make
  the will that was his last (Allen XI 362–5).
7 Bonifacius' wife was Martha Fuchs; Basilius Amerbach was his older brother.

2491
1 Not extant
2 Uutenhove had left Basel to return to the Netherlands on about 18 April (Ep
  2483 n1); by 16 May he had visited Schets in Antwerp (Ep 2494:2–3).

I have nothing new to tell you. In England they have changed again
what had long ago been determined by the authority of Parliament.[3] For once
again the king is eager for the divorce that he has laid claim to for a long   10
time.[4]

They say that the truce between kind Ferdinand and the Turks is ended.[5]
The emperor has obtained from the assemblies of these provinces their assent
for large sums of money.[6] Queen Mary of Hungary will be the ruler and governor of our provinces,[7] and many express and proclaim her praises because   15
of her great virtue and wisdom worthy of a man. The emperor announced
his opinion on the dispute between the pope and the duke of Ferrara. The
duke will retain all the territories claimed by the pope for himself, giving to
the pope the sum of one hundred thousand ducats and an annual tribute of
seven thousand.[8] The French are still at peace with us.[9] The expense of all   20
commodities is reducing us to dire straits; it is by now so universal that it is
making many poor people bemoan their fate.

May God the bestower of all things reward you with his kindness.
Farewell, most beloved Master Erasmus.

From Antwerp, 2 May 1531   25

Your Erasmus Schets

† To the illustrious and most learned Master Erasmus of Rotterdam,
friend and foremost patron. At Freiburg

2492 / From Julius Pflug   Leipzig, 12 May 1531

For Julius Pflug, jurist in the service of Duke George of Saxony, see Ep 2395.
This letter, first published in the *Epistolae floridae*, is Pflug's answer to Ep 2451.
Erasmus' reply to this letter is Ep 2522.

* * * * *

3 This may be a reference to the king's demand (January 1531), granted reluc-
    tantly and with serious reservations, to be acknowledged as supreme head of
    the church in England; see J.J. Scarisbrick, *Henry VIII* (Berkeley and Los Angeles
    1968) 275–6.
4 See Epp 1932 n11, 2211 n11, 2413 n15.
5 The one-year truce between Ferdinand and John Zápolyai signed in December
    1530 was extended for a further year in May 1531; cf Ep 2384 n10.
6 Ie from the estates of the provinces in the Netherlands
7 Mary of Austria, queen of Hungary (Ep 2100), was regent for Charles v in the
    Netherlands from 1531 until his abdication in 1555.
8 Cf Ep 2480:6–10.
9 Since the Peace of Cambrai (1529), which brought a pause in the warfare be-
    tween Charles v and Francis I that lasted until 1536

JULIUS PFLUG TO ERASMUS OF ROTTERDAM, GREETING

I hold to be true what the ancient writers affirmed with great authority, that all virtues are so joined together among themselves that they form one common bond. Indeed you, who are (in my judgment) by far the prince of all men of learning, surpass all others also in your humanity, which, even if it 5 was not unknown to me previously, nevertheless appeared to me somehow with greater clarity from the letter I recently received. If I were confident that I could proclaim this humanity as reality and my duty demand, I would be presumptuous. How you have bound me to you by this very benevolence of yours I prefer to declare by deeds rather than words. 10

If I had achieved what I attempted in the business you know of, namely, that you might have the leisure appropriate to your age and dignity, I would be overcome with incredible pleasure.[1] But however things turn out, I shall console myself by the consciousness of my own good will and by the kindness with which you deem my efforts valid and equitable. I am most grateful 15 that you sent me your book,[2] which I welcome, as I should, as a gift coming from such a great man. And yet I am sorry that this affair is brought out into the open by I know not whom, and that your most respectable old age is called away from peaceful studies to such a conflict. I for my part would wish that as you have deserved well (and you have deserved exceptionally 20 well) of the human race, so should you reap from the good offices of grateful people the fruit that you can rightfully reclaim. But what can one do? These times, inimical to calm and virtue, are such that one can more quickly find someone who stirs up trouble than one who sincerely gives support.

There are nevertheless many – good, outstanding men – who recognize 25 your services and think that a true and just recompense should be awarded to your virtue. Since they both respect and love you to an extraordinary degree, you could find peace of mind in their friendship and cheerfully disregard the gossip for the envious. All good people of the present time very much wish that you would do this, and Christendom itself,[3] if it could 30

* * * * *

2492
1 Clearly a reference to Pflug's effort, on behalf of Duke George of Saxony, to mediate a settlement of the prolonged feud between Erasmus and Heinrich Eppendorf (see Epp 1934 introduction, 2450–1). At this stage, it would still not have been evident that Pflug's effort had been successful and that Eppendorf would not renew his attacks on Erasmus.
2 Presumably the *Admonitio adversus mendacium*; see Ep 2395 n4.
3 Pflug uses the term *Respublica Christiana*, literally 'Christian commonwealth.' In the remainder of the letter he shortens it four times to *Respublica* without changing the meaning.

speak, would insist on it. As a matter of fact, if ever it did in the past, now surely Christendom desires your cooperation. To do this you must bring a quiet mind, free of all perturbation, so that wherever the public good calls, there you will devote your energies with all your heart. You see how far things have sunk. Without question it is to be feared that unless wise and 35 good men arise to provide a remedy for languishing Christendom, it will be completely overturned.

The eyes of all those who look for peace are turned to you alone. Immortal God has accorded to you alone among all men both the authority and the power to bring remedy to these evils, and to persuade our princes 40 that controversy can be removed from religion, or that if, God himself approving, certain prescriptions of the church can be changed, they may be made less severe, and that in this way the princes may be persuaded that it is proper to moderate human laws and institutions in these stormy times for the church. If this could be done by you, perhaps some good man from the 45 other side who is not averse to Christian concord, like Melanchthon, could be moved to intervene and persuade his followers to agree to many things that in themselves are not acceptable but must be tolerated in the circumstances.[4] Even Paul ceded to such contingencies when he made concession to certain rites contrary to what Christian liberty demanded.[5] If both sides are 50 persuaded, Christendom, which is now thrown into confusion, would be reestablished in a short time, with each side diminishing its ardour.

Therefore, since you see that the time has come when your devotion to Christendom must stand out and shine forth in establishing peace, bring it to pass, I pray you, that as you rouse us to piety and study, you may safeguard 55 our peace, without which they cannot be cultivated.[6]

* * * * *

4 Pflug's hopes in Philippus Melanchthon were destined to be disappointed. Melanchthon would indeed be the chief representative of Saxony in the many attempts in the 1530s and 1540s to achieve a negotiated modus vivendi between Lutherans and Catholics in the Empire. Although he was willing to concede much in the area of external ceremonies and institutional arrangements (too much, in the opinion of some of his fellow Lutherans, though not Luther himself; not nearly enough, in the opinion of Catholic conservatives), Melanchthon was stubbornly unyielding in matters of doctrine, and his *De officio principum* (1539) was an unsparing denunciation of the so-called Erasmian *via media*, of which Julius Pflug was a leading champion. See James M. Estes *Peace, Order, and the Glory of God: Secular Authority and the Church in the Thought of Luther and Melanchthon, 1518–1559* (Leiden 2005), chapter 4.
5 Rom 14–15, 1 Cor 8
6 Erasmus would in 1533 respond to this appeal (and others like it) by publishing *De sarcienda ecclesiae concordia* (Ep 2852).

And I have written this not to incite your enthusiasm (for you are sufficiently motivated of your own accord for this cause and for every meritorious enterprise), but because I was drawn to this purpose by love of country
and religion.   60

For the rest, even though you have no need of a recommendation to my
prince (since he favours no one more than you) I will do as you ask, which
will procure me a twofold benefit: one, that I will gratify you, a man more
eminent than I; the other, since my prince knows that I am an admirer of
yours, that I shall enjoy increased favour with him, seeing that he wishes all   65
his followers to have ties with you. I shall pursue the method of cultivating
friendship that you prescribe, and shall see to it that you will not be without
my faithful correspondence.

I will welcome Andreas von Könneritz as you recommend,[7] so that
he will recognize from that gesture that my former love for him has greatly   70
increased.

Farewell. Leipzig, 12 May 1531

2493 / To Duke George of Saxony   Freiburg, 15 May 1531

This is the preface to the posthumous edition of Willibald Pirckheimer's trans-
lation of the *Orations* of St Gregory of Nazianzus, prepared by Erasmus and
Pirckheimer's son-in-law Hans Straub: *D. Gregorii Nazianzeni Orationes* xxx
(Basel: Froben, September 1531). The letter was simultaneously included in the
Epistolae floridae.

ERASMUS OF ROTTERDAM TO THE MOST ILLUSTRIOUS
PRINCE AND LORD, HIS HIGHNESS GEORGE, DUKE OF SAXONY,
LANDGRAVE OF THURINGIA, MARGRAVE OF MEISSEN, GREETING
If one examines rightly the condition of mortals and the lot of human life,
George, glory of Christian princes, he will not judge that the death of Willibald   5
Pirckheimer is greatly to be mourned,[1] since he was granted as much hap-
piness as can fall to the lot of any man. For if we take into account external
circumstances, he was of patrician birth, born and brought up in Nürnberg,
one of the most celebrated and opulent cities of Germany; he had an income
that was not only respectable but splendid; and he had such authority, by   10

* * * * *

7 See Ep 2451:72–7.

2493
1 Pirckheimer (Ep 318) died on 22 December 1530.

virtue of both his popularity and his influence with the greatest monarchs of the world, especially the emperor Maximilian, that he was second to none. He obtained the same honour with Charles, a greater emperor even than Maximilian himself. To both of these he served as a no less prudent than trustworthy councillor. A man both of upright judgment and of a free and resolute mind, whether in saying what he thought or finishing what he had begun, he also gave numerous outstanding proofs of his loyalty, both in war and in peace, shunning no danger for the safety of his fellow citizens.[2] His marriage was neither unhappy nor sterile; he left one female heir, as I hear.[3]

He lived a normal span of life, sixty years, if I am not mistaken, or more.[4] Nor was he lacking in outstanding physical endowments until old age, which does not fail to impair everything, brought gout and the stone. It pleased God to purge his servant with this fire so that the gold would be absolutely pure and tested. Nevertheless, his physical sufferings never exerted such power over him that they took his mind away from serving the interests of the commonwealth, or from promoting liberal studies. He made up with the pen for the diminution of his physical strength. It is true that he rarely attended the meetings of the city council, but his home, frequented by the leading citizens, was a kind of city council, and by writings he fulfilled his role as councilman or counsellor more amply and more fully than others did by their tongue or their feet.[5] For what did he write that does not concern the promotion of the common good or the advancement of studies or the interests of religion?

Moreover, I think it was also a rare blessing that neither the splendour of his fortune nor the fame of his learning nor his liberty of spirit aroused much envy towards him. There were some who tried to shed some darkness

* * * * *

2 Because Nürnberg was a free imperial city, it owed direct loyalty to the emperor and assiduously cultivated good relations with whomever held the office. So Pirckheimer's status as 'imperial councillor' was of a piece with his status as a public servant in Nürnberg (see n5 below).
3 Pirckheimer's only son had died in childbirth, along with his mother, in 1504. He had five daughters, three of whom became nuns and two of whom married prominent citizens of Nürnberg. Erasmus is probably thinking of Barbara, the wife of Hans Straub (see introduction).
4 Born on 5 December 1470, Pirckheimer died a little over two weeks after his sixtieth birthday.
5 Long a member of the Nürnberg city council, Pirckheimer's chief political contribution to the city was as a skilful diplomat, attending meetings of the imperial diet and engaging in direct negotiations with representatives of the cities and principalities of Southern Germany, as well as Austria and Switzerland.

over his name, but the brilliance and radiance, so to speak, of his integrity immediately dispelled the smoke of the calumniators, and the affair came to an entirely different conclusion. For those who spread the smoke were impregnated with their own smoke and the virtue of Willibald shone out more brightly.[6]

Finally death fell to his lot; a more desirable one could hardly be hoped for. He did not fall victim to a contagion or suffer great torment. Only his body became enfeebled; the vigour of his mind remained intact until his last breath. There was a lack of what doctors call the radical humour.[7] Thus he did not so much seem to die as to peacefully fall asleep. The last conversations he had with learned friends breathed nothing else than a marvellous loyalty towards his country, an ardent love of the Christian religion, and a conscientious solicitude for public literary studies. When a certain person paid him a visit at his bedside, he asked him insistently to procure a reliable messenger as soon as possible who would hasten to Freiburg to bring something to Zasius and Erasmus. But while the visitor was diligently seeking someone to set out for earthly Freiburg, he flew off to the heavenly Jerusalem. The last audible words of the dying man were these: 'Would God that after my death all goes well for the country, and that the church be at peace.' Undoubtedly the rest of his words, which death, seizing his tongue, made obscure to our ears but not to God's, were instinct with the same piety.

As to those who think that the death of such a man should be mourned, what do they do but lament that he was born a man? Perhaps someone would more justly shed tears over the public loss to studies because a premature death prevented him from fully completing two exceptional tasks on which he had been working for a long time, namely, the restoration of the *Cosmography* of Ptolemy,[8] which had been corrupted both by the Greeks

* * * * *

6 Doubtless a reference to Pirckheimer's denunciation as a Lutheran by Johann Eck and the consequent insertion of his name into the bull *Exsurge Domine* (1520), which threatened Luther and his followers with excommunication. Eck soon retracted his charges, but Pirckheimer's name had in the meantime been included among those condemned along with Luther in the bull of excommunication *Decet pontificem Romanum* (January 1521). Absolution from the charge of heresy was reserved to the Holy See, and it took pressure from the imperial court to secure it for Pirckheimer (August 1531). See Ep 1182 n2.

7 Erasmus means 'the radical moisture,' which in Greek medicine was the distillate of the four humours (blood, phlegm, yellow bile, and black bile), which circulated in the bloodstream, nourished the body, and sustained life.

8 Pirckheimer published his Latin translation of the *Cosmography*, also known as the *Geography*, in 1525.

and the Latins, and providing us with that eminent herald of Christian philosophy, Gregory of Nazianzus, in Latin translation, in such a way that no   65
one would miss the founts of the Greek language.[9] But when was there a
learned or pious man, born for the public good, who has not left some regrets
to posterity? For since such men never cease labouring at some important
project, and all the more intensely as they approach their final day, it is not
possible that death, whenever it comes, will not interrupt some outstanding   70
enterprise; and since they never cease deserving well of the human race, it is
beyond question that they will come to the end of their life before putting an
end to their projects. I do not say this, most illustrious prince, as if what he
left lacks finish, but that the reader might perhaps notice the absence of the
final touch of so great a master.   75

In Gregory of Nazianzus piety contends virtually on the same level
with eloquence. But he loves subtleties of expression, which, because most
of them are based on individual words, are very difficult to translate into
Latin. The whole sentence, however, resembles somewhat the structure of
Isocrates.[10] Add to this that concerning divine matters, which can scarcely   80
be explained in any human words, he freely and frequently resorts to philosophy. His brother Basil[11] combines piety, learning, intellectual penetration
where it is necessary, clarity, charm, and whatever other virtue one can expect in a Christian orator in a smooth and unaffected flow of language. John
Chrysostom,[12] as much in letters as in the profession of a more perfect life   85
the companion and, so to speak, an Achates of Basil,[13] adapted almost everything he wrote to the understanding of the people; he is more expansive

* * * * *

9 Gregory (330–90), bishop of Nazianzus and (later) of Constantinople, was the
   most rhetorically accomplished of the church Fathers. A few of Pirckheimer's
   translations had already been published, in 1521 and 1528.
10 Isocrates (436–338 BC) one of the most renowned and influential of the ancient
   Greek rhetoricians. His sentence structure was noted for its complexity.
11 St Basil the Great (329/30–379), bishop of Caesarea, lifelong friend of Gregory
   of Nazianzus but not literally his brother (who was Gregory bishop of Nyssa);
   cf Ep 2611:47–8.
12 St John Chrysostom (c 349–407), archbishop of Constantinople, was known as
   an eloquent preacher; cf Ep 2359.
13 Achates was the faithful companion of Aeneas in Virgil's *Aeneid*, his name proverbial for intimate companion. John Chrysostom and Basil the Great were
   not exact contemporaries and did not in fact know one another but, especially in the tradition of the eastern church, the two are regarded figuratively as
   companions in their literary gifts, their theological views, and their piety. Cf
   Ep 2611:47–9.

and simple in style than Basil, and preferred to digress on commonplaces
rather than dwell on very difficult questions. One age produced these three
great men among the Greeks, equal in piety, and not unequal in learning,   90
but dissimilar in the character of their style. If you wish to compare them
with our writers, Chrysostom is not unlike Augustine, nor is Gregory unlike
Ambrose, who, if he had written in Greek, would present much difficulty
to a translator. I have not yet found out whom I should compare to Basil,
unless one were to join Jerome's knowledge of Scripture with the felicitous   95
fluency of Lactantius.[14] In any case, the subtlety of expression, the sublimity
of subject matter, and the rather obscure allusions have certainly deterred me
from translating Gregory. This task our Willibald took upon himself with an
admirable pious ardour, and he died executing it.

This work, most illustrious prince, than whom there is scarcely another   100
more attached to piety, he destined for you while he was alive, and you in
your singular humanity will accept it with all the more gracious favour, since
dying he left it as a last remembrance of himself. Late-born children usually
are more welcome because of the very fact that there is no hope of having
more. Similarly, since his deathbed wish, trusting in your singular humanity,   105
was that this last offspring, so to speak, be commended to your protection,
I do not doubt that you also will be true to yourself in respecting his wish.
If by your favour you recommend to all those who are fond of learning the
books that Willibald has left to us, you will at the same time lend lustre to the
memory of a friend and give no little stimulus to everyone in the attainment   110
of piety. Moreover, those who take piety to heart will not take offence that,
following the ancient Fathers of the church, he does not shrink from using
certain words peculiar to our religion now and then, and that he prefers to
speak Christian rather than Roman; besides, I do not see why words used
five hundred years ago by Roman writers, and not without the example of   115
the Greeks, should not be considered Roman.[15]

Farewell. From the famous University of Freiburg,[16] 15 May 1531

* * * * *

14 Lactantius (c 240–c 320) was an early Christian author who had been trained
as a rhetorician. He was generally deemed a poor theologian, but Renaissance
authors prized him for his Ciceronian eloquence.
15 Clearly a swipe at the Italians whom Erasmus satirized in the *Ciceronianus*; see
Ep 1948 introduction.
16 Although he had been cordially received by the university in Freiburg and
maintained close relations with its faculty, Erasmus did not associate himself
formally with it until August 1533, when he matriculated as 'theologiae professor.' His principal motive appears to have been to secure the professorial

2494 / From Erasmus Schets   Antwerp, 16 May 1531

First published by Allen on the basis of the original manuscript in the Öffentliche
Bibliothek of the University of Basel (MS Scheti epistolae 26), this is Schets' answer to Ep 2487.

†

Around the beginning of this month, I wrote to you,[1] dear Master Erasmus,
a little after I received your letter,[2] brought by your servants Quirinus and
Uutenhove.[3]

I regret that the letter I sent you in the month of December,[4] together
with letters of Molendino and Barbier, did not reach you.[5] I demanded of the   5
merchant of Strasbourg to whom I had entrusted this packet of letters that he
find out what became of them. It is certainly very evangelical to lay traps for
others and intercept the letters of others.[6]

I had written to you in that letter that I had received at that moment
the double pension from Master Jan de Hondt; now two will be due again.   10
After the feast of St John I will go to request them and receive them. That will
make four, and that coincides with your calculation.[7] Barbier did not pay me
anything from the pension which you say he intercepted.[8]

It is good that you have recommended Luis Castro again in England.[9]
He certainly will not fail in his duty. For when they make any payment,   15
he will be pleased to receive it and will then remit the money to me. You
seem to me to have made a not unreasonable offer through Grynaeus, if they

* * * * *

privilege of freedom from taxation. Two months later he entered the uni-
versity senate, with the proviso that no heavy work be imposed on him. See
Preserved Smith *Erasmus: A Study of His Life, Ideals and Place in History* (New
York 1923) 405.

2494
1 Ep 2491
2 Ep 2487
3 Cf Ep 2483 introduction.
4 Ep 2413
5 See Ep 2487:1–4.
6 Cf Ep 2487:4–6.
7 See Ep 2487:12–17.
8 See Ep 2487:9–11.
9 See Ep 2487:18–19.

were to accept and give you a three-year pension as a final settlement.[10] The
rest, which Tunstall and others give you, can be collected and received on
your recommendation by Luis, without expense and without inconvenienc-   20
ing anyone. I have always suspected that there is something in the close
acquaintances of the archbishop of Canterbury that works against your interests; for if they intended to do it willingly, they would not turn away from
Luis in such a way, and would provide the pension of their own will rather
than on demand.[11]   25

Pieter Gillis had some money of yours that Quirinus was not able to
obtain from him.[12] In the end, Quirinus and I devised a subterfuge: that
Quirinus could not remain here any longer, and that he would have to de-
posit this money in your name here and in Holland, and that I would pay
Quirinus, and Pieter in turn would then reimburse me as soon as possible.   30
Pieter promised to do this and Quirinus left. I will ask more openly now that
this money be paid to me, and when I have received it I will add it to the
rest that I recover, and in that way will fill your sponge until you dry it off
(whenever it pleases you).[13]

Farewell, my dearest Erasmus. From Antwerp, 16 May 1531   35
Your Erasmus Schets, in his own hand
The letters that I send you together with this were given to me by
Quirinus to deliver to you.
To the most kind and learned Master Erasmus of Rotterdam. In Freiburg

2495 / To Helius Eobanus Hessus   Freiburg, 17 May 1531

First published in the *Epistolae floridae*, this is Erasmus' reply to a letter that
is not extant in which Eobanus had evidently complained (see lines 2–5) of
Erasmus' response to a still earlier letter, also not extant. For Eobanus, humanist, renowned Latin poet, and staunch adherent of the Lutheran reformation,
see Epp 874, 2446. He was currently (1526–33) teaching in Nürnberg at the St
Aegidius Gymnasium, founded in 1526 by Philippus Melanchthon.

* * * * *

10 See Ep 2487:23–6 with n9.
11 See Ep 2487:19–22.
12 For monies entrusted to Pieter Gillis on Erasmus' behalf, and Erasmus' difficulties in securing from him sums owed, see Epp 2403:63–4 with n14, 2511:7–11,
   2512:1–2, 2527:5–8, 2530:31–9, 45–50, 2552:15–19, 2558:26–31, 2578:3–12.
13 On this frequent image in the correspondence between Erasmus and Schets (eg
   Ep 2552:15), cf Ep 2370 n1.

ERASMUS OF ROTTERDAM TO EOBANUS HESSUS

Your earlier letter, most learned Eobanus, although it was not as toothless
as you would have me believe, I read through rather calmly, because I could
easily detect that it had been written at the prompting of someone else rather
than from your own head. Likewise I answered it with some restraint, and   5
I would not have answered it at all except that I would have been charged
with libel against the city and the magistracy, a weapon that certain persons
alleging adherence to the gospel like to use against me all too often. As for
me, I have never renounced friendship with anyone because of divergence
of beliefs, especially with those whom a rare erudition has rendered accept-   10
able to me. Among the first of these I number you, to whom was given what
was denied to Cicero and which Filelfo arrogantly claimed for himself, the
ability to compose verse as if you had never touched prose, and prose as if
you never had any commerce with the Muses.[1] This gift of the gods you have
brought to the highest point of perfection by study and practice. Therefore,   15
how could my love for you grow cold when what carried me away in admiration increases in you day by day? I have never forgotten your visit to
Louvain.[2] I remember how you came with Sylvius Egranus,[3] not without a
little present, and how you were coldly received. The reason was that because of my unsound state of health I avoided all banquets, and also because   20
at that time pairs of greeters from Germany arrived almost every other day,
none of whom wished to leave unless loaded down with letters. Already in
those days they seemed to be preparing this drama, which I have always
shunned; in whatever way it began and has progressed, I pray that a deus ex
machina will turn it into to a happy ending.   25

Anselmus Ephorinus, a man of exceptional learning and equal moral
integrity, whom you recommended, was a most pleasant boarder, but one
whose company I will not be able to enjoy much longer. At the beginning
of autumn he will set out for Italy.[4] I acknowledge that what you say is very
true: 'If we were to give a complete evaluation of Thraso, he is not worth   30
two farthings.'[5] Nevertheless, Hercules never met up with a more stubborn

* * * * *

2495
1 Cf Ep 2446:115–17.
2 In October 1518; see Ep 870 introduction.
3 Egranus (Ep 1377) from Bohemia, currently a pastor at Chemnitz in Saxony,
  was an ardent admirer of Erasmus. There is no other evidence that he accompanied Eobanus to Louvain in 1518, so Erasmus' memory may be faulty here.
4 See Ep 2539 introduction.
5 'Thraso' (the braggart soldier in Terence's *Eunuchus*) is one of Erasmus' favourite names for Heinrich Eppendorf (Ep 2492 n1). Cf the following note.

monster. I have stomached everything in order that he would not achieve
through me what he seeks to obtain. He feeds on lies as a chameleon feeds
on air, and nothing is sweeter to him than little triumphs obtained by trickery. You would marvel if you knew the whole story. But I am determined to   35
ignore the swaggering soldier from now on.[6]

I have read your *Epicedia*,[7] but none with greater heart-felt grief than the
one dedicated to Willibald.[8] Joachim seems to have more artifice than natural
endowments.[9] Not everyone is capable of everything.[10] He took a new licence
with the scazon, following I know not what author. All the ones I have read   40
always finish the verse with a cretic or a spondee.[11] You see how curious I am
about the affairs of others. But do give my fond greetings to Joachim. If only
you could conveniently come to see me here some time. In Louvain you saw
the shadow of a shadow. Your Theocritus is not yet for sale here,[12] but I shall
try to procure a copy elsewhere. Some people tell me that you have published   45
a huge volume of epigrams, in which there is frequent mention of me. I don't
know if this is true;[13] at any rate, I have so far not been able to find it.

Farewell, most learned Eobanus. At Freiburg, the day before Pentecost
1531

2496 / From Zacharias Deiotarus   London, 1 June 1531

First published as Ep 152 in Förstemann / Günther, the autograph was in the
Burscher Collection of the University Library at Leipzig (Ep 1254 introduction).

* * * * *

6 'Swaggering soldier' = *miles gloriosus*, the principal character in Plautus' comedy of that name.
7 *Illustrium ac clarorum aliquot virorum memoriae scripta epicedia* (Nürnberg: Friedrich
Peypus 1531). An epicedium is a funeral ode.
8 Willibald Pirckheimer, whose death was still recent (22 December 1530). The
epicedium for Pirckheimer begins on folio c5 verso of the *Epicedia* (see preceding
note) and continues for two more unnumbered folios.
9 Joachim Camerarius (Ep 1501) was Eobanus' colleague at the St Aegidius
Gymnasium in Nürnberg, as well as his first biographer (1553).
10 Virgil *Eclogues* 8.63, a much-quoted phrase
11 The scazon, or limping iambic trimeter, differs from the usual rhythm in the
last foot, a spondee instead of an iamb ($\cup \angle \angle -$ instead of $\cup \angle \cup \angle$), which makes
the line come to a jolting stop. In saying that the scazons he has read always
finish with a cretic ($- \cup -$) or a spondee he must mean the last five syllables of a
scazon, which has the rhythm $\angle / \cup \angle / \angle -$.
12 See Ep 2446 n16.
13 It was apparently not true; see Ep 2446 n7.

On Zacharias Deiotarus of Friesland (d 1533), a former servant-pupil of Erasmus who was now in the service of William Warham, archbishop of Canterbury, see Ep 1990 introduction.

Among so many and so great demigods, most honourable lord and master, who from all over the world write to you every day and often send gifts, this poor little man, Zacharias, wishes to be read, to be seen, and to greet you. Even if he is of very humble status in every way, of inferior learning, nonetheless he is not inferior to anyone in his love for you, nor is there any- 5
one who strives to love you to the greatest degree to whom he will yield in love. They give and take away; I have given for a long time, or rather I have surrendered myself, I have vowed myself – how shall I say it? – my whole person to you. You possess me as a slave over whom you will have the power of life and death. I labour and sweat so that my fortune will be more abun- 10
dant, by which one day you will sense an ordinary love from me, for love is commonly assessed by gifts. But in this household there are so many hands, so many lazy gluttons, so many evil beasts,[1] that they hardly leave intact the life-blood owed to you.[2] I only hope that the occasions will be given in which you can see the sentiments of my soul, my mind, and my heart towards you. 15
I hoped to see our Quirinus this year,[3] for the archbishop of Canterbury said two or three times this winter that he had the money ready for you but there was no one at hand to whom he could give it to deliver to you. Grynaeus,[4] a man of incredible learning, wanted by all means that on his initiative I should complain to you in a few words because you did not send greetings 20
to me through him in a single little word or utterance. I did not want to do this, since I judged it unseemly and unfitting that a servant should accuse his master. May your Worthiness be in good health, excellent patron.

London, 1 June 1531

Zacharias the Frisian, your faithful servant　　　　　25

* * * * *

2496
1 Cf Titus 1:12.
2 Ie the income from the livings that Warham had bestowed on him. Cf Ep 2487:19–22, where Erasmus states that many in Warham's entourage resented his gifts to outsiders.
3 Quirinus had paid a visit to Deiotarus in London in the autumn of 1529 (Ep 2237), but had now left Erasmus' service and returned to the Netherlands; see Ep 2488 n1.
4 For Grynaeus' journey to England see Ep 2487 n9.

T. Lupset died in the month of December in his mother's house from an ulcer in the lungs.[5]

To Master Erasmus of Rotterdam, my master, worthy of utmost respect and honour. In Freiburg

2497 / From Johann Löble Stuttgart, 6 June 1531

First published as Ep 153 in Förstemann / Günther, the manuscript, written in German in a secretary's hand but with an autograph signature, was in the Burscher Collection of the University Library at Leipzig (Ep 1254 introduction). The translation, by James M. Estes, attempts to preserve the stilted pomposity of Löble's German.

Johann Löble (d before 24 July 1536), whose surname clearly identifies him as a Swabian, served (1520–1) in the treasury of the duchy of Württemberg during the early years of the Hapsburg occupation of that principality (1519–34). By 1524 he had joined the Austrian Hapsburg treasury. Sometime before January 1530 he took as his second wife Ursula Adler, the widow of Jakob Villinger, who had built the house 'zum Walfisch' at Freiburg in which Erasmus had been living since moving to that city from Basel in 1529. For the somewhat confusing story of Erasmus' ultimately unsuccessful attempt to remain in that house, see Ep 2462 introduction.

Honourable, highly learned, especially dear Herr Roterodamus, [I am] at all times at your disposal with willing and friendly service. I have just recently received from you a letter in which you express the wish to remain, in return for a suitable rent, in the dwelling at Freiburg belonging to my stepson.[1] In addition, my gracious lord of Augsburg has also intervened with me on your behalf concerning the dwelling in question.[2]

* * * * *

5 27 December 1530

2497
1 The letter is not extant. Löble's stepson was Karl Villinger, about whom almost nothing is known other than that he was the heir of his father Jakob Villinger.
2 For the role of Christoph von Stadion, bishop of Augsburg, in these negotiations, and for the proposal that Ferdinand should buy the house (lines 14–18), see Ep 2505:11–31.

I want you to know that previously my most gracious lord, his royal Roman Majesty etc,[3] graciously requested me and my dear wife to lease the dwelling at a suitable rent to you in preference to others, whereupon we replied submissively to his royal Majesty, indicating that in this and in all   10 other matters we acknowledge our duty submissively to oblige him. Since, however, this dwelling was built some time ago at considerable cost by Jakob Villinger for my departed forebears, and it is not feasible for us to lease said dwelling for a yearly rent but are, rather, forced by necessity to sell it, we informed his royal Majesty that if he was disposed to purchase said dwell-   15 ing from us, we would of course respond with appropriate submissiveness to his royal Majesty in this matter. Up to now, however, we have received no further answer or decision from his royal Majesty. Since, as you yourself as a reasonable man must realize, we do not need this dwelling for ourselves and will derive more benefit from it if we sell it, my steward at Heilig Kreutz,   20 Ludwig Praytter,[4] reports to me that he has entered into negotiations with Herr Jakob Stürtzel concerning this dwelling, agreeing to lease it to him for a year.[5] At the same time, said Herr Stürtzel has requested that during that year we come to an agreement with him concerning a purchase. My wife and I are not pleased that our steward, without our prior knowledge, concluded   25 such an agreement with Stürtzel. But now that it is done, and given that we wish to agree with the said Herr Stürtzel on a purchase, we have consented that the dwelling in question shall be made available to the said Herr Stürtzel beginning on the feast of St John Baptist.[6] Although we do not like to eject you from the dwelling, and truly wish we could have allowed you to remain   30 in it, that cannot be done for the reasons stated. We ask you to take this in good part, for we believe that in some other way and at your convenience you will find a good dwelling in Freiburg. I want you to be aware of my

* * * * *

3 Ferdinand of Austria, since 11 January 1531 'king of the Romans,' ie heir-apparent to the emperorship and imperial regent in the absence from the Empire of his brother, Charles v. In the present context it is important that he was also sovereign of the Breisgau.
4 Ludwig Praytter is documented only in this letter. 'Heilig Kreutz' was an estate near Colmar in Upper Alsace that had belonged to Jakob Villinger. It seems that Praytter managed other Villinger properties as well, including the house 'zum Walfisch' at Freiburg.
5 Jakob Stürtzel (d May 1538), was an official of the Hapsburg government of Anterior Austria (including the Breisgau) who often represented Ferdinand i in negotiation with the Swiss. In 1531 he became a citizen of Freiburg.
6 24 June

good will in this. You will always find me willing to show favour and render
service to you.   35
    Given at Stuttgart, on the sixth day of June in the year etc [15]31
    J. Löble
    PMPS[7]
    To the honourable, highly learned Herr Erasm[us] Roterodamus, doc-
tor, in answer to him, my especially dear gentleman and friend, at Freiburg   40
im Breisgau

2498 / To Georg von Komerstadt   Freiburg, 7 June 1531

> This letter was first published in the *Epistolae floridae*. Georg von Komerstadt
> (1498–1559), member of a Saxon noble family of Meissen, was a doctor of both
> laws who from 1525 was a syndic and town councillor at Zwickau as well as an
> adviser and councillor to Duke George of Saxony and his two successors, Dukes
> Henry and Maurice. That being so, Erasmus thought him worth cultivating.

ERASMUS TO GEORG VON KOMERSTADT,
COUNSELLOR OF THE DUKE OF SAXONY, GREETING
There is an old Greek proverb, most distinguished sir, 'tis from seeing love
is born,'[1] which meant that love and benevolence are engendered among humans by a mutual look. Similarly, one could reasonably wonder whence this
mutual love between us arose, although neither one, I think, is known to   5
the other by outward appearance, unless the soul has more perceptive eyes
than the body, and by that look much more pure and stable friendships are
created than from close association. Christoph von Carlowitz,[2] noted no less
for his integrity than for his artistic ability, painted a portrait with his brush
of a pure and at the same time learned man; through him your exceptional   10
services have come to my notice, which I should value all the more since they
are offered spontaneously and not at my request.

        * * * * *

7 The Allen editors suggest plausibly that this stands for *per manum propriam
  scriptum* 'written in my own hand,' which is true at least of the signature (see
  introduction).

  2498
1 *Adagia* I ii 79
2 See Epp 1951 n7, 2085 introduction.

Besides, not to love a man endowed with so many excellent gifts is characteristic of those who do not regard virtue or learning as things to be admired; but not to love in return one who has rendered you a service is so foreign to a grateful spirit as to be unworthy of the human species, and hardly worthy of wild beasts, since they are not only tamed and pacified by the kindnesses of men but also show their gratitude if ever the occasion is presented. Although on the one hand your devotion turned out to be detrimental to me through the prodigious malice, or should I say, stupidity of that Thraso,[3] I do not think it to be the mark of a grateful spirit to evaluate a benefit from the result, but rather from the good will of the one who performed the action. Whatever someone has wished to bestow generously with sincere affection must be set down to his credit. Wherefore I wish you from now on to count Erasmus among those indebted to you; nothing will be more gratifying to him than to be given the occasion to demonstrate in turn that even if the ability to be of help is lacking, the ready and eager will to return the favour will not be lacking.

I count it among my principal instances of good fortune that the most illustrious Prince George deigns to include Erasmus among his clients. Why indeed should I not consider it a great ornament to be praised by a famous, much praised hero? One whom he judges worthy of his favour and even of his friendship is adequately praised. I pray that you continue to promote and increase his favour and benevolence towards me, as is your custom, in timely and friendly conversations, whenever the opportunity presents itself, since you enjoy much good will and influence with him, as I hear, by virtue of your outstanding abilities. Let this letter serve as a pact of friendship concluded among us under good auspices. Farewell.

Given at Freiburg im Breisgau, 7 June 1513

2499 / From Adrianus Chilius   Bruges, 8 June 1531

The autograph of this letter, first published as Ep 159 in Enthoven, is in the Rehdiger Collection of the University Library at Wrocław. Allen assigned the year-date on the basis of the reference in lines 7–10 to the return journey of Simon Grynaeus and Johann Bebel from England. We know from Ep 2502 that Grynaeus reached Ghent by 12 June 1531.

* * * * *

3 Heinrich Eppendorf (Ep 2492 n1). What action of Komerstadt this refers to is not known. For the most recent (and final) phase of Erasmus' controversy with Eppendorf, see CWE 17 xiii–xiv.

Adrianus Chilius, of Maldeghem in Flanders (d 1569), was at this time head-
master of the school of St Donatian in Bruges and had recently been ordained.
From 1533 to 1540 he was at Louvain, presumably studying classical languages
and supporting himself as a private tutor. In 1533 his Latin verse translations of
Aristophanes' *Plutus* and Lucian's *Ocypus* were published at Antwerp. In 1540
he returned to Maldeghem and spent the rest of his life there as parish priest.

ADRIANUS CHILIUS TO THE MOST LEARNED AND KINDLY
DESIDERIUS ERASMUS OF ROTTERDAM, GREETING

O how fortunate and marvellously blessed am I that the opportunity to write
to you, justifiably coveted and sought after by everyone, has not only tempt-
ed but compelled me. O how happy a day it has seemed to me, worthy of be-   5
ing marked with a white stone,[1] on which I was able to make myself known
to some degree to your very learned friend Master Simon and to the most
honourable Bebel,[2] the latter a printer who has contributed great service to
the republic of letters, the former a professor of Greek there[3] and endowed
with remarkable learning and brilliant rhetoric. I owe this, however, to my   10
friend dean Marcus Laurinus,[4] not to my learning, which is too scanty and
trifling to recommend me in any way to those illustrious and exceptional
disciples of the Muses. For in his kindness he invited me to dinner together
with Master Fevijn and your friend Levinus,[5] a dinner more pleasant than
any other that I have experienced, and from which it was very difficult to tear   15
myself away, so completely did I hang upon the lips of your friend Simon,
whose eloquence was so abundant.

During the meal he exhorted everyone without exception to write to
you: the others because they were well acquainted with you, and me, even
though I have never met you, although I am a steadfast admirer, propagator,   20
and imitator of your writings, as far as my feeble powers allow. This happened several times during the meal, and in that way he persuaded almost
everyone to undertake to do so. As for me, I apologized as best I could for my

* * * * *

2499
1 The Romans marked their lucky days on the calendar with a piece of white
  stone (chalk); unlucky days were marked with charcoal.
2 Simon Grynaeus and Johann Bebel were on their way home from their journey
  to England; see Ep 2487 n9.
3 Chilius writes *isthic* (in the place where you are), which in context should mean
  Freiburg, but Grynaeus was professor of Greek in Basel.
4 Dean of St Donatian's at Bruges (Ep 1342)
5 Jan van Fevijn, canon and scholaster of St Donatian's (Epp 1012, 2278); and
  Levinus Ammonius (Ep 2483)

ineptitude in speaking or writing. He, on the contrary, both after the meal,
while taking a walk, and when I had taken them back to the dean's residence, 25
where both were going to have a little rest, never ceased encouraging and
urging me until I promised that I would write. I felt somewhat ashamed to
reject an opportunity that was spontaneously offered to me, lest I seem to
have neglected something that was to be seized at all costs, although I would
reveal my ignorance before the peerless phoenix of all literary learning 30
and thrust my idiocies upon a man greatly occupied with serious matters.
Nevertheless, his discourse conquered my shame, for it was too persuasive
for me not to take up the pen.

Therefore, may you in your kindness take my temerity in good part. I
have written not that I wish or hope that you take any account of me, but that 35
the name of Erasmus, whom I consider my one guide in all my studies, not
seem altogether unknown and of no consequence to a man by far the lowli-
est in the realm of letters. May you be in good health, most learned Erasmus,
and I pray you to judge my sentiments towards you, not my writings, which
are, of course, quite bad. 40

Bruges, at midnight on the eve of Corpus Christi
Your Adrianus Chilius, director of youth at St Donatian
To the most learned and humane man in all the world, Master Desiderius
Erasmus of Rotterdam, the most perfect theologian in every respect

2500 / To André de Resende   Freiburg, 8 June 1531

This letter was first published in the *Epistolae floridae*.

André de Resende of Évora (1498/1500–1573), member of a Portuguese
noble family, studied in Lisbon, Alcalá, Salamanca, and Paris. He entered the
Dominican order and was ordained in Marseille. Along the way he became an
ardent Erasmian humanist and a noted poet. In 1529 he made the journey to
Louvain to continue his studies at the Collegium Trilingue, expecting to find
Erasmus there. Disappointed in this hope, he nonetheless remained in Louvain
to study languages and literature, particularly with Conradus Goclenius,
whose close friend he became. In 1530 his poem in praise of the town and university of Louvain (*Encomium urbis & academiae*) was published by J. Grapheus
at Antwerp. This was soon followed by his *Erasmi encomium* (see n3 below). In
1531, however, the hostility to Erasmus of the Louvain Dominicans, who had
forbidden their members to read Erasmus' works on pain of excommunication, led him to move out of the Louvain convent and place himself under the
protection of the Portuguese ambassador in Brussels, Pedro de Mascarenhas;
see Ep 2570:41–6 with n17. In 1533 he returned to Portugal, where he had close
contact with King John III, who not only sought his advice and employed him
as a tutor in the royal household but also obtained for him a papal dispensation

enabling him to leave the Dominican order and accept a canonry in his hometown of Évora. Resende continued to champion the cause of Erasmian human-
ism in publications and lectures, but eventually, finding his enthusiasm for
Erasmianism unappreciated, he retired to Évora, where he quietly spent his old
age. It does not appear that Resende and Erasmus ever met, and this is the only
extant letter between them. For a fuller account of Resende's life and publications, see Allen's introduction to this letter and de Vocht CTL II 395–403.

ERASMUS OF ROTTERDAM TO THE PORTUGUESE
ANGELO ANDRÉ DE RESENDE,[1] GREETING
Although I sent my secretary Quirinus there,[2] I was so exhausted from writing letters and various domestic tasks that I could hardly care for the health
of this frail body. The result was that I only had a taste of your poem,[3] which   5
was truly elegant, but had absolutely no time to reply. As soon, however, as
I was given a moment to breathe a little from the confusion of activities, I
immediately read your poem attentively and eagerly; in it there was nothing that did not greatly please me, except that it seemed brief and left me
famished and thirsty. But I beseech you, what god or goddess infused in you   10
this ardent love of Erasmus? For since I see no philtres in myself that could
even moderately inflame your soul with love for me, it must be that this
singular good will in my regard is inspired by a deity. I suspect, however,

* * * * *

2500
1 At some point Resende had added the name 'Angelus' to 'Andrea' in his name;
   see the title in n3 below.
2 In April 1531; see Ep 2477 introduction. 'There' is apparently Louvain; cf lines
   20–31 below, which seem to indicate that Resende had not yet departed for
   Brussels. By November, however, he had been living in Brussels for some time;
   see Ep 2570:41–6.
3 Via Goclenius, Resende had sent Erasmus his *Erasmi encomium*, a long poem
   filled with lavish praise of Erasmus and harsh criticism of his opponents, including a number of Resende's fellow Dominicans at Louvain (see n4 below).
   Erasmus was so pleased with it that, without bothering to notify Resende or
   get his permission, he sent it to Froben to be printed. It appeared in September
   1531 under the title *Carmen eruditum et elegans Angeli Andreae Resendii, Lusitani,
   adversus stolidos politioris literaturae oblatratores* (the running heads alternate ir-
   regularly between 'Erasmi Encomium' and 'Erasmi Encomion'). The unauthorized publication of the poem, scarcely in harmony with Erasmus' own advice
   to Resende in this letter (lines 30–1) to stick to literature and not to provoke
   the wrath of the anti-Erasmians, caused Resende a good deal of vexation with
   his fellow Dominicans, and he remonstrated with Erasmus about it. Erasmus
   explained that he had thought Resende was 'a free man,' ie that he had left the
   order, and that otherwise he would not have published the poem; see Allen Ep
   2644:34–6 (Erasmus to Goclenius, 2 May 1531).

that it is some secret affinity that brings us together. For which reason I am
all the more anxious to know you better, although from your verses I seem to 15
recognize your character and nature. It is up to you to find a good place for
this sincerity of heart and vein of eloquence. It is immensely gratifying either
to be loved or to be praised by you, but I regret that there is nothing in me
worthy of your feelings of affection.

As to that giant Stentor, whom you delightfully described to me – al- 20
though in his little book, which was no less unlearned than infantile, he
painted such a vivid picture of himself that no mirror could render a better
image of anyone – I could not help laughing.[4] What made him think of putting on a tragic mask and offering himself as an object of ridicule to children?[5]
It is no secret to me that they are covertly nourishing some monstrosity there. 25
Hence this bravado; as to what happens next, a god will see to it. As for you,
Resende, I would advise you not to provoke this snake against you. There
was once the kingdom of the Assyrians, of the Greeks, of the Medes, of the
Romans; what if some god now wishes there to be a kingdom of monks or
morons? Let them have their turn if it is the will of the Fates. As for you, di- 30
vert yourself with your Muses.

But I wish you to be persuaded that this character and disposition of
yours are not only dear to me, but also delightful. I know nothing more precise than the judgment of Glocenius, and he is not wont to praise anyone
rashly. Furthermore, I so love the man that solely out of affection for him 35
I would be forced to love anyone; I attribute so much to his judgment that
I need no further proof.

Given at Freiburg im Breisgau, on the feast of Corpus Christi 1531

2501 / To Erasmus Schets   Freiburg, 11 June 1531

This letter was first published by Allen, on the basis of the autograph in the
British Library (MS Add 38512 folio 57). Erasmus' answer is Ep 2511.

* * * * *

4 Eustachius van der Rivieren, Dominican, dean of the faculty of theology at
   Louvain, known for his loud denunciations of humanist scholarship in general
   and Erasmus' 'heresies' in particular. His 'little book' was the recently published
   Apologia pro pietate in Erasmi Roterod. Enchiridion canonem quintum (c January
   1531); see Epp 2264 introduction, 2353:15–22, 2443 n12, 2522:83–95, 2566:185–8,
   2629:21–6). According to Allen, it is Erasmus who calls him 'Stentor' (after the
   loud-voiced herald in Homer's *Iliad*); in the poem Resende simply calls him 'a
   tall man with a huge body' and 'an ugly swine,' without naming him.
5 Terence *Eunuchus* 5.8.57

Cordial greetings. I received the letter of Pierre Barbier;[1] God immortal, what a letter! It would be better to deal with a pimp than a theologian. But pretend, accept whatever you can, and make sure that this letter reaches him as soon as possible. The race of men is avaricious. Johannes de Molendino seems prepared to perjure himself for the sake of his friend for money.[2]

I hope everything will be all right, but if something should happen to you I don't know if I can ask anything from your heirs. For I have a good number of letters of yours making mention of money.[3]

They say that a truce has been negotiated between the Turks and Ferdinand, but only for a year.[4] I am more in fear of an evangelical war.[5] Farewell.

Freiburg, 11 June 1531

Your Erasmus of Rotterdam

You complain that there are fewer people going to Freiburg.[6] But be assured that whatever you send to Hieronymus Froben in Basel will get to me quickly and safely. Farewell.

To the excellent gentleman Master Erasmus Schets. In Antwerp

2502 / From Juan Luis Vives   Ghent, 12 June 1531

This letter was first published in volume 2 of Vives' *Opera* (Basel: Episcopius 1555). On Vives see Ep 927 introduction.

VIVES TO ERASMUS

Your friend Grynaeus met me here in Ghent.[1] He seemed to me altogether worthy of your friendship and that of all good people by the moral integrity that shone forth in his countenance and his virginal modesty, by his

* * * * *

2501
1 Ep 2404
2 For Johannes de Molendino, canon of Tournai and close friend of Barbier, see Ep 2407.
3 Cf Epp 2511:17–22, 2530:10–14.
4 The one-year truce that had been concluded in December 1530 was renewed for another year in May 1531; cf Ep 2384 n10.
5 Ie a war between the champions and opponents of the Reformation. The fear was justified, but the threat was not immediate; see Ep 2403 n11.
6 Cf Ep 2413:2–3.

2502
1 Simon Grynaeus was on his way home to Basel from a visit to England; see Ep 2487 n9.

enthusiastic outlook concerning the good arts, and his great achievements in 5
literary studies. According to my usual practice, and also at your direction,
I passed an hour or two with him in familiar conversation, that is to say, as
long as he wished. I was not able to commend him to my friends in England
because he came to see me only on his return from there.

I have written these words in the midst of very well-attended games 10
that are being celebrated in the entourage of the emperor,[2] and consequently
this letter will be shorter than I would wish. I send you letters more rarely
than usual because I have no doubt that, occupied with your affairs and wea-
ried by your age and state of health, you devote yourself less willingly to this
practice of writing letters. But my friendship has no need of the supports that 15
the common crowd requires. I ask you again and again that in future whenever you write to me, you let me know in a few words how you are faring
physically and spiritually, for I consider that in virtue of our mutual affection
this should be a particular concern of mine.

Farewell. Ghent, 12 June 1513 20

2503 / From Johannes Fabri   Vienna, 21 June 1531

First published as Ep 92 in Enthoven, the manuscript is in the Rehdiger collection of the University Library at Wrocław. For Johannes Fabri, since 1530 bishop
of Vienna, see Ep 2097.

Greetings. As was fitting, certainly, I all but annihilated Medardus with invectives, excellent Erasmus, for his blatant impudence, especially towards
you, against whom he employed a coarse and improper wit.[1] For this action
obviously, he has fallen into disgrace with me and with other leading men in
the royal court, and because of his unseemly witticism he has not improved 5
his reputation.[2]

* * * * *

2 Charles v was in Ghent 24 March–2 April 1531, and then again 20 April–14
  June; *Collections des voyages des souverains des Pays-Bas* ed L.P. Gachard and C.
  Piot 4 vols (Brussels 1874–82) II 49–50.

2503
1 For a full account of the incident in question and of the revenge that Erasmus
  took on Medardus, see Ep 2408.
2 According to Horawitz (IV 784) Fabri ordered Medardus to return to his cloister, where, however, he was received in triumph.

But, putting this aside, let us come to Eck.[3] I would not want his vehemence to deter you from your objective. I recently warned him severely by letter that the sow should not teach Minerva,[4] and that he should not interfere with your magnificent labours and your pious and vigorously Christian piety. And really his foolish boasting and comic threats should not distress you, since if in reading through all your works carefully I had found anything amiss, I would have indicated it to you in a friendly way long ago. Accordingly, my advice is – just as you have hitherto been of strong and fearless courage against this kind of men – to regard such Pyrgopolynices with contempt.[5] All the same, I do not doubt that, chastened by my letter, he will recover his reason and will prefer to become famous and illustrious from any other of his writings than his encomium of you in the style of Hipponax.[6]

For the rest, so that you can live for a longer time in the house of Villinger,[7] I have made concerted efforts several times, in royal letters written with great care to the magistracy of Freiburg, to prevent your being dislodged.[8] I would gladly give you my house to live in, in perpetuity, but it is extremely modest and dark.[9] It is fitting that so great man as you should live in a splendid and sumptuous dwelling.

Last of all, I should like you to be assured that your honour, safety, and all your interests are as of great concern to me as I myself and all my possessions.

From Vienna, 21 June 1531

Johannes, bishop of Vienna

* * * * *

3 Johann Maier of Eck, known as Johann Eck (Epp 386:95n, 769, 2357 n1). For his machinations against Erasmus at the Diet of Augsburg in 1530, where Fabri was in attendance, see CWE 17 xiii.
4 *Adagia* I i 40
5 Pyrgopolynices is the name of the *miles gloriosus* 'swaggering soldier' in Plautus' play of that name.
6 A Greek poet of the late sixth century BC, whose coarse and abusive verse survives only in fragments.
7 See Ep 2462 introduction.
8 Cf Ep 2505:11–38.
9 Fabri had taken a degree in both laws at Freiburg (1510 or 1511), and had presumably spent time there now and then in pursuit of his duties as adviser to Archduke Ferdinand of Austria (cf Ep 2196 n31), but we have no information on the circumstances under which he acquired a house there.

Bernhard von Cles

2504 / From Bernhard von Cles Prague, 25 June 1531

First published as Ep 154 in Förstemann / Günther, the autograph of this letter
was in the Burscher Collection of the University of Leipzig (Ep 1254 introduction). For Cles, bishop of Trent, see Epp 1357, 2007.

Venerable, sincere, and beloved friend. Last January, after my most serene
and most honourable lord, Ferdinand, king of Hungary and Bohemia, etc
had been crowned king of the Romans in Aachen, as is the custom,[1] I returned to my church and episcopal see in Trent, for its affairs required it.
After I had remained there for some time, I had to return at the king's order 5
to the court, where I arrived on the 18th of this month, and your letter of
14 March from Freiburg was finally presented to me by Baron Albrecht Slick.[2]
In it you recommend to me a certain Erasmus von Könneritz, a young man
of good family imbued with the study of good letters, who has never been
seen here and still has not made his appearance.[3] But if he had come to see 10
me then or were to come even now, I would have received him in such a way
that you would plainly know and understand that I took due account of your
recommendation, as I would not hesitate to do as often as the opportunity
presents itself, even in much more important matters, in virtue of my good
will and singular affection towards you. 15

No one doubts that Italy is at peace, that France is friendly, and that there
is hope of a truce with the Turks, since that is the current situation.[4] Yet we
must pray God that it be his will that peace and friendship and other things of
this kind be so stable and secure that adversities and misfortunes will not arise
that will unsettle the whole status quo of Christendom, as I could describe 20
more fully and confidentially if we could speak to each other in person.

* * * * *

2504
1 See Ep 2384 n7.
2 The letter is not extant. The baron mentioned was probably Albrecht (I) von
Schlick (d 1548), chamberlain of King Ferdinand and prefect of Lusatia.
3 Erasmus von Könneritz (d 1563) was a younger brother of Andreas and Christoph
von Könneritz (Ep 2450 nn6–7). Little is known of his early life and education,
but from about 1540 he was active as a district official, judge, and diplomat in
the service of the electors of Saxony.
4 The Peace of Cambrai (August 1529) had brought a temporary end to the warfare between Charles v and Francis i in Italy; see Ep 2207 n5. King Ferdinand
had just renewed for one year the truce with the Turks concluded in 1530; cf
Ep 2501 n4.

Concerning the public attacks that Eck and friar Medardus have made against your name,[5] I can affirm that during the whole Augsburg diet, which I attended, I did not hear or deduce anything that could damage your reputation and honour in any way, nor would I have patiently tolerated that in my presence any mention other than honorific be made of such a good man, who has deserved well of our holy faith and religion, and therefore I shall approach both of them by letter concerning this matter to ascertain whether they committed this offence and what induced them to do so. And I will immediately write to you to report what I learned from them.[6]

Moreover, I am annoyed that your letter was not delivered earlier, and accordingly I wish, as is fitting, to apologize that I respond only now. But if it had been delivered in time, what you ask with regard to the house in which you are living in Freiburg would have been taken care of long ago through my doing, and I shall also write to the owner that he allow you to live there longer.[7] I think that if my letter is shown to him in time, he will agree out of regard for me. In addition, if there is anything in which I can be of help to you at the court of his serene Majesty, I strongly urge you to disclose and communicate it to me. When I have learned of your needs I will so plead your cause that it will readily become apparent to you that I am very devoted to you and intently concerned with your interests, since I am intensely desirous of gaining the favour and sympathy of such a great man and wish to convey to him in every way possible my affection for learned and meritorious men (as we know you to be).

Given in the royal castle in Prague, 25 June 1531

Bernhard, cardinal and bishop of Trent

To the venerable Master Erasmus of Rotterdam, whom we love sincerely, celebrated professor of sacred theology. In Freiburg im Breisgau

2505 / From Johann Koler   Augsburg, 26 June 1531

This letter was first published as Ep 155 in Förstemann / Günther. The autograph was in the Burscher Collection of the University Library at Leipzig (Ep 1254 introduction). For Koler, canon of St Moritz in Augsburg, see Ep 2195 introduction. For the current negotiations over Erasmus' occupancy of the house 'zum Walfisch' in Freiburg, which is the principal subject of this letter, see Epp 2462 introduction, 2477, 2497.

* * * * *

5 See Ep 2503:1–18.
6 No such letter has survived.
7 See Epp 2462 introduction and 2497.

Cordial greetings. That I did not go to see you on my return from the baths (as I had promised)[1] came about for two reasons, or rather because of impediments beyond my control, beloved Erasmus. When I was already contemplating and conceiving a plan for my departure, I was suddenly held back by certain personal affairs that arose in my place of birth.[2] It also happened that weakened by the long, drawn out baths, I was so tired and drained of all my strength that nothing was less suitable for me than a journey. And so, returning home, I found your two letters, which had been delivered in my absence, to which you will find response in the present letter, as much as the subject demands.[3]

Today, I received a letter of this same date from the bishop of Augsburg,[4] who again entrusted to me your case, which must be discussed with the treasurer, Johann Löble, and indeed with such assiduity and urgency that hardly anything else could be confided to me with greater care. This was entirely unnecessary as far as I am concerned, because I was about to do for you of my own accord what so eminent a prelate was petitioning at such great length. Therefore I fulfilled my duty and first delivered to the treasurer the letter sent to me by his steward,[5] and to tell the truth, the treasurer seemed deeply to regret that he was not able to put the house freely at your disposal until the feast of St Michael.[6] If in the meantime the most serene King Ferdinand did not wish to buy the house, since on that same feast of St Michael, the provost or his brother, Doctor Stürtzel,[7] could claim it as his property and you would be compelled to cede it to him, etc, your wish seems to have been satisfied, since you asked to stay only until the first of August. Now it seems that a whole month has been added.[8] The treasurer advised the most reverend Christoph

* * * * *

2505
1 Evidently in a letter no longer extant
2 Koler writes *in patria* ('in my homeland' or 'in my native region'), which could be a reference to Landsberg in Bavaria, where he had held a benefice since 1503 and where he may have been born.
3 One of the letters may have been Ep 2470; the other is not extant.
4 Christoph von Stadion (Ep 2480)
5 Ludwig Praytter (Ep 2497 n4)
6 29 September
7 Jakob Stürtzel (Ep 2497 n5). His older brother Andreas (d 1537) was provost of the exiled Basel cathedral chapter.
8 Thanks to this intervention by Bishop Christoph and Koler, as well probably as that by Johann Fabri, bishop of Vienna (Ep 2503:19–21), Erasmus received permission to remain in the house until the end of September; see Ep 2462 introduction.

to write to King Ferdinand and persuade him to buy the house, so that subsequently, once the purchase had been made, the house would be available to
you continuously. But that would seem to me to be advisable only if you were
going to remain in Freiburg for a longer time. Whatever the most reverend
Christoph intends to do, you will learn of it from his letters. For my part, I   30
regret very much that you are moving further away from this region.

I cannot cease to wonder why you are fleeing from our country, or
why you conjure up vain fears and groundless dread of seditions. For the
tumults you fear here among us you will find wherever you go. But if you
were here with us, you would not have to look for a house or any other   35
necessities of life with much trouble.⁹ But I will not try to persuade you of
anything but what will be most agreeable to your intentions and most suitable to your interests.

As for us, I understand from the letter of the most reverend Christoph,
and also from your letter, that you will remain in Freiburg until the first of   40
September, and I do not doubt (if Christ will grant me good health) that I
will visit you in the meantime. For I am expecting from Rome any day now
a brief from the pope, and when I have received it I will immediately set out
from here to see you. I have business in a certain place not far from Freiburg,
because of which I must certainly go there.¹⁰   45

Anton Fugger has withdrawn to his castle with his wife and children
to relax his spirit. I have received your letter to him,¹¹ which I will send to
him immediately, and will see to it that your other letters are duly sent to
Brassicanus and to the others to whom they are owed.¹²

I am eager to see your response to the invectives of Alberto Pio;¹³ when   50
it appears, I beg you to send it to me. He was a truly pious man, who flew
straight up to heaven in his Franciscan cowl, and who, strengthened with
this protection, does not fear the attacks of the devil. When I was thinking of

* * * * *

9 The banker Anton Fugger had repeatedly invited Erasmus to settle in Augsburg
  on generous terms; see Ep 2476 n1.
10 Possibly business related to Koler's position as provost and vicar-general of the
  bishopric of Chur in the Grisons, in connection with which he had journeyed to
  Rome in the winter of 1529–30
11 Presumably Ep 2476
12 The letter to Brassicanus, professor of rhetoric at Vienna (Epp 1146, 2305), is not
  extant.
13 *Apologia adversus rhapsodias Alberti Pii*, which was published by Froben in July
  1531. For Erasmus' controversy with Pio see see Ep 2486 n10.

the Franciscan cowl, your dialogue 'The Funeral,' came to mind.[14] So I had a
good laugh at such great superstition in the great man. 55

My dear Erasmus, I pray you, when you have decided on something
certain, let me know how long you will be living in Freiburg and what you
are doing. I saw your *Apophthegmata*[15] and read them with great delight; they
are rightly approved and read by everyone. What would not be praised that
comes from Erasmus? May God preserve you for us and good letters, so that 60
we may receive many fruits of this type from you.

That person we mentioned wrote me a letter before his departure that
was full of blandishments (all of it pure pretence), attempting to deceive me
with empty words, as if I were not familiar with his tricks.[16] I am convinced
that this affair about your house sprang up with him as the instigator. But the 65
opportunity will come to repay the favour.

Farewell, and continue our mutual love, as you do. May Christ preserve you always for us in good health.

Given 26 June 1531 at Augsburg

Yours sincerely, Johann Koler, provost 70

To the most famous and learned Master Erasmus of Rotterdam, most
distinguished doctor of sacred theology. In Freiburg

2506 / To Bonifacius Amerbach Freiburg, 26 June 1531

This letter (= AK Ep 1535) was first published in the *Epistolae familiares*. The autograph is in the Öffentliche Bibliothek of the University of Basel (MS AN III 15 72).

Greetings. For a long time I have been bidding on a house here, one of good
name but iniquitous price.[1] I will be an owner either today or never. I am
bidding for it for you more than for me. If you think there is someone who is

* * * * *

14 The colloquy *Funus* 'The Funeral' was published in 1526 (CWE 40 763–95). The
colloquy *Exequiae seraphicae* 'The Seraphic Funeral,' which describes the funeral
of 'A. Pius,' was not published until September 1531 (CWE 40 996–1032).
15 Ep 2431
16 Ottmar Nachtgall (Ep 2477)

2506
1 The name of the house that he eventually purchased was 'Zum Kind Jesu,' and
the price was 'almost eight hundred gold florins.' See Epp 2462 introduction,
2512:10–11, 2517:29–30, 2518:25, 2528:53–4, 2530:1–2, 19–21, 2534:24–33.

going to visit Sadoleto,[2] give me an indication. Let me know as soon as you
have pleaded your cause with Mercury at your side.[3] Be in good health with   5
your dear ones.

Freiburg, 26 June
You will recognize the hand.
To the most famous Doctor Bonifacius Amerbach. At Basel

2507 / From Bonifacius Amerbach   Basel, 28 June 1531

This letter (= AK Ep 1536) is Bonifacius' answer to Ep 2506. The autograph is
in the Öffentliche Bibliothek of the University of Basel (MS KI AR 18a 4). The
first part, down to line 13, is well-written; the postscript, on the other hand, is
so illegible that Allen could decipher it only by consulting the letter of Alciati
mentioned in line14.

Cordial greetings. In bidding on the house, illustrious Erasmus, I sincerely
hope that you encounter good fortune, and that it will be sold to you at the
lowest possible price. If you have undertaken to write a letter to Sadoleto, I
shall send it just before August to the Lyons fair, entrusted to men of good
faith, through whom it will be delivered. All my affairs here are now hanging   5
in the balance.[1] While I teach publicly how to win a case for a client, I fear that
in the meantime I have taken few precautions for myself. But the die is cast.
Even if I lose the case, I will be satisfied, since I consider that a significant loss
of one's fortunes is to be preferred to the compromising of one's conscience.

Farewell, illustrious Erasmus. I am prevented from writing more by the   10
haste of the messenger.

At Basel, the eve of the feast of Sts Peter and Paul 1531
Your sincere friend, Bonifacius Amerbach
Our friend Alciati, in his latest letter to me, delivered yesterday,[2] justi-
fies himself profusely for the great sin (that is what he calls it) of having   15

* * * * *

2 For Jacopo Sadoleto, bishop of Carpentras, see Ep 1511, and cf Ep 2611.
3 Bonifacius had been summoned by the Basel city council to defend his claim to
   be exempt from participation in the reformed Eucharist. See Ep 2519 introduction, and cf Epp 2507:5–9, 2541:20–2, 2542:12–19, 2546:9–13, 2551:6–11, 2630:1–
   41, 2631:1–51. Mercury was the god of, among other things, eloquence.

2507
1 See Ep 2506 n3.
2 AK Ep 1534 (15 June 1531)

disturbed you in the interests of and through the prayers of I know not whom, in case Zasius was thinking of a successor.[3] He begs pardon on that account, as if I had ever aspired to succeed this man, or even if I had, that I would not allow those more learned than I to be recommended. What could be more alien to a good man than that? He adds further that he will not 20 write to you now, both because the messenger will not abide any delay, and because you gave him such satisfaction with your letter that he has nothing more to say.[4] He maintains your opinion with might and main.[5] Farewell. More about this when we meet.

To the most famous Master Erasmus of Rotterdam, eminent theologian 25 and father of good letters, incomparable protector. In Freiburg

2508 / To Tielmannus Gravius   Freiburg, [end of June?] 1531

This letter, evidently the answer to one not extant, was first published in the *Epistolae floridae*. The approximate date is based on the known presence of Simon Grynaeus (line 5) in Bruges and Ghent in the second week of June; see Epp 2499:7, 2502:2.

On Tielmannus Gravius, secretary of the Cologne cathedral chapter, see Ep 2103.

ERASMUS OF ROTTERDAM TO TIELMANNUS GRAVIUS, GREETING
There was no need of any excuse, dearest Tielmannus, for you sin in no way except in excessive love. Try to take care of your health, especially because there are many for whom your good health is essential. I am glad that you liked Grynaeus. I have made provisions for the servants,[1] somewhat less 5 learned than the ones I dismissed,[2] but of more agreeable character. I am so busy that I do not have time to finish the *Ecclesiastes*,[3] nor do I feel like doing

* * * * *

3 See Ep 2394:130–9 with n27.
4 Ep 2468
5 Literally 'with hands and feet'; *Adagia* I iv 15

2508
1 Probably Gilbert Cousin (Ep 2381 n1) and possibly Quirinus Hagius, though the first mention of the latter in the correspondence dates from August 1532 (Allen Ep 2644:16).
2 Haio Cammingha and Nicolaas Kan left Erasmus' service in 1530 (Ep 2261 nn1, 34), and Quirinus Talesius in the spring of 1531 (Ep 2488 n1).
3 Cf Ep 2483:54–5 with n9.

it, nor is it useful for this mad century. I congratulate Riquinus on his success.[4] The count of Neuenahr could have lived longer if he had not preferred to take more account of his office rather than of his health.[5] Concerning   10
Bernhard von Hagen and Johann Gropper,[6] your news gives me great joy. I will write to them as soon as I have the time. Alberto Pio is moving the Béda Camarina again with his volume.[7]

Grynaeus told you a nice story about marriage,[8] except that I think you understood it wrongly. In a letter to me he had praised my tolerance of the   15
labours of study at my decrepit age, but he admired particularly my endurance in standing. I in turn jokingly exaggerated my strength, adding that I was at present even looking around for a little wife, and that he should not impede my marriage by referring to my decrepit old age. He, since he is very witty, replied that if another was not forthcoming he would surrender   20
his sweetheart, who was twenty-two years old, to me. I thanked him for his

* * * * *

4 For Simon Riquinus, since 1529 personal physician to Duke John III of Jülich-Cleves, see Ep 2246.
5 Count Hermann von Neuenahr, provost of the Cologne cathedral chapter and chancellor of the University of Cologne (Ep 1926), died on 30 October 1530.
6 Bernhard von Hagen (d 1556) was chancellor of the Cologne cathedral chapter. At the Diet of Augsburg in 1530 he was a member of both the committees that tried to find a formula for religious concord, representing the Catholic cause with notable moderation. Later (1542–3), though still an advocate of moderation and conciliation, he strongly opposed the attempts of Archbishop Hermann von Wied (Ep 1976) to turn his archbishopric into a Protestant principality. Hagen's friend and colleague, Johann Gropper (1503–59), keeper of the seals of the Cologne cathedral chapter, also participated in the theological discussions at Augsburg, and in the years that followed emerged as one of the foremost Catholic advocates, alongside Julius Pflug (Ep 2492), of theological conciliation. In 1536 Gropper prepared the reform statutes for a provincial synod in Cologne (*Canones concilii provincialis Coloniensis*) as well as his principal work of theology, *Institutio compendiaria doctrinae christianae*, both published in Cologne in 1538. Like Hagen, however, he strongly opposed the subsequent attempt to introduce Protestantism into Cologne. In 1551–2 he attended the second session of the Council of Trent. His elevation to the cardinalate was imminent when he died during a visit to Rome.
7 For Alberto Pio, prince of Carpi, see Epp 1634 and 1987. His *Tres et viginti libri in locos lucubrationum variarum D. Erasmi Roterodami* was published on 9 March 1531 (two months after his death) by Josse Bade at Paris. For Noël Béda and his alleged connection with Pio, see Ep 2486 n11. The proverb 'move not the Camarina' is the rough equivalent of 'let sleeping dogs lie' (*Adagia* I 1 64).
8 Cf Epp 2518:23, 2528:49–51, 2534:21–4.

kindness. So much about marriage. From day to day we await our man, who is returning from England.[9] How terrifying is the Virgilian verse: 'Easy is the descent to Avernus.'[10] You know the rest. Farewell.

Freiburg im Breisgau, 1531   25

2509 / To Bonifacius Amerbach

On the basis of good evidence, the AK editor Alfred Hartmann redated this letter to 'spring 1534?' and published it as AK Ep 1810. It will appear in CWE 20 as Ep 2917A.

2510 / From Jakob Sturm   Strasbourg, 6 July 1531

The autograph of this letter, which was first published as Ep 93 in Enthoven, is in the Rehdiger Collection of the University Library at Wrocław.

Jakob Sturm (1489–1553), member of an old aristocratic family in Strasbourg, was an adherent of the Reformation and a leading member of the magistracy of the city. He worked closely with Martin Bucer and the other pastors on the peaceful implementation of reform, and he represented the city in efforts to achieve theological accord and political alliance among the Protestant cities and principalities of Germany in face of the threat from the Catholic emperor and his allies among the princes. Erasmus met Sturm in Strasbourg in 1514 (Ep 302:14), and thereafter maintained cordial relations with him. Indeed, Sturm was the only leader of the Reformation in Strasbourg for whom Erasmus still had a kind word; see CWE 78 326–7 (*Epistola ad fratres Inferioris Germaniae*). This letter is the only one between them that is extant.

Cordial greetings. Most renowned Erasmus, I was scarcely able to speak to Anselmus, who brought your letter to me,[1] because of the occupations that were overwhelming me at the moment, and because he, when he delivered your letter, said that he was already preparing to leave. And so if I did not show him any kindness, both he and you will pardon me.   5

* * * * *

9 Grynaeus was at this point on his way home from England; see Ep 2487 n9.
10 *Aeneid* 6.126. Avernus was the entry to the underworld.

2510
1 The letter is not extant; for the carrier, Anselmus Ephorinus, see Ep 2539 introduction.

I do not think that a copy of your letter, which you sent, was printed here,[2] and I do not know the Peter Schöffer you mention, nor do I know if he lives here.[3] This much I do know, that in the past I have often sweated in vain in curbing the impudence of certain people. I have so far never met Vulturius in person, nor has he ever been admitted to a conversation with me.[4] I have never seen his alluring strains, of which you write,[5] and never liked the tactics of those who tried to drag you into their party against your will, whence originated that tragedy that should never have been aroused. But that was missing from the accumulation of all our woes. May God grant that having learned a lesson from these people and others like them, they will so act in future that no detriment to the cause of Christ or of the truth will result from their stupidity, something that perhaps is more to be desired than hoped for.

I pray God that he will keep you safe for a long time, and that you will be granted your wish, which is to say, as you will understand, that a civil war does not break out in Germany, so that you will not regret your purchase.[6]

Farewell, most distinguished friend, and know that I am at your service.

From Strasbourg, 6 July 1531

Jakob Sturm, your sincere friend

To the most illustrious Master Erasmus of Rotterdam, my very dear friend.

In Freiburg

* * * * *

2 The reference is evidently to Gerard Geldenhouwer's unauthorized edition of Erasmus' *Episola contra pseudevangelicos* 'with scholia,' which had been published in March 1530 without indication of place or publisher. Erasmus correctly suspected that Strasbourg was the place of publication and wanted to discover the name of the publisher. See Epp 2289 n2, 2293.

3 Originally from Mainz, Peter (II) Schöffer (or Schaefer, 1480–1547) was a printer who, after pursuing his trade in Worms (1512–29), set up shop in Strasbourg (1529). In 1527 he had sent from Worms to Basel a pamphlet containing 'defamatory illustrations' showing Luther scoring victories over the pope and Catholic theologians (Ep 1804:161–2 with n32). In 1530, moreover, he had printed Bucer's *Epistola apologetica* (Ep 2312 n2), leading Erasmus to suspect him of being the publisher of Geldenhouwer's edition of the *Epistola contra pseudevangelicos*. Erasmus' suspicions had originally fallen on the printer Johann Schott, but we now know that the actual culprit was Christian Egenolff; see Ep 2293 n2.

4 'Vulturius' was Erasmus' derisive name for Geldenhouwer; see Ep 2358 n6.

5 Presumably the scholia to the text of Erasmus' *Epistola contra pseudevangelicos*, designed to allure the reader to Geldenhouwer's point of view

6 Ie his purchase of a house in Freiburg; see Ep 2506.

2511 / From Erasmus Schets Antwerp, 12 July 1531

First published by Allen, this is Schets' answer to Ep 2501; it will in turn be
answered by Ep 2530. Allen found the autograph (no 58 in the collection 'Des
Réformateurs') in the Bibliothèque de la Société de l'histoire du protestantisme
français in Paris.

Cordial greetings. I believe I last wrote to you in the month of May.[1] Since
that time I have received several letters from you,[2] together with others that
were to be forwarded to Barbier, Molendino, and Goclenius, which I have
duly done.[3] When they have responded and have entrusted the forwarding
to me, I shall follow the procedure that you indicated, that is, include them in 5
an envelope addressed to Hieronymus Froben in Basel.

Pieter Gillis has not yet paid the one hundred and three florins and
eighteen stuivers that he owes you, plus another twelve florins that he received from Quirinus.[4] In all Pieter received in your name one hundred and
fifteen florins and eighteen stuivers.[5] He promises from one day to the next 10
that he will give them to you. I will not relent until I have the money.

Master Jan de Hondt, who now owes two pension payments from
Courtrai, wrote long ago that he would send them soon.[6] I hope he will. I
have received nothing from England. Castro does not write (if he received
anything he would write),[7] and Grynaeus does not come.[8] I have learned 15
from English merchants that the archbishop is still alive.[9]

You seem to have some doubts about the calculation of your money, in
which I serve your interests, and hope that all is correct.[10] I myself have no
doubts about the administration of my affairs and my accounts. They are in
such order that everything is recorded very clearly like a perpetual memorial 20

* * * * *

2511
1 He had written two letters in May, Epp 2491 and 2494.
2 Epp 2487–8, 2501
3 The enclosures for Barbier, Molendino, and Goclenius are not extant. In Epp
  2488:3–4 and 2501:3–4 Erasmus mentions only a letter to Barbier.
4 For monies entrusted to Pieter Gillis on Erasmus' behalf, see Ep 2494 n12.
5 On this sum, which was finally paid by Gillis in October 1531 and remitted by
  Schets via Froben in March 1532, see below Epp 2530, 2558, and 2625.
6 See Epp 2487:7–8, 2494:9–12.
7 Luis de Castro, Schets' agent in London (Ep 2487 n7)
8 Grynaeus had already passed through the Netherlands a month earlier on his
  way home from England; see Epp 2499:7–9, 2502:2, 2508:4–5, and cf Ep 2487 n9.
9 William Warham, archbishop of Canterbury; see Ep 2487 n8.
10 Echoing Erasmus' words in Ep 2501:6

of each transaction. It will be easy for my heirs at my death to review and justify my accounts in whatever way they choose. I was pleased that you received at last those intercepted letters of Barbier and Molendino;[11] I am displeased, however, that Barbier behaves so badly towards you.[12] The avarice of some (or rather very many) theologians in this century is so consuming that through all the means in their power they pillage and ravage whatever they can, and this under the pretext of religion and dignity. And they are not terrified in the meantime by so many threats that hang over them on high.

A young Portuguese, Martín Fernandes,[13] offered me a pot of preserved fruit to deliver to you with the enclosed letter addressed to you.[14] I gave the pot to Martin Lompart here so that he can send it to Basel in a small bundle together with his merchandise to be delivered to Froben.[15] I wrote to him instructing him to forward it to you. Your name is written on the pot.[16]

I see that you are getting tired of Germany. I wish you were here with us! You could not be safer in any other place, in my judgment.[17] I hear that Lutheranism is growing day by day in all of Germany and that Catholics are being expelled and even exiled.[18] I fear that your Freiburg will not escape this faction for long. And where will you stay amidst these tempests? You would surely be safer living among us. We will have here the illustrious Queen Mary as ruler, one of your greatest supporters, as I hear.[19] Here you would be closer to England, France, and whatever other nation is favourable to you, and also closer to their shared friendship for you. The emperor has

* * * * *

11 Epp 2404, 2407
12 See Ep 2527 n8.
13 Martín Fernandes (Mertinus Ferrarius) was the nephew of Rui Fernandes (Ep 1681 n13). Nothing is known of him apart from the incident recorded here.
14 Not extant
15 In other letters (Epp 1651, 1658, 1671) Schets identifies Martin Lompart as the brother of Jakob Lompart, Basel banker and merchant. He is perhaps to be identified with the Martin vom Busch who managed the firm's office at Antwerp.
16 The gift was slow to arrive; see Epp 2530:27–9, 2552:1–3, 2559:31, 2585:1.
17 For the hopes of Erasmus' friends that he would return to Brabant, see also Epp 2243:29–32, 2558:6–8, 2570:31–4, 2582:39–41, 2607:33–57.
18 Despite repeated condemnation by the emperor and the Catholic estates, the process of establishing new evangelical churches that enforced uniformity of doctrine and practice was by 1531 already far advanced in many cities and a few princely territories, and the spread of Protestantism would continue through the 1530s and into the 1540s; cf Ep 2403 n11.
19 In 1531, Mary of Austria, queen of Hungary (Ep 2100), succeeded her aunt, Margaret of Austria, as regent of the Netherlands.

convoked a new diet at Speyer.[20] You could go there safely by carriage, from there down the Rhine slowly by ship to Grave or 's Hertogenbosch, and from there enter Brabant to be with us. May God fortify you in health and provide 45 you with the determination to do what he knows will turn out more successfully for you.

They say that it is a question of prolonging the truce with the Turks.[21] I am not prone to believe, the situation being as it is, that the Turks will be persuaded to consent. There are rumours of great conspiracies between the 50 king of France and the pope against the emperor, whom the king of England will join, they say, although the affair is being conducted in great secrecy.[22]

Farewell, my dear Master Erasmus, happy and fortunate for years to come.

From Antwerp, 12 July 1531 55

Your sincere friend, Erasmus Schets

To the most learned and eminent theologian, Master Erasmus of Rotterdam. In Freiburg

2512 / To Erasmus Schets Freiburg, 17 July [1531]

The surviving manuscript of this letter, first published by Allen, is a copy in the British Library (MS Add 38512 folio 59) bearing the impossible year-date

* * * * *

20 Originally intended for 14 September 1531, the diet had still not begun when, on 15 October, it was postponed to 6 January 1532 in Regensburg, where it finally opened on 17 April; see Epp 2517:25–8 with n9, 2527:67–70, 2534:18–20, 2540 introduction, 2558:71–3, 2559:7–8, 2562:13–17, 2565:19.
21 Ep 2501 n4
22 Following the 'Ladies' Peace' of Cambrai (Ep 2207 n5), Francis I and Charles V were formally at peace. But Francis, whose long-range aim was to recover the duchy of Milan, engaged in intrigues with the emperor's enemies wherever they could be found. In Germany, this entailed cooperation not only with Protestant princes, who had formed the League of Schmalkalden and were prepared to take up arms against the emperor if attacked on grounds of religion, but also with the Catholic dukes of Bavaria, who were more fiercely anti-Hapsburg than they were anti-Protestant. Diplomatic efforts to this end were already under way in May 1531. At the same time, Francis pursued efforts in Italy to persuade Clement VII to approve Henry VIII's divorce and to agree to the marriage of his niece, Catherine de' Medici, to the duke of Orléans, the future Henry II. Nor did Francis shrink from renewed direct contact with the Turks (1530–1) with the aim of encouraging them to weaken the emperor by attacking his interests (and his possessions) in eastern Europe and in Italy. All these efforts would continue throughout the 1530s and beyond. See Knecht 221–6, and cf Ep 2480 n3.

1529. Schets' answer, Ep 2527, is correctly dated August 1531. The reference to Erasmus' purchase of new house (line 10) also confirms the year-date as 1531.

Cordial greetings. Pieter Gillis has written to me that he paid the money that Quirinus was seeking.[1] The archbishop of Canterbury writes that he will remit to Luis de Castro the fifty-five pounds sterling that were due within seven days; I believe this has already been done.[2] Concerning the redemption of my pension he has good hopes.[3] The money coming to me through Luis comes at a great loss to me; how that is so I don't know. A certain Englishman sent me fifty crowns via Bebel. I received them without losing a single farthing for the banker. Another person gave me thirty-five nobles; for these I received forty-nine crowns.[4]

I have bought a house here and paid almost eight hundred gold florins.[5] I will write more copiously during the fair, God willing.[6]

Farewell. Freiburg, 17 July 1529[7]

Your Erasmus, in my own hand

2513 / From Agostino Steuco   Reggio nell' Emilia, 25 July 1531

Agostino Steuco (Ep 2465 introduction) was prior of the convent of San Marco in Reggio nell' Emilia. This is his answer to Ep 2465, which was Erasmus' reaction to Steuco's *Recognitio Veteris Testamenti* (1529). Steuco published the letter, along with Ep 2465, at the end of his *In Psalmum xviii et cxxxviii interpretatio* (Lyon: Gryphius 1533) 198–231.

* * * * *

2512
1 Cf Ep 2494:26–7. The letter is not extant.
2 But cf Ep 2620:13–16.
3 The letter is not extant. For Erasmus' wish to redeem his pension, see Epp 2487:23–7, 2494:16–18.
4 The 'certain Englishman' and the 'other person' may have been John Longland and Thomas Boleyn; see Ep 2576 n7. For Schets' response, explaining the apparent discrepancy in the payment of the second gift in nobles, see Ep 2527 n5.
5 Presumably Rhenish florins. A substantial sum, equivalent, at the official rate, to £188 6s 8d groot Flemish or twenty-one years' wages of an Antwerp master mason/carpenter (CWE 12 650 Table 3, 691 Table 13). See Epp 2462 introduction, 2506 n1.
6 Ie he will send letters (doubtless via Hieronymus Froben) to the autumn book fair at Frankfurt, to be transferred to someone there for delivery to Antwerp
7 On the year-date, see the introduction above.

AGOSTINO OF GUBBIO TO ERASMUS OF ROTTERDAM,
CORDIAL GREETINGS

I could not at this moment have received, most learned Erasmus, any favour
more welcome than a letter from you, that is to say, from a most learned man,
and one whose name I have always held in the highest esteem. Your letter 5
was all the more welcome because many traces of your good will to me are
apparent in it, and I saw clearly there a paragon of modesty and Christian
charity. As far as benevolence is concerned, I would say that it proceeds from
your admonitions to me, as I enter upon such a cruel sea for the first time, to
avoid those great troubles that you now feel you have escaped, as from the 10
cyclopean boulders and the savage Charybdis, and you remind me as I go
forward onto the stage of public opinion what skill I must possess in present-
ing myself to the spectators.[1] It can only be viewed as a divine benefaction
that, as one faces manifold dangers and a variety of perils, one finds someone
who can make one more cautious through his own perils. For that person 15
could very well have kept silent, probably without incurring any blame. For
this service I recognize that I owe you great thanks.

The opportunity to do so was provided to you by my annotations on
the Old Testament, in which, you assert, many things were pleasing to you,
while there were some concerning which it seemed of great importance that I 20
be warned to be more careful in the future. You expressed this exhortation in
many words. I began, therefore, to read your letter very carefully, in order to
comprehend instantly what you had promised at the beginning. After reading
it in its entirety, I concluded that your promises were not fulfilled at all, for instead of admonitions I found criticisms and certain accusations of exceptional 25
gravity. Certainly, if you had written to give encouragement and reassurance
with your usual kindness, you would have demonstrated your good will. But
if you were prompted to write because of some ill temper, I say that you had
no valid reason for behaving in this way towards one who in a secret place in
his conscience silently venerated you and who never openly cited your name 30
to express disapproval. All this criticism on your part I see as originating partly
in your suspicion that I have injured your reputation, and partly because I had
not praised you as much as you would have wished. The result is that your
courtesy both pleased me and at the same time did not quite please me, since
everything was contrived by you to refute a suspected calumny. Although that 35
was your plan, you cleverly concealed it, saying that it was very important for
me and for others that I heed your advice, so that on the surface you would

* * * * *

2513
1 Ep 2465:117–32

appear to be a counsellor but inwardly you would be a censor. You could have fulfilled this duty more sincerely if suspicion and some other emotion had not carried you off in different directions. Everything that you have considered worthy of censure, and all the support of the many people whom you cite in justifying yourself, have this purpose: to make it appear that he who has offended them unjustly has also offended you most unjustly.

I conclude that two things have aroused your suspicion. The first is that I attacked too bitterly the pride of certain people,[2] among whom you suspect that you were also included. The other is that only in one passage do I mention you, but contemptuously, as you interpret it.[3] Concerning those whose insolence is censured, since one kind of insolence in particular had to be censured, namely, the lack of respect for the saints and sacred objects that is so rampant these days, this is how you conduct yourself: ferreting out all the possible passages in my annotations that could serve your purpose, you attempt to make me one of that insolent number, so that either I become involved in the same incrimination or I am forced to admit that those from whose insolence I was not far removed did not deserve my censure. And yet, while you are engaged in this, you say that you are sincerely interested in my good reputation and claim that you have assumed the role of benevolent counsellor. You even cleverly ask that I accept your censures in the same spirit in which they are given. You exert your energies exclusively against the rebuke I directed against the insolent, which is what instigated you to write, and from which you collected the many defects that you impute to me. You plead a case against mockery of old age, inconsistency of language, and a certain juvenile exultation and delirium, in defence of a senile delirium that you suspect me of accusing you.[4] And so, since everything is based on the suspicion that is contained in your letter, I have easily understood that you went hunting for charges you could make against me, imagining them rather than discovering them. I deduced that this was the reason why you interpreted many of my passages differently than I presented them, and that you descended to trifling matters that you could carp at, and that even typographical errors, which had occurred in the printing of the book, furnished you with material that you, a learned man, could point out.[5] Although I was aware of that beforehand, and know that the fault does not lie with me, I accept with good will your calling it to my attention.

* * * * *

2 Ie the reformers, especially Luther, Steuco's criticisms of whom reflected his dislike of Germans in general; see Ep 2465:463–83, and n12 below.

3 Ep 2465:423–4

4 Ep 2465:354–76

5 Ep 2465:73–7

Concerning those points that you interpreted wrongly, and those that I perhaps justly criticized in many places, you defend yourself by twisting and minimizing them – on these points, I say, I will answer with the same moderation and the same frankness that you used towards me. I will make use 75 of that frankness all the more willingly, since you invited me to do so here and there, but especially at the end of your letter.[6] In my turn I implore you, my dear Erasmus, not to suspect that I have said anything unfairly, for your learning has always made you a close friend and an object of veneration, so that even if I have never seen you, I have nevertheless greatly admired you. 80 You must not think that as a young man I ever either held or could have held your grey hairs in contempt; never did such madness enter into my mind. For I have always had the highest regard for your works, and I am of the opinion that your faith and piety have always been irreproachable. My only displeasure was that in your writings you have brought it about 85 that many people suspect that you are different than you are. And this has been your fate because you have led almost your whole life under arms, always engaged with many opponents in gladiatorial combat, now hurling weapons, now repelling those launched at you; indeed in your audacious youth you challenged many people and many things; you took on the heavy 90 burden in those years of severely censuring the morals of everyone. Even if everyone should interpret that this was done by you with good intention, it would have been better to do it with more moderation and less licence.[7] There are many who say that you are partly to blame for the Saxon heresy, not that it was your intention that things would turn out that way, but be- 95 cause, they maintain, it came about through your excessive licence or incautious and imprudent zeal (if I may use that term). And those who say this are not few in number nor altogether uneducated, and they think they can easily demonstrate it from your books.[8] Quite a number of them affirm that if you were aware of wrongdoing and misconduct in the church, it would have 100 been more prudent of you to conceal these things rather than bring them to light before the theatre of the whole world, since all the Scriptures teach that the sins of others should be passed over in silence, lest once they are made manifest they serve as an example of depravity to the wicked or render other aspects of religion worthy of censure. They argue that this would have been 105

* * * * *

6 Ep 2465:696–9
7 This was a common criticism of the *Moriae encomium*; cf Ep 2465:289–93.
8 Of the many who had argued in this way, the one best known to Steuco was Alberto Pio; see lines 681–4 below.

the true method of writing, since from the opposite manner great scandals had risen up among the people. These things, my dear Erasmus, are between us and by letter, for it is not my intent to publish this unless you give me further reason to do so.[9]

But putting these things aside, we must come to your words. At first you 110 congratulate me on my courage and good fortune; you call me very learned, perhaps so that struck with bewilderment by this praise I would not notice your mordant remarks and all the censure that you employed against me. You begin with the much-praised library of Grimani, that is, from your praises of it, and from that beautiful occasion you descend to me: You 'skimmed 115 through, rather than read' my annotations, you say. On the contrary, you read and reread them and carefully scrutinized everything to see if you could find something to criticize, but 'as a counsellor, not a censurer.' This edition, you say, 'abounds with prodigious errors.' This rebounds instead on the heirs of Aldus, but it would have been more appropriate to the friendship that existed 120 between you and them to have spared them this.[10] You say that through some personal resentment I seem to be more cross with certain people, Lyra and the bishop of Fossombrone for example,[11] and you suspect that I inveighed against them through personal animosity because they were Germans.[12] On this point I cannot but require greater openness from you. No doubt it was 125 this sincerity that led you to caution me, saying that I harboured personal resentment. First, when you say that I cite the name of that bishop only to cast blame on him, you would never be able to prove it, since in citing him I have always accorded great praise to his learning. If you had been willing to interpret this correctly, and if another feeling had not drawn you to an- 130 other thought, you would surely have understood it. Moreover, I could have easily taken the opportunity, if I had wished, to mention what he said about

* * * * *

9 Only after Erasmus published Ep 2465 in the *Epistolae floridae* did Steuco decide to publish this letter. See the preface, addressed to Julius Pflug, on pages 2–3 of the psalm commentary cited in the introduction to this letter.

10 Ep 2465:65–75. The first edition of Steuco's *Recognitio Veteris Testamenti* was published by Aldus at Venice in 1529. Erasmus appears to have known that a second edition was in the works; see Ep 2465 n10.

11 Nicholas of Lyra and Paul of Middelburg; see Ep 2465 nn11–2.

12 Ep 2465:78–85. In the preface to his psalm commentary (see introduction above) Steuco had named Julius Pflug the *arbiter et iudex* of his dispute with Erasmus. As he subsequently reported to Erasmus, Pflug took particular offence at Steuco's anti-German sentiments and judged Erasmus the victor; see Allen Ep 2806:56–87.

Giovanni Pico,[13] a man of incomparable learning and sanctity: of this great
man and great Christian, the bishop was not ashamed to say that he was a ma-
gician and a trickster[14] (I think it was because he wrote against astrologers).[15]   135
See what moderation your bishop had. Then, that you think that I, so to speak,
brought him and Lyra before justice because both of them were Germans
came from your conviction that I had attacked you because you were German,
and you make this suspicion known more expressly in other places. It would
befit your moderation and prudence, my dear Erasmus, to examine the truth   140
more carefully. I cited both of them because one discusses Jerome's edition
and the other, knowing Hebrew, wrote following the Hebrew for the whole
Old Testament – for I did not know, may God be my witness, that Lyra was
German.[16] See, therefore, how far removed I was from your imaginings. It is
less grave that you compare the former with Reuchlin,[17] though in your opin-   145
ion the bishop is more distinguished (for me Reuchlin seems to be the more
important of the two); that was because of the polite introduction to Reuchlin,
which I did not add for the bishop, while you thought Reuchlin was worthy of
an apotheosis.[18] You do not see how ridiculous this is, how completely unworthy of a great man like you. But if I wrote a polite introduction to Reuchlin,   150
who is German, you should have seen that I have no personal resentment
towards the Germans, as you seem to suspect.

   And yet in this matter you protest that I am more forceful in asserting
than accurate in proving. You say that I strongly reject the opinions of others,
like that of the bishop of Fossombrone, who thinks that the Latin edition is   155
not by Jerome.[19] But his reasons did not have to be refuted, partly because

* * * * *

13 Giovanni Pico, count of Mirandola (1463–94), the brilliant Italian philosopher
   who was learned in Hebrew and Arabic as well as Latin and Greek, and who
   combined Florentine Neoplatonism with a thorough knowledge of scholastic
   Aristotelianism; cf Ep 126:150n.
14 In *Paulina, de recta Pascha celebratione* (Fossombrone 1513) folio EE iii
15 *Disputationes adversus astrologiam divinatricem* (c 1493–4), first published by his
   nephew Gianfrancesco Pico della Mirandola at Bologna in 1496 (Benedictus
   Hector).
16 Sarcasm at the expense of Erasmus, who had called Lyra, a Frenchman from
   Normandy, a German
17 Ep 2465:83–7
18 In the colloquy *De incomparabili heroe Ioanne Reuchlino in divorum numerum re-
   lato*, published in 1522 and subsequently referred to as *Apotheosis Capnionis* 'The
   Apotheosis of Johann Reuchlin' (CWE 39 244–55).
19 Ie that the Vulgate version of the Old Testament is not by Jerome; see Ep 2465
   n14.

they were not of great importance, and partly because from what preceded it was generally known, in my opinion, that our edition was that of Jerome, and that it was in these prefatory remarks that the solution to the bishop's arguments was contained. You say that I think he should not be heeded. But where is this statement in my book? Where do I say this? What forgetfulness makes you assert that I rejected his opinion, relying on this one argument, that the prefaces are by Jerome, although other reasons are given at the beginning of the work? You propose the example of the two prefaces to the book of Job, and you say that neither of them belongs to this version;[20] how this escaped your eyes and mind bewilders me. Jerome testifies that he sweated over a double labour in Job, one by which he translated the whole book from Hebrew, the other by which he compared the Septuagint with the source the Latins and the Greeks were using at the time, and showed there was a great superfluity of words marked with an asterisk; those that lacked asterisks seemed to have been added from the Hebrew.[21] Of this double labour these are his words in the first preface: 'The two editions, the Septuagint according to the Greeks and mine according to the Hebrew, have been translated into Latin by my efforts.'[22] Therefore Jerome reveals that the Hebrew text translated into Latin is his work, which is the one read today, if you compare it with the Hebrew. Therefore you cannot say that neither of these prefaces corresponds to this edition, since the first preface openly indicates that it is the preface of this edition and of that book, not of the other.

You will say that this edition does not come from the Hebrew, but if you compare the Septuagint and the Hebrew, you will easily understand what is very evident to me. I truly cannot see for what reason many people are persuaded that the Latin version of the Old Testament is not by Jerome, which has always seemed to me to be a mark not only of ignorance but also of supreme ingratitude. I am not referring to those whom I would not name without praise. If one important part of the Bible, that is, all the prophets, is clearly the edition of Jerome (since in his commentaries he cites his edition from the Hebrew, which is the one the church uses today, and opposes it to the Septuagint), how is it possible that the other books are not from

* * * * *

20 Erasmus had actually said that the two prefaces correspond to two different versions of Job, but he speculated that the second version was a corruption of the one Jerome had made from the Hebrew; see Ep 2465:95–9 with n16.
21 See Jerome's preface to his translation of Job from the Hebrew (Stuttgart *Vulgata* 731:1–14).
22 Stuttgart *Vulgata* 732:51–2

his edition, since it is also clear that it is not the Septuagint? Therefore the
prophets are the edition of Jerome; how can the other books not be, since our   190
edition differs almost everywhere from the Septuagint? How can it be a combination of the two where there is such diversity between them? Then, who
were those eminent personages who dared to pervert the edition of Jerome,
that is, change some things? And if they changed some things, why did they
not change everything? Where are those passages that are interpolated? This   195
is what you should have proved, most learned man, who did not hesitate to
protest that others loudly make known their views.[23]

But I pass over these things rapidly, as being unimportant and well
known. With all due respect there is a twofold error in what you infer. 'It is
highly probable,' you say, 'that when Jerome's edition had been accepted in   200
practice, church leaders changed certain passages translated by him and restored some of them either from the old translation or from the Septuagint.'[24]
First of all, it cannot be highly probable, since it is not true. Those things that
are manifestly untrue cannot be probable. Why it is not true is sufficiently
apparent from the whole edition; or rather, if anything has been added or   205
changed, it must be supposed that it slipped in by error from other editions,
as in this passage: 'And the Lord had regard for Abel';[25] certain manuscripts
had 'And the Lord was inflamed,' although that is not altogether an error.[26]
But this kind of thing is extremely rare. Then you distinguish the old edition
from the Septuagint edition, although the old edition that the church used   210
was the Septuagint,[27] out of respect for which Augustine did not want Jerome
to make innovations.[28] Jerome can teach you this abundantly. If, therefore,
to return to a previous argument, I seem to be rather irritable with certain
people for very trivial reasons, you for the same reasons seem to be irritable
not with some people, but with everyone, since you have spoken quite freely   215
everywhere. Who is there among mortals or divinities about whom you have
not pronounced your opinion as you pleased?

* * * * *

23 Modern biblical scholarship has amply justified Erasmus in his detection of
   hands other than Jerome's in the text of the Vulgate.
24 Ep 2465:96–9
25 Gen 4:4
26 *Recognitio* 35 recto
27 Erasmus had made a distinction between the Greek Septuagint and the old
   Latin translation (*Vetus Latina*), which was a translation of the Septuagint; see
   Ep 2465:98–9.
28 Augustine *De civitate Dei* 18.43

But let us put this aside. You continue in this way. 'At times you mention the Averroists in a very hostile manner, so that you give the impression of
condemning Aristotelian philosophy altogether.'[29] Who would not wonder at   220
this inference, most learned man? For who does not perceive that condemning the Averroists is very different from doing away with the philosophy of
Aristotle? I would say that it is truer that those who wish to have a more accurate philosophy of Aristotle should remove his bad interpreters. And you
think that the philosophy of Aristotle is abolished together with Averroes,   225
for no other reason, I think, than to accumulate more things to criticize in
me, as if you were my Aristarchus.[30] Furthermore, it is even more offensive
to say that he who condemns Averroes abolishes the philosophy of Aristotle,
although you are not ignorant of philosophers of this type; if it were you who
had attacked them, you would think that you had performed a praiseworthy   230
deed. But because they have been condemned by someone else, you do not
approve, and what you have done everywhere with the greatest licence dis-
pleases you in others. Since, therefore, I do not eliminate the philosophy of
Aristotle, nor do my words suggest it, it follows that what you say in that regard has no place here and has rather been introduced by a desire to calum-   235
niate. It is no less alien to my mind and to the truth that because I said that
certain Platonists erred in the philosophy of Plato, I would do away with the
philosophy of Plato. With the same witty language that you used previously
you say: 'You condemn Averroists, therefore you abolish Aristotelian philosophy; you condemn Platonists, therefore you also do away with Platonic   240
philosophy.'[31] Who would deny that this kind of argumentation originates
from a certain ignorance of these very disciplines (although nothing escapes
you) and an inordinate desire to criticize? Those who know the philosophy of
the Platonists know how far their principles are from the philosophy of Plato.
The same thing must be said of the Averroists; the argumentation ends up   245
with the opposite meaning. For those who abolish Averroes abolish a strange
kind of philosophizing in the teachings of Aristotle; they abolish many false
opinions into which he drew Aristotle without his consent. In the same way

* * * * *

29 See Ep 2465:102–3.
30 Aristarchus of Samothrace (c 216–144 BC) compiled critical recensions of the
    texts of Homer, marking questionable passages with an obelus. His name be-
    came proverbial for severe and unsparing criticism.
31 Ep 2465:108–10 (a paraphrase rather than a direct quotation)

the Platonists extracted many perverse beliefs from the philosophy of Plato. When these interpreters of both philosophies have been abolished, the phi- 250 losophy itself is not abolished but affirmed and enhanced. If this type of argumentation pleases you, what prevents you from reasoning in this way: Jerome condemns bad Christians, therefore, he also condemns Christ and the Christian religion – because in your judgment he who condemns bad philosophizers condemns philosophy. 'You state openly that you will write against 255 Platonic philosophy.'[32] But where did I say that? That is a patent deformation of my words; I spoke about certain Platonists, not about Plato.[33]

I will pass over in silence certain other things of the same import that you also said, because they are completely irrelevant. Certainly there is no one who has carefully assessed what you have said so far who would not 260 desire more fair-mindedness in you. You make someone into an accuser of everyone who is not even your accuser, but whom you suspect to be your accuser. With this same kind of incrimination you call one who reproves those who abuse the good disciplines an accuser of those same disciplines. What if someone were to say that you despised all theology because you perse- 265 cute theologasters everywhere? What if someone were to call you a scorner of the Christian religion because you have condemned superstitious worshippers, as you call them, everywhere? What if someone were to call you the enemy of all cenobites in general because you have mercilessly vilified certain lazy and corrupt monks? You have become accustomed to excusing 270 yourself by saying that you are in the habit of reprimanding not the good, but the bad. You should have interpreted my words in the same way, if you had any good will. And so it necessarily followed that in defending yourself you explained away false accusations with false accusations. I say false accusations because you suspected that I found fault with you; and all of this, 275 may it please the gods! in the guise of an admonitory letter. Your accusation is threefold. You call one anyone who criticizes those who present the good disciplines wrongly a critic of the good disciplines.[34] You call one who censures those who lead an evil life in a region a critic of the whole region.[35] With

* * * * *

32 Ep 2465:108–9
33 *Recognitio* 6 recto
34 This appears to be a generalization based on Erasmus' accusation that Steuco's hostility to the Averroists amounted to the rejection of Aristotelian philosophy altogether; cf lines 218–20 and n29 above.
35 Ep 2465:463–502

this same loftiness, a little further on, you call one who compares different   280
translations with each other a critic of translators, so that if someone should
show that Jerome's translation differs from the Hebrew, you would say he is
a critic of Jerome;[36] yet Jerome calls those who criticized his translations and
comparisons of the old translators calumniators. As to what you say about
navigation,[37] I hope I shall never experience an unfortunate navigation, for I   285
shall avoid with all my strength the reefs on which your little ship crashed,
whether willingly or not, I do not know. Nevertheless what you say is excellent, and in this regard I owe you a great deal. You say I 'devoured many
things in haphazard reading.'[38] This too, in whatever spirit it was said, I take
in good part. In fact a little later you call me very learned. You know in what   290
spirit you said these things; they are received with serenity even if they were
not said with peaceful intention.

I come now to what provided you with the occasion and the motivation
to write. It was what I had said as a digression in my annotation on the name
of Adam. On which subject let me say this in advance. You know, esteemed   295
Erasmus, and you cannot deny it, by what fates and ill fortune our times
have been beleaguered, so that together with the excellent studies that had
lain buried for so many years there emerged also a huge swarm of evils. We
can only attribute this to those minds that by their impudence and blindness
exploited these studies, which should have been used to good purpose, and   300
produced disaster. And even if this evil began with them, it is certain that it
was not their fault but rather the fault of passionate feelings and audacious
tongues. When the tongue is the servant and the interpreter of an evil mind,
what havoc it can create! It can happen sometimes that even if the intention is not evil, the tongue is not aware of it, or is incapable of interpreting   305
the mind's thoughts, and so it says other things than what was intended.
They say that in writing not only a good intention but also proficiency is
absolutely necessary, which things certainly can be disconnected. Many are
skilled in expressing themselves and very clever in concealing the wickedness of their intentions. On the other hand, you will find others who, if you   310
live on familiar terms with them, will turn out to be straightforward, loyal,
and guileless. But it often happens that the better someone is, the more he is

* * * * *

36 Ep 2465:589–675
37 Ep 2465:117–22
38 Ep 2465:122–3

prone to anger.[39] If such a person dedicates himself to writing, he will appear quite different than he is.

This is what I have to say about language, which has been the mother 315 of many evils in our day, of which we have seen a very clear example in what orators have said about the art of speaking. The greatest orator of all said that many cities were founded, many wars ended, solid alliances and inviolate friendships established through language, and that on the other hand, no inconsiderable part of disasters were created by very eloquent men.[40] There 320 have been many well-known and clear examples of this in our day. With the resurgence of studies and eloquence, which were long hidden in darkness, a great multitude of disasters has arisen, and much greater than in other times, since language encompasses not only earthly but heavenly things.

But, you will say, where is all this leading? Evidently, to demonstrating 325 that I, who am a man far removed from any insulting language, have for good reason been much distressed about this. No one is of such a complaisant and forgiving character as not to have been exasperated by the language of those (and they are not few in number) whose crimes you, Erasmus, excuse or pretend not to notice. You say that the Saxon sometimes disregards 330 the authority of the saints,[41] although he does this all the time; you ignore the blasphemies in the books of those people, although they are filled with blasphemies and vituperations against the divine majesty. It is not necessary to enumerate them; Eck recently made this known by collecting more than three hundred of their blasphemies into a little pamphlet (giving the names 335 of the authors, who number, plus or minus, fifteen heresiarchs).[42] They are too abominable for me to mention without horror; among them are these: that when Christ, in despair, called out with great cries, 'My God, my God,'[43] his soul descended to the underworld to suffer punishment for his sins, like everyone else; that if the writings of Jovinian, Helvidius, and Vigilantius 340 were extant, it would become clear that they contributed much to the

* * * * *

39 *Apologia adversus Petrum Sutorem* LB IX 740C–D; cf lines 657–9 below.
40 Cicero *De inventione* 1.1
41 Ep 2465:276–7
42 Johann Eck (Ep 2503 n3) had brought with him to the Diet of Augsburg in 1530 a pamphlet containing no fewer than 404 errors found in the writings of 'those who disturb the peace of the church' and announced that he was prepared to discuss them in the presence of the emperor. Most of the errors were attributed by name to Luther, Zwingli, or other reformers, but four were attributed merely to 'Someone,' in whom Erasmus recognized himself. See Ep 2365 n5.
43 Matt 27:46

writings of Jerome and that he criticized them unjustly;[44] that the mass has no value for the living or the dead; that fasts, since they were instituted by the church, need not be observed; that it is permitted to consecrate otherwise than in the mass; that it is permitted to priests and monks to marry and that 345 nuns may marry. There are a thousand articles I could cite if I had the time, far more stupid and disgraceful. And these doctrines are taken so seriously that they have been proposed as a subject of discussion before the most wise and Christian emperor. And all these fanatics are so much in agreement in subverting religion that they seem to have conspired together to bring about 350 its destruction. Do these not seem to be blasphemies to you, my excellent and learned friend? But you defend or wittily excuse them, introducing another kind of blasphemy that you heard about in Rome,[45] which of course has nothing to do with the matter under discussion, as you well know yourself, as if it were a matter of ethnic customs, or the depravities of the common 355 people, not of heresies, not of wrongdoing, not of pernicious dogmatists. You yourself see with what hostility you, who find the moderation you speak of to be lacking in others, vilify Rome, both here and elsewhere.

But I will return to what I had suggested earlier. All that conduct displeased me. But if I seem to have spoken anywhere too harshly against those 360 people, it was up to your kindness and great humanity to interpret it in such a way that the rebuke was not aimed at an entire nation or at men of moderation. Rather you should have thought that I was motivated by Christian zeal, like those who become infuriated when they hear some obscenity. I think it is the indication not of a perverse and ungenerous or proud spirit, but of one 365 who is indignant for the sake of Christian fairness and integrity. You will say perhaps: 'But you have me as a just interpreter; you have to have regard for others.' I admit it, but the more just one's indignation, the greater it is. At that point men of virtue are transported with fury, and the indignation that breaks forth from their soul and their heart forces them to exceed the ordinary rules 370 of propriety, as in the case of Moses, who broke the tablets of the law,[46] and Phinehas, indignant for a similar reason, killed two people.[47] I don't know

* * * * *

44 Jovinian's denial that virginity and monastic asceticism were superior to marriage elicited from Jerome his *Epistola adversus Jovinianum*. Helvidius' denial of the perpetual virginity of the Virgin Mary provoked Jerome's *De perpetua virginitate beatae Mariae adversus Helvidium*. Vigilantius' criticisms of (among other things) celibacy and monasticism produced Jerome's *Contra Vigilantium*.
45 Ep 2465:471–76
46 Exod 32:19
47 Num 25:6–9

if presumptuous language can be expressed more fittingly than by a corresponding effrontery. What names could I use to express the madness of those people, if not by calling these arrogant, supercilious men Cyclopes 375 and cruel and inhuman giants? And these words that reproach shameless conduct are not abuse, otherwise Isaiah, who said, 'O sinful nation, people laden with iniquity, wicked children,'[48] would be an utterer of abuse. Christ would be an utterer of abuse, when he called the Jews hypocrites;[49] Paul likewise, when he called the high priest a white-washed wall.[50] Would you not 380 be such a one yourself?

And that has to do only with language. For in my annotations I almost never challenge their doctrine. Therefore, there was no reason for you to demand proofs, arguments, and refutations, and to say that it is easy for anyone to hurl insults, and that a solid doctrine is required against such beliefs. You 385 say these things with contempt. But if you evaluate the question correctly, this was not the objective of that book. I have presented elsewhere solid arguments against several of their dogmas.[51] Therefore, there will be no dispute here with you or with them about confession,[52] of which you have undertaken the defence, though you were the first to make war against it.[53] And 390

* * * * *

48 Isa 1:4
49 Matt 6:2
50 Acts 23:3
51 Especially in his *Pro religione christiana adversus Lutheranos* (Bologna 1530)
52 In his *Pro religione christiana* (see preceding note) 7 verso, Steuco had placed Erasmus by name among the reformers who had 'erred grievously' and done great harm by saying that confession was a recent institution (ie not an institution founded by Christ himself and practised in the ancient church). For his part, Erasmus, without mentioning the *Pro religione christiana* (which he may not have known), had taken Steuco to task for the inadequacy of his defence of sacramental confession against Luther in the *Recognitio,* urging him to do a more effective job in their common struggle against error (Ep 2465:503–60).
53 Cf lines 391–6 below. This half-hearted concession that Erasmus had finally arrived at an acceptable view of confession may well indicate that Steuco had read the greatly expanded second edition of the *Exomologesis sive modus confitendi* (Basel: Froben 1530), in which Erasmus did his best to mollify his Catholic critics and distinguish his views from those of Luther and the other reformers. Though insisting that conclusive proof was still lacking, he indicated that he was now inclined to side with those who believed that confession had been instituted by Christ. He stated further that, for the sake of the peace of Christendom, confession as currently practised should be preserved as a valid ecclesiastical custom and an effective means of pastoral care. Moreover, while repeating his earlier warnings about the dangers of abuse, he emphasized the

would that your words now coincide with your thoughts on this subject. Yet your *Colloquies* and what we have witnessed in the last few years forcefully demolish what we forcefully affirm.[54] If it is your wish that I had remained silent, it was much more to be desired that you had never uttered a word on this subject. For confession was first subjected to suspicion by you. But it is good that you have changed your opinion – or your words. 395

Now that I have wounded your feelings, Erasmus, I return to a previous consideration. I confess that at one time many things displeased me in your books, those in particular that produced many scorners of divine things who, certainly not interpreting your words correctly but relying on your learning and authority, attacked viciously everything that they saw despised and condemned by you, and began to spurn these things not only in their lives but with their tongues, and (following your lead) everywhere labelled as superstition the external forms of religion. For when you, whatever your intentions may have been, maligned the way of life of monks, calling them potbellies and whatever other opprobrious term you used; when you frequently denounced fasting, abstinence from meat, the eating of fish, judging others by your own stomach; when you expressed your disdain for psalmody,[55] which we know was held sacred from the apostles up to the time of the ancient writers; when you often derided the relics of the saints and those who venerate them; finally, when you hissed off the stage and rejected this piety as ordinary and second-rate, you stirred up many people greatly devoted to these practices to despise them as well as greater things. Imitating your continuous derision, they constrained simple folk to despise everything, and in our times, at your instigation, there has been an extreme contempt for fasts, chastity, and psalmody. The books of the Saxon and others who despised these same practices could not be sold publicly in Italy. How 400 405 410 415

* * * * *

benefits to the believer of the sacrament if properly administered by adequately trained priests. For a survey of the controversy from its inception in 1516 through to the end of Erasmus' life, see Michael J. Heath's introduction to the *Exomologesis* in CWE 67 2–15; see also John B. Payne *Erasmus: His Theology of the Sacraments* ([Richmond, Va] 1970) 197–209.

54 The subject of confession is touched on in several of Erasmus' colloquies, most significantly in the *Confabulatio pia* 'The Whole Duty of Youth' (literally 'A Pious Conversation'); see CWE 39 96:31–97:36 with nn53–70. The colloquy was first published in 1522. Steuco's point here is that the colloquies in question, as well as all the other works in which Erasmus had defended his view of the human origin of confession and heaped scornful criticism on the shortcomings of confessors, were still in print and available to be read.

55 Steuco presumably means the chanting of psalms by monks in choir.

great was the belief that your books were prejudicial to the life of monks
is amply testified in that, by public consent and edict, it was forbidden to
some of them to read or possess those books.[56] This, however, was not your   420
fault, but that of those who did not read your writings correctly and with
discernment, and who really did not grasp your thought (for I believe that
you did not condemn holiness itself, but only superstition and ignorance).
Nevertheless, some people say that you should have acted more moderately
and more discreetly. For what purpose (to give an example) did you attack   425
the vices of certain people, as you did in your colloquies? What poisonous
cups you offered for a toast! What springs of blasphemy did you open up! Is
this your foresight, Erasmus, in your role of grave censor? Sorrow penetrates
to your inmost entrails if you think something has been detracted from your
reputation; you prepare defences and responses. And do you not think that   430
others feel sorrow when you wound them so savagely? You say that I should
be more temperate in attacking the name of a whole nation. How do you
observe this advice, who, when you attack one or two individuals, discredit
a whole order, and you tacitly allude to a defiler of sacred virgins, but you do
not keep silence in your *Exomologesis*.[57] I ask you, when you do this, do you   435
not provide a pretext for condemning everyone? But what a great scandal
this is for the Christian people! Witnesses to this were the governments that,
saturated with documents of this kind, conspired to suppress monasteries.[58]
I saw and read with my own eyes your letter in which you reply to a certain
religious who was calling you back to the religious life. There you openly say   440

* * * * *

56 The reference is not clear. The language may well refer to a proscription imposed on an entire monastic order by its central authority, but the only monastic
bans on Erasmus' works that we know of appear to have been local in scope. In
Ep 1275:62–4 Erasmus reports that in 1522 the Dominicans at Cologne decreed
the banishment from their libraries of all books written by him. And in 1531
André de Resende left Louvain because his fellow Dominicans had banned the
reading of Erasmus' books on pain of excommunication (Ep 2570:44–5).
57 Allen cites LB V 154A–B (= CWE 67 39–40). Steuco's point seems to be that Erasmus
had discredited priests in general by criticizing the few who reveal the secrets
confided to them in the confessional. We have not succeeded in tracking down
the allusion to the defilers of sacred virgins (presumably nuns).
58 Presumably a reference to Protestant rulers, who missed no opportunity to appropriate monastic property and use the income to support their new ecclesiastical establishments, to finance schools, universities, hospitals, and other
measure of social welfare, or just to pay off their accumulated debts. By 1531
this process was already well advanced in many German territories and Swiss
cantons as well as in Denmark and Sweden.

that no greater evil could be found in the Christian religion than the invention of those religious orders.[59] But you will say the letter is not yours. I shall
be glad if that is the case. Many people wonder why in these tragic years you
silently inserted so many foul things into your *Colloquies* (which otherwise
smack of your eloquence and cleverness). I do not defend in opposition to   445
you the life and morals of inert and superstitious monks, but I say that there
is another way of remedying these evils than exposing the crimes of particular individuals to the people as a spectacle.

These are the things that displeased me among the outstanding gifts of
God that you possess, dearest Erasmus. I am disposed to honour and vener-   450
ate you with great affection, and I esteem that your character is irreproachable. The immense praise you have received, both in other places and in Italy,
I not only do not envy but proclaim and extol as much as possible in the
presence of everyone, and often I revive my spirits by reading your writings.
I am not one to seek out pretexts for disparaging anyone, not to say a most   455
learned man, to whose labours and erudition everyone is hugely indebted.
My character is completely foreign to all hatred and envy. Nothing is further from my mind than conceiving personal resentment against anyone, as
you suspected.

To return, then, to the previous subject: concerning Augustine, in the   460
earlier editions,[60] when you differed with him on the interpretation of some
passage or other, you expressed your exasperation in this way: 'I ask you,
reader, does he not seem to be living in some other world?'[61] You mitigated
this outrageous insult in later editions, as I see.[62] What clever dissembling
you employ at this point! I will not argue about the etymology of the name   465
[Adam], except to say that you failed to mention, through forgetfulness, that
it was Cyprian who said that.[63] I admit, not to appear too much on the defen-
sive, that the comment on the name Adam is frigid.[64] But you cannot deny
that this etymology does exist. That is what I said, and I am surprised that you

* * * * *

59 Clearly a reference to Ep 296 (8 July 1514), the letter to Servatius Rogerus, prior
     at Steyn, justifying Erasmus' failure to return to his home monastery; see espe-
     cially lines 79–81. Erasmus never published the letter himself, but copies of it,
     including perhaps two in print, circulated before his death.
60 Steuco is referring to the editions of Erasmus' Annotations on the New Testament.
61 Annotation on Romans 14:5 CWE 56 372; cf Ep 2465:25 with n43.
62 Not that we can find
63 Ep 2465:145–50
64 On Erasmus' use of the word *frigidus* ('cold,' 'insipid,' 'absurd'), see Ep 2465
     n20.

did not see that kind of etymology in Plato's *Cratylus*.[65] Isn't it similar to what   470
he said about the name Ζεύς Διός, as if to say δι' ὃν ζωή [through whom comes
life]?[66] And Apollo, from ὃς ὁμοπολῶν [he who moves together],[67] changing
the letters, and other examples of that kind? And this occurs very frequently
with those who profess the Cabala, if you accept the example. Nowhere do
you find this kind of argument: 'This sheep is sick, therefore there are no   475
healthy sheep.' How far removed I am from this kind of reasoning I leave to
your judgment and the judgment of others. These are bagatelles and child's
play, which you drew out longer than is reasonable. Therefore, in this angry outburst, which you say was so vehement, so harsh, so diversified, you
can easily understand who are the objects of my attack and what motivated   480
me. But if I seem to have said anything against you that was unworthy of
your prestige, you must consider that I said it not with the intention of doing
harm, but rather through indignation and in the interests of Christian dignity. I saw that a respectable form of piety was regarded with contempt, I saw
that everything that Jovinian tried to introduce in his time was being revived,   485
and the most powerful incentives came from your books.[68] But if at your advanced and venerable age you were to revoke many things, as is natural, and
tone down some of your statements, then I would render infinite thanks to
God, and from this moment on promise to be the promoter of your piety and
learning everywhere. Therefore, there is no place here for the many things   490
you uttered in a frenzy of indignation. It is not against your age, as you think,
that these things have been said; it is sufficiently clear to what they refer. For
the *Colloquies* and the *Exomologesis* are works of your old age. There is another thing, too, altogether foreign to my character, which I laugh at rather than
refute, since I introduced my own person in these words: 'Therefore, it is not   495
that we are boasting about our erudition; whether we equal or surpass those
saintly men in learning, we are surely inferior to them in sanctity, so much
so that we cannot evoke it without tears.'[69] 'Here' you say, 'you express your
own personal feelings.' See with what fairness you interpret these words,
Erasmus, as if I likened myself to them in learning, whereas I meant only to   500
show my failings, which I share with many others. What an occasion you
chose for invectives! And you do not allow your eyes to see what is being

* * * * *

65 *Cratylus* 396
66 ζῆν is both the accusative of 'Zeus' and the infinitive 'to live.'
67 *Cratylus* 405
68 See n44 above (Jovinian).
69 Ep 2465:399–402

referred to, namely, that I of course teach that primary importance is given
to piety, not to learning. There are many people who, spurning piety, devote
all their enthusiasm to letters and philosophy. There are those who persuade 505
themselves that godlike perfection resides in the knowledge of many things,
not in a hallowed sanctity. How many you would find who, if given the op-
tion, would choose the learning rather than the sanctity of Jerome! I do not
think it is wrong to dissent from the saints if it is done without arrogance,
without offence, without the boastfulness of those who dissent, without too 510
great a scandal, if you dissent genuinely, instinctively, not for personal reasons, and in the case of extreme necessity. If you ponder these conditions,
Erasmus, you will find them in the heresiarchs rarely, in you not so rarely. If
you think you are despised by me because I dissented from you, are not the
saints from whom you dissent despised? When you attempt to show that I 515
dissent from them (to make me resemble you), it is very different; neither
the intention nor the examples correspond. If it is true that Augustine did
not know Hebrew, if he translates some passage in a way that is inconsistent
with the character of that language, how shall I express it in any other way
than by saying 'Augustine, not knowing Hebrew, misconstrued it,' or some- 520
thing similar? If Jerome translates differently from what is in the Hebrew
context, with what words will I demonstrate it? This is clear reasoning for
those who are open-minded. Often, with you, defamation takes the place of
prefaces. You say that Augustine lives in another world;[70] you assert that he
is sometimes too credulous.[71] These words are in your early editions, which I 525
see you later mitigated.[72] With what colour you sometimes paint Jerome! All
this is sufficiently well known, since many people have written pamphlets
containing insults of this sort, excerpted from your writings.

What differences exist between me and you on this point I leave to im-
partial judgments. But before I descend to those subjects, I would like to dis- 530
cuss that one passage in which you say that I mentioned you disparagingly
and in disagreement.[73] Here, as in almost all cases, you ignore the reason for
my disagreeing with you and interpret my intentions and my words wrongly. First of all, you have no reason to suspect that I disparaged you because

* * * * *

70 See lines 462–3 with no 61 above.
71 This assertion first appeared in the 1516 version of Erasmus' Annotation on
John 21:22; see CWE 72 228 (*Responsio ad annotationes Eduardi Lei*).
72 We know of no mitigation of the comment on living in another world (cf n62
above), but the passage on Augustine's credulity was considerably toned down
in the Annotations of 1519; see CWE 72 228 n917.
73 Ep 2465:423–45

I was in disagreement with you. Do you not understand how this suspicion   535
of yours negates everything you said? You tried to argue that if someone
disagrees with another, it does not follow that he despises him. Here are
your words: 'Are we to understand that one who disapproves of something
in the writing of Augustine automatically holds his piety and erudition in
contempt?'[74] You thus argue against yourself. If you dissent, you therefore   540
despise. You do not name me except in dissent, therefore only in contempt,
because there is no other word there except that which implies contempt.
This argumentation is plainly inferred from your words. You used the same
kind of argumentation at the beginning also, when you thought that I despised the bishop of Fossombrone and Nicolas of Lyra because I disagreed   545
with them on the ground that they were Germans (something deserving of
a laugh and resulting from an old man's suspicions).[75] I disagree with you
and I cite you, not contemptuously, as you think, nor because I have any less
esteem for your learning, but rather for the following reason. Although the
Hebrew text says that Joseph was in the habit of accusing his brothers, and   550
Jerome's translation in our manuscripts, as well as all the other Greek translators, have this text, and those who explain the Sacred Scriptures demonstrate that this is the correct reading, you, unaware of this or pretending not
to know it, not only disagree in the *Paraphrase*,[76] but in your *Lingua* you say
expressly that the Septuagint reading is more correct than what is contained   555
in our version.[77] When you said that you did not know what the Hebrew text
read, I said that I wondered why you did not know that the Hebrew text has
what our version has. I said in many places that not only in the *Lingua* but
also in the *Paraphrase* you had reaffirmed this. It is necessary that the figurative sense depends on the literal sense; the figurative cannot exist if the literal   560
sense is wrong. No one, I believe, would prefer the Septuagint to the Hebrew
truth.[78] If I sometimes prefer the Septuagint to Jerome, I do so following the
Hebrew, not contrary to that same source. You see how different we are.
Jerome reports what they translated, because this version was the received
version when he had not translated from the Hebrew himself. In another   565
place, where you say I attacked you, may I perish if I ever even dreamed of
doing you harm. My words are these at Genesis, chapter 46: 'Therefore this

* * * * *

74 Ep 2465:391–3
75 See lines 121–4, 136–44 above.
76 *Paraphrase on Luke* 24:27 CWE 48 261
77 ASD IV-1A 110:765–83
78 *Hebraica veritas*, Jerome's term for the Hebrew text of the Old Testament

is the solution of the knot that they say Jerome tied but did not loose.'[79] I ask you, dear Erasmus, if you said that Jerome tied the knot but did not untie it, what should I have said of you? In what way could I express myself with more moderation? If I had been a familiar friend of yours, if I had sometimes conversed with you, I would have said something like this: 'My dear learned Erasmus states that Jerome tied, but did not untie,' and any suspicion that I had profaned your name would have been removed.

I come now to those passages that you looked for everywhere so that you could defend yourself against me. For since you suspected that my reproof was in great part directed at you, although I had improvised it in general terms in a fit of anger against detractors of sacred things (it took its inspiration from your words, in which you dissented insultingly from Augustine), you tried to show that I dissented from Augustine and others in many places, so that I often fell into that same vice that I had attributed to you. You did this magnanimously and with great charm, it is true, but it had nothing to do with the question. I do not criticize the occasional straying from the words of the saints, but rather the caustic remarks, the mockeries, and, if I may use the expression, the contempt, such as your remark about Augustine that he lived in another world. What else is this than to say he was raving mad? Your books are full of this kind of witticisms. If you were to criticize something of the sort in my books, I confess that I would be just like you and those others. For which reason, when I say on the subject of paradise, 'Therefore I consider to be mere fable the ideas that men have concocted about this paradise, that if Adam had not sinned, men would always have lived in that paradise,' and what follows, you say, 'Augustine was one of those who believed this, and you are not afraid to call them fables?'[80] It is obviously a manner of speaking, my dear Erasmus, and you, who keep looking for the opportunity to cast aspersions at the slightest pretext, cannot find here anything to serve your mordant wit. For I do not name anyone; sometimes I appear to defer to everyone, sometimes I draw back in doubt, if I do not understand it well. Who except Momus in person would find something to carp at in this case?[81] You alone, in your eagerness to contradict, found something to censure in order to show yourself the master. Besides, Augustine is definitely not among these. In my opinion, in fact, he would not have believed that the earth would never have been inhabited if man had not sinned. You continue: 'From time to time you

570

575

580

585

590

595

600

* * * * *

79 Ep 2465:446–62
80 Cf Ep 2465:572–83.
81 Momus was the god of carping criticism.

burst forth into praise of Jerome, but not without insulting the church, which
you write somewhere would have fallen into very great errors if that great
man had not translated from the Hebrew sources.'[82] First you say: 'It is a   605
harsh sound to pious ears to hear that the church is susceptible to error, especially in Scripture.'[83] Listen to how you have distorted everything, honoured
sir, how you have exploited the least opportunity to calumniate, how there is
nothing that you have not twisted into the opposite meaning. If anything is
praised, you carp at it; if it is justly criticized, you don't put up with it, which   610
demonstrates that you are clearly convicted of having wished to exacerbate
everything. Errors against the faith are of two kinds: one in dogma, the other in the Scriptures, as when something is read otherwise than it should be
read. It is certain that the first kind cannot exist in the church, for the church
cannot err. The second kind can be found, as it is found sometimes that the   615
manuscripts are read otherwise than they should be read. Jerome found that
this kind of error was very frequent in the Septuagint in his day, as anyone
who wishes can find out both in Jerome and in the Septuagint. The whole
church now reads, 'The whole earth was destroyed because of their blood,'[84]
whereas it should read 'was polluted.'[85] And everywhere it is sung, 'For forty   620
years I was close to this generation,'[86] whereas it should say 'I loathed this
generation,' or something of that nature. It is sung, 'That I may see the will of
the Lord,'[87] when it should say 'the joy.'[88] The Greek word is τερπνότητα, the
Hebrew נעם. Therefore this type of error can exist in the church. But you not
only wanted this latter kind of error, which does not lend itself to scandal,   625
to exist in the church, but also the former, and you affirmed in many places
that it exists. Because of this the whole world has risen up against you. For
whether deliberately or unintentionally, I do not know which, you have severely weakened fasts, celibacy, confession, and the seven sacraments. I do
not say these things by way of reproach, but to answer you in a friendly   630
manner, and with the same freedom that you employ indiscriminately with
a friend.

　　As for the other things that you pursue belligerently everywhere, which
you have hunted down so zealously (even if you do not wish to give that

*　*　*　*　*

82 Ep 2465:589–91
83 Ep 2465:592–3
84 Ps 105:38
85 The mistake was reading *interfecta* for *infecta*.
86 Ps 94:10
87 Ps 26:4
88 Reading *voluntas* instead of the correct *voluptas*

impression), feigning that they presented themselves to you – although they   635
are frigid in the extreme[89] and you make them more harsh and more repre-
hensible through your penchant for contradiction; when you distort many
passages in your interpretations and divert many to the opposite meaning;
when you accuse me of despising the Septuagint and Jerome with the same
kind of licence that you are accustomed to use in matters of this sort – these   640
things, I say, I will neither bother to refute, nor will I answer you on these
subjects. For I have rendered to Jerome the honour that the sanctity and
learning of this preeminent and incomparable man deserve. Accuse of this
crime only those who preferred to him the insane heretics whose morals and
doctrine he had most justly attacked. There are no grounds for your making   645
this false charge against me, which is and always will be far removed from
my character.

Thus far, with God as my witness, I have responded to you in a very
friendly manner. Now since you indicate in your modesty that I will have a
share in your friendship if I make some recommendations to you, that I may   650
obtain what you promise, listen to me, I pray, not as to a counsellor, but as
to a son, if you wish, or at least as a friend, and accept what I propose in
the name of Christian charity. For this will be useful to many people in general, and at the same time it will enhance your glory considerably. It would
be better, first of all, that you be less prone to anger. If you are excessively   655
inclined to that by nature, you must strive to eliminate every trace of anger from your language. For although we read that people who are more
inclined to anger are better,[90] nevertheless it would not be proper to expose
in writing a person's way of living and habitual behaviour. Then, as many
learned men advise you, you must not defend yourself in everything, just as   660
you should not submit to all the blows. Nor should you think that a man of
your importance should retort to everyone's grumblings, but that there are
many that you may disregard with good reason. In that way others will be
less inflamed, and they will act more peaceably with you; in that way the
time spent in writing apologias will be dedicated to more serious studies.   665
To attain that more easily, it would be better to pass over many things in
your writing, which, since they do not accomplish anything but rather are
a source of scandal, should be entirely passed over in silence, and so much
perturbation removed from your life. In the meantime I would wish that
you be more moderate in answering the accusations that you think have   670
been made against you, that you would avoid many abusive names, insulting

* * * * *

89 See n64 above.
90 See lines 312–14 above with n39.

remarks, and sarcasms, and would remember the words 'Do not repay evil
with evil.'[91] For what would be shameful for the profane must be deemed
much less fitting for a Christian, even less for a priest, and least of all for
a very learned man, and one who demands such moderation from others.   675
Not to mention other things, whoever vented his rage so savagely against
anyone that he cast the man's destiny and his death in his teeth, as if they
were crimes, as you did against Alberto, prince of Carpi, whom you condemned after his death, and whom you insulted because he was expelled
from his principality?[92] Do you think, Erasmus, that there would be anyone   680
who would not shudder reading this? What kind of moderation was it to say
that he was first prince of Carpi, then exiled to France, then a sycophant, and
finally a Franciscan?[93] A sycophant, obviously, because he called you to account. And are you not ashamed to preach moderation to others? Are you
not also ashamed, if it please the gods, to demand it so often from St Jerome?   685
You become angry, you rush to your apologias if anyone even barely grazes
your skin; you interpret it as a mortal wound if anyone does not adorn you
with praises. But I think you must have read that it is bad enough not to pick
up a man when he has fallen by accident, but to press him down when he
is lying on the ground or push him when he is falling is inhuman.[94] Would   690
it not have been sufficient simply to render an account to men of his faith
and piety rather than to mention his Franciscan habit, his exile, and his re-
versal of fortune and death? Wherefore, my celebrated friend, it would also
be most laudable if you would put less trust in biting sarcasm, witticisms,
and jesting, and made more spare use of them, because they weaken your   695
case. Jest and sarcastic remarks are not at all becoming in a Christian, and
besides, we should not wish to defend our cause by them alone. For while
you ridicule one, denigrate another, while you insult everyone with your wit
and jests, it has greatly detracted from your reputation. Lastly, what I propose to myself and other Christians, we must not make so much of the glory   700
derived from literature that for its sake we think we must 'plunge into arms
and the sword,'[95] as if this will make us immortal. Every kind of knowledge

* * * * *

91 1 Peter 3:9
92 For Erasmus' controversy with Alberto Pio, prince of Carpi, which had just come
    to an end with the publication Erasmus' *Apologia adversus rhapsodias Alberti Pii*,
    see Ep 2486 n10.
93 Steuco is evidently quoting Erasmus' remark in Ep 2522:68–9, thus indicating
    that he incorporated subsequently published material into the text of this letter
    before publishing it in 1533 (cf introduction above).
94 Cicero *Pro Rabirio postumo* 1.2
95 Virgil *Aeneid* 2.353

is an excellent thing, but far more illustrious is meekness and humility and expressing the life of Jesus Christ in our lives. The time will come when all the monuments of books will be destroyed by fire, when only uprightness in 705 every human activity will be glorified. I do not say this to prohibit anyone from writing, but to show that this good is a preparation for a greater good. There are some who say that while you desire to be unique in the whole human race, while you allow no one to be equalled to you or preferred to you, while you claim to be of the first rank among men of learning, you have 710 receded greatly from moderation and have done certain things that reveal an open jealousy. I would wish also that you would be less inclined to quibbling, and would ponder more carefully what befits a Christian and a man of learning. Not to speak of other things, so great is this quibbling that anyone who does not have a magnificent opinion of you despises all of Germany! For 715 example, I know that Germany is full of learned men who are also Christian, and I know many whose probity and learning are for me an object of admiration, among whom are Julius Pflug,[96] Jakob Ziegler,[97] the famous mathematician Johannes Marquardus,[98] the illustrious Georg Boëmus,[99] and others. Thus I use the word 'quibbling' correctly to indicate that in not praising you 720 and in venting my anger upon certain impudent Lutherans I have supposedly insulted Germany.[100] I do not acknowledge this offence at all. In fact, factious people and those eager for novelties have not even pleased prudent Germany. Certainly there has been no one in our day imbued with any degree of Christian piety and doctrine who has not been compelled to voice 725 some outcries against the shallowness of these people. What I did everyone should account to be fair and equitable, especially you, who arrogated great freedom to yourself in this regard.

The same quibbling is true of interpretations,[101] of philosophy,[102] and shows that in all your discourse you seem to be fighting with yourself, so that 730 the conflict is not so much with me as with yourself. You almost resent that

* * * * *

96 Ep 2492; see also n12 above.
97 Ep 1260
98 Neither Allen nor CEBR could identify Marquardus, and neither can we.
99 Probably Georg Beham of Nürnberg (c 1461–1520), who for the last seven years of his life was provost of the chapter of St Laurence (Sankt Lorenz) in Nürnberg. If the identification is correct, it must mean that Beham visited Italy at some point.
100 See n2 above.
101 Ie Erasmus' comments on what he called Augustine's 'interpretation' of the name 'Adam.' See Ep 2465:137–8, 192–3, 277–9, 625–7.
102 See n104 below.

I praised Reuchlin, whom you, I know not on what authority, placed among the saints.[103] You chastise me because I reproach the Averroists,[104] whom you in all your books reviled to the point of becoming hoarse. You say that the edition used by the church is not by Jerome,[105] and in your Annotations and 735 other books you say that Jerome translated from the Hebrew. You would have wished me to defend confession more vigorously, while your *Colloquies* declare plainly how you treat it.[106] You say that I display some kind of ill feeling towards Nicolas of Lyra,[107] whom you, when you were able to do so, criticized, mocked, and tore to shreds. Therefore, my most learned man, re- 740 flect more carefully on what is proper for you to do: disregard many things, pass over many things in silence in your writing; do not regard as enemies all those who reprehend you for something.

    There are many other things that I willingly pass over, lest I seem to have wished to teach an old and most erudite man. As far as I am concerned, 745 know that I have the highest opinion of your learning and your morals and your faith. I never liked those who published infamous little books against you. I wish, however, that with great prudence you would succeed in pre-venting hatreds from increasing in intensity and from small beginnings greatly multiply. You must confront them with mildness. For immediately 750 the mouth of the adversary is blocked and the readers are entranced by a marvellous pleasure. I recommend with great ardour that Christians admon-ish one another with Christian charity, but I cry out that the display of in-solence and insulting language is absolutely incompatible with the religion that we profess. O miserable age of ours if learning, which is a heavenly gift 755 and the glory of the human race, either breeds heresies or sunders the sacred alliances by which all of us are joined in Christ! Farewell, letters, if this is the case. Better to sweat over the rakes and the hoes, as far as I am concerned. Therefore I beseech you to put an end at last to your contention with me and with others. Disputes must not be stirred up for just any reason at all. We 760 must not fear for our reputation to the extent of thinking that if someone has mentioned our name without due respect or was completely silent about us, he has put our reputation at stake or disgraced it, nor should we struggle with the false suspicions and imaginations of our own mind. It is not the

* * * * *

103 See n18 above.
104 See lines 218–20 with n29 above.
105 See n19 above.
106 See n54 above.
107 See lines 121–3 and n11 above.

mark of a Christian to think that if he has been the victim of unjust accusa- 765
tions, he should avenge the injustice in the same way. If it is your intention
to conduct yourself with me in a conciliatory manner, I spontaneously accept
and welcome your friendship, and in addition to friendship I proffer to you
the honour and respect that is owed by me, a young man, to you, an old
man, a recruit to a veteran in Christian philosophy. And so that you cannot 770
complain that I was the initiator of discord, I will be the first to pursue the
moderation that I preach – and to which you invited me – and to this end I
finish the letter. As I pardon all the injuries you may have inflicted, so I ask
and beseech the same of you, so that if I have involuntarily offended you
in any way, either in this letter or elsewhere, you may pardon it in turn and 775
interpret it as coming from an intention that was not in the least prejudicial
or eager to do injury. May the Lord Jesus Christ increase your glory in this
world and in the next. Farewell.

Given at Reggio nell' Emilia, 25 July in the year 1531 since the Virgin 780
birth

2514 / To the City Council of Besançon   Freiburg, 26 July 1531

This letter was first published in the *Epistolae universae = Des. Erasmi Rot.
Operum Tertius Tomus epistolas complectens universas quotquot ipse autor unquam
evulgavit aut evulgatas voluit, quibus praeter novas aliquot additae sunt ...* (Basel: H.
Froben and N. Episcopius, c February 1538) 1110. It is striking that, at precisely
the time when he had just completed the purchase of an expensive new house
in Freiburg (Ep 2506 n1), Erasmus was giving thought to moving to a presumably safer place.

ERASMUS OF ROTTERDAM TO THE CITY COUNCIL OF BESANÇON,
GREETING
Magnificent and most honourable lords, when the altered situation in Basel
forced me to leave the home in which I had lived for a long time and was therefore dear to me,[1] I was thinking of moving to Besançon, having experienced at 5
one time your kindness and that of the canons.[2] But then the canons intimated
to me that there was some kind of dissension existing there and that it would
be better to put off my change of abode to another time.[3] Thus it came about

* * * * *

2514
1 See Epp 2090 introduction, 2097 n1.
2 In 1524; see Epp 1440:4–6, 1610, 1679:100–15, 1956.
3 See Epp 2112:5–11, 2410:48–50.

that, with the approval and recommendation by letter of King Ferdinand, I
took refuge in nearby Freiburg,[4] where I have been living for two years and   10
more, welcomed by everyone, but especially by the university. During all that
time I was not a financial burden to anyone, subsisting on my own resources.

But since I see that everything hangs in the balance, and I even see
forebodings of wars and tumults, which I hope will be groundless, I would
prefer to be anywhere else than in Freiburg if anything of that sort should   15
occur. Those who left Basel out of hatred for the sectarians, by whom they
are suspected of inciting monarchs to defend ecclesiastical interests by force
of arms, have come together here and continue to do so today. The town
is elegant and attractive, but deficient in basic commodities, and this frail,
aged body of mine, stricken with poor health, has need of many supports,   20
but especially wine from Burgundy, because German wines do not suit my
stomach.[5] When, however, I undertake to have it brought here from there, it
is, despite the excessive expense, either not the kind I want or spoiled in the
journey by the drivers.

I hope that everything will be peaceful, but if something should arise   25
that I do not want, I would be much obliged if I could avail myself of the
hospitality of your city temporarily. I would not be a burden to anyone. I
have, thanks be to the gods above, the wherewithal to nourish this frail little
body. I have no connections with any sect. I have no disciples except for those
I have in common with Christ, nor will I have, God willing. I have published   30
some admonitions about the vices of men, which cause some offence to certain difficult individuals, although it would have been more fitting that they
correct the vices rather than become angry with one who gave good advice.
I seek only a port and a tranquil abode for my age and my health. I have
been invited, and I am invited elsewhere under splendid conditions,[6] but it   35
is not my intention to stray beyond the boundaries of the jurisdiction of the
emperor, by whose singular favour I have stood firm against the attempts of
the malevolent.

But if in your wisdom you think it would be relevant in the circumstances, I shall most easily obtain letters of recommendation both from the   40
emperor and from Ferdinand.[7] Your kindness being what it is, however, I
do not think that either their recommendation or my letter will be necessary.

* * * * *

4 See Epp 2090 introduction, 2149 introduction.
5 For Erasmus' dependence on wine from Burgundy, see Ep 2348:7–12, 2397:3–17.
6 See Ep 2360 nn5–6.
7 The emperor obliged with Ep 2553.

Nonetheless, because of the varied opinions and sentiments of men, I thought it best not to attempt anything without first ascertaining your views, for without your favour I do not know whether it would be possible for me to   45
have a tranquil sojourn there. Wherefore, I hope your illustrious Highnesses, to whom I profess that I shall always be a devoted servant, no matter what province it will be that receives Erasmus, will not be reluctant to answer this letter in a few words. May the Lord Jesus protect you all and prosper your possessions.   50

At Freiburg im Breisgau, on the day after the feast of St James 1531

2515 / From Bernhard von Cles   July–August 1531

For Bernhard von Cles, bishop of Trent and chancellor to King Ferdinand, see Ep 2504.

This letter was first published by Allen. The manuscript, a rough draft in the bishop's hand, is in the 'Corrispondenza clesiana' collection of the Archivio di Stato di Trento: 'Minute, copie e originali di lettere di Bernardo Clesio, 1514–1539.' According to Allen, the present letter is found in a bundle labelled, in the bishop's hand, 'month of July to 10 August 1531.' The letters are arranged in the order in which they were written, and this undated one is near the end of the bundle. Allen designated Vienna as the probable place of writing, but there is no firm evidence for or against that. We know that Cles was in Budweis (Ceske Budejovice) in Bohemia from 6 to 19 July, and that he spent 17–22 August in Linz before proceeding to Trent. His whereabouts in the period 20 July–16 August are undocumented. See Renato Tisot *Ricerche sulla vita e sull' epistolario del cardinale Bernardo Cles (1485–1539)* (Trent 1969) 112.

TO ERASMUS
Your letter was delivered to me, from which I learned that you had responded to my last letter in the preceding days: which letter, however, did not reach me.[1] I saw also a copy of your letter to the bishop of Vienna,[2] and I am grieved that in these times so many troubles and disturbances are inflicted   5
upon such an unassuming man as you, not accustomed to suffering such things. I shall report all this to his royal Majesty, who we know will never fail you at any time in all your necessities. And I ask earnestly of you that in the future you will have confidence in me in this, namely that I ardently desire to

* * * * *

2515
1 Neither of these letters is extant.
2 Not extant, but answered by Ep 2503

gratify your wishes in whatever way I can, and I hope that I may be in a place   10
to which you will be able to repair if necessary,[3] or where at least letters can
be delivered more conveniently from one place to the other.

2516 / To Johann von Botzheim   Freiburg, 5 August 1531

For Botzheim (1480–1535), canon of the cathedral chapter of Constance, which
in 1527 had moved to Überlingen, see Ep 1285.

   This letter, the response to one no longer extant, was first published in the
Epistolae palaeonaeoi, which (like all subsequent editions before Allen's) gives
'Sigismundus Questenbergius' as the name of the addressee. Allen's text is
based on the autograph rough draft in the Royal Library at Copenhagen (MS
GKS 95 Fol, folio 199), which clearly identifies the recipient as Botzheim.

TO JOHANN BOTZHEIM

I am glad, dearest Botzheim, that you have been granted respite from the
annoyances and unrewarding labours that were occupying you in your role
as coadjutor to the dean.[1] I am more happy that you are safe and sound,
especially in these pestilential times, than unhappy that you have suffered   5
material losses. There can be nothing in excess for people like you who either
spend whatever they have on necessities or hold it in reserve for a noble
charity. But none call upon the faith of gods and men more than those who
have enough means of subsistence to provide nurture for horses, birds, dogs,
gambling, and mistresses, to live like satraps and Luculluses,[2] although there   10
is not a sacred text to be found in their house. Complaints from people like
these carry no conviction.

   What the emperor is doing has never been more secret than now, and
nowhere more secret than in Brabant, where he is now living. Certain friends
of mine have purposely mingled with high dignitaries to seek out informa-   15
tion, but they were not able to sniff out anything. Everyone knows that he

* * * * *

 3 Bernhard had repeatedly invited Erasmus to settle in Trent on generous terms;
   see Epp 1409, 1771:13–16, 2097:13–20, 2159:12–24, 2299:33–9, 2383:3–4.

   2516
 1 Botzheim was still coadjutor to the dean as late as 1533, so it appears that in his
   letter he had made reference to a journey or some other welcome respite from
   his duties.
 2 Lucius Licinius Lucullus (c 116–57 BC) was a Roman general and consul, proverbial for his wealth and luxurious banquets.

loves to hunt, for his health, I think, which is exhausted by so many long journeys and so many consultations. The journey from to Bologna is long.[3] There, besides the religious ceremonies, carried out to perfection, there were familiar discussions about no ordinary domestic affairs with Clement VII.[4]   20 The diet at Augsburg followed on this, attended by an incredible number of princes.[5] From there the emperor traveled to Aachen, where King Ferdinand was crowned king of the Romans.[6] After so many tasks successfully accomplished, he relaxed his mind for a while with his fellow Flemings, in the place of his birth.[7] An incredible amount of money is being demanded, but I hear   25 that assent has not yet been given in many parts of his dominions.[8] There are various conjectures about the uses that will be made of this money, but nothing certain. There are some who predict that in the autumn he will go through France on his triumphant return to Spain; others think that these military resources are being prepared for war against the Turks; some conjec-   30 ture there will be a sudden attack against supporters of the sects.[9] God knows the outcome.

As for us, certainly, as the Hebrews of old exiled to Babylon, to whom it was not allowed to sing the canticle of the Lord in a foreign land,[10] we await our Messiah, who will restore us to our previous condition; may he   35 succeed in restoring us to a sincere piety. There are some who demand a general council, but I think this will never come about while this pope is alive.[11] Nor do I see any good that would come from this council, if it takes place, especially in the present state of affairs. One faction does not accept relinquishing any of their power, the other faction would rather make additions   40

* * * * *

3 See Ep 2208:45–52 with n12.
4 See Ep 2240 n6.
5 20 June–19 November 1530
6 See Ep 2384 n7.
7 Ghent
8 An apparent reference to demands for money from the estates of the Netherlands provinces
9 The Protestant estates had left the Diet of Augsburg convinced that the emperor intended to make war on them, and they immediately took measures to prepare for their defence; see Ep 2403 n11.
10 Ps 136:4 (Vulgate)
11 Fearing a general council that would be dominated by the European monarchs, make too many concessions to heretics, and attempt to limit the powers of the papacy, Clement VII consistently evaded the demands of Charles V (among others) that he call one. There would be no real progress towards a council until the reign of Clement's successor, Paul III (1534–49).

to dogmas. If anyone begins to whisper something about compromise, he hears immediately 'author of a new heresy.'[12]

A few days ago a man was here from the court of King Ferdinand, not extremely learned but most cordial and of rare honesty.[13] He told us a new, scarcely believable story that there was in your city a certain two-horned 45 Momus (this is the term he used)[14] who is in the habit of raving with great boldness against all lovers of good letters, and especially against Erasmus, not only at banquets but also in public meetings. I tried to discover who this Momus was, but he did not wish to give his name. Only when I guessed that it was the suffragan of your bishop[15] did he smile slightly, but shaking 50 his head in disagreement. I would think, however, that I had divined correctly, were it not that the story was so absurd that it could apply to no one except a man who is so singularly stupid and demented that it would be impossible for your bishop to have such a man as his suffragan, or that your church would have him as a preacher. Moreover, I could not be persuaded 55 that there was anyone there with such an unbridled tongue and so devoid of any judgment that he could utter such nonsense even at drinking parties. To the contrary, however, he continued to claim that he was not simply recounting something he heard, which like dreams that fly through the gate of ivory are often accounted as false,[16] but rather things seen with his own eyes and 60 heard by his own ears. He added the place and the day and cited by name several witnesses absolutely worthy of belief who had seen and heard the same things.

But for a long time now, I suspect, you are dying to hear the story. You will hear it, but only that one, for he told several. He said the man bawled 65 at the top of his voice, taking particular aim at the New Testament translated by me from the Greek manuscripts. So when, on the feast of St James the Apostle,[17] he was explaining the gospel of that day to the people,[18] he tossed before the ignorant crowd, and by his words exaggerated as much as he could, my blatant temerity, since in the Gospel of Matthew, chapter 70

* * * * *

12 Cf Epp 2343:4–6, 2346:8–12, 2347:10–11, 2353A:34–7.
13 Unidentified
14 Momus was the god of carping criticism. 'Two-horned' is doubtless to be understood as referring to a bishop's mitre.
15 Melchior Fattlin (c 1490–1548), suffragan bishop of Constance since 1518, a vigorous opponent of Erasmian scholarship and of the Reformation
16 *Odyssey* 19.563; *Aeneid* 6.893
17 25 July
18 Matt 20:20–8

20 I had added on my own 'to be baptized by the baptism by which I am
baptized,' whereas our translation mentions only the cup he was about to
drink.[19] He added that I did the same thing in other passages when I shamelessly remove, add, and change many things in the divine Scriptures arbi-
trarily, sometimes in a heretical way, whenever it pleases me, to the great 75
detriment of the Christian cause. Then he scrupulously warned one and all
to be on their guard against such novelties. These were his words to the more
than illiterate common crowd, who believed that what he said was true.

Certainly whoever would dare to do what he claimed I did would be
worthy of public hatred. But far removed from this audacity is he who, leav- 80
ing the reading of the Vulgate unchanged, translates into Latin for the use
of scholars what is found in the Greek manuscripts, not any ones at all, but
those that Origen, Chrysostom, Basil, and Theophylact, as well as other celebrated and orthodox men, notable also for the sanctity of their lives, followed. With what effrontery is that man who does not change one iota in the 85
Vulgate manuscripts said to add and remove? Or what does he remove or
add if in the role of a translator he renders in good faith what he finds in the
books he undertook to translate? If what I rendered into Latin is not in the
Greek manuscripts, there would be reason to find fault with the accuracy of
the translator. There would be more just cause to protest against me if, pro- 90
fessing to be a translator, I had omitted what is invariably in the best Greek
manuscripts. Furthermore, I am so far from condemning the Latin edition
accepted by the church that in my Annotations I suggest that it could have
happened that this phrase was taken from Mark and added here.[20] We find
that this happens sometimes with us, but more frequently with the Greeks, 95
in my opinion. The reason for this was the rules according to which Origen

* * * * *

19 By 'our translation' Erasmus means the Vulgate. When the mother of the apostles James and John asked Jesus to promise that her sons would sit at his right
hand in his kingdom, Jesus replied (Matt 20:22): 'You do not know what you
are asking. Are you able to drink the cup that I am to drink?' The Vulgate text
does not include the words 'or to be baptized with the baptism with which I am
baptized,' but Erasmus added them because, as he notes in lines 80–5 below,
they were in the best Greek manuscripts known to him.
20 See Mark 10:38. Luther's Bible and the King James Version still have the reference to baptism not found in the Vulgate text of Matthew but included by
Erasmus in his translation. Modern biblical scholars, however, have concluded that those words were indeed an interpolation into the Greek texts that
Erasmus used. Revised Standard Version and other modern translations are
in accord with the Vulgate in excluding the phrase in question from the text of
Matthew's Gospel.

and after him Eusebius determined what was in agreement and what was discordant in each of the evangelists, what was missing and what was in excess. For what a particular scholar had noted in the margin, an inattentive scribe transferred into the text. And although certain cases of this sort are detected in Origen, Chrysostom, and Theophylact, it was possible that they did not change anything in the text but in translating wove in what had been added by others.

What the ancients allowed themselves is not very clear to me; in any case I would wish that no one should change one iota in the divine writings, especially in the language in which they first appeared. If it was done on occasion, it matters not by whom and with what right; it certainly cannot be reckoned as a fault in me, who makes no other claim than being a translator. But if he condemns all the labour I employed in transmitting the Greek text to Latin ears, let him read the Apology in which I responded to Pierre Couturier.[21]

I still cannot convince myself that your suffragan behaves in that way, but I would like you to provide more information. If the person at the court told me the truth, I will advise the man by letter to refrain from such impudent language, especially before people who are not only ignorant but rustic, as I hear. But if he does not cease after being warned, I will be forced to speak German myself.[22] I hope the situation is different from what he recounted to me, or if it is as he says, I think the man, if he possesses a Christian spirit, will, once he has been warned, abstain from this licentious frenzy against one who does not deserve it. Farewell, my most sincere friend.

I pray you to greet affectionately and courteously on my part Laurentius Merus, a true theologian, as I am told, and a man of simple and pure heart, in accordance with his name, the pastor of your flock.[23] Farewell.

Given at Frieburg im Breisgau, 5 August 1531

* * * * *

21 See Ep 1571 n10.
22 The apparent meaning is that Erasmus would defend himself in German. Although he frequently denied knowledge of German (see Ep 1313:93–4 with n16), Erasmus occasionally resorted to the use of it, as, for example, in his Letter to the Swiss Confederation (Ep 1708), and in the German translation of his *Detectio prestigiarum* (Ep 1708 n2). See also his remark in the *Purgatio adversus epistolam Lutheri* (CWE 78 418): 'If I had written for the unlearned, I would have written in German, not Latin.'
23 Parish priest in Überlingen, Merus (documented 1521–46) had evidently sent greetings to Erasmus via Botzheim. *Merus* is Latin for 'pure,' 'genuine.'

2517 / To Caspar Ursinus Velius   Freiburg, 7 August 1531

First published in the *Epistolae palaeonaeoi*, this is Erasmus' reply to a letter in which Ursinus, professor of rhetoric at the University of Vienna and official historian of King Ferdinand (Epp 1810 n6 and 2008 introduction), had commented on some points in Ep 2453 (see lines 2–3, 6–7, 19–20, 37–8 below).

ERASMUS OF ROTTERDAM TO CASPAR URSINUS VELIUS, GREETING
I have never been greatly preoccupied with my style, most learned Velius, nor do I envy the Budéists, who hold first place in this regard, as you write.[1] In this I am not unlike Ovid, who liked any kind of girl, whatever her attraction. Wherever there is soundness of mind, acute sensibility, profound 5 thoughts, the mode of expression is amply satisfactory to me. It was wise of Budé not to publish any letters whatsoever to anyone at all.[2] As for myself, either to comply with the wishes of my friends or to defer to the urging of the publishers, I often take little thought for my reputation. On the other hand, although I was never anxiously ambitious for this praise, nevertheless, with 10 good letters now reigning everywhere, I bear with great resignation being thrown off the bridge at age more than sixty,[3] and I experience the same joy as that Spartan who, when he was defeated in his attempt to be admitted to the number of the three hundred,[4] went away cheerfully and laughing. When he was asked why he was so elated, he said: 'Why should I not rejoice that 15 there are three hundred men better than I in this city?'[5]

Because you strive with all your energies to restore the human race, afflicted as it is with so many calamities, I praise your devotion; that your efforts are successful, I congratulate you. You have a correct and judicious opinion of your prince,[6] but I hope that one day fortune will respond to his 20

* * * * *

2517
1 Ursinus had evidently made some reference to the *Ciceronianus* and the controversy over Erasmus' alleged belittling of the Latin style of Guillaume Budé; see Ep 1948 introduction,
2 Erasmus surely knew that a volume of *Epistolae Gulielmi Budaei Regii Secretarii* had been published by Josse Bade at Paris in 1520, and that Andreas Cratander had brought out a reprint at Basel in 1521. One surmises that Ursinus had made some reference to the complete silence that Budé himself maintained throughout the uproar over the *Ciceronianus*.
3 *Adagia* I v 37
4 Ie the three hundred knights of the royal bodyguard
5 *Apophthegmata* 1.327, citing Plutarch *Moralia* 231B; CWE 37 145–6
6 Ferdinand of Austria

aspirations. The emperor does nothing but collect; when he will disburse I do not know. They say that it is fatal for the imperial crown always to be in need, to be the empty jug of the Danaids, no matter how much you pour in.[7] A far from happy rumour is circulating about the Turks,[8] and another rumour is being propagated about the convocation of another diet.[9] About the   25 emperor's plans, nowhere are they less known than where he lives. I know what proverbs say about the diets of Germany,[10] but what will happen I do not know.

Lest you think there is no news to report, I bought a house of honourable name, but dishonourable price. I have used up whatever money I had   30 on hand and I am still building. I have experienced so much weariness in making bids, contracting, seeking guarantees, moving out, moving in, wrangling with workers and thieves, that I would prefer to spend ten years in my books than a single month swallowing those pills. My little body lives

* * * * *

7 Of the fifty daughters of Danaus, mythical king of Egypt, forty-nine killed their husbands and were condemned to spend eternity carrying water in perforated jugs.

8 Ie that a renewed attack was imminent. It would materialize in April 1532.

9 Erasmus' language here is ambiguous. In this sentence he uses the word *synodus*, which can mean either '[church] council' or '[imperial] diet.' In the following sentence he uses the word *concilium*, which has the same ambiguity; see Ep 2347 n5. Both sentences appear to refer to the same thing, so the passage can be read either way. It is true that for more than a decade German rulers, lay and ecclesiastical, had been calling for a church council (cf Ep 1372 n6) and that Charles v himself wanted the religious schism to be settled by a council. Since, however, there had been no church council since the fifth Lateran (1512–17), and since there was no immediate prospect of one (see Ep 2516 n11), German imperial diets had repeatedly taken on the task of attempting to deal with the religious schism, usually by postponing any decisive action. Under the circumstances, the reference to 'another' *synodus* appears to refer to the rumoured plan to convoke another diet hard on the heels of those at Speyer in 1529 and Augsburg in 1530. A diet had in fact already been summoned to meet at Speyer in September 1531, but it was soon postponed to January 1532 and then transferred to Regensburg, where it opened on 17 April; see Ep 2511 n20.

10 German diets were famous for concluding with the announcement that they would reconvene soon because they had not been able to reach a decision on the business at hand. This caused Enea Silvio Piccolomini (1405–64), who spent much time in Germany before his election as Pope Pius II in 1458, famously to compare German diets to rabbits: one always had the next one in its body, ie every diet was pregnant with its successor; see Karl Friedrich Wilhelm Wander *Deutsches Sprichwörter-Lexikon* (Leipzig 1867–1880) III 1623 sv 'Reichstag,' 1: 'Deutsche Reichstage und Kaninchen haben immer Junge im Leibe.'

here, my mind elsewhere.[11] Now there is also the danger that the plague, 35
which is already emitting disturbing sparks,[12] will drive me away from a
well-furnished house. With regard to the bishop of Olomouc, I will do what
you so often advise as soon as the opportunity presents itself.[13] This is my
response to your letter written in Vienna on 26 June. Farewell.

Freiburg, 7 August 1531 40

2518 / To Johann Herwagen   Freiburg, 9 August 1531

This is the preface to the *Epistolae floridae* (Basel: J. Herwagen, September 1531),
comprising 112 letters, all hitherto unpublished, from the period 3 April 1523–
21 August 1531. As Erasmus explains in lines 40–5, his criterion for choosing
letters for inclusion was that they should be 'flowery' (*floridae, florulentae*) in the
sense of 'lively,' 'beautiful.'

ERASMUS OF ROTTERDAM TO JOHANN HERWAGEN, GREETING
Many indeed, dear Herwagen, were the virtues in Johann Froben of happy
memory,[1] which commended him greatly to my affection, but nothing bound
my spirit more closely and steadfastly to him than that throughout his life
he considered nothing more important than to promote public studies by 5
publishing the most respected authors at no matter what cost of fatigue and
money, a magnificent undertaking in which that excellent man died. I do not
see what more beautiful death could have fallen to his lot. Thus it came about
that he enriched literary studies more than his family fortune, and left his
heirs more good fame than money. Likewise, since I see that not only have 10
you become the host of the very distinguished wife that he left behind, but
also have taken upon yourself the duty of continuing the desire he manifested

* * * * *

11 See Epp 2506 n1, 2525:4–7, 2531 n2, 2533:7–10, 2535:5–6, 2558:6–7, 2563A:33–6.
12 See Ep 2472 n4.
13 The bishop of Olomouc was Stanislaus Thurzo (Ep 1242). Ursinus had evi-
    dently suggested that Erasmus once again dedicate a book to Thurzo (he had
    already dedicated the Froben edition of Pliny's *Naturalis historia* to Thurzo in
    1525; see Ep 1544). In 1532 Erasmus complied with the suggestion by dedicat-
    ing to Thurzo his commentary on Psalm 38, mentioning Ursinus in the dedica-
    tory letter (Ep 2608:17–31). In his letter of thanks for the dedication, Thurzo
    mentions Ursinus' good offices in arranging it (Allen Ep 2699:1–3).

2518
 1 The Basel publisher Johann Froben died on 26 October 1527; see Ep 1900.

to promote and enhance literary pursuits,[2] I cannot but transfer to you a good part of the benevolence with which I honoured him. Would that I could bring to your enterprise as much assistance as my heart desires and your ability deserves. But my age and my health demand, if not my retirement, at least a remission from my labours, and rightfully so. You taskmasters, therefore, to whom I was often more compliant than was necessary, should not expect comparable tasks from me.

At the present time I am in such a situation that even if the excuse of age or of health were entirely lacking, I would be absolutely estranged from all commerce with the Muses. You will ask me what are the new circumstances. Did I too get married? Truly, I am doing something that is no less bothersome, no less painstaking, no less foreign to my character and my nature. I have bought a house here, of honourable name, but dishonourable price. And so Erasmus, accustomed to pay for his literary leisure at the expense of all his possessions, now makes bids, contracts, seeks guarantees, makes provisos, takes counsel, demolishes, erects, has dealings with stonemasons, carpenters, blacksmiths, glassworkers – you know what kind of men they are – with such boredom that he would prefer to spend three years in any grueling studious pursuits whatever than to be occupied with this kind of anxieties for a single month.[3] I never understood until now how wise Diogenes was in preferring to take refuge in a barrel rather than contend with such people.[4] To this degree of misery this ill-fated century has reduced me, and the hypocritical dishonesty of certain people, whom some day perhaps I will not defraud of the praise they deserve. And among these evils the continual lavish spending of money is the least of my woes. You can guess the rest.

I mention these things, dear Herwagen, so that you will take in good part what I now send to you, not the kind of thing I wish, but the kind of thing I can. I had to send this or nothing. I send you a number of flowery letters. I know you will wonder what kind of a title this is. But it is of no importance, do not be deceived. It was barely possible, in the midst of the turbulent occupations of moving in and moving out, to undertake this trivial task of marking with a small flower those letters out of a huge pile that were

* * * * *

2 Herwagen, the Strasbourg publisher who moved to Basel in 1528, married Froben's widow. Gertrud Lachner, in that same year. Originally a partner in the Froben press, he had now gone into business for himself. Cf Ep 2033 n24.
3 See Epp 2506 n1, 2517 n11.
4 The Greek philosopher Diogenes (c 412–323 BC), indifferent to physical comfort, made his home in a *pithos*, a large vessel used to store oil or wine.

DES·ERASMI ROTE

RODAMI, EPISTOLARVM FLORIDARVM LIBER

unus, antehac nunquam excufus.

HER   VAG.

BASILEAE IN OFFICINA IOANNIS HERVA
GII MENSE SEPTEMBRI
AN. M.D.XXXI

Title-page of the *Epistolae floridae*, showing one of the two versions of Johann Herwagen's printer's device (cf page 132)

worth printing, although I hardly ever write any for that purpose. Whatever   45
this little book is worth,[5] such as it is, I hope it turns out well for you; it will,
if in the sales you find that your three-headed Hermes has been propitious to
you,[6] and I pray that he will show you a short cut to the plutopolis to which
almost everyone is hastening now, but not with equal success. But pleasantries aside, I pray that the Lord, the true protector, who makes all things pros-   50
per, will bless your holy enterprise, to which I will not fail to contribute my
part, however small it may be, as soon as I return to my former tranquillity.

Farewell to you and to those dear to you.

At Freiburg im Breisgau, the eve of the feast of St Lawrence 1531

2519 / From Bonifacius Amerbach   [Basel], 14 August 1531

First published by Allen, the autograph rough draft of this letter (= AK Ep 1544)
is in the Öffentliche Bibliothek of the University of Basel (MS C VIa 73 293).

By an ordinance of 1 April 1529 the Basel city council made attendance at
reformed Sunday worship compulsory (see Ep 2248 n5). Bonifacius demanded
and received exemption from the law as one of the conditions of his continuing
as professor of law at the university (see Ep 2180 n5). In January 1530, however,
he complained that the agreed conditions were being honoured in the breach
(Ep 2248:22–9). On 23 April 1531 the city fathers issued an *Edictum de non com-
municantibus* (text in Burckhardt 375–6), which threatened with excommunication all who failed to heed three admonitions to participate in the reformed
sacrament. On 25 April 1531 Bonifacius was summoned before the *Bannherrn*,
the committee charged with enforcement of the edict. Second and third hearings followed on 8 June and 2 August. Meanwhile, on 11 May he had submitted
to the city council a statement of his position (the booklet [*libellus*] referred to
in line 4), and at his third hearing he appears to have contented himself with
repeating the arguments found in the booklet. By 5 September he had been informed that the city council had decided to take the matter into its own hands
(AK Ep 1556:1–8), and on 9 September he appeared before that body (Burckhardt
Epp 75, 79). His request for a delay in proceedings until the following Easter appears to have been granted, judging by his several references to himself as *inter*

* * * * *

5 A much quoted phrase from Catullus 1.8
6 Herwagen had adopted as a printer's device an image of three-headed Hermes
   (Mercury). On three-headed Mercury as the god who shows one the road to
   take, see *Adagia* III vii 95. From Ep 2524:16–17 it appears that there was some
   misunderstanding about the design of the image.

ampliatos reos 'among the defendants whose hearings have been postponed' (Burckhardt Ep 79; Ep 2551:7–8, and cf Ep 2630:16–20). On 23 November 1531, Johannes Oecolampadius, the driving force behind the campaign to exact conformity (Ep 2312:6–17), died. The course of the controversy to that point can be traced in Bonifacius' diary entries for 25 April–22 November 1531 (text in Burckhardt 327–72). The case would drag on until 1534, when Bonifacius finally produced a statement of his faith that satisfied the city fathers (cf Ep 2248 n6).

This is the first of Bonifacius' extant letters to Erasmus that reports in any detail on his dispute with the city council, despite his reference to it as being in the last act (line 1). There is no surviving detailed comment from Erasmus before Ep 2631 of 25 March 1532.

Cordial greetings. We are now in the last act of the obligatory presence at the supper. Whether this will turn into a tragedy or a comedy I do not know. Soon, however, it will become clear. When recently I was given a third warning, I resorted to the booklet I presented to the city council a long time ago, in which I clearly showed, unless I am greatly mistaken, that according to the 5 decrees of the magistracy itself, no one can or ought to be forced to the communion table against his will.[1] Moreover, I once again solemnly testified that it was not through hatred or spite – what more can I say? – not through contempt for anyone that I did not take part in the rite, but rather because I do not yet firmly believe in the doctrine of our good friends. At the same time I 10 affirmed my respect for the magistracy in civil matters and my affection for my fellow citizens, and said that I was prepared to match anyone in services and generosity, indeed with my goods and even my life, if ever necessity demanded it. As far as the spiritual eating alone is concerned,[2] I maintained that the principle of my faith consisted in being of the opinion that everyone 15 who firmly believes that he has been delivered from the bonds of Satan by the death of Christ, and that through it satisfaction has been made for the sins of men, placing all his confidence in it forever, eats and drinks spiritually the body and the blood of Christ; moreover, in the supper, which was meant to augment and quicken faith, the body and blood of the Lord are truly pres- 20 ent for us and distributed by the simple signification of the words. In order not to approach the supper unworthily, it seems to me that two things are

* * * * *

2519
1 Text, dated 11 May 1531, in Burckhardt 376–85; also in AK IV 474:149–57.
2 Ie the official position of the Basel reformers that the body and blood of Christ were present in the bread and wine only spiritually, not really (as Catholics and Lutherans believed), and thus could only be consumed spiritually

necessary: one, to be mindful that we do this in memory of the Lord, that is, with the intention of proclaiming his death; the other, that we believe in the words signifying that the body and blood of the Lord are there present. How 25 this happens cannot be understood by human reason but is known to faith alone, which comes from the word of God.[3]

Finally, subjecting myself respectfully once again to the magistracy, I exhorted them to the charity that Paul represents as patient and kind and always hoping for the best,[4] and I asked for a delay until Easter for further 30 deliberation on this matter. I stated openly that in the meantime I would implore the Lord that, if my opinions are incorrect, he in his immense goodness will not refuse to instruct one who is in error, since he promised that he would give to those who seek and open to those who knock.[5] Then I promised also to consult learned men both here and elsewhere, from whom, if I 35 were in error, which I do not believe, I could be instructed. Lastly, I said that if I do not find any reason why I should abandon my long-standing opinion, I would, packing my belongings, depart from here immediately, so that I would not be a stumbling block to anyone. I do not know what I will achieve. I will let you know on what side the scales fall. 40

I do not think my father-in-law has arrived yet; otherwise nothing would please him more than if you would not refuse to spend some days at his home for your diversion.[6] What of all your services and kindnesses to me, what of those duties of hospitality that you displayed recently?[7] The more you do not want these things publicized, the more they are fixed at the 45 bottom of my heart. Since I cannot do more, would that I could present you with a token of my gratitude towards you.

The eve of the Assumption of the Blessed Virgin 1531

* * * * *

3 Bonifacius' language here, with its insistence on the real presence without mentioning transubstantiation, is strikingly similar to that of the Lutherans. Cf the similar passage in Ep 2630:1–16.
4 1 Cor 13:4 and 7; cf Epp 2538:7–8, 2546:9–11.
5 Matt 7:7, Luke 11:9
6 Bonifacius' father-in-law was Leonhard Fuchs, burgomaster of Neuenburg am Rhein, a small town halfway between Basel and Freiburg. At least since April, Erasmus had been contemplating a visit to Fuchs in Neuenburg (Ep 2490:11–12), and would continue to do so (see Epp 2531:4–5, 2532:4–5, 2536:6–7, 2538:4–5, 2539:74–6) until an outbreak of the plague in Neuenburg made the visit impossible (Epp 2541, 2542:1–10, 2543, 2546:1–8, 2547:1–2, 2556:5–7).
7 The reference is to Erasmus' hospitality to Anselmus Ephorinus (Ep 2539), who lived with him April–September 1531; see AK Ep 1546:7 with n2.

2520 / From Sigismund I   Cracow, 17 August [1531]

This letter was first published as Ep 12 in Miaskowski, using an eighteenth-century copy in the Czartoryski Museum at Cracow (MS CN 46 175). Allen was also able to make use of notes on a copy in a sixteenth-century manuscript volume in the Imperial Library at St Petersburg that had been made before World War I by the Polish historian Jan Nepomuk Fijalek, who subsequently communicated them to him. The manuscript volume, which contained copies of this letter, Epp 2521 and 2533, and fifteen other letters to or from Erasmus, was (like the manuscript that included Ep 1954) one of those returned to Poland in the 1920s and '30s and placed in the National Library of Poland at Warsaw, only to perish in 1944 when German SS troops burned down the library (cf Ep 1954 introduction, which incorrectly attributes the fate of the library to 'German bombardment'). Information generously provided by Dr Olga Bleskina, Curator of West European Manuscripts, Russian National Library, St Petersburg.

The manuscript has the year-date 1530, but that is inconsistent with the added regnal date; see lines 9–10. Sigismund was crowned on 24 January 1507, which makes 1531 the twenty-fifth year of his reign. The year 1531 is also confirmed by the reference of the visit of Jan Boner in lines 1–3.

For Sigismund I, King of Poland see Ep 1819.

We have learned that the son of the noble Seweryn Boner, burgrave and prefect of our salt mines in Cracow, a faithful friend, has been entrusted to your domicile and care.[1] Since it is our wish that in virtue of all that his father has merited of us he will progress in all virtues, we recommend him and his studies to you and we pray and exhort you to see to it that for our sake he will be educated in such a manner that he will one day be an honour to his father and family and of service to us; in this way you will show yourself no less worthy than gratifying to us.   5

Given in our city of Cracow, 17 August 1530, the twenty-fifth year of our reign.[2]   10

Personal commissary of his august royal Majesty.

* * * * *

2520
1 For Seweryn Boner and his son Jan, see Ep 2533 introduction.
2 The year-date is wrong; see introduction above.

2521 / From Piotr Tomicki Cracow, 17 August 1531

This letter was first published in Wierzbowski I 325–6. The manuscript is a rough draft in a secretary's hand in the Zamoyski Collection of the Polish National Library at Warsaw (MS BN BOZ 2053 vol 13 no 1494). For Tomicki, see Epp 1919, 1953.

PIOTR TOMICKI, BISHOP OF CRACOW, VICE-CHANCELLOR
OF THE KINGDOM OF POLAND, TO ERASMUS OF ROTTERDAM
Even if I have not received a letter from you in a long time, Erasmus, most distinguished man of our time,[1] I have heard from dependable people that you are in good health. This gives me great pleasure, for I have no friend ex- 5
cept you of such outstanding renown and accumulation of virtue. The reason that I too write to you less often is not my will but rather the miserable condition and turbulent situation of the present times, to which I often apply my energies so vigorously that it is necessary for me to neglect my duties to my friends, however unwillingly. Now that I have happened upon a messenger, 10
I did not want to let him go without giving him a letter for you, especially since I am moved to write by the duty I owe to the illustrious lord, Seweryn Boner, a man of great renown and authority here, father of the young Jan, who is now living under your roof.[2] Indeed, when he learned from certain people that you are a good friend of mine, he asked me to write a letter to you 15
recommending his son. Since I was conscious of the high esteem I had for you, and had experienced your benevolence towards me, I willingly agreed to do so. Therefore I commend to you with great enthusiasm this boy, whom I fondly love because of his splendid character and the distinction of his father as well as the bond of friendship that exists between us, and I strongly 20
wish that through your renown and the honour of his parents he will be eminently adorned with learning, good morals, and all virtues, which I have no doubt will come to pass, since you will not fail him in authority and precept. You cannot possibly fail him if you consider that in keeping with the gracious and generous disposition of his father you will reap the reward that you are 25
accustomed to expect from the generosity of honourable men. For I can assure you that he will be most grateful for your services and good will, which he will reciprocate to the fullest, since he is first among those who have access to the favour and resources of the most serene king, and he is not only

* * * * *

2521
1 Erasmus' most recent extant letter to Tomicki is Ep 2377.
2 For Seweryn Boner and his son Jan, see Ep 2533 introduction.

an honourable and respected man, but also prudent and obliging. Farewell,   30
and continue as you have begun to earn praise for your virtue and learning
from our age and from posterity.

Cracow, 17 August 1531

2522 / To Julius Pflug   Freiburg, 20 August 1531

This letter, Erasmus' reply to Ep 2492, was first published in the *Epistolae floridae*.

ERASMUS OF ROTTERDAM TO THE MOST DISTINGUISHED
DOCTOR JULIUS PFLUG, GREETING
To that felicitous sequence of virtues that you in your goodness attributed to
me, my incomparable friend, I have nothing to respond except in the most
laconic fashion: if only! Nor do I see what praise for my humanity I merit   5
in this instance, since I will be simply inhuman if I judge the good offices of
friends by their outcome, which is in the hands of fortune, not ours. What
happened to you through experience has happened to all who made a similar attempt, and I knew it would happen. Let him bask in his glory,[1] the only
glory by which he decided he would become famous, since the remedies   10
themselves also end up contrary to expectation. He approaches on his own
initiative any learned or upright person who he thinks is known to me, at-
testing that he wants to repair a friendship with Erasmus, in order to make it
appear through that very fact that it is of some value to have differences with
Erasmus. If he had even the faintest glimmer of being one who is inclined   15
to mutual agreement, we would have had a peaceful solution to this trifling
affair long ago. As I would not wish to be involved in a dispute with such
people, so neither would I wish to be bound to them by a pact of friendship.
But among so many monstrous forebodings I must put up with this also. I
should wish, however, that from now on that inauspicious name would be   20
completely absent from your letters, in which I find the greatest delight myself and am accustomed to show them gladly to my learned friends, so that
I often renew the great pleasure I receive from them.

I confess that there was hardly ever a more insane century than this
one; you would say that a thousand Furies had flown up from hell; no part of   25
it, neither the secular nor the ecclesiastical, is sane. It is an utterly fatal evil, to

* * * * *

2522
1 Heinrich Eppendorf. For the history of Erasmus' feud with Eppendorf see Ep
1934 introduction and CWE 78 370–8. For Pflug's role in bringing the feud to a
conclusion, see Ep 2400.

which I see no remedy, not even an ecumenical council, so far is it that I, who
am a nonentity, can lend aid, although you seem to have formed an astonishing opinion of me. The pope's intentions are not clear to me, but I see nevertheless that certain priests are aiming at settling the matter by war, since so   30
far there has not been much progress by fire.[2] Whether this would be feasible
or not, even if we were at peace with the Turks, I have not decided. The evil
would be more curable if the rulers of both realms would consent with sincere hearts to the restoration of evangelical piety.[3] The matter would then
be confided to one hundred or five hundred men, chosen from each nation,   35
recommended by their holiness of life, outstanding learning, and capacity of
judgment. Their decisions would be reduced to a compendium by a selected
few. The opinions of theologians would be discussed within the walls of the
schools and not all opinions would be indiscriminately considered articles
of faith. Certain constitutions would be abrogated, others would be turned   40
into exhortations. The principal care of princes and cities would be that those
who are put in charge of the Lord's flock should be instructed in the word of
God and trained to teach, encourage, console, censure, refute. How many satraps the revenues of monasteries or churches maintain! In the meantime the
people are tossed about among the sects, like dispersed sheep, destitute of   45
their shepherd; although here also – Oh sorrow! – I see few sheep who simply
wander off rather than go astray with deliberate malice. I fear that the same
thing will happen to us as happens in wars, namely, that when both sides are
saturated with calamities, then finally they will begin to negotiate for peace.
One side aims at suppressing the ecclesiastical estate altogether, the other   50
does not wish to improve it. We all carry the world around in our hearts, and
as we are terrestrial beings, so we understand and speak of terrestrial things.
Would that the Lord would implant a new heart in both parties.

There are other things that it is not safe to commit to letters, and besides
are of a nature that they are more to be wished than hoped for. I am tired not   55
so much because of my age as because of my health, and because of all the
quarrels, disputes, calumnies, and strident criticism, I have long thought of
retiring from the scene. But what I must seek to obtain from my spirit is, as
you wisely and lovingly recommend, that I find peace of mind, in accordance
with Christ and the consciousness of good intention, in the judgment of good   60
men. The Fates will find a way, and I hope that all these tumults of the church
will eventually result in a good ending through the supreme ability of that

* * * * *

2 Ie by burning people at the stake
3 By 'rulers of both realms' Erasmus means princes and bishops.

stage director by whose inscrutable wisdom the affairs of men are regulated.
If that happens while I am alive, I will say farewell with a tranquil spirit and
'give your applause.'[4] But if I do not merit this, he is the Lord, and may he do   65
what his eternal will has decreed. It is right that we regard as best whatever
he has decided, since nothing can be better.

An enormous volume of Alberto Pio, once prince of Carpi, then an exile
in France, next a sycophant, finally a Franciscan, has appeared.[5] For he put on
that sacrosanct habit three days before he died. He deals with me as if I con-   70
demn everything he does, or everything the church teaches, and this prince,
this old man on the point of death as the result of a long illness, and finally
destined for the seraphic community,[6] was not ashamed to spread with manifest lies a pernicious calumny against his neighbour. Admittedly, he shares
this with almost all those who sharpen the point of their pens against me;   75
they permit themselves to utter manifold lies in the most shameless manner
while they profess to be defenders of the truth, as if fire could extinguish fire.

I was not going to answer him except that I was greatly disturbed, first
of all, by the reputation of the author, next, that the book was published in
Paris, and lastly by the pact with the seraphic band. At any rate, I responded,   80
but in very few words,[7] and I would have responded more copiously and
more bitterly if the man had not departed from the earth in the middle of
his work. Moreover, I will not deign to answer the Dominican theologian
from Louvain who wrote in such a way that he would not have been able
to make himself more ridiculous to children, more detestable to all good   85
and learned men, [8] and finally to imprint a stain on his cherubic order more

* * * * *

4 Formulaic admonition to the audience at the end of a play
5 For the volume in question (*Tres et viginti libri in locos lucubrationum Erasmi*), and
   for Erasmus' controversy with Pio, see Ep 2486 n10. Agostino Steuco quoted
   this description of Pio in the published version of Ep 2513; see lines 681–3 and
   n93 of that letter.
6 Ie for the Franciscans. Pio's burial in the habit of a Franciscan is satirized in
   the colloquy *Exequiae seraphicae* 'The Seraphic Funeral' (CWE 40 996–1032),
   which was about to be published; see Ep 2505:53–5 with n14. As was his custom, Erasmus here makes sarcastic use of the traditional designation of the
   Franciscans as the 'seraphic' order.
7 *Adversus rhapsodias Alberti Pii* (Ep 2486 n10)
8 Erasmus did not reply to the *Apologia pro pietate in Erasmi Roterod. Enchiridion
   canonem quintum* of the Louvain Dominican Eustachius van der Rivieren, but he
   did persuade Froben to publish the *Carmen ... adversus stolidos politioris literaturae oblatratores* of André de Resende, in which Rivieren is ridiculed; see Ep 2500
   nn3 and 4.

indelible than a shoemaker's blacking.[9] I have not yet found anyone with enough patience whom I could persuade to read through this little book, slight as it is. I tried myself three or four times but had to put it down, over- come by nausea. This man, who is self-love incarnate, did not want anyone   90 not to know that he was a theologian from Louvain,[10] a title that I know has merited him great unpopularity among the theologians of that academy. Not content with this, he dedicated this ridiculous, insipid, prodigiously fatuous nonsense by name to the cardinal of Liège, an illustrious prince adorned with every distinction.[11]   95

If, perchance, you would like to know the general sense of the argu- ment, he postulates that all who are eloquent are heretics, and on the basis of the fifth rule of the *Enchiridion*[12] he teaches that I condemn all ceremonies indiscriminately, although it is pious to adore God also through external rites, and in addition, since the life of monks consists in great part in ceremo-   100 nies, that I totally disapprove once and for all the many venerable rules of monks and nuns. Elsewhere he concludes very stupidly that I surpass by far the impiety of Luther and am no less shameless a liar. But among all other things he thinks nothing is more impious than what I advise, towards the end of the *Enchiridion*, that it is expedient that no one should bind himself by   105 those adamantine bonds of vows before the age of thirty.[13] Then he threat- ens that if I do not summon back the young men who were turned aside by my words from such a holy way of life, which produces such doctors of the church, he will perform the duty that is owed to piety. If I should wish that this whole breed of men be completely annihilated, what more could I   110 wish them to do than to reveal themselves as they are in good faith? No one would believe that such stupid individuals are thought of as great theolo- gians among these Cherubs.[14] Some years ago there issued from that same press a little book, put together by a considerable number of these cherubic

* * * * *

9 While Franciscans were the 'seraphic' order, (see n6 above), Dominicans were traditionally known as the 'cherubic' order.
10 On the title-page and again on the first page of the treatise Rivieren proclaims himself 'Professor of Theology, Order of Preachers, at Louvain.'
11 Erard de la Marck (Ep 738)
12 CWE 66 65–84
13 See CWE 66 127 where, however, there is no mention of the age of thirty. For that, cf Ep 447:708–15. Cf also CWE 66 174 (*De contemptu mundi*).
14 Ie the Dominicans; see n9 above.

souls.[15] No one could imagine anything more inane, insipid, ignorant, or in-   115
sane. And they are not ashamed of such stratagems, so great is the dullness
of their minds, and such is their blind self-love. How could the church of
Christ exist if it were not supported by such pillars?

I think that by now I have for the most part answered the part of your
letter in which, with great testimony of your pious intentions, and with great   120
wisdom and equal eloquence, you encourage me to assume the role of mediator in these irresolvable divisions within the church. Though in other respects judicious, in this one alone you are very much deluded in believing
that I have the capacity to deal with such an arduous task. If I had even
average capabilities, I would not have desisted, although I have not alto-   125
gether desisted. From the very beginning of the play I advocated that the
matter should be discussed among learned men in a restrained manner. But
it seemed much more advisable to the very saintly monks to conduct the dispute by outbreaks of hostility. In a letter I tested the intentions of the emperor
and the chancellor Gattinara,[16] to see if they would allow unsolicited advice   130
to be given by letter. They responded to other matters but not to that. Adrian
favoured the scholastic disciplines, and it is not surprising that he did, since
he was educated in them from his earliest years, but he favoured them in
such a way that the role of piety took precedence, while at the same time he
was fair and benevolent towards good literature and languages.[17] He had   135
great respect for the papacy, as is indicated in his commentaries on the fourth
book of the *Sentences*,[18] and it was for that reason, if I am not mistaken, that he
was enrolled in the college of cardinals by Leo vii[19] and soon afterwards was
elevated to the triple crown. If, however, he had been able to sit in the chair
of Peter for ten years, that city would be considerably less defiled, if I am   140
not in error. I indicated to him through a certain person that I would gladly
communicate my opinion to him, provided I could do so with impunity.[20] He

* * * * *

15 *Apologia in eum librum quem ab anno Erasmus Roterodamus de Confessione edidit*
   (1525), the authorship of which was attributed on the title-page to 'Gotfridus
   Ruysius Taxander.' As Erasmus soon learned, this was the pseudonym for four
   Dominicans: Vincentius Theodorici, Cornelis of Duiveland, Walter Ruys of
   Grave, and Govaert Strijroy of Diest. See Epp 1571 n14, 1581A introduction.
16 The letter is not extant.
17 Pope Adrian vi (1522–30); see Ep 1304 introduction.
18 *Quaestiones in quartum Sententiarum librum* (Paris: Josse Bade 1516)
19 A surprising slip; it was Leo x who made Adrian a cardinal.
20 The 'certain person' was probably either Pierre Barbier or Theodoricus Hezius;
   see Ep 1324 introduction.

demanded that I do it quickly;[21] I think you read it. He was not offended, but he did not respond. Thus I readily divined that he did not like what I thought was desirable.   145

In addition, if you read my letters, both those addressed to others, and in particular the one to Vulturius,[22] you will see that I suggested certain remedies to calm these troubles, remedies that were not useless, as it seemed to me. The favour I won for this service is evidenced in a book, or I should say several books, that were immediately hurled at my head from both sides. 150 Philippus Melanchthon, besides his exceptional learning and rare eloquence, has a certain irresistible charm, which he owes more to his nature than to his genius, by which not only is he most popular with all good men, but even among his enemies there is no one to whom he is an object of hatred. At Augsburg he diligently attempted what you advise. If my malady had 155 permitted me to be present,[23] I would gladly have joined my efforts, however humble, to his enterprise. But what he accomplished is clear to all.[24] There were people there at the time who branded as heretics certain men of unblemished character and of distinguished rank for no other reason than that they had sometimes engaged in conversation with Melanchthon. What 160 would they have said if Erasmus had often conferred with him? For that was inevitable. Imagine that we had devised methods of allaying these dissensions; what would we do if neither the leading citizens nor the common people of both factions accepted what we had proposed?

In Cologne, when this pestilence had not yet progressed to this point, 165 a plan emerged suggesting some moderate measures for calming the storm, without infringing on the authority of the pope and of theologians.[25] The rejection of it was such that I was almost overcome by the suspicion that it was based on no other proof than that the language was better than average Latin. What if I should suffer the same fate as did a certain monk named 170

* * * * *

21 In Ep 1338, to which Erasmus replied with Ep 1352
22 Ie the *Epistola contra pseudevangelicos*, addressed to Gerard Geldenhouwer, to whom Erasmus applied the epithet 'Vulturius'; see Epp 2219 n5, 2358 n6.
23 See Ep 2339 n6.
24 On the failure to reach a negotiated settlement and the unhappy conclusion of the diet, see CWE 17 xi–xii.
25 The reference is to the *Consilium cuiusdam ex animo cupientis esse consultum et Romani pontificis dignitati et christianae tranquillitati*, published anonymously at Cologne in 1520. It proposed that the examination of Luther's works be entrusted to a scholarly commission appointed jointly by Charles v, Henry viii, and Louis ii of Hungary. Instantly attributed to Erasmus, *Consilium* was in fact the joint effort of Erasmus and the Dominican Johannes Faber; see Ep 1149 introduction.

John, if I am not mistaken, who is mentioned in the *Tripartite History*? Since he was a man ignorant of polite behaviour, having been brought up in the country, it happened that when by chance he was dragged into the amphitheatre and there saw two gladiators joining battle, the pious man leaped into their midst, crying out, 'What are you doing, my brothers, why are you 175 rushing headlong to kill one another for no reason?' Why say more? While he was separating the gladiators, he was killed by their swords. This fate did not befall him alone, but happens to many others who try to separate mortal enemies.[26] Of this sort was the battle between Hector and Achilles, whom only death could separate. Some people fight in such a way that they pray 180 for someone to separate them.

How could I be unaware of the kind benevolence of your illustrious prince towards me, having experienced it so many times?[27] But it was, nonetheless, gratifying that it was confirmed by your vigorous testimony. I do not require the courtesy of your recommendation unless a convenient opportu- 185 nity presents itself. There would be no need of this remedy if there were not so many evil tongues.[28] I read with incredible pleasure that the prince wishes that all his citizens be sympathetic to my cause. As to what you add, that if he knows that you are my devoted friend, there will be an appreciable increase of his favour towards you, who would deny that he said this in all sincer- 190 ity? May this also come true. The duke, who is by far the most judicious of all men of this century, not only sees the outstanding endowments of your intelligence but admires them as well, and they give him cause to love you in a special way and revere you. This is quite clear in his letters, which make mention of you in the most honorific terms.[29] 195

I ask that you give my fondest greetings to your colleague, Simon Pistoris, who is much like you.[30] I do not write to him at the moment, not that my love for him has cooled, but since I had nothing to write about, I did not want to annoy a very busy man. Although your letters, on the other hand, bring me much solace, I would nevertheless not wish you to be burdened 200

* * * * *

26 Cassiodorus *Historia ecclesiastica tripartita* 10.2; cf Ep 1400:217–29, where 'John' is called Telemachus.
27 Duke George of Saxony
28 The word translated as 'remedy' is *baccar*, which occurs in Virgil *Eclogues* 4.19 and 7.27. It is the name of a plant from the root of which an aromatic oil was pressed that was thought to have potent medicinal, even magical, powers. In his *Commentary on the Eclogues of Virgil*, at 4.19, Servius observes that *baccar* was a plant that could drive off evil spirits.
29 These letters have not survived.
30 Ep 1125 n6

by this obligation. That Andreas von Könneritz has become an even greater
friend through my recommendation, I am most gratified, and also grateful.[31]

Moreover, since my audacity in making requests is turning out so well,
I will ask one more thing of you, namely, that you signify to me by letter in
what way I can oblige the excellent prince who has deserved so well of me.   205
You know the proper approaches and propitious moments and are familiar
with his character, since you are closely acquainted with him. Farewell.

At Freiburg in Breisgau, 20 August 1531

2523 / To Alonso Ruiz de Virués   Freiburg, 21 August 1531

First published in the *Epistolae floridae* (September 1531), this letter answers one
(not extant) that was written on 20 August 1530 and not delivered until almost
a year later (lines 3–4). Ep 2641 makes clear that in April 1532 Virués had still
not received the present letter and was unaware that it had been published.

On Virués, a Spanish Benedictine monk who admired Erasmus and defended him against his hostile critics in Spain, see Ep 1684 introduction.

Even if no letter comes from my Virués that is not most welcome, nevertheless, none was more welcome than this last one, which you entrusted to Guy
Morillon. It was delivered rather late, just to let you know, since it was written on 20 August 1530 and arrived here around 1 August 1531. Obviously I
do not think Morillon is to blame, although it was his fate that his name is   5
derived from the word 'delay,'[1] and besides, he is a remarkable Callipides,[2]
having prepared his trip for six whole years and left Spain only now.[3] But it
is a long journey from Spain to Flanders and then from Flanders to Freiburg,
so that it is a matter of luck if any letters can reach here even late.

I mention these things partly so that you will not accuse me of tar-   10
diness, for it is possible that this letter may be held up further en route,

* * * * *

31 See Ep 2492:71.

2523
1 *Moror, -ari*
2 Ie someone who is constantly in motion but never gets anything done; see
   Adagia I vi 43.
3 Morillon (Epp 582, 1287) had gone to Spain in 1517 in the entourage of the
   imperial chancellor Jean (I) Le Sauvage, and after the latter's death (1518) was
   taken into the service of Charles v as one of his secretaries. He appears to have
   been in Spain without interruption from sometime in 1522 to the end of 1531,
   when he returned to the Netherlands and lived in Louvain.

and partly so that you will not expect the consolation that you demand of
me. What Cicero wrote is true, that belated congratulations are usually not
criticized,[4] but there is nothing more lame than a late consolation. I do not
doubt that remedy for the cruel wound you suffered at the death of your   15
excellent brother Jerónimo Virués will long ago have been brought,[5] if not by
reason (the best of remedies, in my opinion), then at least by time, and that a
scar will have formed over it. Consequently, it would have been a futile gesture to apply a remedy, and an inhuman one to rub again a wound that had
ceased to be painful. But if it is still bleeding and fresh, you have neverthe-   20
less depicted the man in such a way that it is more gratifying to congratulate
you on your good fortune to have had such a brother than to console your
grief for losing such a one.

        Yet it is fitting that this word 'lose' should be completely eliminated
from the language of Christians. Is it not exceedingly bold to say that he who   25
has preceded you into the heavenly kingdom, where you are soon to follow,
is lost to you? You might rightly say that he was sent off or sent ahead, but
by no means lost. All the more so when I consider the many ways in which
he was your full brother, born of the same parents, professing the same life of
monastic piety, brought up in the same monastery under the same teacher of   30
religion, instructed in the same literature and disciplines in the same school,
equally dedicated to the sacred function of teaching the people, engaged in
it with the same fervour and the same good results, and finally so similar to
you in physical characteristics and intellectual ability and even in the way he
spoke that those who did not yet know that there were two Viruéses were   35
often uncertain whether they had heard Alonso or Jerónimo preaching. If the
old proverb 'Like rejoices in like' is correct,[6] I can easily imagine with what
affection such likeness in everything joined you together.

        Moreover, although I know you have been so long involved in Christian
philosophy with such great zeal and success that there is no danger of any   40

                * * * * *

4 *Ad familiares* 2.7
5 Jerónimo Ruiz de Virués (1489–1530) was the older brother of Alonso and his
   fellow Benedictine. In March 1527 he represented the Benedictines at a meeting
   of delegates of the religious orders that was called to draw up a list of propositions taken from Erasmus' writings in preparation for their examination by a
   conference of theologians at Valladolid that summer. His advocacy of Erasmus
   at the meeting is described in Ep 1814:255–66. Although there is no evidence
   that Erasmus ever had any direct contact with Jerónimo, he here displays a
   good knowledge of his life, most of it evidently drawn from the letter to which
   this is the answer.
6 *Adagia* I ii 21

human occurrence deterring your spirit from its noble ideals, nevertheless, since we carry around this treasure in clay vessels,[7] I can easily see what a cruel blow your natural feelings have inflicted on your heart. Yet I think now that both through time itself, which heals even the most incurable of evils, and much more so through reason and piety, the wound has long ago been healed 45 or so mitigated that you feel much more spiritual joy from the remembrance of your excellent brother than distress from your longing for the deceased. Of what importance was it to have lived longer if, after having reached perfection in a short time, he completed many lifetimes? He has lived long who, though in a few years, has gained many talents for the sake of Christ.[8] 50

I admire your brother in all respects but especially in this, that even if he was not Seraphic or Cherubic (for they love to be called by these names),[9] but from the posterity of St Benedict, he devoted all his zeal to this task, than which there is no other more apostolic or more pleasing to Christ or more salutary to Christ's flock.[10] Benedict taught poor farmers; your Jerónimo pre- 55 ferred to work in the Lord's vineyard, and using a language taught by the Spirit instead of the ploughshare, the hoe, the mattock, the rake, and the weeding hoe, he preferred to tear out impious beliefs from the minds of men, dissipate carnal affections, insert the cuttings of evangelical piety, and gather the copious harvests into the granaries of the Lord, of whom he knew he was 60 the tiller. You write very truly, my Virués, that there is a great crowd everywhere of those who preach to the people, but according to the old proverb 'Many bear the wand, few feel the god,'[11] that is, few teach Christian philosophy purely and sincerely.

Therefore the first merit of Jerónimo is that he was amply prepared 65 for the most sacred of all functions. The second is that he did not rush into it of his own, but waited until, after the example of Paul, he was called by God. I interpret the word 'called' to mean one who was drawn to this position by order of the abbot and the demand of the people, whose voice is the voice of God, and through the entreaties of that most esteemed woman, the 70 Empress Isabella.[12] His third merit is that in accepting this apostolic office he

* * * * *

7 1 Cor 4:7
8 Matt 25:14–30
9 Ie neither a Franciscan nor a Dominican; cf Ep 2522 nn6, 9.
10 Ie preaching, to which Franciscans and Dominicans devoted themselves, with results that were frequently the butt of Erasmus' sharp criticism
11 *Adagia* I vii 6
12 Isabella of Portugal, wife of Charles v and his regent in Spain during his many absences. It was at her invitation that in 1527 Jerónimo took a position at the court and served there until his death three years later.

strove to emulate not just any apostle at all, but the greatest of the apostles, namely, the magnanimous and generous Paul, who glories in no other title more than that he taught the gospel free of charge,[13] that is, he undertook, carried out, and saw through to the end and at his own expense so many labours, dangers, and afflictions. The pious man knew for whom he invested those labours, he knew his reward was secure in the hands of the just judge, or rather the most beneficent Lord, who renders a hundredfold in this world and life eternal in the next.

How pleased I was with those words of yours in your letter: 'He sets out for the court, he begins to preach, not about himself but about the remarkable achievement of his order, not about the commentaries of men but of Christ.' As I read these words, how many things came to mind that I often heard from preachers, with great repugnance. I do not feel like mentioning them here. They all reeked of boastful glories and financial gain. Nowadays those who are invited, not to say who force their way, into the courts of monarchs, though professing to be beggars, aspire immediately, for the most part, to the mitre, then the cardinal's hat, then the triple crown. But your Jerónimo went hunting for Christ, not for himself. From the pomp, riches, and delights of the court he contracted no more vice than fish do from the salt of the sea. In the midst of luxury he consumed his body by fasting and reduced it to servitude, lest perhaps in preaching to others he might become depraved.[14]

The last act of the apostolic drama drew nigh, in which he outdid himself as an outstanding performer. The emperor Christ furnished his soldier with the opportunity by which he could demonstrate his exceptional virtue to everyone. The centurion Cornelius solicited an interview with Peter and his request was granted.[15] A different' centurion was provided for Jerónimo: Stephen, a Genoese by birth, who thirsted for the gospel. The violence of a persistent fever banished his shyness; he sent emissaries. But when appeal was made to him, Jerónimo, undeterred by fear of infection with the pestilential illness, more than once went to visit the bed-ridden man. He taught, counselled, encouraged, consoled, and heard the secrets of his heart, why say more? While he was to him the food of the soul, he drew in the death of the body from the last breath of the sick man.

At this some evil-minded commentator will cry out in protest: 'He did nothing new, many others do the same thing – he sought a reward from the dying man.' But in this too he imitated Paul, who collected money from

* * * * *

13 2 Cor 11:7
14 Cf 1 Cor 9:27.
15 Acts 10:1–33

Asians to help the poor in such a way that not only did he not touch any part
of it, but he also took care that no shadow of suspicion could fall upon him.[16]
Stephen left about ten thousand ducats, and he entrusted them to the hands   110
of Jerónimo, not as to the executor of his will, but that he should spend them
for pious uses as he saw fit. If this man, so useful to the commonwealth, had
saved a good part of this sum of money for himself, who would have denied
that it had been devoted to pious uses? But he did not take a farthing for himself, since, generally speaking, there is scarcely any contagion more deadly   115
than that which comes from money. If he had given the entire sum to his
monastery, which I learn from your letter is bountiful in works of piety but
has slim financial resources, well established in religious discipline but di-
lapidated physically, who would not approve the charity of the man towards
his confrères? But he did not leave them a single farthing from that huge sum   120
even if they complained about it. He took care with a Pauline generosity not
to give any opportunity to the suspicions of men who are always inclined to
see the worse side of things. He donated the whole sum of money immediately to the poor, and did not allow any discussion about those to whom it
had been devoted. For whoever is slow to give gives the impression of being   125
unwilling to give. He was such a sincere Christian that he was more in fear of
money than of pestilence. The first he gave away immediately, the other remained. If what you write is true, on the fourth day after the centurion died,
Jerónimo began to burn with fever, and he who refused to inherit the money
became heir to the malady.   130

It was not an ordinary death, but a favour of the propitious divinity,
who called his vigorous athlete at an early age to receive his reward, lest a
longer sojourn on earth stain his pure soul with some blemish or failing. For
this reason he foresaw and even predicted his death and, not unlike his Lord,
he at first shuddered in the face of death (this was part of Christ's human   135
nature), but then his spirit rose up with marvellous confidence against death
and at this point recalled the words of Christ: 'Father, if it be possible, let this
cup pass from me,'[17] and he also said: 'Do not weep for me.'[18] And consider
also that the cause and the time were fitting: while he was intent on saving
his neighbour, he expended his soul; he died for the gospel during the same   140
days on which Christ was killed for us.[19] There was no great difference of age
either; he died at the age of forty-one, for there are some ancient writers who

* * * * *

16 2 Cor 8:18–21
17 Luke 22:42
18 Luke 23:28
19 CEBR says 'Easter 1530.'

say that Christ died at that age.[20] He spent three years in his evangelical function, the same amount of time it is thought that Christ spent in preaching.
In all the time in which he was confined to his sickbed he never ceased from
the fervour of his preaching. The vigour of his spirit shook off the languor
of his body. He kept giving advice, exhorting, adjuring whoever was present
and, after the example of the Saviour, without uttering a cry, he expired. You
would recognize a true, genuine disciple of Christ who resembled the master
in so many external qualities that one cannot doubt his interior endowments;
you would recognize also the disciple of Paul, who completed in his body
what was lacking in the sufferings of Christ.[21]

For the rest, to play for a moment the role of Momus and find something to criticize in Venus' sandal,[22] I am surprised at the solicitude, to my
mind unnecessary, with which he admonished his confrères not to let a woman touch his dead body. If he feared for himself, surely it was a baseless fear;
if it was for women, he attributed excessive fragility to that sex. But we must
not think that he was a misogynist, since the Lord did not shun contact with a
sinful woman.[23] You will say that it was an immoderate concern for chastity,
and I gladly concur.

Since you had such a brother, dearest Virués, you ask of me a new and
unusual consolation. What would you say if I were to console you the way
the delegates of the Gauls consoled Nero? I pray you, Virués, to support your
happiness bravely.[24] For what greater happiness could have befallen you than
to be able to glory safely in such a brother, not according to the flesh, but in
the Lord. I hope that his spirit will find its equivalent in you; in that way all
who now mourn his death will feel his absence with less sense of loss. But
while we congratulate the community of monks on Jerónimo alone, an immense sorrow occupies my mind when I think of the scarcity of such monks
and what a great multitude exists everywhere of those who are slaves of the
belly and the abdomen.[25] May the Lord deign to inspire them with his spirit.

* * * * *

20 The common view is that Jesus died at the age of thirty-three, but the church
Father Irenaeus argued that he died between his fortieth and his fiftieth year
(*Against Heresies* 2.22.5–6).
21 Col 1:24
22 Momus was the god of carping criticism.
23 Luke 7:36–50
24 Julius Africanus, a Gaul, remarked to Nero concerning his mother's death (he
had had her murdered): 'Your provinces of Gaul beg that you will bear your
happiness bravely.' See Quintilian 8.5.16. The inappropriateness of this example is striking.
25 On Erasmus' habit of referring to monks, particularly members of the mendicant orders, as slaves of their own bellies, see Ep 1980 n1.

For the kindness you showed Frans Dilft I am much indebted to you.[26]
Farewell.

Frieburg im Breisgau, 21 August 1531

2524 / From Johann Herwagen   Basel, 21 August 1531

This letter was first published as Ep 156 in Förstemann / Günther. The autograph was in the Burscher Collection at Leipzig (Ep 1254 introduction).

I send you the rest of the letters that were printed,[1] and I could have given
you all of them if the others that I am waiting for had not been delayed.
Whatever you wish to add please send via Hieronymus,[2] and if some care-
less error slipped in that will not meet with your approval, let me know, for I
am prepared to change it. The copy you sent will return to you as you sent it. 5

Concerning a return to our B,[3] I have consulted with Hieronymus, as
you will hear from him in person. If there is anything that you wish to have
done in Frankfurt or on the way or even elsewhere,[4] you have every right to
ask it of me, and I shall carry it out with the same diligence as I conduct my
own affairs. At this point we must stop the presses completely because I do 10
not know what to commit to them. I ask you as our chief patron what you
think Herwagen should do so that he may throw out the old and make room
for the new. Be in good health.

Basel, 21 August 1531

Your sincere friend Johann Herwagen   15

* * * * *

26 On his second journey to Spain (c January 1530) Frans van der Dilft had carried
   letters, of which none of those that survive (Epp 2250–5) is addressed to Virués.

2524
1 Ie in the *Epistolae floridae*; see Ep 2518.
2 Froben
3 The Latin is 'nostra B.', in which, as the Allen editors point out, 'B.' might well
   stand for 'Basilea' (Basel). Given, however, that Basel was still in the process of
   consolidating the religious changes that had led Erasmus to move to Freiburg
   (see Ep 2519 introduction), it is difficult to imagine him contemplating a return there at this time. When, fearing that plague or war might make Freiburg
   unsafe, Erasmus considered the pros and cons of moving somewhere further
   away from the disorders of Germany and Switzerland: Brabant (Ep 2582 n9),
   Besançon (Epp 2514, 2553), or Italy (2479:52 with n11).
4 Ie during the autumn book fair at Frankfurt

QVARTVS TOMVS
IN QVO

MARCI TVLLII CICERONIS OPERA PHILOSO
phica, uigilantissima cura, fide uetustissimorum exem,
plarium, recognita, quorum catalogum se,
quens indicabit pagina.

BASILEAE EX OFFICINA HERVAGIANA
ANNO M. D. XXXIIII.

Second of the two versions of Johann Herwagen's printer's device (cf page 112)

With regard to the Mercury that I have placed on the frontispiece of
books, I had already had it made when you made mention of the medallion.[5]
If you do not approve of the medallion, we shall endeavour to make a suitable adaptation of it.

To Erasmus of Rotterdam, his lord and revered patron. In Freiburg   20

2525 / To Anton Fugger   Freiburg, 22 August [1531]

First published by Allen, this letter is Erasmus' reply to one now lost (see
lines 14–15) in which Anton Fugger once again invited Erasmus to settle in
Augsburg at his expense (cf Ep 2476 n1). The autograph is in the Staatsbibliothek zu Berlin (Sammlung Darmstaedter, 2d 1508, Erasmus, Desiderius). The
contents of the letter make the year-date obvious.

Cordial greetings. Just as it is supremely pleasing, day after day, to recognize more and more the singular predisposition of your spirit towards
me, so I am grieved that some fate or other prevents me from enjoying the
company of such an amiable friend. If I had had such a response about the
house, I would not have involved myself in so many miserable anxieties   5
of making bids, buying, building, from which I have recoiled to a marked
degree throughout my life.[1] Now I have hidden myself in a nest and accumulated provisions for the winter, and I do not see how I can change my
residence, especially since Augsburg is quite cold in winter. I must await the
new swallow. In the meantime we shall see what the emperor is planning,   10
of whom various rumours are circulating,[2] and how the war in Switzerland

* * * * *

5 'Mercury' was the image of three-headed Mercury that Herwagen had adopted as his printer's device; see Ep 2518 n6. The word here translated as 'medallion' is *clipeus*, the word for a Roman soldier's shield or for the medallion
   image of a god in the form of a shield. In his publications Herwagen used two
   versions of the three-headed Mercury: one, like that in the *Epistolae floridae*
   (see illustration page 112), had Mercury's three heads atop an undecorated
   column. In the other, the column was decorated with a medallion (see image
   on preceding page).

2525
1 This seems to indicate that, in a letter no longer extant, Fugger had advised
   against Erasmus' purchase of a house in Freiburg; cf Epp 2506 n1, 2517 n11.
2 Cf Ep 2511 n20.

is going,[3] and finally where your commonwealth is heading, which I hope
will be as peaceful as possible.[4] For I see that human affairs are in a dangerously unstable state. For the rest, I thank you for the kindness that you offer
me so sincerely. There is, however, no cause for you to demolish or build   15
anything for my sake unless I write a detailed account of what I have decided. I would not wish to be a burden in any way either to your household
or your fortunes.

Farewell.

Freiburg, 22 August, the day on which I received your letter[5]   20
Erasmus of Rotterdam, in my own hand
To the most illustrious gentleman Anton Fugger. In Augsburg

2526 / To Reginald Pole   Freiburg, 25 August 1531

This letter was first published in the *Epistola palaeonaeoi*. For Pole, cousin of
Henry VIII, humanist scholar, and future cardinal, see Ep 1632 introduction.

ERASMUS OF ROTTERDAM TO REGINALD POLE OF ENGLAND,
GREETING
On his return from England, Simon Grynaeus remonstrated with me not a little because while I wrote to other friends, I had omitted you, to whom is owed
with good reason a privileged place among the privileged.[1] But, most es-   5
teemed Pole, this came about neither through my forgetting you nor through
my laziness. I imagined that you had returned long ago to your Muses, from
which I heard you had been torn away much against your will when you

* * * * *

3 Political, economic, and religious tension between the Protestant and Catholic
   cantons in Switzerland were at this point moving rapidly towards military conflict, which in October would break out in the so-called Second Kappel War,
   in which Huldrych Zwingli would lose his life on the battlefield (11 October
   1531); cf Ep 2173 n10. Erasmus was prone to worry that religious war in Switzerland would spill over into the nearby Breisgau and perhaps further; see for
   example Ep 2193:28–9 with n12.
4 This is a renewed expression of Erasmus' fear that in Augsburg tensions between the Catholic city government and the burgeoning evangelical movement
   would lead to disorder; cf Ep 2406:70–1.
5 Not extant

2526
1 For Grynaeus' journey to England in the spring of 1531 see Ep 2487 n9.

REGINALDVS, CARD. POLVS.
Creat. Anᵒ. 1536 Jnoſt. 1558 .   F.N.W f.

Reginald Pole

were leaving Padua.[2] Your Chrysostom is in a safe place, and I shall send it to
you at the time of the next fair if I know to whom you wish me to deliver it. 10
The whole manuscript was copied some time ago by my amanuensis.[3] It has
been two years since a complete Greek Chrysostom was promised us from
Verona on the initiative of Matteo Giberti, once the papal datary, now the
bishop of Verona, but I still see no sign of it.[4] At my suggestion Hieronymus
Froben will print a complete Greek Basil,[5] whom I particularly like among 15
the writers of that period. For while Chrysostom has a certain rather annoying prolixity and Gregory of Nazianzus a kind of affected subtlety, princi-
pally in his choice of words, in Basil there is nothing displeasing.

I think that Leonico, an excellent man, has departed this earth.[6] About
four months ago someone returning from Padua reported that he was con- 20
fined to his bed at the time and that the doctors had given up hope. I pray
that through the mercy of the Lord he is safely in his hands. I hear also that
our Lupset has departed to a better life.[7] It gave me great pleasure to learn
from Grynaeus that you are there and in good health and that you occupy a
position, which, leaving aside the fame of your ancestors, your moral integ- 25
rity and learning deserve.[8] It will give me much more pleasure, however, if
I will learn more fully from your letters about the state of your affairs.

Farewell.

Freiburg im Breisgau, on the day after the feast of St Bartholemew, 1531

2527 / From Erasmus Schets   Antwerp, 28 August 1531

This letter, Schets' reply to Ep 2512, was first published by Allen. The autograph is in the Öffentliche Bibliothek of the University of Basel (MS Scheti epistolae 27).

* * * * *

2 Pole had returned to England in 1527 after having lived since 1521 at Padua,
  where his home was a haven for young humanists. But the business of the royal
  divorce, to which his opposition was obvious, had made residence in England
  increasingly uncomfortable for him, and in 1532 he would return to Italy, not to
  return until the reign of Queen Mary in 1554.
3 It seems that Pole had lent Erasmus a manuscript for his Latin edition of
  Chrysostom (Ep 2359).
4 For the never completed Verona edition of Giberti, see Ep 2340:2–12.
5 See Ep 2611.
6 Niccolò Leonico Tomeo (Ep 1479 n70) died on 28 March 1531.
7 Thomas Lupset (Ep 270:69n) died on 27 December 1530.
8 In 1527 Pole had been elected dean of Exeter, but he had since refused Henry
  VIII's offers of the archbishopric of York and the bishopric of Winchester.

†

Cordial greetings. I wrote you last, my very dear master and friend, on
12 July.[1] I addressed the letter to Froben at Basel. I hope that it will reach you
in the more usual way. I have just received the letter that you wrote to me on
the seventeenth of that month.[2]

Pieter Gillis wrote one thing but did another, for up to now I have re-   5
ceived nothing but fine words. He promised me twenty times that he would
send you the money, but nothing came of it.[3] I will not hesitate to go see him
myself from now on.

I have heard nothing from England. But I know that when something
is paid to Castro he will let me know immediately and will send it to me by   10
letters of exchange. If the English buy back that pension you will be rich, and
you will be relieved of the worry about the annual payment.[4]

I am surprised that you complain about a loss suffered from the sums
you received via Castro.[5] You add two examples by which you apparently
wish to prove that you received more through others. You say that Bebel was   15
paid fifty crowns and that you received them intact with no loss. In addition,
you say that another person exchanged thirty-five nobles in England and
received forty-nine crowns in return.[6]

* * * * *

2527
1 Ep 2511
2 Ep 2512
3 For the monies deposited with him by Erasmus, see Ep 2494 n12.
4 Cf Ep 2512:4–5.
5 Erasmus believed that he was being cheated by Luis de Castro, Erasmus Schets'
   factor in London, who remitted a gift of thirty-five angel nobles, possibly from
   Thomas Boleyn (see Ep 2512 n4), as forty-nine rose crowns instead of the fifty-
   six Erasmus reckoned it was worth. As Schets explains, however, the gift was
   clearly in 'nominal' nobles, worth 6s 8d (80d) or three to the pound sterling,
   the traditional ratio. But Henry VIII's debasement of 1526 had raised the official
   value of the angel-noble by 12.5 per cent to 7s 6d (90d), and therefore in terms
   of real coins three nobles represented £1 2s 6d (270d) (CWE 12 573–4 and 650
   Table 3; on Henry's debasement, see also CWE 14 423–76). Schets suggests that
   Erasmus' benefactor retained the difference in the value between nominal and
   real nobles, some 17s 6d. The sum paid over in crowns was roughly equivalent
   to the amount delivered by Bebel, for a total of ninety-nine crowns; Erasmus
   complains in Ep 2552 that about half the coins were defective.
6 The rose crown, a gold coin which, after Henry VIII's debasements of 1526,
   was worth 60d. Fifty crowns were equivalent to 500 days' or almost two years'
   wages for an Oxford master mason (6d per day, 230 days per year) (CWE 12 650
   Table 3, 688 Table 11). As Schets explains, because the sum was both awarded
   and paid in rose crowns, Erasmus received the full amount with no discrepancy
   that might arise in converting it to another denomination.

I was sure that I had explained this matter to you a year ago. I will do it again, using the two examples you gave, if I can. The fifty crowns received 20 by Bebel were correctly paid in coin, for you received money for money. But as for those thirty-five nobles, which another person gave, if they were given in the form of nobles they would be equivalent to fifty-six crowns, for which you say you received no more than forty-nine. Therefore, I easily deduce that they were given in nominal nobles, of which there are three to the pound. 25 These nominal nobles were created by the increase in the value of gold. I remember that I wrote to you once, in quite clear language, that while at one time three nobles in coin made a pound, now, because of the said increase, they make a pound, two and a half shillings sterling.

Thus it turns out also that the thirty-five nobles received in England 30 were not worth and were not exchanged for more than forty-nine crowns, which at the rate of three nobles in coin would have to be exchanged for fifty-six crowns.

And so that you may understand the matter more clearly, note that the increase in the value of gold in England brought it about that ordinary 35 people kept the name of noble and they count three of these per pound following the old custom, but when they pay or reckon in cash they give as much more money as the value and price of gold has increased, which is to say that for the noble in coin, which formerly was worth six shillings and eight pence sterling, they will pay seven and a half shillings sterling. Thus 40 those who pay you pounds or nobles in England do not give nobles in coin but three nominal nobles per pound, and the three that they pay out in coin they give in place of twenty-two and a half shillings, retaining for themselves the difference dictated by the value of gold, to their own benefit and your disadvantage. 45

That is why Castro received the money you complain about, when your Quirinus was present, because of the devaluation of pounds and nobles at the present moment; perhaps you think that he was paid nobles in coin. I would wish that you had more understanding of this matter than I observe. I could not, however, explain it to you more clearly. In the two 50 aforesaid examples you have before your eyes what the difference is and where the error that concerns you lies hidden. For just as from crowns received in coin you collect all of what was given, so also from nominal pounds or nobles what you collect varies with the price of gold and the devaluation of the pound. And so Castro gave you the value of the mon- 55 eys received in pounds and nominal nobles accordingly. In any case, he is certainly to be regarded as innocent of what you wrongly suspected him. If it had been otherwise, I would have known about it and I would not have remained silent.

A few months ago I had ordered through a banker of Courtrai that a   60
half-pension be demanded from Jan de Hondt.[7] He said that he would send
two pension payments at once at the time of the fair. Now he has informed
me that he will first meet Barbier, and he contends that he is no longer bound
to pay this pension.[8] I wrote to Barbier and Molendino,[9] instructing them to
clarify the matter so that you will be compensated for this pension and they   65
will fulfil their duty as good men. I hope they will do so.

The emperor is preparing a trip to Germany to meet with the princes of
the Empire at Speyer.[10] They say he will set out before October. I don't know
whether it is to be hoped that this meeting will be more successful than the
preceding one in Augsburg.[11] May God provide that it turn out well.   70

Farewell, dearest Erasmus, and may you long be happy and prosper.
From Antwerp, 28 August 1531
Sincerely yours, Erasmus Schets

† To the eminent and most learned Master Erasmus of Rotterdam, honoured friend. In Freiburg   75

2528 / To Alfonso de Valdés   Freiburg, 29 August 1531

This letter, which is Erasmus' reply to one from Valdés that is now lost, was first
published in the *Epistolae palaeonaeoi*. The manuscript, an autograph with the
address page missing, is in the University Library at Leiden (MS B P L 293 B). For
Valdés, who as secretary to Emperor Charles was with him in the Netherlands
at this time, see Epp 1807, 2469.

ERASMUS OF ROTTERDAM TO ALFONSO VALDÉS, GREETING
'The falling-out of lovers is the renewal of love,' said the comic writer.[1] May
no ill feeling, however, occur between us, joined together by the bonds of an

* * * * *

7 See Epp 2404, 2487:7–8, 2494:9–12, 2511:12–14.
8 The income from Erasmus' Courtrai prebend had to be paid by Jan de Hondt to
Pierre Barbier and then to Erasmus; see Ep 1993 n11. Since Barbier, who was heavily in debt in consequence of the prolonged litigation at Rome over his deanery at
Tournai (cf Ep 2404 n8) owed de Hondt money, the latter no longer felt obligated
to make payments to the former for the benefit of Erasmus (cf Allen Ep 2704:24–5).
9 For Molendino see Ep 2501 n2.
10 See Ep 2511 n20.
11 The Diet of Augsburg in 1530; see Ep 2403 n11.

2528
1 Terence *Andria* 555

uncommon friendship. Yet it sometimes happens that even among the closest of friends some slight suspicions or complaints may arise that renew the 5
vigour of good will. For it is hardly possible that the ardour of love can last
continually among human beings unless it is roused from time to time by
certain stimulants. It is, after all, too well known how powerful is the malice
of pernicious tongues. Furthermore, if you had slackened somewhat the in-
tensity of your singular good will (or as you call it, your piety) towards me, 10
since you are separated by such a long distance and occupied by the affairs of
the court, what else would it be than something that occurs between one human being and another? And besides, if you had not been born of the Graces
themselves and nourished by their milk, how would you have been able constantly to protect your pure and sincere soul amidst the venom of so many 15
malicious slanderers? And further, by that perfidious name, since you wish
to know it, I meant Aleandro.² Concerning yourself, I suspected nothing else,
excellent Valdés, than that you had perhaps made up your mind not to join
battle with these hornets in future, and I strongly approved this decision.
One who is not oppressed by hatred himself more easily allays the anxieties 20
of one who is weighed down by hatred. Nor do I always like to know what
this person or that person says or writes about me. There is nothing more
frenzied or more talkative than this world of ours. You are accustomed not
only to writing to me in detail about the tumult fermented by certain lawless
men but also to transmitting letters of others of a similar nature. This novelty 25
has not diminished in any way my long-standing good will towards you
but has increased my admiration for your wisdom.³ I have recognized your
greatness of soul, which is above not only money, but all desire for glory, and
I acknowledge that what you write is the absolute truth, that you have never
given any indication that you wished one of my works to be dedicated to 30
you. I am in agreement with you on that score. But I do not quite understand
the reason you allege: 'It is not that I fear envy,' you say, 'but that I value
your works too highly to have them dedicated to me.'⁴ I have preferred, as
becomes a true friend, that more consideration should be given to their immortality than to my petty glory. If only my labours could be of such worth 35

* * * * *

2 See Ep 2469:22–3 with n4.
3 Without the text of Valdés' letter, it is not possible to say what the 'novelty' was.
4 In Ep 2469:28–31 Erasmus says that he would have dedicated a book to Valdés
   were it not for his fear of thereby arousing envy against him. Although this passage seems to renew the offer of a dedication, no work of Erasmus' was ever
   dedicated to Valdés, perhaps because he died in 1532.

that they could transmit the name of such a friend to posterity. But you are greatly in error, most loyal friend, if you think that I suppose that more distinction would accrue to my writings from the name of any prince whatsoever than from the name of Valdés. You have within you what is necessary to consecrate your name to immortality, and outstanding virtue does not pay   40
heed to the praise of men, but it is important to others that rare talents born for virtue should be transmitted to posterity.

While your whole letter was wonderfully enjoyable, the last part, in which you hold out the hope that soon we will discuss matters together in each other's presence, was the most enjoyable of all. Hardly anything else   45
could be more desired than that. But I have grave fears that the inextricable chains of your affairs will deny us such great happiness. In the meanwhile, however, we will prepare accommodations for you.

Well, if anyone should tell you that Erasmus, half-dead and almost a septuagenarian, has taken a wife, wouldn't you make a big sign of the cross   50
and cry out: 'Ye gods! I hear a prodigy!' But that you may not be unaware, I have done something no less troublesome or less foreign to my inclination and my temperament.[5] You will ask what it is: I bought a house here, of good reputation, but of inequitable evaluation.[6] You will say, 'What happened?' It's a long story, my friend,[7] which it is better to reserve for our conversation.   55
I am merely afraid that the newness of the place and the unfamiliar tasks may be detrimental to my health, for already, not to mention other things, I had an attack of gout in my left foot. Undoubtedly these things are the messengers of all-powerful death. Today dysentery was added.[8] My Lieven Panagathus is seeking to obtain some kind of employment with Queen Mary.[9] I would   60
like to know what you think of the young man's character. I would like to converse further with you, but at this same moment I have to write to several others. Farewell.

Freiburg, 29 August 1531

You will recognize the hand and the spirit of your friend.   65

* * * * *

5 Cf Ep 2534:21–6.
6 Ep 2506 n1
7 See Ep 2462 introduction.
8 Cf Epp 2534:39–40, 2536:1–3, 2541:22–3, 2582:31–2.
9 Lieven Algoet ('Panagathus' is a Hellenization of 'Algoet,' meaning 'all good') had left Erasmus' service and was seeking employment at the court of Mary of Hungary, regent of the Netherlands; see Ep 2469:43–4 with n5.

2529 / To Georgius Agricola   Freiburg, 29 August 1531

This letter was first published in the *Epistolae palaeonaeoi*. For Georgius Agricola, see Ep 1594 n23. His *Bermannus sive de re metallica dialogus* was published by Froben in 1530 with a prefatory letter by Erasmus (Ep 2274).

ERASMUS OF ROTTERDAM TO GEORGIUS AGRICOLA, GREETING

My little expostulation with Plateanus had good results.[1] It won for me merited letters from both of you,[2] although you prefer that yours be considered an acknowledgement of debt rather than a letter. Nevertheless, it certainly gives me much more pleasure to be able to make known through the af- 5
fixed documents that Agricola, a man of eminent learning and, unless I am completely mistaken, soon to occupy a prominent place among the leading literary figures, is allied to me by the laws of gratitude. That my support, or rather my acquiescence in having the book published, for it was accomplished through the recommendation of Andreas von Könneritz,[3] was not 10
displeasing to you is very pleasing to me.

   Certain learned friends have written to me from Brabant concerning Cornelius Agrippa, but in such a way that they seem not to approve the aggressiveness of the man and attribute to him more zeal in accumulating than judgment in choosing.[4] Some are not displeased that he mocks the theolo- 15
gians and the monks, up to now successfully, under the protection of the emperor, whom he serves as counsellor,[5] and of Cardinal Campeggi.[6] But I fear that the audacity of the man breeds hatred for good letters, if what my

* * * * *

2529
1 Petrus Plateanus (Ep 2216 introduction), friend of Georgius Agricola, had sent the manuscript of Agricola's treatise *De re metallica* to Erasmus, soliciting his good offices in persuading Froben to publish the work. Erasmus did as requested, and the success of the book made Agricola a well-known author; see Ep 2216:5–10 with nn3–4. There is no documentary record of the 'little expostulation' with Plateanus mentioned here.
2 Not extant
3 Erasmus' dedicatory letter for Agricola's treatise (Ep 2274) is addressed to Andreas von Könneritz and his brother Christoph, both of whom lived for a time with Erasmus after his arrival in Freiburg (1529). Their father, Heinrich von Könneritz, was superintendent of mines at Jáchymov (Joachimsthal) in the Erz Mountains, where Agricola acquired his knowledge of mining and metallurgy (Ep 2274 introduction).
4 For Henricus Cornelius Agrippa of Nettesheim see Ep 2544 introduction. The reference here seems to be to his treatise *De incertitudine et vanitate scientiarum et artium declamatio*, which had just been published.
5 In 1530 Agrippa had become court historian and archivist.
6 Lorenzo Cardinal Campeggi (Ep 2366), the papal legate at the imperial court

friends tell me in their letters is true. I have not had the opportunity of seeing
his book and he has never written to me.[7]   20

I would be very eager to read the book concerning weights and measures that you are working on as soon as you send it to me.[8] I predict, my
dear Georgius, that it will bring you great renown. And you should have no
fear of envy, since the subject is of such a kind that it will never be exhausted,
partly because of its antiquity, partly because of the various regional cus-   25
toms, and partly because of the subtle obscurity of the material itself, not to
speak for the moment of the corrupt texts. I hear that Portis is no less kindly
than learned.[9] Alciati is endowed with a very good-natured disposition, so
that you have nothing to fear from him.[10] Budé, though rather blunt in manner, is too good a man to take offence at someone engaged in these studies.[11] 30
Even if he were to do so, which I think will never be the case, he will do
harm to his own name, not yours. Finally, even if some rivalry should arise
between you, provided that it is not disrespectful, these words of Hesiod will
console you: 'This kind of struggle is good for mortals.'[12]

You need not congratulate me on my *Against Lying*,[13] since I greatly   35
regret that project. I would have composed a wholly different Iliad, but it is
worthy of that monster, who is a combination of mere banter, subterfuges,
lies, empty boasting, and chicanery. Your letters will always be most welcome. Return my greetings to the burgomaster, Lucas Scuppegius, and to the
clerk of the town council, Bartholomaeus Bach.[14]   40

Farewell.

At Freiburg im Breisgau, 29 August 1531

* * * * *

7 Erasmus would initiate the correspondence with Agrippa; see Ep 2544.
8 *De mensuris et ponderibus*, which would be published by Froben and Episcopius
   at Basel in 1533
9 Leonardo de Portis, author of a book on ancient coinage and measures (*De ses-
   tertio, pecuniis, ponderibus et mensuris antiquis*) published at Venice circa 1520,
   and reprinted by (among others) Froben at Basel in 1524 and 1530; cf Ep 648:58n.
10 Andrea Alciati (Ep 1250) published a *Libellus de veterum ponderibus et mensuris* in
   1530 (Haguenau: J. Setzer). In a 1550 edition of his *De mensuris* Agricola would
   append a section entitled *Ad ea, quae A. Alciatus denuo disputavit de mensuris et
   ponderibus, brevis defensio.*
11 Guillaume Budé's groundbreaking work on ancient coinage, *De asse et partibus
   eius*, was published in 1514 (Paris: Josse Bade).
12 Hesiod *Works and Days* 24
13 *Admonitio adversus mendacium*, Erasmus' final reckoning with Heinrich Eppendorf; see Ep 2400 introduction.
14 For Scuppegius see Ep 2216 n10. Bartholomeus Bach (documented 1522–36) was
   clerk of the town council in Jáchymov (Joachimsthal) and a good friend of Agricola.

2530 / To Erasmus Schets   Freiburg, 30 August 1531

This letter was first published by Allen on the basis of the autograph in the
British Library (MS Add 38512 folio 61). Starting at line 27 it is Erasmus' reply to
Ep 2511. Schets' reply to this letter is Ep 2558.

I have bought here a new house for seven hundred gold florins, and I am
still building at great expense.[1] It was necessary. I paid in cash. But I suffered a great loss in florins. Among them there were many that Maximilian
coined there.[2] Here they value them as twelve batzen.[3] There are many of less
weight.[4] I experienced the same disadvantage with crowns. There are some   5
that have the symbol ℍ, which they do not accept except at a loss for me.[5] I
write this to you so that you will be more careful, although I know that I am
instructing the instructed and reminding the mindful.

I think fifty pounds will have reached you by now, with others that
Mountjoy and More promised.[6] You will do me a great favour if you note sep-   10
arately on the written contract how much you have. For if anything should
happen to you, which, please God, will not, I would not be able to negotiate
with your heirs on the basis of letters. I have many letters of yours that make
mention of the money I have received, which would now be useless.

Concerning the bundle of letters for England,[7] see to it that you do not   15
entrust them to anyone without due care. I cite this caution not without

* * * * *

2530
1 See Epp 2506 n1, 2517 n11. In Ep 2512:10–11 Erasmus puts the price of the house
  at c 800 florins, which may well include the sum spent on new building. In a
  letter of 12 September 1535 Erasmus states that the actual cost of the house was
  '624 gold florins in proven gold' (Allen Ep 3036:6–7).
2 'There' is presumably the Netherlands.
3 Basel coins; cf Ep 2477:10–11.
4 The florin of St Andrew (St Andries florin), issued from 1466 to 1496 in the
  Burgundian Low Countries, was of the same weight and fineness as the gulden
  or florin of the Rhine (CWE 1 317). The batzen officially represented 1/15 of
  the Rhenish florin, but Erasmus complains that several St Andries florins issued between 1477 and 1482 by Duchess Mary of Burgundy and her husband
  Maximilian of Hapsburg were currently valued in Freiburg at only twelve batzen. The age of the coins meant that they had suffered considerable wear and
  tear or clipping and therefore did not retain the official weight and fineness
  ('There are many of less weight'; on this phenomenon, see CWE 1 312).
5 Probably a reference to the gold rose crown, initially issued by Henry VIII in
  August 1526 with a value of 4s 6d (54d) sterling but revalued in November
  1526 at 5s 0d (60d). See CWE 12 574 and 650 Table 3. Possibly the coins with the
  distinctive symbol traded at the lower value.
6 For the fifty pounds, see Ep 2512:2–4; for the others promised, cf Ep 2576:21–2.
7 Only one of them, Ep 2526 to Reginald Pole, is extant; cf Ep 2258:1–4.

reason. But if it is not convenient for Luis de Castro to transmit them all, have
him the give the rest to the apostolic notary Zacharias Deiotarus, the Frisian.[8]

We will soon see where the evangelical business is heading. If war
breaks out, I did not buy the house at the right time. I have moved with great   20
peril to my life and I am frequently ill. I would prefer to live anywhere at all
rather than here, if necessity did not constrain me.[9]

I was hoping that the emperor would return from here to Spain fairly
quickly but, as I see, this is not the end of his travels.[10] Keep well, my excellent friend, with your wife and children and all those dear to you.   25

Freiburg, 30 August 1531

After I had written this, your letter written on 12 July arrived,[11] which
makes mention of the fruit preserves that a Portuguese sent,[12] although
Hieronymus has not received it yet.[13] In this letter there are things that I do
not understand. I had sent via Quirinus a letter of Pieter Gillis, together with   30
his promissory note, in which he testified that he had received via my servant Lieven 117 florins and some pence as part of the Courtrai pension. If
Quirinus did not deliver this letter and promissory note to you, he behaved
like a scoundrel, as I suspect he has done on many occasions. And then I still
lose twelve florins here, for thirty florins were owed in addition to a hun-   35
dred. Therefore, where are those one hundred and three florins you mention?
What Gillis gave Quirinus is not important. He wrote to me that he had paid
you that money. And perhaps he has paid you by now.[14]

I do not question your faith in any way, but if anything should happen
to either of us, there would be a dispute among the heirs. What is more, I do   40
not know how much you have. Who would give anything to someone who
asks for it without a promissory note and when the one who asks does not
know the amount?

I cannot marvel enough at the ingenuity of Pieter Gillis. He asked me
for a receipt so many times, although he never paid me the whole amount.   45

* * * * *

8 See Epp 2487 n7 (Castro) and 2496 (Deiotarius).
9 See Epp 2506 n1, 2517 n11.
10 Emperor Charles was at this time preparing to attend another meeting of the
   imperial diet in Germany (Ep 2511 n20) and would not leave Germany again
   until November 1532, going first to Italy.
11 Ep 2511
12 See Ep 2511:29–33.
13 Hieronymus Froben, the Basel publisher via whom much mail reached Erasmus
14 Schets in fact puts the total owed by Gillis at 115 Carolus florins, 18 stuivers
   rather than the '117 florins and some pence' that Erasmus specifies (line 52
   below). See Epp 2511, 2552, 2558, 2578 and 2593.

I gave it to him and he thanked me. He was afraid that after sending letters I would initiate a suit against him, although the letter in which he testified how much he possessed had sixteen perforations of his pen. There is no fear that that man will squander his money. Be careful not to put much faith in Grynaeus and Bebel.[15]

Again farewell, my dearest friend Schets. Remember that Pieter Gillis owes 117 florins and some pence.

To the distinguished gentleman Erasmus Schets, merchant. At Antwerp

2531 / To Bonifacius Amerbach [Freiburg, summer 1531]

The manuscript of this letter (= AK Ep 1560), first published in the *Epistolae familiares*, is in the Öffentliche Bibliothek of the University of Basel (MS AN III 15 73). Allen assigned the date 'Summer 1531' because of the reference to Erasmus' apparent intention to visit Bonifacius' father-in-law at about this time; see lines 4–6. AK dates the letter 'Sept. 1531?'; this corresponds more closely to Erasmus' efforts to get his new house ready for occupancy at the end of September 1531; see n2. For our purposes the letter can safely be left where Allen put it.

Cordial greetings. Have a look at your father-in-law's house.[1] Can a fireplace be finished within two days, at least to the point that it is usable? I will not make any certain decision until you return here.[2]

* * * * *

15 For reasons that are not clear, Erasmus had become suspicious that Grynaeus and Bebel had not conducted themselves properly as his agents in the effort to redeem his pensions from Archbishop Warham (Ep 2487 n9) and had cheated him of money owed; see Ep 2558:38–42. Grynaeus protested his innocence and, with the help of Bonifacius Amerbach, cordial relations were restored between him and Erasmus (Epp 2574–6, 2580:18–19), though later reports of Grynaeus' indiscretions on delicate religious matters during his visit to England would bring a renewal of Erasmus' misgivings about him (see especially Allen Ep 2878:15–35). Erasmus also cleared Bebel of any suspicion of wrongdoing (Ep 2576:14–15), and in the years 1533–6 would again entrust him with letters and commissions on his trips to England and Italy. But he never really trusted the printer again and was given to making belittling remarks about him, as in Epp 2541:18–20, 2542:3–5.

2531
1 Bonifacius' father-in-law was Leonhard Fuchs, burgomaster of Neuenburg am Rhein, a town about halfway between Basel and Freiburg.
2 This seems to reflect Erasmus' anxieties about the 'building' that he was obliged to undertake to get his new house in Freiburg ready for occupancy (Epp 2506 n1, 2517 n11). Given his aversion to the fumes from 'stinking German stoves'

If I stay with your father-in-law, I will make sure not to cause him any
disturbance.³ I shall dine with my own companions, and I will do nothing 5
save at my own expense. Farewell.

2532 / To Bonifacius Amerbach   [Freiburg, August–September 1531?]

> This letter (= AK Ep 1553) was first published in the *Epistolae familiares*. The manu-
> script is in the Öffentlich Bibliothek of the University of Basel (MS AN III 15 83).
> The postscript (lines 8–10) is on a small piece of paper that was perhaps slipped
> inside the already closed letter. The approximate date can be inferred from
> Erasmus' reference to Bonifacius' father-in-law's not having returned (lines 4–5).

Cordial greetings. What is more pitiful than this age? What more iniquitous?
I hope that fortune will give favourable answer to your wisdom and integ-
rity.¹ And you even thank me? You will always be the same.² You seem not
to be aware of my intention.³ I am thankful that you let me know that your
father-in-law has not yet returned.⁴ But I am puzzled that there has been such 5
a long delay. I suspect that he is busy at the court of the emperor, making use
of some other pretext. I wish you and your family the best of health.

After sealing this letter I received another letter of yours, which was not
very cheerful.⁵ But be of philosophic mind and being born a human man bear
up with human vicissitudes.   10

To the excellent doctor Master Bonifacius Amerbach. At Basel

* * * * *

(Epp 1248 n5, 1258 n18, 1399:4–7, 2055 n7, 2112:4 and 23–4, 2118:45–6), he was
determined to have a fireplace with chimney installed in his new house; cf Ep
2534:35–6.
3 Ep 2519:39–41 indicates that Erasmus had recently been contemplating a visit
to Leonhard Fuchs at Neuenburg, possibly in connection with the making of a
new will (Ep 2490:11–12).

2532
1 Probably a reference to Bonifacius' difficulties with the city fathers at Basel; see
Ep 2519 introduction.
2 Cf Ep 2490:12.
3 Probably a reference to Erasmus' intention to make a new will during a visit to
Bonifacius' father-in-law in Neuenburg am Rhein; see Ep 2490:11–12.
4 Cf Ep 2519:41–3.
5 Possibly Ep 2519; otherwise not extant

2533 / To Seweryn Boner   Freiburg, 1 September 1531

This letter was first published as Ep 15 in Miaskowski, using an eighteenth-century copy in the Czartoryski Museum at Cracow (MS CN 46 191). For his text, Allen also used a sixteenth-century copy at Leningrad (Ep 2520 introduction) as well as a seventeenth-century copy in the Raczynski Library at Poznan (MS 310 folio 5).

Seweryn Boner (c 1486–1549) was born into a German family from Landau in the Palatinate that settled in Cracow early in the sixteenth century and prospered there. A brilliant financier, Boner established a banking house that had extensive connections in Germany and Italy. By 1523 he had become court banker to King Sigismund I, amassing a profusion of titles and possessions as the reward of his services as well as becoming a generous patron of the arts and of humanist scholarship. From his marriage to Zofia Bethmann, daughter of a wealthy Cracow merchant, he had two sons, Jan (1516–62) and Stanisław (c 1523–1560) Boner. In April 1531 Jan, whom his father had sent abroad to study in Germany and Italy in the company of his tutor Anselmus Ephorinus (Ep 2539), paid a visit to Erasmus at Freiburg and ended up living with him until September. Learning of this, the elder Boner arranged for the dispatch to Erasmus of letters of recommendation for the boy from King Sigismund (Ep 2520) and Piotr Tomicki (Ep 2521). This letter is Erasmus' report to the proud father of the pleasure he had derived from the visit of Jan and his tutor. In December 1531 Erasmus dedicated his edition of the comedies of Terence to Jan and his brother Stanisław (Ep 2584). The presentation copy did not reach Cracow until 1535. When it did arrive, Boner sent a letter (Ep 3010) explaining the delay and enclosing two gold medals, one with the image of King Sigismund I and the other with his own likeness (Major 72, plate 24).

ERASMUS OF ROTTERDAM TO SEWERYN BONER, CASTELLAN OF
ŻARNOWIEC, ADMINISTRATOR OF THE SALT MINES OF CRACOW
Cordial greetings. I consider it truly the work of some good and friendly divine spirit, Seweryn Boner, foremost glory of Poland, that your friend Anselmus Ephorinus, as he was passing through Germany on his way to Italy, deviated 5 somewhat from his planned itinerary and stopped off at this city of Freiburg im Breisgau. For five months he showed himself to be not only an obliging, friendly, accommodating, and pleasant guest but was also of no little comfort to me, more than usually oppressed by domestic cares because of the purchase of a new house and the transactions involved in moving and making repairs.[1] 10

* * * * *

2533
1 See Epp 2506 n1, 2517 n11.

He is a man as varied in learning and versed in literature as he is cautious,
skilful, and circumspect in every kind of activity that is usually abhorred by
those who are carried away by love of studies. Antiquity called a person of
affable character a man of all seasons;[2] this man deserves the appellation of
a man of all actions; on that account I declare openly that I owe him a great   15
deal. I cannot but have confidence in such a man, who affirmed that he was
prompted to extend his stay in Germany beyond what he had planned for no
other reason than to enjoy Erasmus' company for a few months. If you also
approve the man's intention, as I am sure you will, there will be reason for me
to thank you also for your sympathy. Let us hope that our friendly associa-   20
tion brought as much benefit to him and to your son Jan Boner as it brought
pleasure to me, and that this will not have been an instance of the old Greek
proverb 'I looked for treasure but found coals.'[3] If he erred in this, he deserves
an excuse; rumour, which sometimes makes an elephant out of a fly,[4] has been
unfair to an unassuming man.   25
　　As for your Excellency, I judge you fortunate not so much because you
abound in riches, or because you stand out for the renown of your ancestry,
or because you are preeminent in dignity, popularity, and authority in your
flourishing kingdom, as because you received such a son as your portion. For
among all one's possessions there is nothing more precious, among all one's   30
distinctions nothing more beautiful, among all one's gratifications nothing
more agreeable than loyal children worthy of succeeding to the blessings of
fortune. Through them, when parents arrive at old age they are rejuvenated;
when that fatal day is at hand, they depart from life with tranquillity and in
them they live, though they are dead. I beg you, do not think that I say this   35
just to please you; with Christ as my witness I speak from the heart. These
too are the gifts of a benevolent divinity, which cannot be better safeguarded
than by considering that they proceed from the gratuitous munificence of
God. The greater his liberality towards us, the more we should distance ourselves from insolence and confine ourselves more closely within the bounds   40
of modesty, for fear that Nemesis will take away from the insolent what she
gave to the undeserving.
　　I have often admired how your son at this tender age, in which most
children can barely read with any facility, has produced some worthwhile
efforts in writing. Believe me, such natural talent does not give promise of   45
something common or mediocre; he displays an alert, tractable, docile, and

* * * * *

2　*Adagia* I iii 86
3　*Adagia* I ix 30
4　*Adagia* I ix 69

versatile character. There are some who you would say were born for literary studies but in everyday matters are completely inept. In this boy's behaviour you can detect nothing puerile or inept. In some boys an excessive modesty leads to stupor, while in others boldness leads to an unseemly impudence. 50 Your son has a liveliness tempered with a certain polite respect. But though it was entirely through good fortune and the gift of God that such a son was born to you, yet no little praise is owed to your singular wisdom in that you took care that the young child from earliest infancy was trained both by honourable teachings and exemplary morals and also with a Ulysses-like and 55 vigorous prudence, and was armed against the adversities of fortune. In vain did Thetis dip the infant Achilles in the swampy waters of the Styx.[5] Nothing arms a man against all the blows of fortune more than philosophy, especially that which is acquired in exploring reality and examining things at first hand.

How few parents have the courage to allow sons of this age to be sepa- 60 rated from them in remote regions rather than pampering them in their embraces and as the object of their affection, and holding on to them almost to the age of puberty. But you, just as if you raised him not for yourself but for the common good, take the trouble to have him immediately introduced to those skills by which he may be both an honour and an asset to his friends 65 and to the kingdom, and you did not allow this best part of his life to slip by amidst the kisses of his mother and the caresses of nurses, since you were not unaware that, as Quintilian says, there is nothing that we understand better or remember more tenaciously than what we imbibe during those first tender years, which are responsive to every situation.[6] What we learn 70 when we are grown up, we discern in our mind as if through a mist, so to speak, and we remember these things as if they were seen in a dream. It was a mark of extraordinary foresight on your part that you entrusted the wet, rich clay to an expert modeller, and the good soil to an experienced farmer. What good is it to be well born if the proper education is lacking? It is to 75 your credit that you sought out such an education, and it was your good fortune that you found it. We sometimes see that this blessing does not fall to the lot of great monarchs.

* * * * *

5 When Achilles was born it was predicted that he would die young. To prevent this his mother, Thetis, dipped him in the river Styx to make him immortal. But in doing so she held him by the heel, which did not become immersed in the water and thus did not become immortal, with the result that Achilles was eventually killed by a wound to his heel.
6 Quintilian 1.1.5

Once again I must ask you, excellent sir, not to think that I am saying anything merely to please you or to flatter the ears of a father with words 80 of this kind. I do not deny that such behaviour is widespread, but just as it is completely foreign to my nature and repugnant to me, so there is no need of any pretence on this subject and no reason for being insincere. I have known many educators of youth, but among those who are highly esteemed I have seen up to now no one more vigilant, honest and more skilful than 85 Anselmus. He obtains more from boys with a mere nod than many do with imprecations, wrangling, threats, shouting, and blows. Quintilian thought that nothing should be more recommended to teachers than that they should show the affection of a parent to their pupils.[7] Parents should retain the good will of their children through restraint and liberality rather than through fear. 90 With good reason men of former times attributed much importance to the forehead, which they said was more important than the back of the head, and to the eyes of the master, by which they said the horse grew fat more than in any other way, and the ground became more fertile.[8] But I think that the eye of the parent is no less efficacious for his son than that of the master for 95 his stable or his land. Anselmus fulfils the role of parent and teacher marvellously well and does not depart from it in the least, and the boy is attached to no one more willingly. Anselmus would not do this unceasingly if he had not transferred your affection for your son into himself, nor would the boy enjoy the unceasing presence of the man if he did not love and venerate him 100 as taking the place of his father.

Of the boy Stanislaus,[9] faithful attendant and study companion of your son, I do not know in what family he was born, but he is of such generous nature that I would strongly desire that no children of qualities inferior to his be born to any monarch. He gives excellent hope of learning himself. And so I 105 think that each should be congratulated: your Jan, who had the good fortune of having such a suitable companion of studies, and Stanislaus, for having such a benign patron, through whose generosity he will be able successfully to complete the course in good letters that he has begun.

* * * * *

7 Quintilian 2.2.4
8 *Adagia* I ii 19: *Frons occipitio prior* 'Forehead before occiput.' As Erasmus explains at some length (citing Cato, Pliny, and Aristotle), the words of the ancients about foreheads versus occiputs (the back part of the head) as well as those about the master's eye meant that a man's business is most successfully conducted when he himself is present.
9 Stanisław Aichler (Ep 2545)

I see and rejoice that the happiness which Plato desires for citizens has 110
come to your Poland, in which the rulers embrace philosophy.[10] I call philosophy not the method of discoursing on the beginnings of things, on matter, time, motion, and the infinite, but that wisdom which Solomon judged
to be more precious than all riches and for that reason the one thing that he
desired from God above all others.[11] Its virtue is that man can both regulate 115
his own life more correctly and consult properly the interests of his country
in time of war and of peace. Since the renowned kingdom of Poland has King
Sigismund as an outstanding example and teacher of this philosophy, it is
no wonder if the stars follow their sun.

With this letter, excellent sir, it seemed proper to me to congratulate 120
you and your most noble wife on your exceptional good fortune and to give
thanks to you on my part for the consolation derived thus far from my association with your family; would that it had continued longer, but nothing is
permanent in human affairs; nor is it courteous, if we are to believe Homer,
to detain a guest who wishes to depart, especially if either expediency or ne- 125
cessity compels him to do so.[12] The plague began to glimmer here,[13] but only
faintly, and the oracle of the doctors who advise flight as the best remedy is:
'soon, far, late.'[14] I pray to the Lord that he may will this happiness to continue without interruption for you and your family. As for me, I should like
you to be assured that there is no service that a most deserving patron can 130
demand from the most obligated client that I shall not render most eagerly
at the merest indication of your wishes, provided that it is within my power.
Farewell.

Given at Freiburg im Breisgau, 1 September 1531

2534 / To Johann Rinck   Freiburg, 4 September 1531

This letter was first published in the *Epistolae palaeonaeoi*. For Johann Rinck,
jurist of Cologne, see Ep 2285 introduction.

* * * * *

10 Plato *Republic* 6.484A–502C
11 1 Kings 3:1–15
12 Homer *Odyssey* 15.74
13 Cf Ep 2517:35–6.
14 In a letter of 1565, cited in Allen's note (at lines 125–6), Gilbert Cousin (Ep 2381
   n1) quotes this passage and compares it to a French proverb: 'Remede contre la
   peste par art, Fuir tost, et loing, et retorner tard.'

DESIDERIUS ERASMUS OF ROTTERDAM TO THE MOST HONOURABLE
MASTER JOHANN RINCK, GREETING

Most honourable sir, although there was nothing serious to write about, I
could nevertheless not allow my matchless friend Johann Rinck, whose continued company, if I could but enjoy it, would render me quite happy, to re-   5
main without a greeting at the time of the present fair.[1] But we are driven by
the Fates, and to the Fates we are forced to succumb. I often feel that there is
not much thread left to me for the Fates to spin, but however little time there
is I would prefer to spend it in a celebrated and populous city, where there
would be a greater number of friends and a more abundant supply of goods.   10
But the tempest has deposited me on this shore.

This place is not unpleasant, but since it is somewhat distant from the
Rhine it is less populated and there is a meagre supply of commodities. The
town had its beginnings, it is said, from mines, which are now depleted. It is
possible even now to see some vestiges of the customs of the country. When I   15
was preparing to move last summer, I was told by my friends at court, especially by the bishop of Augsburg, that I should wait until the end of the Diet
of Augsburg.[2] Now, when I was ready to take wing again, anxious to fly off
somewhere, I was again ordered to await the outcome of the Diet of Speyer,
about the future course of which there are various prognostications.[3]   20

But listen to something about me that will make you laugh. If someone were to tell you that Erasmus, now almost a septuagenarian, had taken
a wife, would you not make the sign of the cross three or four times? You
would, I know, and not without good reason. But now, my dear Rinck, I have
done something no less burdensome, no less troublesome, no less foreign to   25
my character and pursuits. I bought a house, outwardly impressive, but not
fairly priced. Who would now give up hope of seeing the rivers reversing
their course and flowing back to their source after Erasmus, who through
his whole life thus far subordinated everything to the leisure of literature,
has become a bidder at an auction, a buyer, one involved in contracts, a   30
guarantor, a builder, and in place of the Muses, engaged with carpenters,

* * * * *

2534
1 The autumn book fair at Frankfurt
2 The letters giving Erasmus this advice are not extant, but cf Epp 2370:16–18 and
  2371:24–6.
3 For the diet see Ep 2511 n20. The 'order' mentioned here is not documented in
  any other letter.

blacksmiths, masons, and glaziers?[4] These concerns, my dear Rinck, from which my character has always recoiled, almost killed me with boredom. And I am still wandering around in my own house, which, spacious as it is, has no nest to which I can entrust this little body. I have fitted out one 35 refuge by constructing a fireplace[5] and panelling the floor and the walls, but because of the acrid smell of the lime I would not yet dare enter there.

In a little while, nonetheless, I will have to move in, and may it be auspicious and favourable. This has not been the case so far. After severe pain in my left foot, diarrhea has followed, which has been with me for six days.[6] But 40 this is enough about my problems. I could have easily gone down to Cologne if the Rhine permitted, but when my friends dissuaded me I remained here, and, as far as I can see, I will have to wait for the spring swallows. The purchased house will not hold me back if everything else goes as I wish. I hope all is prosperous for you and your family. I have reason to rejoice greatly, and 45 I hope it will be lasting.

Given at Freiburg im Breisgau, 4 September 1531

2535 / To Simon Grynaeus [Freiburg, beginning of September 1531]

This letter was first published in the *Grynaei Epistolae*, that is, *In librum octavum Topicorum Aristotelis Simonis Grynaei commentaria doctissima. Adiectae sunt ad libri calcem selectiores aliquot eiusdem S. Grynaei Epistolae* (Basel: J. Oporinus 1556) page 146. A date shortly before 6 September 1531 is clearly indicated by Ep 2536:4–5, where the departure of Anselmus Ephorinus, imminent in Ep 2533, is mentioned as already having taken place.

Simon Grynaeus, professor of Greek at Basel, had recently returned to Basel from a trip to England in the company of the Basel publisher Johann Bebel; cf Ep 2487 n9.

ERASMUS OF ROTTERDAM TO SIMON GRYNAEUS, GREETING
Cordial greetings. Admiration for your learning and rectitude attracted Anselmus Ephorinus to go there,[1] on which account I should be rather resent-

* * * * *

4 See Epp 2506 n1, 2517 n11.
5 Cf Ep 2531 n2.
6 See Ep 2528 n8.

2535
1 To Basel

ful towards you, if I were a potter,[2] since you tore away from me half of my
soul. I would have perished if amidst the cares and troubles of moving and   5
building, to which, through some mysterious natural instinct, I have always
been averse all my life, if he had not alleviated my distress.[3] He cajoled me
with the hope of his return, but I know that he will never return here. As soon
as he has a taste of you, he will say immediately, 'Acorns have had their day.'[4]
Bebel has been here.[5] I hope that you and your family are in the best of health. 10

2536 / To Bonifacius Amerbach   [Freiburg], 6 September 1531

This letter (= AK Ep 1557) was first published in the *Epistolae familiares*. The autograph, written in a shaky hand, is in the Öffentliche Bibliothek of the University
of Basel (MS AN III 15 31).

Greetings. The severe pain in my foot, which caused me some fear, has left
me, but that was followed by diarrhea, without any harm to my stomach. I
still have it today, but I hope it is the end.[1]

Anselmus, tired of my miseries, took refuge with happy people;[2] I almost envy him, but I remain here willingly.   5

I had decided to visit Neuenburg, but I think it is more advisable to wait
until I am a little stronger.[3] That will be soon, I hope. I wish you were here.
There is something I should like to discuss with you in person. Farewell, and
write to me about what you are doing.

6 September 1531   10
Your friend Erasmus of Rotterdam
To the most honourable Master Bonifacius Amerbach. In Basel

* * * * *

2 See *Adagia* I ii 25: *Figulus figulo invidet, faber fabro* 'Potter envies potter and smith
  envies smith.'
3 See Ep 2533:4–25.
4 Said of those 'who have left behind a squalid way of life and proceeded to a
  more polished and wealthier one'; see *Adagia* I iv 2.
5 See introduction.

2536
1 See Ep 2528 n8.
2 Anselmus Ephorinus (Ep 2539) who had lived with Erasmus since April, had
  now gone to Basel, with Italy as his ultimate goal; cf Epp 2533:4–25, 2535:2–8.
3 See Ep 2519 n6.

2537 / From Thomas Venatorius   Nürnberg, 6 September 1531

First published as Ep 94 in Enthoven, the autograph of this letter is in the Rehdiger Collection of the University Library at Wrocław (MS Rehd 254 157).

Little is known of the early life and education of Thomas Venatorius of Nürnberg (c 1488–1551). By 1520 he had an established reputation in humanist circles, had found in Willibald Pirckheimer a friend and patron, and was known as a great admirer of Johann Reuchlin as well as a follower of Luther. In June 1522 the Nürnberg city council appointed him preacher at the Hospital of the Holy Ghost. Together with other preachers (Andreas Osiander, Dominik Schleupner, and Wenzel Linck), he was adviser to the council on its measures to implement the Lutheran reformation in Nürnberg, a process, already far advanced in 1528, that would reach its culmination with the publication of a church ordinance (*Kirchenordnung*) in 1533. Venatorius published numerous theological and pastoral works in both Latin and German, but also found time to devote himself to humanistic scholarship. In these endeavours his friends and companions were Eobanus Hessus (Ep 2495) and, despite obvious theological differences, Pirckheimer, who arranged for his papers to be entrusted to Venatorius after his death. This letter, the only known communication between Venatorius and Erasmus, is the product of the former's responsibility for Pirckheimer's epistolary legacy.

Cordial greetings. At last I have broken down the barrier of my obstinate and almost perpetual timidity, which so many times held back the pen and the desire of one who wished to write to you. But now I am compelled, just as elsewhere in cases of doubt, and rashly rather than courteously, to make a decision and of necessity to face up to my timidity, and, no matter what the 5 consequences, seize whatever opportunity presents itself to write to you. For until now the learned and numerous letters, full of friendship and affection, sent by you to Willibald Pirckheimer, allayed in some measure the ardour of my desire. That great man, magnanimous as he was, gladly lent me these letters to read (confidentially, of course). Several years ago he had already 10 formed such a good opinion of me that he kept no secrets from me. Hence, when recently I had spent not less than six days in listing and affixing seals to his books, I began to apply myself to reading his letters, the huge number of which no one other than myself has yet seen (if you except one daughter and his nephew, the first-born of his sister).[1] Because it seemed laborious to read 15

* * * * *

2537
1 Of Pirckheimer's five daughters, three became nuns and two married; the one referred to here is probably Barbara, husband of Hans Straub, who cared for her father in his old age. As for Pirckheimer's eight sisters, seven of them became

through all of them, we decided to consign a great part of them to Vulcan for
fear that many would read publicly what learned men had written in friendship to only one individual privately.[2]

He himself was preparing to put everything in order after duly drawing up his will before he passed from this life, and he would have accom-   20
plished this if our God had not decided otherwise and if his spirit had not
failed him sooner than we expected.[3] I hope that his relatives will present
you with some gift so that you may always remember him. I know that they
will do this unless all my surmising and reason fail me. And certainly they
will do it with good reason. For the great esteem you had for him while he   25
was alive is attested by your letter to our Eobanus that was brought to him
a few days ago, which I read and reread with great joy.[4] The whole letter
pleased me, but especially the part in which I perceived not only your admiration for the Muse of Eobanus but also the sincerity of your loyal sentiments
towards the spirit of Pirckheimer. You write also that you read not without   30
pleasure the epicedium that Eobanus wrote for the funeral.[5] Since it has virtue itself as its author, it admits of no falsity.

As to what you add in that same letter, that Eobanus would see the
shadow of a shadow if he saw you now,[6] I interpret it as the sign of a soul
that entertains humble feelings of itself, in accordance with the grave saying   35
of a wise man: 'The greater you are, the more you must humble yourself in
all things.'[7] If you are a shadow, what do you think we are, who compared
to you cannot even be the dream of a shadow?[8] Do you not surpass us by
a distance as great as that by which the sun surpasses all the other stars by
the power of its light? Of myself I dare to assert firmly: Whoever will have   40
known me in my private life and seen how wanting are my resources will
call me one of the atoms of Epicurus or any other minute particle rather than
a shadow.

*****

nuns, but one, Juliana, married Martin Geuder and had a son. See Allen's note,
and on Martin Geuder cf Ep 1085 n1.
2 Vulcan was the Roman god of fire. The letters that survived this conflagration
are available in a modern critical edition begun by Emil Riecke and completed
by Helge Scheible: *Willibald Pirckheimers Briefwechsel* (Munich 1940–2009) 7 vols.
3 On 22 December 1530. Ep 2493 is Erasmus' obituary for him.
4 Ep 2495
5 See Ep 2495:37–8.
6 Ep 2495:43–4
7 Jerome *Against Jovinian* 1.18
8 Pindar *Pythian Odes* 8.95–6

Moreover, I am not playing a game in this matter. At any rate, if it is a game, it is, as far as I am concerned, more serious than I myself would wish. I am therefore astonished by the judgment of Anselmus Ephorinus,[9] a learned man and devoted to your cause, who to make me more happy through the acquisition of your friendship, was not ashamed, if not to lie about me to Erasmus, then certainly to praise me more generously than befitted my station. I discount his praises, since I know he is excessively friendly towards me. Love is blind as far as the loved one is concerned. For that reason, however, I should not call such a respectable man a liar, nor such a sincere friend a flatterer, to whom nothing is more important than that saying of Homer: 45 50

> Hateful is that man, like the gates of Hades,
> Who hides one thought in his mind, but saith another.[10]

55

Thus, if my audacity in seeking your friendship has offended you, do not be angry with me, but with Ephorinus, who often urged me on and even compelled me to come forward, though I hesitated and was unwilling to do so. Farewell.

From Nürnberg, 6 September 1531

With sincere devotion, Thomas Venatorius

To the most eminent Erasmus of Rotterdam, greatest of theologians, his respected master

60

2538 / From Bonifacius Amerbach   Basel, 15 September 1531

This letter (= AK Ep 1561) was first published by Allen on the basis of the autograph in the Öffentliche Bibliothek of the University of Basel (MS C VIA 73 247). The letter was apparently not sent, since it is crossed through and the rough draft of Ep 2542 is written on the back, which would explain the almost exact repetition of lines 7–9 in Ep 2546:9–13.

Greetings. What happened in my father-in- law's house has already been made known to you through my wife's brother.[1] Our position is so precarious

* * * * *

9 Who had paid a visit to Nürnberg before going to Freiburg; see Ep 2539 introduction.
10 *Iliad* 9.312–13, cited in Greek

2538
1 See Epp 2542, 2543, 2546.

that we cannot promise ourselves anything certain even from hour to hour;
apart from that, nothing could be more pleasing to my father-in-law than
your arrival.[2] About my own affairs I will inform you in person. I have the   5
wolf by the ears,[3] to tell the truth. What is there not to be feared everywhere?
Would that we had that charity in our heart that Paul calls patient and kind,
not envious and insolent.[4] We complained in times past about Babylonian
servitude under the pope; now, of course, we are free.

But these things are for your eyes alone. The haste of the messenger   10
prevents me from writing more. Farewell, most illustrious Erasmus.

In a rush at Basel, the day after the feast of the Holy Cross, 1531
Yours, Bonifacius Amerbach
To Master Erasmus of Rotterdam, consummate theologian and glory of
all good disciplines, incomparable patron. In Freiburg   15

2539 / From Anselmus Ephorinus   Basel, 15 September 1531

First published as Ep 157 in Förstemann / Günther, the autograph of this letter
was in the Burscher Collection of the University Library at Leipzig (Ep 1254
introduction).

Anselmus Ephorinus of Friedeberg in Silesia (c 1505–1566) began his studies
at the University of Cracow in 1515, taking a BA in 1522 and an MA in 1527. As
member of the Erasmian circle that had formed around Leonard Cox (Ep 1803),
he contributed to the success of the publishing industry in Cracow, writing
prefaces and verses for various works. In 1528 he himself published editions of
Erasmus' *Epistola consolatoria in adversis* and *Precatio ad Virginis filium Iesum*. At
the beginning of 1531 Ephorinus became the private tutor of Jan Boner (Ep 2533
introduction), who at his father's behest was setting out for study abroad in the
company of Stanisław Aichler (Ep 2545). Passing through Germany on their
way to Italy, the trio stopped for a time at Nürnberg and then, at Ephorinus'
behest, proceeded to Freiburg, carrying a letter of introduction from Eobanus
Hessus (Ep 2495:26–8). Arriving in April 1531, they stayed in Erasmus' house
for nearly five months, Ephorinus earning Erasmus' respect as a scholar and
his gratitude for practical services rendered (see Ep 2533). At the end of August
1531 Ephorinus and his charges moved to Basel where, as Ephorinus reports
in the present letter, they were well received and generously accommodated

* * * * *

2 See Ep 2519 n6.
3 *Adagia* I v 25, which 'is said about people who become involved in some affair
   which it would not be honest to abandon, and yet cannot be borne.'
4 1 Cor 13:4

by Erasmus' friends. In April 1532 Ephorinus and his two charges set out once
again for Italy, travelling via Constance and Augsburg, where Ephorinus delivered a letter from Erasmus to Anton Fugger and made the acquaintance
of Johann Koler (see Ep 2658). In May or June 1532 the trio arrived in Venice
and then settled in Padua, where Ephorinus studied medicine, receiving his
doctorate in April 1534. Ephorinus and his two charges remained in Italy, first
Bologna and then Rome, until the spring of 1537, and then returned to Poland
via Paris, the Netherlands, and Germany, arriving at Cracow in the autumn
of 1537. Ephorinus set up a medical practice in Cracow, becoming a much-
esteemed town physician. But he also maintained his contacts with many humanists, some of them Protestants, though he himself remained a loyal Catholic.
Relations between Erasmus and Ephorinus remained cordial until 1533, when
they became somewhat strained because of Ephorinus' failure to forward to
Seweryn Boner the copy of the edition of Terence (dedicated to Boner's two
sons) that Erasmus had entrusted to him, with the result that it did not reach
Boner until the spring of 1535; see Ep 2584 introduction.

Greetings in Christ. To avoid being charged with impudence, most illustrious and learned sir, I asked you, after our last delightful conversation, to
pardon me if ever you were to receive a letter from me that was illiterate. For
almost five months I admired, with the highest veneration, love, and devotion, the brilliance, sincerity, and especially the piety of your life (in which   5
you surpass all famous men of learning of this century), as well as the charm
of your manners in conversation, joined with maturity of judgment and dignity. All these qualities persuaded me to reject as utterly false the reports I
had heard from some deceitful friends before I set out for Freiburg, who told
me concerning one whom the whole world cherishes that I would not be able   10
to bear his forthright character – said of one who, I must insist, surpasses
without any ostentation everyone in the most refined learning and divine
judgments, a man dear to the Muses, to the Graces, to Apollo himself and,
most important of all, to Christ, who not only readily admits all scholars into
his company but can even put up with those totally unfamiliar with polite   15
society and offer them every gesture of hospitality.

If I were to say that I and my companions did not leave your house
more learned and more instilled with piety, I would be plainly lying. There is
no place for idleness, shameful indolence, no place for impiety where you are
in command, and may our enterprise commend itself to you in every way, as   20
your holy calling does to us. Whatever you do, who will deny that you do it
for the sake of the republic of letters, not for your private advantage? I offer
myself and all my support as a permanent herald of your fame and praise,
and you may with every right order me, command me, and compel me to do
whatever you wish. I shall never be found wanting in any way to one who   25

has so benefitted me and my charges. I do this all the more willingly because all your exterior qualities correspond to your interior character. Antiquity tells us that Cato the Censor was an excellent orator, an excellent general, and an excellent senator.[1] But I rightfully (God forbid there be any suspicion of adulation) dare to call you the most learned among learned men, the most kindly among kindly men, and the most famous among famous men.

If I had not sincerely been a great admirer of your renown, neither the prestige of the university there, nor the pleasantness of the location, nor anything else would have detained me for so long a time; I would certainly have left Freiburg a month earlier if your most genial company had been denied me. I must confess that I am much indebted on that account to Glareanus,[2] who first established close acquaintance between us, something for which I shall be forever grateful to him. And although he declined me an interview as I was leaving, informing me through my friend Stanislaus,[3] whom I had sent ahead, that he was busy, nevertheless there will be no lessening of my affection for him both because of you and because of his learning, by which he is of assistance to scholars. That he played Davus at table,[4] frequently calling me the fox and himself the crane,[5] I don't mind; I have no difficulty in suffering and putting up with insults as long as they do not injure my reputation.

Luckily, thanks to Amerbach, a man of great integrity, we found here a host who was kind-hearted and hospitable, not associated with any sects, a lover of true piety and an admirer of scholars, with whom we are living and taking our leisure.[6] In addition, during the day, a spacious and pleasant

* * * * *

2539
1 Marcus Porcius Cato, commonly known as Cato the Censor (234–149 BC), was a renowned military commander who won praise for his role in the battle of Metaurus in the Second Punic War (207 BC) and suppressed a major rebellion in Spain (195 BC). After his retirement from the army he entered politics, where his speeches in the senate and elsewhere proved him the greatest orator of his day. In 184 BC he was elected censor, in which office he was a stern defender of traditional Roman virtues against the influence of 'decadent' Greek culture and morals.
2 Henricus Glareanus (Ep 440), friend of Erasmus and since 1529 lecturer in poetry at Freiburg; see Ep 2105:25–6.
3 Stanisław Aichler (Ep 2545)
4 In Horace Satires 2.7 the slave Davus takes advantage of the freedom allowed to slaves on the feast of Saturnalia to speak without inhibition to their masters.
5 In the fable (Phaedrus 1.26) it is a stork, not a crane, who outwits the fox and tells him he must grin and bear it.
6 In a letter to Ephorinus (AK Ep 1547:1–17) Bonifacius regrets that he had no room for Ephorinus and his party in his own house but says that he has found an honest citizen ready to take them in, although the price seems high: a crown

house, with a fireplace and a garden worthy of the Muses and Apollo, has
been provided for us by Canon Peter Reich.[7] In the meanwhile we are await-   50
ing our master's letter.[8] I have nothing new to tell you. It is a story without a
beginning here: preachers in frequent sermons vigorously defend the Lord's
Supper,[9] people are dragged, not led, to their teachings, and recently it was
decreed by the city council that people either receive communion or leave.[10]
To send people into exile for something that should be achieved not by tyr-   55
anny, not by violence, but by persuasion and conscience divinely given, is
not to save the commonwealth but to destroy it. There is a novel invention
here in the field of education. Grynaeus,[11] a learned man, who because of
his sound erudition deservedly presides over the activities of several others, explains the Gospel of Matthew in Greek, Oecolampadius in Latin, and   60
some deacon or other in German. They do this sharing a single hour among
themselves.[12] In that way the literary approach is used to incline the hearers
to the study of virtue. For the rest, I commend myself and my charges to your
innate generosity. May your Lordship be in good health for a long time and
enjoy good fortune.   65

    At Basel, 15 September 1531
    Yours sincerely, Anselmus Ephorinus of Silesia

* * * * *

a week each for board, lodging, and bedding. The 'honest citizen' was Johann
Gross, the cathedral organist; see AK Ep 1547 n1, and cf Ep 2606:51–3 (where
Allen confuses Gross with Peter Reich).
7 Peter Reich von Reichenstein (d April 1540), canon of the cathedral at Basel,
  moved with the cathedral chapter to Freiburg in 1527 in consequence of the victory of the Reformation in that city, but he kept ownership of the house at Basel
  mentioned here. When Erasmus left Freiburg in 1535 to return to Basel, Reich
  purchased from him the house 'zum Kind Jesu' (Epp 3056, 3059; AK Ep 1989).
8 'Our master' is evidently Seweryn Boner (Ep 2533).
9 Ie the recently instituted evangelical celebration of the Lord's Supper, which
  included communion in both kinds and the denial of the Real Presence
10 See Ep 2519 introduction.
11 Ep 2535
12 This multilingual approach to the education of both clergy and laity was introduced in 1523 by Johannes Oecolampadius, following his appointment as
  professor of theology. In his lectures on Isaiah, he commented on the original
  Hebrew text, as well as the Greek Septuagint and Latin Vulgate translations of
  the passage under discussion. He followed this with a sermon on the text in
  German for the benefit of the laypeople who had come to hear him. Following
  the introduction of the evangelical church order of 1529, daily lectures on the
  Bible were introduced that followed this same pattern, but with the added participation of other scholars qualified in Greek, Hebrew, or theology. In 1531 the
  practice was modified so that the lectures would alternate weekly between the

After finishing and sealing the letter, my most beloved and learned patron, I decided to meet with Amerbach, since he had taken it upon himself to find a messenger. Behold, by chance he appeared at the bridge over the Rhine 70 with a messenger. After rereading the letter I sent him on his way immediately. I address to your Lordship not the thanks that I owe you, but as much as I am able, for your most solicitous efforts on my behalf.

I gave your greetings dutifully to the burgomaster of Neuenburg, who looks forward to your visit with great enthusiasm and was very happy when 75 I told him that you would come soon.[13] He seems to be hospitality itself.

The letter to me from Poland is dated the beginning of May, but presents nothing corresponding to my wishes. Our master did not yet know whether we were still staying with you.[14] I would like to know who the messenger was who brought it. 80

Neither I nor Amerbach have been able to find a fuller.[15] My pupils send you greetings with greatest esteem, etc.

If my letter offends Glareanus,[16] I pray that you will act as reconciler, for I love him sincerely.

To the most illustrious and learned Master Erasmus of Rotterdam, emi- 85 nent friend and protector. At Freiburg

2540 / From Bernhard von Cles   Stuttgart, 14–18 September 1531

This letter was first published by Allen. For the manuscript, an autograph rough draft, see Ep 2515 introduction. Allen took the date from the label on the packet of rough drafts in which the letter is found. Erasmus' response to this letter (and to three others not extant) is Ep 2555.

For Bernhard von Cles, bishop of Trent and chancellor to King Ferdinand, see Ep 2504. He was in Stuttgart on his way to Speyer, where an imperial diet was scheduled to take place but in the end did not; see Ep 2511 n20.

* * * * *

Old and the New Testaments. See Amy Nelson Burnett 'Preparing the Pastors: Theological Education and Pastoral Training in Basel' in *History has Many Voices* ed Lee Palmer Wandel (Kirksville MO 2003) 131–51, here 135–6.

13 For Erasmus' plans to visit Bonifacius Amerbach's father-in-law Leonhard Fuchs in Neuenburg, see Ep 2519 n6.
14 Cf n8 above; the letter in question is not extant.
15 The word is *fullo, -onis*, doubtless used in the Roman sense of a cloth launderer, not in the medieval sense of someone who cleans wool before it is made into cloth.
16 See lines 42–4 above.

TO ERASMUS OF ROTTERDAM

When I learned that the royal messenger was going there, I did not wish to miss the opportunity of sending a letter to you, informing you both that I would come to visit you and at the same time that you would be assured of my ardent desire to be able to enjoy your sweetly flowing conversation and   5
pleasant company before my departure.

If it were possible without any inconvenience to you, I exhort you again and again to make haste to come to Speyer where, in addition to my personal affection for you, your presence would be of no less benefit for the Christian religion (for that will be the principal subject at the imperial diet) than if you   10
were to devote all the time that is left to you to writing and research. And if in the meantime I learn that you have decided to heed my desire, I shall arrange that all your needs will be most suitably looked after. But (as I desire nothing but your convenience) I leave everything to your discretion, since I wish to please you in every way.   15

2541 / To Bonifacius Amerbach   Freiburg, 17 September 1531

This letter (= AK Ep 1562) was first published in the *Epistolae familiares*. The autograph is in the Öffentliche Bibliothek of the University of Basel (MS AN III 15
32). Bonifacius' reply is Ep 2542.

I very nearly made it to Neuenburg.[1] A canon who has a house there offered me a horse, a covered coach, hospitality – and what did he not offer? He had gone there before me on Tuesday; I was to follow in a coach on Wednesday. On the preceding day I was given notice to be ready at noon. It was done. Later I was told that the coach would not depart before 2:00. I ate an egg.   5
Again news came that I would not depart until 6:00. I had already sent my baggage. It was brought back to me and the servants told me that the coach would not be going anywhere that day. So, weary of the trip before setting out on it, I stayed at home, for several reasons. I was not certain whether your father-in-law had returned,[2] and if he had returned, I was afraid that he might   10
be somewhere in his vineyard. Then I wondered if I would be a welcome guest, coming from a place infested with the plague.[3] For people are dying here, and the rumour is usually more frightening than the reality. There was no lack of things to do at home either. I am still dealing with the workers. I am

* * * * *

2541
1 For Erasmus' plans to visit Neuenburg see Ep 2519 n6.
2 See Ep 2519:41–3.
3 See Ep 2472 n4.

still a stranger in my own house.[4] You will say: 'I had let you know that my 15
father-in-law had returned and that you would be a most welcome guest.' I
know that you told me, dutifully, as is your custom. But I did not know what
you had said. 'How is that?' you will say. Bebel,[5] having drunk his fill, had left
three letters, among which was yours, at the inn, which is between Basel and
Freiburg.[6] I finally received them two days ago. I wish to know whether your 20
affairs are going according to your wishes.[7] For rumour brings unpleasant
stories here. I have recovered successfully from the severe pain in my foot and
from diarrhea, thanks be to Christ.[8] Farewell. Give my greetings to Basilius.[9]

Freiburg, 17 September 1531
Your Erasmus of Rotterdam 25
To the most illustrious doctor of laws Bonifacius Amerbach. In Basel

2542 / From Bonifacius Amerbach [Basel, c 19 September 1531]

The manuscript of this letter (= AK Ep 1563), which is in the Öffentliche Bibliothek
of the University of Basel (MS VIA 73 247 verso), is an autograph rough draft hast-
ily scribbled on the back of Ep 2438. It could be a first draft of Ep 2546, but it could
just as well be an independent letter, mentioned in Ep 2546:13–14 as written a
day earlier. In any case, it responds directly to the content of Ep 2541.

Cordial greetings. Not so much dutifully as truthfully, most illustrious
Erasmus, I had written that nothing would be more pleasing to my father-in-
law than your visit.[1] I had in fact explicit orders to tell you this. But in truth I
am glad now that, as you write, you were prevented by the negligence of Bebel
and the foolishness of the coachman from undertaking the journey. But you will 5
have been informed about what happened in the meantime at my father-in-
law's house by his son, who was sent to you for that purpose. He had provided
hospitality for a day or two to a certain nobleman, a counsellor of Ferdinand,
who went there to flee the plague. On the very day he arrived, one of the daughters of this nobleman was seized by the plague and died within three days. 10

* * * * *

4 See Ep 2517 n11.
5 The Basel printer Johann Bebel, whose name Erasmus here distorts to 'Bobellius'
6 Not extant
7 See Ep 2519 introduction.
8 Cf Ep 2528 n8.
9 Basilius Amerbach, Bonifacius' elder brother

2542
1 See Epp 2519:41–3, 2538:4–5, 2542:2–3.

Concerning my affairs I do not know what I should write.[2] To speak
frankly, I have come to a standstill at the crossroads of my deliberation. What
is there not to be hoped here, what is there not to be feared there? What is
reasonable in either case? One is at fault both within and without the walls of
Troy.[3] If I leave it to my conscience, since there is some ray of hope, I will not   15
move away at this point, especially at the approach of winter, and to a place
stricken by the plague, of which the one is not fitting for the father of a family,
and the other, if I am not mistaken, not fitting even for a madman.

But we will speak of this when we meet. Lack of time prevents me from
writing further. I am most gratified that you are enjoying better health.   20

2543 / To Bonifacius Amerbach   Freiburg, 19 September 1531

This letter (= AK Ep 1564) was first published in the *Epistolae familiares*. The autograph is in the Öffentliche Bibliothek of the University of Basel (MS AN III 15 33).

Greetings. I have written to you via Caspar Velius.[1]

If you want to give me any news, write via this messenger, whom I
personally hired. I expect a favourable answer from the city council.[2] Your
father-in-law wrote to Baer that a certain person came to stay with him together with his family in fear of the plague. One member of the family died   5
immediately.[3] He did not want me to be unaware of this, lest I regret my decision after having gone there. I had already abandoned the idea, but in view
of this solicitude I esteem this man even more than I did before.[4] Farewell.

Freiburg, 19 September 1531
Your Erasmus of Rotterdam   10
To the most illustrious Doctor Bonifacius Amerbach. At Basel

* * * * *

2 See Ep 2519 introduction.
3 Horace *Epistles* 1.2.16

2543
1 Possibly Ep 2541. The only visit of Caspar Ursinus Velius (Ep 2517) to Freiburg
   that would fall into this period is mentioned in Allen Ep 2664:1–2 (26 June
   1532); cf Epp 2546:14–15, 2608:16–31.
2 Ie a favourable decision of the Basel city council in their dispute with Bonifacius;
   see Ep 2519 introduction.
3 Cf Ep 2542:3–10.
4 Ludwig Baer (Ep 488), who in 1529 had moved with the Basel cathedral chapter
   to Freiburg (Ep 2087 introduction).

2544 / To Henricus Cornelius Agrippa   Freiburg, 19 September 1531

The letter was first printed in *Agrippae Opera* II 993, which is the only source for it.

    Henricus Cornelius Agrippa of Nettesheim 1486–1535) studied law, medicine, and theology at Cologne and Paris and then embarked on a wandering existence too complicated to be summarized here. He is remembered largely for his early, abiding, and controversial interest in magic and the occult, including hermetic literature and the Hebrew Cabala. Among his chief works were *De occulta philosophia*, a study of magic and esoteric knowledge (c 1511) that circulated in manuscript before finally being published in revised form at Antwerp in 1530 (first book only), and at Cologne in 1533 (complete work). In the meantime he had caused a furore by publishing at Antwerp in 1530 his *De incertitudine et vanitate scientiarum atque artium declamatio*, which emphasized the tension between human knowledge and the content of Scripture. Although Erasmus had no interest in magic or the occult and shunned the study of the Cabala, he and Agrippa had in common their desire for a Christianity based on the Bible and the Fathers and their dislike of scholastic theologians. Agrippa's works contain frequent references to the *Adagia*, the *Apophthegmata*, and the *Antibarbari*, and he is known to have owned a number of other works, including the *Spongia* against Hutten. Although Erasmus had heard of Agrippa as early as 1523, direct epistolary contact seems to have begun only in 1531 with this letter, and to have lasted until 1533, most of the surviving letters having been written by Agrippa (Epp 2589, 2626, 2692, 2737, 2739, 2748, 2790, 2796). They deal primarily with Agrippa's controversy with the theologians of Louvain, in which Erasmus urged Agrippa to be cautious, lest he suffer a fate like that of Louis de Berquin (Epp 2158:94–126, 2188).

A FRIEND, TO AGRIPPA

Cordial greetings, illustrious sir. For some time now you are on the lips of everyone here, especially because of the new work you have published, *On the Vanity of the Disciplines.*[1] Although many learned men have written to me about it, I have not yet had the opportunity to see it.[2] They all agree that it is   5 quite outspoken; about other aspects opinions vary. I shall be sure to procure a copy as soon as possible, and I will devour it entirely.

* * * * *

2544
1 Ie *De vanitate scientiarum ... et artium* (see introduction), which Erasmus here refers to as *De vanitate disciplinarum*
2 See Ep 2529:12–20.

Henricus Cornelius Agrippa of Nettesheim

This Andreas,[3] a modest and pious priest in my judgment, came here
to see Erasmus, but hoping for treasure, he found coals.[4] He wishes now to
meet you, to imbibe from your breast a draft of more limpid wisdom. He   10
seems to love your genius to a singular degree, and he has your book *On
Occult Philosophy* as his constant companion in his journeys.[5] I do not recommend him to you but would rather be recommended to you by him. When
I have read through your book I will write to you about it at length.[6] In the
meanwhile I pray that you fare most prosperously.   15

Given at Freiburg im Breisgau, 19 September 1531

2545 / From Stanisław Aichler   Basel, 19 September 1531

This letter was first printed as Ep 16 in Miaskowski. The autograph is in the
Rehdiger Collection of the University Library at Wrocław (MS Rehd 254 13).

Little is known of the early life and education of Stanisław Aichler (c 1519/20–
c 1585), who was the son of an alderman of Cracow. In 1531 he left Poland in the
company of the young nobleman Jan Boner, whose father had sent him abroad
for study under the guidance of Anselmus Ephorinus (Ep 2533 introduction).
Proceeding slowly through Germany on their way to Italy, the trio lived for five
months with Erasmus at Freiburg (April–August 1531) and then spent several
months (until the spring of 1532) in Basel before making their way to Padua.
Erasmus formed a good opinion of Aichler (Epp 2533:103–10, 2584:69–71), and
the two kept in touch by letter until 1534 (Epp 2658, 2718; AK Ep 1739), after
which no trace of contact between them is found. Aichler stayed on in Italy with
Boner and Ephorinus, acquiring a doctorate in both laws at Bologna in 1535,
and then in 1537 returned with them to Cracow, where he became a highly
esteemed lawyer and public official. Around 1550 he became a supporter of the
Reformation and served as an elder of the Calvinist church in Cracow.

Greetings. If I have not written to you recently, together with my preceptor,
most learned sir, it is partly through modesty and partly through meagreness of talent; the former cautioned me, the latter dissuaded me altogether. I

* * * * *

3 Ie the bearer of the letter, an otherwise unknown French priest who had travelled to Germany to visit Erasmus and was now on his way to Brabant to visit
   Agrippa
4 *Adagia* I ix 30
5 At this point only the first book of *De occulta philosophia* had been published; see
   introduction.
6 If such a letter was ever written, it did not survive.

feared that my audacity would be treated as a fault, since as one who is still
an unsophisticated votary of the Muses and with barely a first taste of them, 5
who has not thumbed Aesop,[1] I dared importune with my nonsense the most
learned man the sun has looked upon and who is occupied with so many
demanding labours, although my sense of shame would easily have given
consent if my literary talents, which are still much in need of a graceful style,
had not failed me. 10

But in the end my love for you tossed all of this aside and drove me
to the point where I now write to your Excellency utterly without shame.
Accordingly, if this bold temerity should offend your taste, I ask in the name
of the Muses that you impute it to my love for you, to whom I commend
myself ever more urgently with love and gratitude. 15

Be in good health for as many years as Nestor.[2]

Basel, 19 September 1531

Your most devoted servant, Stanisław Aichler

To the most learned gentleman Erasmus of Rotterdam

2546 / From Bonifacius Amerbach   [Basel, 20 September] 1531

First published by Allen, the autograph of this letter (= AK Ep 1565) is in the
Öffentliche Bibliothek of the University of Basel (MS C VIa 73 246). Lines 9–13
are an almost verbatim duplication of Ep 2538:7–9, and it is not clear whether
the two documents are independent letters or first draft and final version of
the same letter; see Ep 2538 introduction. The sentences in square brackets are
crossed out in the manuscript. The contents of the letter make Bonifacius' date,
21 August 1531, impossible; see line 16 with n7 below.

Cordial greetings. My father-in-law afforded hospitality for a short time to
a certain noble, one of the royal counsellors, until he could rent a house. But
not very auspiciously. For on the day of his arrival one of his daughters was
seized by an illness during the night and died within three days.[1] My father-
in-law also is away from home now, but there is nothing more important to 5

* * * * *

2545
1 See Aristophanes *Birds* 471, where birds are described as ignorant because they
have not read Aesop.
2 Ie to a very great age; see *Adagia* I vi 66.

2546
1 Cf Ep 2542:3–10.

him than to inform you of every calamity as soon as possible, and he sent his
son as far as Krotzingen, in case you had already set out.[2] [He did that on the
day on which the canon had said that his family would arrive.]

In my negotiations the inquiry is still being postponed.[3] May they give
heed to Christian charity, which does not seek its own interests, but is pa-   10
tient and kind, believing all things and hoping all things.[4] We formerly complained of a Babylonian servitude under the pope. Now, if they continue in
this direction, we will all, doubtless, be free. [Yesterday I sent you a letter,
which I think you received. I hope I can visit you soon.] Velius delivered your
letter,[5] to which I responded yesterday.[6]   15

21 August 1531[7]

2547 / To Bonifacius Amerbach   [Freiburg, September 1531]

This letter (= AK Ep 1570) was first published in the *Epistolae familiares*. The autograph, which is in the Öffentliche Bibliothek of the University of Basel (MS AN
III 15 79), lacks a signature, but Bonifacius noted 'D. Eras. Rot.' above 'At Basel'
in the address (line 6). This is perhaps Erasmus' reply to Ep 2546. The contents
of the letter indicate a date in late September 1531.

Greetings. Half-dead myself, I am sincerely grieved at the calamity that has
come upon your father-in-law's house.[1]

Consider my home your own. As soon as it is convenient, I shall gladly
discuss certain matters with you in person.[2]

Keep well.   5

To the most illustrious Doctor Bonifacius Amerbach. At Basel

* * * * *

2 Bad Krotzingen, midway between Freiburg and Neuenburg
3 See Ep 2519 introduction.
4 1 Cor 13:4–7
5 See Ep 2543:1 with n1.
6 Possibly Ep 2541; see Ep 2543 n1.
7 The manuscript bears the date '12 Cal. Septembri 1531' (21 August 1531), which
   is earlier than the events described in the letter. Allen reasoned that Bonifacius
   had mistakenly written 'September' for 'October' and that the actual date was
   thus 20 September 1531.

2547
1 See Ep 2546:1–8.
2 Possibly Bonifacius' difficulties with the Basel magistrates (Ep 2519)

2548 / From Jan Boner   Basel, 20 September 1531

First published as Ep 158 in Förstemann / Günther, the original manuscript of this letter, probably autograph, was in the Burscher Collection of the University Library at Leipzig (Ep 1254 introduction).

Sent by his father to study abroad, the Polish noble Jan Boner of Cracow (1516–62), together with companion and fellow student Stanisław Aichler (Ep 2545) and tutor Anselmus Ephorinus (Ep 2539), had spent five months as a guest in Erasmus' home (April–August 1531); see Ep 2533 introduction. The trio were now in Basel, where they would remain until departing for Italy in the spring of 1532. In 1537, after five years spent in Padua, Bologna, Rome, and Naples, Boner and his companions returned to Cracow. Boner embarked on a career in royal service, becoming castellan of Żarnowiec (1546), Chełm (1552), and Biecz (1555), as well as governor of Cracow Castle (c 1551). Early attracted to the Reformation, he became a devout Calvinist, and in 1556 was one of those who invited the reformer Jan (II) Łaski to return to Poland. He died suddenly and left no heirs. Contact between Boner and Erasmus is documented only until 1532: in December 1531 Erasmus dedicated his edition of Terence to Jan and his brother Stanisław (Ep 2584); the last of the letters to pass between them (Epp 2548, 2549, 2550, 2658, 2717) was written from Padua in September 1532.

Greetings. I fear, most learned man of all those the world has known, that my lack of eloquence may offend rather than please you when I, still a stranger to the Muses, dare to assault and deafen your learned ears with my idle talk although you are intensely occupied with weighty studies. But my love and admiration for you, which admit that they owe you more than they can re- 5 pay for the benevolence shown to us, will justify my temerity. You deigned to admit us who are unworthy of your acquaintance not only to be your table companions but also to share your lasting friendship; you satiated us not only with banquets but with daily learned conversations, which we will fondly remember. For this I give you thanks and I will make requital through 10 my parents, to whom in all my letters I have commended your gracious kindness and hospitality towards us.

Farewell and consider the Boner family most dedicated to your Muses.
From Basel, 20 September 1531
Your most devoted friend, Jan Boner   15
To the most learned Erasmus of Rotterdam, his most worthy master and teacher

2549 / To Jan Boner   Freiburg, 21 September 1531

This letter, which responds to one now lost, was first published in the *Epistolae palaeonaeoi*. Boner's reply is Ep 2550. For Jan Boner, see Epp 2533 introduction, 2548.

ERASMUS OF ROTTERDAM TO JAN BONER, GREETING
I don't know how it happened that Stanisław's letter was delivered to me without yours;[1] I do not think it was through negligence on your part. I am entirely persuaded that Boner will never yield to Stanisław either in recipro- cated love for me or in his enthusiasm for study, but will rather strive in both   5 endeavours to leave the other behind no matter what efforts he employs. For it is fitting that you, who excel him in the nobility of your ancestors, wealth, and the other advantages of fortune, should emerge even more superior in those true blessings to which fortune has no claim. The renown of your fam- ily and the splendour of your fortune shine forth before you so that there   10 is no room for idleness, from which you long ago removed yourself, since at such a tender age you have advanced with such success into the green meadows of the Muses. It would be shameful, my dear Boner, if when God and your excellent parents have provided you with all that is necessary for a superior education and the acquisition of virtue – a docile nature, innate   15 good qualities, an adequate supply of money, which is no less the support of studies than of wars, and finally a teacher (it would be difficult to find one more learned, more attentive, and more devoted than he) – you alone were to fail to do your part. Since for all these reasons you arouse such expectations, therefore, you must not prove them vain. But if now your studies have some   20 disagreeable aspects, think how much pleasure, how much glory will accrue to you from them when, like an avid merchant, after traversing the commer- cial centres of both Germanies,[2] Italy, and France, after enjoying the company of so many learned men, you return to your Poland marvellously enriched with the commodities of all the disciplines and virtues. Farewell.   25
Freiburg, on the feast of St Matthew 1531

* * * * *

2549
1 Stanisław Aichler's letter is Ep 2545; Boner's letter is not extant.
2 Ie of Upper and Lower Germany, *Germania superior* and *Germania inferior*; see Ep 1998 n6.

2550 / From Jan Boner   Basel, 25 September 1531

> First printed as Ep 18 in Miaskowski , this is Boner's reply to Ep 2549. The manu-
> script, apparently autograph, is in the Rehdiger Collection of the University
> Library at Wrocław (MS Rehd 254 32).

Greetings. I received with great delight, distinguished sir, your most learned
letter, in which you acknowledge that it was not through any negligence on
my part that Stanisław's letter arrived without mine.[1] By Hercules, this was
not caused by my negligence, for I was away when the messenger collected
the letters. I sent it through your theologian's servant,[2] who brought to us   5
those from Poland that had been kept there in Freiburg for a long time. I
think you will have received it recently, because he left on 21 September.

Moreover, most learned sir, since you exhort me so good-naturedly and
so charmingly not to employ my diligence in anything but good letters, citing numerous examples, and since you even deigned to write me in your   10
own hand, mentioning that the gods and my parents had furnished me in
abundance with whatever is necessary to attain to eminent virtue, namely, a
docile character, innate good qualities, a good supply of money, which is no
less useful to students than to soldiers, I will see to it – by Hercules, I will see
to it – that the goods of the spirit and not riches will take precedence with me.   15

For I see that many learned men have gone from dire poverty to great
riches, which are venerated everywhere above all other things. I shall make every effort that my youth and my parents' expenditures are not squandered. In the
meantime, farewell and keep me in your favour together with my Anselmus.[3]

At Basel, 25 September 1531   20
Jan Boner, always most devoted to you in every way
To the most learned Erasmus of Rotterdam, his most worthy master
and teacher

* * * * *

2550
1 See Ep 2549 n1.
2 'The theologian' or 'my theologian' was Erasmus' habitual way of referring
  to Ludwig Baer (Ep 2225 introduction), who had also abandoned Basel for
  Freiburg in 1529, and on whom he relied for advice on difficult theological matters. Cf Epp 2598:5, 2606:1–2, 2631:80–1.
3 Anselmus Ephorinus (Ep 2539)

2551 / From Bonifacius Amerbach   Basel, 27 September [1531]

This letter (= AK Ep 1568) was first published by Allen. The manuscript, a much-corrected rough draft, is in the Öffentliche Bibliothek of the University of Basel (MS C VIa 73 244). The year-date is established by the movements at this time of Viglius Zuichemus (Ep 2101). In his autobiography Viglius reports that on his way to Italy in the autumn of 1531 he visited the universities of Basel, Freiburg, and Tübingen. In Basel he met, among others, Bonifacius Amerbach, who provided him with this letter as he set out for Freiburg. In Freiburg he finally met Erasmus in person. See C.P. Hoynck van Papendrecht *Analecta Belgica* 3 vols in 6 (The Hague 1743) I/1 9–11.

Cordial greetings. I would recommend Viglius to you with great solicitude, most illustrious Erasmus, if his benevolent nature, as is manifest in the exchange of letters between the two of you, had not long ago commended him to you. Consequently, not to waste my effort, I prefer to congratulate both of you on embracing one another at last. I am well aware of the joy that the   5
two of you will derive from it. About my affairs there is nothing to report as I write, because I am still numbered among the defendants whose hearings have been deferred.[1] Whether the judgment will be gracious or severe, that is, whether they will acquit or condemn me, is uncertain. Whatever is finally decided about my fate, I will let you know in person.   10
    Farewell. In haste, from Basel, 27 September

2552 / To Erasmus Schets   [Freiburg, September–October 1531]

This letter, Erasmus' reply to Ep 2527, was first published by Allen on the basis of the undated autograph in the British Library (MS Add 38512 folio 63). Schets' reply to this letter is Ep 2593. Only an approximate date can be assigned. It is clear from lines 5–7 that Erasmus had not yet received Schets' letter of 18 October (Ep 2558); and it is equally clear that when Schets wrote that letter, he had not received this one. A date in September or early October is suggested by the first mention in the correspondence (line 19) of the *Determinatio* of the Paris theologians, published July 1531.

* * * * *

2551
1 See Ep 2519 introduction.

Title-page of the *Determinatio … super quam plurimis assertionibus*
D. Erasmi Roterodami

Cordial greetings. The sweets that the Portuguese fellow sent have not arrived.[1] I ask you to give me the name of the merchant to whom you entrusted
them, so that we can hunt him down. Things have a tendency to be held up
at Strasbourg.[2]

I would like to know what was done about the letters addressed to 5
England. I had ordered that a considerable number of them be given to you
together, and I would not want them to go astray.[3]

I am very grateful for your instruction about nobles of nominal value and
nobles in kind. I see that Bebel is a great scoundrel. In 99 crowns there were almost 40 that were defective, either in weight or minting or in some other way.[4] 10

Goclenius, by now a canon, is there with you.[5] Find out from him how
much money Haio Cammingha spent so that I can determine what is missing in the account.[6] Here three crowns are worth four golden florins in gold.[7]
Farewell, dearest Schets, and fill the sponge with good results.[8]

Pieter Gillis has finally paid his debt, I think. He owes, as he testifies 15
in his own hand, 117 florins. If there should be some loss coming from that

* * * * *

2552
1 See Ep 2511:29–33.
2 Seemingly an expression of Erasmus' belief that 'Evangelicals' were intercepting
  mail addressed to him; cf lines 20–1 below with n11, and Ep 2487:3–5 with n2.
3 The letters were safe: see Ep 2558:1–5.
4 That is, they were either clipped or worn and thus did not retain their official
  weight and fineness; on this, see CWE 1 312 and Ep 2527. During his trip to
  England with Simon Grynaeus in the spring and summer of 1531 (Ep 2487 n9),
  Johann Bebel had been given sums of money, an equivalent value of which was
  to be paid to Erasmus on his return. Erasmus was now convinced that Bebel
  had short-changed him; cf Ep 2530 n15.
5 Conradus Goclenius (Epp 1209, 1994A), professor of Latin at the Collegium
  Trilingue in Louvain and one of Erasmus' closest friends. In 1525 Goclenius
  had been appointed to a canonry of Our Lady's at Antwerp, but it took a lawsuit of eight years duration before he could defeat the rival claim of a candidate
  backed by the curia. A seemingly favourable development in the case had caused
  Erasmus to conclude prematurely that Goclenius had won it; cf Ep 2573:58–63.
6 On Haio Cammingha and his debt to Erasmus, see Epp 2325 n1, 2364:10–14,
  2403:35–41 and 69–71, 2413:24–8, 2573:66–7, 2587:47–52, 58–62, 2593:37–41.
7 Erasmus is presumably speaking of the gold rose crown of England, whose official value in 1531 was 76d Flemish; the Rhenish gold florin was worth
  59d groot Flemish. Three crowns were therefore officially valued at 228d groot
  Flemish, four florins at 236d groot Flemish (CWE 12 650 Table 3). The slight discrepancy can probably be put down to local fluctuations in the value of bullion,
  to which Erasmus seems to be referring ('four golden florins in gold').
8 See Ep 2494 n13.

money, it would be his loss since he received my money without my permission and held on to it against my will.[9]

A *Determinatio* has appeared in Paris, extorted by Béda.[10] Act cautiously, lest confiscation occur there.[11] There are harpies everywhere. Be in good   20
health, together with your family.

To Master Erasmus Schets. In Antwerp

2553 / From Charles v to the City Council   Brussels, 1 October 1531
       of Besançon

This letter, written in French, was first published by A. Castan in the *Revue Historique* I (1876) 125. The manuscript, a contemporary copy made c 25 November 1532, is in the Bibliothèque municipale at Besançon (MS BB 14 folio 449). For Erasmus' contemplated move to Besançon, see Ep 2514. Ep 2563A:3–5 confirms that Erasmus had requested the letter from Emperor Charles.

BY ORDER OF THE EMPEROR

Dear and faithful subjects. We have no doubt that you are well aware of the great virtues, wisdom, knowledge, learning, and laudable qualities that exist

* * * * *

9 See Ep 2494 n12.
10 *Determinatio facultatis theologiae in schola Parisiensi super quam plurimis assertioni-bus D. Erasmi Roterodami* (Paris: Josse Bade, July 1531). Based on the Paris faculty of theology's formal censures of Erasmus' *Colloquies* (September 1526) as well as the New Testament Paraphrases and other works (December 1527), the *Determinatio* condemned a total of 175 propositions excerpted from Erasmus' works. The reason for the long interval between censure and publication is not clear, but the man behind the publication was the syndic (presiding officer) of the faculty of theology, Noël Béda, who since 1523 had waged a campaign to prove that Erasmus' works and his kind of humanist scholarship were the sources of Luther's heresy (cf Epp 2558:61–8, 2561:3, 2600:9–16). Erasmus, who had already published several works defending himself and humanist scholarship against Béda, now had to respond to this renewed attack. His *Declarationes ad censuras Lutetiae vulgatas sub nomine facultatis theologiae Parisiensis* (Basel: Froben) was in print early in 1532. An extensively revised and augmented edition appeared the following September. It was Erasmus' final word in the long controversy with Béda. For the history of the controversy, see Farge *Orthodoxy and Reform* 186–96, and CWE 82 ix–xxxiv (introduction to the *Declarationes*).
11 Erasmus here returns abruptly to the theme of the opening paragraph, namely the failure of a gift of sweets to be delivered and his suspicion that letters and parcels addressed to him are being intercepted or confiscated by his enemies. Hence the reference in the following sentence to 'harpies,' monsters who (among other things) steal food from their victims.

in the person of our dear and well-beloved councillor, Doctor Master Erasmus
of Rotterdam, for which he is to be esteemed and loved, and he has our af-   5
fectionate and particular commendation, and we desire to show our favour to
him. For this reason and because, as we hear, seeing the reprobate and heretical sects, Lutherans and others, who reign and daily increase in the cities and
places where he resides, for the repulsion, reprobation, and contradiction of
which he dare not or cannot write as freely as he would wish, he would like to   10
retire to some secure and free place not infected by the said errors, and indeed
to our imperial city of Besançon, knowing of its stability and steadfastness in
our holy Catholic faith. And since we believe that in the event of his coming
to the said city, he will be welcomed by you and you will show him every
courtesy, favour, and pleasure for the comfort of his residence and sojourn, we   15
have wished to write you this, asking affectionately that you will do so, and
in everything that concerns him you will assist and aid him, as a personage
of such quality deserves. And further, confident that he will contribute to the
honour and glory of the said city, we will most happily keep him in our service. Dear and faithful subjects, may our Lord keep you in his holy protection.   20
    Written in our city of Brussels the first day of October 1531
    Charles and Perrenin[1]
    To our dear and faithful rectors and governors of our imperial city of
Besançon[2]

2554 / From Anselmus Ephorinus   Basel, 9 October 1531

First published as Ep 159 in Förstemann / Günther, the autograph was in the
Burscher Collection of the University Library at Leipzig (Ep 1254 introduction).
For Ephorinus see Ep 2539.

Greetings. I had already given my letter for you, most illustrious and learned
patron, to Trübelmann,[1] who had told me that he was leaving from here to-

* * * * *

2553
1 Antoine Perrenin (documented 1525–38), imperial secretary
2 In Ep 2563A:4–5 Johannes Dantiscus describes this as a letter 'to the city and
  clergy of Besançon.'

2554
1 Georg Trübelmann (Tribelmann, Truffelmann) of Bamlach in the Breisgau (documented 1513–56) first appears in the historical record as a member of the Basel
  contingent at the battle of Novara (1513), where his bravery won him Basel citizenship and a pension for life. He is frequently mentioned in the sources as a
  messenger and letter carrier between Basel and Freiburg; cf Epp 2747, 2827, 3051.

day and setting out in your direction, and behold, he had hardly left the city
when I received the letter in which you give me your anxiously awaited advice about my trip to Speyer.[2] I embraced it with open arms as if it had come 5
from the tripod,[3] and I thank you for it.

I am grief-stricken that Sebastian,[4] who was very attached to me, as
was apparent in his last letter, suffered an untimely death (may his soul be
with God), but who will not succumb to irrevocable fate? We are all destined
there. It would please me if you would diligently look after your own health, 10
at least for the sake of all pious and scholarly men, and, I pray you, do not
allow anything to disturb or harm it in any way. You will take no heed of
those foolish calumnies of the followers of Oecolampadius concerning your
letters,[5] if you consider the motivation for their actions. Herwagen, who is
involved in the matter, has made you too anxious about this business. 15

I decided to postpone my trip to Speyer until Trübelmann returns
with the surety,[6] so that it will not be necessary for the canon of Würzburg
to give me a letter.[7] But I would like to present it to your friends as a recommendation for me. I do not wish, however, that this be a burden to your
health for my sake. 20

I see that the junk-dealer is a Proteus and a master of trickery.[8] He
agreed on five florins, not six. I wish that the enclosed letter be given to him,
and he will see that what was agreed upon is not according to his wishes. I
will warn the man to have some regard for his reputation, at least.

* * * * *

2 Not extant. No letters of Erasmus to Ephorinus survive. For the projected trip
to Speyer to attend the imperial diet, see Ep 2559.
3 The tripod of the Pythian Sibyl in Delphi
4 Possibly the 'friend' mentioned in Ep 2555:13–14; cf line 41 below.
5 Ie the *Epistolae floridae*, published by Johann Herwagen in September 1531.
Johannes Oecolampadius took offence at some of the indiscretions in the letters
(Ep 2559:27–8), and Erasmus subsequently expressed his regret for them (Ep
2615:31–41).
6 Ephorinus uses the word *vas, vasis* (vessel, dish) but doubtless means *vas, vadis*
(surety, security). It seems that he was expecting Erasmus to provide him with
a document in which he would stand surety for Ephorinus' expenses in Speyer.
7 The canon of Würzburg was probably Daniel Stiebar (Epp 2069, 2303), who
had lived with Erasmus at Freiburg in 1529–30 and had now embarked on his
career as an administrator of the imperial bishopric of Würzburg. In that capacity he regularly attended imperial diets, including the one at Regensburg in
the spring of 1532 that replaced the one originally intended for Speyer in the
autumn of 1531.
8 Unidentified

I cannot but greatly appreciate your good will towards me in offering   25
us a part of the first floor of your house to live in.[9] Would that I could do
whatever I wished; I call upon Christ as my witness that I would desire no
one's hospitality more than yours. I have two brothers who are priests.[10] Both
of them would easily accommodate themselves to your way of life. How
much I would like one of them to become your servant! But one is in his fif-   30
ties and the other in his forties. I could command them, even though I am
younger, if the difficulty and length of the journey were not an obstacle. You
would certainly be free of all domestic cares.

Understand that Stanisław, aged seven, is the brother of Jan, not my
brother.[11] He is a boy noble in his behaviour and character, whom his par-   35
ents adore, and he is very interested in literature. In the dedication of your
Terence I pray that you mention my solicitude for Jan and exhort the two
brothers to follow the example of the young King Sigismund,[12] who exhibits
a truly kingly nature and frame of mind. In this way you will do nothing
more pleasing to their parents.   40

If Sebastian left unsold anything that belongs to me, it will be given
to the poor. In other matters he gave satisfaction in the most friendly way. I
would like to know if you received the cup from Strasbourg.[13] You said nothing about the quince preserves; if you wish anything else for your health
from the medicine-vendors, say but the word and the matter will be properly   45
taken care of.[14] Whatever I have or will have I am prepared to spend in your
behalf. I wish you the best of health.

* * * * *

9 Erasmus had very much wanted Ephorinus to remain with him in Freiburg; see
   Ep 2533:7–20.
10 Nothing is known of these brothers.
11 Ephorinus had suggested that Erasmus dedicate his edition of Terence (Ep
   2584) to the brothers Jan and Stanisław Boner (cf lines 36–8 below). Erasmus
   had somehow misunderstood Stanisław to be Ephorinus' brother, not Jan's.
   (Both Allen and Gerlo say that Erasmus took 'Stanisław' to be a reference to
   Stanisław Aichler, but that makes no sense. During the five months that Aichler,
   Jan Boner, and Ephorinus lived in his house Erasmus must have figured out
   that Ephorinus and Aichler were not brothers.)
12 The son of Sigismund I, born in 1520 and crowned king in 1530, while his father
   was still living, reigned as Sigismund Augustus until 1572.
13 This is apparently the cup referred to in Ep 2559:31, the delivery of which via
   Nürnberg is mentioned in Ep 2606:5–7, 53. It appears to have been a gift from
   one of Erasmus' Polish patrons.
14 The quince preserves were doubtless the still undelivered preserves sent by
   a Portuguese via Erasmus Schets (Ep 2511:29–30); see Ep 2559:31. Their delivery is reported in Ep 2606:46–7. As the reference to 'anything else for your

Basel, in all haste, 9 October 1531

Your devoted Anselmus Ephorinus, Silesian, not a Pole[15]

To the great Erasmus of Rotterdam, his eminent master and patron. At   50
Freiburg

2555 / To Bernhard von Cles   Freiburg, 9 October 1531

This letter, Erasmus' reply to Ep 2540, was first published in the *Epistolae palae-onaeoi*. Cles' response is Ep 2557.

ERASMUS OF ROTTERDAM TO THE REVEREND LORD BERNHARD
VON CLES, BISHOP AND CARDINAL OF TRENT, GREETING
I received in recent days four letters from your most reverend Highness, not
dissimilar in content.[1] This makes clear to me your extraordinary affection
for me, already well known and verified over a long period of time, but it is   5
gratifying to renew the memory of it from time to time.

In your kind invitation to the diet at Speyer[2] I see that you greatly over-
estimate the state of my health. In my new house I am struggling against
death for the fourth time. The battle was going well enough while the benign
summer weather favored the struggler. But as soon as autumn began to rage,   10
I could barely draw in a feeble breath, confined as I was indoors sitting by
the fire. Around the feast of St Michael[3] a northeast wind suddenly came
up that confined me to bed. A friend and neighbour of mine contracted the
malady that same day for the same reason and died within four days.[4] The
oak was knocked down but, as in the apologue, the reed, though shaking,   15

* * * * *

health' in this sentence makes clear, fruit preserves were intended to serve a
medicinal purpose, namely as a remedy for certain intestinal disorders, such
as Erasmus' recent bout of diarrhea (Ep 2536:1–2), because of their astringent
effect. Cf Ep 2740 (26 November 1532), in which Bonifacius Amerbach mentions
a prescription that was concocted from dried fruits on Ephorinus' instructions
and offered to Erasmus. For other evidence of Ephorinus' role as a prescriber of
medications, see Ep 2559:34–7.
15 It seems that at some point Erasmus had referred to Ephorinus as a Pole.

2555
1 Only Ep 2540 is extant.
2 The invitation is in Ep 2540:7–15 ; for the diet see Ep 2511 n20.
3 29 September
4 See Ep 2554 n4.

stood firm.[5] How I could be useful there to the common good, I do not know; in any case it would be just as important for me to be there as it was for me not to be absent from the Diet of Augsburg.[6] But what can I do with this frail body, more fragile than glass, for which a change of bed or wine or a little draught means death? It is no secret to me that there will be people at the diet who have a very bad opinion of me and who even plot my death. If it becomes possible for me to go there, you can learn of it from the reverend lord Johann, bishop of Vienna.[7]

I am not worried about money; the Lord has provided it up to now and will provide, as I hope. I merely wished that I would be permitted to live in peace in my extreme old age; not even that has been granted. The purchase of this house has involved me in inextricable woes,[8] and yet there is still no place in the whole house comfortable enough for this frail body. Many people wonder what will be the outcome of this diet. The spirit of Christ will deign to suggest to the intelligence of princes what will be most salutary. We must use great circumspection in this matter, lest while we suppress one party we vindicate not the rights of the other, but tyranny. I see whom I should flee, but see only vaguely whom I should follow. That is all my health has allowed me for now. When I have more strength, I will write more copiously. May the Lord preserve your Highness unharmed.

Given at Freiburg in Breisgau, 9 October 1531

2556 / To Bonifacius Amerbach   Freiburg, 11 October 1531

This letter (= AK Ep 1573) was first published in the *Epistolae familiares*. The autograph is in the Öffentliche Bibliothek of the University of Basel (MS AN III 15 34).

You need not be tormented by my troubles. Such is my destiny. I wish all happiness for you and hope it will be so.

Your arrival will be most welcome,[1] but I would not wish you to hurry, thereby causing yourself inconvenience. Pay attention to the weather. The

* * * * *

5 *Aesopica* 179
6 Cf Ep 2339 n6.
7 Johann Fabri (Ep 386)
8 Epp 2506 n1, 2517 n11.

2556
1 For Erasmus' expectation of a visit from Bonifacius, cf Epp 2559:1–4, 2561:8–14, 2564:15–18, 2574:20–2, 2631:89–90 with n33.

matter does not require great speed.[2] Take care that you do not get involved   5
with your father-in-law prematurely.[3] It appears that the pestilence is violent,
it kills its victims so quickly. And these are the worst months. Farewell, incomparable friend, together with all your dear ones.

Freiburg, 11 October 1531

We have room and hay in the stable, so you do not have to deal with inns.   10

Your friend Erasmus of Rotterdam

To the eminent doctor Master Bonifacius Amerbach. At Basel

2557 / From Bernhard von Cles   [Speyer], October 1531

This letter was first published by Allen. For the manuscript, an autograph rough
draft, see Ep 2515 introduction. The approximate date is deduced from the presence of the letter in a small packet of correspondence labelled 10 September to
21 October 1531. If, as seems the case, this is the answer to Ep 2555, it cannot be
earlier than 9 October.

TO ERASMUS OF ROTTERDAM

For many reasons it was distressing to hear of your state of health, especially because for the public good of the entire Christian commonwealth
it is important that you be able to provide for its needs without harm to
yourself. This is what we would have hoped for if, at the time when the im-   5
perial diet was to have been held, as decreed and in accordance with general
expectation,[1] you had been able to be present. In the meantime, if there is
anything we can do for your comfort and honour, we earnestly desire that
you call upon us, since we will not refuse for your sake to do whatever an
excellent friend would expect of us.   10

2558 / From Erasmus Schets   Antwerp, 18 October 1531

This letter, Schets' answer to Ep 2530, was first published by Allen on the basis
of the autograph in the Öffentiche Bibliothek of the University of Basel (Scheti
epistolae 23). Erasmus' reply is Ep 2578.

* * * * *

2 Presumably the matter that Bonifacius wanted to discuss with Erasmus; see Ep
  2547:3–4.
3 For the case of the plague in the home of Bonifacius' father-in law, Leonhard
  Fuchs, see Ep 2519 n6.

2557
1 Ep 2511 n20

†

Cordial greetings. Immediately after the Frankfurt fair I received your letter, together with many others that were to be sent to England.[1] I sent them off immediately to Luis de Castro,[2] with instructions not to entrust them rashly to anyone at all and to take care that they were delivered, since you saw fit to recommend this, not without reason.   5

That you have bought a house in Freiburg and are busy rebuilding it lessens our hope that you will return here.[3] But when necessity demands it, and you esteem yourself happy and safe there, it cannot be bad for us.

I cannot see the cause of your complaints about losses incurred in the money you have received. When in the month of December in the year 1529 I   10 gave Quirinus by your order all the money in my possession, I received from him an acknowledgement of receipt.[4] And I paid him in Carolines and other good currency of ours one thousand five hundred and twenty-five florins and five stuivers.[5] You had said in your letter[6] that this Quirinus had instructions from you and that you had indicated to him how he should dispose of this   15 money. How he disposed of it I don't know; nothing was indicated to me. That is what I wrote to you at the time. I suggested that he wait for the fair and I would have given him the equivalent of the entire sum in gold florins in Frankfurt. He refused. You now complain that you suffered a loss and remind me to be more careful on that point as if I were at fault for your loss. That is   20 certainly not the case, my dear Erasmus. I did what you commanded. I gave your Quirinus your money in good currency, money which he perhaps exchanged or disposed of – I do not know, nor am I at fault, and I should not like to remain under such suspicion. I am not the type of person who would wish to seek my own advantage at your loss. I love you more sincerely than that.   25

While he was here lately in the month of May, Quirinus could not extort any of the money that Pieter Gillis received here in your name,[7] except

* * * * *

2558
1 See Ep 2530 n6, and cf Ep 2552:5–7.
2 Schet's agent in London
3 On the house see Epp 2506 n1, 2517 n11; for the hopes of Erasmus' return to Brabant see Ep 2511:34–47 with n17.
4 See Ep 2243:7–13.
5 That is, Carolus florins. This represented a very large sum, equivalent to almost thirty-one years' wages of an Antwerp master mason/carpenter at 9.05d per day and a 230-day year (CWE 12 650 Table 3, 691 Table 13).
6 Not extant; answered by Ep 2243
7 See Ep 2494:26–31.

for twelve florins, giving me a written receipt which stated that Pieter had received twenty angelets, twenty-four Philips, one rose noble, one gold Rhenish florin and twenty Carolines. That money made 115 florins and 18 stuivers in all.[8] Deducting the twelve florins that Pieter paid Quirinus, that left 103 florins and 18 stuivers. I have now wrested them from Pieter. Therefore Quirinus also refunded the twelve florins. Thus I now have the full said 115 florins and 18 stuivers. I informed you of this in a letter to which you answered that you did not understand. And you say that I should remember that 117 florins and some stuivers are owed. From my calculations and reasoning I do not find this to be so.

From England I do not receive anything. I wrote recently to Luis asking him to find out whether they can procure the money from other sources or whether perhaps they sent it through Grynaeus or Bebel.[9] I have not set eyes on them.[10] You warn me that I should not trust them at all.[11] Good, I shall be careful.

From the last account of your money, which, as said above, I gave to Quirinus at your order, who gave me a receipt for them, I received in your name, in the month of June in the year 1530, 65 florins from Master Jan de Hondt; around the month of December in the same year I received another 65 florins, and now from Pieter Gillis 115 florins and 18 stuivers. Taken all together, they make the sum of 245 florins and 18 stuivers.[12] Please see to it

* * * * *

8 On the coins mentioned here and their official values, see CWE 1 311–47, CWE 12 650 Table 3, and CWE 14 442–7. The angelet or half angel was worth (after Henry VIII's debasement of 1526) 3s 9d (45d) or 59.5d groot Flemish; the Philippus florin (after 1521) 54d groot Flemish; the rose noble (after 1526) 11s 0d (132d) or 174.5d groot Flemish; the Rhenish florin 59d groot Flemish; the Carolus florin (Caroline) 42d groot Flemish for a total of £14 1s 7d groot Flemish at the official rates. Schets' total of 115 Carolus florins, 18 stuivers was worth £20 5s 6d groot Flemish, presumably reflecting the rising price of gold in this period. This was equivalent to just over two years' wages of an Antwerp master craftsman (CWE 12 691 Table 13).
9 Luis is Luis de Castro (n2 above); 'they' are presumably those who assist him in the collection and transmission of Erasmus' pensions.
10 Although Simon Grynaeus and Johann Bebel passed through the Netherlands on their way home from England in the summer of 1531 (Epp 2499:5–10, 2502:1), they evidently did not visit Schets at Antwerp; cf Ep 2487 n9.
11 See Ep 2530:49–50, and cf Ep 2552 n4.
12 The total sum of 245 Carolus florins, eighteen stuivers was equivalent to £42 11s 6d groot Flemish, or five years' wages of an Antwerp master craftsman (CWE 12 650 Table 3, 691 Table 13). See also Ep 2625.

that you send me a receipt for this money through Hieronymus Froben at
the next Frankfurt fair, so that I shall be absolved by you of this sum together   50
with the other money previously received in your name. In that way I will
be freed from the burden of rendering account for all these monies in my
letters. In that same meeting I will have the aforementioned money given to
Hieronymus by my agents in full in gold florins or another equivalent currency at the discretion of Hieronymus.   55

If I receive anything over and above that from England, I will add it.
I have decided to give you at every fair whatever money has been received
through me in your name in the intervening period. That will be more reas-
suring for you and for me and will not lead to any disputes between us or
our heirs. May God ordain that there be no dispute between us, alive or dead.   60

The inane, nonsensical criticisms against you that Béda published under
the authority of the faculty of theology at the University of Paris (so that they
will have more weight than they deserve), arouse great interest among good
and learned men.[13] I think you will not let this matter go by, and that it will be
easy for you to shut this gaping and malicious mouth with just refutations. This   65
Béda has made it quite clear how much he favours the sects. While he himself
does not dare lift a little finger to touch Luther, he babbles against the only man
who treads him under foot, so blinded by envy of you that he has gone mad.
You have the advantage of being so clear and irreproachable in writing as you
are and in possession of the truth that you do not spare our masters.[14]   70

The emperor, hearing of the obstinacy of the Germans, has postponed
the meeting of Speyer to the month of January, and it is to be held in
Regensburg.[15] That is not the end of the calamities: may God prevent it, but I
fear that in the end an evangelical or religious war will break out. It would already have begun if the monarchs were not so exhausted. The king of France   75
is eager to have a colloquy with the emperor,[16] and they would already have
met if the death of the king's mother had not interrupted it.[17] People think
they will still meet, and that for the great good of the world, or its great loss.

* * * * *

13 See Ep 2552 n10.
14 In *Praise of Folly* Erasmus makes fun of the delight of theologians in being addressed with the grandiose title of *magister noster* ('our master'); CWE 27 130.
15 See Ep 2511 n20.
16 In September and early October 1531 there had been talk of a meeting between
   Charles v and Francis I in September 1531, but nothing came of it; see LP 5 nos
   437, 462, 472, and cf Ep 2565:18–19.
17 Louise of Savoy, who died on 22 September 1531.

Here life is very expensive. Cereals are sold at three times the usual price. My field produced nothing but straw this year, and hoping for a harvest we were completely deluded by fate. Keep well, my master, dearest Erasmus, happy and prosperous for many a year. 80

From Antwerp, 18 October 1531

Yours sincerely, Erasmus Schets.

† To the excellent and supremely learned Master Erasmus of Rotterdam, most exceptional friend. At Freiburg 85

2559 / From Anselmus Ephorinus Basel, 19 October 1531

This letter was first published as Ep 160 in Förstemann / Günther. The autograph was in the Burscher Collection of the University Library at Leipzig (Ep 1254 introduction). For Ephorinus see Ep 2539 introduction.

Greetings in Christ. I was hoping that Amerbach, a man both learned and upright, more humane than humanity itself, would go to see you,[1] for I saw that he needed no other motivation for his trip than love for you and solicitude for your health. But though God heard our wishes, in which we never cease in our humble prayers to watch over you, he changed his mind,[2] and in the meantime no appropriate messenger presented himself to deliver my answer to your last letter.[3] Frequent rumours that few people are going to the diet keep me here longer than I had thought.[4] A persistent rumour here is that Ferdinand has gone to Heidelberg and that all the delegates of the princes have gone in haste to the emperor. If I could have more certain information from you, I would be very happy. The business of the gospel does not allow me to stay here any longer; it leads to tumult. The place is reasonably safe from pestilence, but many suffer from a pestilence more pestilential than the plague, namely those who proclaim tyrannically in public meetings 5 10

* * * * *

2559
1 See Ep 2556 n1.
2 See Ep 2561A:3–5.
3 Not extant; cf Ep 2554 n2.
4 On Ephorinus' planned visit to Speyer, where the imperial diet was supposed to meet, cf Ep 2554:4–5. On 15 October, after receiving news of the battle of Kappel (see n6 below), King Ferdinand suspended the diet and ordered it to reconvene at Regensburg in the new year; see Ep 2511 n20. Ephorinus would not yet have known this, but confused rumours about the diet (see the following two sentences) had reached him in Basel.

that the papal realm must be eliminated without further thought. The people   15
of Zürich, with their Glaucoplutus,[5] have been crushed by the cantons and
were driven into a shameful flight.[6] Glaucoplutus fell in the first lines with
all the best and most learned men, like Karlstadt and others;[7] our people are
downcast because they hear nothing but the sound of the trumpet summon-
ing them to battle. The common people are beginning to speak badly about   20
the Oecolampadians,[8] who they say are the cause of this bloodshed. Soldiers
are pushed into the war. Oecolampadius mounted the pulpit recently to give
a sermon in such a fit of madness as can hardly be imagined.[9] He began to
exhort to penitence, to preach that a great disaster menaced this commonwealth; he seemed to shriek, not to preach, inciting the people to public sup-   25
plications and fasts.

Oecolampadius was offended by some of your letters published in the
great work published by Herwagen.[10] When Amerbach comes to visit you,
he will give you a true picture of the situation, which is not of such great
importance as to increase your anxiety.   30

I have no news about the cup or the Portuguese preserves.[11] I will await
your letter, from which I am very eager to have information from you about
the diet;[12] as soon as I receive it, there will be no delay.

If you wish me to send you some remedies against the plague in tablets,
pills, or powder, either for yourself or your servants (although your female   35

* * * * *

5 'Owl-rich' in Greek, which would be 'Eul-reich' in German, a play on 'Ulrich,'
   the putative first name of the Swiss reformer Huldrych ('Grace-rich') Zwingli. It
   is the invention of Erasmus in the *Colloquies*; see CWE 40 624:40 (*Peregrinatio reli-
   gionis ergo* 'A Pilgrimage for Religion's Sake'), and cf CWE 40 713:233 (Ἰχθυοφαγία
   'A Fish Diet'), where Glaucoplutus is the name given to Udalricus Zasius.
6 At the battle of Kappel (11 October 1531), which brought an end to the Second
   Kappel War between Zürich and the Catholic cantons of Switzerland. For the
   causes and outcome of the conflict, see Ep 2173 n10.
7 Zwingli, serving as chaplain, was indeed killed at the battle, but the reports that
   Andreas Karlstadt (d 1541), Conradus Pellicanus (d 1556), and others had also
   been killed were false; see Burckhardt 354:17–18 with n2.
8 Ie Johannes Oecolampadius and the other leaders of the newly reformed church
   in Basel
9 Apparently the sermon of 15 October referred to in Bonifacius' *Tagebuch*; Burckhardt 353–4
10 The *Epistolae floridae*; see Ep 2554 n5.
11 For the cup see Ep 2554 n13; for the preserves see Ep 2554 n14.
12 Cf lines 10–11 above.

servant is more pestilential than the plague and has no fear of sickness),[13]
let me know. I will not spare the expense.[14] This one thing I ask of you, most
learned Erasmus, that when you incur the calumnies of the impious, who
we see were born to write defamatory books, try to bear the offence with
resolute spirit. For it is thus that one achieves immortality.[15] May Christ Jesus   40
deign to preserve you unharmed for us for years to come. I gladly offer and
dedicate myself to you as to a father, ready to fulfil your every wish.

In haste from Basel, 19 October 1531
Your Anselmus
To the great Erasmus of Rotterdam, his eminent master and patron   45

2560 / From Bonifacius Amerbach

This letter has been redated to 'after 24 October 1531' and appears below as
Ep 2561A.

2561 / To Bonifacius Amerbach   [Freiburg], 24 October 1531

This letter (= AK Ep 1577) was first published in the *Epistolae familiares*. The autograph is in the Öffentliche Bibliothek of the University of Basel (MS AN III 15
35). Bonifacius' reply is Ep 2561A.

Cordial greetings. My stomach has come back to life, fortunately, and so far
in these physical disorders nature has acted so appropriately that I do not ask
for more. What is lacking is a charming guest at table and a mind free from
cares. Béda will not desist.[1] But since we have come by chance into this mad
age, the mind must be fortified against every eventuality. I fear that the spark   5
of this war will grow into a great fire.[2] Zwingli has his judgment among men;
may he find a milder one with God.[3]

Whenever you come, you will be most welcome, provided that it is
done at your convenience, but I advised you not to hurry, so that, as you

* * * * *

13 Undoubtedly Erasmus' fearsome housekeeper Margarete Büsslin (Ep 2202 n4)
14 On Ephorinus' role as a prescriber and supplier of medications, cf Ep 2554 n14.
15 Virgil *Aeneid* 9.641

2561
1 See Ep 2552:19 with n10.
2 Ie the Second Kappel War; see Ep 2559 n6.
3 See Ep 2559:17–18 with n7.

are so conscientiously obliging, you would not come here with any inconve-   10
nience to yourself. From a letter of Anselmus I understand that he does not
intend to return as my guest.⁴ Therefore I must welcome another house guest
to relieve the boredom of solitude. This house is big enough to welcome you
and your entire household.

Two days ago Anton Fugger sent me his personal messenger to an-   15
nounce to me that his home and fireplaces are ready;⁵ he offers all his fortunes, if I should wish to come, and all of this with wondrous affection.
Would that he had written this to me before I bought this house.⁶ I put the
matter off until the next swallow. I could not do otherwise. Winter is upon us
and all through Germany vapours hostile to me are boiling.   20

It is not my place to counsel you, excellent friend. You have your Pallas
Athena at home to suggest to you what is best to be done.⁷ Farewell.

24 October 1531

Your Erasmus of Rotterdam

To the most illustrious doctor of laws Master Bonifacius Amerbach. In   25
Basel

2561A / From Bonifacius Amerbach   [Basel, after 24 October 1531]

The manuscript of this letter (= AK Ep 1578) is an autograph rough draft in the
Öffentliche Bibliothek of the University of Basel (MS C VIA 73 241 verso). Allen,
who was the first to publish the letter, took it to be Bonifacius' answer to Ep
2556 and published it as Ep 2560 with the date 'c 19 October 1531.' But the AK
editor, Alfred Hartmann, has argued persuasively that the letter has to have
been written after 24 October. It is in a letter written on that date (Ep 2561:1–3)
that Erasmus first describes his health in terms justifying the optimism expressed by Bonifacius in lines 1–3 of this letter. It is, moreover, in the same letter
(lines 13–14) that Erasmus invites Bonifacius to move with his whole family
into his new house in Freiburg. This renders comprehensible Bonifacius' remark in lines 13–14 of this letter that some would accuse him of flight or worse
if he were to go to see Erasmus, an accusation that would make no sense if it
were just a matter of one of Bonifacius' occasional brief visits to Erasmus.

* * * * *

4 Ep 2559
5 The letter is not extant. For Fugger's earlier invitations to Erasmust to settle in
   Augsburg see Ep 2476 n1.
6 See Ep 2506 n1.
7 Presumably a reference to his wife, Martha Fuchs

Cordial greetings. Your letter brings good news.[1] For 'since love is a thing full of anxious fear,'[2] I was worried that you were feeling worse than you now are, as I learn from your letter. Therefore, if there is no hurry, as you write, I will remain at home for a few days because of troubles that have in the meantime suddenly arisen again among the Swiss.[3] I myself was enrolled   5
in the militia by my countrymen, who, I think, were trying their hardest to make a soldier in arms out of a soldier in a toga (as Justinian somewhere calls lawyers).[4] But I obtained my discharge by supplying a replacement, unskilled as I am in nothing as much as military service.

What a wretched age, dear Erasmus! May Christ grant that we give an   10
example of his meekness, not so much in words as in reality, lest while we enjoy being called Evangelicals we perhaps be regarded as good talkers.[5] Without a doubt there will be no lack of those who accuse me of flight, not to say something worse, if I were to move there, just as there is nothing now that is not seized upon for calumny. But confident of my innocence, I will   15
easily tolerate all of it if you think I should set out as soon as possible. I ask you all the more urgently to inform me about this by the first courier. Look after your health as much as possible, I pray you, and be assured that nothing more pleasing could happen to me than to know that you are in the best of health. Farewell.
                                                                          20

2562 / From Alonso de Fonseca   Alcalá, 31 October 1531

This letter was first published by Allen from a manuscript (an eighteenth-century copy) that was in a private collection assembled in Spain (1846–7) by Dr Gottfried Heine of Berlin. In 1907 the then owner of the collection gave Allen permission to examine, copy, and publish the letters. The subsequent fate of the collection is not known. See Allen IV 620–3 and CWE 8 336.

For Alonso Fonseca, archbishop of Toledo, see Ep 1748 introduction.

* * * * *

2561A
1 Ep 2561
2 Ovid *Heroides* 1.12
3 Ie the Second Kappel War (Ep 2559 n6), in which no troops from Basel had taken part, but as a result of which all the Protestant cantons were for a time fearful of further military conflict in the confederation
4 *Codex* 2.4.14
5 For 'good talkers' Bonifacius uses the Greek word χρηστολόγοι (*chrestologoi*), a play on words with Χριστός (*Christos*).

ALONSO DE FONSECA, ARCHBISHOP OF TOLEDO, PRIMATE OF SPAIN,
ETC TO HIS FRIEND DESIDERIUS ERASMUS OF ROTTERDAM, GREETING
For a long time now no letter of yours has been sent to me, but neither have
you received a letter from me; therefore it is fitting that we mutually pardon
a mutual neglect.[1] I wish you to be assured that nothing in my earlier senti-   5
ments towards you has for this reason been diminished or changed, and I
hope that this is true reciprocally. The occasion that prompted me to write
now was the departure of your friend Dilft,[2] whom I did not wish to leave
for a visit to his native country without a letter from me to you. I have seen
with pleasure the works of Augustine which you refashioned, so to speak, by   10
your toils.[3] I shall take care that you understand how gratifying your dedication was to me, especially if I shall be given the opportunity of visiting you,
as I had recently decided, in compliance with the authority of the emperor,
who wished me to attend the Diet of Speyer, which, so it was believed, was
imminent at the time. As I was preparing my departure, I was surprised by   15
a message that the date of the diet had been put off to a later time, and that
it would be held in Regensburg on the Epiphany of the Lord.[4] That message
has caused a delay in my plans until I receive definite information about the
departure of the emperor; I will make my decision based on that. Let us hope
at any rate that public affairs will progress to the point that some fruit will   20
result from their labours. I was of the opinion that these labours were of very
great importance, but I fear that we must await something greater than human powers. At any event, however, I would like to see you and men who,
like you, are of outstanding learning, eloquence, and piety, ready to extinguish the widespread fire. I would hope that God will support your efforts.   25

* * * * *

2562
1 Fonseca's most recent surviving letter to Erasmus is Ep 2003; Erasmus' to
   Fonseca is Ep 2353A.
2 After an unsuccessful visit to Spain in 1528 in search of employment, Erasmus'
   famulus Frans van der Dilft (Ep 1663) returned to Spain in 1530, carrying letters of recommendation from Erasmus, and this time secured employment
   with Fonseca (Ep 2348). The final paragraph of this letter makes clear that he
   was expected to return to Spain, which he evidently did, only to return to the
   Netherlands for good in 1533.
3 The Froben ten-volume edition of the *Opera omnia* of St Augustine was published in the autumn of 1529, with a dedicatory letter addressed to Fonseca (Ep
   2157).
4 See Ep 2511 n20.

Your friend Dilft, whom we first admitted to our service on your recommendation and then through personal acquaintance, we have held and will continue to hold in great esteem as a good and learned man, and we will make every effort to confer benefits on him when he returns, for we have found him to be most worthy of your recommendation and our generosity.[5] Farewell. 30
From our city of Alcalá, 31 October 1531

2563 / From Juan de Vergara Alcalá, 31 October 1531

The manuscript of this letter, which is in the Biblioteca Nacional at Madrid (MS C 38 no 16), is an eighteenth-century copy written in the same hand as that found in some of the letters of the Heine Collection (see Ep 2562 introduction). On the back the same hand has written: 'To Desid. Erasmus per Dilft' (cf Ep 2562:7–9). The letter was first published by A. Bonilla y San Martin in *Clarorum Hispaniensium Epistolae ineditae* 72–3 = *Revue Hispanique* VIII (1901) 246–7.

For Juan de Vergara, secretary to Alonso de Fonseca, archbishop of Toledo, and a faithful friend and champion of Erasmus in Spain, see Epp 1277, 1814.

JUAN DE VERGARA, THEOLOGIAN, TO ERASMUS OF ROTTERDAM, GREETING

If I were to plead in excuse to you either my official occupations, with which, for that matter, I am continually distracted, or the paucity of couriers, I know that I would be wasting my time. You are well acquainted with these ordi- 5 nary excuses.

First of all, however, I have the highest regard for you, as I have always had, and I am confident that I have your love as well.

Association with your friend Dilft has been most gratifying, so that we are much indebted to you for your recommendation. He is an upright, 10 loyal, and well-born man.[1] Since you will learn from him all that pertains to us, there is no necessity for my dwelling on it at present. Merely keep in mind that I shall cede to no one in loyalty and duty to you when the occasion presents itself.

Farewell. Alcalá, 31 October 1531 15

* * * * *

5 Cf Ep 2563:9–11.

2563
1 Cf Ep 2562:26–30.

2563A / From Johannes Dantiscus   [Brussels, end of October 1531]

The manuscript of this letter, which was unknown to Allen, was discovered by Henry de Vocht in a collection of the letters of Johannes Dantiscus in the Czartoryski Museum at Cracow (DE 230: CCM, 1615, 13015). De Vocht published a summary of its contents, with brief excerpts, in *John Dantiscus and His Netherlandish Friends* (Louvain 1961) 104–8. The manuscript, which has no date and is signed only 'J,' is a copy in the hand of a secretary. Given the available information, there is no reason to doubt de Vocht's identification of the author as Dantiscus: there was no one else at the imperial court at the time who had a history of friendly correspondence with Erasmus (see lines 1–3), who would have used the initial 'J,' and whose letter would likely have turned up in an archive in Cracow. The approximate date assigned by de Vocht is confirmed by the contents of the letter. In lines 3–5, 31–3 Erasmus is said to have announced the purchase of a new house in a letter of 17 July, the answer to which 'J' postponed until it could accompany a copy of Charles v's letter of 1 October 1531 to the city council of Besançon on Erasmus' behalf. The reference (lines 92–3) to the intended meeting of the imperial diet at Speyer, which on 15 October had been postponed until January 1532 at Regensburg, makes it likely that the letter was written in the second half of October, at which time the imperial court was still in Brussels (cf Ep 2567:21). This is the first publication anywhere of a complete text of the letter. The Latin original is reproduced on pages 392–4 below.

For Johannes Dantiscus cf Ep 2163 n34 (where it is stated without warrant that this letter was never sent). In 1524 Dantiscus was sent as Polish ambassador to the imperial court in Spain. He accompanied the court on its journey to Italy and Germany in 1529–30, went with it to the Netherlands in 1531, and stayed with it until recalled to Poland in 1532. The reference in lines 95–111 to a possible meeting with Erasmus in Speyer indicates that Dantiscus expected the imperial court to be there on its way to Regensburg. This is the only letter of Dantiscus to Erasmus to have survived; Erasmus' only surviving letter to Dantiscus is Ep 2643, the dedicatory letter to Basil's *De Spiritu Sancto*.

Cordial greetings. Even though I do not dedicate myself to any task more willingly or with greater pleasure than reading your letters or writing my letters to you, I nevertheless deferred answering your letter of 17 July so that I could add to it the letter of the emperor to the city council and clergy of Besançon (which you had requested).[1] I should not wish that my fidelity   5

* * * * *

2563A
1 Erasmus' letter of 17 July is not extant. The emperor's letter is Ep 2553.

appear suspect on the grounds of negligence. Now at last I write back to you
and send the letter of the emperor, which he willingly granted, a gesture that
exceeded the expectations and surmises of many, so that you may make use
of it when circumstances and necessity demand it. You would hardly believe,
my dear Erasmus, how perverse are the judgments of men here also, how   10
depraved their minds and ever more prone to evil, how ignorance reigns
everywhere, how tongues, dipped in poison, inveigh against men's reputa-
tions, no matter how well deserving they are, and declare all lovers of good
letters heretics or, at all events, the patrons of heretics. With what weapons
do they not stab you, as if you were the originator of all the dissensions in   15
Germany, immortal God! and not only within the confines of their homes but
also in the crowded assemblies of men, and not only among their fellow bab-
blers, but sometimes even in the presence of the emperor. But the singular
good will of the emperor triumphs over all this, as you will readily gather
from his letter, if you will have it translated from French into Latin. I did   20
not want it to be written in Latin, but in French, that is, the emperor's own
language, lest the favourable opinion he has formed of you be attributed to
my affection for you, and that what he proclaims in the most honorific terms
concerning your virtues seem to be composed by me (which I also would
love to do). Consequently, you ought to preserve it as a symbol of his un-   25
wavering good will towards you and of his high opinion of your virtue and
erudition. I have said this not to prove my devotion to you (I know that you
are perfectly aware that this person, in his entirety, is yours), but so that you
may recognize more and more through many examples how manifest the
emperor's favour has been towards you for a long time.   30

I come now to your letter, in which you write that you have bought
a house in Freiburg and that you are building an Italian fireplace and preparing a winter nest.[2] But what is this I hear? Erasmus the philosopher and
almost seventy years old has bought a house? And yet Diogenes was happy
with a jar,[3] and perhaps you will experience more troubles with your house   35
than he suffered with his jar. But, I ask you, for what heirs, or how is it possible that a house can be divided among so many heirs? I call heirs of Erasmus
not those related to him by blood but those whom you generated for Christ,
whom you adorned and enriched with virtues; now consider whether your
house will suffice for so many heirs. But, joking aside, what spirit persuaded   40

* * * * *

2 See Epp 2506 n1, 2517 n11.
3 See Ep 2518 n4.

you to buy a house, and in Germany, full of discord; do you not see into what times we have fallen? Does it not come to mind how many evils all these events portend for us? What do the two comets mean? What of the rainbow appearing in the sky in the second hour after sunset and forty-three […] seen after the full moon.[4] Sinister voices were heard in the Vatican. There were   45
three suns in the city of Troia in Apulia. There were three moons in Liège, fountains of blood, rains of bread, and twins of whom, they say, as soon as they were born, one said, 'Where will we put so much wheat?' and the other, 'But where will we store so many cadavers?' Three fiery diadems were seen for nine days over Jerusalem, which then fell with great impetus and   50
destroyed the part of the temple that faces east. What if I were to write about the other portents that were seen here and there, which I will omit, lest we stir up a hornets' nest. In whom would these things not inspire the greatest terror, including one to whom the twelfth hour is already at hand, as I read Crassus said to King Deiotarus in Plutarch?[5] You are buying a house, and in   55
Germany? And is this not like a portent? And is that which the Parisian faculty writes against Erasmus not much different from a portent?[6] And is this not the greatest portent of all, that this faculty, to which all had recourse, as if it were the oracle of Apollo, gave such an example of itself? Believe me, to speak frankly, at first sight the censure of the Parisian faculty struck fear into   60
me, not because I feared that it had detected something less than Christian in your books, but because I was sad that the monks of the faculty, celebrated for its authority, would mount a triumph. But when I looked into the matter with care, so help me God, I could not refrain from laughter when I saw that so many men had collected so much ignorance, so much nonsense, calumny,   65
and humbug, and that while they attempted to make you into a heretic, they betrayed their own malice and ignorance and added further recommendation of your learning to all learned and good men. I remember that I often tried to persuade you to abandon those who write against you to their own malady and to judge them unworthy of your response. At this point I think   70

* * * * *

4 It appears that a word or phrase is missing from he manuscript at this point. Among these portents would have been Halley's comet, which appeared in 1531.
5 Plutarch *Life of Crassus* 17
6 Dantiscus writes *Academia Parisiensis*, but he is clearly referring to the Paris faculty of theology and its recently published *Determinatio* against Erasmus; see Ep 2552 n10.

you must deal differently with these Parisian rabbis of yours.[7] You should first examine the matter discreetly, and if you discover some comments that are not altogether inappropriate, you may thank them for this friendly office and correct this in your works, even if it seems to you that there is no great need of correction. For there is no more effective weapon for delivering a mortal blow than conceding to them in some insignificant matters so that they will not be able to accuse you of obstinacy. When you have done that you can treat them as you wish, disregarding from then on people like Zúñiga, Lee, Béda, Duchesne, Cousturier, Egmondanus, Carvajal, and all other creatures of that ilk who never cease to rave against you,[8] and contending with these rabbis.[9] Treat these men as they deserve and show them who Erasmus is, what kind of scholar they have provoked, into what stone they have stumbled, and then – as you have often demonstrated on other occasions in much less important matters – show them what kind of man you are. Their shamelessness and insults will shed lustre (believe me) on your dignity. But in writing this to you, I must not myself be impudent with someone who has employed or will employ these tactics far better and more prudently than I am able to devise, let alone give written advice.

If you will forgive my audacity, I should like to know how things stand with you after the uprising of the Swiss,[10] and whether the situation is more tranquil there. I am afraid that you cannot take up residence elsewhere, leaving your winter nest. We hoped that the emperor would assemble a diet at Speyer,[11] and that you would come to us or we to you, so that the friendship initiated through letters could be confirmed through conversation and a formal handshake. But as you see, this opportunity has been denied us, for a meeting at Regensburg has been announced, and if it is not inconvenient for you, let us see each other in Speyer. As far as I am concerned, I would prefer to come to Freiburg rather than that you undertake such hardship

* * * * *

7 'Rabbis' was a term often applied derisively to conservative theologians; cf Ep 1334 n26.
8 See Epp 1260 n36, 2172 (Diego López Zúñiga); 1341A:823–30, 2094 n8 (Edward Lee); 2552 n10 (Noël Béda); 1188 n15 (Guillaume Duchesne); 1804 n65 (Pierre Cousturier); 1254 n6 (Nicolaas Baechem, known as Egmondanus); 2110 n10 (Luis de Carvajal).
9 Dantiscus appears to have forgotten, or perhaps not yet to be aware, that Noël Béda was the chief 'rabbi' in this case.
10 Se Ep 2559 n6.
11 See Ep 2511 n20.

and disturbance for our sake. However, because of my public engagements
I doubt that I shall be able to come. There are so many of us who very much   100
desire to see you: the patriarch of the Indies, patron of all good men;[12] the
distinguished commander of the equestrian order of Calatrava, a man of
great moral integrity and authority with the emperor;[13] then the archdeacon
of Toledo, a young man devoted to you and endowed with talent and intelligence far beyond his years, on whom Fortune and the Graces have show-   105
ered their gifts in great abundance.[14] We are also expecting the archbishop of
Toledo, whose admiration for you is too well known to need my testimony.[15]
There are many other nobles who would be reluctant to leave Germany without greeting you. If you join us in Speyer you will do something very pleasing to us and not without profit or gratification for yourself (not, however, at   110
the risk of your health). Again and again I beg you to come. Farewell. J.

* * * * *

12 Estéban Gabriel Merino (c 1472–1535), since 1513 archbishop of Bari, and since
    1523 bishop of Jaén, the diocese of his birth. Esteemed for his services as an
    administrator and diplomat and for his loyalty to Charles v, he was admitted
    to the emperor's council of state in 1526 and accompanied the emperor to Italy,
    Germany, and the Netherlands in 1529–32. In September 1530 he was given
    the honorific title of patriarch of the West Indies, and in 1533 he was created
    cardinal. See J. Goñi 'Merino, Esteban Gabriel' *Diccionario de historia eclesiástica
    de España,* Supplement 1 (Madrid 1987) 483–9.
13 García de Padilla (d 1542), about whom little is known apart from the long list
    of his offices and titles in the service of Charles v and his signature on impor-
    tant state documents. Clearly someone who had studied law at a university,
    he was (from 1523) knight-commander of the military order of Calatrava (the
    title by which he was known), president of the council of the military orders
    of Calatrava and Alcántara, member of the council of Castile (1526–42), and
    the emperor's countersigner (*referendario*). He accompanied the emperor on his
    journey to Italy, Germany, and the Netherlands in 1529–32. In the list of the
    participants in that journey, he is described as 'a man of great learning and
    integrity, worthy to be at the side of such a prince.' See Pedro Girón *Crónica
    del Emperador Carlos v* ed Juan Sanchez Montes (Madrid 1964) 9; Fernando de
    Cotta y Márquez de Prado *Descripción del Sacro Convento y Castillo de Calatrava
    la Nueva ...* ([Madrid s n] 1961) 28 n92; Aurelio Espinosa *The Empire of the Cities:
    Emperor Charles v, the Comunero Revolt, and the Transformation of the Spanish
    System* (Leiden 2009) 148, 170 n138. Judging by what Dantiscus says about him
    here, the name Garcia de Padilla is to be added to the list of Erasmus' admirers
    at the imperial court.
14 Francisco de Mendoza y Bobadilla (1508–66), future cardinal, patron of the
    Jesuits, and leading representative of Spanish humanism; cf Ep 1805 n82.
15 Alonso de Fonseca (Ep 2562)

Julius Caesar Scaliger

2564 / From Bonifacius Amerbach   [Basel, c beginning of November 1531]

This letter (= AK Ep 1583), first published by Allen, is Bonifacius' reply to Ep 2561. The manuscript is an autograph rough draft in the Öffentliche Bibliothek of the University of Basel (MS C VIa 73 239 verso). Allen assigned the approximate date on the basis of Ep 2574:1–2, where Bonifacius mentions having sent Scaliger's book (n2) 'recently'; Ep 2565:23–4, which indicates that by 7 November Erasmus had already seen the book; and the references to Erasmus' health and Bonifacius' proposed visit, which indicate that the letter has to have been written later than Ep 2561 of 24 October.

I received yesterday evening from Paris, from one of your admirers,[1] the oration of a certain Scaliger,[2] who from a first sampling seems worthy of the

* * * * *

2564
1 Not Philippus Montanus, as assumed by Allen (who calls him 'Jo.'), but Johann Sphyractes (AK Ep 1490 introduction), a native of Basel who had taught briefly (1529–30) in the city's Latin school and was now studying law at Paris. See his letter to Bonifacius, 1 October 1531 (AK Ep 1571:21–5), which accompanied the copy of Scaliger's *Oratio* (see following note).
2 *Julii Caesaris Scaligeri Oratio pro M. Tullio Cicerone contra Des. Erasmum Roterodamum* (Paris: Gilles Gourmont and Pierre Vidoue, September 1531). Julius Caesar Scaliger (1484–1558) claimed to have been born into the prominent della Scala family of Verona, but he was in fact the son of a manuscript illuminator in Padua named Benedetto Bordon. After earning a doctorate in arts at Padua (1519) and working for a time on an Italian translation of Plutarch, Scaliger settled at Agen in southern France (1524) as the physician to the bishop, Antonio delle Rovere. In 1528 he became a naturalized French citizen and married a well-to-do French woman who bore him fifteen children, one of whom, Joseph Justus, became a far more famous scholar than his father. In 1529, enraged at what he took to be Erasmus' denigration of Cicero in the *Ciceronianus*, Scaliger wrote his oration, in which he denounced Erasmus for slandering not only Cicero but the Christian religion as well. It took Scaliger two years to find a printer, finally doing so with the help of Erasmus' ancient foe in Paris, Noël Béda. Shown the work, Erasmus instantly concluded that 'Julius Caesar Scaliger' was a pseudonym for his old adversary Girolamo Aleandro, and continued to believe that Aleandro was behind the work even after being assured that Scaliger was a real person; see Ep 2565 n12. Despite his resentment of the *Oratio*, Erasmus never deemed it worthy of a public response. When, however, Scaliger came across the 1536 reprint of the preface to Cicero's *Tusculanae disputationes* that Erasmus had written for Froben's 1523 edition of the work, he read Erasmus' praise for Cicero as evidence that the author of the *Ciceronianus* had seen the error of his ways and declared his readiness to be reconciled with

Gemonian steps.[3] I send it to you so that in case you do not yet have it, you may read this nonsense, if you have the time. But if you do have it, send it back to me so that I can employ some good hours badly in reading it. I will 5 keep it safe and will not lend it to anyone. But take care, my dear Erasmus, not to be perturbed by this kind of rubbish. The reputation of your name, with that of all the best men of every nation, has taken root too deeply to be violated, still less extirpated, by anyone's slander; the recognition of your valour is too great for any slander to have any rights over it. Remember 10 what is said of most good and saintly men, and that Jerome did not lack his Rufinus[4] nor our Saviour – he who was the most perfect being that the world has ever seen – the Pharisees. What is so strange if you too suffer in your turn? Envy attacks greatness and, as the poet said: 'Envy is better than pity.'[5]

In other matters, the reason I have not come to see you is that in your 15 letter you gave me the opportunity of staying here longer, saying that there was no need for hurrying,[6] and also because Enyo is still sounding her trumpet among the Swiss.[7] Our envoys returned. It is uncertain what the outcome of this affair will be.[8] Although I would not willingly leave here at the moment for the reasons about which I wrote to you recently,[9] nevertheless, if 20 you wish to call upon my aid now, I will be there immediately. Farewell.

* * * * *

him. But it was too late. Scaliger subsequently earned much greater fame for more important works of scholarship, particularly his systematic treatments of Latin grammar, poetics, and natural philosophy.

3 This is a play on the name Scaliger, which derives from *scala*, the word for 'step' in both Latin and Italian. The Gemonian steps were on the Aventine in Rome; the bodies of executed criminals were dragged down them into the Tiber.

4 As translator of Origen and champion of his orthodoxy, Rufinus of Aquileia (c 345–410) became involved in a bitter dispute with St Jerome, who found his translations tendentious, a view that Erasmus shared (see Epp 1844:72–8, 2569:18–19, 2611:117–18).

5 Pindar *Pythian Odes* 1.64

6 Epp 2556:3–5, 2561:8–11

7 Enyo was a Greek goddess of war.

8 Following the battle of Kappel (11 October 1531), which brought an end to the Second Kappel War (Ep 2525 n3), there were negotiations that produced (24 November 1531) the Second Peace of Kappel, by which the Swiss Confederation became the first polity divided by the Reformation to establish religious peace on the basis of the principle later formulated as *cuius regio eius religio*, in this case the right of each canton to choose and maintain its own form of worship, free of outside interference. It would take the Holy Roman Empire another twenty-four years to achieve a similar settlement.

9 Presumably a reference to Bonifacius' difficult negotiations with the city authorities of Basel; see Ep 2551:7–10.

2565 / To Johann Koler   [Freiburg], 7 November 1531

The letter was first published as Ep 18 in Horawitz I. The autograph is in the
Austrian National Library at Vienna (Cod 9737c folio 9). For Koler see Ep 2505.

Cordial greetings. Curses on this gout of the hand, and may it migrate to
those worthy of such an evil. I have never had any doubts about the sentiments of Fugger.[1] I have to pass the winter in this nest. I expect a terrible tragedy. The archbishop Girolamo Aleandro is now with the emperor
as legate with full powers,[2] and I do not doubt that he went to Paris and   5
moved Camarina among the theologians so that they would publish the
Determinationes.[3] At the same time Eck was there;[4] that he suddenly began
to rage ferociously against me is owed, no doubt, to a letter of Aleandro.
When Aleandro brought the bull against Luther here about nine years ago,[5]
he came with the intention to destroy Erasmus rather than to do anything   10
against Luther, nor did he try to quell these rumours. And at that time he
did all in his power to annihilate me, but he did not succeed. Now he is more
exasperated because in my response to Alberto Pio he is often referred to as
the 'bull-bearer.'[6] A certain courtier, close to the emperor, has intimated to me
that these meetings of princes and consultations with scholars are nothing   15
other than ceremonies, but in reality everything is done by order of the pope

* * * * *

2565
1 See Ep 2476.
2 Aleandro (Ep 2482 nn3–4) departed from Rome as papal nuncio to the imperial court around the beginning of September 1531, arriving at Brussels on 2
   November. On 17 January 1532 he left Brussels with the emperor, reaching
   Regensburg on 28 February. See Allen's note and *Lettres familières de Jérôme
   Aléandre* ed J. Paquier (Paris 1909) 142 n1.
3 On the *Determinatio* of the Paris theologians see Ep 2552 n10. Erasmus' accusation that Aleandro had been at Paris and was behind the *Determinatio*, repeated in Epp 2578:31–2 and 2587:12–13, was entirely unfounded. In July 1532
   Aleandro would write to Erasmus that he had not seen Paris for eighteen years
   (Allen Ep 2679:25–6). On 'moving Camarina,' ie stirring up needless trouble,
   see *Adagia* I i 64.
4 In Ep 2587:11–12 Erasmus repeats this charge that Johann Eck (Ep 2503 n3) had
   been at Paris, but the 'Itinerarium Io. Eckii' in Theodor Wiedemann *Dr. Johann
   Eck, Professor der Theologie an der Universität Ingolstadt* (Regensburg 1865) 435–44
   records no visit by Eck to France.
5 In 1520, in his capacity as papal nuncio to the imperial court, Aleandro had
   been responsible for the publication and execution of the bull *Exsurge Domine*,
   which gave Luther sixty days to recant his errors or face excommunication.
6 *Diplomatophorus*; see Ep 2443 n43.

HIERONYMVS ALEANDER ARCHIEPISCOPVS
BRVNDVSINVS, ET ORITANVS, ETC.
M · D · XXXVI

Girolamo Aleandro

through secret emissaries.[7] Alberto Pio and Aleandro were of one mind, and the pope has great esteem for both of them.[8] Charles is preparing a meeting with the French and English kings.[9] The diet at Speyer faded away,[10] and there is no doubt that all these things are done by order of the pope, who   20
summoned all the cardinals to Rome for Christmas. This seemed to him the best way to lull to sleep the dissensions of the world.

A defamatory and simply mad book has been published in Paris under the fictitious name of Julius Caesar Scaliger.[11] But I recognize the style of Aleandro no less than I know the face.[12] I am not so stupid as not to under-   25
stand what these preambles are aimed at. I have Aleandro with the emperor,[13] Béda in Paris, Lee in England, Eck in Germany,[14] Nachtgall with Ferdinand,[15] monks and theologians everywhere. We are waiting for the end of the play; may God will that it be a happy one. They made sure that the censures of the faculty of theology of Paris, inept and purely slanderous as they are,   30
were published so that they could say to the princes: 'Here is the judgment of the most prestigious faculty on Erasmus.' Nachtgall last summer visited France, and he spoke with Sadoleto, bishop of Carpentras.[16] He shared with Nachtgall some secret plan to oppress the sects. Nachtgall boasted of this in Basel. I suspect that on this occasion he was summoned to Ferdinand. I   35
have already responded to the censures of the theologians. I will see to it

* * * * *

7   Cf Ep 2366:20–2 with n7.
8   See Ep 1987 introduction.
9   Cf Ep 2558 n16.
10 See Ep 2511 n20.
11 Ep 2564
12 Erasmus repeats this accusation in Epp 2575:6–8, 2579:34–7, 2581:4–5, 2613:43–8. Even after Aleandro's lengthy denial of the charge (Epp 2638, 2639), and assurance from François Rabelais that Scaliger was a real person (Ep 2743), Erasmus refused to be budged from his conviction that Aleandro was behind the *Oratio* (Epp 3005, 3127).
13 See n2 above.
14 See Epp 2552 n10 (Noël Béda); 1341A:8, 2094 n8 (Edward Lee); 2357 n1, 2503 n3, 2513 n42 (Johann Eck).
15 Ottmar Nachtgall, whom Erasmus had come to dislike and distrust as a result of a quarrel over their joint occupancy of the house in which Erasmus first lived after his move to Freiburg (Ep 2166 n3)
16 Nachtgall appears to have carried a letter no longer extant to Sadoleto at Carpentras, along with other letters entrusted to him by Erasmus in the spring of 1531; cf Ep 2472 introduction. It is not known what substance there may have been to the suspicions expressed in the following sentences.

that they are published,[17] although there is nothing there to which I have not responded ten times, to Lee, Béda, Pio, etc.

I do not want these things to be divulged to the populace; if you wish, however, you may communicate them to the reverend lord bishop of Augsburg.

Farewell. 7 November 1531

Give my affectionate greetings to the Rems,[18] to whom I will write soon, if Christ so wishes it.

Your friend, Erasmus of Rotterdam, extempore   45

To the honourable Master Johann Koler, provost of Chur. In Augsburg

2566 / From Maarten Lips   [Croix-à-Lens, November 1531]

This letter was first published by Allen, using the undated and unsigned autograph in the Öffentliche Bibliothek of the University of Basel (MS KI AR 25a folio 114). There is also an abstract of it (incorrectly dated at 1519) in Horawitz III 4–9, based on a copy in the Simler Collection of the Zentralbibliothek at Zürich. Maarten Lips (Epp 750, 1837, 2045) was Erasmus' friend, fellow Augustinian canon, and valued collaborator on many scholarly projects. Once a member of the priory of St Maartensdal in Louvain, where conflicts had arisen because of his friendship for Erasmus, he was now chaplain of the Augustinian nunnery of Croix-à-Lens at Lens-Saint-Rémy in the province of Liège.

This letter, the last one to survive from the correspondence between Erasmus and Lips, is the latter's reply to a letter from Erasmus that is no longer extant. The assigned year-date 1531 is evident from the references (lines 44–5, 210–11) to the Paris *Determinatio* and Erasmus' expected answer to it (Ep 2552 n10). As for the month-date, Lips excuses the tardiness of his reply on the grounds that he had been away from home (lines 3–5), and then mentions (line 44) that he was on a visit to Louvain 'in October,' which makes clear that the letter was not written before November. On the other hand, he refers (lines 201–2) to the expected arrival of Aleandro at Brussels, which took place on 2 November (Ep 2565 n2). Since Lips would not long have remained unaware of the nuncio's arrival, the letter has to have been written in the early days of November. It appears that 'towards the end of November,' before receiving the present letter, Erasmus wrote Lips another letter, also not extant, which reached Lips only after he had written this reply to the first letter; see Ep 2587:68.

* * * * *

17 See Ep 2552 n10.
18 Ie to Wolfgang Andreas Rem (Ep 2419) and his father, Wolfgang Rem (Ep 2269 n2)

Greetings. If I reply a little late to a letter of my friend Erasmus, neither sloth-
fulness nor diminished affection are to blame, but a firm mental resolution
that I wanted to write more fully and more abundantly about various things
that pertain to you, but I was not able to have exact knowledge of these
things until I had completed my journeys. Now therefore let us turn to your 5
letter, leaving aside for a moment the introduction, in which you attempt to
win my good will by wishing for poor little me liberty, a library, fortune, and
the acquaintance of learned men.

ERASMUS *The passage that displeased you about Jesus, who, sitting on the*
mountainside, mourned the fall of Jerusalem, is found at Mark 13, etc.[1] I looked 10
at Mark but did not find any of this. It was not when he was sitting on the
mountainside that he said, 'Not one stone shall be left,' etc, but when he
was coming out of the temple and was making his way to the mountain.
Matthew describes the same scene a little more clearly in chapter 24, saying
that Jesus, coming out of the temple and going to the Mount of Olives, said 15
to his disciples, 'Amen, I say to you, not one stone shall be left, etc.'[2] Then,
seated upon the mountain, he wove a long sermon about the last days, unless
perhaps you interpret a single brief phrase – 'when you see the abomination
of desolation' – as referring to the fall of the city of Jerusalem.[3] But even if I
grant that Mark wrote that these things were said by Jesus on the mountain, 20
I will not concede at the same time that he wrote that Jesus mourned the
fall of Jerusalem there. The fall of Jerusalem is described in Matthew 21 and
Luke 19.[4] But in Mark 13 and Matthew 24 the ruin of the temple is predicted.
You seem to identify the fall of the city and the destruction of the temple,
when obviously in one place the disaster of the city is described and in an- 25
other place the destruction of the temple. When Jesus saw the destruction of
the city of Jerusalem he wept bitter tears; when he predicted the ruin of the
temple we do not read that he wept. There is nothing so carelessly written
that it does not admit of an excuse, and I well see your objection to what I
wrote. But I would prefer that you write in such a way that there is no need 30
of such excuses. And, unless I am mistaken, you could accomplish this if
you wrote that Jesus on the mountain wept at the destruction of the temple,
for that is what the gospel says explicitly, while there is no clear mention

* * * * *

2566
1 Mark 13:1–2
2 Matt 24:1–2
3 Matt 24:15
4 Luke 19:41–4 (cf Luke 21:20–4). There is nothing in Matthew 21 about the fall of
Jerusalem. Lips is probably thinking of Matt 23:37–9.

of the city.⁵ This is the gist of the matter. I have no other request but that
you write with circumspection, if possible. You have not found me to be   35
an obstinate or contentious person. I simply note down whatever occurs to
me. If you do not acquiesce, if you disagree, I will not take it badly, nor will
I take exception to it defiantly or in an insulting manner. Besides, to speak
truthfully, I don't know now what I wrote to you either about Jesus sitting
on the mountainside, or Judas son of James, or James the Righteous,⁶ or the   40
investigation of genealogies. I do not save copies of my annotations.

ERASMUS *Winghe is true to himself. He does not hate Erasmus, etc.* Since
you mentioned this man,⁷ I will report to you what happened between us
when I was in Louvain in the month of October. We were discussing the
censure of the faculty of Paris,⁸ which your enemies call the Condemnation   45
of Erasmus. When I said that I was fed up with responses, and that I wished
that you would come to a holy agreement with one another once and for
all, Winghe responded, 'This will never happen until Erasmus yields,' in-
sinuating that you were obstinate and did not want to concede to anyone.
I answered, 'In what things do you want him to yield? You undermine the   50
good together with the bad.' 'Ja,' said Winghe,' is this what you say?' indicating that everything that the Parisians criticized was to be condemned. I also
found a letter in his cell in which he shows why I and others who favour
you do not have the right frame of mind in examining your works, while he

* * * * *

5 Having just insisted, with ample citation of biblical texts, that Jesus did not
   weep over the destruction of the temple but only over the destruction of the
   city of Jerusalem, and that on the mountain his sole concern was the destruction of the city rather than that of the temple, Lips concludes by advising
   Erasmus to say exactly the opposite, namely that Jesus on the mountain wept
   over the destruction of the temple, with no clear reference to the city. Without
   the text of the letter to which Lips is responding we cannot know for sure
   what, if anything, there may have been in it that would dispel this glaring
   contradiction.
6 The apostle Judas son of James (also known as Thaddeus, not to be confused
   with Judas Iscariot), and James the brother of Jesus (also known as James the
   Righteous). For Erasmus' interest in the thorny problem of identifying the various Jameses and Judases in the New Testament and distinguishing them from
   one another, see the introductions to Epp 2181 and 2184.
7 Nicolaas van Winghe (c 1495–1552), Augustinian canon of St Maartensdal in
   Louvain, was an unswerving opponent of Erasmus and thus a thorn in the side
   of his fellow monk Maarten Lips. He is remembered chiefly for his Flemish
   translation of the Bible (1548).
8 The *Determinatio* of the Paris theologians (Ep 2552 n10)

and his followers are very well suited for it. We, in discussing your books, 55
are either totally blinded by love or have no powers of discernment or, if we
use our judgment when our conscience stimulates us to a love of truth, our
judgment is naïve, not exact, not rigorous. But Winghe maintains in that letter that your books are to be read with judgment, rigorous judgment. I have
aroused your annoyance by my use of such judgment, but my judgment was 60
not rigorous according to the prescription of Winghe. To the contrary, it was
unsophisticated, insipid, puerile, sweeping together many trivialities that
provoked your disgust.

ERASMUS *Willem seems quite sincere, but at the same time, while I am judged
by everyone, I antagonize the feelings of many people, etc.* If you suspect that letter 65
was Willem's you are wrong.[9] He found it in the house of one of our confrères
and sent it to you. But I sometimes permit myself more things than Willem
would wish.

ERASMUS *How many times they bring up the Retractations of Augustine,
etc.*[10] May I die if you have not hit the nail on the head, and I have the same 70
experience every day. Whoever holds a middle ground between Zoilus and
his friends[11] repeats it and wishes it. More correctly, even among those who
were thought to be your close friends, there are those who wish the same
thing, adding that there are many things that they would wish you had either
never written or at least had written differently. Since that cannot be done, 75
they think that the only remaining possibility is a retractation, which, as you
say rightly, they think is a palinode.[12]

ERASMUS *At this point, according to whose judgment do they want me to
correct my works? etc.* The majority of your enemies will answer 'according

* * * * *

9 Probably Willem Gheershoven (d 1547), Augustinian canon at the monastery of
   Groenendal at Hoeilaart near Brussels, where he was librarian for twenty years.
   He is remembered for the seven letters preserved from his correspondence with
   Lips (1525–6) concerning two manuscripts of St Augustine in the Groenendal
   library, one of which Erasmus studied as a young man.
10 On Augustine's *Retractationes*, cf Epp 2424:329–31 with n51, 2443:51–4, 2466:
   206–17.
11 Zoilus, a sophist of the fourth century BC, whose books attacking Homer made
   him proverbial for the kind of critic eager to belittle the achievements of their
   betters; *Adagia* II v 8. Lips does not identify the 'friends' between whom and
   Zoilus there was a middle ground.
12 Strictly speaking, a retractation (*retractatio*) is a reconsideration, not necessarily a retraction. A palinode, on the other hand, is a poem in which the author
   retracts a view or sentiment expressed in an earlier poem.

to the judgment of the Parisians or Pio,[13] who wrote against you.' I said the   80
majority, for not even your adversaries are agreed on this.

ERASMUS *A certain Medardus, a Franciscan, etc.* With the addition of the
Merdardus the *Colloquies* were increased again.[14] I am uncertain whether I
ought to say that this was felicitous or not. I was unaware of the augmenting
of the *Colloquies,* but Rutgerus Rescius showed me the latest edition, as well   85
as the poem of Resende.[15] There are three books that have a bad name: *Folly,*[16]
The Eating of Meat,[17] and the *Colloquies.*[18] To these some add the *Exomologesis,*[19]
but I have not heard anything about that for a long time, and for that reason
omit it.

ERASMUS *Johann Eck has poured out so much poison, etc.* I have often won-   90
dered to myself that you had such an ingenuous opinion of Eck, who was
always suspect in my eyes, but when I saw that you were well disposed
towards him, I condemned my suspicion as contrary to Christian charity.[20]
Now I read with sadness what you add: *He wrote a book on heretics, etc.*[21] Many

* * * * *

13 For Alberto Pio see Ep 2486 n10.
14 The colloquy *Concio, sive Merdardus* 'The Sermon, or Merdardus' was first
   published in the September 1531 edition of the *Colloquia.* For the Franciscan
   Medardus, his sermon denouncing Erasmus in Augsburg during the diet of
   1530, and Erasmus' transformation of his name into Merdardus ('Shitty') for
   the colloquy, see Ep 2408:5–19.
15 For the poem see Ep 2500 n3. For Rescius, professor of Greek at the Collegium
   Trilingue at Louvain, see Ep 1882.
16 *Moriae encomium;* see Ep 337.
17 *Epistola de esu carnium;* see Epp 1341A:1306–13, 1353 n13.
18 Cf lines 207–10 below. A favourite target of the Paris theologians (cf Epp 2552
   n10, 2600 n5, 2613:39–43, 2633:50–1), but of many others as well. For a survey of criticisms of the colloquies and Erasmus' defence of them, see Craig
   Thompson's introduction to CWE 39 sections V and VI and also his introduction
   to *De utilitate Colloquiorum* 'The Usefulness of the Colloquies' in CWE 40 1095–7:
19 Erasmus' treatise on confession; cf Ep 2513 nn52–4.
20 One cannot know what Erasmus may have said to Lips to give him the impression that he had ever been well disposed towards Eck. Nowhere else in the
   surviving record is there evidence of anything but hostile relations between the
   two (cf following note). It may be, however, that Erasmus had recently sought
   through intermediaries to achieve friendlier relations with Eck; see Ep 2437:73–
   6, where Johann Koler tells Erasmus that Matthias Kretz is a 'good friend of
   Eck' and 'will reconcile Eck to you whenever you wish.'
21 This could well be a reference to Eck's *Articuli 404* (1530), as Allen thought,
   even though Eck did not use the word 'heretics' in the title; see Ep 2365 n5.
   On the other hand, in 1530 Eck had also published the first volume of his collected writings against Luther (*Prima pars operum Iohan. Eckii contra Ludderum*

people blame you for being too to ready to form friendships, as if you do not 95
distinguish between a true and a false friend. But I cannot interpret this facility as a fault, because if you were not endowed with this quality you would
never have numbered Lips among your friends.

ERASMUS *If the pope does not recommend anything unless it is worthy of*
Christ, we will be happy under this emperor, etc. I am afraid that will never hap- 100
pen. If only the pope were guided by the spirit of Christ rather than of the
flesh or the world!

ERASMUS *I know what the monks are doing to have my works condemned,*
etc. They will deny it and say with Winghe that they do not nurture hatred
for Erasmus, but merely desire and strive to make you retract your faulty 105
writings. Whatever challenges their customs, their constitutions, and their
ceremonies they consider bad, even if it is not contrary to the gospel. They
think those things were superadded to the gospel according to the passage
'When I come again, I will repay you whatever more you spend.'[22]

ERASMUS *I wonder why that fellow (presumably Berselius) is angry with you,* 110
etc.[23] He was anxious to enter into your good graces and form a new friendship with Erasmus, and he thought he had happened upon an ideal occasion
here. Moreover, he had persuaded himself that I had received a considerable
remuneration from Froben. But after returning to Louvain, I departed for
Liège and paid the man a visit. He denied that he had been angry with me 115
but he acknowledged that he was upset that for the significant amount of labour he had employed in transcribing and correcting these works, the glory,
credit, and profit had been granted to another. He asked me to inform you
that he possessed things that would be of great interest to you and for that

* * * * *

[Ingolstadt: Georg Krapf]), book four of which consists of Eck's confutation of
'the teachings of the heretics' on confession; see folio 189 recto. After twenty-
four chapters devoted to the errors of the eminently heretical Martin Luther
and Johannes Oecolampadius, Eck devotes the final four chapters to Erasmus
(folios 216 verso–220 verso). The first of them bears the heading 'Erasmus of
Rotterdam defended against the [charge of] Lutheran heresy: and certain du-
bious statements of Erasmus concerning confession resolved.' Eck employs
the conceit of defending Erasmus against the accusation of holding heretical
views on confession – thus acknowledging Erasmus' formal acceptance of the
church's teaching despite his own doubts (see Ep 2513 nn52–3) – as the prelude
to picking apart a number of the arguments he had advanced in order to demonstrate that they are misinterpretations of the evidence. (Thanks are due to
Timothy J. Wengert for calling this seldom-noticed work to our attention.)
22 Luke 10:35
23 For Paschasius Berselius of Liège (1480–1535) see Ep 674.

reason he asks that if ever you send a servant here, you should see to it that   120
he stops in Liège. He showed me Victorinus on the *Rhetoric* of Cicero, written in the old style, but I don't know if it has been published yet.[24] He also
has an Alcuin, which in elegant verses describes the sacred books, beginning
with Genesis.[25] The rest, he said, he would communicate to the servant when
he arrives. He met with the legate Campeggi,[26] whom he found to be very   125
favourably disposed towards you. He hopes for similar sentiments from his
prince, the bishop of Liège.[27] The latter dares to say to Paschasius face to face
that Erasmus is the torch and seedbed of all Lutheranism. But I wonder if the
bishop is speaking ironically.[28]

ERASMUS *I have not read completely Augustine's Quinquagenas.*[29] *I assigned*   130
it to a certain semi-learned person, etc. I had pretty well concluded that myself,
and I patiently accept your excuse, but the Erasmus floggers sneer at this
kind of excuse.

ERASMUS *If it is feasible, I will send you your notes on Augustine, etc.* I
do not refuse. On the contrary, if you send them, both what I corrected in   135
Augustine and in the *Interpellations*,[30] my life will be more secure.[31] I will
make sure that it is clear how much has been added to Augustine through
the work of Erasmus in this last edition.[32] And whatever defects remain I will
try to amend as much as I can, provided I have a printer available.

* * * * *

24 Caius Marius Victorinus, known as Victorinus Afer (fourth century), Roman
grammarian, rhetorician, and Neoplatonic philosopher. The work in question
was *Commentarius sive expositio in libros de inventione*, which had been published
at Venice (Zarotus) in 1474.
25 Alcuin of York (c 735–804), poet and scholar at the Carolingian court, principal
figure in the Carolingian Renaissance. The work in question is *In sacrum biblio-
rum codicem* (*Monumenta Germaniae Historica* 21/1 288–92).
26 Lorenzo Cardinal Campeggi (Ep 2366), papal legate to the imperial court, had
travelled with it from Italy to Germany in 1530, and thence to the Netherlands
in 1531.
27 Erard de la Marck (Ep 738)
28 For Erasmus' difficult relations with Bishop Erard, see Ep 2590 n6.
29 Ie Augustine's *Expositio super tres quinquagenas psalterii*, an exposition· of the
Psalms arranged into three groups of fifty
30 Probably a reference to *De interpellatione Job et David* of St Ambrose
31 As Gerlo (IX 503 n23) points out, Lips in this passage expresses the hope that
Erasmus' work on Augustine, together with evidence of Lips' contribution
to it, will contribute to better relations between him and the members of his
Augustinian order who disapproved of his friendship with Erasmus.
32 The ten-volume Froben Augustine of 1529 (Ep 2157)

But, as I indicated in another letter,[33] which I doubt that you received,   140
I do not completely approve of your preface to these works of Ambrose.[34]
For you say in your preface that one of these works treated of David, the
other of Job, but in fact both books are about David. You say that these
books were not written by Ambrose. Winghe is displeased by that, and he
has discussed this problem in letters with our friend Willem.[35] I wish that   145
you would say that only about the *Apologia*. It cannot be shown, unless I am
mistaken, that Ambrose wrote two apologias about David. It seems more
probable that he wrote only one. About the book of *Interpellationes*, since it
is certain that Ambrose published four of them, and it is clear to everyone
that only three exist in print, and since the one I discovered is found in the   150
three or four manuscripts that I have seen, and no one else has seen another
book of the *Interpellationes*, and the style is not altogether at variance with
the Ambrosian style, I wish that you would mitigate this criticism a little so
that we might have in their entirety all the books of the *Interpellationes*, which
up to the present day were mutilated. Concerning the *Apologia*, as I said, I   155
do not disagree with you. If, therefore, you would be willing to change the
preface slightly and correct the error indicated above, all the books of the
Interpellationes, among which, as you know, several have been restored by
me, could be published together with the apocryphal but learned *Apologia*.[36]

ERASMUS *What is Willem of Haarlem doing? etc.*[37] I spoke to the man. He   160
justifies himself in every way, asking to be forgiven if he has sinned through
weakness, and promises that he will not be guilty of such things in the future.

* * * * *

33 Not extant
34 Ep 2190, the preface to two short works, attributed to St Ambrose, that were
   unknown at the time of the publication of his edition of Ambrose in 1527 (Ep
   1855): a second *Liber de apologia David*, and the missing second book of *De interpellatione Iob et David libri quatuor*. Erasmus published both works with *De
   pueris instituendis*, but rejected their authenticity on grounds of style. Lips, who
   had discovered manuscripts of the works and sent transcripts to Erasmus, had
   tried in vain to persuade Erasmus that they were genuine; see Ep 2076. He tries
   again here with respect to *De interpellatione*, but with no more success. The two
   works were included in an appendix to Erasmus' second edition of Ambrose,
   published by Froben in 1538. See also n36 below.
35 See nn7 and 9 above.
36 The introduction to Ep 2076 states incorrectly that modern scholars have accepted the authenticity of both the second book of *De interpellatione* and the
   second *Apologia David*. They have accepted the former but not the latter; the
   pages cited there (PL 14 929–60) include only one *Apologia David*.
37 See Ep 2352:366–77.

He added that there were some students who consorted with prostitutes, drink-
ers, ran away from his school into the city, came to see you, and denounced
him to you, reporting many things worse than he said. The man is afraid of   165
becoming a laughing stock, together with Christian the Hieronymite,[38] whom
many call the preacher (I have sent you his idiotic criticisms, copied down by
our friend Willem).[39] 'If you do that,' he says, 'it will be the object of public
derision by all the students.' He fears this all the more because he knows that
he is not very well liked but is in fact hated by many.   170

ERASMUS *I heard that it was forbidden in that school, etc and that this was*
the work of Theodoricus Hezius, to whom I wrote, etc.[40] Since I could not learn
anything certain from others, I approached Hezius himself. I told him that I
had received a letter from Erasmus in which he indicated that he had written to Hezius, and I added on my own that you doubted whether the letter   175
had reached you since you had not received a response. 'Erasmus' letter
was delivered to me,' he said, 'but I have not responded yet, fearing that I
might offend Erasmus' feelings.' 'How could you offend him,' I said, 'if you
answered him politely, not offensively?' 'Far be it from me,' he said, 'that I
should wish to answer him offensively. On the contrary, if I write to him,   180
I will write as to a father.' 'If you do this,' I said, 'there will be no reason
why Erasmus should be angry with you.' He seemed to intimate that he disagreed with you in certain things and was afraid that if he mentioned this,
you would take offence.

ERASMUS *I gave that book of Eustachius to a theologian to read, etc.* Among   185
the theologians of Louvain Eustachius has a certain reputation; they say there
is more learning in the preface to the book than in the book itself.[41] The story
about the priest who was whipped provoked laughter from many.

ERASMUS *I am in Germany and I have long ago become tired of it, etc.* Stop
writing such things, I beg you. Proof of how much aversion you have for   190

* * * * *

38 No positive identification is possible; see CEBR I 303 'Christianus Hieronymita.'
39 Probably the Willem of n9 above
40 In 1530, Hezius, a former friend who had gone over to support of the Louvain
    theologians against Erasmus and now functioned as inquisitor in the diocese
    of Liège, had ordered the removal of all of Erasmus' books from the library of
    the school of the Brethren of the Common Life at Liège; see Ep 2369:35–61. The
    letter Erasmus wrote to Hezius on the subject, to which he received no answer,
    is not extant. It appears that he wrote again at the end of November 1531; see
    Ep 2587:69–71.
41 For Eustachius van der Rivieren and his book against Erasmus (to which the
    latter did not reply), see Ep 2500 n4.

Germany is the house that you bought, repaired, and renovated with no little trouble and expense.[42] It was Master Maarten Davidts who told me that.[43]

ERASMUS *This letter has lingered with me for a long time, etc.* Nonetheless there is no reason why I should not count myself among the fortunate because it finally arrived. Let us hope that mine reaches you also.   195

ERASMUS *We see the position of the sects getting stronger day after day. What the princes are contemplating I don't know, etc.* Nor do I know what the princes have in mind. The emperor seems to do hardly anything except pile up treasure.[44] I hear that Ferdinand is rather well disposed towards the Lutherans.[45] The supreme pontiff, as the Friars Minor say, would sooner renounce the   200 pontificate than permit a council.[46] Others maintain that Aleandro will come here with full authority against the Lutherans.[47] I had dinner with Rutgerus,[48] who for my benefit had invited Clenardus and some theologians. I said goodbye to Clenardus, who was leaving soon for Spain.[49] When mention was made of the censure of the Parisians,[50] a certain person alleged that many   205 things noted by them were of little importance, while at the same time there were many things that were not at all to be taken lightly. Good gods! How your *Colloquies* were spat upon by certain people: 'It is full of obscenities!'[51] It corrupts not only youth, but adults and decrepit old men as well. With these eulogies the Zoiluses honour the *Colloquies*. And I think they derive   210 this mainly from the *Censure* of the Parisians.[52] During the conversation, Conradus Goclenius remarked that the bishop of Bressanone (I believe), the bastard son of the late Maximilian, reported that Erasmus' answer to the Parisians was in press.[53] Others think that a response is useless, and that only

* * * * *

42 See Epp 2506 n1, 2517 n11.
43 For Davidts see Ep 2571.
44 By taxing his subjects in the Netherlands; cf Epp 2491:13–14, 2516:25–6.
45 This can only mean that Ferdinand was willing to make limited concessions to the Lutherans in return for their active support against the Turks; cf Ep 2384 n9.
46 See Ep 2516 n11.
47 See Ep 2565 n2.
48 See n15 above.
49 For Nicolaus Clenardus of Louvain and his career in Spain and Portugal see Ep 2352 n51.
50 See Ep 2552 n10.
51 Dutch in the text: 'Het is vol rabbauwerie!'
52 See n18 above. For Zoilus, see n11 above.
53 George of Austria (Ep 1938), bastard son of Emperor Maximilian I, bishop of Bressanone (Brixen), admirer of Erasmus. What he reportedly said about Erasmus' rejoinder to the *Determinatio* of the Paris theologians was mere rumour;

a formal appeal remains, but Berselius disagrees with them.[54] I have learned   215
by experience that you have friends who are more sensible and more coura-
geous than I. They dare to jeer at the *Censure* and its authors, but I am more
timorous than I should be. I walk in silence with my head down because of
Winghe and his like, who are already celebrating a triumph.

I was about to send you some annotations, but since the Parisians took   220
my place, as it were, I do not want to add a burden to someone who is already burdened down, or an affliction to one afflicted. Nevertheless, I finished what I had begun in the *Paraphrases*.[55] But if you refuse to believe it,
here are a few examples:

Chapter 11 Pagi. g. 7 fa. 2. ver. 5: ERASMUS *To recognize with the eyes of faith,*   225
etc. You make reference here to the name of Israel as if it means 'man seeing
God,' although most interpreters deny that.[56]

Chapter 12 Pa. h. 2. fa. 1, penultimate and last verse: ERASMUS *Faith, which*
is the only thing God respects, not other merits, etc.[57] You are not surprised if I
interpret this piously, because you know I am one inclined to praise faith.   230
But Béda and the other anti-Lutherans consider it a blasphemy; according to
them God considers not only faith, but also other merits.

[Chapter 13] P. k. 5, fa. 1 ver. 8: ERASMUS *So also the justice of the law [arises*
from God], etc.[58] You understand this as the law of the pagans, but others do
not understand it that way. It would be different if you said 'the justice of   235
laws.'

From the letter to the cardinal of Liège,[59] most people take exception to
these things:

* * * * *

but Erasmus would in fact finish his reply in December 1531 (Epp 2579:57–9,
2587:3–4), and by 4 February 1532 it would be in print (Ep 2600:24–5).
54 For Berselius, see n23 above.
55 In February 1525 Erasmus had written to Lips (Ep 1547:18–19): 'If you produce
any notes on the *Paraphrases*, I shall be deeply grateful.' Lips may have owned
a copy of the *Paraphrases* given him by Erasmus; see Ep 1473:10–11. The three
quotations that follow are all from the *Paraphrase on Romans*.
56 CWE 42 67
57 CWE 42 70–1
58 CWE 42 74. Lips failed to note that this is from chapter 13.
59 Ep 916, the preface to the *Paraphrase on Corinthians*

P. k. 8. fa. 1 ver. 10: ERASMUS *Who were called Essenes, etc.* Josephus
speaks of them with great praise,[60] and most people esteem them and their   240
teachings greatly, but you seem to think of them as heretics.[61]

P. k. 8 fa. 2 ver. 5, 6, etc: ERASMUS *Do they [souls separated from the body]*
enjoy the glory of immortality, are the souls of the wicked in torment even now, do
[our prayers] provide relief, etc, or does an indulgence [from the pope free them all
of a sudden from punishment]?[62] What is it you are saying? Is it permitted to   245
doubt that pious souls enjoy glory from this moment on? That impious souls
are already suffering? It seems impious to inquire how our prayers come to
the aid of those impious souls when it is firmly accepted that he who prays
for the damned commits a sin, because in hell there is no redemption. If there
is no way back from hell, it seems altogether absurd to say that papal indul-   250
gences can immediately deliver the souls of the impious. If these questions
concerned the souls in the fire of purgatory, I would not be astonished, but
you say expressly 'the souls of the wicked.' Which are the souls of the wicked
but those of whose salvation we despair because they have been irreparably
damned in Tartarus?   255

To the eminent professor of theology Erasmus of Rotterdam

2567 / From Cornelis de Schepper   Brussels, 17 November 1531

The autograph of this letter, first published as Ep 161 in Förstemann / Günther,
was in the Burscher Collection of the University Library at Leipzig (Ep 1254
introduction). Cornelis de Schepper (Ep 1747 n23) was a trusted administrator
and diplomat in the service of Charles v.

Cordial greetings. When I returned to the court on the thirteenth of this
month, Lieven found your letter there,[1] and he immediately insisted to me
that I recommend him to the most serene queen. But I, who have no influence
and am not known to her except by some services I have rendered to her,
sought out Olahus to see if there was any hope for the young man, whom   5

* * * * *

60 Flavius Josephus *Jewish Antiquities* 2.8.2–13
61 Ep 916:303–5
62 Ep 916:324–8. Erasmus continues (lines 328–30): 'I observe that many men are
   in doubt on these points, or at any rate dispute about them, which would have
   been needless had Paul left us clear definitions.'

2567
1 Not extant

I have aided up to now at my own expense, and would wish more than for any other person that he be well looked after.[2] For as you justly write, I do nothing but perform a play full of intrigue, and I am of little benefit to myself or my friends. This is my fate. As for Olahus, on the other hand, although he said he would be willing to lend his services, especially for your sake but also   10
with some consideration for me, he was of the opinion that if your recommendation interceded with the queen, Lieven would be well provided for. Therefore, it is up to you to render service or not to the young man.[3] So great is your reputation for virtue and learning that you will easily obtain whatever you wish. I have to set out again on a difficult and unrewarding mission,   15
as all of them have been. If, however, my commendations have some value, they will be proffered most willingly. I commend myself most highly to your dignity and do not wish to detain you any longer with my banal style of writing, since you are occupied with so many tasks.

Farewell, most honoured teacher.   20

From the court, which is at Brussels in Brabant, 17 November 1531

Yours sincerely, Cornelis de Schepper

To the most famous Master Erasmus of Rotterdam, my venerable teacher

2568 / From Viglius Zuichemus   Padua, 18 November 1531

The letter was first published as Ep 13 in VZE. The surviving manuscript is a late sixteenth-century copy in the University Library at Ghent (MS 479. 20). Erasmus' reply is Ep 2604. For Viglius Zuichemus, see Ep 2484.

TO ERASMUS OF ROTTERDAM
In Augsburg I left at the home of Anton Fugger the letter that I wrote to you as I was setting out for Italy,[1] and in it I informed you about his most generous disposition towards you in wishing to oblige you, and how all the

* * * * *

2 In 1530 Erasmus' famulus Lieven Algoet, in Augsburg during the meeting of the imperial diet, had attached himself to de Schepper in the hope of finding employment. With much effort and strong support from Erasmus, he was eventually (1532) appointed personal secretary to Nicolaus Olahus (Ep 2339), the chief minister of Mary of Austria, regent of the Netherlands; see Ep 2278 n2.
3 Erasmus followed de Schepper's advice by writing Ep 2583 to Queen Mary.

2568
1 Not extant

conveniences of his house would be at your disposal if only you would bring   5
yourself to accept it.[2] I completed my journey to Italy according to my wishes.
In Venice I paid a visit to Giambattista Egnazio,[3] a very eloquent and cheer-
ful old man, not only in his private life but also in his public business. He
asked very affectionately about you and spoke of you with great respect, for
which reason I esteem and love him all the more. Others here who pretend to   10
some knowledge take glory for the most part in heartily despising Erasmus
and the Transalpines, admiring only Cicero and deeming worthy of praise
only those who studiously compose their books in imitation of him. I have
had some skirmishes with them but without insulting language. I am often
provoked to that by a certain German,[4] who knows a lot, in his opinion, and   15
glorifies himself remarkably with his own eulogies, even if in the opinion of
everyone else he sometimes seems to be in need of a dose of hellebore.[5] He
has so sworn himself to praise Lazzaro Bonamico that no scholar, no matter
how outstanding, can be cited without his chiming in immediately: 'But he's

* * * * *

2 See Ep 2476 n1.
3 Ep 2448
4 Georg von Logau (or Logus), d April 1553, a Silesian nobleman born in
  Świdnica (Schweidnitz). He matriculated at the University of Cracow (1514)
  and then at Vienna (1516), where he became closely associated with Caspar
  Ursinus Velius (Ep 2517), another native of Świdnica. He continued his stud-
  ies in Italy, registering at the University of Bologna in 1519 and again in 1526.
  In 1527 he returned to Cracow, and two years later he entered the service of
  Ferdinand I, in whose entourage he attended the Diet of Augsburg in 1530.
  From Augsburg he returned to Italy, and by September 1530 he was in Padua.
  The journey was financed by his patron, Stanislaus Thurzo (Ep 1242), whose
  brother Johannes (II) Thurzo (Ep 850) had sponsored his years as a student in
  Vienna. In Padua he met Viglius Zuichemus and his circle of friends, as well
  as the Polish Erasmians Jan Boner (Ep 2548) and Stanisław Aichler (Ep 2545).
  After visits to Rome (1534–5) and Naples (1535–6) he left Italy and spent the
  remainder of his life at Wrocław as canon and then provost of the Holy Cross
  and canon of St John's. The identification of him as the unnamed German referred to here is based on Allen Ep 2657:16–25, where Viglius describes 'the
  German' as someone from the same 'patria' as Anselmus Ephorinus (Ep 2539),
  ie Silesia, and living in Italy on funds supplied by Stanislaus Thurzo. In Allen
  Ep 2716:9–25 Viglius refers to Logau by name and describes his differences
  with him in much the same terms as are applied to 'the German' in this paragraph, ie as an obstinate champion of the Italian Ciceronians and critic of
  Erasmus. In 1534 Erasmus would learn that a tract attacking the *Ciceronianus*
  was circulating in manuscript at Rome and that Logau was its author; see
  Allen Epp 2906:15–16, 2961:158–62.
5 Ie in need of a cure for his insanity; see *Adagia* I viii 51.

nothing compared to Lazzaro.'[6] And he said that I would change my opinion, 20
for the same thing happened to Herman the Frisian.[7] 'Those who do not share
that opinion do not have any judgment at all,' he said. Isn't that the height
of effrontery? If this is not impudence or arrogance, it surely has to be the
utmost stupidity. As for me, I am re-reading your *Ciceronianus* more carefully
if for no other reason than to quash this kind of men, even though I engage 25
unwillingly in quarrels with people of this mentality. Their obstinate attitude
cannot be modified by any argument, but rather they become more irritated,
and the dispute gives them the opportunity to attack more violently those
whom they should venerate. But not everyone agrees with them. And among
the Italians themselves there are those who, more moderate and not at all 30
pretentious, do not deprive you of the praise owed and attributed to you by
the approval of the whole world and the applause of all truly learned men of
genuine discernment, who await you here with great longing. A Pole,[8] I think,
gave some hope of your arrival, which I dare not hope for. Even if the weather
here is milder than in Germany, I fear that you cannot support such a long 35
journey. Nor did his recent trip to Italy did not turn out well for Gregorius
Haloander, who was a great asset to our profession, although some say that
he died because of the inexperience of an apprentice doctor.[9] But if this visit
could materialize at your convenience and in agreement with your wishes,
nothing would be more pleasing to me than to be able with my personal 40
assistance to testify my devotion to you in your presence. In all these disturbances in Switzerland I do not know how safe the situation is there for you.[10]

May the good and great God grant a happy end to this tragedy and
vouchsafe to you all joy and prosperity in compensation for your merits.

* * * * *

6 Lazzaro Bonamico of Bassano (Ep1720 n10), an eminent champion of Ciceronianism, had been appointed lecturer in Latin and Greek at the University of
Padua in September 1530.
7 Haio Herman, who was thought to have been offended by Erasmus' failure to
mention him in the *Ciceronianus*; see Ep 2586:40–2 with n11.
8 Possibly Jan Boner, Stanisław Aichler, or Anselmus Ephorinus; see n4 above.
9 Gregorius Haloander of Zwickau studied law in Italy (1525–7), where he en-
deavoured to apply humanist methods of textual criticism to the *Corpus iuris
civilis*. In 1527 he journeyed to Nürnberg, where Willibald Pirckheimer persuaded the city council to underwrite the publication of Haloander's pioneer-
ing edition of the *Corpus*, the four parts of which (*Digest, Institutiones, Codex, and
Novellae*) were published at Nürnberg between 1529 and 1531; cf Ep 1991 n4. In
1531 he returned to Italy, hoping to complete a doctorate, but fell ill and died at
Venice on 8 September 1531, greatly mourned by his fellow German scholars.
10 Ep 2525 n3

Do not cease to love Viglius, who will never cede to anyone in his love   45
for you.

Farewell, immortal glory of good letters.

Padua, 18 November 1531

2569 / To Georges d'Armagnac   Freiburg, 19 November 1531

This letter was first published in the *Epistolae palaeonaeoi* where, as in all subsequent editions until that of Allen, it is addressed to 'the bishop of Rieux,' ie
Jean de Pins (Ep 2628). As Allen pointed out, however, this letter is addressed
to a complete stranger, whereas Erasmus had been well acquainted with Jean
de Pins at Bologna in 1506–7 (Ep 928:43n). The confusion is dispelled by the
content of three subsequent letters: that of Erasmus to Jean de Pins of 20 March
1532 (Ep 2628), Jean de Pins' reply to it of c July 1532 (Allen Ep 2665:30–65), and
François Rabelais' letter to Erasmus of 30 November 1532 (Allen Ep 2743:1–
7). Taken together these letters document the following sequence of events.
Erasmus wrote the present letter to Georges d'Armagnac, bishop of Rodez, in
the mistaken belief that he owned a Greek manuscript of Josephus' *Jewish War*
and asking for the loan of it for use by the Froben press. The real owner of the
manuscript, however, was Jean de Pins, to whom d'Armagnac duly forwarded
this letter (which may account for the false address in the early editions). At the
same time he wrote to Erasmus explaining that he had borrowed the manuscript from de Pins but had already returned it. Erasmus then wrote directly
to de Pins, who responded by sending the manuscript back to d'Armagnac for
safe delivery to Erasmus. D'Armagnac in turn entrusted it to François Rabelais,
who sent it to Erasmus (together with the only surviving letter between the
two men). Curiously, the dedicatory letter to the 1534 Froben Latin edition of
Josephus identifies d'Armagnac as the owner of the manuscript.

Georges d'Armagnac (1500–85) belonged to the family of the counts of
Armagnac. In service to the French crown he accumulated a long list of ecclesiastical preferments, beginning with the bishopric of Rodez in 1530 and culmi-
nating with a cardinal's hat in 1544. A man of learning and a patron of letters, he
corresponded with Guillaume Budé and other scholars. Contact between him
and Erasmus appears to have been confined to this letter and d'Armagnac's
reply to it (alluded to in Ep 2628:5–7).

ERASMUS OF ROTTERDAM TO THE BISHOP OF RODEZ, GREETING

With good reason one would impute to temerity, most honoured prelate,
that an unknown person should address an unknown person, to audacity
that an insignificant little man should introduce himself to such an eminent
prince, resplendent with distinctions of every order; but as indigence dispels   5

reserve, so charity, according to St John, casts out fear.[1] Of your outstanding virtues so many things are made known to me by many that I cannot but have great love for you. What gave me more confidence was the admirable affability of your character, as I am told, but most of all, the marvellous patronage you accord to the polite disciplines that we see flourishing felici-   10
tously in this age among all nations under the auspices of the languages and the ancient authors, who emerge everywhere from the darkness to the light, although of those who survived some have perished to no less a degree than those who seemed to have been completely lost. A book teeming throughout with monstrous errors is more of a cross than a book.   15

The Froben firm has struggled for a long time to restore Josephus, a historian of the first rank,[2] but we have found that the text is so hopelessly corrupt that we have must have recourse to the Greek original. Rufinus indeed never translated anything trustworthily,[3] but many seem to have amused themselves as they wished with this author.[4] We have learned that a Greek   20
text exists in your library.[5] If you would not object to putting this codex at our disposal for a few months, you will place not only us but also all scholars under obligation to you for this benefit. The book will be returned to you intact and unharmed at whatever time you prescribe.[6]

* * * * *

2569
1 1 John 4:18
2 Flavius Josephus (c 37–c 100), Jewish historian and Roman citizen, was highly esteemed by the church Fathers and later Christian scholars for his *Jewish War*, an eyewitness account of the struggle that ended in the siege of Jerusalem and the destruction of the temple (70 AD), and for his *Antiquities of the Jews*, a history of the Jews from creation to the fall of Jerusalem. Both works supplied a wealth of information, sometimes supplemented by unwarranted interpolations, that was easily exploited for the purpose of Christian apologetics.
3 The extant Latin translation of the *Jewish War* was that commonly attributed to Rufinus of Aquileia (c 345–410), otherwise known as a diligent translator of Origen. (Erasmus shared St Jerome's view that Rufinus was tendentious and unreliable as a translator; cf Ep 2564 n4.) Most modern scholars reject the attribution of the translation to Rufinus; see G. Ussani 'Studi preparativi ad una edizione della traduzione latina in sette libri del *bellum iudaicum*' *Bollettino del comitato per la preparazione della edizione nazionale dei classici greci e latini* (1945) 85–102.
4 Ie the translation attributed to Rufinus has itself been corrupted by other hands
5 Allen Ep 2757:7 makes clear that the manuscript in question was that of the *Jewish War*.
6 Froben's Latin Josephus of 1534, edited by Sigismundus Gelenius (Ep 1702), included Rufinus' translation of the *Jewish War*, extensively corrected by Gelenius on the basis of two Greek manuscripts, one of which was the one being requested here.

You will say with Ennius: 'Will there be some recompense?'[7] Of course,   25
that which mortals pay to the immortal gods. We will give thanks, we will
celebrate the author of this benefaction, and what we cannot repay materi-
ally we will requite with the ardour of grateful devotion. For this reason we
have sent this notary to ensure that the codex will be delivered to us safely.
I know that the city of Basel does not enjoy a good reputation these days,[8]   30
but nonetheless it has many honourable men who would prefer to live elsewhere if it were possible to move away without great inconvenience. In any
case, we have taken great care that nothing issues from the press except all
the best authors. Up to this point I have pleaded a cause common to me and
Hieronymus Froben and all scholars; now I shall treat of my own affairs.   35
'What is that?' you will ask. I ask earnestly that you deign to enrol Erasmus
among the humblest of your clients. Farewell.

Freiburg im Breisgau, 19 November 1531

2570 / From Jakob Jespersen   Brussels, 19 November 1531

This letter was first published as Ep 162 in Förstemann / Günther. The autograph was in the Burscher Collection of the University Library at Leipzig (Ep
1254 introduction).

Nothing is known of the early life of Jakob Jespersen of Aarhus (documented
1526–49). He matriculated at Louvain in 1529 and was a student of Rutgerus
Rescius (Ep 546) at the Collegium Trilingue. He taught Greek privately for a
time at Louvain, and was employed in that capacity at the court of Lorenzo
Cardinal Campeggi (lines 54–6 below). Then, unwilling to accompany the
Campeggi entourage back to Italy, he entered the service of Nicolaus Olahus
(lines 27–9 below),whom he tutored in Greek and whom he accompanied back
to Austria and Hungary in 1539. From 1541 he appears to have lived continuously in Antwerp, where he published a series of poems of no great merit praising famous men and women. In the spring of 1531 he attempted to initiate
correspondence with Erasmus by sending him a selection of his poems (lines
1–8 below). When he received no reply, he wrote the present letter in a renewed
attempt to establish contact. Again, no response from Erasmus has survived.
Instead, in letters to Conradus Goclenius and Nicolaus Olahus in May 1532,
Erasmus accused Jespersen of offending Johannes Dantiscus (on whom see Ep
2563A) by showing one of Erasmus' letters to him to Girolamo Aleandro (Allen

* * * * *

7 Ennius *Annals* 10 fragment 327, a passage quoted in Cicero *De senectute* 1.1
8 Ie not since it adopted the Reformation and banned Catholic worship (1529)

Epp 2644:24–5, 2646:12–13, 2849). Olahus apologized for Jespersen (Allen Ep 2693:146–52), but Erasmus continued to distrust him (Allen Epp 2762:1–3) and heaped scorn on his poetry (Allen Ep 2792:52–6). In May 1533 Jespersen wrote Erasmus to protest his innocence (Ep 2849), a gesture that succeeded to the extent that Erasmus sent him greetings in subsequent letters to Olahus (Allen Epp 2877:22, 2898:20–1, 2922:33). Following Erasmus' death Jespersen composed an epitaph for him that is included among the preliminary pieces in LB I (under the name Jacobus Danus Arusiensis). No letter of Erasmus to Jespersen is extant; of Jespersen's letters to Erasmus, only this one and Ep 2849 survive.

Cordial greetings. I wrote to you previously, when the emperor was in Ghent,[1] dearest Erasmus, fervently wishing to be enrolled in the list of those whom Desiderius Erasmus of Rotterdam considers his friends. I included three poems that I had written on the revered sacrament, together with several epitaphs,[2] some of which were composed by Doctor Frans van Cranevelt[3] and some by me, on the deaths of Jacobus Ceratinus and Nicolas Wary,[4] hoping that you were not the kind of person who would refuse to accept the friendship of one who is devoted to you, though he is unknown. I gave the letter to our harbinger (as he is called),[5] Johann of Sélestat,[6] who returned but did not bring me even a trace of a letter. It is impossible that he did not deliver it to you, since he brought your letters to Valdés and Hilarius.[7] I my-

* * * * *

2570
1 The letter is not extant; on the presence of the imperial court at Ghent, see Ep 2502 n2.
2 It does not appear that the poem or the epitaphs were published; see *Bibliotheca Belgica: Bibliographie générale des Pays-Bas* ed Ferdinand van der Haeghen, reed Marie Thérèse Lenger 7 vols (Brussels 1964–75; repr Brussels 1979) III 600 item J36.
3 Ep 1145
4 Jacobus Ceratinus (Ep 1843) died on 20 April 1530; Nicholas Wary (Ep 1756) on 30 November 1529.
5 The word Jespersen uses is *forarius*, a medieval word meaning 'quartermaster' (an officer responsible for the provision of food and lodging to an army, a princely court, or some other entity), or 'harbinger' (someone who goes on ahead to announce the arrival of an important person and his entourage and to secure suitable accommodation for them); cf French *fourrier*. If we knew more about this particular *forarius* than his name (cf following note), Jespersen's use of the word to describe a letter carrier might make more sense.
6 Unidentified. Lines 19–23 below seem to indicate that he was attached to the court of Cardinal Campeggi.
7 The letter to Alfonso de Valdés is Ep 2528; that to Hilarius Bertholf (on whom see Ep 1712) is not extant.

self gave the letter to each of them, since the harbinger did not know Valdés, and they both read to me all that you had written. I asked the man what had become of my letter. He answered that he had presented the letter to you but you responded that there had never been any ties or relationship between us. But that is why I wrote to you, dearest Erasmus, so that our letters might bring about not only a mutual acquaintance but a friendship. I was not too disturbed that you did not write. I ascribed it to your many labours, although it would not have taken much time to write a few words in reply. But I was very annoyed that that little fool at the court of Campeggi spread the word at table and on the street corner that I had written to you but that you had not given him anything to bring back to me.[8] 'Ah,' he said, 'the famous Erasmus, who is so highly praised, does not deign to answer?' For that reason I pray you to answer, just a few words, if you have the time, but if not, write to Hilarius or Lieven[9] so that I can demonstrate that you answered me and shut the mouths of those scoundrels.

I am, dearest Erasmus, at the home of Master Olahus, the secretary of Queen Mary,[10] to whom I am teaching Greek at the moment, and of whom you wrote to Lieven.[11] He seems to be a man of utmost sincerity; he not only seems to be but is in fact entirely philo-Erasmian,[12] who would do whatever he can for your sake. The day before yesterday at dinner he expressed the wish that you were here. I told him that you had bought a house at great expense.[13] 'He could re-sell it,' he said; 'the queen would gladly have him live in Brabant.'

There is nothing new save that our illustrious King Christian sailed forth from Holland with 14,000 men on the day after the feast of St Crispin in the attempt to win back his country.[14] In the meantime we know nothing certain about what happened to him. The emperor and everyone expect news

* * * * *

8 Lorenzo Cardinal Campeggi (Ep 2366) was the papal legate at the imperial court. The 'little fool' would appear to be the harbinger of line 9.

9 Lieven Algoet (Ep 2528 n9)

10 Ep 2339

11 Letter not extant

12 Greek in the text

13 Ep 2506 n1

14 In April 1523 Christian II, king of Denmark and Sweden (Ep 1228 n6), had taken refuge in the Netherlands with his brother-in-law, Charles V, after being expelled from both his kingdoms by his rebellious subjects. The expedition referred to here, financed by Charles V, ended in disaster, and Christian spent the rest of his life (d 1559) in captivity. The feast of St Crispin is 25 October.

from him. Master Gotskalk, chancellor of the king, is now explaining your
Apophthegmata to his son.[15]   40

The Dominicans of Louvain have prohibited, at least in the chapter room,
the reading of your books, under pain of excommunication, even if someone has the authorization of the pope. That is what Rescius and Conradus
Goclenius told me the day before yesterday. Therefore, André de Resende,
your Portuguese friend, left that sect.[16] He now lives in Brussels with the am-   45
bassador of the king of Portugal, to whom he is teaching Greek and Latin.[17]
I am glad our friend Hilarius Bertholf has become reconciled to Dantiscus
again; he is now living with him.[18]

There are a great many people in the court of Campeggi who have purchased an enormous quantity of your books and have had them transported   50
to Italy; but they were always curious to know if there might be something
heretical in them. I wonder why it is that because many say that Erasmus
entertains views of this kind we must therefore always believe the multitude
and the monks. I have left the court of Campeggi; I decided not to go to Italy.
Master Jacopo Canta of Asti,[19] to whom I taught Greek, engaged Jacobus   55
Alostensis in my place.[20] He was staying with you more than a year ago,
sent by Goclenius. He used to live with Dirk.[21] Now he has been sent to Italy,
where he is in charge of a printing house.

My lord, Master Nicholas Olahus, promises to do all in his power to
help Lieven, even if you had not recommended him. Everyone wonders –   60

* * * * *

15 Gotskalk Eriksen (d 1544), born in Schleswig, probably matriculated at Cologne
   in 1507, and by 1513 was secretary to King Christian II. He shared his master's
   exile in the Netherlands and became his chancellor. At the request of Margaret
   of Austria, he also served as tutor to Christian's children, including Prince John,
   referred to here. In 1532, following King Christian's failed attempt to regain his
   kingdoms, Eriksen entered the service of Charles v, whom he served on diplomatic missions to Germany. He had close contacts with a number of Erasmus'
   friends, including Frans van Cranevelt and Johannes Dantiscus.
16 See Ep 2500 introduction.
17 The ambassador was Pedro de Mascarenhas (1484?–1555), who in August 1532
   would send Erasmus a gift of sugar (Allen Ep 2704:7–12).
18 Bertholf (Ep 2581) had recently entered the service of Dantiscus; nothing is
   known of the events leading to the reconciliation referred to here.
19 Canta (dates unknown) was Cardinal Campeggi's chamberlain. One letter to
   him from Erasmus, praising his devotion to learning, survives (Ep 2636).
20 Doubtless the Jacobus of Ep 2369:15–16, who had been ten years in the service
   of Dirk Martens (Ep 2352:321–8)
21 Dirk Martens; see preceding note.

Goclenius, Valdés, and my master – what you mean in writing: 'If your letter of recommendation arrives with their letters,' since you recommend Lieven to them.[22]

Girolamo Aleandro, the archbishop of Brindisi, has arrived here.[23] I introduced myself and made mention of you to him, namely, that you had a 65 high opinion of him as expressed in the adage 'Make haste slowly,'[24] in the *Ciceronianus*,[25] and in other places. He uttered not a grunt, neither good nor bad, but diverted the conversation and his words to something else. His secretary, Domenico Mussi,[26] a man exceptionally skilled in Greek and Latin, whose acquaintance your friend Hilarius wishes to make through my inter- 70 vention, smiled. On the following day I met the said secretary again at the court of Campeggi. I asked him how things were going between you and Aleandro. 'I know that there were close ties between them at one time,' he said. 'Indeed there still are,' he added. 'The most reverend has a good opinion of Erasmus and speaks well of him.' I don't know whether he said this just 75 to be nice. I hear, however, that after being elevated to high office, Aleandro has become a troublemaker with the pope and Christian princes, and on that account seeks favour and more benefices, as did Pious Albert himself, Prince of Carpi,[27] if in fact one can be called Pious who writes against Erasmus so impiously and in a manner so foreign to a Christian.[28] It is astonishing 80

* * * * *

22 Erasmus had indeed lent his strong support to Lieven's efforts to secure a post at the court of Queen Mary, writing letters of recommendation to Valdés (Epp 2469:43–4, 2528:59–61) and (via Cornelis de Schepper) to Olahus (Ep 2567). No letter of recommendation to Goclenius survives.
23 On his arrival in Brussels see Ep 2565 n2.
24 *Adagia* II i 1, where Erasmus mentions that Aleandro was one of the scholars who provided him with valuable manuscripts when he was in Venice working on the first edition of the *Adagia*; see CWE 33 14.
25 The one reference to Aleandro in the *Ciceronianus* (CWE 28 419–20) is the none too complimentary observation that by wasting his fine linguistic skills on 'profane concerns' such as 'civil administration and wartime diplomacy' he had failed to develop into an accomplished Ciceronian.
26 Little is known about Domenico Mussi (documented c 1525–c 1533), who was Aleandro's private secretary. His dismissal for gross incompetence over accounts in 1527, and his attempt, after reinstatement a year later, to stab Aleandro's nephew to death in a quarrel over a plate of plums, suggest that he had an unstable character. Yet he somehow retained Aleandro's favour and received a benefice in Louvain through his good offices, disappearing from sight thereafter.
27 Alberto Pio, whom Jespersen here mocks by calling him 'Pius Albertus' and denying that he was really 'Pius.'
28 See Ep 2486 n10.

how much confidence is placed in these Jews and expropriators of the faith among Christians.[29]

Listen, there is one thing that I do not want you to be ignorant of. Jan van Campen, professor of Hebrew, has written a work on the whole Psalter, which everyone commends.[30] Recently at a dinner the cardinal of Liège and 85 the bishop of Palermo were present,[31] as well as many others. Dantiscus himself asked the bishop of Palermo for the privilege of printing the annotations of van Campen. An apathetic theologaster answered, 'There are enough commentaries on the Psalms.' Dantiscus immediately cut the man short, asking for the explication of certain passages. He did not know how to comment 90 on them. In the end the bishop of Palermo gave permission for five hundred copies to be printed, but not without remuneration. Dantiscus, bishop of Chemno, then responded: 'Fine people you are to envy such a benefit to the Christian world. If Titelmans,' he said, 'or Eustachius of Zichem or some other unlearned monk were to write it,[32] there would be no need to ask you 95 that it be published, because they wield the pen against Erasmus. So I shall not insist further, but I shall have not five hundred, but five thousand copies printed at my own expense, and I shall send free copies to all the bishops, ambassadors, universities, and kings of all Christendom. I shall have them printed by people who do not prize your privileges.' They were silent and be- 100 came more mute than fish,[33] after they understood that he was willing to pay for the printing himself. Last week, when I was going to Louvain, Dantiscus gave me a letter and some money to give to Rescius for certain things he printed for him. 'I admire,' I said, 'that your Magnificence spoke so courageously to the cardinal of Liège and the bishop of Palermo.' 'What do I have 105 to do with them?' he said 'they are bishops and I have the emperor, who is no less favourable to me than to them, and I have my king, the king of Poland.'

* * * * *

29 For the allegation that Aleandro was Jewish, see Ep 1166:93–4 with n24. No such suspicion adhered to Pio.

30 Jan van Campen (1491–1538) was professor of Hebrew at the Collegium Trilingue in Louvain from 1521 to 1531. He had just resigned his post and entered the service of Johannes Dantiscus; see Ep 2573:37–43. The psalm commentary in question, *Psalmorum omnium iuxta Hebraicam veritatem interpretatio*, was published at Nürnberg (J. Petreius) in May 1532, dedicated to Dantiscus.

31 The cardinal of Liège was Erard de la Marck (Ep 2054); the archbishop of Palermo was Jean (ii) de Carondelet (Epp 1275, 2055).

32 For Frans Titelmans see Ep 1823 introduction; for Eustachius of Zichem, better known as Eustachius van der Rivieren, see Ep 2500 n4.

33 *Adagia* i v 29

There is a certain religious in the monastery of Bethleem near Louvain by the name of Johannes of Athens or of Rome,[34] who has great love for you. He would have gladly written to you if he had known in time. I know that   110 he wrote to you once; he does not know whether you received the letter. He studies Greek at night so that the other monks do not notice it, as your friend Levinus Ammonius once did.[35] If you write to me, make mention of him in your letter; I will show it to him. I will speak with my master and the queen so that we can at last attract you here. Re-sell your house, come   115 and be well.

Brussels, 19 November 1531

My master Nicolas Olahus greets you; he will also write to you himself.

Your friend Jakob Jespersen, Dane of Aarhus, with all my heart

To the most distinguished Master Desiderius Erasmus of Rotterdam,   120 my honourable friend. In Freiburg

2571 / From Maarten Davidts   Brussels, 19 November 1531

> This letter was first published as Ep 163 in Förstemann / Günther. The au-
> tograph was in the Burscher Collection of the University Library at Leipzig
> (Ep 1254 introduction). For Maarten Davidts, canon of the collegiate church
> at Brussels, see Ep 1997A. This is the second of the two letters of Davidts to
> Erasmus to have survived, the other being Ep 1254; Erasmus' only surviving
> letters to Davidts are Ep 1997A and (perhaps) Ep 1258.

Greetings, first of all. I recently received the letter written on 19 August in the hand of the master of Freiburg,[1] from which I learn that the master found his Brussels host agreeable, just as I have often experienced.[2] I received some

* * * * *

34 Unidentified. The monastery was a house of the Augustinian Canons in Herent.
35 For Ammonius, see Ep 2483.

2571
1 Not extant; perhaps written and dispatched at the same time as letters to other
   friends in the Netherlands (Epp 2528, 2530). In July 1530 Conradus Goclenius
   informed Erasmus that Davidts complained much that he had not heard from
   Erasmus in a very long time (Ep 2352:382–4).
2 In the winter of 1516–17 Davidts lodged Erasmus in his house in Brussels (Ep
   532:35n), and thereafter Erasmus referred to him as 'my host Maarten,' and
   their common friends referred to him as 'your former host.' See, for example,
   Epp 1437:160–1, 2352:382.

time ago the epitaph of the lord and master Philippe Haneton, for which I
do not remember whether I thanked you, and so I render thanks now.[3] At 5
Mechelen there is a certain Lambert de Briaerde, who is a counsellor in the
council of the emperor.[4] He was once married to the daughter of the aforementioned Master Philippe Haneton, who died, so that now he has as a wife
the daughter of Master Jean Micault, receiver-general of the emperor for the
Low Countries.[5] Briaerde saw Master Erasmus in Paris, and he finds great 10
pleasure in the writings of Master Erasmus. Thus he asked me, unworthy as
I am, to exhort the master to write something on Psalm 50, 'Have mercy on
me, O God.'[6] For, as he informed me, he cannot have his fill of reading what
the master has written on several other psalms.[7] He is a very good and kind
man, who should be promoted to higher things, as I hope. He could be of 15
great advantage in the future, through the aforesaid receiver-general, as far
as the imperial pension is concerned.[8]

Do not be dismayed that I dare to write or give advice in such an un-
couth and shameless manner. Master Jean Le Sauvage, son of the deceased
grand chancellor, has just died, and Antoine Le Sauvage, the sole surviving 20

* * * * *

3 For Haneton and the epitaph that Erasmus composed for him in 1528 at
Davidt's request, see Ep 1997A.
4 Lambert de Briaerde of Dunkirk (c 1490–1557) obtained a doctorate in law,
probably at Paris. In 1521 he became master of requests in the grand council of
Mechelen, subsequently becoming privy councillor. In November 1532 he was
made president of the grand council. He undertook several important missions
on behalf of Charles v and Mary of Hungary, and wrote a treatise on legal procedure that was published after his death.
5 Jean Micault (d 1539), first documented in 1506 as *argentier* and keeper of accounts at the court of Philip the Handsome, was made receiver-general of the
Netherlands in 1507, a position that he held until August 1531, when he became a deputy auditor-general in the Brussels audit office. He became auditor-
general the following year. His daughter Marguerite married Lambert de
Briaerde in 1526.
6 Vulgate numbering; Psalm 51 in other versions
7 Erasmus ignored this request. He ignored it again when it was repeated by
Conradus Goclenius in 1533 (Allen Ep 2851:60–2).
8 Micault had paid Erasmus his first salary as a councillor to the emperor. Payment
of the pension had, however, been long in abeyance, and Queen Margaret
had made its resumption conditional upon Erasmus' return to Brabant; see
Ep 2192:97–104. In 1533 Viglius Zuichemus would echo Davidt's advice that
Micault could be helpful to him in securing the payment of his pension from
Queen Mary; see Allen Ep 2767:9–13.

son, is residing in Sterrebeek.[9] He is a great admirer of yours and he asked
me, his curate at Sterrebeek, to recommend him warmly to Master Erasmus.
My brother and my whole family most respectfully commend themselves to
you.[10] Master Jo. Jacobi and Busleyden are both well.[11]

From Brussels, through your humble host and servant, 19 November   25
1531

Maarten Davidts, your most obedient servant, at your command
To Master Erasmus of Rotterdam. In Freiburg

2572 / From Jakob Spiegel   Strasbourg, 23 November 1531

This letter was first published as Ep 164 in Förstemann / Günther. The manuscript, in a secretary's hand, was in the Burscher Collection of the University
Library at Leipzig (Ep 1254 introduction). For Jakob Spiegel of Sélestat see Ep
323:13n. A member of the imperial chancellery under Maximilian I and Charles
v, in 1523 he became secretary to Ferdinand of Austria, with the help of a warm
recommendation from Erasmus (Ep 1323). In 1526 he retired to Sélestat, where
he was a long-standing member of the literary society as well as a practising
lawyer. As this letter and Ep 2590 indicate, however, Spiegel continued to have
some connection with the court of Charles v, and he was (as ever) prepared to
use his connection to be of service to Erasmus.

Cordial greetings. Erasmus, you who are to me like a venerable father, I send
to you a letter of the cardinal of Trent,[1] which my brother Maius,[2] en route to

* * * * *

9 Jean (II) and Antoine Le Sauvage were the sons of Jean (I) Le Sauvage (on
   whom see Ep 301:38n). The younger Jean was a member of Charles v's privy
   council and master of requests. Antoine inherited from his father the lordship
   of Sterrebeek, where Davidts was his chaplain.
10 Davidt's brother, Zeger (Sigarus) was a priest.
11 'Jo. Jacobi' may possibly be the Jan Jacobj who was said to be a canon of
   Mechelen at this time, and who reportedly played host to the recipient of a letter from Johannes Dantiscus that was delivered by Hilarius Bertholf, Erasmus'
   former amanuensis; see Henry de Vocht *John Dantiscus and His Netherlandish
   Friends* (Louvain 1961) 123. For Gilles de Busleyden see Ep 2352 n53.

2572
1 Possibly Ep 2557
2 Johannes Maius (Maier, Meier), Spiegel's half-brother (1502–36). After study
   at Heidelberg and Freiburg he entered the imperial chancellery in 1520, and
   in 1526 succeeded his brother as secretary to King Ferdinand. Like his brother,

Innsbruck with King Ferdinand, gave to me as he was leaving. It was given
to me in Speyer,[3] from which I came directly here. Tomorrow I head for my
native city of Sélestat.   5

In Speyer I made mention of you to the cardinal of Trent; I was the
first to tell his Lordship what you wrote about him in the *Epistolae floridae*.[4]
He spoke very affectionately of you. With Aleandro also, bishop of Brindisi,
I purposely brought up your name. I am accustomed to discuss whatever
I wish familiarly and even somewhat freely with him. We prolonged for a   10
lengthy hour our conversation on the dissension in the church, with him
supplying the subject matter. Among other things he said that it was a scoundrel who persuaded you that the prince of Carpi wrote against you at his
instigation,[5] or rather that the prince allowed his name to be used because it
seemed to carry great weight with schoolmasters and petty pedagogues. The 15
prince of Carpi was a man of restless spirit, and of a cunning and perfidious
character, which I easily discovered when I was occupied with the prince's
papers.[6] May God have mercy on him; if he had removed him from the land
of the living twenty years earlier, an accord would easily have been reached,
I am sure, among the monarchs of Christendom. He was truly the henchman   20
of the Furies while he was alive.[7] I have no doubt that you will answer ap-

* * * * *

he was an enthusiastic admirer of Erasmus, but there is no record of personal
contact between him and Erasmus.

3 Where an imperial diet was supposed to meet but did not; see Ep 2511 n20.

4 See Ep 2299:33–9.

5 For Erasmus' belief that Aleandro was behind Alberto Pio's attacks on him,
see Epp 2329:103–4, 2371:35–40, 2375:81–2, 2379:110–11, 2385:65–7, 2411:50–2,
2414:10–20, 2421:55–6 with n13, 2443:264 with n34.

6 As a member of the imperial chancellery (1520–3)

7 Alberto Pio, prince of Carpi, had a brilliant but checkered diplomatic career
during two decades of the warfare in Italy between the Hapsburgs and the
Valois (1506–27). After several years in the service of Louis XII of France, Pio
became Emperor Maximilian's ambassador at the papal court (1512–19). But
Maximilian's successor, Charles V, did not renew the appointment, and when
Pio, at the request of Pope Leo X, served reluctantly as the informal agent in
Rome of Charles' enemy, Francis I, Charles accused him of treachery and (as
his feudal overlord) deprived him of his principality of Carpi (January 1523).
Despairing of reconciliation with the emperor, Pio formally entered the service
of Francis I as his ambassador to the Holy See. During the sack of Rome by the
emperor's mutinous troops in 1527, Pio took refuge with Clement VII in the
Castel Sant' Angelo. Clement subsequently sent him to France as papal ambassador to the royal court. Most contemporaries were kinder in their judgment of
him than is Spiegel here. See CWE 84 xxv–xxxvi.

propriately those denizens of the Sorbonne, that font of universal ignorance, who have spawned for us the magisterial *Determinatio*.[8]

The emperor transferred the diet to Regensburg until Epiphany;[9] if it takes place, and provided that, as I suppose, I am summoned there by the king or his grand chancellor, the cardinal of Trent, you will have me there ready to accomplish your commands and wishes, whatever they may be, to the best of my ability.[10] Many people know how much I esteem you. I will never be able to repay all that I owe you; I candidly acknowledge it both because of the memory of my uncle,[11] whom you rescued from oblivion, and because of your honourable mention of my name.[12]

When you write to Rhenanus sometime in the future (discretion does not allow me to demand a response from you),[13] inform me in a few words about delivery of the letter from the cardinal of Trent. For my brother is very anxious to learn of this from me.[14] Even if the favour and beneficence of the cardinal of Trent have never ceased – as the proverb of Polidoro (not yours) 'Honours change behaviour'[15] suggests – since some time ago, when he was one of the counsellors of Maximilian, he derived a great benefit from a small effort on my part, nevertheless it would please me if you would mention me affectionately in a few words at the end of your letter,[16] for he is glad to support those whom you love. May God watch over you, who undoubtedly

* * * * *

8 See Ep 2552 n10.

9 Cf n3 above.

10 There is nothing to indicate that Spiegel did in fact attend the Diet of Regensburg.

11 Jakob Wimpfeling (Ep 224)

12 Allen says that this is a reference to the *Encomium Selestadii*, a poem in praise of Sélestat that Erasmus wrote in gratitude for his hospitable reception by the humanists of the city as he was travelling to Basel in August 1514. Wimpfeling and Spiegel are both mentioned briefly in the poem (CWE 85 124:21), but hardly in a way calculated to rescue anyone from obscurity. This sentence makes much more sense if read as a reference to the encomium of the recently deceased Wimpfeling in the letter to Johann von Vlatten that was published with the second edition of the *Ciceronianus* in 1529 (Ep 2088:64–122), in which Spiegel does indeed receive honourable mention (lines 112–13). Text also in CWE 28 339–41.

13 Beatus Rhenanus had retired to Sélestat in 1526.

14 See lines 1–3 above.

15 Polidoro Virgilio *Adagiorum liber* (Basel: Froben 1521) no 207. In the Froben edition of 1525 it is no 202.

16 There is no record of Erasmus having written to Beatus Rhenanus, but on 27 December 1531 Spiegel gratefully acknowledged the receipt of letters (not extant) to him and to Bernhard von Cles (Ep 2590:2–3).

wished, for the benefit of his church, that while you are still alive those frenzied sophists would finally spew out their venom.[17]

In haste. Strasbourg, from the house of the provost of Young St Peter,[18]
23 November 1531   45

Your servant Jakob Spiegel

To the lord and master, whom I revere like a father, Desiderius Erasmus
of Rotterdam, ardent champion of Christian piety and strong and energetic
defender of genuine theology

2573 / From Conradus Goclenius   Louvain, 23 November 1531

The autograph of this letter, first published by Allen, is in the Öffentliche
Bibliothek of the University of Basel (MS Goclenii epistolae 5). Erasmus' an-
swer is Ep 2587. For Goclenius, professor of Latin at the Collegium Trilingue in
Louvain, see Epp 1209, 1994A.

Cordial greetings. When I reflect on how your courage in the noble cause of
studies and true piety has hitherto always remained invincible, and how it has
not only never succumbed to adversity but shown itself stronger day by day,
I am totally astonished by your last letter,[1] which seemed to betray some kind
of fear because of the *Determinatio* of the Sorbonnists;[2] if you only knew how   5
few people this affects, you certainly would be very little disturbed by it. Add
to this that those who wish evil to the humanities, in particular those to whom
the truth discovered by your divine labours and introduced to the world has
brought famine, had expected something quite different from the prolonged
birth-pain of the Sorbonnic heroes. Their virtue and wisdom became known   10
not long ago through their *determinatio* on the divorce of the king of England,[3]

* * * * *

17 See n7 above.
18 The Young Church of St Peter, known simply as Young St Peter (Jung Sankt
   Peter), was so called to distinguish it from Old St Peter's church, a much
   earlier foundation. The provost from 1531 until his death in 1551 was Jakob
   Schmidhäusser of Molsheim, who had been a member of the chapter since
   1506. (Information generously provided by Louis Schaefli, Conservateur de la
   bibliothèque du Grand Séminaire de Strasbourg, and Milton Kooistra, co-editor
   of *The Correspondence of Wolfgang Capito* [Toronto: 2005–   ]).

2573
1 Not extant
2 See Ep 2552 n10.
3 See Ep 2413 n15.

not without great discredit to themselves, and now will become even more
well known if you will hold fast to your long-standing principle of not yield-
ing to the enemy in a cause that has so often been victorious but considering
the truth worthy of your usual advocacy. Be assured that this is expected   15
of you by all those who wish you well, and that your enemies ask nothing
more than that you seem by your silence to acknowledge the errors of which
the Sorbonne falsely accuses you. If that happens, they will consider that
the foundations have been laid for what they have been planning for a long
time, that under the pretext of religion they will overturn all good studies   20
while you will be branded with an everlasting stigma of disgrace. Therefore,
see to it that you do not allow the glory of your previous benefactions to be
obscured, and be mindful of the furious courage[4] that we expect to be as
unflinching, to judge from the fierce battles you have endured in the past.
This much I can promise you in the meantime, that there is nothing for you   25
to fear in these regions, since the emperor himself and the queen of Hungary,
as well as the leading personages of the court, are, to speak jokingly, in no
way ill disposed towards you, as I myself have deduced with unmistakable
proof from my conversations with many of them. Therefore dismiss from
your mind not only the groundless fear[5] concerning the imperial treasury,[6]   30
but also all anxiety, and do what the situation demands, if you wish to preserve the authority you have thus far acquired, so that the Sorbonnic sophists
do not flaunt their great insolence with impunity.

But since your wisdom is too great for you to be given advice by anyone, and since your dedication and indefatigable zeal in defending the   35
truth do not require anyone to encourage you, I will leave these things
aside and pursue another subject. First of all, there is the matter that Gilles
de Busleyden avidly awaits your response concerning the new professor
of Hebrew,[7] if perhaps you have found someone suitable for this position.
For in the absence of your advice they have not decided that another take   40
the place of van Campen, who some time ago resigned from his post at the
college because, he said, he could not put up with the solitude or, at any
rate, the small number of students.[8] The other professorships are thriving

* * * * *

4 Greek in the text; a Homeric phrase (*Iliad* 7.164; *Odyssey* 4.527)
5 Greek in the text (Plato *Symposium* 198A)
6 Ie Erasmus' imperial pension, the payment of which had been made conditional on his return to Brabant; see Ep 2571 n8.
7 Ep 2588
8 Jan van Campen had just resigned his post as professor of Hebrew at the Collegium Trilingue and entered the service of Johannes Dantiscus; cf Ep 2570 n30.

more than ever, and I do not know why our compatriots have always been
rather indifferent to Hebrew studies. But they would change their mind   45
if, as we hope, there were someone who would show the persistence and
diligence in teaching that everyone, not without just complaint, found lacking in our friend van Campen. It will fall to your kindness not to fail your
college, which to this point owes its development above all to your advice.
At all events, make it known that I informed you in the name of Master   50
Busleyden and his administrators, lest they infer that I did not wish to undertake the task assigned to me.

   What the emperor is achieving against the heretics, about stabilizing
the value of money, which is in a state of perpetual flux, about restricting
luxury in clothing, preventing drunkenness, lowering the high price of grain,   55
feeding the poor of the country, restoring the municipal rights of each city
to a form corresponding to the laws, and other things of that sort, you will
learn from the ordinances that I am sending you. Your congratulations on
my victory in Antwerp were most gratifying, and it seemed that now 'peace
was attained and the port was within reach,'[9] when suddenly a new litiga-   60
tion arose, fomented by my enemies, who, not being able to deprive me of
my reward, will in any event render it unfruitful for several years, since the
profits and revenues will be given to the chapter as long as the trial lasts.[10] I
am being maltreated by these stratagems, but I hope in a short time to find a
way to reciprocate this spiteful treatment, without any risk to myself.   65

   Haio Cammingha sent four gold coins to add to the previous sum,[11] but
he is angry, I think, because they were returned without a letter. Girolamo
Aleandro has made his way to the emperor, passing this way fewer than
twenty days ago;[12] we do not know the reason except that they say he was
sent by the pope to the German diet, and when the emperor hesitated,[13] he   70
preferred to spend the winter in Brabant rather than in the German heated
rooms. This messenger comes to you hired by either Lieven or Valdés, so you
will not have to pay him anything.[14] In my last letter[15] I asked you, in virtue

* * * * *

9 Virgil *Aeneid* 7.598
10 On Goclenius' lawsuit over his contested appointment as a canon of St Mary's
   at Antwerp, see Ep 1994A n17.
11 See Ep 2552 n6.
12 See Ep 2565 n2.
13 Ie when the emperor cancelled the meeting of the diet that was to be held in
   Speyer and transferred it to Regensburg; see Ep 2511 n20.
14 Cf Ep 2587:84–8.
15 Not extant

of your long-standing good will towards me, that in writing to Valdés you would indicate that you would be grateful to him if he would oblige me in 75 that matter that he had taken upon himself to do in the interest of Master Dantiscus.[16] But I do not doubt that you had good reasons to refuse or to put it off. So it is not proper for me to question you about this again.[17] Your young Erasmius is in Lille,[18] a city situated about five miles north of Hainaut. He is studying French there. I enclose a letter to Hieroynmus Froben and Nicolaus 80 Episcopius,[19] thanking them for the present they sent and the care they employed. I ask that you transmit it to them when you have access to a courier. The second one is a letter from Arnold Birckmann, containing some of their accounts.[20] Keep well.

    Louvain, 23 November 1531   85
    Your friend Conradus Goclenius
    To Master Erasmus of Rotterdam. At Freiburg im Breisgau

2574 / From Bonifacius Amerbach   [Basel, 23 November 1531]

> The autograph rough draft of this letter (= AK Ep 1585), which was first published by Allen, is in the Öffentliche Bibliothek of the University of Basel (MS C VIa 73 237 verso). The date is determined by the reference to the death of Oecolampadius in line 20. Erasmus' reply is Ep 2575.

* * * * *

16 Frustrated in his attempts to gain the canonry in Antwerp (see n10 above), Goclenius in 1531 disclosed his financial difficulties to Johannes Dantiscus, who promised to intervene with the emperor's secretary, Alfonso de Valdés, in search of a benefice to which the emperor had the right of nomination. He did so to good effect. In 1534 Valdés' efforts bore fruit with Goclenius' appointment to a canonry at St Gorgonius in Hoegaarden; see de Vocht CTL III 97–8.
17 In Ep 2587:42–3, Erasmus reports that he had indeed written to Valdés as requested, but the letter does not survive.
18 Erasmius Froben; see Ep 2229 introduction and n3.
19 On Episcopius see Ep 2233A n4.
20 Together with his brother Franz (Ep 258:14n), Arnold Birckmann (documented 1508–d 1541/2) had built a flourishing book business with branches in Antwerp and London and extensive contacts elsewhere. Erasmus had had dealings with them both in connection with the collection of his Aldington annuity, and had come to distrust them; see Ep 892:21n. Following the death of his brother in 1530, Arnold was sole head of the business. The letter referred to here (not extant) was evidently addressed to the Froben firm concerning business that Arnold had with them.

I sent you recently, at the behest of our friend Ephorinus,[1] the nonsense
of a certain Scaliger;[2] I would not want it to fall into the hands of strangers. I would therefore appreciate it if you would let me know whether you
received it or not. I found out today that as a result of your recent letter,
which repeated something about empty boasters,[3] Grynaeus is still smart-   5
ing from the injury that he thought had been done to his sense of honour.
Indeed, with the interjection of a religious oath he declared, in fact swore
with such emphasis that I was completely convinced, that everything he
had reported to you on his return from England in the name of More and
the archbishop of Canterbury he had received directly from them. He is dis-   10
tressed that you have called into question his good faith, which he wishes
to be regarded by everyone as inviolable. I, on the contrary, maintain that
you have confidence in his words but that you call into question the vain
promises of those who had given this to you in commission. I ask you, dear
Erasmus, to remove this cause of anxiety from the man so that he will un-   15
derstand that he is not being accused of lying but is numbered among men
of good faith who are not given to empty boasting. He is certainly, to put it
briefly, an extraordinary panegyrist of your virtue and, in my opinion, not
unworthy of your friendship.[4]

Oecolampadius migrated to heaven today.[5] If you wish to make use of   20
my humble assistance in person, since with the advent of peace we are finally
reconciled,[6] so indicate with a mere word and I will be there immediately.
Farewell, in haste.

* * * * *

2574
1 Ep 2539
2 See Ep 2564:1–4.
3 The letter that had caused offence to Simon Grynaeus is not extant, but on 30
  August 1531 Erasmus had warned Erasmus Schets not to trust Grynaeus or
  Johann Bebel, whom he suspected of improper behaviour as his representatives
  on a journey to England; see Ep 2530:49–50 with n15.
4 Erasmus responded to this request with Ep 2576.
5 According to the chronicle of Fridolin Ryff, Oecolampadius died on the morn-
  ing of 23 November 1531; see *Basler Chroniken* ed Wilhelm Vischer and Alfred
  Stern I (Leipzig 1872) 138.
6 The Second Kappel War had come to an end on 20 November 1531; the Peace
  of Kappel was concluded on 24 November (see Ep 2564 n8), though Basel's
  peace with the victorious cantons came only on 22 December. The hostilities
  had been among the reasons for Bonifacius' reluctance in recent weeks to pay
  a visit Erasmus; see Ep 2564:15–21.

2575 / To Bonifacius Amerbach   [Freiburg], 29 November 1531

This letter, Erasmus' response to Ep 2574, was first published in the *Epistolae familiares*. The autograph is in the Öffentliche Bibliothek of the University of Basel (MS AN III 15 36). Bonifacius' reply is Ep 2580.

Greetings. What are you saying? Grynaeus convinced you with an oath? May I die if even the slightest suspicion of his good faith ever touched my spirit. And I cannot adequately express my astonishment that he should conceive of this suspicion on my part except that this world does not allow anything to be at peace. I think that this anxiety has now been removed from him.[1] 5 If anything has remained, you banish it. I received the venomous attack of Scaliger.[2] Aleandro is the author of it. I recognize the style of the man as well as I know his face.[3] I see it clearly: they are converging on me with gladiatorial spirit, Béda with his followers, Eck, and the archbishop Aleandro,[4] now a legate at the imperial court, invested with full powers and an equal amount 10 of insanity. Now he thinks he will complete what he vainly tried to do eight years ago.[5] He gives himself the name Scaliger and threatens to set things on fire. There is nothing too defamatory to be published in Paris, provided it is against Erasmus. It is not enough for them to cut down Erasmus; they must entirely obliterate him, robbing him of his reputation as well. The Lord will 15 provide. The matter I wished to discuss with you is not of great importance and is not pressing. Your arrival will be most agreeable, provided it causes you no inconvenience, and will be even more agreeable if you wish to stay for a few weeks; a stable for the horse will also be available. Farewell.

The eve of the feast of St Andrew 1531   20
You will recognize the hand.
To the illustrious doctor of laws Bonifacius Amerbach. In Basel

* * * * *

2575
1 By Ep 2576, written on the same day as this letter
2 Evidently the copy mentioned in Ep 2574:1–4
3 See Epp 2564 n2, 2565 n12.
4 Cf Ep 2565:4–12 with nn3–5.
5 Presumably a reference to *Racha*, the treatise attacking Erasmus as a heretic that Aleandro wrote in 1524. It was never published, but it circulated anonymously at the papal court, and reports of it infuriated Erasmus; see Ep 1717:38–42 with n18.

2576 / To Simon Grynaeus Freiburg, 29 November 1531

This letter was first published by Allen. The manuscript, a copy made by
Bonifacius Amerbach, at whose urging it was written (see Ep 2574:14–16), is in
the Öffentliche Bibliothek of the University of Basel (MS A IX 74).

Cordial greetings. As I read your letter,[1] I was affected by two contrary sentiments: by sorrow, because I perceived once again that you were upset by
my letter,[2] and by laughter, because I saw and wondered all the more at this
suspicion that arose from nothing and remained so tenaciously implanted in
your mind. May Christ never show his favour to me if it ever came into my 5
mind, whether I was awake or asleep, to suspect that you ever did anything
in England or on your return from England reported anything that was not
of the utmost reliability. I took note of the usual custom of courtiers who
promise more generously than they give. If I had the inclination to argue justifiably with a friend, I could more justly remonstrate with you for conceiv- 10
ing such an ungenerous opinion of me. Who could be more heartless than I
if, concerning a man whose exceptional learning I admire, whose integrity,
equal to his learning, I esteem, I were to harbour a suspicion of infidelity,
especially since I have never found you lacking in good faith. Not even with
Bebel did a thought of this kind ever enter my mind.[3] And yet between him 15
and you I think there is no less difference than between glass and a precious
stone. Concerning your accounts, how could I have questioned your good
faith, since they tallied exactly with what each one stated in his letters? What
reason would there be for you to report something different from what you
had ascertained? You know that in drawing conclusions the first thing to be 20
investigated is to whose benefit it was. I see no deviation and do not think
any exists. Mountjoy in his letters promised what you reported.[4] The same
is true of the archbishop of Canterbury.[5] I know how dilatory Mountjoy is.
I think the archbishop has already given what he promised. Or if that has
not been done, the reason is that no one complained to him about it, since 25
there are so many people around him making their own claims. It is also

* * * * *

2576
1 Not extant
2 See Ep 2574 n3.
3 But it did; see Ep 2530:49–50 with n15.
4 See Ep 2530:9–11 for mention of sums of money promised by Baron Mountjoy
and Thomas More.
5 Cf Ep 2512:2–4.

possible that the money has already been paid, although Schets, who lives
in Antwerp, has not yet been informed about it. I had written to More tell-
ing him not to send anything,[6] and I do not expect anything from him. What
he said to you he said in order to send you on your way in better spirits,   30
since perhaps he sensed that you were waiting for him to send some present.
I have no doubt that the bishop of Lincoln and the count of Ormond said
what you reported.[7] The reason why they did not write anything is obvious.
They wished to compensate for the meanness of their gift with more generous promises. They did not wish to commit these words to writing, either to   35
have the freedom to give or not give, or to avoid the appearance of rewarding
my praises with simoniac payments.

   But no matter how things stand, my dear Grynaeus, consider it as said
from the tripod of Delphi[8] that not even the slightest doubt about your good
faith ever entered into the mind of Erasmus. And I have such a low opinion   40
of your good faith that if it were a question of three thousand florins, I would
not hesitate to lend it to you without a receipt, so far am I from suspecting
anything, since you would have no interest in deceiving me, and I would not
have the slightest reason to suspect you. Perhaps someone painted a false
picture of my character to you, since our day is the reign of evil tongues.   45
There remains my letter, which seems to you to be written in such a manner that it seems to everyone except me to cast suspicion on you. Show it to
our mutual friend Bonifacius. If he judges that there is a single syllable there
that censures you, I will confess that I was drowsy when I wrote it, or if you
prefer, that I was drunk. And I will not refuse to hand it over for punishment 50
so that you have the right to destroy it by throwing it into the fire or into the
Adriatic Sea. And in fact no copy of it exists with me.

   But listen! Make sure that together with the letter you destroy all that
suspicion which is absolutely groundless, believe me. That you strive with
great effort never to be lacking in good faith makes you all the dearer to me, 55
and on that account I more easily overlook that you conceived this suspicion

* * * * *

6 Letter not extant
7 John Longland (bishop of Lincoln) and Thomas Boleyn (earl of Ormond) may
   be the two Englishmen mentioned in Ep 2512:6–9 as sending gifts. In 1525
   Erasmus had dedicated *In Psalmum quartum concio* to the bishop (Ep 1535); and
   in 1530 his *In psalmum 22 enarratio triplex* to Boleyn (Ep 2266).
8 The seat from which the priestess at the temple of Apollo in Delphi delivered
   the oracles of the god

of me and feared things that presented no danger, that is, a groundless fear, according to the proverb.[9]

The death of Oecolampadius will affect people in different ways, according to each one's opinion.[10] I pray for the mercy of God upon him, of   60 which we all have need. Farewell.

Freiburg, the eve of the feast of St Andrew 1531

Erasmus of Rotterdam, unfeignedly yours

To the most learned Master Simon Grynaeus. At Basel

2577 / To [Jean Morin]   Freiburg, 30 November 1531

The manuscript of this letter, which was first published by Allen, is an autograph rough draft in the Royal Library at Copenhagen (MS G K S 95 Fol, folio 181). The person addressed is not named, but the royal licence printed with Scaliger's book (see lines 1–3) identifies him as Jean Morin, 'Lieutenant du Bailliage de Paris, conseruateur des priuileges royaulx de Luniversite de Paris.' Little is known of Morin (documented 1523–35) apart from the record of his official duties. In 1534, when Francis I inaugurated a wave of suppression against religious dissidents, Morin personally led the hunt for 'heretics' and pronounced death sentences upon them, thus earning the hatred of Protestant chroniclers.

Cordial greetings, honoured sir. A little book has appeared in Paris, printed by Guillaume Gourmont under the false title of *For Cicero against Erasmus, [an Oration] by Julius Caesar Scaliger*,[1] a book that is not only defamatory but simply raving mad, stuffed full of the most impudent lies and more than scurrilous abuse, and with the most criminal accusations, among which was this   5 one, that with my accomplices I tried to cast down the Roman pope from his elevated rank, although I have hitherto fought constantly in defence of the pope and the Catholic church against the advocates of the sects, and continue to fight, not without peril to my fortunes and my life. I omit for the moment

* * * * *

9 Greek in the text; see Ep 2573 n5.
10 See Ep 2574 n5.

2577
1 On the book, which Erasmus immediately concluded had been written by Girolamo Aleandro under a pseudonym, see Ep 2564 n2. The publisher's name was Gilles Gourmont, not Guillaume. There is a detailed summary of its contents in Vernon Hall, Jr *The Life of Julius Caesar Scaliger (1484–1558)* Transactions of the American Philosophical Society, new series 40/2 (1950) 99–105.

that he reproaches me for wishing to obliterate the glory of Cicero, that he   10
accuses me of drunkenness, although those who live with me know that the
exact opposite is true, that I functioned as a reader with Aldo, although I
served as Aldo's instructor.[2] But I am foolish to continue to enumerate these
charges, since the whole book contains nothing but insane insults that one
clown would hardly let fly at another. They published this in violation of   15
the edict of the king and the authority of the theologians,[3] but with your
permission; nor does anyone bring forward a reason why this little book
should seem worthy of publication. I suspect, moreover, that your name was
fraudulently inserted there, or if it is true that the business was carried out
with your permission, that they convinced you that it was something quite   20
different from what it really is. It would have been more in keeping with the
prestige of your university, which is justly famous, if such an example were
not to go forth from it to studious youth throughout the Christian world. I
know the author, a mitred buffoon,[4] and I could take revenge against this
man as he deserves, not with false, but with true accusations, but I have no   25
desire to imitate a madman. I will not mention here the services I have rendered to studies or to the Christian religion; but even if this were not so, and
I were worthy of this scurrility worse than that of a wagoner, he should have
given careful thought to what befits your university. I admit to being a man of
very humble condition, yet the emperor acknowledges this humble subject as   30
his councillor, and King Ferdinand acknowledges him as his teacher,[5] which
they state openly in many letters. And the mitre would not have been lacking

* * * * *

2 Erasmus spent about a year in Venice (1507–8) as a member of the circle of scholars around the renowned publisher Aldo Manuzio, and in that capacity provided him with expert advice and assistance in his publication of classical texts.
3 Presumably a reference to the decree of 21 March 1521, issued by the Parlement
  of Paris in the name of the king, authorizing the Paris faculty of theology to
  examine, approve, or prohibit all books dealing with religion; see Ep 1815 n16.
  Erasmus' point is apparently that the book contained no indication that it had
  been authorized in the way thus prescribed. In Ep 2587:17–19 he reiterates his
  charge that the book had not been properly authorized by the theologians but
  had instead been approved 'by some lieutenant or other.'
4 See n1 above.
5 Erasmus was made councillor to the future Charles v in about January 1516
  (see Ep 392:17n), and retained the largely honorific title for the rest of his life.
  As for Ferdinand, as a young prince he read Erasmus' *Institutio principis christiani* with his tutor, reportedly knew it almost word for word, and thanked
  Erasmus for it in person; see Epp 943:26–7, 970:25–8, and LB IX 371E (*Apologia
  ad prodromon Stunicae*).

to me if I had not preferred to serve Christ rather than men.[6] I did not wish your Excellency to be unaware of these matters, so that if this thing was done without your knowledge, the temerity would be punished, and if, on the contrary, it was done with your knowledge, you would understand that you were led by the false insinuations of dishonest men into an inappropriate course of action.[7] May the Lord watch over you, most esteemed sir.

Given at Freiburg im Breisgau, on the feast of St Andrew 1531

2578 / To Erasmus Schets   [Freiburg, end of November 1531]

First published by Allen, this is Erasmus' answer to Ep 2558. The autograph is in the British Library (MS Add 38512 folio 64). Schets' answer is Ep 2593.

Greetings. I am sorry that you were so upset by my letter, which you seem not to have understood, or else I did not express my feelings well enough.

I was not aware that my servant Quirinus had received some money from Pieter Gillis. He had given me no indication of this. Nor did I impute to you any loss regarding the sums of money that you entrusted to Quirinus at my bidding, nor did such a thought ever enter my mind. But in the letter of Pieter Gillis to me a sum of money that my Lieven had given to him is specified, as also in the receipt he sent with the letter;[1] he estimated the sum to be 117 florins and a few stuivers. I instructed Quirinus to present this letter and the receipt, which he did not do, as far as I can see. It was him I accused, not you. In addition, the pension, as you know, is 130 florins, and only 117 florins and a few stuivers have been paid. Here, again, I lose almost fifteen florins. But this does not pertain to you at all. It is the fault either of Lieven, or of the dean,[2] or of those who remit the pension. I complained about this matter to you as to a friend, not about you. So dismiss this suspicion altogether from your mind.

* * * * *

6 Ie he could (with the help of the emperor or the pope, or both) have become a bishop (or better) had he wanted to do so

7 This letter to Morin seems to have had some positive result, for in the spring of 1532 Erasmus sent Morin an effusive letter of thanks (Ep 2635), in which he restated his conviction that approval for the publication had not been provided by the Parlement or the faculty and that Morin has been misled into licensing it. Cf Ep 2615:524–7.

2578

1 The letter is not extant.

2 Pierre Barbier, dean of Tournai; see Ep 2487:9–17.

Now you know what I did not understand and what I complained of. None of these things pertain to you, my dear Erasmus. I will write to Quirinus, now that I understand the situation. This is in answer to your letter of 18 October.

The house gives me no motivation for wishing to stay here for any length of time.[3] As to what you write about a receipt that would absolve you, I will do as you ask, although I made no such demand.[4] And I do not see how a receipt can be made, since it is uncertain what you will receive from the English. But I will send you a general receipt that will free you from any anxiety, since that is what you wish. You can accept it or not accept it, as you wish. But concerning your suspicion about what you have received in the past, it is pure fantasy, as far as I am concerned. Quirinus did not act honestly, since he did not show you Pieter Gillis' letter. Therefore I warned you to be more careful and not readily believe my servants when they present nothing but their word. There is among you a Jew who has stirred up a furor in Paris, and I have no doubts that he will stir up an even more dreadful one.[5] I wonder what the pontiffs are contemplating who think such a universal evil can be allayed by lunatics. Farewell.

You will recognize my hand.

To the honourable Master Erasmus Schets. At Antwerp

2579 / To Lorenzo Campeggi   Freiburg, 2 December 1531

This letter was first published in the *Catalogue raisonné de la collection de livres de M. Pierre Antoine Crevenna [Pietro Antonio Crevenna], négociant à Amsterdam* (n p 1776) iv/2 239–41. Unable to locate the original manuscript, Allen printed the text as found in the *Catalogue*. Lorenzo Cardinal Campeggi (Ep 2366) was at this time papal legate at the imperial court.

* * * * *

3 Cf Ep 2558:6–8.
4 In Ep 2558:48–53 Schets had asked that a receipt be sent via Hieronymus Froben at the Frankfurt fair for monies received in Erasmus' name, which would free him from the burden of rendering account for these sums in his letters. Erasmus promises to comply but denies that he had ever demanded such an accounting from Schets. In Ep 2593:20–1 Schets says that Erasmus need not send a receipt to Frankfurt.
5 The reference is to Girolamo Aleandro; for Erasmus' belief that he was behind the *Determinatio* of the Paris theologians and that he was the author of Scaliger's *Oratio*, see Ep 2565 nn3, 12. For his arrival as papal legate at the imperial court in Brussels, see Ep 2565 n2. On Erasmus' habitual charge that he was a Jew, see Ep 2570 n29.

Cordial greetings. The two main pillars of the Sacramentarian sect have collapsed.[1] Zwingli, as befitted a brave man, was slain in battle; his body was found in the slaughter cut up into four parts and then burned.[2] This news so shocked Oecolampadius that he fell ill, and tortured by an abscess on his spinal cord near the kidneys, which was accompanied by a burning fever, he   5 departed from this earth within about a fortnight.[3]

The change in people's minds is hard to believe.[4] The turn of events seems clearly to be governed by divine agency; would that he who has begun it will bring it to completion. For the Lord is the only one who can remedy these fatal evils, and he wishes that praise for this be attributed to   10 him rather than to human plans or strength. I fear, however, that after this setback they will recover their spirits and return to their course of action with greater vehemence.

As for me, with Christ as my witness, I conducted myself with a sincere conscience in these tumults, not only scrupulously abstaining from   15 their company, but also frequently engaging in conflict with them in open warfare by publishing books. Your most reverend Lordship easily perceived that this was no game if he read at least my *Diatribe*,[5] and *The Enslaved Will*, which Luther published against it;[6] again, in opposition to the latter, my two *Hyperaspistes*,[7] then my epistle against Vulturius,[8] and my answer to his scur-   20 rilous annotations,[9] then the book of the Strasbourg preachers and my *Apology*

* * * * *

2579
1 'Sacramentarian' was the epithet applied by Luther and his followers to Huldrych Zwingli, Johannes Oecolampadius, and others who denied the Real Presence in the Eucharist and insisted that the bread and wine were mere symbols. This appears to be the first use of the word by Erasmus, at least in the correspondence; cf Ep 2631:17.
2 See Ep 2559:17–18 with n7.
3 See Ep 2574:20 with n5.
4 Cf Epp 2582:43–4, 2583:18–20, 2585:14.
5 *De libero arbitrio* (1524)
6 *De servo arbitrio* (1525)
7 *Hyperaspistes* 1 (1526) and 2 (1527)
8 The *Epistola contra pseudevangelicos*, addressed to 'Vulturius Neocomus,' Erasmus' elaborately contrived nickname for Gerard Geldenhouwer; see Epp 2219 n5, 2238 n1.
9 In March 1530 Geldenhouwer published an unauthorized edition of the *Epistola contra pseudevangelicos* with his own annotations; see Ep 2289 n2. What Erasmus calls his answer to it is presumably the second authorized edition of the *Epistola* (Freiburg: Johannes Faber Emmeus 1531).

against them,[10] not to mention a good number of letters. If I had stirred up this Camarina against my own person in order to please men,[11] I would completely regret the role I played; but since it was all done for Christ and with a good conscience, I do not regret it at all. There is no happiness that I can henceforth   25 hope for from this world; I am often exposed to danger through illness and struggle with death, and I am well aware that my last day is very near.

Although that is the present state of affairs, there are those in the party that I defend who through personal hatred never cease to plot my destruction, fulminating against my name with defamatory and mad little books.   30 They prevailed on the prince of Carpi to write against me, despite his protests.[12] Béda, whose hatred cannot be sated by any of my misfortunes, sent to press the censures of the theologians, at the instigation or at least the connivance of the faculty.[13] At the same time a little book appeared under the false name of Julius Caesar Scaliger; nothing more groundless, more insolent, or   35 more frenzied could be imagined. And the real author is not unknown to me. I recognize the style of the man no less than I recognize his face.[14] I answered Pio some time ago,[15] the theologians recently,[16] but without doing any injury to the faculty, who blamed not what I had written, but what was denounced by my malevolent accusers. If I had been tainted by perverse dogmas, it was   40 the duty of Christian charity to make every attempt to lead me back to the right path. But since I have persistently adhered to the church, there is nothing they can concoct to make me into a heretic, nor will they ever do so, even if they stone me with a thousand little books. I will rather imitate David, who did not allow Shimei, a relative of Saul, to be punished even though he   45 uttered the most outrageous abuse against him and threw stones and dirt at the afflicted king.[17] And I will think to myself: 'Let them curse me; perhaps

* * * * *

10 Martin Bucer's *Epistola apologetica*, published in the name of all the preachers at Strasbourg, and Erasmus' *Epistola ad fratres Inferioris Germaniae*; see Ep 2312 nn2–3.
11 On 'stirring up Camarina,' ie stirring up needless trouble, see *Adagia* I i 64.
12 Erasmus persistently maintained that Pio had been duped into writing against him by others, the chief suspects being Paris theologians and monks, the Spanish theologian Juan Ginés de Sepúlveda, and Erasmus' favourite scapegoat, Girolamo Aleandro; see Ep 2486 nn9–10; CWE 84 xcix–c, cxxiii; and Erika Rummel *Erasmus and his Catholic Critics* 2 vols (Nieuwkoop 1989) II 122.
13 See Ep 2552 n10.
14 See Epp 2564 n2, 2565 n12.
15 *Apologia adversus rhapsodias Alberti Pii* (Basel: Froben, July 1531)
16 See n20 below.
17 2 Sam 16:5–12

the Lord has ordered them to do so.'[18] And who knows whether he will have
mercy on me? What if it seemed best to him to purify me, since I am polluted
by so many accusations? But a single Shimei cursed Saul; against me so many   50
Shimeis vent their rage with tongues and stones.

Ten years ago there were some who undertook to alienate somewhat
the sympathies of the emperor from me.[19] If anyone should arise who would
once more contrive similar plots against me, I ask that your most reverend
Lordship show himself to be the protector he has hitherto always most gra-   55
ciously shown himself to be. It will weigh heavily upon one, I know, because
of the faculty of theology, but I beg you not to find it burdensome to inspect
my *Declarations,* which are now in the hands of the printer and will appear
very soon.[20] May the Lord keep your most reverend Highness safe and sound.

Given at Freiburg im Breisgau, 2 December 1531   60
Erasmus of Rotterdam, at your service
Erasmus of Rotterdam. I have signed it with my own hand.
To the most reverend doctor of theology Lorenzo Campeggi, his most
reverend lord, cardinal, apostolic legate to the emperor

2580 / From Bonifacius Amerbach   Basel, 9 December 1531

First published by Allen, this letter (= AK Ep 1591) is Bonifacius' reply to Ep 2575.
The autograph rough draft is in the Öffentliche Bibliothek of the University of
Basel (MS C VIa 73 256).

Greetings. What you write is true, most illustrious Erasmus. Nothing can
be said so honestly and prudently these days that it cannot immediately be
interpreted as calumny. But whether that is the result of the iniquity of the
times or of men, we must resign ourselves to the inevitable. Your excellence
has, to be sure, so sunk its roots into the hearts of all good men that no injus-   5
tice of the times (I pass over in silence the virulence of the Ecks, the Betas,[1]

* * * * *

18 Cf 2 Sam 16:11.
19 In 1522 Erasmus was much exercised by reports that Aleandro and others were
    campaigning against him at the emperor's court, but he noted with satisfaction
    that they had not succeeded; see Ep1302:57–66.
20 *Declarationes ad censuras Lutetiae vulgatas* (Basel: Froben 1532). The month of
    publication is not indicated, but Erasmus sent a copy of it to Piotr Tomicki on
    4 February 1532; see Ep 2600:24–5.

2580
1 Turning 'Béda' into 'Beta,' ie 'Beet'

the Cacandroses,[2] and their like)[3] can uproot it. The ancients passed on to us
the saying that envy is the companion of virtue.[4] What happiness was ever so
great that it was not attacked by the tongues of tell-tales and slanderers?[5] Do
you remember that the rabbis and the Pharisees brought Christ the Saviour to   10
trial? The disciple is not above his teacher nor the servant above his master.[6]
Thus one ascends to the stars.[7] Let them snarl, let them erupt, let them throw
everything into confusion, the name of Erasmus will be transmitted to posterity unharmed by any injury and worthy of applause, while these vermin
(if indeed any memory of them survives) will live on only for punishment   15
and disgrace. In truth I am bringing owls to Athens in writing this to you,[8]
to whom Pallas Athena and greatness of soul are the resident counsellors.
You dispelled entirely the cloud of suspicion that Grynaeus had conceived, a
common human failing, as you will be amply informed in his letter to you.[9]
What temperament is so savage as not to be pacified by your warmly affec-   20
tionate letter?[10] In my opinion, at least, he persuaded me of nothing else by
his oath except that he had reported to you in good faith what he received in
commission; in this we are agreed. Since the matter is of no great urgency, as
you write,[11] I will be there at Christmas. Farewell, most illustrious Erasmus.

At Basel, the day after the Conception of the Blessed Virgin 1531   25
Cordially, Bonifacius Amerbach

2581 / To Hilarius Bertholf   Freiburg, 10 December 1531

This letter was first published by Allen on the basis of the autograph in the
Staatsbibliothek at Berlin (MS Acc MS). For Hilarius Bertholf, Erasmus' former
servant and courier (1522–4), see Ep 1712. He was now married and had just
recently entered the service of Johannes Dantiscus (Ep 2563A); see Ep 2570:47–8.

* * * * *

2 Turning 'Aleandro' into a combination of κακός 'bad' and ἀνήρ, ἀνδρός 'man,'
   with *kakos* echoing *kacke* (German for 'shit') and *cacare* (Latin for 'to shit')
3 Cf Ep 2575:8–11.
4 See, for example, *Ad Herennium* 4.36 (once attributed to Cicero but now regarded as an anonymous work).
5 'Talebearers' in Greek, as in Aristotle *Rhetoric* 2.6 1384b11
6 Matt 10:24
7 Virgil *Aeneid* 9.641
8 'Bringing owls to Athens' is the ancient equivalent of 'carrying coals to
   Newcastle'; see *Adagia* I ii 1.
9 Not extant
10 Ep 2576
11 See Ep 2575:16–17.

As this letter makes clear, Erasmus had stayed in touch with Bertholf and was concerned that he find suitable employment.

Cordial greetings. This dissimulator has gone there mainly to cause my ruin and to display his own greatness.[1] He published a little book in France as raving mad as it is defamatory, full of scurrilous insults and manifest lies. The title is *[An Oration] of Julius Caesar Scaliger for Cicero against Erasmus*. But I recognize the style and the character no less than I know the man's face.[2] 5
Here is an example. He says that I made it my aim to destroy Cicero's renown so that I would be chosen to take his place; that I served as a menial, that is, a reader, with Aldus; that when I lived with Aldus I never rose from table without being drunk, although they never served anything that could make you drunk and I never had the time to indulge in wine; that I had never read 10
Aristotle, although there is no work of his from which I have not made some citation. Orestes in the paroxysm of his madness would speak more sanely.[3] But conceal your reactions and observe.

I would like you to change your way of life. As long as you frequent the court, your financial situation does not improve and your time grows short- 15
er. You know the popular saying: 'A young courtier, an old beggar.'[4] And what about the fact that in the meantime she who depends on you grows old alone? If you move to Lyon, having a few students will supply you with a livelihood, and you will earn some money from the printers. The court does not bring success to everyone. You must think this over carefully.[5] Farewell, 20
dearest Hilarius. For the moment I could not write further.

Given at Freiburg, the tenth day of December 1531

Your Erasmus of Rotterdam, in my hand

Concerning the publication of your epigrams, you decide; see to it, however, that they are inoffensive. If you want your writing to be read, write some- 25
thing that will be well-worn in students' hands, on the elegance of the Latin language, the precepts of rhetoric, or something similar.[6] Once again, farewell.

To the learned Hilarius Bertholf. At the court of the emperor

* * * * *

2581
1 Aleandro was with the imperial court at Brussels; see Ep 2565 n2.
2 See Ep 2565 n12.
3 For having killed his mother Clytaemnestra to avenge the death of his father Agamemnon, Orestes was hounded by the Furies and driven mad.
4 Dutch in the text: 'Een ionck houeling, een out schoueling.'
5 Bertholf followed Erasmus' advice and settled in Lyon, where he, his wife, and his three children died of the plague in 1533 (Ep 2865).
6 There is no record of the epigrams having been published, or evidence that the book on Latin elegance was ever written.

2582 / To Nicolaus Olahus Freiburg, 11 December 1531

This letter, which is Erasmus' reply to a letter no longer extant, was first published in Ipolyi, page 174. The manuscript is page 228 in the Olahus codex of the Hungarian National Archives in Budapest (Ep 2339 introduction). For Nicolaus Olahus see Ep 2339.

ERASMUS OF ROTTERDAM TO NICOLAUS OLAHUS,
TREASURER OF SZÉKESFEHÉRVÁR

I have never doubted the singular benevolence of my friend Olahus towards me, and it is not my custom to measure friendship by the dutiful exercise of letter-writing. Those who have little love for Erasmus also write to him. Just 5 as it is most agreeable to receive letters from friends like you, so do I easily bear it if letters do not arrive, assured as I am of their good sentiments towards me. Polyphemus, as he was about to leave Augsburg, wrote me a detailed letter about his current circumstances;[1] I do not know where he has gone.[2] He promised that he would let me know, but he has not yet done so. 10 He extorted letters from friends as if he was setting out directly to see me, but he has not come. He entrusted letters to a certain Dominican in Ulm, which by some happy chance were delivered to me via Dominicus.[3] Polyphemus indicated that you would also write, but nothing has been received from Olahus. I imagine you promised to write but something happened that pre- 15 vented you from doing what you had in mind.

But in this regard, dear Nicolaus, there is no reason for you to excuse yourself. Be absolutely assured that your loyal character is never remiss in the fulfilment of good offices whenever there is need. While you exaggerate in words my services to you, you do not retreat from your innate loy- 20 alty. If I had at the present time merited some outstanding recompense from you, I would not be able to ask anything in return save that you continue to be Olahus. For this name expresses in a single word all the good offices of friendship, just as a famous man thought that everything was contained in the one adverb 'royally.'[4] 25

* * * * *

2582
1 Not extant; possibly the letter left with Johann Koler in Augsburg (see Epp 2437:21–3, 2438:3–4). For Polyphemus (Felix Rex), see Ep 2475 n1.
2 He had gone to the court of Elector John of Saxony and would not reappear in Freiburg until February 1532; see Ep 2609 introduction.
3 Unidentified
4 Reference unidentified

I have recommended my Lieven to Queen Mary, into whose entourage he desires with astonishing eagerness to be enrolled, for what reason I do not know exactly. I ask that you do not cease your support for him, if he seems apt for the post to which he is aspiring; to me he seems, by virtue of his temperament and literary experience, more suited to the role of secretary.[5] 30

The severe pain in my foot left me after three days, but a stomach diarrhea followed, which, thank God, turned out well.[6] For the rest, not being able to devote myself to the needs of my frail little body because of many visitors, I fell victim to another illness, which went away of itself. After that my stomach began to comport itself a little better than previously. I hope this 35 house will be a little more favourable to me from now on.[7]

I did not write more often because I was uncertain whether you were still in the service of the queen. Lieven's letter was delivered to me too late.[8] I have thought more than once of returning to Brabant. But certain friends suggested that I should stay here for as long as was necessary for matters 40 there to be settled by the emperor.[9]

We have been liberated from a great fear here with the death of the two preachers, Zwingli and Oecolampadius.[10] Their deaths have brought an incredible change of mind to many people.[11] This is no doubt the sublime hand of God; may he complete what he has begun for the glory of his name. 45 Farewell.

Given at Freiburg im Breisgau, 11 December 1531

* * * * *

5 Cf Ep 2587:71–4, where Erasmus professes his astonishment that Lieven is trying to be appointed chamber valet to Queen Mary despite being more suited to the post of secretary.
6 See Ep 2528 n8.
7 See Epp 2506 n1, 2517 n11.
8 Not extant
9 Erasmus had indeed often given thought to returning to Brabant. Payment of his imperial pension had been made conditional on his doing so (Ep 2196:154–8), and he would have been welcomed with open arms by many old friends (Ep 2192:97–104). But the presence there of the Louvain theologians with their enduring hostility, combined with the danger to his freedom and independence of becoming entangled in the affairs of the imperial court, invariably defeated whatever temptation there was to exchange the Breisgau for Brabant (Epp 2196:158–61, 2328:57–62). He did not need the advice of 'certain friends' to persuade him to stay where he was. As the purchase and extensive refitting of a new house at great expense indicates, he was not seriously considering moving anywhere unless circumstances compelled him to do so; cf Ep 2566:189–92.
10 See Ep 2579:1–7.
11 See Ep 2579 n4.

2583 / To Mary of Hungary   Freiburg, 12 December 1531

This letter was first published in Ipolyi, page 175. The manuscript is page 230 in the Olahus Codex of the Hungarian National Archives in Budapest (Ep 2339 introduction).

Mary of Austria, sister of Charles v and Ferdinand of Austria, was the widow of Louis II, king of Bohemia and Hungary, who had been killed at the battle of Mohács in 1526. She had used her considerable influence and impressive political skills to aid Ferdinand in his claim to succeed her husband as king of Bohemia and Hungary, and she acted as his regent until 1527. Steadfastly rejecting her brothers' efforts to manoeuvre her into a new, politically advantageous marriage, she remained single and childless. But in 1531 she agreed to succeed her aunt, Margaret of Austria, as regent of the Netherlands, in which capacity she served with distinction until the abdication of her brother Charles in 1556. Informed of Mary's admiration for his works, Erasmus wrote his *Vidua christiana* for her and dedicated it to her (Ep 2100). Of the direct correspondence between Mary and Erasmus, only six letters are extant, four from him to her (Epp 2100, 2350, 2583, 2812), and two from her to him (Epp 2820, 3034). Through her secretary Nicolaus Olahus (Ep 2339), however, Mary maintained a lively correspondence with Erasmus. As regent of the Netherlands, moreover, she made a sustained effort to persuade him to return to his native country, but by the summer of 1533, when her personal invitation to him to do so (Ep 2820) was delivered to him in Freiburg, his health had deteriorated to the point where he could no longer undertake the journey.

ERASMUS OF ROTTERDAM TO MARY OF HUNGARY, QUEEN OF
BOHEMIA AND IMPERIAL VICE-REGENT OF LOWER GERMANY, ETC,
GREETING
Do we not clearly recognize in you, most eminent of women, a divine goodness, which after the wine and bitterness of tribulation[1] has poured out the   5
oil of consolation, and after the violent storms of raging fortune has generously granted a longed-for serenity? Through adversity he has both tested and exalted your piety: he tested it in order to crown it more richly; he exalted it so that by the example of a woman men would learn patiently to suffer the hand of the Lord, who scourges us, not for our destruction but for our   10
salvation.[2] Now the winter of desolation is passed, the flowers of joy have

* * * * *

2583
1 Cf Rev 14:10: 'the wine of the wrath of God, which is poured out full strength.'
2 Cf Hebr 12:6–11.

appeared, the cruel tempest belongs to the past, and pleasant good fortune
has succeeded it, which for you we pray will be unending. And so we who
were in anguish for you with good cause render thanks to God for you. But
we congratulate not so much you as our country, which will have such a sov-   15
ereign; governed under her auspices, it will flourish much more in piety and
the liberal disciplines than in riches.

Here the death of Zwingli, who perished in battle, and that of Oecolampadius, who was carried off shortly afterwards by an abscess and a fever,[3]
have brought about among many an incredible change of mind.[4] If God will   20
deign to stretch out his hand, I hope to see the end of this evil. The Lord, however, will moderate the ardour of the invincible emperor, so that the weeds
will be torn out in such a way that the wheat will not be eradicated with it.[5]
Thus impiety will be suppressed in such a way that the victory will redound
to the glory of Christ rather than arouse the tyranny of certain people. Many   25
who run to help put out this fire in the church are corrupted by private am-
bitions and pursue their own interests, just as it often happens that when a
house is on fire some hasten not to lend aid but to pillage. Many take care of
their hair and their nails but leave untouched the ulcers from which all this
tumult of the world arises. But the Lord one day will deign to put an end to   30
these evils.

Lieven Panagathus,[6] a young man of clever mind and sufficiently com-
petent in both literatures, who was in my service for almost six years, is most
eager to be a member of your household, whether your Majesty deigns to
receive him into the number of chamber valets or any other service, however   35
humble. He wishes to be among your devoted servants, whatever his position. He is known to Alfonso de Valdés, and is not unknown to Nicolaus
Olahus.[7] If on their advice your Benevolence will deign to give him a place
on your domestic staff it will be most pleasing to me, and I shall consider
what you bestow on him to be bestowed on me as well. May the Lord Jesus   40
keep your illustrious Majesty safe and sound and flourishing in all good
endeavours.

Given at Freiburg im Breisgau, 12 December 1531

* * * * *

3 See Ep 2579:1–7.
4 See Ep 2579 n4.
5 Matt 13:24–30
6 Ie Lieven Algoet; see Ep 2528 n9.
7 See Ep 2582:26–8.

2584 / To Jan and Stanisław Boner   Freiburg, 12 December [1531]

This is the preface to the Froben edition of the comedies of Terence: *Terentii comoediae, cum scholiis ex Donati, Asperi, et Cornuti commentariis decerptis* (Basel: March 1532). For the brothers Boner and the circumstances of the dedication see Epp 2533, 2539 introductions. The date in line 115 (1532) is clearly a mistake for 1531.

DESIDERIUS ERASMUS OF ROTTERDAM TO THE POLISH BROTHERS
JAN AND STANISŁAW BONER, GREETING
'In the tender years,' said the famous poet, 'it is important to form habits,'[1] just as it is advisable to become accustomed immediately to that which is best. In that way it will come about that what is best by nature will also be- 5 come most pleasant through practice. There is nothing better for man than piety, the seeds of which must be instilled in young children immediately from early infancy. The liberal disciplines come next, which, though they are not virtues in themselves, prepare the character for virtue, transforming it from rustic and coarse to mild and tractable. Moreover, when Aristotle says 10 that adolescents do not have the right qualities to learn moral philosophy, perhaps he is not altogether wrong.[2] This, however, does not occur so much through a defect of the subject matter or of the human spirit as through the fault of those who transmit it too late to souls that have already been cor- rupted by a perverted education and seized by evil desires, or who trans- 15 mit it in a tiresome and pedestrian way, trying more to appear sophisticated themselves than to improve their students. Otherwise, there is nothing more in accordance with nature than virtue and learning; if you take these two things away from a man, he has ceased to be a human being. Every living thing is responsive above all else to what nature has predisposed it: the horse 20 to run, the dog to hunt, the bird to fly, the monkey to play. There is no reason to find fault with nature, but it is of great importance to know from what source the basic principles of piety and learning are imbibed, and then what guide the child will obtain for this purpose, especially in the early years, in which the character is free of faults, and like soft wax is pliant and amenable 25 to the configurations of the modeller.

Therefore I consider you fortunate on many accounts, distinguished young men: First, that you were born in this age, in which the purity of true

* * * * *

2584
1 Virgil *Georgics* 2.272
2 Aristotle *Nicomachean Ethics* 1.3 1095a2–5

piety and of better literature has miraculously come back to life. For when
I was a boy religion contained much superstition, and in the schools ado-   30
lescents learned with great torture almost nothing, only to unlearn it. Then,
because you have been given a father who considers that his children will
not be very happy if he has prepared them to be heirs of the wealth and status by which he holds a privileged position among the leading men of the
Polish nation but has not also rendered them rich and adorned with the true   35
assets of the spirit. He does not think that he has discharged the role of parent to the full if, just as he brought you into being, he does not also fashion
your souls, knowing full well that this is the best part of man, that this is a
man's primary possession. Your father, a virtuous man, educates you not
so much for himself as for Christ and the commonwealth. That he fathered   40
you is a natural thing; that he makes sure that as soon as you have left the
breast of the wet nurse you are imbued with the most noble disciplines is
the mark of a true sense of duty. He shows his wisdom because he chose
Anselmus Ephorinus for this role, a man known and recognized for his integrity, wisdom, loyalty, learning, and vigilance.[3] Wherefore, since everything   45
has been provided for your success, you must strive all the more diligently
not to seem to have been found wanting. There is great expectation of you,
especially you, Jan Boner. This is made known to me in numerous letters
sent to me by prominent men, letters in which they scrupulously commend
your talents, especially those of the wise king Sigismund,[4] then of the distin-   50
guished prelates of Cracow and Płock,[5] the famous Krzysztof Szydłowiecki,
chancellor of the Polish kingdom,[6] not to mention Doctor Antonin and the
royal secretary, Justus, men inferior in rank, it is true, but equal in good will.[7]
They understand that there are no better ornaments to do honour to a kingdom than men who excel in learning and wisdom. This element of glory is   55
no less coveted by the most wise of the kings of this age than the delight he
experiences in so many victories over the enemy.[8] And up to now, certainly,
your Poland has flourished happily in studies, and if there was some degree

* * * * *

3 For Seweryn Boner and Ephorinus see Epp 2533 and 2539 introductions.
4 Ep 2520
5 The letter of Piotr Tomicki, bishop of Cracow, is extant (Ep 2521), but that of
   Andrzej Krzycki, bishop of Płock, is not.
6 Letter not extant; for Szydłowiecki see Ep 1593 introduction.
7 Letters not extant. For Jan Antonin, physician to Piotr Tomicki, see Ep 1602 introduction. For Justus Ludovicus Decius, secretary to King Sigismund, see Ep
   1341A n210.
8 A recent war between Poland and Moldavia had ended with a Polish victory at
   Obertyn on 22 August 1531.

of native barbarity, it has been eradicated by contacts with good letters. But there is good hope that it will be able to vie with any country whatever in 60 this type of literary adornment, particularly under the leadership and auspices of the young King Sigismund,[9] who, besides other qualities worthy of an excellent prince, is preparing himself for his reign with the finest literary accomplishments.

But to encourage you I have both written something to you previously,[10] 65 and will do so again in the future, whenever the opportunity arises. To spur you on at present, although you are already racing ahead, I have decided that the *Comedies* of Terence, but corrected with much greater care than they were previously, should appear under the auspices of the name of Boner. It is your ability and that of your servant Stanisław Aichler that motivated me to do 70 this,[11] since you are accustomed, from time to time, to perform some scenes so successfully that all those who watched the spectacle with us greatly admired both your gift of imitation, the first sign of intelligence in a child, according to Quintilian,[12] and your memory. The purity of Roman speech is not better learned from any other writer, nor is there any other more pleasant 75 to read or more suited to the character of children. For the rest, the kindly help of your teacher, Ephorinus, will serve to make this study useful for eloquence and good morals. And as a good part of wisdom consists in knowing the diverse morals and character of men, so decorum and the manner of treating the passions, which are the principal qualities that lend charm to a 80 speech (the Greeks call these qualities ἤθη), are not better learned with any of the rhetoricians. In addition, since the invention of arguments is of primary importance among the functions of oratory, the reading of Terence also contributes enormously to the acquisition of this faculty in every kind of subject. It is not without reason that the recommendations of critics have attributed 85 technical skill to this author. There is more precise judgment in one comedy of Terence – may Nemesis be far removed from my words – than in all the plays of Plautus. But in the case of such an author, as for any painting of Apelles, the one who elucidates it is of great importance.[13] If he happens to be an excellent artist, this reading will serve not only to gladden the mind, not 90

* * * * *

9 See Ep 2554 n12.
10 The reference seems to be to letters of encouragement, like Ep 2549, published in the *Epistolae palaeonaeoi*.
11 For Aichler, see Ep 2545 introduction.
12 *Institutiones oratoriae* 1.3.1
13 Apelles (fourth century BC) was considered the greatest painter of ancient Greece. Erasmus may be alluding to the tale of the cobbler who proved himself an ignorant critic of one of Apelles' paintings; see *Adagia* I vi 16.

only to express oneself correctly, not only to enrich the faculty of elocution, but also it will bring no small portion of moral philosophy, which Socrates considered to be the one thing a man must learn to lead a happy life.

Therefore, if I did not see you running of your own will, my dear Jan, I would exhort you again and again to consider how much you owe to God, by whose munificence you have received as your portion such a prolific intelligence and receptive character and to whom you owe also your father Seweryn Boner and Anselmus, a second father; then what great hopes are entertained for you by such distinguished men and how all eyes are fixed on you; lastly, how your present age is most suited to the noble disciplines. You have not yet passed your fourteenth year, as I understand. For in the acquisition of learning a single year at a tender age is worth ten when the mind, already absorbed by other cares, has become hardened in its ability to learn. Add to this that it is what we assimilated as boys that lasts most tenaciously throughout our lives. I shall dismiss you after having first urged you to exercise yourself diligently in all types of poetry, for the reason that those who have neglected this part of learning engage themselves with less profit and less pleasure with authors who have composed poetry. These same people let themselves be deceived more easily by the defects of manuscripts, which are often revealed by the rules of metrics. And since in this author the structure of the verse is often disorderly and quite free, I have supplied a few notes, which will provide some light for those who are not well trained.

Farewell, and make good use of my advice.

Freiburg im Breisgau, 12 December 1532[14]

2585 / To Erasmus Schets   Freiburg, 13 December 1531

This letter was first published by Allen on the basis of the autograph in the British Library (MS Add 38512 folio 66). Schets' reply is Ep 2593.

Greetings. I have received the preserves.[1] Since my papers are in disorder because of my move, I have not been able to find the letter of the person who sent them. Let me know. In the meantime I pray you to thank him in my

* * * * *

14 On the year-date see the introduction above.

2585
1 See Ep 2511:29–33.

name.[2] Aleandro, who has long been plotting my destruction, is there.[3] And I
have no doubts that he is now doing the same thing. A rumour is flying about   5
concerning the diet at Regensburg,[4] but I think the emperor will pass the
winter there.[5] I am astonished about Pieter Gillis and Barbier.[6] If such friends
deceive us, whom are we to believe and what are we to believe? I await your
letter concerning affairs in England. I wish you and yours the best of health.

    Freiburg, 13 December 1531   10
    Your Erasmus, in his own hand
    You know, I believe, that Zwingli perished in battle and Oecolampadius
in bed.[7] There is a great change of attitude, one hopes for the better.[8] We await
the diet at Regensburg.
    To the honourable gentleman Erasmus Schets. In Antwerp   15

2586 / To Hector van Hoxwier   Freiburg, 13 December 1531

    First published in the *Epistolae palaeonaeoi*, this is Erasmus' response to a let-
    ter of self-introduction that is not extant. Born in Mantgum, near Leeuwarden,
    into a noble family related to that of Viglius Zuichemus (Ep 2101 introduction),
    Hector van Hoxwier (1502–47) studied with Conradus Goclenius, professor of
    Latin at the Collegium Trilingue in Louvain (see line 3). Returning home, he
    became a councillor of Friesland, in which capacity he delivered an oration
    to Charles v in 1531, congratulating him on his recent coronation as emperor
    in Bologna. In 1534 he resigned his office to go to Italy and study law under
    Andrea Alciati, to whom Erasmus had recommended him (Allen Ep 3022:1–7).
    Having completed a doctorate in both laws in 1536, he resumed his career in
    Friesland and was sent on several important missions to Charles v, who also
    made similar use of him an emissary. In 1541 he became president of the council
    of Utrecht, and in the year before his death his services were rewarded by ap-
    pointment as knight of the Golden Fleece. This is one of the three letters in the
    correspondence between Erasmus and Hoxwier that survives (the others being

    * * * * *

2 The sender was Martín Fernandes (Ep 2511 n13). In Ep 2593:8–10 Schets says
    that he has already conveyed Erasmus' thanks to Fernandes.
3 Ie there in the Netherlands, having arrived at the imperial court in Brussels on
    2 November 1531; see Ep 2565 n2.
4 See Ep 2559:7–11.
5 Ie in Brussels
6 See Epp 2494 n12 (Gillis), 2527 n8 (Barbier).
7 See Ep 2579:1–7.
8 See Ep 2579 n4.

Epp 2624 and 3022); three other letters are mentioned in line 3 below and in
Allen Epp 2851:40, 2972:5–6.

ERASMUS OF ROTTERDAM TO HECTOR VAN HOXWIER
OF FRIESLAND, GREETING

From your letter[1] I clearly recognized a true disciple of Goclenius, to such
an extent do you recall him both in elegance of language and singular modesty. Assuredly, you must have a very high opinion of Erasmus, seeing that   5
although you had no fears whatsoever to approach the emperor,[2] monarch of
the whole world, nevertheless even at the exhortation and the assurance of
Goclenius, you could scarcely be prevailed upon to address yourself to me in
writing. And yet they say that a letter does not blush.[3] Who could not greatly
admire the remarkable modesty displayed in someone with such outstand-   10
ing endowments of character and of fortune? But at the same time I am somewhat offended by this modesty, which delayed my getting to know a person
of such loving heart. The truth is that your letter of 26 May was not delivered
to me until 2 November, so you may not accuse me of negligence or discour-
tesy because you have received my answer so tardily. There is no need, my   15
distinguished young man, to request that the name of Hector van Hoxwier
be inscribed in the list of my friends; on the contrary, I am most grateful that
you have wished to enrich me by the addition of such an exceptional friend.
I am fully convinced that, as you say, you were drawn by some mysterious
impulse to feel this affection for me. If that had not happened, what qualities   20
does this poor little man possess that anyone could love or admire? I rejoice,
however, that many persons have risen up who by their renown will obscure my good name, if such exists. I congratulate also your native Friesland,
which, though previously considered more closely associated with Komos
or Bacchus than with Pallas Athena,[4] has now begun to be the home of the   25
Muses, since so many prolific talents are flourishing there. What is more able
than the intelligence of the councillor Haio Herman, more affable than his

* * * * *

2586
1 Not extant
2 Perhaps a reference to the oration mentioned in the introduction
3 Cicero *Ad familiares* 5.12.1, cited in *Adagia* II i 70 *Pudor in oculis* 'Shame is in the
   eyes'
4 Komos was the Greek god of revelry and merrymaking; Bacchus (the Roman
   equivalent of the Greek Dionysus) was the god of wine and drunken revels;
   Pallas Athena was the goddess of reason, wisdom, and civilization. Cf the same
   description of Friesland in Allen Ep 2681:14, in which Erasmus recommends
   Viglius Zuichemus to Pietro Bembo.

character, more pure or refined than his style?[5] With the addition of Viglius Zuichemus, whose immaculate style I have admired in his letters to me, there would be a triple rope, which, as the wise Hebrew said, is not easily bro- 30 ken.[6] But my affection for him increased after he came here to visit me, even though only for a short time,[7] for he found one who was languishing and exhausted by the fatigue of moving house.[8] He manifested a marvellous affection for me not only in his words, but in his eyes, countenance, and every movement of his body. He also left with me an exquisite souvenir. It is a ring 35 engraved with astrological signs, which depicts the rotation of the heavenly sphere, so that I can carry the universe on my finger.[9] Either I am completely deluded or, if the gods grant him life, he will one day be a great ornament of Friesland. He was on his way to Italy at the time to finish a course of studies in Padua.[10] I have not received any letters from Haio Herman for a long 40 time, perhaps because there is no one to whom he can safely entrust a letter, although he is generally very sedulous in the fulfilment of this duty.[11] Please be sure to greet him in my name, since I have had no opportunity at the present time to write to him. Please greet also the other colleagues who wish us well, and may no viper slither its way into their midst that would vitiate our 45 friendship with its venomous hissing. An eye contorted with envy can effect very baneful spells. If there is anything I can do for you, you may ask it by right of friendship. I will not offer resistance to Hector, whom Achilles could barely match. I do not doubt that you will live up to your name in friendship also, as you so wittily promise. Farewell. 50

At Freiburg im Breisgau, 13 December 1531

2587 / To Conradus Goclenius   Freiburg, 14 December 1531

First published in the *Vita Erasmi*, this is Erasmus' response to Ep 2573.

* * * * *

5 For Haio Herman of Emden, since 1528 member of the council of Friesland, see Ep 1978 introduction.
6 Eccl 4:12
7 In the autumn of 1531; see Ep 2551 introduction.
8 See Epp 2506 n1, 2517 n11.
9 See Major 39 with n16 on page 40, 54 with n66 on page 63.
10 Viglius had already completed a doctorate in both laws at Valence in 1529. In 1532 he accepted a one-year appointment to lecture in civil law at Padua.
11 Cf Ep 2587:57–8, where Erasmus says that Haio had conceived a mortal hatred of him because he was not included for honourable mention in the *Ciceronianus*.

ERASMUS OF ROTTERDAM TO MASTER CONRADUS GOCLENIUS,
GREETING

I have now responded to the censures of the Sorbonnists;[1] the work, of which
I send you a sample, is almost printed.[2] And yet I had, as a matter of fact, already responded to most of their accusations. They are almost all propositions 5
of Béda. I knew what that conspiratorial fraternity deserved, but I restrained
the impetus of my pen for fear that the faculty, more than sufficiently irritated,
would burn my books, which would be suitable and agreeable to them, since
Béda reigns there together with a number of conspirators and has the favour
of the president of the Parlement,[3] as they write. All the same, the *Censures* 10
would never have appeared unless someone had poured oil on the fire. Eck
was in Paris and, as I suspect, Aleandro.[4] who, I suspect, went there principal-
ly for the purpose of encompassing the ruin of Erasmus. I am as certain that
the book of Julius Scaliger is his as I am that I am alive,[5] but we must conceal
this lest, if his trickery is revealed, he become even more frenzied. I know 15
that the followers of Béda will never desist. Yet Béda, however hostile, did
not approve that this raging nonsense should be published. It was printed
clandestinely and suppressed for a while until they could obtain permission
from some lieutenant or other.[6] I have nothing to reply about the imperial
treasury[7] except for the saying of jurisconsults: 'Abundant caution does no 20
harm.'[8] I know I have to do with very devious beasts. And there are also
certain Evangelicals, whose master is that diabolical Geldenhouwer,[9] who use
incredible stratagems to provoke the feelings of the emperor and Ferdinand
against me. In Strasbourg they have published a book in German against his

* * * * *

2587
1 *Declarationes ad censuras Lutetiae vulgatas*, Erasmus' response to the *Determinatio*
  of the Paris theologians (Ep 2552 n10)
2 It was in print by 4 February 1532; see Ep 2579 n20.
3 Erasmus calls him *regii Senatus praeses*, but he is referring to the president (since
  1529) of the Parlement of Paris, Pierre Lizet (c 1482–1554). A councillor in the
  Parlement since 1514 and a royal advocate since 1517, he was notably severe in
  his attitude towards the evangelical cause.
4 See Ep 2565 nn3–4.
5 See Ep 2565:24–6 with nn11–12.
6 Jean Morin; see Ep 2577.
7 Ie Erasmus' imperial pension; see Ep 2573:29–30.
8 *Abundans cautela non nocet*, a familiar legal maxim, still cited in Latin in English
  dictionaries of legal terms
9 Gerard Geldenhouwer (Ep 2238 n1)

imperial Majesty,[10] in which they often cite the authority of Erasmus, excerpt- 25
ing some passages from the proverb about the dung-beetle and the eagle and
the preface to Suetonius.[11] I have no doubt that this is the work of Capito and
Bucer, perhaps with the secret help of Eppendorf.[12] I have not yet seen the book,
but I learned of the affair today in a letter from the cardinal of Trent,[13] who presides over the privy council of Ferdinand and is a very close friend of mine. 30
In Strasbourg no one hatched any schemes against me until Geldenhouwer
moved there; he is now in Augsburg and teaches poetry there with a salary of
sixty florins, as rumour has it. It is a good thing that the two chieftains died,
Zwingli in battle, Oecolampadius shortly afterwards from a fever and an abscess.[14] If Mars had favoured them, that would have been the end of us. About 35
a professor I cannot promise anything.[15] There was only one here, the teacher
of our Erasmius.[16] He secretly moved to Strasbourg, through love for a sect.
All studies here are inadequate except for jurisprudence. I saw only the titles
of the ordinances.[17] These money-experts do this so that they will not seem
to have done nothing. What is this I hear? We have sung a song of triumph 40
before the victory.[18] I was surprised, obviously, but I did not dare disbelieve it
when you were so confident.[19] This is a game played by courtiers. I had recom-

* * * * *

10 Sebastian Franck *Chronica, Zeytbuch vnd Geschychtbybell* (Strasbourg: Balthasar
   Beck, 1531); see Ep 2615:350–88.
11 The proverb is *Adagia* III vii 1, the meaning of which, according to Erasmus,
   is that 'not even the more powerful prince can afford to provoke or disregard
   even the humblest enemy' (*Institutio principis christiani* CWE 27 211–12). In his
   preface to Suetonius (Ep 586) Erasmus emphasizes that the emperors whose
   lives he recorded were mostly vicious monsters and enemies of the human race,
   in every way the opposite of what a Christian prince should be.
12 Cf Ep 2615 introduction; Wolfgang Capito and Martin Bucer were the two principal leaders of the Reformation in Strasbourg. Erasmus' old adversary Heinrich
   Eppendorf (Epp 2384 n15, 2400), whom Erasmus never ceased to believe was
   plotting against him, had settled in Strasbourg in the mid-1520s.
13 Bernhard von Cles (Ep 2504). The letter is not extant, but see Ep 2615:353–4, and
   cf Ep 2622:1–10.
14 See Ep 2579:1–7.
15 Ie a professor of Hebrew to replace Jan van Campen at the Collegium Trilingue:
   see Ep 2573:37–43.
16 Erasmius Froben (Ep 2229 introduction and n3); the teacher has not been
   identified.
17 See Ep 2573:53–8.
18 *Adagia* I vii 55, cited in Greek
19 Ie his confident expectation of victory in his suit over the Antwerp prebend; see
   Ep 2573:58–65.

mended you enthusiastically to Valdés,[20] although I still don't know who was to decide the matter. I would gladly recommend you to Campeggi also,[21] if I were not afraid of impeding your cause. But I expect that I shall soon hear the words as I awake: 'We won.' 45

Cammingha paid four in all? But he owed an additional fourteen, if I am not mistaken.[22] I have never seen anyone more unreliable or more difficult than that young man. I suspect he was offended by my last letter,[23] in which I indicated to him that I was not unaware of his trip to Italy, although 50 in the meantime he wrote to me as if he were in Friesland. I said this in jest. But I also exhorted him to deal openly with a straightforward friend. The other Haio, Herman, writes nothing, thanks to Alaard, if I am not mistaken, who recently wrote to Hieronymus Froben that he would come to Basel with his commentaries on Rodolphus Agricola,[24] if Hieronymus was willing to 55 send him the money for the journey and settle on a fair payment for the rest. Haio has conceived a mortal hatred for me because he was passed over in the *Ciceronianus*.[25] What monsters this age brings forth! Cammingha is not to be bothered or worried about. Keep the four florins for yourself, seeing that you sent the doctor here, the servant of Theodrinckus,[26] at your own 60 expense, and Hieronymus did not give you anything,[27] although the whole matter was his concern.

I do not know what you mean by what you call your last letter. Not all of them reach me.[28] The one in which you ask about it was delivered to me towards the end of November, although it was written on 17 July.[29] I 65 answered it via Gualterus, once a canon of Maastricht and Liège.[30] I did not write to Valdés because it did not seem that he was going to the court in the

* * * * *

20 See Ep 2573:73–8 with nn16–17.
21 Lorenzo Campeggi, papal legate at the imperial court (Ep 2579)
22 Haio Cammingha had sent 'four gold coins' in partial payment of his debt to Erasmus; see Ep 2573:66–7 with n11.
23 Not extant
24 For Alaard of Amsterdan and his edition of Rodolphus Agricola (1539), see Ep 433 introduction.
25 See Ep 2586:40–2 with n11.
26 Unidentified
27 Presumably Hieronymus Froben
28 No letter from Goclenius is extant between Ep 2369 (28 August 1530) and Ep 2573 (23 November 1531). Erasmus' most recent surviving letter to Goclenius is Ep 1890 (15 October 1527).
29 Not extant
30 Unidentified

near future.[31] By this same courier I wrote to Maarten Lips,[32] and since he himself asked me repeatedly, I wrote to Hezius, who was exceedingly fond of me when he was in Rome but now that he has returned to his country 70 seems to have become a different person.[33] I wonder why Lieven is so anxious to have the position of chamber valet to Queen Mary, since the office of secretary would be more fitting for him. I acceded to his request, but my spirit cried out in protest.[34] He was previously in the service of Schepper, to whom, as I hear, he lent 50 crowns. Now Schepper hands him over to me, 75 writing that he cannot be of any help to him.[35] I still do not have enough confidence in his ability. I would have preferred to give him a good sum of money rather than that recommendation. I feel sorry for our Erasmius, who after enduring such labours in the study of letters is now thinking of becoming a merchant, so that one day he will become the servant of those of whom 80 he could be the master. Hieronymus has firmly established his business. I hope that Erasmius, who is so faltering in his speech, succeeds in learning the language[36] and that he who could not learn in so many years to write two words correctly becomes a good merchant.[37] Lieven writes that he hired this rustic, but the man complained from the first that he did not receive 85 a cent.[38] I recognize Lieven's ways. He should have written at what price and on what terms he had hired the man. Otherwise these people have the habit of demanding double payment. Through this same rustic I sent two letters to Hieronymus, one to you and the other to Arnoldi,[39] in case he would like to send something to Brabant. In the meantime, while the messenger is 90 in Basel I am preparing packets of letters. I blurted out to Cammingha that

* * * * *

31 Alfonso Valdés, secretary to Charles v (Ep 2528 introduction)
32 Letter not extant
33 The letter to Hezius is not extant; cf Ep 2566:171–85 with n40.
34 See Epp 2582:26–30, 2583:32–40.
35 See Ep 2567.
36 Erasmius Froben, Erasmus' godson, was now in Lille, attempting to learn French; see Ep 2573:78–80 with n18.
37 A hopelessly inept student, Erasmius soon moved back to Basel and seems to have spent the rest of his short life (d 1549) working without distinction, and without leaving much of a documentary record, in the great Froben publishing firm.
38 The letter is not extant. For the 'rustic' messenger, who was supposed to deliver Ep 2573 at no cost to Erasmus, see Ep 2573:72–3.
39 Possibly Jan Aerts (Arnoldi) of Nossegem, (d 1537), Augustinian eremite and friend of Maarten Lips, to whom Erasmus sometimes sent greetings in letters to Lips; see Epp 1190:5–7, 1547:33–4.

Haio Herman suffered from the French pox in Italy.[40] Perhaps he conveyed that news to several others more offensively. This may have upset Herman. Viglius paid us a visit here on his way to Italy.[41] There is no one more amiable than this young man. I instructed that the whole packet be given to you so that you can, if you wish, forward those that seem suitable. 95

Farewell. Freiburg, 14 December 1531

2588 / To Gilles de Busleyden   Freiburg, 15 December 1531

This letter was first published in the *Vita Erasmi*. The autograph is in the library of the University of Leiden (MS Vulc. 108). For Gilles de Busleyden and his services to the Collegium Trilingue at Louvain, see Ep 2352 n53.

Cordial greetings, most honourable sir. Goclenius informed me in his letter that Campen has resigned his post as professor, which I regret. But Goclenius' letter, written on 15 July, was not delivered to me until 13 November.[1] There is no one here whom I would dare to recommend to you, to such a degree has this pestilence of opinions corrupted studies.[2] I will look into it more 5 carefully and write to you in detail. Unless the diligence of the professors is maintained, I fear that in the end this college will be a failure. The apathy of the human spirit is astonishing. It falls asleep unless it is roused from time to time by pleasure or novelty. I have warned the professors of this in a letter.[3] I wish you and yours the best of health. 10

Given at Freiburg, 15 December 1531

Erasmus

A crazed ambassador is there with you again,[4] who instead of one fire will kindle many for us. There is nothing more deranged than the present age.

To the most honourable Master Gilles de Busleyden. In Brussels 15

* * * * *

40 Haio was in Italy from 1521 until sometime in 1525, obtaining a doctorate in civil and canon law at Padua.
41 See Ep 2586:28–40.

2588
1 The letter in question is not extant, but see Ep 2573:36–41.
2 Cf Ep 2587:35–8.
3 Ep 2456
4 Probably a reference to Girolamo Aleandro, who had recently arrived in Brussels as papal legate to the imperial court; see Ep 2565 n2.

2589 / From Henricus Cornelius Agrippa   Brussels, 20 December 1531

This letter, Agrippa's reply to Ep 2544, was first published in *Agrippae Opera* II 999.

AGRIPPA TO ERASMUS

The letter you wrote on 19 September, most esteemed Erasmus, I received on 1 November. I can scarcely say – and perhaps you would not believe it if I told you – what incomparable happiness I experienced from this extraordinary kindness of yours towards me, namely, that you deigned not only to   5
honour me, a person unknown to you, with your letter, but also to offer me more than I could hope to obtain. You promise to read my *Declamation on the Vanity of Knowledge and the Excellence of the Word of God* and to write your detailed opinion of it. Therefore I pray you, dear Master Erasmus, for Agrippa's sake do not refuse such a small task, and signify what your Highness thinks   10
of my declamation. I am yours, and having sworn an oath to your word, I dedicate, surrender, and commit myself to you as a faithful soldier. I will always regard your judgment as if it were ancient and venerable wisdom, and I am so persuaded of your kindness that I think you will take in good part my open and frank manner of speaking. For you know what a declamation   15
is. But I also want you to be aware that in matters concerning religion I hold no opinions that do not coincide with those of the Catholic church. I offered hospitality for several days to the priest Andreas, the bearer of your letter, a pious and modest man, who was highly commended by his own virtues and your letter.[1] Would that I could satisfy his aspirations or live up to his   20
opinion of me!

I wish you the best of health, and know for certain that nothing more pleasing can be granted to me than that my sentiments, which are consecrated to you, may be accepted with the same magnitude of soul as they are offered. Again, farewell.   25

From the imperial court, that stepmother of all good letters and virtues, at Brussels, 20 December 1531

2590 / From Jakob Spiegel   Sélestat, 27 December [1531]

This letter was first printed as Ep 106 in Enthoven. The manuscript is in the Rehdiger Collection of the University Library at Wrocław (MS Rehd 254 141).

* * * * *

2589
1 See Ep 2544:8–13 with n3.

For Jakob Spiegel see Ep 2572 introduction. The contents of the letter indicate
that the year-date (see line 35) has to be interpreted as 1531.

Greetings and respects, honoured sir, whom I honour as a father.

The courier delivered your letters, one to me and one to the bishop of
Trent, today, 27 December after the Nativity of the Lord 1532.[1] I shall see to
it as soon as possible that your letter is sent to my brother,[2] who will send it
by post, as they say,[3] to the bishop of Trent, if he is not at court, from which,   5
however, he will not be absent for long. You did well to advise me, for if the
diet takes place and I am called to it, I will direct my conversations and my
words in support of your cause to those clad in purple and mitred.[4] May the
gods exterminate those inarticulate theologians and verbose sophists who
can persecute you but will never overwhelm the evangelical truth that you   10
profess in an evangelical manner. I know their plans and what they have
been plotting for six years, but their attempt was in vain and will remain that
way through the favour of God, whose spirit is with you.

Aleandro came straight from Rome to Speyer through the Veneto; he
did not visit France, I am certain of that.[5]   15

About the Sardanapalus of Liège,[6] whom we would have seen as
a wretched burden hanging from a tree if he had fallen into the hands of

* * * * *

2590
1 Neither the letter to Spiegel nor that to Bernhard von Cles, bishop of Trent, is
   extant. Erasmus had written to Cles on 9 October (Ep 2555), but that letter can
   scarcely have taken so long to get to Sélestat.
2 Maius; see Ep 2572 n2.
3 On the word 'post' (*posta, -ae*), which had come into Latin from the vernaculars
   following the establishment of regular postal services in the late fourteenth century, see Ep 1540 n2.
4 The imperial diet, originally summoned to meet at Speyer in September 1531,
   had been postponed to January 1532 and transferred to Regensburg; see Ep
   2572:24–8.
5 For Erasmus' conviction that Girolamo Aleandro had recently been at Paris and
   was behind the attacks on him by Béda, the Paris theologians, and Julius Caesar
   Scaliger; see Ep 2587:3–15.
6 Erard de la Marck, prince-bishop of Liège (Ep 738). Sardanapalus was a fic-
   tional king of Assyria (seventh century BC) notorious for the decadent luxury
   of his private life. By now Erasmus' frequently strained relations with the
   prince-bishop (cf Ep 2222 n14) had reached the point of complete and final
   breakdown. In Ep 2566:127–9 Marten Lips suggests that the bishop may not be
   well disposed towards Erasmus. Moreover, when Eustachius van der Rivieren,
   the Dominican of Louvain, dedicated his sharp attack on Erasmus, *Apologia
   pro pietate*, to Bishop Erard (Ep 2522:83–95), Erasmus refused to take seriously

Maximilian,[7] I am not surprised that the earth still bears his weight, since there is someone from the flock there who sings the same tune, but I stood up to him in person in the presence of Rhenanus three years ago.[8]

I know nothing certain about the little book in German published in Strasbourg[9] because my nature recoils from the vernacular. Except for your writings and those of Melanchthon I pass over the rest.

This Julius Scaliger, worthy, whoever he is, of the Gemonian steps,[10] is unknown to me. If I am called to the court, I will do for you what you would do for me if the occasion presented itself, with all the discretion and prudence to which you invite me in a single word. I shall meet Rhenanus this evening; the bearer of your letter hardly gave me enough time to answer you in this letter. I asked him to pass the evening and the night at my house, but he was unwilling. As a result, I cannot respond to all the points of your letter. I express my great thanks to your Lordship for your commendation of me;[11] as long as I live I shall honour and defend you to the best of my abilities in the presence of ecclesiastical dignitaries, whose favour the Aristotelian theologians try to alienate from you.

In haste from Sélestat, 27 December 1532[12]

Your servant, Jakob Spiegel

To the most reverend and most illustrious gentleman, whom I respect as I do my own father, Master Erasmus of Rotterdam

2591 / From Bernhard von Cles   Innsbruck, c 30 December 1531

This letter was first published by Allen. For the manuscript, an autograph rough draft, see Ep 2515 introduction. The bundle in which the draft is found is dated 'from 26 November 1531 until 25 January 1532.' This letter is one of a group of three having no month-date; the letters preceding it are dated 28 and 29 December; the one following it is dated 30 December.

* * * * *

Erard's vehement denial (Ep 2629) that he had had anything to do with the book; cf Allen Epp 2906:74–5, 2961:48–9, where he is described as a 'two-faced' friend.
7 At the time of his election as bishop of Liège in 1505, Erard was an ally of Louis XII of France, and would remain an ally of the French crown until 1518 when, in a grand switch, he allied himself with the future Charles v. See Ep 738 introduction.
8 Circumstances unknown. Beatus Rhenanus had retired to Sélestat in 1526.
9 See Ep 2587 n10.
10 See Ep 2564 nn2–3.
11 In Ep 2572:35–41 Speigel had asked Erasmus to mention him favourably to Bernhard von Cles.
12 On the year-date see the introduction above.

For Bernhard von Cles, bishop of Trent and chancellor to King Ferdinand, see Ep 2504.

TO ERASMUS

Your letter of the tenth of this month,[1] which I recently received, was most welcome. But I was displeased to learn that the letter of his royal Majesty and mine were delivered to you tardily,[2] and I cannot understand the reason. It is equally unpleasant to hear that in return for all your services to Christendom 5 you are harassed daily by the insults of many people. But since it is not unknown to us that nothing inspires envy more than learning, and that your prudence and circumspection are such that they render you invulnerable to hostile attacks, we suffer these things with resignation.

Although we were aware of what you wrote about the Swiss, your con- 10 firmation of what is taking place there was appreciated;[3] and would that a fitting end would finally be imposed on so many disturbances and troubles; our fervent wish is that everyone will repent of his errors. And the more we rush headlong day by day to a worse plight, the sterner will be God's vengeance against us. 15

But we will speak of this at another time. In the meantime it will be our task to look after your well-being; it is you we wish to oblige.

Given at Innsbruck, December 1531

2592 / From Christoph von Stadion   Dillingen, 2 January 1532

This letter was first published as Ep 19 in Horawitz I. The autograph is in the Württembergische Landesbibliothek Stuttgart (MS Hist Fol 47 folio 5). For Christoph von Stadion, bishop of Augsburg, see Ep 2029 introduction.

Cordial greetings. Koler sent me the letter that you wrote to him, from which I learn that the theologians of Paris have issued some determinations against your writings.[1] I have so far not been able to find a copy. I ask you one thing,

* * * * *

2591
1 Not extant
2 The letter from King Ferdinand is not extant; it is not clear which of the recent letters from Cles is referred to.
3 Erasmus had presumably written to Cles of the deaths of Zwingli and Oecolampadius in much the same terms as in Ep 2579:1–7.

2592
1 See Ep 2565:4–8 with n3.

that in your response you treat them as they deserve and paint them in their
true colours. I do not see anything good that they have written in so many   5
disputes about the faith. And I do not think that in these calumnies against
you they have written anything but conclusions, deductions, and corollaries.

In your last collection of letters,[2] on page 132, you write among other
things these words to Cuthbert Tunstall: 'Moreover it is agreed that in the
time of the apostles there was a divine service that the laity conducted among 10
themselves involving prayers and a blessing; and it is likely that they called
the bread at that service "the body of the Lord," etc.'[3] There are some who
doubt this: would you therefore please indicate the passage from which this
can be proved? Various rumours are spread here concerning the death of
Oecolampadius.[4] Several people maintain that he perished in the course of a   15
tumult, others that he was killed by women; certain others that he died of an
illness. The diversity of the rumours demonstrates that none of them are based
on the truth. About the pope and the emperor we know absolutely nothing; we
will wait to see what the Diet of Regensburg will produce for us.[5] May Christ
deign to be present so that finally something worthy of the Christian name   20
will be concluded; may he deign to assist you always. Farewell.

From our house in Dillingen, 2 January 1532
Your friend, the bishop of Augsburg
To the theologian Erasmus of Rotterdam, his eminent friend

2593 / From Erasmus Schets   Antwerp, 16 January 1532

This letter, which was first published by Allen, is Schets' reply to Epp 2552,
2578, and 2585 (see n1). The autograph is in the Öffentliche Bibliothek of the
University of Basel (Scheti epistolae 28). Erasmus' reply is Ep 2620.

†

Cordial greetings. Reassured now by your three letters,[1] I was most pleased
to know that you are safe and sound, and that, having received my letters,[2]

* * * * *

2 *Epistolae floridae*
3 Ep 2263:77–80
4 See Ep 2579:3–6.
5 See Ep 2511 n20.

2593
1 This seems to indicate that Epp 2552, 2578, and 2585 had all arrived together.
2 Epp 2511, 2527, 2558

you may now be more tranquil concerning the sums of money received in your name, about which you seemed to be concerned. I did not know that the money received by Pieter Gillis came from the Courtrai pension. If Pieter himself or your servant Quirinus had told me this, I would have inquired about the rest, because they gave me less than 130 florins.[3]

I thanked Martín Fernandes the Portuguese, a generous young man, for the preserves;[4] he returns your greetings and entrusted the accompanying letter to be transmitted to you.[5]

With Zwingli and Oecolampadius dead, I think half of the sects have now perished.[6] Let us hope that things get better.

The emperor is prepared for his trip to Germany.[7] All the baggage has been sent ahead. May God bring it about that this diet, which is about to begin in Regensburg, will be more successful than previous ones.

The Turks have made a truce in Hungary,[8] and in the meantime are plotting something in the Mediterranean.[9] The rumour is that they are fitting out a fleet in Valona.[10] I think they wish to threaten the emperor's passage to Spain.[11]

* * * * *

3 The precise sum was 115 Carolus florins, 18 stuivers; see Epp 2511, 2530, 2552, 2558, 2578.
4 See Ep 2585:1–3.
5 Not extant
6 Cf Ep 2585:12–13.
7 To attend the imperial diet at Regensburg (Ep 2511 n20). Charles left Brussels on 17 January 1532 and entered Regensburg on 28 February; see *Deutsche Reichstagsakten, Jüngere Reihe* (Gotha / Stuttgart / Göttingen 1896–) 10/1 123–5.
8 See Ep 2501 n4.
9 Cf *Lasciana* page 125 where, in a letter dated 9 February 1532, Jan (II) Łaski reports that even while preparing to attack Austria once again (cf Ep 2606 n21), the Turks were preparing 'a huge expedition against Italy, such as has never been seen before,' with 800 ships, each able to hold 300 men. Not until 1537, however, would the Turks actually undertake a short-lived invasion of Italy (Apulia).
10 Valona (Vlorë), a town on the Mediterranean coast in Albania. On these rumours of a Turkish fleet, cf Pastor 10 193.
11 The emperor would leave the Empire in November 1532, travelling overland by slow stages via Mantua and Bologna to Genoa, whence he sailed to Spain. By 11 May 1533 he was in Barcelona. See *Correspondenz des Kaisers Karl v* ed Karl Lanz 3 vols (Leipzig 1844–6; repr Frankfurt 1966) II, Epp 306–7, 325, 332, 345.

About sending a receipt to Frankfurt,[12] that is not necessary, dear   20
Erasmus. Place your confidence in me, and give me the power always to
pay whatever money I have of yours in your name to Hieronymus Froben
in Frankfurt (he is a faithful friend of yours, I believe). When I have received
from him an acknowledgment of what I have given him, there will be no
need of another receipt or, as they say, quittance.   25

In England Luis de Castro has received money for you.[13] From day to
day he was hoping to receive more. Whatever I accumulate I will take care to
give to the same Hieronymus in Frankfurt. I prefer that your money be with
you rather than with me (to avoid having any obligations to fulfil).

Goclenius, who is a very good friend of mine, made me very happy   30
when he told me of your response to the censures of the Sorbonne.[14] God is
so benevolent towards the right of heart that in order to shut the mouths of
calumniators he always supplies innocence with an abundance of eloquence,
which I know you do not lack, to defend itself. There are many people looking forward to your making a clean sweep of them. Happy the booksellers   35
who will first put the result on display.

In accordance with your wishes I have exhorted Goclenius to furnish
an account of the monies he received in your name from Haio Cammingha.[15]
He answered that he had sent satisfaction to you for this and other sums via
a trustworthy messenger. He sent me a letter from you addressed to Reginald   40
Pole,[16] which I transmitted to Castro.

Farewell, dearest Master Erasmus, and may you enjoy success and
prosperity.

From Antwerp, 16 January 1532
Your Erasmus Schets   45
† To the most learned Master Erasmus of Rotterdam, most loyal friend.
In Freiburg

2594 / From Viglius Zuichemus   Padua, 17 January 1532

This letter was first published as Ep 22 in VZE. For Viglius Zuichemus, who had
recently gone to Italy to continue his studies, see Ep 2568.

* * * * *

12 See Ep 2578:22–7.
13 Castro was Schet's agent in London.
14 Ep 2552 n10
15 See Ep 2552 n6.
16 Ep 2526; cf Ep 2530 n7.

Your letter, most learned Erasmus, which you wrote to me in the month of
November, was delivered to me on the calends of January.[1] I interpreted it
as a most welcome New Year's gift, from which I even predict that this year
will proceed auspiciously in preserving and strengthening your affection for
me. For my part, I shall not knowingly omit anything that could nurture and   5
increase your benevolence towards me. I wrote you previously about my
journey.[2] In Venice, while still involved in various matters and, in addition,
unknown and ignorant of the language, I met only Egnazio.[3] I heard him
teach, however, but much of it fell on deaf ears because he has the habit of
frequently inserting anecdotes in Italian, although he is no less eloquent and   10
fluent in Latin. But in this he seems to be able to win over the good will of
his noble auditors, with whom, obviously, the vernacular language is highly
prized. In the Asulanus workshop a sordid opulence proclaims itself.[4] They
are so lacking in discrimination,[5] or if they have a sense of smell, they surely
confirm the truth of what you have written, namely that the smell of this   15
kind of wealth seems good to them. Lazare de Baïf still discharges the role of
ambassador there and he is working on a book about ships.[6]

* * * * *

2594
1 January; the letter is not extant.
2 Ep 2568
3 Ep 2568:7–10
4 The 'Asulanus workshop' was the household (family, workers, guests) of the
   Venetian printer and (from 1507) partner of Aldo Manuzio, Andrea Torresani of
   Asola (hence the surname Asulanus), whose heir and successor after his death
   in 1528 was his son Gianfrancesco. During his visit to Venice in 1508 Erasmus
   had lived with Andrea. Although his relations with Andrea then and later were
   cordial, Erasmus remembered him as greedy, stingy, and without real sympathy
   for pure scholarship, a view shared by many others who had known Andrea.
   In the colloquy Opulentia sordida 'Sordid Opulence' ('Penny-Pinching' in CWE),
   which was first published in the edition of September 1531, Erasmus satirized
   Andrea as the rich skinflint Antronius, who provided rotten, evil-smelling
   food, musty wine, and little of it, just to save money; see CWE 40 979–95. It appears that while in Venice Viglius became sufficiently well acquainted with the
   Asulanus workshop to be able to assure Erasmus that his description of it in the
   colloquy was still accurate.
5 Literally 'in nose,' which accords with the olfactory imagery of the rest of the
   sentence
6 For Baïf, currently the resident ambassador of Francis I in Venice, see Ep 1962
   introduction. His work De re navali was published in 1536 (Paris: R. Stephanus).

I have decided to return to Venice in the next few days; I will then set about investigating everything more thoroughly. I find it pleasant living in Padua, and the professors of civil law give me ample satisfaction, for with great diligence and through competition among the auditors they rouse enthusiasm, although they are clearly ignorant of humane letters. There is talk of inviting a certain Ludovico Cato, a man very learned in law and, if not expert in humane letters, having at least some rudimentary training. He was ambassador of the duke of Ferrara to the Most Christian King while I was in France, and I got to know him somewhat.[7] Alciati has returned to Bourges, where he was displeased by the scarcity of auditors resulting from a recent outbreak of the plague, and by the perfidy of the citizens, who were evasive about his salary.[8] So he wrote to us saying that he was ready to return to Italy if there was hope of a just and sure honorarium.[9] We diligently attended to this and have brought things to the point that the Venetian Senate has offered terms. But I am afraid our efforts are in vain, and that he is acting in this manner so that he may more easily force the people of Bourges to keep their promises when he shows them the offers of their rivals.[10] Matteo Corti,[11] brother of the man who is regarded as the prince of jurisconsults

* * * * *

7 Ludovico Cato of Ferrara (1490–1553) became doctor of civil and canon law at Ferarra in 1516, and some years later became procurator at Ferrara and lector in civil law at the university, posts that he held until his death. In the 1520s he served the duke on important diplomatic missions to Charles v, Francis i, and Pope Adrian vi (among others). Allen cites evidence (vze Ep 20) that Cato was in Padua in October 1532 and conferred doctorates in law on two of Viglius' former pupils. But if he did actually accept a post at the university in Padua, he did not stay long. By 1534 he was back in Ferrara as secretary to the new duke, Ercole ii d'Este, and remained there until his death.
8 This was in 1529; see Ep 2209:72–5 with n19.
9 The letter is not extant. It is not known who besides Viglius himself was included in the 'us ... we' of this passage.
10 In 1533 Alciati would return to Italy at the invitation of Francesco ii Sforza, duke of Milan, to teach at Pavia. This occurred at the same time that Pietro Bembo (n15 below) was negotiating with the Venetian authorities to secure Alciati an appointment at Padua.
11 Matteo Corti of Pavia (c 1475–1544?) taught medicine at Padua, Bologna, and Pisa, becoming one of the most sought-after professors of medicine in Italy. At various times he was also personal physician to Pope Clement vii and Cosimo i de' Medici. He left behind numerous medical treatises, many of them still in manuscript.

here,[12] taught medicine here some time ago. He consecrated his late but not fruitless efforts to the study of Greek literature, and in that field easily attained to the first rank among the initiates. But when he was called to Rome some time ago, no one whose learning would attract students of medicine was appointed in his place.   40

You know that Niccolò Leoniceno departed this life last year.[13] Lazzaro Bonamico is especially commended among the professors of Greek and Latin literature, but his following is not numerous among the sworn devotees of the Ciceronian faction.[14] Their patron here is Pietro Bembo,[15] whom I went to visit several times, but he has become accustomed to speaking Italian   45 more frequently, and for that reason I cannot enjoy his company very often. I have learned that our friend Sucket, who was on his way here, stopped in Turin.[16] I have rented a magnificent house here, together with young men from Augsburg.[17] It belongs to the Contarini family, a name that comes from little birds.[18] Would that you had the intention to come to this city, as rumour   50

* * * * *

12 Franceschino Corti of Pavia (1463–1533) taught law at Pavia until 1512, at Pisa in 1514, and then again at Pavia. In 1527, when Pavia was sacked by French troops, Corti was taken hostage by imperial troops but ransomed by the Venetians to teach at Padua, where he died.

13 It was not Niccolò Leoniceno, professor of medicine at Ferrara (Ep 1587 n46), who died in 1531 (28 March), but rather Niccolò Leonico Tomeo (Ep 1480 n70), who taught Greek at Padua. Even at the time, as is evident here, the two were often confused with one another; cf Ep 1595 n8.

14 Bonamico, professor of Latin and Greek at Padua, was in fact an ardent Ciceronian, though this does not appear to have caused any quarrel between him and Erasmus; see Ep 1720 n10.

15 Pietro Bembo, with whom Erasmus had recently established a friendly correspondence, was the advocate of a kind of Ciceronianism that was very much to Erasmus' taste; see Ep 2106 introduction. Besides being an excellent Latinist, he was instrumental, through his *Prose della volgar lingua* (1525), in establishing Tuscan as the literary language of Italy.

16 After completing a doctorate in law with Andrea Alciati at Bourges (October 1530), Karel Sucket departed for Italy, where he was appointed to a lectureship in law at Turin; see Ep 2191 introduction.

17 Viglius had been accompanied to Italy by young members of prominent Augsburg patrician families whose studies he supervised: Johann Georg Hörmann, Johann Georg Paumgartner, the brothers Heinrich and Quirin Rehlinger (nephews of Anton Fugger's wife), Claudius Pius Peutinger, and Leonard Langenmantel. For Hörmann, Paumgartner, and the Rehlingers see CEBR II 204, III 62 and 135. For Peutinger and Langenmantel see VZE Ep 20 n4.

18 Viglius appears to be punning on 'Contarini' by implicitly turning it into 'Cantorini,' which, if it existed, would mean 'little singers.'

has it. I would hope that our house would not be displeasing to you, and I am
convinced that I can bring it about that Fugger would not hesitate to grant
you here what he offered in Augsburg.[19] He wishes nothing more than to do
you some good service. The relatives of Rehlinger[20] are most grateful for the
greetings you imparted to them, and together with me pray that everything 55
is favourable and propitious for you.

Padua, 17 January 1532

2595 / From Bernhard von Cles   Innsbruck, 17 January 1532

> This letter was first published by Allen. For the manuscript, an autograph
> rough draft, see Ep 2515 introduction. On 10 December 1531 Erasmus had
> written a letter to Cles that is not extant but that was answered by Ep 2591
> (c 30 December). Meanwhile, Erasmus had written again on 19 December but,
> fearing that that letter had gone astray, he sent a copy of it on 3 January. The
> copy, which is not extant, arrived first, and was answered by this letter. The
> original letter, which is also not extant, was answered by Ep 2596.
>
> For Bernhard von Cles, bishop of Trent and chancellor to King Ferdinand,
> see Ep 2504.

We cannot but greatly wonder that our letters were received late, and since
we cannot understand the reason for this, we will have to devise a remedy
for sending letters when I have occasion to write to you.

In the remaining pages of your letter we perceived that you are profoundly distressed that rivals of your learning or, I should say, detractors of 5
your name, are fulminating against you with unbridled violence, and that
they teach your writings, published in more peaceful times, to the ignorant
multitude in these turbulent times, interpreting them in a way that is at variance with your intentions and contrary to the truth, so that from these insinuations there is nothing left for you to hope for but your obvious downfall, 10
since the minds of kings and the multitude will be moved to anger against
you. Although all this has tormented our spirit time and time again, we do
not wish, on the one hand, to justify ourselves or, on the other hand, to relieve your anxieties, except to inform you, as much as we can, about the present state of affairs. As far as his most serene Majesty is concerned, we wish 15

* * * * *

19 For Fugger's offer to Erasmus, see Ep 2476 n1. For the idea of Erasmus moving
     to Italy, see Ep 2479 n11.
20 See n17 above.

you to be assured that nothing has ever been brought to his ears that would lessen your reputation, and as for our role, in whatever way we can, both with his royal Majesty and all others, whenever the opportunity presents itself, we have been a protector of your name. And in future we will see to it that you know that we will diligently do everything possible to protect your 20 well-being, dignity, and honour. We exhort you to apply yourself to matters concerning the faith, as you have done hitherto.

Given at Innsbruck, 17 January 1532

2596 / From Bernhard von Cles   Innsbruck, 24 January 1532

This letter was first published by Allen. For the manuscript, an autograph rough draft, see Ep 2515 introduction. For the sequence of the letters between Erasmus and Cles in December 1531–January 1532, see Ep 2595 introduction.

Your letter, dated the nineteenth of last month, and the second letter, a copy of the first, which you sent us on the third of this month, we received in inverse order. We will not reply differently in the present letter, since response was made lengthily in our other letter, and we have taken care that it be brought back to you by the same messenger who brought yours. We have 5 nothing more to add to our previous response. In the meantime we wish you the best of health.

Given as above

2597 / To Bonifacius Amerbach   Freiburg, 25 January [1532]

This letter (= AK Ep 1598) was first published in the *Epistolae familiares*. The autograph is in the Öffentliche Bibliothek of the University of Basel (MS AN III 15 88). The year-date is determined by the connection to Ep 2605. Judging by this letter, Ep 2598, and Ep 2605, it seems that Erasmus had offered Bonifacius a loan of five hundred florins on generous terms, for a purpose not stated.

Cordial greetings. As I see, I thought you were more well off than you really are. I had no doubt that you had three thousand florins in your house.[1] At

* * * * *

2597
1 A very large sum to hold in cash, presumably chosen simply to express great wealth. If Erasmus is thinking of Rhenish florins, it was equivalent to 85 years' wages of an Antwerp master mason/carpenter (CWE 12 650 Table 3, 691 Table 13).

any rate, you deserve to have one hundred thousand. If the adversity of the
times or any other reason prevents you from thinking that it is to your advantage to accept what I offer, I will not importune you further. There is no   5
reason to worry about a fixed date.² It is sufficient if the first payment is two
hundred florins, the same amount for the second, and one hundred for the
third. If there is any interest involved, I would prefer that it be transmitted to
you and your family rather than to anyone else. But if something else stands
in the way, I will not opportune you further. I will not negotiate with anyone   10
else before receiving your letter. There is no reason for you to thank me. I
consider all that is mine to be yours. I wish you and yours the best of health.
Give my fond greetings to Grynaeus,³ and to Basilius.⁴

Freiburg, 25 January

To the most illustrious Doctor Bonifacius Amerbach. In Basel   15

2598 / To Bonifacius Amerbach   [Freiburg, beginning of February 1532]

This letter (= AK Ep 1599) was first published in the *Epistolae familiares*. The
autograph is in the Öffentliche Bibliothek of the University of Basel (MS AN III
15 75). The date derives from the connection with Epp 2597 and 2605, since all
three letters deal with Erasmus' offer of a loan to Bonifacius. This letter appears
to have been written before Erasmus received a reply to Ep 2597.

Cordial greetings. For many days now a terrible cough has been disturbing
me, and it won't let up.¹ May great Jupiter do away with that fickle tribune
who thrust me into these tribulations.² He lay ill with a kidney stone and was
in danger of death, but he returned to life. For the stones in the fireplace he

* * * * *

2 Erasmus uses the expression *oculata die* 'a date with eyes,' taken from Plautus
  Pseudolus 301. The meaning is 'ready cash here and now,' as opposed to *die caeca*,
  literally 'blind date,' meaning an indefinite date in the future. Cf Ep 2605:1–2.
3 Simon Grynaeus (Ep 2535); for a recent episode of strain in Erasmus' relations
  with him, see Epp 2574–6, 2580.
4 Bonifacius' older brother Basilius

2598
1 Cf Epp 2603:26–7, 2604:42–3, 2605:11.
2 Erasmus puns on *turbunus* (for *tribunus*) and *turbas*. The tribune referred to is
  probably Ulrich Wirtner (Ep 2462 n2).

asked eighteen Basel pounds.[3] But I overheard him saying to my theologian:[4] 5
'They will not cost very much, four or five florins.' A master of trickery.

If you were to move here,[5] my offer would not be disadvantageous. But
I do not see any great hope of this; therefore, another plan must be sought if
you reject what I offered in my last letter.[6]

I would be pleased to know if you and your dear ones are in good 10
health. Give my fond greetings to Basilius.[7]

To the most illustrious doctor of laws Bonifacius Amerbach. In Basel

2599 / To Germain de Brie　　　　　　　Freiburg, [January–February?] 1532

This letter, seemingly the answer to one now lost, was first published in the
Epistolae palaeonaeoi, which means that it was written before September 1532. In
lines 61–3, on the other hand, Erasmus writes as though he had not yet heard of
the death of Lodovico Canossa, which occurred on 30 January 1532. So the letter can with some confidence be placed in the first part of the year. For Germain
de Brie see Ep 2021 introduction.

ERASMUS OF ROTTERDAM TO GERMAINE DE BRIE, GREETING
You have decided, as I see, to consecrate to immortality the name of Canossa.[1]
I met the man several years ago in England, but I knew him without really
knowing him.[2] Rumour was that he had come there as papal cardinal-legate,

* * * * *

3 According to an annuity agreement drawn up in 1522 between Amerbach and
  the Basel Carthusians, one Rhenish florin was equivalent to 276 Basel pennies
  (that is, £1 3s 0d or 23s). If the same rate prevailed in 1532, Erasmus paid almost
  sixteen florins for his fireplace, more than triple the price quoted to Baer by
  Wirtner ('four or five florins'); see AK Ep 1599 n1.
4 Ludwig Baer; see Ep 2550 n2.
5 Ep 2561:13–14 seems to indicate that Erasmus had offered to take Bonifacius
  and his entire family into his new house.
6 Presumably Ep 2597
7 Bonifacius' older brother

2599
1 In 1528 Brie had dedicated his edition of Chrysostom's homily *Contra gentiles*
  (Paris: S. de Colines) to Lodovico Canossa, bishop of Bayeux, for whom see Ep
  489 introduction (where he is incorrectly referred to as 'Luigi').
2 The meeting, also mentioned in Ep 2421:33–40, took place between Canossa's
  arrival in London in June 1514 and Erasmus' departure from England for Basel
  in the following month (see Ep 294 introduction). The present letter is Erasmus'
  only extended account of the meeting.

but in civilian dress. Andrea Ammonio had invited me to dinner.[3] I came, not   5
suspecting any ambush; I was very fond of him as a close friend. I found at
his home someone dressed in a long mantle, but with his hair gathered into a
net, and he was accompanied by a single servant. I was chatting about various
things with Andrea, suspecting absolutely nothing of Canossa. I wondered,
however, at the military ferocity of the man, and so I asked Andrea in Greek,   10
'Who is this man?' He answered: 'A famous merchant.' And I answered in
turn: 'He certainly gives that impression,' and convinced that he was a merchant, I completely ignored the man. We took our places at table. Canossa
sat at the head of the table and I next to him. All through the meal I traded
stories familiarly with Andrea in my usual way, not concealing my contempt   15
for the merchant. Finally, I asked whether the rumour was true that a legate
had come at the command of Leo x to compose the differences between the
kings of France and England. Andrea nodded assent. 'The sovereign pontiff,'
I said, 'has no need of my advice; if, however, he had summoned me here, I
would have given different advice.' 'What?' said Ammonio. 'It is not expedi-   20
ent,' I said, 'to make mention of peace.' 'For what reason?' 'Because peace
cannot be agreed upon at short notice. And in the meantime, while monarchs
are dealing with conditions, the soldiers, at the mere suggestion of peace, contrive worse things than in war. In a truce the hands of soldiers are restrained.
I would prescribe a truce for three years, which would make it possible to ex-   25
amine adequately the necessary conditions for a long-lasting peace.' Andrea
expressed his approval and said: 'That is what this legate will do.'

After discussing these matters I returned to what Ammonio had not answered clearly. 'Is the legate a cardinal?' I said. 'Where did you get that idea?'
he said. 'Because this is what the Italians say,' I said. 'And where did they   30
get that knowledge?' he said. 'I met you here,' I said. 'If I saw you after some
years in Brabant, would you ask me where I met you?' They smiled at each
other, while I still did not have the slightest suspicion. A little later I returned
to the attack, asking whether the legate really was a cardinal. Ammonio hesitated. Finally, he said: 'He has the character of a cardinal.' I then said, with an   35
amiable smile: 'In these circumstances it is something to show the character
of a cardinal.'

Canossa heard these and other remarks in silence. Finally he said something or other in Italian. Later he mixed in some Latin words, but in such
a way that you could see he was a clever merchant. When I made no an-   40
swer he turned to me and said: 'I am astonished that you wish to live in this

* * * * *

3 For Ammonio, Latin secretary to Henry VIII and one of Erasmus' closest friends
   in England, see Ep 218 introduction.

barbarous nation, unless perhaps you prefer to be without rivals here rather
than the first among many in Rome.' Marvelling at this subtlety in a merchant, I answered that I lived in a region that had many markedly learned
men, among whom it was sufficient for me to occupy the last place, while   45
in Rome I would have no rank at all. I said this and other things, somewhat
annoyed with the merchant. I think some good genius came to my aid at this
point; otherwise Ammonio would have dragged me into great peril, since
he was not unaware of my habit of blurting out with great freedom among
friends whatever came to mind.   50

We rose from the table. Andrea and I took a walk in the garden that
separates the two parts of the house, and after a long conversation he conducted me out of courtesy to the land gate (for the part of the house in which
we had dined faced the Thames river); I preferred to return by foot rather than by boat. When, after a few days, we returned to our conversation,   55
Andrea explained the background of the story, and zealously urged me to
accompany Canossa to Italy, testifying profusely how highly he spoke of me
and what a high opinion he had of me. But he was singing the tale to a deaf
man.[4] Meanwhile, he was not behaving like a friend, since he knew my out-
spokenness. I could have blurted out something either against the pope or   60
against the legate, which afterwards could have caused me some trouble. If
now Canossa is not very well disposed to Erasmus, it is nothing new. A love
spurned often turns to wrath.[5] And I see that there are some who try to inflict
the same plague on studies that they they did on religion. Among the Italians
the Ciceronian faction is seething with activity, since none are of less worth 65
than those who shout the loudest.[6] I was not unaware of your good fortune;
I have confidence in your loyalty and I congratulate you. I think a position of high rank will accrue to you even if you did not seek it.[7] Concerning

* * * * *

4 *Adagia* I iv 87
5 In 1516, after being made bishop of Bayeux, Canossa invited Erasmus to come
   live with him in his diocese on generous terms (Ep 489), but Erasmus replied
   evasively, and that appears to have been the end of it (Ep 538). Erasmus here attributes Canossa's alleged coldness towards him to this case of 'love spurned,'
   But other factors may have been at least as important. The two none-too-clear
   sentences immediately following may indicate that Erasmus now viewed
   Canossa as a member of the 'Ciceronian faction,' which he had attacked in the
   Ciceronianus. It may also be relevant that Canossa was a friend of Erasmus'
   most formidable Italian critic, Alberto Pio (Ep 2486 n10).
6 Cf lines 63–6 here with Epp 2600:17–23, 2604:15–25.
7 We have no information about this stroke of 'good fortune,' which apparently
   had something to do with acquiring 'high rank.'

Chryostom, I would have preferred that you were less of a Callipedes,[8] for
that results in a conspicuous loss to the printer.[9]   70
     Farewell. Freiburg im Breisgau, 1532

2600 / To Piotr Tomicki   Freiburg, 4 February 1532

This letter was first published in Wierzbowski 1:326. The autograph is in the
Zamoyski Collection of the Polish National Library at Warsaw (MS BN BOZ 2053
vol 13 no 1561). For Tomicki, see Epp 1919, 1953.

Cordial greetings. Most honoured prelate, although there was nothing new to
write to you, nevertheless, after the unexpected arrival of the eminent Erazm,
abbot of Santa Clara, who in his kindness spontaneously invited me to send
greetings to my friends through him,[1] I did not think I should allow him to return home without letters from me, especially since for that reason he did not   5
object to spending a night here. Since your last letter, in which you had commended to me the son of Seweryn Boner,[2] nothing has arrived here from you.
     Perhaps there was disseminated among you also what Alberto Pio, a
man who made ill use of his free time, wrote against me in Paris.[3] This was
followed by censures of the Sorbonne, under the title of the faculty, although   10
in reality the business was conducted by Béda,[4] a man completely deranged

* * * * *

8 Ie someone who promises great things but never gets them finished (*Adagia* I
  vi 43). In 1526 Brie accepted Erasmus' invitation to contribute translations of
  works by St John Chrysostom to Froben's five-volume Latin edition of the Greek
  Father, which was published in 1530. But his translation of the *Comparatio regis
  et monachi* was so long delayed that Froben had to substitute one by Johannes
  Oecolampadius, while that of the first eight homilies on Romans had to be omitted altogether and be published separately in 1533; see Ep 2359 introduction.
9 Cf Epp 2405:210–12, 2422:19–22.

2600
1 Erazm Ciołek (d 1546) was abbot of the Cistercian monastery of Mogiła (*Clara
  Tumba*, but here called *Santa Clara*). Returning to Poland from a trip to Rome on
  a mission from King Sigismund I, Ciołek visited Erasmus at Freiburg and made
  the offer recorded here. In 1533 he wrote to Erasmus a letter that is now lost
  (see Allen Ep 2811:10–11), and sent him as a gift a knife and fork of gilded silver
  (see Major 54 with n55 on page 62).
2 Ep 2521
3 See Ep 2486 n10.
4 See Ep 2552 n10.

by hatred, with three theologians whom he had conscripted.⁵ Everywhere personal passions vitiate the public interest. I know that many theologians are ashamed of this publication. I knew what Béda's malice deserved, but I·wanted to render honour to the name of the faculty by replying with the   15 utmost moderation,⁶ although answer had already been given to the greater part of the criticisms.⁷ Girolamo Aleandro, bishop of Brindisi, now apostolic legate at the imperial court, has long breathed an uncontrolled hatred against me, and he would not be able to say why; now he is all the more moved to anger because I am said to have impaired the majesty of Cicero in   20 a dialogue entitled the *Ciceronianus*. There are, especially among the Italians, those whose aim it is to create no less discord among those who cultivate humanistic studies than that which exists among those who profess dogmas.⁸ I send to your most reverend Eminence the little book that answers both the

* * * * *

5 Allen's suggestion, on the basis of Ep 2134:146–8, that the three theologians were 'perhaps' Pierre Cousturier, Jérôme de Hangest, and Jacobus Latomus is wide of the mark; none of these three participated in any way in the deliberations of the Paris faculty in the years that Erasmus' works were under investigation. To whom, then, is Erasmus referring? If one assumes that 'the business' referred to was not that of getting the *Determinatio* of the faculty into print in 1531 but rather that of the condemnation of Erasmus' works by the faculty in 1527 and (in the case of the *Colloquies*) by the entire university in 1528, then Erasmus' correspondence yields the names of at least four, possibly five theologians whom he had at one time or another designated as Béda's allies against him. Uppermost in his mind at the moment was Josse Clichtove, a major apologia against whom was about to issue from the Froben press (see Ep 2604 n12). Three other theologians are mentioned by name in letters of 1528: Jacques Berthélemy, who in the summer of 1528 reportedly had in his possession the only copy of the faculty's censures (Ep 2027:33–5 with n18); Nicholas Le Clerc, whose support for Béda had been reported to Erasmus (Ep 2043); Guillaume Duchesne, who until his death in 1525 had been Béda's chief collaborator in the proceedings against Erasmus (Ep 2043 n1). To these should perhaps be added the theologian Nicolas Boissel, to whom Erasmus refers only as 'the rector of his own stamp' whom Béda had 'obtained,' and who presided over the condemnation of Erasmus' *Colloquies* by the entire university; see Epp 2037:165–8 with n23, 2126:154–5.
6 The reference is to Erasmus`s *Declarationes ad censuras Lutetiae vulgatas*, a copy of which accompanied this letter; see lines 24–5 with n9 below.
7 Most thoroughly and completely In the *Supputationes errorum in censuris Natalis Bedae* (March 1527); see Ep 1804 n14.
8 Cf Epp 2599:63–6, 2604:15–25. Erasmus was firmly convinced that Aleandro was the author of Julius Caesar Scaliger's *Oratio pro Cicerone contra Erasmum*; see Ep 2565 n12.

censures of the Sorbonne and the calumnies of Alberto Pio.[9] I opposed the 25
sects in Germany with more force than six hundred theologians, and for this
service this is the gratitude rendered to me by these pillars of the church, as
they think of themselves. But Christ, our superintendent of the games, for
whom we are fighting, lives; it is from him that we hope for a reward, and
that in a short time. For this dwelling collapses day by day. May the Lord 30
deign to preserve your Highness unharmed for a long time. We applaud the
magnificent victories of your Poland with all our heart.[10]

Given at Freiburg im Breisgau, 4 February 1532

Erasmus of Rotterdam, servant of your most reverend Lordship, in my
own hand extempore 35

To the most reverend lord Piotr, bishop of Cracow, chancellor of the
king and the kingdom of Poland. In Poland

2601 / From Jan Benedykt Solfa · Cracow, 4 February 1532

The manuscript of this letter, in a secretary's hand but signed and corrected by
Benedykt, is in the Rehdiger Collection of the University Library at Wrocław
(MS Rehd 254 23). A fragment of it (lines 12–16, 148) was published in LB III/2
1750 *Appendix epistolarum* no 363. The complete text was first published as Ep
23 in Miaskowski.

Jan Benedykt Solfa (1483–1564), of Trzebiel in Lower Lusatia, normally
signed his name Johannes Benedictus or Benedicti. After taking his BA (1507)
and MA (1512) at Cracow, he acquired a doctorate in medicine at Bologna (1516).
Returning to Cracow, he won such fame through his medical practice that in
1523 he was made court physician to King Sigismund I. He devoted much effort to the study of syphilis, the English sweat, mental illness, hallucinations,
and prophecy, but was also deeply interested in theological problems, particularly the fate of the soul after the death of the body, which is the subject of this
letter. No other letter of Benedykt to Erasmus survives, and there is no evidence
that Erasmus responded to this letter.

I have found out for certain that there is no literary genre in which you, a
man most learned and cultured in every respect, take less pleasure than

* * * * *

9 For the Froben volume (1532) of several of Erasmus' shorter works, including
the scarcely known *Brevissima scholia* against Alberto Pio (CWE 84 cviii–cix) and
the *Declarationes ad censuras Lutetiae vulgatas* (Ep 2552 n10), see CWE 84 cxl no 6.
10 The victory of the Poles under JanTarnowski over Peter Rareş (Petryllus), the
voivode of Moldavia, in August 1531; cf Ep 2606 n18.

letters of praise, since your outstanding virtue together with your singular learning are well known throughout the world. Having verified his kindness through the reports and writings of many people, I was not afraid to   5
address such a man, even in a crude and uncultivated style, in the hope that he would conduct himself towards me in the same way as he is accustomed to show himself towards others. And I do this especially because I shall treat of matters that are very important in these terrible times, in which no one does anything, even with impunity, which the prophets did not foresee, at   10
least through divine inspiration. But the philosophers also predicted human events long before they happened, and Master Jan of Głogów, in particular, once the ornament of our university, burst out publicly forty years ago with these words: 'There will come a black monk, who will throw the church into turmoil, and our people of Wrocław will be worse than those of Prague.'[1]   15
That this has happened, alas! is clear to the eyes of all.

They boast that the gospel was hidden for so many centuries and generations, even when there were saints who performed miracles, claiming that now for the first time it has been revealed to Luther, Hess,[2] and their followers because of their virtues, as if Christ our Lord had permitted his spouse, the   20
Catholic church, to err for so many centuries. Consequently there are many roads that seem good to men, and the newest of these end up in the depths of hell. Therefore Solomon said: 'Do not go beyond the old boundaries that

* * * * *

2601
1 Jan of Głogów (Johannes Glogoviensis, 1445–1507) was from 1468 a professor at the University of Cracow. He was the author of many works on grammar, logic, philosophy, and geography, and also published numerous astrological prognostications. We have not been able to trace the quotation given here. 'Black monk' generally means a Benedictine, but Luther's order, the Augustinian Eremites, also wore black robes. As for Wrocław, it had succumbed to Lutheranism (see following note) just as Prague had succumbed to Hussitism a century earlier.
2 Johann Hess of Nürnberg (1490–1547) studied at Leipzig and Wittenberg and then in 1513 became the secretary of Johannes (II) Thurzo, bishop of Wrocław (Ep 850). In 1517 he returned to his studies, attending the universities of Erfurt, Bologna, and Ferrara, where he received a doctorate in theology. In 1519 he returned to Wittenberg, where he spent several weeks and formed a close friendship with Philippus Melanchthon. He then returned to the service of Thurzo, who died in 1520 and was succeeded by Jakob von Salza, a man unsympathetic to Hess' Lutheran views. Hess was forced to retire to Nürnberg, but in 1523 the city council of Wrocław, in defiance of the bishop, appointed him parish priest of St Mary Magdalen, in which capacity he led the Reformation to victory in the city and won general recognition as the principal leader of Lutheranism in Silesia. This is the only reference to him in Erasmus' correspondence, and there is no record of personal contact between the two men.

your fathers established.'[3] But let us cross over onto the right road, which
was trodden by the footsteps of all the saints who worshipped the true God,   25
and the paths trodden by the holy Fathers, according to the prophet: 'Stand
at the crossroads and look, and ask for the ancient paths where the good way
lies, and walk in it, and you will find purification for your souls.'[4] And elsewhere: 'He will show his path to you.'[5] But if we go astray and, as humans
are wont to do, get lost on the wrong road, God will reveal it to us, just as he   30
promised through the apostle Ezechiel: 'I will give them one way and one
heart.'[6] But let us speak well of those who persecute us,[7] and, on the advice
of Gamaliel, 'Let us stay away from these people and leave them alone, because if this plan or this undertaking comes from man, it will be destroyed.'[8]
'Every plant which my heavenly Father has not planted will be uprooted.'[9] 'If   35
it comes from God, you will not be able to destroy it,'[10] for man has no power
against the spirit that would enable him to restrain the spirit. The Lutherans
claim that they have this spirit, as if the spirit would never depart from men
through human fragility, ignoring that once the prophecy has been fulfilled,
the prophet becomes an ordinary man, and that the Holy Spirit has remained   40
in no one except Christ, our Saviour, and ignoring that the Lord does not
rest except with the humble and the quiet and those who stand in fear of his
commandments. Among the Lutherans, therefore, there is neither the spirit
of sanctification nor the Holy Spirit, who is a spirit of mildness and appeared
to the apostles in the form of a dove, who is not the author of confusion but   45
of peace,[11] as in all the associations of the saints. 'For he is our peace.'[12] If,
then, Christ is the peace of believers, whoever is without peace does not have
the spirit of Christ. For, according to the testimony of David, 'Great is peace,
which belongs to those who love your law, O Lord, and nothing can make
them stumble.'[13]   50

* * * * *

3 Prov 22:28
4 Jer 6:16
5 Jer 42:3
6 Not Ezechiel, but Jeremiah 32:39
7 Rom 12:14
8 Acts 5:38
9 Matt 15:13
10 Acts 5:39
11 1 Cor 14:33
12 Eph 2:4
13 Ps 118:165 (Vulgate)

Of this Holy Spirit the Lord said in the gospel: 'If you love me, keep my commandments, and I will ask the Father, and he will give you another Paraclete, to be with you forever, the spirit of truth.'[14] For all his commandments are truth. If, therefore, we love one another, God dwells in us. And again: 'He who hates his brother is in darkness, and he walks in darkness, and does not know where he is going, because the darkness has blinded his eyes.'[15] And in such people, the Lord says in Genesis, 'my spirit will not remain because they are flesh, doing their own will and not God's.'[16] And for that reason they cannot please God, because a contrary spirit is discerned in them, whose pleasures are mixed with bitterness to their undoing, and who prophesy not through divine inspiration but from their own heart, and they see nothing. They interpret the Scriptures as the devil interpreted it in Matthew 4,[17] as can be seen in a thousand and more passages taken falsely from the original text.

Their wisdom does not descend from the heavens but is terrestrial, animal, demonic; they do not observe charity or oneness of spirit through the bond of peace, contrary to the teaching of the Apostle, where he teaches that all bitterness, wrath, anger, wrangling, slander, and foul language should be taken from you,[18] and in 1 Peter three times,[19] and in Colossians 4: 'Put away wrath, indignation, slander, and foul language from your mouth.'[20] The lips and deceitful writings of the Lutherans abound with such things, giving sure testimony that they do not have the spirit of Christ but the deceptive spirit of the devil, by which they seduce the people of God and by which also they fall suddenly into all kinds of errors and plunge into impiety and filth. Thus there will no longer be reason for saying to the seers, 'Do not see,' and to the prophets, 'Do not prophesy what is right; tell us things that please us, prophesy illusions for us, take away the road from us.'[21] We have despaired, 'We have come to love strangers and we will follow after them.'[22]

* * * * *

14 John 14:15–16
15 1 John 2:11
16 Gen 6:3
17 Matt 4:1–11
18 Eph 4:31
19 1 Pet 2:1, 3:8–9, 4:2
20 The reference is to Col 3:8.
21 Isa 30:10–11
22 Jer 2:25

Hearing this, the Apostle, 'bound in the spirit,'[23] said: 'Persevere in the faith, established and steadfast,'[24] 'without which it is impossible to please God,'[25] and John:[26] 'Let no one deceive you with empty words, for because of these things the wrath of God comes upon those who are disobedient.'[27] According to the psalmist, 'If his children forsake my law,'[28] to which the Apostle adds, saying: 'the fire will test each man's work, whatever it be, and it will be revealed in the fire.'[29] For this is the Catholic faith: those who have done good things will have eternal life. But 'the faith has perished,' as Jeremiah says, 'and has disappeared from their mouth,'[30] and they no longer believe in purgatory for, they say, Scripture in no way expresses it, although they know that not everything is written in this book, but some things were laid down by the apostles, as Paul writes to the Corinthians: 'For my part, what I received from the Lord I have handed on to you. As for the rest I will give instructions when I come.'[31] Augustine, however, wrote to Casulanus: 'In those things about which the divine Scripture gave no certain opinion the custom of the people of God and the teachings of our ancestors must be considered as law.'[32] Jerome supports this, writing to Lucinius: 'Let us consider the precepts of the ancients as apostolic laws because of the authority of the church,'[33] that is, the assembly of the faithful who heard and saw Christ and were his witnesses. Thus, for example, Peter confesses 'an elder myself and a witness of the sufferings of Christ,'[34] and the evangelist Luke said, 'just as it was handed down to us by those who saw and were ministers of the word,'[35] and John writes: 'What we have seen with our eyes, what we have looked at and touched with our hands concerning the word of life.'[36] His

* * * * *

23 Acts 20:22
24 Col 1:23, where the text actually says *If* you persevere ...'
25 Heb 11:6
26 Mistake for 'Paul'
27 Eph 5:6
28 Ps 88:30 (Vulgate)
29 1 Cor 3:13
30 Jer 7:28
31 1 Cor 11:23 and 34
32 Ep 36.2.101–21
33 Ep 71.435
34 1 Pet 5:1
35 Luke 1:2
36 1 John 1:1

victorious cross and blood were beneficial not only to the angels and virtues in heaven,[37] but also to us men on earth.

But the rite of the church approves the suffrages of the living for the   105
dead, as does Augustine in his *On the Care to be Taken for the Dead*, and in his *Enchiridion*,[38] as well as Chrysostom in Homily 69 on Philippians: 'It is not by chance' (among other things) 'that it was prescribed by the apostles that a commemoration of the dead should be made in the awe-inspiring mysteries, for they knew there was advantage and profit to be gained from   110
them.'[39] Damascene affirms the same thing in his sermon on the suffrages for the dead,[40] according the blessed Dionysius (who was a contemporary of the apostles and a disciple of Paul), in the last chapter of the *Ecclesiastical Hierarchy*, where he mentions the custom according to which one prayed for the dead in the primitive church, saying: 'Drawing near, the venerable bish-   115
op recites the sacred prayer over the dead man.' And he adds: 'This prayer makes appeal to divine clemency, that it will efface all the sins committed by the dead man as a consequence of human weakness and that it will place him in the light and the land of the living, in the bosom of Abraham, Isaac, and Jacob, in a place where sorrow, sadness, and mourning are absent.'[41]   120

These are the distinctive, rich rewards of the saints, beyond all doubt. But I have recently come upon the third homily of Chrysostom on Lazarus, newly translated,[42] a homily that makes little of the suffrages that are made for the dead,[43] as well as Homily 39 concerning chapter 8 of Matthew, where Chrysostom says that the soul separated from the body cannot wander   125
among us.[44] We see the contrary of this, as Master Joachim,[45] deceased last year at Thorn, demonstrated, troubling the priests with whom he had lived.

* * * * *

37 On the basis of Eph 1:21 and Col 1:16, medieval theologians had devised a hierarchy of angels into three spheres of three ranks each. 'Virtues' (or 'strong-holds') were in second place in the second sphere, after 'dominions' (or 'lord-ships') and ahead of 'powers' (or 'authorities').
38 PL 40 596 (*De cura pro mortuis*), 283 (*Enchiridion*)
39 John Chrysostom *Homilia in epistolam ad Philippenses* 3 PG 62 204
40 John of Damascus *De his qui in fide dormierunt* 3 PG 95 250
41 Dionysius the Areopagite *De ecclesiastica hierarchia* 7.4 PG 3 559
42 The four homilies *De Lazaro et divite* were among the works of Chrysostom translated by Erasmus in 1527; see Epp 1800:113 with n20, 2283:176.
43 It is actually the fourth homily; see *De Lazaro concio* IV PG 48 1019.
44 Not Homily 39 but 28; PG 57 353
45 Unidentified

After being implored many times, he said: 'Read Psalm 63;[46] you will see where I am, how I am faring, and what I want. Why do you not distribute the books I left as a legacy?' A certain Pole, a Master Matthias, said to him: 'Of what concern are your books to us? Go to the German executors of your will.' But he answered: 'Recite to them yourself chapter 14 of Ezechiel: "They will save their souls by their righteousness."'[47] But when we come to the tribunal of Christ, neither Job, nor Daniel, nor Noah will be able to pray for anyone. In order that the contradiction that arises everywhere in the homilies and in this saying of Ezechiel be understood, perhaps you would not find it a burden, if you have the leisure, to explain these things to me and the whole world, since I appreciate your unerring judgment, which is greater than that of all the mortals I know. Let us hope that no one throws in my teeth the passage of Matthew: 'Do not throw pearls before swine,'[48] or the one from Isaiah 39, when Hezekiah had shown to strangers the riches he had acquired as a gift from God, and there was nothing that he did not show them.[49] God was justly angry with him, saying: 'Behold the days will come, etc.'[50] But the little dogs eat their masters' crumbs,[51] and those who are initiated into sacred things should not be kept away from hidden things, so that they may be ready to give answer, with politeness and respect, to anyone who asks them about their faith. Farewell, most shining light of letters.

From Cracow, 4 February 1532

The servant of your Lordship, Jan Benedykt, most devoted physician to the king of Poland, Sigismund I

To the excellent and most learned Desiderius Erasmus of Rotterdam, eminent theologian

2602 / From Udalricus Zasius　　　　　　　　Freiburg, 6 February 1532

First published as Ep 165 in Förstemann / Günther, the autograph was in the Burscher Collection of the University Library at Leipzig (Ep 1254 introduction). For Zasius, professor of law at Freiburg, see Ep 303.

* * * * *

46　Vulgate numbering
47　Ezechiel 14:14 and 20
48　Matt 7:6
49　Isaiah 39:2
50　Isaiah 39:2–6
51　Matt 15:27

My greetings, great Erasmus, most celebrated man in the world. When I sent
you last year a carafe of the wine that Johann Paumgartner,[1] a man of great
distinction, had given me as a present in Augsburg, this excellent gentleman
wrote to me that you liked this wine and that, among other things, you made
mention of him to your friends.[2] Seizing this opportunity, he wishes to win   5
your friendship, to ingratiate himself with you, on the condition that, when
the occasion presents itself, you publish a little work with a dedication in
his honour, in praise of his merits, in such a way, however, that no one will
know that this was done at his request, but rather that you were inspired to
sing his praises of your own accord. He solemnly promises that you will not   10
have written in vain, but will discover in a profusion of gratitude that your
labours have borne fruit.

He is a man of great renown, surpassing all mortals in generosity; he
abounds in riches, and he alone directs the mine operations in Innsbruck
in such a way that he has a surplus of a thousand florins every year after   15
expenses;[3] he is a man of such integrity that he is spoken of, if not as God, at
least as Mercury,[4] by his workers; in this year when, commodities are very
expensive, solid in the Christian faith, he supports the poor in a remarkable
manner, so as to be a model. His father was a man of honourable distinction,
namely, councillor to the divine Emperor Maximilian and of King Matthias of   20
Hungary, and, if I may add, he held the highest rank with the pope.[5] Through
the privileges granted by the divine Charles, our Paumgartner was elevated
above the condition of a private citizen as councillor among the leading men
of our King Ferdinand; he lives under their protection as if they were his
patrons. In a word, nothing is lacking to him to be immortal save that he is   25
not immortal by nature.

* * * * *

2602
1 Johann (II) Paumgartner; see Ep 2603 introduction.
2 Cf Ep 2438:25–31.
3 A substantial profit; if Zasius is referring to Rhenish florins, it was the equivalent of 28 years' wages of an Antwerp master mason/carpenter (CWE 12 650
Table 3, 691 Table 13).
4 Mercury was the Roman god of, among other things, commerce and financial
gain.
5 Johann (I) Paumgartner (1455–1527), Augsburg merchant who prospered from
the sale of silver and copper mined in the Tirol. He repeatedly lent money to
Emperor Maximilian I, who ennobled him in 1499 and named him councillor
in 1502, entrusting him with the financial administration of the Tirol. We have
no information concerning his services to Matthias Corvinus of Hungary or to
the pope.

Summoned to aid him in his affairs, I was of some help to him; he showered so many benefits upon me, who asked nothing of him, that if such a Jupiter had not come to my rescue I would hardly have been able to maintain my family in this time of scarcity. He is now preparing the way that 30 may afford you opportunities beyond your fondest desires. He fails no one. If justice, if virtue is to be operative among mortals, they will find hospitality with this hero, as Cybele once did with Nasica.[6] I pray, in virtue of our mutual friendship and through the immense affection that binds me to you, that you will not disregard this offer, but when the occasion arises, will write 35 some little book in his honour.[7] Now I ask for even the semblance of a letter, so that you give him the hope of your friendship.[8]

Farewell. From my home, on the third day after Sexagesima Sunday 1532

Your Zasius   40

Pardon the erasures; I am impeded by many tasks.

To the great Erasmus, the ornament of our age, prince of theologians and of all learning, most respected master and teacher

2603 / To Johann (II) Paumgartner   Freiburg, 8 February 1532

Written at the suggestion of Udalricus Zasius (see Ep 2602:36–7), this letter was first published in the *Epistolae palaeonaeoi*.

Johann (II) Paumgartner (1488–1549), brother-in-law of Anton Fugger, assumed the direction of the Paumgartner firm when his father, Johann (I) Paumgartner (Ep 2602 n5) retired in 1520. Continuing his father's close association with the Hapsburgs, Paumgartner advanced them loans that were important in securing the election of Charles v as emperor and in financing the wars against the Turks. He was rewarded with much of the silver mined in the Tirol as well as with influence at the court. In 1541 he was made an imperial councillor and in 1543 became 'Freiherr von Paumgarten zu Paumgarten.' After the victory of the Reformation in Augsburg and the expulsion of the Catholic clergy from the city, Paumgartner resided at the imperial court or on one of

* * * * *

6 Cybele, the great Asian mother-goddess, was officially welcomed to Rome when her sacred stone was transported from Pessinus in Asia minor in 204 BC. Cornelius Scipio Nasica was chosen to receive it at the Porta Capena on the west side of the Tiber. The episode is recounted in Ovid *Fasti* 4.305–350.

7 In 1533 Erasmus fulfilled this request by dedicating to Paumgartner his *Aliquot homiliae divi Joannis Chrysostomi*; see Ep 2774.

8 Erasmus complied with Ep 2603.

his many estates. Further loans to Charles v helped the latter prepare for the
Schmalkaldic war of 1546–7, in the wake of which Augsburg had to surrender to the emperor on harsh conditions. In July 1547 Paumgartner entered the
city in the entourage of the emperor and in 1548 helped him impose a form of
government that put power in the hands of the patricians at the expense of the
guilds, which had been sources of support for the Reformation and resistance
to imperial authority. He died in Augsburg the following year.

In 1532, aware of Anton Fugger's friendship with Erasmus, Paumgartner exploited his friendship with Udalricus Zasius to establish his own connection with
the celebrated humanist; Ep 2602 is the first surviving evidence of that effort, and
this letter is the first fruit of it. Paumgartner responded with a gift of pure gold,
for which Ep 2621 is the letter of thanks. There followed a lively correspondence,
some of it via third parties. In August 1532 Erasmus praised Paumgartner in a
letter to his son, Johann Georg, that served as the preface to Johann Herwagen's
edition of Demosthenes (Ep 2695), and in March of the following year he dedicated to Paumgartner himself Froben's *Aliquot homiliae divi Joannis Chrysostomi*
(Ep 2774), in return for which Paumgartner sent him a gold goblet (Ep 2809).
These cordial relations ended only with Erasmus' death. The very last letter in
Allen's edition of the correspondence (Ep 3141) is one from Bonifacius Amerbach
to Paumgartner, responding to the latter's request for copies of all of Erasmus'
works. Paumgartner apparently disappointed the hopes that he would make a
substantial contribution to the cost of publishing the Basel *Opera omnia* (1540),
but he did order copies for each of his three sons (AK Epp 2115, 2156).

ERASMUS OF ROTTERDAM TO JOHANN PAUMGARTNER, GREETING
Almost two years ago Ulrich Zasius, a man to be admired for his many great
gifts, yet in nothing more lovable than in the generosity of spirit that he
shows towards his friends, gave me a sample of Paumgartner wine, which
could not fail to please the most refined palate.[1] But in addition he recently   5
gave me a more substantial sample of Paumgartner, which was much more
agreeable to my taste.[2] For in his letter to me he included such praise of you,
honourable sir, that not only did he carry me away with affection for you, but
he also brought it about that I consider myself in no small way attached to
you, and more attached to him, although hitherto I had been most attached   10
to him. Who would not love a man born for the benefit of the common good,
in whom eminent virtues of soul match his impressive fortune, or rather do
not match, but surpass them? I have nourished such deserved affection for

* * * * *

2603
1 See Ep 2602:1–3.
2 The reference is to Ep 2602:13–33.

Zasius for many years that, according to the rule of Pythagoras,[3] I have considered absolutely everything to be possessed in common with him. Since   15
your generosity has been bestowed on him so lavishly, know that Erasmus
is attached to you for as many reasons as Zasius is attached to you. If by this
rule you receive me into the number of those indebted to you, by this same
rule it is proper that you admit me into the number of your friends. For if it is
the law of friendship that all else is common among friends, it is much more   20
fitting that friends themselves be shared in common, since there is nothing
more precious than this possession. Furthermore, Zasius significantly increased the number of his many kindnesses to me from the moment that he
introduced an old friend into this community of friendship.

      But we shall discuss these matters more fully at another time. It was   25
hardly possible for me to write this since I am weakened by a cough, an ail-
ment that has afflicted many people here.[4]

      Farewell. In Freiburg in Breisgau, 8 February 1532

2604 / To Viglius Zuichemus   Freiburg, 8 February 1532

> This is Erasmus' reply to Ep 2568; Viglius' reply to it is Ep 2632. The letter was
> first published in the *Epistolae palaeonaeoi*; the manuscript, written and signed
> by a secretary, is in the City Library of Rotterdam (Erasmuszaal 94 D 3).

I have received the letter that you left at Augsburg,[1] full of the most friendly
sentiments towards me, which you had manifestly declared when you were
here, most loyal Viglius. I answered via a Frenchman with the most auspicious name of Pierre Mondoré, if I am not mistaken.[2] He seemed to be a
sensible, upright man; he was not en route to Padua, but to Rome, passing   5
through the Veneto.[3] I entrusted other letters to him also, but I suspect that

* * * * *

3 Ie that between friends all is common. As Erasmus explains in *Adagia* I i 1,
   Cicero 'seems to attribute this adage to Pythagoras.'
4 See Ep 2598 n1.

2604
1 Cf Ep 2568:1–2; neither Viglius' letter nor Erasmus' reply (line 3) is extant.
2 Pierre Mondoré (documented 1532–5) was a French student on his way to Italy.
   Little else is known of him. His surname (Monsaureus in Latin) means 'golden
   mountain.'
3 Viglius later reported that Mondoré had changed his plans and had come to
   Padua instead; see Ep 2632:1–2.

he did not deliver any of them.⁴ I received another letter of yours via Anton
Fugger, written in Padua on 19 August. If this date is not erroneous, you
flew there rather than went on horseback: I suspect that by a slip of the pen
September was written instead of October.⁵ However that may be, I congrat-   10
ulate you that the beginnings of your trip to Italy went well, and I pray that
the rest will correspond to these good auspices.

Concerning Egnazio you tell me there is nothing to report, but that
everything is proceeding satisfactorily. I have such affection for this truly
refined man that I am cheered by any mention of him. What is this I hear?   15
Are you engaged in skirmishes with the bands of Ciceronians and preparing yourself for a showdown with them? But I would first like to know in
what you agree with them and in what you are at odds. They want young
men to strive to imitate Cicero. On that point we are in perfect agreement
with them. I would not object if they recommend that he should be imitated   20
more than anyone else. If they do not permit us ever to depart from Cicero
in any way or to borrow anything at all from other approved authors, I do
not think that they themselves do what they exact from others, if there really are any who require this. But some evil genius is attempting to inject
this plague into studies, as they did long ago into religion.⁶ Haio Herman   25
of Friesland always seemed to me to try to emulate the pleasing facility of
Cicero,⁷ and I think you have done and continue to do the same, for your
last letter breathes a certain something of Tully, not beyond the ordinary,
but more than the ordinary. But you must take care that in your aspiration
to be a Ciceronian you do not gain approval in the ears of the jurisconsults   30
and lovers of Bartolo.⁸ Joking aside, my Viglius, I would advise either that
you do not engage in conflict with such people or else that you do not allow the disputes to end up in bitterness. If they require the brilliance of a
Tullian style from me, they are twice unfair: they are asking this first of a

* * * * *

4 He had in fact delivered them all (Ep 2632:2–3), but none of them appears to
  have survived.
5 Ep 2568 was dated xiv Calends of December, ie 18 November 1531. Erasmus
  appears to have misread December as September.
6 Cf Epp 2599:63–6, 2600:18–23.
7 See Ep 2568:20–1 with n7.
8 Bartolo of Sassoferrato (1313–55) the most famous of the medieval commenta-
  tors on Roman law. His name is used here to represent all jurists, whose prose,
  in the opinion of the humanists, caused the Muses to freeze to death; cf Ep
  134:29–33. Viglius will take a kinder view of the style of Bartolo and the jurists;
  see Ep 2632:77–100.

Dutchman and second of a theologian.[9] In other respects I am of that num- 35
ber who think that the eloquence of Cicero is divine rather than human. So
far am I from disapproving his style.

Here we are embroiled in wrangling. The censures of the Sorbonne have
come out, of which I think the theologians themselves are now ashamed. I
responded to them, but with unvarying moderation.[10] With the same oil, as 40
they say,[11] I have responded to the old absurdities of Clichtove.[12] The emperor
is expected at Regensburg to resume the diet,[13] but he is playing Callipedes to
an amazing degree,[14] although this is nothing unusual. I have been stricken
with a cough for many days now.[15] This malady is common here. I am astonished that you make no mention of Bembo, who I hear plays the role of chief 45
patron of all gifted writers there.[16] You ought to be known and endeared to
him by now, unless I do not know either of you very well. Farewell.

Given at Freiburg, 8 February 1532

Your Erasmus of Rotterdam

To the most learned young man Viglius Zuichemus of Friesland. In 50
Padua

2605 / To Bonifacius Amerbach   Freiburg, 9 February 1532

This letter (= AK Ep 1600) was first published in the *Vita Erasmi*. The autograph
is in the Öffentliche Bibliothek of the University of Basel (MS AN III 15 38).

* * * * *

9 Dutchmen were 'not ... outstandingly erudite, particularly in ancient studies' (*Adagia* IV vi 35), while theologians were obliged to use words that are not
   found in Cicero (see Ep 1805:88–98).
10 See Ep 2552 n10.
11 Ie with the same waste of time and effort; see *Adagia* I iv 62, citing Cicero *Atticus*
   13.38.1.
12 For Josse Clichtove, a close ally of Noël Béda, and his attacks on Erasmus, particularly his views on marriage, see Epp 1609 n8, 1642:8–10, 1679:91–6. Already
   in 1527 Erasmus had responded briefly to Clichtove in the *Appendix de scriptis
   I. Clichtovei*, published with *Supputatio errorum in censuris Natalis Bedae*. But just
   at this time (February 1532), moved by the publication of the *Determinatio* of the
   Paris theologians, Froben published Erasmus' much more detailed response to
   Clichtove: *Dilutio eorum quae Iodocus Clichtoveus scripsit adversus declamationem
   suasoriam matrimonii* (Basel: Froben 1532).
13 See Ep 2511 n20.
14 Ie someone who undertakes great projects but never seems to get them finished
   (*Adagia* I vi 43)
15 See Ep 2598 n1.
16 Erasmus had not yet received Ep 2594, in which Viglius reports (lines 44–6)
   having visited Bembo several times.

Cordial greetings. If you either had a home here or had intended to have a home here, we would come to some agreement about the specified date.[1] Now, since the situation advises against it, I will not continue to be bothersome while I try to be helpful.

I don't know what news the emperor is going to announce. His silence is astonishing.[2] Something extraordinary is being prepared. Everything is done now by secret deliberation.

If only the fertile talent of Grynaeus had remained at the disposition of liberal studies. For I hear that he has been appointed to take the place of the dead Oecolampadius.[3]

I am still coughing, but a little less violently.[4] We have to wait for the end of winter. I hope that you and all those dear to you are in the best of health.

Freiburg, 9 February 1532

To the most illustrious doctor of laws Bonifacius Amerbach. In Basel

2606 / From Anselmus Ephorinus   Basel, 10 February 1532

The autograph of this letter was in the Burscher Collection of the University Library at Leipzig (Ep 1254 introduction). Allen lists the first publication as Ep 166 in Förstemann / Günther (1904), but the letter had already been published as Ep 24 in Miaskowski (1901).

Greetings. Your theologian's servant was sent to us at the most propitious moment.[1] But I fear, Erasmus, excellent ornament of all centuries, that you

* * * * *

2605
1 Cf Epp 2597:1–6, 2598:7–9.
2 The imperial diet, which was supposed to open on 6 January 1532 in Regensburg, was still not in session, and would not be so until 17 April; see Ep 2511 n20.
3 Simon Grynaeus (Ep 2487 n9) was indeed the initial choice to succeed Oecolampadius (d 23 November 1531) as chief pastor (*antistes*) and professor of divinity, but he declined to do so, preferring to devote himself to his professorship of Greek, to which a special professorship of theology was now added. As a result, Osvaldus Myconius (Ep 861), who in 1531 had moved from Zürich to Basel to become pastor of St Alban's, was in August 1532 appointed Oecolampadius' successor. See Karl Rudolf Hagenbach *Johann Oekolampad und Oswald Myconius, die Reformatoren Basels* (Elberfeld 1859) 338–9.
4 See Ep 2598 n1.

2606
1 'Your theologian' was Ludwig Baer; see Ep 2550 n2.

may say that my promises are like cypresses, which, rising up magnificently, splendidly, and with their towering summits shaped like a cone, neverthe-less do not bear fruit.[2] Your cup, which I send now through Melchior,[3] was faithfully brought to me;[4] it is an unfruitful cup, however, for I see that it did not produce a second cup, as I had hoped.[5]

I have received a letter from Poland written at the beginning of Novem-ber, from which I learn with great chagrin that four letters sent from here have not yet been delivered to my Maecenas.[6] But, most learned Erasmus, the time and the hour will bring you the recompense of your virtue, especially for the dedication of the Terence,[7] do not doubt it. I will not allow it to be said that the Boner family was unmindful of your kindness and benevolence, and this delay, whatever its cause, will not be of any harm to you. My Maecenas will compensate with a fitting reward the fame that he will recognize has come to him through your lucubrations.[8]

Eobanus Hessus and Venatorius,[9] very renowned for their erudition and their honesty, and very devoted to your person, enjoined it upon me to relay to you their respectful greetings. They write that Petrus Apianus, not so much a student as an expert in this subject, has undertaken to publish in Ingolstadt the *Geography* of Ptolemy in Greek and Latin.[10] I always thought that he was the only one able to make those books available to scholars in a

* * * * *

2 *Adagia* iv iii 10
3 Unidentified
4 See Ep 2554 n13. Lines 51–3 below indicate that it was delivered from Nürnberg.
5 Ephorinus appears to have expected the second cup to come from the Boner family; see the following paragraph.
6 Seweryn Boner (Ep 2533). The name of Maecenas, confidant of Emperor Augustus and the patron of Virgil and Horace, became (and remains) the by-word for a generous and enlightened patron of the arts.
7 Ep 2584
8 The presentation copy of the Terence had not yet reached Cracow, and would not do so for another three years, at which point a generous gift (gold medal-lions rather than a cup) was dispatched to Erasmus; see Ep 2533 introduction.
9 For Eobanus Hessus see Ep 2495; for Thomas Venatorius see Ep 2537.
10 Petrus Apianus (Peter Bienewitz, 1495–1552) studied mathematics at Leipzig and Vienna, and then taught mathematics at the University of Ingolstadt from 1527 until his death. His first major work, *Cosmographia seu descriptio totius orbis* (1524), which was based on Ptolemy, became one of the most popular texts of his time and was translated into all the major European languages. See *Dictionary of Scientific Biography* 1 178–9. The proposed bilingual edition of the *Geography* of Ptolemy was never completed.

fitting manner. He was provided with Ptolemy's work translated into Latin
by Willibald Pirckheimer in Nürnberg.[11] The maps will not be drawn with
curved lines, but with parallel straight lines crossing at right angles;[12] the ex-   25
planations for this by Johannes Regiomantanus will be added.[13] It will be evident that whoever supplied Ptolemy's *Geography* with maps in Rome made
many errors.[14] Apianus himself will make all the maps with his own hands,
since he knows where the original passages were corrupted and where we
were deceived. I would like Glareanus to know this,[15] as a friend among   30
friends, but for the very reason that I began to love him more intensely and
evangelically, for we must make some allowance for his weakness.[16] I would
like to have the opportunity to render him some service, so that he may know
how inappropriate it is for a Christian to seek discord among friends in a useless and fabricated matter that never entered my mind.[17] He who is faithful   35
conceals the fault of a friend. But I will return good for evil, etc.

* * * * *

11 See Ep 2493:62–3 with n8.
12 The use of terrestrial grids in maps was a major topic in Apianus' *Cosmographia*
    (n10 above).
13 Johannes Regiomontanus of Königsberg in Franconia (1436–76) received a thor-
    ough training in mathematics and astronomy in Vienna and then in 1461 went
    to Italy, where he mastered Greek in order to study the works of Ptolemy and
    other ancient writers on mathematics and science. While in Rome he completed
    the *Epitome* of Ptolemy's *Almagest* begun by his teacher in Vienna, Georg von
    Peuerbach (published 1496). Some of the observations in it later proved useful
    to Copernicus. After several years (c 1471–75) in Hungary, in the service of King
    Matthias Corvinus, he moved to Nürnberg, where he set up a press devoted to
    turning out accurate editions of mathematical and astronomical texts. In 1475
    he went to Rome at the invitation of Pope Sixtus IV to consult with him on the
    reform of the calendar, but he died the following summer. He had long been
    working on a new edition of Ptolemy's *Geographia*, which was never published.
    But his notes on the errors in the earlier translation by Jacopo Angeli (see fol-
    lowing note) were appended to Willibald Pirckheimer's Latin translation of the
    Geographia (see n11 above).
14 Jacopo Angeli's Latin translation (1406–10) of Ptolemy's *Geography* was pub-
    lished at Rome in 1478 (Arnoldus Buckinck).
15 Because of his interest in geography. In 1510 Henricus Glareanus (Ep 2539 n2)
    had published a map of the world that was remarkably accurate for the time. In
    1527 he published *De geographia* (Basel: J. Faber Emmeus), a description of Asia,
    Africa, and Europe.
16 The language is unclear, but this seems to be a reference to behaviour at which
    Ephorinus decided not to take offence; see the following note.
17 For Ephorinus' quarrel with Glareanus see Ep 2539:37–44, 83–4.

Our Poland triumphs over the defeated foe.[18] Even during the winter months, frequent incursions were made into their territories, bringing rich and abundant booty. The grand ambassador of the Turkish sultan was sent to settle the dispute between the Wallachians and our king.[19] Hieronim Łaski has returned from an embassy to the Turks,[20] unloading a profusion of threats against Germany.[21] I am glad the emperor will come to Regensburg.[22] I am enormously distressed by your poor health, but with the aid of Christ your former physical vigour will return. Jan and Stanisław, who greet you in return most respectfully as a father, are suffering from the illness about which I wrote to you, especially Stanisław.[23] I send to your theologian,[24] in your name, the quince preserves.[25] We all wish that from this new cup you will drink long-lasting health.[26] Farewell, most learned Erasmus.

* * * * *

18 In 1529 Peter Rareş (Petryllus), *voivode* (or *hospodar*) of Moldavia, a vassal of the Ottoman sultan, invaded Polish territory without the sultan's permission. On 22 August 1531, a Polish force under the command of Jan Tarnowski won a decisive victory over Rareş at Obertyn on the Dniester and incorporated the defeated portion of Moldavia into Poland. The sultan congratulated King Sigismund on this great victory. See *Lasciana* 128 n7.

19 The ambassador was Alvise Gritti (1501–34). Born in Constantinople, the son of a Venetian father and his Greek mistress, Gritti rose to great prominence in Ottoman service. He was the pivotal figure in the Turkish attempt to pacify Hungary under John Zápolyai, Ferdinand of Austria's rival for the kingship of Hungary. This letter appears to be the sole evidence that Gritti was involved in an attempt to restore peace between King Sigismund I and the princes of Wallachia, who were Turkish vassals.

20 While Poland remained neutral in the conflict over the kingship of Hungary between Ferdinand of Hapsburg and John Zápolyai, the Polish diplomat Hieronim Łaski (Ep 1341A n310) sided with John, was instrumental in negotiating the treaty (1528) that brought John the support of the sultan against Ferdinand, and was at this point still conducting difficult missions on John's behalf.

21 In April 1532 Suleiman, who had failed to capture Vienna in the autumn of 1529, would launch another, similarly unsuccessful attempt to take Vienna and drive Ferdinand of Austria out of Hungary. In June 1533 Suleiman and Ferdinand, having fought one another to a standstill, signed a truce by which Ferdinand acknowledged John Zápolyai as king of Hungary but was left unmolested in his possession of the fragment of the kingdom known as Royal Hungary.

22 To attend the imperial diet; see Ep 2511 n20.

23 The letter is not extant. For Jan Boner and Stanisław Aichler, see Epp 2533 introduction, 2545 introduction.

24 See n1 above.

25 For the preserves, which had a medicinal purpose, see Ep 2554 n14.

26 See n4 above.

Basel, 10 February 1532

Completely at the service of your Highness, Anselmus Ephorinus   50

My host,[27] an aged and pious man and admirer of your fame, prays for nothing more from the gods than a greeting from Erasmus, for doing us the service of faithfully bringing you the cup from Nürnberg.

2607 / From Nicolaus Olahus   Brussels, 12 February 1532

This letter, Olahus' point-by-point reply to Ep 2582, was first published in Ipolyi, page 196. The manuscript is page 229 of the Olahus codex in the Hungarian National Archives in Budapest (Ep 2339 introduction). Erasmus' reply is Ep 2613.

RESPONSE OF NICOLAUS OLAHUS TO ERASMUS OF ROTTERDAM

You will learn from the enclosed letter of the current state of the matter of Lieven.[1] Prompted by your wishes, as well as by his good character and native endowments, which are not to be despised, I will do all I can so that he may finally realize his ambition.   5

I am happy and rejoice that you have now been liberated from that severe pain in your foot and also from the other physical afflictions that you have suffered. I wish earnestly that the great and good God will allow you to enjoy for a long time this desired freedom from physical impairment. But I cannot imagine how, after leaving your native country, you can enjoy hap-   10 piness and physical well-being under a foreign sky. Others strive hand and foot[2] to be able to lead a quiet life in the land where they were born and brought up and in which they were adorned with all blessings and advantages, and wish only to adorn and honour their country with all the virtue and knowledge that is in them. To speak frankly and in my usual manner,   15 dear Erasmus, you seem for many years now to have done otherwise. For even if, because of your outstanding virtues and gifts, you were, wherever you lived, no less an ornament and honour to your native country than if you had lived there all your life, nevertheless, your country seems in a certain sense to complain of you that it did not receive any ornament or any benefit   20

* * * * *

27 Johann Gross; see Ep 2539 n7.

2607

1 The letter is not extant. In Ep 2582:26–30 Erasmus had solicited Olahus' support for the effort of Lieven Algoet to secure a position at the court of Mary of Hungary, regent of the Netherlands.

2 *Adagia* I iv 15

when you deserted it and did not adorn it with your presence. But you have in readiness many reasons why you were absent for so long and deprived your countrymen of your presence. I do not deny that heretofore perhaps you could have had some reasons. But since I see no great impediment now that could divert a man from an honourable leisure, and nothing that would 25 fail to please a man of great renown, I do not think it is fitting for you to be absent any longer, all the more since, as I myself am aware, our most serene queen is an admirer of your talent and learning, as well as wholeheartedly well disposed towards you. You seem in your letter to approve my candid and sincere sentiments towards my friends. It is with the same candour that 30 elicits your praise that I write these things to you, I who dare wish that my friends will be no different towards me than I am towards them.

You write that you have bought a new house in Freiburg, even though you contemplated more than once returning to Brabant, but that certain friends urged you to remain there until things were brought under control by 35 Emperor Charles. The house should not detain you from your purpose, for in my opinion it will be easy to find a buyer without any loss to you whenever you put it up for sale. I do not see that the situation here is so turbulent and troubled that it would deter you from returning. The emperor, after resolving things that he had to resolve and could resolve, left the rest in the hands of 40 the queen. I offered my cooperation even earlier, which you are free to make use of, insignificant though it may be. Provided that I know your intention, I have no doubt, if you have decided to return, that I can support and accommodate you in that matter. For even without your instruction, both while I was here and while I was elsewhere, I made mention of you more than once 45 to the right people. I omitted nothing that pertained to enhancing or contributing to your reputation. If the opportunity presents itself some day I would prefer to make known my sentiments to you in person rather than by letter, as I do now. If therefore you wish to hear the advice of a friend who loves you, give thought to visiting your native land, in which, besides the love of the 50 country itself, you have many friends and a prince who honours you with his benevolence, and I see nothing that would be lacking here to your peace and tranquillity and literary leisure. Unless perhaps you fear the Franciscans and Dominicans! There is no one among them who, the gods being favourable to you, could harm you with their loquacity. As for their impudence, you will 55 easily repress it, thanks to the many other circumstances here in your favour as well as your own presence. That you have been liberated there from the plague of Zwingli and Oecolampadius is cause for rejoicing, not only to me but to all good men. Would that the church of believers were liberated from other persecutors as well! There would be less feeling of weariness and dis- 60 tress among good men.

Farewell, and let me know if you have something in mind, or rather when I can expect you here. You will excuse my frankness and freedom of language, if it annoyed you. I am accustomed to use this freedom with my sincere friends. Farewell, love me, and write back.

Brussels, 12 February 1532

2608 / To Stanislaus Thurzo

Freiburg, 13 February 1532

For Stanislaus Thurzo, bishop of Olomouc in Moravia, see Ep 1242 introduction. This is the preface to *Enarratio psalmi trigesimi octavi* (Basel: Froben, March 1532). Thurzo's letter of thanks is Ep 2699.

TO THE MOST REVEREND PRELATE AND ILLUSTRIOUS PRINCE
LORD STANISLAUS THURZO, BISHOP OF OLOMOUC,
DESIDERIUS ERASMUS OF ROTTERDAM SENDS GREETINGS
Silence destroyed Amyclae,[1] but lack of communication has destroyed many friendships,[2] if we are to credit the adages of the ancients. Now, since among all possessions there is none that can compare with a loyal friend,[3] I did not think, most honoured prelate, that I should risk that a prolonged intermission in our correspondence might appear to have deprived me of such an excellent patron. Indeed, my beloved Thurzo has never faded from my mind. How could that be possible, unless I were, alone of all mortals, not only the most inhuman but also the most ungrateful? But from time to time I heard that you had changed your episcopal see, at times I wondered if you were safe and sound in the midst of such great tumults, at times the suspicion nagged at my mind that perhaps one of that number who carry venom about on their tongue had either obliterated or at least dampened your long-standing good will towards me.

* * * * *

2608
1 *Adagia* I ix 1
2 See *Adagia* II i 26: *Multas amicitias silentium diremit* 'Many's the friendship that silence has undone.' The Greek word ἀπροσηγορία, translated as 'silence' in the adage, really means 'prolonged absence and lack of communication.' See Aristotle *Nicomachean Ethics* 8.5 1157b10–13. The idea is often expressed in English as 'out of sight, out of mind.'
3 Ecclus 6:15

But when Caspar Velius,[4] once the protégé of your Grace, paid me a
visit on his way to the imperial diet that had been summoned to Speyer,[5]
he removed all doubts, confirming both that everything was proceeding according to your wishes, and that you had not deviated from your inveterate   20
attachment to me. On the other hand, as he had often done previously by letter, he upbraided me in my presence that I did not refresh such an excellent
friend's memory of me with some token of my studies. When I answered that
I had always had the desire to do so but that so far nothing had come forth
that seemed worthy of such a great prelate, he reprimanded me even more   25
sharply for not being well enough acquainted with the bishop's humane
character. 'There is no little work' he said, 'so insignificant that he would
not welcome it as a great gift, as long as it was a genuine offspring of the
Erasmian genius.' Again, when I protested that my genius was exhausted by
labours, misfortunes, maladies, and old age, he did not accept any evasion   30
and did not relent until I promised what he demanded.[6]

And so I have done what the British are accustomed to doing: when
they are absent from one another symbols (they call them tokens) are exchanged between them. No one gives thought to the price; it is the intention
of the sender that lends charm to the gift, even if it is a piece of cloth no   35
bigger than a fingernail. Stirred by this example and by the hope of success
inspired by Velius' words, I send you the thirty-eighth Psalm, which writers
of old treated in various ways, but in such a way that, in my opinion at least,
they seem to have distorted certain passages and to have had little understanding of certain others.[7] What I have contributed I will leave to your judg- 40
ment. Let me state openly, however, that I expended no little effort to ensure
that the tenor of the argument would be consistent.

Whatever the value of this little gift, if you in your benevolence will accept it with serene countenance, it will give me great pleasure; but you will
redouble my pleasure if you will be kind enough to indicate by letter if you   45
wish something to be treated differently. I have no doubt that many such

* * * * *

4 Ep 2517
5 Ie the diet that was supposed to open at Speyer on 14 September but was
  posponed and transferred to Regensburg (Ep 2511 n20). For Caspar Ursinus
  Velius' visit to Erasmus in September 1531, see Ep 2543 n1.
6 Cf Ep 2517 n13.
7 In the commentary Erasmus several times criticizes the ancient exegetes for
  excessive use of allegory in their interpretation of certain verses; see CWE 65 5–6,
  32, 44, 123.

things will come to your attention. But in this little commentary you will
see in passing an image of these times, in which among the untold disasters
of human life there is none more pernicious, among many pestilences none
more pestilent than the tongues dipped in deadly poison that tyrannize our 50
age more than any other. You will also get some idea of my activities and
perhaps you will wonder that this half-dead old man still holds the tiller on a
straight course amidst so many storms and tempests that assail him on every
side. 'But the Lord is the protector of my life; before whom will I tremble?[8]
I feel free to write to you in Greek, since I am told that for some time now, 55
though already on the threshold of old age, if I am not mistaken, you have
been a philhellenist and have been devoting your energies vigorously to
Greek literature, to the great shame, no doubt, of many who as young men
neglect this essential part of their studies and rush into the mysteries of theology with unwashed feet, as they say.[9] Farewell. 60

Given at Freiburg in Breisgau, 13 February 1532

2609 / From Christian Beyer [Torgau], 18 February 1532

First published as Ep 167 in Förstemann / Günther, the manuscript of this letter (in a secretary's hand but dated and signed by Beyer) was in the Burscher
Collection of the University Library at Leipzig (Ep 1254 introduction). Christian
Beyer (c 1482–1535) was from c 1511 a member of the faculty of law at Wittenberg,
from 1513 a councillor at the Electoral Saxon Court, and several times burgomaster of Wittenberg (1513, 1516, 1519, 1522, 1525). An early supporter of
Luther, he advised the electoral court on legal resistance to efforts of the papacy
and the imperial government to condemn and punish the reformer. In 1528
he became chancellor to Elector John the Steadfast of Saxony, and at the Diet
of Augsburg in 1530 it was he who read out to the emperor and princes the
German text of the Augsburg Confession.

It appears that the Saxon court was at this time resident at Torgau
(Förstemann / Günther page 299), hence Allen's designation of it as the place
from which the letter was probably written.

Both this letter and Ep 2610 are letters of recommendation for Erasmus' wayward servant Felix Rex, known as Polyphemus (Ep 2130 introduction), who
was about to return to Erasmus after a period of wandering that began at the

* * * * *

8 Ps 26:2, quoted in Greek from the Septuagint
9 *Adagia* I ix 54

Diet of Augsburg in 1530 and had now come to an end at the electoral court in
Saxony; see Ep 2334 n1. Polyphemus' last mission for Erasmus before being dismissed from his service would be to deliver Epp 2679, 2685, and 2687 to the diet
at Regensburg in 1532. He eventually settled at Königsberg (now Kaliningrad),
where he became librarian to the duke of Prussia. He died of the plague in 1549.

TO HIS GREAT FRIEND ERASMUS OF ROTTERDAM, GREETING
Last year, once the Diet of Augsburg had come to an end,[1] your friend – or
rather our friend – Polyphemus came to see me, bearing letters of recommendation from Martin Luther, Justus Jonas, and Philippus Melanchthon,[2]
in which they asked me to lend support to Polyphemus' petition to be admit- 5
ted into the staff of courtiers of the Duke Elector of Saxony. I gladly undertook
this task, not so much because of their recommendation as for your sake. For
I would wish that you be convinced that you, the father of all scholars, the
champion of humane letters, and the restorer of a more authentic theology,
are loved, honoured, and revered by all the learned and good men that our 10
Saxony possesses. As far as I am concerned, I confess that whatever learning
I have – and its meagreness is proved by this letter – I must attribute to you.
I therefore submitted the matter concerning Polyphemus to the prince, and
since I made mention of your name, he assigned an important position in the
court to Polyphemus. He so fulfilled his role that he was highly esteemed 15
by all the good men at court, and would have been of great benefit to the
prince had he been able to endure the Saxon climate. But after he began to
suffer pain in his feet, no less seriously than unceasingly, I took care that, by
leave of the prince and through his munificence, he was allowed to betake
himself elsewhere, where a milder climate would be more suited to his na- 20
ture. Although Polyphemus is very well regarded and liked by you, I have
nevertheless wished to bear witness before you and before everyone to his
honesty, candour, and loyalty. I therefore ask that he find undiminished the
favour with you that he enjoyed when he departed. If I were to gain more
favour with you through my recommendation, I would have reason to re- 25
joice immensely. Farewell, revered father, and impute my audacity to the
love with which I embrace Erasmus.
   Given 18 February 1532

* * * * *

2609
1 The formal conclusion of the diet took place on 19 November 1531.
2 Melanchthon's letter is MBW Ep 1104A, dated at 'November / December 1530.'
  The others appear not to have survived.

Your friend Christian Beyer, doctor in canon and civil law and chancellor of the duke of Saxony, imperial elector, has affixed his signature.   30

To the eminent man of rare learning the great Erasmus of Rotterdam, his master and most loved patron

2610 / From Georgius Spalatinus   [Torgau, 18 February] 1532

First published as Ep 168 in Förstemann / Günther, the autograph of this letter was in the Burscher Collection of the University Library at Leipzig (Ep 1254 introduction). For Spalatinus see Ep 501. There is no trace of any correspondence between Erasmus and Spalatinus since Ep 1497 (6 September 1524), and this is the last extant letter of either man to the other. For the circumstances of its composition, the presumed date, and the probable place of writing see Ep 2609 introduction.

†

Although I know that our Polyphemus has no need of a recommendation to you, most learned Erasmus (why should I recommend someone well known to you?), nevertheless, at least in order not to be failing in my duty, I gave this letter of praise as a gift to a friend who was departing. For I see that he leaves with a letter of our excellent prince, the Elector of Saxony, which testifies   5 highly to his honesty and probity, which I think will please you greatly,[1] and also with a letter of my lord the chancellor and doctor Christian Beyer,[2] my very dear compatriot. And I do not know of anyone whom our Polyphemus offended, whether at our court or elsewhere. He is so obliging, a gift perhaps of the Graces, that is, of good letters themselves, the mothers of the Graces.   10 These words in behalf of our Polyphemus. I gladly oblige those I can, with God as my witness. 1532.

Georgius Spalatinus

2611 / To Jacopo Sadoleto   Freiburg, 22 February 1532

This is the preface to Froben's large folio edition of the works of St Basil the Great in the original Greek, the first such edition ever published (Basel: March

* * * * *

2610
1 Not extant
2 Ep 2609

1532). Although Erasmus denied editorial responsibility (see lines 3–5), it appears that he directed the project (see Ep 2526:14–16). Erasmus' interest in Basil was evident early in his career. In 1511 he took William Grocyn's manuscript of the commentary on Isaiah with him to Cambridge and set to work translating it, only to anticipate modern scholarship by concluding that it was not genuine (Epp 227:21–5, 229:7–20). He nonetheless published his translation of it with Froben's new edition of the *Enchiridion* in 1518. Erasmus' interest in Basil continued. In 1528 he asked Willibald Pirckheimer to send him a Basil manuscript (Epp 1997:13–14, 2028:1–3). Allen's speculation that this might have been the manuscript sent to Levinus Ammonius with the request that he make a copy of it is unfounded; see Ep 2214 n5. A significant by-product of Erasmus' work on this edition was the publication of his own translations of Basil's *De Spiritu Sancto* (see n22 below) and *De laudibus ieiunii* (see n26 below).

For Jacopo Sadoleto, bishop of Carpentras, see Ep 1511.

DESIDERIUS ERASMUS OF ROTTERDAM TO THE MOST REVEREND
LORD JACOPO SADOLETO, BISHOP OF CARPENTRAS, GREETING

I had thoroughly made up my mind, Sadoleto, glory of this age, and had decided for the future to refuse absolutely, no matter how relentless the demands of the printers, to contribute prefaces to the works of others. But I was 5 carried off course from this adamantine (as I thought) decision by St Basil, a man justly called the Great, but more worthy of the surname of the Most Great. From what I had read in translation, as if through a mist, I admired the obviously divine gifts of genius and the heart that transcended the human condition. But as soon as I had the opportunity to read the Christian 10 Demosthenes, or rather the heavenly orator, speaking in his own language, the truly persuasive eloquence of the divinely inspired prelate so overwhelmed and enflamed my whole being that I thought I should give priority to nothing else than to ensure that this inestimable treasure was made available in print for the common good. For if it so moved me, myopic and torpid 15 as I am, to a love of piety, how much more would it carry away those who by reason of their natural endowments and more abundant learning have eyes more discerning than others and are more spontaneously drawn to the study of piety. And this passion, in my opinion, was not engendered in me by some arcane affinity for gifted writers, as Horace for example thrilled me 20 long ago when I was a boy and not yet aware of what charmed me so greatly, for what affinity is there between the most abject of mortals and that incomparable hero? But that omnipotent Spirit, exercising its power through an elect instrument, so stirs up our minds. This is indeed that most beautiful of all things, wisdom, which Plato saw only in a dream, which when it is seen 25 with spiritual eyes, excites incredible love for it.

For my part, I think it is an affront to compare the oratorical talent of
Basil with any of those whose eloquence Greece admired excessively and
Italy emulated with more moderation. Who among them so excelled in all
the oratorical virtues that something was not lacking in him or might give   30
offence? Pericles thunders and lightens but without art.[1] Lysias virtually falls
flat with his Attic eloquence.[2] They attribute charm to Demetrius Phalereus,
but they deny him a sense of gravity.[3] Isocrates, a closeted orator, lost the
charm of natural diction through the studied rhythms of the arrangement
of words and periodic sentences.[4] In the case of Demosthenes, whom Cicero   35
presents as the perfect model in every detail, the charge was that his orations
smelled of the lamp, and there are some who complain that he lacks feeling
and urbanity.[5] But even granted that there was someone whom you did not
find lacking either in natural gifts, art, or experience, whom will you name
who I will not say equalled but even came close to equalling the soul of St   40
Basil, filled with divine power? Whom can you name who joined so much
philosophy and the sum total of all the disciplines with the utmost skill in
speaking? But, as I said, it is a kind of insult to compare a man divinely inspired with profane, ordinary mortals.

It is more appropriate to compare a saint with saints. That same age,   45
approximately, produced some great men of the greatest eloquence and similar in knowledge as in piety: Athanasius, bishop of Alexandria;[6] Gregory of

* * * * *

2611
1 Pericles (495–429 BC), Athenian statesman and general, also known for his
   oratory
2 Lysias (445–c 380 BC) was the paragon of the pure, simple 'Attic' style that was
   the opposite of the florid 'Asian' style.
3 Demetrius of Phaleron (c 350–c 280 BC) was an accomplished Athenian orator
   and lawgiver. His works are not extant, but Cicero judged his style to have been
   somewhat lacking in force though nonetheless charming (*Brutus* 10.37–8).
4 Because of his weak voice, the Athenian rhetorician Isocrates (436–338 BC) did
   not speak in public, but he wrote eloquent speeches for those who had to defend themselves in court, as well as pamphlets that contributed to the discussion of public affairs. He was an enormously influential teacher of rhetoric who
   had an enduring influence on the history of rhetoric and education.
5 Demosthenes (384–322 BC), the Athenian statesman, was the greatest of the
   Athenian orators, lucid in exposition, flexible in style, and forceful in delivery.
   'Smelled of the lamp' (*Adagia* I vii 71: *Olet lucernam*) means that his orations
   were all carefully written and thought out before he gave them.
6 Athanasius (c 296–373), opponent of Arianism and defender of the doctrine of
   the Trinity proclaimed at the Council of Nicaea in 325

Nazianzus, the Pylades of Basil and his companion in studies;[7] John Chrysostom, himself also close friend of a Basil;[8] and the brother of Basil, Gregory, bishop of Nyssa.[9] Each of these was eminent for his talents: Athanasius was most gifted 50 in teaching; Nazianzus seems to have embraced a florid and clever style of oratory; Chrysostom, while living up to his name,[10] is at times over-exuberant and seems to be immoderate in his digressions; Gregory of Nyssa was content with a pious simplicity. But Philostorgius preferred Basil to Athanasius to such an extent that he wrote that this great man, eminent in other respects, looked 55 like a child when compared to Basil.[11] Gregory of Nazianzus seemed to be on a par with Basil except that some defects were intermingled at times with his many ornaments. A striving after subtleties and exotic wisdom, as well as a stylistic configuration that was not unlike the style of Isocrates, are reminiscent of the rhetorical school.[12] If one wishes to be convinced of this, he will see 60 in the *Monodia*,[13] which Nazianzus himself does not deny was elaborated with great care, an abundance of fables taken from the poets; he will also see that the comparison he makes of Basil with the famous heroes of the Old Testament is a little lame.

* * * * *

7 Contemporary of Basil, Gregory of Nazianzus (329–89) was, together with Basil and Gregory of Nyssa (n9 below) one of the Cappadocian Fathers, who together were the chief influence leading to the final defeat of Arianism and the triumph of the Nicene doctrine of the Trinity at the Council of Constantinople in 381. Pylades was the inseparable friend of Orestes, his name synonymous with loyal friendship.

8 The Latin, *et ipsum Basilio familiarem*, can be read as 'himself also a close friend of Basil,' but, as explained in Ep 2493 n13, that was not literally the case. Alternatively, the phrase can be read as 'himself also close friend of a Basil.' John Chrysostom had, in fact, a friend from boyhood named Basil, who is his interlocutor in *De sacerdotio*, an allusion that probably would not have been lost on Sadoleto. So we have adopted the second reading.

9 The younger brother of St Basil, Gregory, bishop of Nyssa (c 330–c 395) was a theologian of great learning and originality and an ardent defender of Nicene orthodoxy concerning the Trinity.

10 Chrysostom means 'golden-mouthed.'

11 Philostorgius (c 368–c 439) was an Arian church historian at Constantinople whose *History of the Church* survives only in an epitome by Photius, patriarch of Constantinople, in the ninth century. The opinion expressed here appears in book 8, chapter 11 (PG 65 563).

12 Ie of the style of rhetoric taught by Isocrates at his school in Athens; see n4 above.

13 Ie the *Panegyric on St Basil* (Oration 43), the funeral oration delivered a few years after Basil's death in 379

But in Basil I do not know what even the most exacting reader could 65
find lacking. There flows from a most holy heart, purified of all human desires, a simple and natural language. All that art can accomplish is in evidence, but nowhere is there any sign of pretence; you would perceive there a
consummate acquaintance with profane philosophy, but no ostentation. You
would sense that he is thoroughly experienced in all the liberal disciplines 70
and all the mathematical sciences, but they are employed only in the service
of piety. He incorporates the testimonies of the divine Scriptures so harmoni-
ously into the body of the discourse that you would say that the gems were
not sewn into the purple but born there.

Nor does he excel in only one genre. So great was the versatility of his 75
genius that wherever he directed his energies he achieved the greatest success. In commenting on the mysteries of the sacred books he was remarkably didactic, conscientious, circumspect, lucid, and not at all assertive. He
is thought to have been most gifted in the panegyric genre, in which he so
adapts his language to the minds and ears of the multitude that he is both 80
clear to the unlearned and a source of wonder to the learned. In his controversy with Eunomius, although he displays wonderful subtlety, he never de-
parts from clarity of language, and limiting himself to the defence of Catholic
dogma, he never resorts to verbal abuse that has nothing to do with the question.[14] He remains true to himself in his work dedicated to Amphilochius on 85
the Holy Spirit;[15] but whatever argument he treats, a consistent soundness
and charm of diction never failed him, and this quality was not borrowed,
but native. There is present everywhere in his writings, matching his name,
a certain royal majesty joined with an admirable humanity.[16] He inveighs

* * * * *

14 Eunomius, Arian bishop of Cyzicus (d 394), whose theology was Anomoean, ie
   it held that the Son was 'unlike' (*anomoios* in Greek) the Father in essence. His
   ideas are known to us chiefly through Basil's refutation of them in his *Against
   Eunomius*. In lines 213–15 below Erasmus observes that he had been unable to
   obtain a Greek text of the work and so could not include it in this edition. It was
   first printed by S. de Sabio at Venice in 1535. Here Erasmus is presumably referring to the translation of the third book of the work by George of Trebizond (see
   n22 below).
15 Amphilochius (c 340–c 394), cousin of Gregory Nazianzus and from 373 bishop
   of Iconium, was a strong proponent of the divinity of the Holy Spirit. Basil, in
   his treatise *On the Holy Spirit*, supports Amphilochius' defence of the divinity
   of the Holy Spirit against the Macedonian heresy (named after Macedonius
   [d 362], bishop of Constantinople).
16 The name Basil is derived from the Greek *basileus* 'king.'

against men's morals in such a way that you can love him even when he   90
is reprimanding.

As was his speech, so was his life. Through his adroitness of spirit he
turned the bishop Eusebius, who through his ambition was prone to discord, from a rival into a good friend.[17] He so cleverly disregarded Modestus,
the emperor's prefect, that by the radiance of his virtue he won the admira-   95
tion of the impious man.[18] Thanks to this cleverness he defeated and cast
down Eusebius, prefect of Pontus, and then came to his aid when he was cast
down.[19] Thanks to this cleverness he reduced the emperor Valens himself to
a state of stupefaction when he entered the church, and later in a sagacious
conversation he deterred him from the cruelty he had in mind; and he would   100
have even recalled him from Arianism if what his persuasive frankness of
speech had constructed had not been destroyed by the intransigent perversity of others.[20] His mind was so prepared to suffer martyrdom that he desired it as a reward. Nowhere in his writings do human emotions stand in the
way, nowhere does he defend his own interests. Finally, there is something in   105
them for which I cannot find a name. There is present a particular charm that
never satiates the reader but always leaves him thirsting.

And so when I had convinced myself that it would be of great ben-
efit to sacred studies and to Christian piety if not the shadow of Basil but
Basil himself would be available to everyone,[21] I persuaded Hieronymus   110
Froben and his associate Nicolaus Episcopius to publish whatever works of

* * * * *

17 In 362 Eusebius, a recent convert, became bishop of Caesarea in Cappadocia.
    Tensions between him and Basil caused the latter to withdraw from Caesarea
    for a time, but they were reconciled in 365, and Basil was chosen to succeed
    Eusebius in 370.
18 Flavius Domitius Modestus, praetorian prefect of the East (369–77) in the
    reign of Emperor Valens (364–78), who sent him to Caesarea to bully Basil into
    submission to the imperial policy of imposing Arianism as the religion of the
    Empire. See Gregory of Nazianzus *Panegyric on St Basil* 48–51, 55; Theodoret
    Ecclesiastical History 4.16.
19 For Basil and the prefect of Pontus, see Gregory of Nazianzus *Panegyric on
    St Basil* 48–52, 55 (where, however, there is no indication that his name was
    Eusebius).
20 Valens (see n18 above) visited Caesarea in 371, intending to exile Basil, but he
    was so impressed by the splendor of the divine liturgy on the feast of Epiphany
    at which Basil presided, and so impressed by Basil in private conversation, that
    he abstained from all hostile action; see Gregory of Nazianzus *Panegyric on
    St Basil* 51–4; Theodoret *Ecclesiastical History* 4.16.
21 Ie not translations but the original texts

his could be tracked down. In what we possess under the name of Basil in
Latin translation, the greatest part of Basil is absent. George of Trebizond,[22]
a learned man, admitted frankly that he was unequal to the task because he
did not have sufficient skill in the Roman tongue to render the grace and elo-   115
quence of the Greek, nor did he have enough knowledge of theology always
to understand the subtlety of the matters discussed. Rufinus never showed
himself to be either an elegant or a conscientious translator.[23] In order to make
trial of some translations of Raffaele Maffei I thought I would compare the
first passage I happened upon with the Greek.[24] The homily *On Fasting* turned   120
up, which treats a familiar subject and does not present any difficulties. I will
set aside elegance of style for the moment and examine the reliability of the
translation. Immediately, in the first line, he omitted the words ἐν νεομηνίαις,
that is, 'at the beginning of the month.' But to make up for it he added on
his own 'because it is a prescription in Israel,' which is not appropriate, since   125
shortly afterwards follows 'this prescription comes from the prophets.' Then
in another place the Greek reads τὴν προάγουσαν τῶν ἡμερῶν ἑορτήν, that is, 'a
feast day surpassing all other days,' which he translates as 'the celebration
of these days.' But Basil makes allusion to a particular day that preceded this
feast day. And again, the Greek is ὑποσημαίνει τὰ ἀναγνώσματα, that is, 'the   130
readings indicate,' which he translates as 'they seem to indicate,' weakening
what Basil wanted to be important, since he said previously, 'more sono-
rous than any trumpet and more expressive than any musical instrument.' I
will pass over in silence some minutiae, namely, for ἐγνωρίσαμεν, that is, 'we
learned,' he translates 'we know,' and for παρωσαμένου, that is, 'rejecting,' he   135
translates 'criticizing.' And here again the translator added from Isaiah: 'On
the day of fasting you meet debtors and you engage in business and quarrels,' although the Greek text is μὴ εἰς κρίσεις καὶ μάχας νηστεύετε, ἀλλὰ λύε, etc,
that is, 'do not fast in disputes and quarrels.'[25] A little further on, the Greek is
μὴ σκυθρωπάσῃς θεραπευόμενος, that is, 'do not be gloomy when you are being   140
healed'; he translates 'no one who is treated and set free is gloomy.' Again,

* * * * *

22 See Ep 36:3n. His translation of *Magni Basilii contra Eunomium de Spiritu Sancto
    liber tertio* was published at Rome in 1526 (Antonio Blado); cf n14 above.
    Erasmus would be the first to publish a complete translation of Basil's *De
    Spiritu Sancto* (Basel: Froben 1532).
23 Rufinus of Aquileia (c 345–410) translated Basil's *Regula* and eight homilies. For
    Erasmus' negative view of him as a translator, see Ep 2464 n4.
24 Raffaele Maffei of Volterra (1452–1522) published a Latin translation of the
    Opera Basilii at Rome in 1515 (J. Mazzocchi).
25 Isaiah 58:4

εὐθύμησον, that is, 'be of good cheer,' he translates 'rejoice if you are wise.'
A little further on, ἡ γε ἀληθῶς ταύτης τῆς προσηγορίας ἀξία ['the true dignity
of this term'] he left out altogether because, I think, he did not understand
that this referred to the etymology of the word νηστεία ['fast']. And he does   145
the same later with ὁ ἀλειψάμενος ἐχρίσατο, ὁ νιψάμενος ἀπεπλύνατο ['he who
is anointed with oil is christened, he who is washed is cleansed']. Next, the
Greek ἐπὶ τὰ ἔνδον λάμβανε τῶν μελῶν τὴν νομοθεσίαν, that is, 'adapt the divine
law to your inner life,' he translates as 'within, within, anoint your head with
holy oil.' Likewise in the phrase ἵνα μέτοχος γένῃ Χριστου ['so that you   150
may become a partner with Christ'], he missed the allusion to Christ
from the word 'chrism.' Then, καὶ οὕτω πρόσελθε τῇ νηστείᾳ, that is, 'approach fasting in this way,' he translates as 'in this way you will be of service
to the fast.' I will purposely skip over many things, so as not to become tiresome to the reader. πρόσδραμε that is, 'hurry,' he translates as 'give up.' A little 155
further on, the Greek reads πατέρων ἐστὶ κειμήλιον πᾶν τὸ ἀρχαιότητι, διαφέρον
ἐστὶ αἰδέσιμον, that is, 'a treasure was handed down to us by our ancestors;
whatever excels in its antiquity is venerable'; he omitted the first part and
rendered the last part thus: 'there is a saying: Everything becomes nobler
through its antiquity.' Then what follows immediately, δυσωπήθητι τὴν πολίαν   160
τῆς νηστείας, that is, 'revere the antiquity of fasting,' he translates as 'investi-
gate carefully the antiquity of fasting.' Again, a few lines further, concerning
the passage φειδοῖ τῆς σαρκὸς τὴν βρῶσιν ὑποτιθέμενον, that is, 'suggesting food
for the indulgence of the flesh' (for there was previous reference to the ser-
pent), he isolated it and translated thus: 'avoid procuring food for the flesh,'   165
thinking that φειδοῖ was a verb when it is a noun in the dative case, otherwise
it would be φείδου. Why pursue this any further, since from these comments
it is abundantly clear that there is as much difference between the translation
of Basil and Basil speaking in his native tongue as there is between the croak-
ing of a crow and the trills of a nightingale.[26]   170

For my part, I acknowledge that we owe some gratitude to the industry of Raffaele and Francesco Aretino and Anianus and other writers of this
sort,[27] but what do we imagine would happen when grave theologians, making use of authors translated in this way, bring these testimonies in good
faith before the public and make pronouncements on the Catholic faith?   175

* * * * *

26 Erasmus' own translation of the homily De laudibus ieiunii (On Fasting) was
   published in 1532 (Freiburg: Johannes Faber Emmeus).
27 For Aretino see Ep 2226 n19, and for Erasmus' criticisms of him as a translator
   see Epp 2263:53–65, 2291:13–15. For Anianus see Ep 1558 n22.

Consequently, in every formal pronouncement, especially in theology, I think it is necessary that they either prefer to draw on the original sources rather than on deficient versions, or be absolutely certain of the reliability of the translators. And yet among the innumerable people who have undertaken this task how few there are who have not fallen into error in places either   180
through incompetence or negligence? For this reason the Froben firm richly deserves, in my opinion, the applause of all men of learning, for the Frobens were the first among the Germans to print a Greek author who had never previously been published, inaugurating their enterprise with Basil, the most lauded of such authors.   185

If the enterprise succeeds, as I hope it will, I have determined to dedicate one press to this project every year. Afterwards, what was tried in *Plutarch's Lives* by a certain person skilled in both languages[28] will be undertaken for Basil, Chrysostom, Athanasius, Cyril, Gregory of Nazianzus, and similar authors, although some will seem to be translated in such a way that   190
the one who translates anew from the original will give evidence of less toil than the one who corrected the corrupt translations. Are they, therefore, who expend all their resources and the greatest care and vigilance for the benefit of studies and religion not worthy of the public favour of all good men? But here too Homeric Ate[29] seems not to slumber, she who through Eris[30] strives   195
to foment evil and discord among Italians, French, and Germans. But how much wiser it would be if we helped each other by mutual services, so that he who is behind would not envy but applaud the one who is in front of him, and he who is in front would lend a hand to the one who attempts to follow.

There would be no need of this admonition if everyone had the gener-   200
osity of spirit and sincerity that you have. I have no doubt that you will favour this honourable project eagerly or, to put it more aptly, with your whole heart. And it was for this reason particularly that it seemed best to me that Basil the Great should appear under the auspices of your name, since you discuss the arcane volumes with such eloquence that one could justly call   205
you the Latin Basil. May your good will be indulgent towards me if I cannot conceal what I think.

* * * * *

28 *Vitae Graecorum Romanorumque illustrium, autore Plutarcho* (Basel: Johann Bebel 1531), edited by Simon Grynaeus (Ep 2487 n9).
29 Ate, described by Homer (*Iliad* 19) as the eldest daughter of Zeus, was a goddess who caused mental aberration leading to disaster.
30 Eris, said by some to be the mother of Ate, was the Greek goddess of chaos, strife, and discord.

But as I write this, the intense sorrow that I experienced at the complete loss of your library wells up in me again.[31] It could have been of great advantage to this project, which cannot be carried out without an ample supply of   210
Greek books. If by chance your library does not have a Greek Basil, we will at least increase its resources with the accession of this volume. But would that it had been possible to give you all of Basil. Despite our search, we were unable to obtain the books he wrote with such divine inspiration against Eunomius. I pray that the Lord will preserve your revered Highness safe and   215
sound for the good of studies and Christianity.

Given at Freiburg, 22 February 1532

2612 / To Bonifacius Amerbach   [Freiburg], 26 February [1532]

This letter (= AK Ep 1606) was first published in the *Epistolae familiares*. The autograph is in the Öffentliche Bibliothek of the University of Basel (MS AN III 15 17). Allen supplied the year-date by comparison with Epp 2605:5–7 and 2620:1–2, where Erasmus expresses the same fear concerning the emperor's intentions found in lines 7–8 of this letter. Ep 2620:30–2 also mentions, as does this one (lines 5–6), the reply to the Paris theologians.

Cordial greetings. Jacopo Sadoleto complains in his letter to me that letters coming from you and me are rare.[1] He said he had read everything that Pio wrote against me.[2] I pray you that if you have the opportunity, you see to it that my letter be brought to him,[3] and that you send at the same time, if you can, the books in one of which I responded to Pio and in the other to the   5
faculty of theology.[4] I will look for an opportunity to send these same books

* * * * *

31 Lost at sea on Sadoleto's journey to France in 1527, his library included precious Greek manuscripts; see Ep 2059 n8.

2612
1 Sadoleto's letter is not extant.
2 See Ep 2486 n10.
3 Probably Ep 2611, the dedicatory letter for the Froben Greek Basel, which Bonifacius probably dispatched to Sadoleto on 7 March 1532; see AK Ep 1610:49 with n9.
4 For the response to Pio see n2 above; for that to the Paris faculty see Ep 2552 n10. For the actual dispatch of the books by Bonifacius at the beginning of March, see AK Ep 1610:35–41.

to him, if by chance they can reach him. He asks this in his letter. I fear the emperor may provoke some new tragedy for us. Farewell.

26 February

To the most honourable Master Bonifacius Amerbach. In Basel   10

2613 / To Nicolaus Olahus   Freiburg, 27 February [1532]

This letter, Erasmus' reply to Ep 2607, was first published in Ipolyi, page 200. The manuscript is page 232 of the Olahus codex in the Hungarian National Archives in Budapest (Ep 2339 introduction). Olahus' reply to this letter and to Ep 2646 is Ep 2693.

ERASMUS OF ROTTERDAM TO NICOLAUS OLAHUS,
SECRETARY OF THE MOST SERENE QUEEN

In your letter, dear Olahus, I cherished your exceptionally candid spirit. I am most pleased that you came to the aid of Lieven. I hope that with the help of your advice he will show himself worthy of such a famous court and of the   5
service to a most sagacious queen.[1]

My native country cannot complain of me; whether I am an ornament to it I do not know; at any rate it has not brought much in the way of ornament or emolument to me. Persuaded by Le Sauvage, I disregarded a fortune in England.[2] When I had alerted him beforehand not to expect any services   10
from me and he had accepted what I said, he later complained about me that I did not frequent his company or have dinner or supper with him. On the contrary, I often waited for him to the last moment and then would return home hungry or late at night in the middle of winter, which at that time was not safe because of the Spaniards. As for the imperial pension, I received it   15
for only a year and a half. In my absence I was not paid a cent, although the emperor had twice written from Spain to his aunt Lady Margaret to look out for my welfare with exceptional care.[3] As for the pension from the prebend at Courtrai, Pierre Barbier, dean of Tournai, the theologian who was such a

* * * * *

2613
1 See Ep 2607:1–2 with n1.
2 It was evidently Jean (1) Le Sauvage (Ep 301:38n), chancellor of Burgundy, who in 1515, when Erasmus was hoping to return to England for the rest of his life, secured his appointment as a councillor to the future Charles v; see Ep 1437:378–82. On Erasmus' high hopes for fortune in England at that time, see Ep 296:115–50.
3 For the history of Erasmus' difficulties with the collection of the pension due him as imperial councillor, see Ep 1380 introduction.

friend that I would not have hesitated to entrust ten lives to him if I had ten, 20
intercepted it with incredible impudence.[4] How I was treated by certain people in Louvain I will not mention.[5] Either I had to leave or I had to exercise
the office of hangman, which they were planning to thrust on my shoulders.[6]

Nevertheless, I am not complaining about the court, to whose favour
I owe it that my books were not burned there. Nor do I have there any truly 25
sincere friend except one, Conradus Goclenius,[7] while in England I found
friends who showed me tactful and unfailing good will. The monks rule
there, especially in Brabant,[8] and nothing is more stupid, nothing more implacable than this race of men. They imagine me as their enemy because I
have reminded them of what true piety consists. They would prefer that the 30
people know nothing at all. 'But my presence will impose silence on them,'
you will say. On the contrary, it will stir up a clamour. They are armed with
horrible edicts. I saw the edict printed in Antwerp.[9] Aleandro, the archbishop
of Brindisi, at one time stopped at nothing to bring about my downfall, and
I do not doubt that he is plotting to do the same thing now, no matter how 35
he tries to hide it.[10]

* * * * *

4 For the complicated business of the income from the canonry at Courtrai that
   Jean Le Sauvage had procured for Erasmus in 1516, and for the difficulties of
   collection that had caused Erasmus to doubt the honesty of his friend Pierre
   Barbier, see Epp 2404 and 2527 n8.
5 Ie the Louvain theologians
6 Ie by demanding that he attack the reformers and approve of their execution
   as heretics
7 Ep 2573
8 On the 'tyranny' and 'villainy' of the monks in Brabant, see Ep 2249:30–2 with
   n8.
9 An ordinance of Charles v for the 'extirpation and expulsion of the Lutheran
   and other reprobate sects' was published several times, in both French and
   Flemish, at Antwerp in 1531 by Michaël Hillen and Willem Vorsteman. The
   Dutch version was dated in the title at 7 October 1531. See *Netherlandish Books:
   Books Published in the Low Countries and Dutch Books Printed Abroad before 1601* ed
   Andrew Pettegree and Malcolm Walsby 2 vols (Leiden 2011) I 335 nos 7565–70
   (French), 7572–8 (Flemish). The ordinance was essentially a reiteration of the
   one of 14 October 1529, concerning which see Ep 2249 n8. Lapsed heretics were
   to be burned at the stake; otherwise men were to be beheaded, women buried alive, and their goods were to be confiscated. Thanks are due to Victoria
   Christman for supplying the information for this note.
10 Aleandro was currently papal legate at the imperial court; see Ep 2565 n2. For
   his past efforts against Erasmus see Ep 1553 n9. For his supposed current efforts, cf lines 43–8 below.

They have cleverly prepared the way for what they are devising. An incredibly stupid book of Alberto Pio appeared,[11] but the renown of his name nonetheless weighs heavily upon me. The censures of the Sorbonne followed, to the great disgrace of the theologians, but among a great many people the 40 name of the faculty is weighted with hatred against me, although the affair is not being conducted by the faculty, but by a crazed dean and Béda, who is simply a raving madman.[12] I made answer to Pio and to the faculty.[13] Another little work followed in Paris under the fictitious name of Julius Caesar Scaliger, teeming with so many manifest lies and wild invectives that even mendac- 45 ity itself could not lie more impudently, and none of the Furies could rage more furiously. The whole style proves, just as if it were the man's face, that Aleandro is the author. Both of them are well known to me.[14]

The singular wisdom as well as the piety of Queen Mary are proclaimed by all, and I am well aware of her sentiments of good will towards me, for 50 which I owe her the greatest thanks.[15] But she has only recently assumed the helm and is in need of many things (although the emperor, as I hear, having harvested the crop, has left her the gleanings). My health, however, is such that it is unsuitable not only for any service but even for social intercourse. I can barely sustain my life while living at home. The emperor himself was 55 not able to impose silence on the Spanish monks.[16] Therefore I doubt that the queen can do so there. But whatever my feelings, I fear that this extremely frail little body cannot support the cold and windy climate of that region.

I will not be able to resell the house without a loss of one hundred and fifty florins.[17] But I can easily disregard that. I shall await the return of the 60 printers from Frankfurt. At Easter perhaps I shall send another of my servants, who will bring me back definite news and will prepare a nest for the one who will come, should I decide to return to my country. In the meantime,

* * * * *

11 See Ep 2486 n10.
12 See Ep 2552 n10. The 'crazed dean' was perhaps the rector Nicolas Boissel, whom Béda had supposedly recruited to preside over the condemnation of Erasmus' *Colloquies* by the university; see Ep 2600 n5 (final sentence).
13 See nn11–12 above.
14 For Scaliger's book and Erasmus' attribution of its authorship to Aleandro, see Epp 2564 n2, 2565 n12.
15 See Ep 2583.
16 For the hostility to Erasmus of the mendicant orders in Spain and the theological conference at Valladolid (27 June–13 August 1527) that was summoned to examine their charges of heresy against him, see Ep1814 introduction.
17 In Ep 2512 Erasmus puts the price of the house at 800 florins, but this might include renovation costs of about 150 florins, since in a letter of 1535 he records the actual price as 624 gold florins; see Ep 2530 n1.

I beseech you to continue to maintain the favour of the queen as you are
wont to do. The Zwinglians are a little more placid now, but I fear that the   65
evil will break out again.[18] Oecolampadius now has a successor, and his wife
a husband.[19] I don't know what the people of Zürich are doing.

There is no reason, dear Olahus, to beg pardon for your audacity; your
very forthright frankness of speech is most pleasing to me, since it bespeaks
a benevolent mind free of pretence. I answered the censures of the Sorbonne,   70
but with great moderation.[20] I await the result. I received your letter and that
of Lieven on 26 February through someone whom the grand master of couriers sent here for that sole purpose, immediately after Speyer.[21]

I wrote this yesterday, that is, on 27 February. Farewell. Freiburg im
Breisgau.   75

2614 / From Johann Albrecht Widmanstetter   Naples, 1 March 1532

This letter was first published as an appendix to a composite volume of works by
the Spanish humanist Alonso Enríquez (Naples: Johann Sulzbach of Haguenau,
3 March 1532). The volume opens with an *Epistola dedicatoria* addressed to
Charles v and dated at Naples on 25 February 1532. This is followed by *De matrimonio Reginae Angliae*, and finally by *Defensiones pro Erasmo Roterodamo, contra
varias theologorum Parrhisiensium annotationes*. Widmanstetter's remarks in the final paragraph of the appended letter (see lines 43–4, 49–50, 55–60 below) assume
that Erasmus has seen and read the three works in the volume, which would
lead one to suspect that a copy of the volume was sent to him. There is, however,
no evidence that Erasmus ever saw the volume or the letter, or that he became
aware of Enríquez' *Defensiones* via any other source. For Enríquez see n4 below.

Johann Albrecht Widmanstetter (1506–57) was born in Nellingen, near
Ulm. After studying philosophy, Greek, and Hebrew at Tübingen (1526–7),
Widmanstetter travelled to Italy via Heidelberg and Basel, where he presumably

*****

18 Following the deaths of Zwingli (11 October 1531) and Oecolompadius (23 November 1531)
19 Oecolampadius' successor in Basel was Osvaldus Myconius (Ep 861). Wibrandis
Rosenblatt, whom Oecolampadius had married in 1528, married the Strasbourg
reformer Wolfgang Capito (Ep 459) on 11 April 1532. After Capito's death in
1542 she married Martin Bucer.
20 See Ep 2552 n10.
21 The Latin is *juxta Spiram*, ie 'near or immediately after Speyer,' which may mean
simply that the letters went from Brussels to Freiburg via Speyer. Lieven's letter
is not extant.

met Erasmus. He continued his studies in Turin, where he also lectured on Greek literature, and at Bologna, where in February 1530 he attended the coronation of Charles V as emperor. From 1530 to 1532 he was in Naples, where he lectured on the *Iliad* and, through contact with Jewish scholars, deepened his knowledge of the Talmud. In 1532, at the invitation of Cardinal Egidio Antonini of Viterbo (cf Ep 2447 n4), he went to Rome, where he studied Arabic and Syriac, acquired a wide circle of friends at the papal court, and served popes Clement VII and Paul III as secretary and diplomat. After leaving Rome in 1539, Widmanstetter became a councillor to Duke Louis of Bavaria, who sent him to the Diet of Regensburg in 1541. There he met a number of evangelical reformers, including Martin Bucer, to whom he showed a Latin translation of the Koran, presumably his own. In 1546, after another visit to Rome (1543–4) he became chancellor to Cardinal Otto von Truchsess, bishop of Augsburg. By 1552 he was in the service of King Ferdinand, who made him chancellor of Lower Austria. In 1556 he became a canon at Regensburg, where he died the following year. He published few works, the most notable being his edition (with the French scholar Guillaume Postel) of the Syriac version of the New Testament (Vienna: Zimmermann 1555). It was followed by his Syriac grammar, *Syriacae linguae prima elementa* (Vienna: Zimmermann 1556). Widmanstetter acquired a remarkable library of printed books and manuscripts that eventually went to the ducal library at Munich. Most of the printed volumes were destroyed in World War II, but the manuscripts, which include texts in Hebrew, Arabic, Syriac, and other languages, as well as Widmanstetter's biblical translations and his commentary on the *Iliad*, survive at the Bayerische Staatsbibliothek in Munich.

IOANNES LUCRETIUS OESIANDER TO MASTER ERASMUS
OF ROTTERDAM, GREETING[1]

That I left off writing to you after my departure from Turin, most learned Erasmus, I will not attempt to excuse,[2] since I think the blame is to be attributed more to the wickedness of the times than to me. There was nothing of   5
all that went on publicly or privately that could have pleased you very much, because of the continued disturbances of the wars in Italy, the doubtful hope

* * * * *

2614
1 Like many German humanists, Widmanstetter adopted a classicized form of his name. 'Oesiander' is a Hellenization of the first two syllables of Widmanstetter: *oisos* 'osier' or 'willow' (*weide* or *wide* in German) plus *aner*, *andros* 'man' (*mann* or *man* in German). To this he added 'Lucretius' during his sojourn in Naples.
2 This is the sole surviving letter in whatever correspondence there was between Erasmus and Widmanstetter.

of an uncertain peace, the new fear of external enemies, which was confirmed by the conversations of many people, and by letters that arrived here from Thrace.[3] For all these reasons it came about that hardly anyone found it agreeable to discuss his studies, and this is still the case at present. But now I rejoice that a splendid occasion has been offered to me to write to you, and it will be a pleasant occasion for you in that you will sense, as will everyone else, that I have properly remembered my duty, as I should have.

I thought I would do something most gratifying to you if I were to write a few words to you concerning Alonso Enríquez, who, because of our similar interests, has shown incredible good will to me.[4] In this way you will become more familiar with this enthusiastic extoller and fervent defender of your merits, and you will understand that he can help you, not only by his intelligence and learning, by reason of which he has demonstrated his superior abilities, but also by his authority and wealth. For he is descended

* * * * *

3 'Thrace' was the ancient name for the area that included what is now European Turkey, southern Bulgaria, and a strip of northeastern Greece. This appears to be a reference to the rumours of a planned Turkish naval assault on Italy; see Ep 2593 n9.
4 Alonso Enríquez (d 1577) was born into a wealthy and highly influential noble family, from which had come several admirals of Castile, including his uncle, Don Fadrique Enríquez (cf n8 below). Alonso studied theology at Alcalá (BA 1523), and by 1526, when he became a 'formed bachelor of theology,' he was the abbot of Valladolid, a title that went with the chancellorship of the University of Valladolid. In this capacity he participated, as a member of the pro-Erasmus faction, in the conference of theologians at Valladolid (1527) that was supposed to pronounce on the orthodoxy of Erasmus (Ep 1791 introduction). In 1531, on a visit to Rome to resolve some difficulties over his benefices, Enríquez undertook to write De matrimonio Reginae Angliae, an attack on Henry VIII's attempt to divorce Catherine of Aragon. But after an encounter with a theologian who vehemently denounced Erasmus as a heretic, he also decided to write a defence of Erasmus' orthodoxy. The publication of the Determinatio of the Paris theologians (Ep 2552 n10) provided a convenient occasion for doing so, and he set to work on what became known as Defensiones pro Erasmo Roterodamo contra varias theologorum Parrhisiensium annotationes. These two works were still unpublished when Enríquez, who had made himself unpopular in Rome, found it prudent to move to Naples, where he and Widmanstetter became friends, and where the two works were published in March 1532 (see introduction above). No correspondence between Erasmus and Enríquez, if indeed there was any, has survived. Nor, as noted in the introduction, is there any evidence that Erasmus received this letter from Widmanstetter, or that he ever heard of Enríquez' Defensiones. See Bataillon I 261–3, 265, 453–6.

from ancient kings, as Horace writes of his Maecenas,[5] and, established by
the origin of his birth at the pinnacle of fortune, he consecrated his surpassing intelligence not only to those things in which the children of noblemen
are usually instructed, but also to the sublime knowledge of divine and hu-   25
man subjects. In this he is so eminent that he seems to have spent his whole
life devoted to learning within the walls of his own house and never to have
departed from the side of the philosopher.[6] Indeed, in all other things that
we do not so much require of princely men as praise in them, if those things
are of outstanding quality, he so trained himself that all of them are found in   30
him to an astonishing degree. What shall I say of his extraordinary generosity and most charming disposition? Through them he has bound everyone to
him in such a way that all who have had some association with him in their
lives affirm with one accord that they have never experienced in the life of
mortals anything more gracious or more profitable than his company. Nature   35
fashioned him so nobly that he would have been able to excel even without
any instruction; to these virtues were added immense learning, admirable
zeal, and practical experience of such magnitude as others could scarcely
hope to achieve.

Now, with how much praise did he recently depart from Rome! when,   40
sensible man that he is, he had seen that because of the unjust hatred many
nurtured towards him a public massacre and catastrophe threatened the city
if he had remained there any longer, as you were able to discern from his letter to the emperor.[7] There is hardly anyone who does not know with what solicitude, diligence, and equity he governs and protects those under his care,   45
an exceptional proof of which is that, even in these troubled times, he decided to sail to Sicily to rouse and strengthen that part of the kingdom which
belongs to his family[8] against the terrors of the wars that are reported from

* * * * *

5 Horace *Odes* 1.1.1. Cf Ep 2606 n6.
6 Presumably Aristotle, though the word is not capitalized
7 Ie the *Epistola dedicatoria* to Charles v (see introduction), in which Enríquez was
   actually not very explicit about the circumstances that made his stay in Rome
   untenable; all that is known is that he was ordered by an imperialist cardinal,
   in the name of the emperor, to leave; see Bataillon i 453.
8 From 1481 to 1530, Enríquez' uncle, Fadrique de Enríquez (c 1465–1538), admi-
   ral of Castile, was, by virtue of his marriage to Ana de Cabrera (c 1459–1526),
   count of Modica (on the southern tip of Sicily). In 1530, Fadrique ceded rule
   over Modica to his nephew Ludovico Enríquez, who had married Ana (ii) de
   Cabrera, the niece of Ana de Cabrera. It appears then that Alonso Enríquez's
   visit to Sicily was one undertaken for family reasons. See Paolo Monello *Federico
   Enriquez e Anna Cabrera Conti di Modica* (Chiaramonte Gulfi 1994) 45–9, 137.

Byzantium.⁹ I pass over in silence the pious zeal he displayed in the highest degree in defending the cause of the queen of England. Lastly, omitting   50
many other things which, if the epistolary genre did not prohibit it, could
have been brought forward in his praise, I would like you to be persuaded,
dear Erasmus, that he is as concerned for your well-being as he is for his
own, since he understands that the everlasting glory of your name is tied to
the interests of the church and makes no secret of it. For that reason he has   55
not suffered this glory to be harmed by the spoken word or by the writings
of your detractors. On the contrary, by his learning and authority he has at
length succeeded in bringing it about that you have an unimpaired reputation among innumerable people. Farewell.

Naples, 1 March 1532   60

2615 / To Martin Bucer   [Freiburg], 2 March [1532]

> The letter (= MBB Ep 564) was first published by Allen. The manuscript is an au-
> tograph rough draft in the Royal Library at Copenhagen (MS G K S 95 Fol, folios
> 170–7). There is no heading, but according to Allen, 'Bucero' is found written on
> the verso of the final folio. The year-date is also missing (cf n121 below) but the
> contents of the letter leave no doubt that it is 1532. There is nothing to indicate
> that the letter was ever sent. In the opening paragraph (line 7) Erasmus asks
> Bucer to treat the letter as confidential, and if Bucer received it, he did as asked,
> for there is no reference to it or echo of it in any of his letters or other works.
>
> The occasion for correspondence between Erasmus and Bucer at this time
> was, it seems, the publication of Sebastian Franck's *Chronica, Zeytbuch vnd
> Geschychtbybell* (Strasbourg: Balthasar Beck, August 1531), a work in which
> Erasmus is quoted approvingly in support of opposition to the execution of
> heretics, and is himself hailed as one of the great and unjustly persecuted her-
> etics of Christendom (cf n20 below). Even worse, Erasmus is quoted by name
> in support of Franck's harsh criticisms of the imperial house of Hapsburg, the
> good will and support of which Erasmus could not afford to lose. See Peter
> G. Bietenholz *Encounters with a Radical Erasmus* (Toronto 2009) 21–2, 30, 69–70.
> Alerted to the publication of the work by Bernhard von Cles, chancellor to King
> Ferdinand, Erasmus described it as 'a book in German against his imperial
> Majesty, in which they often cite the authority of Erasmus,' and he immedi-
> ately blamed its publication on Wolfgang Capito and Bucer (see Ep 2587:24–8).

* * * * *

9 Possibly another reference to the fears of a Turkish invasion by sea; see n3
above.

Abcontrafactur des Ehrwürdigen vnd hochgelehrten Herzen / Martin Butzer / Diener des Euangelions Jhesu Christi zů Straßburg.

Ich/ weyß nichts dann Christum den gecreutzigten/ 1.Cor.2.

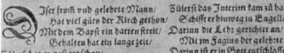

Dieser fromm vnd gelehrte Mann/
Hat viel gůts der Kirch gethon/
Mit dem Bapst ein harten streit/
Gehalten hat ein lange zeit/
Zületst hat er gefliger schon/
Helffen stellen die Confession.

Zületst das Interim kam zů handt/
Schiffet er hinweg in Engellandt/
Darinn die Lehr gerichtet an/
Mit im Fagius der gelehrte Mann/
Darinn ist er in Gott entschlaffen/
Der ist sein Burg/ Wehr vnd Waffen.

Getruckt zů Straßburg/
Anno 1586.

Martin Bucer

In a letter to Capito, now lost, he repeated the charge, assigning primary responsibility to Bucer (see lines 350–3). At about the same time, he addressed a
complaint to the Strasbourg magistrates (see lines 384–6 with n93). Bucer then
wrote the letter, also lost, to which this is Erasmus' response. In it Bucer not
only denied responsibility for the publication of Franck's *Chronica* but also reviewed the whole history of Erasmus' relations with the Evangelical reformers,
who, conscious of how much they owed to Erasmus, were convinced that he
should be on their side (cf Ep 2219 n5). In reply, Erasmus withdraws what he
had said about the publication of Franck's book (lines 355–7, 530–3), but only in
the context of an unconciliatory, paragraph-by-paragraph (see line 41) response
to Bucer's letter that emphasizes the doctrinal differences between himself and
the Evangelical reformers.

Cordial greetings. Since the official courier of the city council brought three
letters, I did not have time to answer yours,[1] and even if I did have the time, it
dealt with a subject of such a kind that I strongly doubted that it was expedient to answer. In complaints and altercations of this kind, I am oppressed by
hatred among those who favour your teachings, while at the same time I do   5
not see what advantage accrues to your cause. But since you want me to believe that you are a good man and give a guarantee of silence, I will disclose
freely and without pretence what I think; I am quite astonished that it is not
clear to you already.

Nowhere do I treat your cause with hostility, but I so temper my pen   10
that I prefer that your cause be refashioned to a moderation that is salutary
for the church rather than utterly suppressed. In any case, the material for
railing against your teachings is more abundant than I would wish. When
you say 'we ourselves' you return again to your pronouns, as if there were
agreement among you, although you are divided by fierce hatreds.[2]   15

So it is, dear Bucer, that one's own point of view is beautiful.[3] In responding to your apologia, I see that in your view I am not equal to you

* * * * *

2615
1 Not extant. One of the others would presumably have been a letter from the
 Strasbourg magistrates. The third may have been from Jakob Sturm (cf n93
 below).
2 Erasmus reminds Bucer that while the Strasbourgers may be of one mind, there
 are serious differences and much bad blood between them and the Lutherans
 of Wittenberg and elsewhere; cf *Epistolola ad fratres Inferioris Germaniae* CWE
 78 380.
3 *Adagia* I ii 15

in courtesy or sincerity,[4] and here you even appeal to my conscience, if it please the gods. But in my opinion, and in that of many others who are by no means stupid, I surpass your sincerity by many miles.[5] I would never have   20
answered you a single word if I had not read such splendid lies there.[6] If you had meticulously defended your cause, whatever it is, you would not have offended me in the least. It may be that here and there something appears correct to me that is not correct. In any case I did not answer you with false pretences, but in every detail I envisaged the hope of redirecting these truly   25
dangerous tumults to some good outcome.

If you wrote the apologia so that I could think better of you and your cause, it turned out exactly the reverse. You accuse me of suspecting you, when everyone knows what you are doing and what you are writing. You must remove suspicions from them, not from me.   30

But you say the *Epistolae floridae* breathe a Vatinian hatred against you.[7] I admit there are things in them that I would rather not have divulged. Herwagen insisted endlessly on having something of mine to inaugurate his Mercury,[8] and through gifts thrust at me rather than given he made it impossible for me to refuse. Since I had nothing at hand I went through fascicles of   35
letters. Out of these I saw that some could be printed; I rejected most of them, and some I corrected, removing things that might cause annoyance. But when I saw them in print there were many things that made me wonder that they had not been omitted; they had either escaped my notice or, because of the carelessness of the secretaries, some were copied out in place of others.[9]   40
But I will come back to that later, for I am following the order of your letter.

You say that you are convinced that what you profess is the doctrine of Christ. If I had also been convinced, none among you would profess it more openly than I. But if that is apparent to all of you, how is it that you are in

* * * * *

4 Bucer's apologia was the *Epistola apologetica*, and Erasmus' reply to it was the *Epistola ad fratres Inferioris Germaniae* (Ep 2312 nn2–3).
5 Literally 'by many parasangs,' parasang being the Persian name for thirty stades (c 5.4 km); see *Adagia* II iii 82.
6 Cf *Epistola ad fratres Inferioris Germaniae* CWE 78 272–3. Cf n26 below.
7 Publius Vatinius was a corrupt and scheming politician so detested by the Roman people that his name became proverbial for someone cordially hated; see *Adagia* II ii 94 and Catullus 14.3. Oecolampadius in particular had taken offence at some of the letters in the *Epistolae floridae*; see Ep 2554 n5.
8 The new printer's device adopted by Johann Herwagen when he went into business on his own, separate from the Froben press; see Ep 2518 n6.
9 Erasmus had in fact had plenty of time to make editorial changes to the letters that he chose for inclusion in the volume; see Epp 2518:38–45, 2524:1–5.

such disagreement with one another? Besides, the doctrine of Christ knows   45
no artifice, nor does it contain oblique barbs, but it is simple, and it is not
forgetful of its mildness when it fights against declared enemies. Concerning
your conscience, on which you swear, the knower of hearts will judge.[10] Yet
those who know you well, even if they profess the same dogmas, do not
make proud profession of the sincerity to which you testify.[11] The heart of a   50
man can be discovered in nothing better than in his style.[12] It is in this mirror
that I seem somehow to have seen you.

I would not wish to claim that you intend to incite princes against me;[13]
but in your apologia at any rate, there were many words that tended in that
direction. While I had written that people of little consequence gravitated to   55
your sects, referring to vagabonds and disreputable people, your apologia
enumerates a profusion of princes of Germany and of famous cities.[14]

The argument that princes are so devoted to me that even a Cicero
could not draw them away from me is harsh, not to say impudent.[15] Only an
evil tongue in a faint whisper is capable of this, particularly in the presence of   60
the emperor, who is young as well as pious; especially since those who wish
me evil are raised up to the highest offices by those very princes. Aleandro is
the archbishop of Brindisi and now the apostolic legate.[16] Edward Lee is archbishop of York and primate of England.[17] Standish, long a bishop, is now in

* * * * *

10 'Knower of hearts' in Greek; see Acts 1:24.
11 Most likely a reference to Wittenberg theologians' criticisms of Bucer; see n56
    below.
12 Cf Donatus *Commentum Terentii: Andria* praefatio 14.4.
13 Erasmus had made precisely that claim in 1529 in response to Gerard Gelden-
    houwer's publication of three pamphlets in which he cited passages from
    Erasmus' works in support of the proposition that princes had no right to in-
    flict capital punishment on heretics; see Ep 2219 n4. This not only associated
    Erasmus with the views of a group that he detested, but also threatened to dis-
    credit him in the eyes of Emperor Charles, King Ferdinand, and other Catholic
    princes, who, at the Diet of Speyer in 1529 and elsewhere, had decreed the
    death penalty for Anabaptists. Erasmus responded angrily and at length in
    the *Epistola contra pseudevangelicos*; see CWE 78 224–8. In the *Epistola apologeti-
    ca* Bucer denied any hostile intent on the part of Geldenhouwer or the other
    Strasbourgers; BOL I 128.8–129.6.
14 See *Epistola ad fratres Inferioris Germaniae* CWE 78 278 n87.
15 Since no such argument is found in Bucer's *Epistola apologetica*, it is presumably
    something said in Bucer's missing letter.
16 See Ep 2565 n2.
17 Edward Lee (Ep 765) had become archbishop of York in 1531.

favour at court.[18] Alberto Pio, after having denigrated me to his fill in Rome, 65
has now infected France with his sycophants.[19] The loyalty of the king of
England is well known to me, but not that of others. I do not know what is
hidden in my letters. Even good words can easily provoke the spirit of princes if a malevolent and dishonest interpreter intervenes. Furthermore, since
nothing is more ignoble than to collect here and there and publish in these 70
vicious times what was said to friends, whether in jest or in earnest, when the
world was at peace, I had no fears of this from you and your followers, who
profess evangelical sincerity; and yet your famous Sebastian is not entirely
exempt from this blemish, whether he did it out of stupidity or malice.[20] Who
ever provoked me to the point that I exposed to an enemy what had been 75
said in private conversation or entrusted to a friend in confidence? But if every time you say 'we, we,' you answer in the name of everyone, I could point
out with my finger those who in secret armed my mortal enemies with information they had learned through close friendship. Moreover, your language
here seems to threaten me covertly, just as at other times your blandishments 80
often conceal some attack or menace.

As to your promise of providing me with a safe refuge there if some
danger from my enemies should threaten me, though I readily believe that
you are speaking sincerely, I wonder if you can provide what you promise,
although I am well aware that your authority carries great weight in that 85
community. It would seem that I have deserved well of the city of Basel,

* * * * *

18 For Henry Standish, bishop of St Asaph, see Ep 608:15n.
19 See Ep 2486 n10.
20 The reference is to the publication at Strasbourg of the *Chronica* of Sebastian
   Franck (cf the introduction to this letter). Born in Donauwörth, Franck (1499–
   c 1543) was one of the great religious individualists of the sixteenth century.
   After disappointing experiences as a Catholic and a Lutheran he became an
   Anabaptist, but by the time of his arrival in Strasbourg in 1529 he had become
   a radical Spiritualist who rejected all religious parties and all attempts to orga-
   nize churches that imposed conformity on individual consciences. He greatly
   admired Erasmus and quoted him extensively in his works, but in so doing,
   particularly in the *Chronica*, embarrassed him by making him sound more radical than he was, as in the attribution to him of denial of the right of princes to
   execute heretics (cf n13 above). It was a letter of complaint from Erasmus to the
   Strasbourg magistrates that led to their banning of the book and to the expulsion
   of Franck from the city; see n93 below. In 1532 Franck set up a printing shop at
   Ulm, where he aroused the wrath of the Lutheran preachers and was eventually
   expelled in 1539. In 1541 he arrived at Basel, where he acquired citizenship and
   again set up a printing business, only to die after little more than a year.

even by the testimony of Oecolampadius in person,[21] while I have not rendered any service to your city; and yet the former seems to protest if I should
wish sometimes to lend support to Froben when the situation requires it.[22]
Besides, if the general tumult that we feared should take place – and we still   90
have not ceased to fear it – would one who is within those walls continue to
be safe? It would be an extraordinary gesture of kindness if you would deign
to receive into your protection one who is not in agreement with what you
teach, or rather not only disagrees with you but opposes you. But if I had
to move there on the condition that I profess your teachings, know that I   95
would sooner face an inevitable doom than profess things about Christianity
of which I have not yet been persuaded. But I do not understand what you
mean when you say it would be an act of extreme perversity if I were not to
believe what you promise. Certainly this thought never came into my mind.

Concerning what I wrote to Cardinal Campeggi, namely, that I would   100
be among the first victims of the partisans of Zwingli if an uprising took
place,[23] I am astonished if you think this pertains to you and your community.

It is no secret what the people of Zürich had in mind had Enyalios been
favourable to them.[24] That Oecolampadius was not unsympathetic to this
plan was revealed by the fact that his deacon perished in the conflict.[25] As for   105
me, I was of the opinion that I had less to fear from Zwingli or Oecolampadius
than from the villains who involve themselves in such evils.

* * * * *

21 Doubtless a reference to Oecolampadius' attempt (April 1529) to persuade
   Erasmus to remain in Basel rather than move to Freiburg; see Epp 2158:53–62,
   2196:90–9.
22 This may be another reference to the resentment of Oecolampadius and others at some of the content of the *Epistolae floridae*; cf lines 31–2 above. Erasmus
   had compiled the collection reluctantly, as a favour to Johann Herwagen, who
   in 1528 had married the widow of Johann Froben and gone into business with
   Johann's son and heir, Hieronymus Froben; see lines 32–40 above. The *Epistolae
   floridae* (September 1531) was the first of Herwagen's ventures as an independent publisher in Basel. It is possible that Erasmus had reason to feel that he was
   doing Hieronymus a favour by lending a hand to Herwagen with the project.
23 See Ep 2411:43–4.
24 *Enyalios* 'warlike' is the epithet of Ares, the Greek god of war. Zürich and its
   allies were determined to defeat the Catholic cantons and compel them to
   permit the free preaching of the gospel, thus opening the door to the complete
   victory of the Reformation in the Confederation as well as its spread into
   adjacent areas of Germany.
25 Hieronymus Bothanus (d 24 October 1531), of Massevaux in Upper Alsace, was
   Oecolampadius' deacon at St Martin in Basel from 1525, and in 1529 became
   minister at St Alban. In the Second Kappel War he was appointed chaplain to
   the Basel troops and, like Zwingli two weeks earlier, died on the battlefield.

Nowhere did I criticize the lies of your apologia, except to show the futility of them.[26] You say: 'I would say that it is the work of a madman if I had written such things.' But I do not write such things, nor would I wish to write them.

But you go further and lay to my charge certain things that can in no manner be explained away. I write to Marius: 'Now a load of prosy trash has come out with the printer's name, but without mentioning the city. I have read none of it except the headings, nor do I intend to read it. He says that at Basel everything happened without any kind of disturbance and in complete calm.'[27] At this point, just as if a god were terrorizing me, you press on: 'If you did not read it, why do you affirm that I said what I said?' I will resolve this difficulty with a word. Certain reliable persons of your party in Basel had written this to me. I had faith in them. You admit there was a tumult, but one that originated with the Catholics.[28] This is not altogether false, if you consider the matter from the day armed warfare began. But you amply conceal the fact that the tumults first arose among the Evangelicals, who in the end compelled others to defend the authority of the city council by force of arms. It had been agreed that there be no unauthorized assemblies.[29] Everyone swore fidelity to this edict.[30] But when such assemblies took place from time to time against the oath, in spite of the vain appeals of the magistracy, only then did those who prefer the old religion take up arms, for which the city council expressed their thanks.[31] I never heard anything about

* * * * *

26 An odd statement indeed; Erasmus' criticism of Bucer's 'lies' is vehement and extended. See, for example, Ep 2324 and *Epistola ad fratres Inferioris Germaniae* CWE 78 317.
27 Ep 2321:29–33
28 BOL I 141:11–17, 164:3–5, 165:15–18
29 Erasmus uses the word *conventiculum* (literally 'a small assembly'), a term that came to be widely used for the unauthorized (and often secret) meetings of Anabaptists and other dissident groups. Here the meaning is unauthorized gatherings of evangelicals to put pressure on the government for reforms.
30 A reference to the 'Mandate of the council concerning the removal of images from five churches,' 15 April 1528 (AGBR III 67–8). Having decreed the orderly removal under government supervision of images from five specified churches, the council declared that images (along with the celebration of mass) were to remain undisturbed in the other churches of the city and that neither party was to engage in disorderly public demonstrations against the other.
31 Cf *Epistola ad fratres Inferioris Germaniae* CWE 78 325–6.

a book of supplication.[32] But what value would a book of supplication have   130
against a public edict confirmed by oath? Furthermore, that they unleashed
their fury only against statues is owed perhaps to those who preferred to
give ground rather than bathe the city in blood.[33]

What followed concerning the statue that was struck by a spear was
recounted to me in a letter written by a learned and far from unreliable man,   135
who wrote it to me after reading your book.[34] I believed him. But if a joke
directed against your story irritates you, your whole story was openly ridiculed by those who had been present at all these troubles and tumults, and
nowhere, if you will allow me to say so, did you seem more foolish than
in your euphemisms.[35] But here you engage me in battle from a position   140
of safety in your tower, whereas it is not safe for me even to tell the truth.
Otherwise you would hear an entirely different story. But you are fighting
with me while I report what was written to me. If they have written me false-
hoods, I cannot be accused of lack of judgment.

To continue, what I added about the schoolmasters and Scopegius I   145
had learned from one of the most vigorous supporters of your enterprise,
who told me for a fact that this work was not by the Evangelicals but by the
schoolmaster Scopegius.[36] And perhaps someone had purposely persuaded
him of this so that he might transfer the suspicion to others.

* * * * *

32 'Booklet of supplication' (libellus supplex) is Bucer's somewhat inflated rendering of the German word Bittschrift 'petition'; see BOL I 164 @ n410, ASD IX-1
384:259). The reference is to the Bittschrift that twelve of the fifteen guilds in
Basel presented to the city council on 23 December 1528, calling for the abolition
from all the city's churches of Catholic preaching and the mass (AGBR III 197–
203). Armed conflict between the two sides was narrowly averted, but peace
did not last for long. The final triumph of the Reformation, accompanied by
violent iconoclasm in the cathedral and other churches, came on 8–9 February
1529; see Ep 2097 n1.
33 Cf Ep 2201:47–9.
34 The letter is not extant, but for Erasmus' account of the incident see Ep 2321:33–
8 and Epistola ad fratres Inferioris Germaniae CWE 78 328–9.
35 As Erasmus notes in Ep 2321 (see preceding note), Bucer in his Epistola apologetica
had attributed the iconoclasm at Basel on 9 February 1529 to someone acciden-
tally touching with his spear a statue that soon afterwards crumbled, whereupon
others attempted the same thing with similar effect. Taking this as a sign of divine favour, the crowd demolished the rest of the statues; see BOL I 165:6–18.
36 Cf Ep 2321:38–40, where Erasmus reports the rumour that two schoolmasters,
one named Scopegius, were involved (with the Strasbourg ministers) in the
writing of the Epistola apologetica. Here he reports having been informed that
Scopegius was the sole author.

As for the name of the place of publication, how could I have supposed 150
that it had been omitted through the carelessness of the printers when that
is usually among the first things to attend to,[37] especially when the book is
published with the permission of the city council?[38] And these days many
books take wing without a name. Therefore, if I had some suspicions, you
should direct your anger at the printer rather than at me. The novelty of the 155
title increased my suspicions. If you had added your name, I would have
answered Bucer, but now if I offend anyone, I offend the one who I thought
was the author of the book, not you.

As for what I wrote to Duke George,[39] I wonder why you should take
it as directed against you personally. It was said in general and pertains to 160
Noviomagus,[40] who proclaimed this dogma in letters based on the laws, unless perhaps you think that there is a great difference between fraud and
trickery and lies.[41]

I have not read your translation of the Psalms, but if you have translated conscientiously what Pomeranus wrote, dogmas that are now regarded 165
by most people as condemned will certainly be included.[42]

To the examples that you cite of Abraham and Paul I make no answer.[43]
Neither of the two lied and both were in danger of death. You are in safety.

* * * * *

37 Erasmus had received a copy of the *Epistola apologetica* from which 'the conclusion,' indicating the place of publication and the names of the printers, was
missing; see Ep 2324:5–6.
38 Erasmus was aware that the Strasbourg magistrates exercised control over the
publication of books in the city, and he had written to them (Ep 2293) to protest the publication of Gerard Geldenhouwer's annotated edition of the *Epistola
contra pseudevangelicos*.
39 Ep 2338
40 Ie Gerard Geldenhouwer; see Ep 2219 nn4–5.
41 The 'dogma' was that it is permissible in law to use fraud and deceit in a good
cause; see Ep 2338:56–65, and cf *Epistola ad fratres Inferioris Germaniae* CWE 78
269–70. For examples of such 'trickery and lies,' see nn43–4 below.
42 See n56 below.
43 Ie their use of ruse and deception. In the case of Abraham, the reference is
clearly to Gen 12:10–20, which Bucer cited to justify publishing books without
the author's name or with a fictitious name; see BOL I 128:2–3. The reference to
Paul is more difficult to identify. Acts 9:23–5 records an incident in which Paul
escaped by night from Jews who plotted to kill him, but Bucer is not known to
have cited this or any other incident in Paul's career as an example of the use of
deception in a good cause.

I would pardon you a ruse of this kind if you were to demonstrate equal
virtues.[44]   170

Concerning the dialogue about people versed in three languages,[45] even
if I should grant what you seem to suspect,[46] there is no ruse there to persuade people to accept the gospel; all the same, what ruse can there be if no
name is attached to it?

Concerning commentaries on the *Folly*,[47] I am surprised that you men-   175
tion them. It was agreed that Listrius should add annotations to the *Folly*.
Since he did nothing but promise, and since time was pressing, I, to show
him the way, began to annotate briefly certain things that were to be treated
more at length by him. Since not even this roused him to action, and the press
was already demanding a copy, I was forced to continue until he finally put   180
his hand to it.[48] Therefore, since the work was partly his, and I felt that the
young man sought some glory for his career, what kind of generosity would
it have been to frustrate his desires and to claim as my own what in part belonged to another? But what does this deception, if such it is, have to do with
the gospel and who would care a fig about it?[49]   185

* * * * *

44 Erasmus probably has in mind Bucer's publication in 1529, under the pen
    name Aretinus Felix, of the book *S. Psalmorum libri quinque ad ebraicam veri-
    tatem versi, et familiari explanatione elucidati*, which he dedicated to the son of
    Francis I of France, and in which he pretended to be a Frenchman writing from
    Lyon. Erasmus found similarly duplicitous Bucer's translations of Johann
    Bugenhagen's Psalm commentary and Luther's *Kirchenpostille* (n56 below); see
    Epistola ad fratres Inferioris Germaniae CWE 78 239–40 with nn122–3.
45 *Dialogus bilinguium ac trilinguium* (Paris: Josse Bade for Konrad Resch 1519),
    a fierce satirical attack on Edward Lee and the Louvain theologians; English
    translation in CWE 7 329–47 (introduction and text), 430–6 (notes). The title-page
    attributes authorship to Konrad Nesen, the brother of Erasmus' friend Wilhelm
    Nesen, who was undoubtedly the principal author (CWE 7 330–1). Many people
    assumed that Erasmus had written the work himself or had caused it to be writ-
    ten. He contented himself with denying that there were any grounds for this
    assumption (CWE 7 332).
46 Probably that Erasmus had written it himself but published it under the name
    of another; see preceding note.
47 For a new Froben edition of the *Praise of Folly* in 1515, Gerardus Listrius (Ep 495)
    took on the task of writing an extensive commentary, one major aim of which
    was to explain to readers the Greek passages and references in it.
48 In every other reference to the commentary, Erasmus attributes exclusive au-
    thorship of it to Listrius; see Epp 337:940–2, 641:5–6, 1341A:697–9. Only here
    does he reveal that he had a hand in writing it.
49 It appears that Bucer had cited Erasmus' concealment of his role in the prepa-
    ration of Listrius' commentary as an example of the sort of 'deception' that
    Erasmus criticized in Bucer and the other Evangelicals.

But concerning the *Julius exclusus* you say that you can show, providing witnesses, where it first came from.[50] The one who first copied it out in his own hand is not necessarily the author,[51] even if you provide the authors of this conjecture as witnesses. At the same time you will brand with a mark of perfidy those whom you wish to regard as most faithful. If I had never had friendly relations with Nesen,[52] I would have escaped many annoyances in which he involved me. Of ferocious letters I have absolutely no memory, unless perhaps you are thinking of the life of Stupid Nicholas.[53] Some people conjectured that this little work came from me. But what has this to do with Bacchus, as they say?[54] I do not harry you because you resort to trickery but because, although you have taken upon yourself an extremely arduous task and have conferred upon yourself an apostolic role,[55] you nevertheless think you must indulge in deception. If I had come forward on this stage where you are now playing a role, I would be extremely careful not to say, do, or write anything unworthy of the sincerity of the gospel. And if I had added my name to your sodality, I would have sharply censured ruses of this kind, all the more so if I had wished a happy outcome for the sake of your good reputation.

I have read neither the accusation brought forward by Luther and Pomeranus, nor your justification.[56] I simply believed what was said by everyone who had read them.

* * * * *

50 The dialogue *Julius Excluded from Heaven* circulated in manuscript for several years before it was finally printed at Louvain in 1518 by an unidentified publisher. The overwhelming majority of contemporaries and modern scholars have attributed the work to Erasmus. Erasmus himself always denied any connection to the publication of the work, while carefully avoiding explicit denial of authorship. Silvana Seidel Menchi has recently demonstrated conclusively that Erasmus both wrote the work and arranged for its earliest circulation in print; see ASD I-8 5–131.
51 On the existence in 1516 of a manuscript of the *Julius exclusus* in Erasmus' hand, see Ep 502:11.
52 See n45 above.
53 For Wilhelm Nesen's *Vita S[ancti] Nicolai sive stultitiae*, a spirited attack on Erasmus' bitter critic Nicolaas Baechem, see Ep 1165:42–4 with n17.
54 Ie 'what does this have to do with the matter at hand?' See *Adagia* II iv 57.
55 See *Epistola ad fratres Inferioris Germaniae* CWE 78 271 with n43.
56 Cf lines 164–6 above and *Epistola contra pseudevangelicos* CWE 78 239 n123. In January 1526 Bucer published a German translation of the Psalm commentary of the Wittenberg theologian Johann Bugenhagen, known as Pomeranus ([Basel: Adam Petri]). In translating, Bucer took great liberties with Bugenhagen's text, creating the impression that the Lutheran party and his own were in agreement on the Eucharist. This was followed in July 1526 by Bucer's Latin translation of the fourth volume of Luther's *Kirchenpostille* (Strasbourg: Johann Herwagen), in

It was your own little book that convinced me of your hypocrisy;[57] it succeeded in making me have a little less excellent opinion of your sincerity than I had previously, for there were many things in it that were not worthy of those who vaunt a faultless piety, your resolution to be of benefit to everyone, to harm no one, to have Christ alone in view and to be prepared to suffer death and punishment for Christ.

And yet there are some in your camp who proclaim clearly that you and Capito manage your affairs in a slothful way. Most people said the same thing about Oecolampadius. But it is the Lord who judges everyone's heart.[58] Zwingli gave sufficient proof that he was ready for martyrdom.[59] How truly evangelical it is to fall armed in battle, especially when it is those who profess the gospel who attack you!

You have tempered[60] your language in the rest of your letter as though I had never shown any kindness or sincerity towards your fellow initiates. But it seems to me that I served you in many ways, as when at the beginning I recalled Luther to more moderate ideas,[61] or when to the best of my ability I restrained princes and theologians from cruelty, or when I warned many people to refrain from an action that seemed destined to end in sedition.[62]

* * * * *

which he again created the illusion of agreement on the Eucharist. Bugenhagen responded with *Oratio Johannis Bugenhagii Pomerani, quod ipsius non sit opinio illa de eucharistia, quae in psalterio, sub nomine eius Germanice translato, legitur* ([Nürnberg: Friedrich Peypus] 1527). Luther responded with a vehement denunciation of Bucer in a letter to Herwagen (13 September 1526) that was published at Haguenau by Johann Setzer in 1527 under the title *Martini Lutheri Sermo elegantissimus, super sacramento corporis & sanguinis Christi, in quo respondetur obiter & eiusdem sacramenti calumniatoribus.* Bucer attempted to justify himself in letters to Bugenhagen and Luther, dated 25 and 29 March 1527 respectively, that were published in *Praefatio M. Buceri in quartum tomum Postillae Lutheranae* ([Strasbourg: Johann Herwagen] 1527).

57 Presumably a reference to Bucer's *Epistola apologetica*
58 Cf Ps 7:9.
59 Zwingli was killed at the battle of Kappel on 11 October 1531.
60 Erasmus' word is *temperatus* 'tempered,' 'restrained,' moderated.' It may well be that Bucer himself had used the word in his letter to describe his language in dealing with Erasmus. At all events, Erasmus' use of the word here is clearly ironic, his point being, both here and elsewhere, that Bucer and his Evangelical colleagues had been immoderate in their criticisms of him and of the Catholic church.
61 See Epp 980:41–58, 1415:54–62.
62 See *Epistola ad fratres Inferioris Germaniae* CWE 78 310, and cf Epp 1352, 1418, 1422, 1526:146–59.

I denied the token of friendship to no one.[63] I helped some people with recommendations, others with money. I would rather not mention or remember   225
what recompense I received from the Evangelicals. If I were to enumerate
them, you would cease to wonder that I find lacking in certain Evangelicals a
spirit worthy of the gospel. I nourish a private hatred against no one, unless
someone wounds me deeply.

I read with great astonishment that I share your opinion regarding the   230
whole of religion.[64] If that is true, then I have been a perfect stranger to myself all my life. What living creature could be more base and abject than I if
I had fought with the pen against those with whom I have been in complete
agreement concerning the whole of religion? You adduce my writings as
proof; but where do my writings lessen the number of sacraments, where do   235
they abhor the mass, where do they do away with purgatory, where do they
deny that the substance of the Lord's body is present in the Eucharist, where
do they teach that it is not permitted to invoke the saints, where do they
teach that man has no free will? I shall omit the rest. I have demonstrated
that I was displeased that many of their opinions were passed on in a rath-   240
er peculiar way, that some of them inveighed insolently against popes and
princes and against those who were of a contrary opinion, and that against
the will of monarchs they altered public rites and ceremonies. These things
displeased me, I admit, but not only these, which you prudently pretend not
to notice. But I said that I did not like the performance of the play to such   245
an extent that even if it were a pious programme it would have been necessary to conduct the affair with different methods, given that a play, good in
itself, is often hissed off the stage because of the incompetence of the actor.[65]
You know that this is said figuratively, not unequivocally. Otherwise who
would be more perverse than I, who more inconsistent, if in published books   250
I would impugn the dogmas to which I adhere? As far as the actual performance is concerned, you admit that some things were proposed to engender
hatred, you admit that monarchs were unjustly attacked in irreverent books.
And yet in such activities that you think are of such importance to the whole
church, it is no small fault to render a good cause unpopular in pleading it.   255
Again I speak figuratively.

* * * * *

63 Cf *Epistola ad fratres Inferioris Germaniae* CWE 78 344–5.
64 This presumably refers to something said in Bucer's missing letter.
65 For Erasmus' summation, in the *Epistola contra pseudevangelicos*, of his reasons
    for disliking the Evangelicals, see CWE 78 229–45.

As for the new rites, you allege necessity as an excuse.[66] But of what profit was it for the advancement of the gospel to knock down statues and smear paintings, no matter how pious they were? I am silent about the rest. I see a pit into which I do not want to go any deeper. Many things could have been corrected gradually, some could have been ignored. If the reign of the pope was an obstacle to the gospel, his tyranny should have been broken first, which was not at all difficult if certain people, in opposition to the proverb, had not preferred the whole to the half.[67] This too you will remember was said figuratively, so as not to believe that something was said against your city, of which I have never complained, nor have I heard others complain. As to the people of Zürich and Basel, many are complaining even today. But there is no time to report their complaints, because they are endless, nor is it prudent, because the matter belongs to the jurisdiction of the magistracy. Let us come to the dogmas.

You say: 'On the subject of the sacraments we have no dogmas other than what you teach. We do not contend that there is nothing in the Supper but bread. The manner of the presence, which is the only thing we deny, you wrote long ago was not to be required of anyone, as you do not acknowledge that it has been defined by the church, even if you are unwilling to join those who oppose it.'[68] Here, dear Bucer, I challenge the sincerity of which you boast so often and even swear to. Why do you not cite the passage in which this is written? In the *Epistolae floridae* I have found one passage where I say something like that, namely, that it is not necessary to require of ordinary people to know how the body of Christ is present in the Eucharist, but I add, whether beneath the actual substance of the bread or beneath the accidents, that is to say, under the species as some call them.[69] The passage you refer to is among the *Floridae* in the letter to Cuthbert Tunstall. Here are my words: 'The old authorities talked about the Eucharist with proper reverence [before the subject became a matter of debate]. Perhaps even now [the church] has not clearly defined how the body is present beneath the accidents or beneath the actual bread.'[70] Here I appeal to your conscience, Bucer: does this passage show that concerning the Eucharist I think the same thing that you teach?

* * * * *

66 Again a reference to Bucer's missing letter
67 Alluding to the proverb 'The half is more than the whole'; *Adagia* I ix 95
68 This can only be a citation from Bucer's missing letter.
69 Ep 2263:71–94
70 Ep 2263:74–7. The words omitted by Erasmus have been enclosed in square brackets.

I have doubts about the definition of the church, but this doubt retains the fundamental belief that the true body of the Lord is present in substance. 290 And I believe this relying on the authority of the Scriptures and the church, and never have I written or thought the contrary. Who does not know that it has been defined by the church that in the consecrated bread there is the true body of the Lord, in the wine the true blood?[71] My answer concerning the pamphlet of Oecolampadius testifies that I never forgot it.[72] And in this 295 respect, of course, you thank me for my outstanding services rendered to the church. Is that one of my outstanding services? If the church did not demand it, one could call it into question. But at the present moment one is not free to do that. On the other hand, suppose I said something of the kind, which was never my intention; if it is not required, why do you demand the other 300 part of the alternative with great hue and cry? If you had left the matter in suspense, the disorders in the world would have been fewer and you would have more followers.[73] There are, in fact, many people who, while approving or tolerating everything else, turn away in horror from your bread and your chalice. But let us grant, although it is entirely false, that there is agreement 305 between us on the subject of the Lord's body; does it follow immediately that you teach nothing except what I teach? And that there are things in me which neither you nor I approve? If you speak of morals, I profess to be nothing else than a man. If it is about dogmas, it is very annoying to me to be justified by you, more annoying to be praised. In the meantime I hear 310 endlessly: 'We, we.' If you speak in the name of everyone, Hutten criticized nothing, Otto nothing, Geldenhouwer nothing,[74] Luther nothing. Otherwise, you say, we would have written a different apologia – as if it were not venomous enough! And if the prayers of some part of Lower Germany have such influence over you that you wrote such a wordy and, in my opinion, 315 cleverly mordant apologia, what kind of men do you think instigated me to sharpen keenly the point of my pen against you? To them things that seem ruthless to you seem watered down and mild. And it is not unusual that I am buffeted by insults because I seem to be colluding rather than fighting

* * * * *

71 Cf Ep 2284, Erasmus' preface to his edition of Alger of Liège's *De veritate corporis et sanguinis Dominici in Eucharistia*, a classic summary of the arguments in favour of the doctrine of the Real Presence against Berengar of Tours, the spiritual ancestor of the sixteenth-century 'sacramentarians,' who denied it.
72 Ep 1636
73 Cf *Epistola contra pseudevangelicos* CWE 78 245–53.
74 See Epp 1341A:1020–1106 (Ulrich von Hutten), 1405 (Otto Brunfels), and n40 above (Gerard Geldenhouwer).

with you. If I were convinced (I have to shout this out more often) that what   320
you do is the work of Christ and that this is all carried on with the sincerity
that you affirm and swear to, I would not wait three days before going over
to your side. What is it that deters me from that purpose? I have lived for a
long time; what is left, exposed to continual maladies, is not life but a slow
death. I am not suitable for high office or any grand function. Pleasures have   325
long ago deserted me, if ever I desired them. To what purpose should I store
away riches, a man who is truly but a bubble?[75] Nothing is left to me but this
little soul, which I wish to remain unharmed. Although it is more than sufficiently laden, I would weigh it down with an intolerable burden if I were to
profess what you profess. Even if I had less aversion for your dogmas, there   330
is something else that would prevent me from giving my name to them: once
enrolled in your militia, I would never be free to abandon my adherence to
you. Obviously the fame by which I am weighed down stands in the way.
And new dogmas continue to appear, to which I would have to subscribe,
willing or not, once I had given my name. How far has Luther progressed from   335
his humble beginnings? How much did you add to his dogmas? And some are
still kept secret that are planned to be made public. You know what passed
between Marius and Oecolampadius in handwritten books,[76] and how much
Oecolampadius differs from Jovinian[77] and the Anabaptists.[78] A book on the

* * * * *

75 *Adagia* ii iii 48
76 On 16 May 1527 the Basel magistrates ordered Johannes Oecolampadius, leader
   of the evangelical clergy, and Augustinus Marius (Ep 2321), outspoken leader
   of their Catholic opponents, to submit within thirty days memoranda explaining, on the basis of Holy Scripture, their view of the mass. Oecolampadius
   and his colleagues appear to have complied by the imposed deadline; the
   memorandum of Marius and his colleagues was submitted on 16 July. On 23
   September the magistrates decreed the establishment of evangelical worship in
   three churches; otherwise, Catholic worship was to remain, but no one was to
   be forced to participate. See Staehelin 352–8.
77 Jovinian (d c 405) was an opponent of Christian asceticism. He taught, among
   other things, that a virgin is no better than a married woman, that fasting is no
   better than partaking of food in the right disposition, and that Mary did not remain perpetually a virgin. As seen by Catholics, moreover, he came perilously
   close to teaching justification by faith alone, without works. On all accounts he
   could be seen as a precursor of the heresies of the reformers.
78 Augustinus Marius (n76 above) viewed Oecolampadius as a *Freitäufer* ('free
   baptist'), ie someone who asserted that the Bible neither commands nor forbids
   the baptism of infants; see Marius' statement to that effect to the Basel magistrates in July 1527 (AGBR ii 580:1, 36). On the meaning of the rarely used word
   Freitäufer, see *The Mennonite Encyclopedia* 4 vols (Hillsboro, Kansas 1956–9)

Trinity is said to have been printed there recently with Capito's full approba- 340
tion. They add that Oecolampadius would have permitted it to be printed
again in Basel, if the author had been willing to make a few corrections.[79] You
will say that I am repeating hearsay. I admit it, but these reports were heard
by your associates and by those whom you think are eminently trustworthy.
You say, 'You could have declared yourself unfavourable to our faction in a 345
different way.' On the contrary, so far I am able to persuade neither you nor
the opposing party of this. But in the meantime you falsely insinuate that I
disapprove of your dogmas[80] for no other reason than to declare myself alien
to your faction. What drives me to this is the fear of hell.

At this point, evidently, you come to the letter written to Capito, but 350
against you.[81] It was your apologia that caused me to conceive this suspicion.
I did not, however, suspect that the book was written by you, but published
thanks to you.[82] I had not yet seen the book, but the Cardinal of Trent had
informed me that it was very seditious and dangerous for me.[83] Yet what
I wrote to Capito could not damage your reputation. He is another you. I 355
asked pardon from the city council for this error and now I ask it of you also.[84] It seems to me that old men are suspicious, not so much because of age
as from the experience of suffering many evils that they had never believed
would come about. Thus it happens that while they think a scorpion is sleeping under every stone,[85] they are sometimes mistaken. The letter from the 360

* * * * *

11 392. Oecolampadius' position was in fact that infants *may* be baptized, and
he harshly criticized the Anabaptists for calling infant baptism blasphemy and
insisting that it must be forbidden; see Staehelin 384–6.
79 The book in question was Michael Servetus' *De trinitatis erroribus libri septem*,
published in July 1531, not at Strasbourg, as Erasmus here assumes, but at
Haguenau by Johann Setzer, though with no indication of place or publisher.
Concerning the rumours that Capito and Oecolampadius, both of whom had
afforded hospitality to Servetus, shared his views, see MBB VII 148 (Ep 529) n10.
For Oecolampadius' harsh criticisms of Servetus' book, see his letter to Bucer of
18 July 1531 (MBB VI 34:7–35:4 (Ep 437).
80 The object of 'your' is missing from the sentence. We are guessing that the reference is to the 'dogmas' of line 333 above.
81 The letter is not extant.
82 Erasmus had jumped to the conclusion that Capito and Bucer were responsible
for the publication of Franck's *Chronica* at Strasbourg; see Ep 2587:24–8.
83 See Ep 2587:28–30.
84 No letter to the city council on this matter has survived, but see n93 below.
85 *Adagia* I iv 34

cardinal, who is not in the habit of rashly writing just anything, had instilled this misgiving in me.

You make light of what that numbskull of yours did, as you do in everything, but he wrote not only at the wrong time but also perversely.[86] What was said jokingly in a moral fable he distorts into something serious; often he skips the passages that mitigate the hostility. Then the theologian mentions which articles in my writings were condemned as heretical, as if whatever is censured immediately qualifies as heresy. Then the fool responds in my place.[87] I have never expressed the least suspicion concerning the city council, but there is a nest of starved numbskulls there who from time to time obtrude this kind of nonsense. Otto's little book, printed three times, contrary to the edict of the city council,[88] was followed by the epistles and the *Comet* of the scholiast Geldenhouwer.[89] Immediately after this came the *Seven-headed Image*,[90] and soon afterwards your querulous apologia. Next was my letter written to Cardinal Campeggi, a letter that was not delivered to him, but through the treachery of that Evangelical was printed in your city, as those testified who recognized the typeface of the printer. It was printed again in the same place with certain ridiculous additions falsely attributed to me. The typeface is unknown to me but there is no doubt that it is the work of the same artisan.[91] Now the ill-omened rubbish of your Franck has appeared, who wrote to me, apparently from prison, but more probably, I think, from a tavern, not to ask pardon for his crime but to demand thanks from me for the honour he had bestowed on me.[92] This kind of effrontery does not come from other cities. And yet: 'What penalty did he deserve if he presented his manuscript to the examiners and if he published it with their

365

370

375

380

385

* * * * *

86 The 'numbskull' was Sebastian Franck.
87 In book three of the *Chronica*, folios cccxc verso–cccxciiii verso
88 The 'little book' was Otto Brunfels' *Pro Ulricho Hutteno defuncto ad Erasmi Roter. Spongiam responsio* (Ep 1405 introduction). For the charge that it was published three times illegally at Strasbourg, see Ep 2293:7–9.
89 Gerard Geldenhouwer is here referred to as 'the scholiast' because of his unauthorized edition of Erasmus' *Epistola contra pseudevangelicos* with his own annotations (*scholia illustrata*); see Ep 2289 n2. For 'the epistles and the *Comet*' see *Epistola contra pseudevangelicos* CWE 78 222–4.
90 Erasmus is not thinking of the famous *Septiceps Lutherus* of Johannes Cochlaeus (Ep 2120 n31) but rather of a lost publication in which Charles v was displayed as a monster with seven heads; see Ep 2375:64–5 with n15.
91 See Ep 2366 introduction.
92 The letter is not extant.

approbation?'[93] I excused the city council to the cardinal even before I had seen the book. I did this also in more detail in another letter. The cardinal answered that nothing had yet been reported to King Ferdinand.[94]

Putting these things aside, there is one thing I should like to learn from you. Since there are so many people who speak so badly of you and have such a terrible opinion of you, who castigate you in published books, who openly plot your ruin, why are you so upset if my writings barely graze you? Towards the Ecks, the Fabris, the Clichtoves, the Pios, and many others you are mute.[95] Against me only do you show your teeth. But you, Bucer, keep playing the same wrong note,[96] because if anything is said in general against the pseudoevangelicals, either you take it as aimed at you, or you think it is directed at everyone without exception;[97] and if someone lets fall a rather free remark, immediately it begets a Vatinian hatred.[98] You wish the emperor to be favourably disposed to you. But what did the one who published the *Seven-headed Image* want?[99] What did that new historian want?[100] When I expressed my fears to certain members of your band that the emperor, if moved

390

395

400

* * * * *

93 This appears to be the citation of a passage from Franck's letter (see preceding note), or perhaps one from Bucer's letter. In mid-December 1531 the Strasbourg magistrates received from Erasmus a formal complaint that books 'against his imperial Majesty,' in which certain of his works were quoted, had been published in Strasbourg without the required approval of the city authorities. The task of investigating and reporting the results to the magistrates and to Erasmus was assigned to Jakob Sturm (Ep 2510 introduction). After examining Franck's book, Sturm concluded that in addition to its seditious content it contained a libellous description of Erasmus as a heretic. Whereupon Franck was imprisoned and questioned concerning his claim that he had sought and received permission to publish the book. The conclusion was that the title of the book had deceived the authorities concerning its content and that much new material had been added in the process of printing. On 30 December the magistrates banned further sale of the book and banished Franck from the city. See L. Dacheux 'Annales de Sébastien Brant (suite et fin)' *Bulletin de la société pour la conservation des monuments historiques d'Alsace*, 2nd series, vol 19 22–260; here page 203, items 4956–7.
94 This series of letters between Erasmus and Cardinal Bernhard von Cles, chancellor to King Ferdinand, is not extant.
95 See Epp 2387 (Johann Eck), 1926 n10 (Johannes Fabri), 2604 n12 (Clichtove), 2486 n10 (Pio).
96 *Adagia* I v 9, citing Horace *Ars poetica* 356
97 See, for example, *Epistola ad fratres Inferioris Germaniae* CWE 78 350 (after n577).
98 See n7 above.
99 See n90 above.
100 Sebastian Franck

to anger, might treat some of the cities harshly, they laughed at my words
with incredible contempt. But we have seen what happened to the people
of Zürich, while the emperor did nothing.[101] Concerning your city, as I have
said, I heard no particular complaints. But in other places your followers   405
regard with hatred those who are of a different opinion. It is to these hated
individuals that they owe it that the princes have not attacked any city. New
complaints about Basel are brought here every day.[102] Often by force of affir-
mations and oaths you attempt to prove your sincerity, but it would be necessary to do this both by actions worthy of the gospel and by books redolent of   410
the apostolic spirit. It is up to you to judge whether Luther himself does it.
And you answer in the name of all: 'We desire the emperor to be benevolent,
not irate.' I will refrain from saying with what moderation certain persons of
your confession behaved at Augsburg, and with what reverence they speak
of him.[103]   415

What prince would desire the form of government that seems to be
arising in certain cities where, for those who cannot renounce the religion
received from their forefathers, the mass is denied, the Eucharist is denied
(and those who are convicted of having received it elsewhere are fined),
where Catholic preaching is forbidden, where Catholic confession is forbid-   420
den, where, finally, the churches are closed and one lives not much better in
his own city than Jews live among Christians; where, even worse, people are
forced by threats to participate in a communion that they abhor (with your
indulgence, I narrate things that I have heard, but they are many and from

* * * * *

101 Charles v was far too preoccupied with matters elsewhere, particularly the
    Turkish threat on the eastern borders of the Holy Roman Empire, to come to
    the aid of the Catholic cantons in the Swiss civil war that ended with the cata-
    strophic defeat of Zürich in October 1531. The same was true of Ferdinand of
    Austria, who in 1529 had concluded a 'Christian alliance' with the Catholic can-
    tons, promising substantial military aid if they were attacked; see Potter 354–5.
102 See lines 416–26 with n104 below.
103 Presumably a reference to the Diet of Augsburg (1530), which ended with a hos-
    tile confrontation between the emperor and the Protestant estates; see Ep 2403
    nn10–11. The word Erasmus uses for 'confession' is *professio*, not *confessio*,
    which seems to indicate that he is not referring specifically to the adherents of
    one of the written confessions (Augsburg, Tetrapolitan) presented at the diet.
    He may indeed be alluding to Landgrave Philip of Hessen, the most aggres-
    sively anti-Hapsburg of the Protestant princes, who thumbed his nose at the
    emperor by secretly leaving the diet months before its unhappy conclusion; see
    Ep 2363 n4.

many mouths, and from very close by);[104] where, on the other hand, those   425
who approve or pretend to approve the new dogmas can do as they wish:
they do not obey the laws, they do not observe conventions, either public or
private (I will cite one example from among many: they affirm that it is stated
expressly in the treaty of alliance that the people of Basel concluded with the
Swiss that if hostilities arose between regions of Switzerland, the people of   430
Basel would maintain their neutrality but would fulfil the role of peacemak-
ers, yet now it is well known with what ferocity they rushed into war to come
to the aid of General Zwingli);[105] where priests are so treated that they go
into exile of their own will;[106] where monks are either expelled or besieged,
as they tell of the Carthusians in Basel;[107] where faith is not kept with signed   435
documents and certificates; where a citizen who has moved away because of
religion or fear is not allowed to be a guest in his own house but is forced to
go to a public inn;[108] where monasteries are turned into barns and churches
are deserted; where the liberal arts and good letters are totally extinct. I see
learned men who are induced to join sects; I see no one in a sect who has   440
learned letters or has any desire to learn them. Professional titles are made

* * * * *

104 Erasmus is thinking primarily of the situation in Basel following the victory
    of the Reformation there in January–February 1529, and in particular of the
    pressure exerted on Bonifacius Amerbach to participate against his will in the
    evangelical celebration of the Eucharist; see Ep 2519 introduction.
105 According to the treaty (9 June 1501) by which Basel joined the Swiss Confed-
    eration, the city was to remain aloof from any conflict between other members
    of the confederation and play the role of mediator; see Hans R. Guggisberg
    *Basel in the Sixteenth Century: Aspects of the City Republic Before, During, and
    After the Reformation* (St Louis 1982) 4. So Basel's alliance with Zürich in the
    Christian Federation and its consequent participation in the war against the
    Catholic cantons was in fact a violation of its constitutional obligations to the
    Confederation. After the catastrophic defeat of Zürich, however, Basel did take
    a lead in the search for the terms of settlement that were included in the Second
    Peace of Kappel. See Gottfried W. Locher *Die Zwinglische Reformation im Rahmen
    der europäischen Kirchengeschichte* (Göttingen and Zürich 1979) 353, Potter 415,
    and cf Ep 2173 n10. Erasmus here makes heavily ironic use of the word *dux*
    (military commander, leader of an army) to describe Zwingli. We have trans-
    lated the term as 'general' (cf Ep 1342 n33).
106 The entire cathedral chapter, for example, abandoned Basel and settled in
    Freiburg; see Ep 2097 n1.
107 On the harrassment of the Carthusians and other religious orders at Basel see
    Roth 50–2.
108 The Basel magistrates issued a decree to this effect in November 1529; see
    Roth 49.

up, but where is the audience? Recently I sent my famulus to Basel.[109] He
listened to a sermon in the cathedral. I asked how many listeners there were.
'Three men and ten women,' he said. And among those there was no sign of
true piety. Almost all those who are members of a sect immediately conceive   445
a fierce hatred against those who are of a different opinion, scant evidence of
an evangelical spirit. I will repeat what I said: I have seen no one who became
better through this gospel, that is, no one who became less inclined to consort
with prostitutes, carouse, or gamble, no one who became more tolerant of
wrong done to him, less given to revenge, less attentive to his own interests.   450
On the contrary, I know many who have become worse than they were. I do
not pass judgment on those I do not know. All we hear is: 'gospel, gospel,
faith, faith.' I wish nothing more than to see that this affair, whatever it may
be, have a happy outcome; but as far as I can foresee by conjecture and from
its beginnings divine the sequel, the affair will end up as the greatest disaster   455
in Christendom, not only in external things but also in the goods of the soul.
What will this life be when literature and the arts are taken away? And since
piety is languishing now, what can we expect but paganism? If in every city
the fate of piety depends on the preacher, and there is no one who can govern
many cities, it is to be feared that we will have as many sects as we have cit-   460
ies. What would be more deplorable than this state of affairs? Hence princes
too are afraid that in the end they will suffer the same fate as bishops and
abbots in some places. And no small part of this hatred is brought about by
these scoundrels or senseless fools who disguise themselves under the cover
of the name of evangelical. Since the preachers do not dare to reprove these   465
people severely, they either encourage them with blandishments or turn a
blind eye to them. Thus it happens that the preachers themselves are not
free, fearing that they may be deserted by the people. But even if this risky
venture succeeds, what else will come of it but schism? unless perhaps you
think that the whole world will come running to adopt your beliefs. I don't   470
see with what audacity you hope for this, seeing that you are so divisive
among yourselves.

The complaint about the curriculum of studies, about the morals of
those who govern the church, is an old one by now, even if it was perhaps
never more just than it is in this century. But things will never be so fortunate   475
in human affairs that there will not be many complaints about many matters.
Yet if the evil was bearable, one should have distinguished with great care
that the good not be removed together with the bad. There are many among

* * * * *

109 Gilbert Cousin (Ep 2381 n1)

you who want nothing to be left, who were ready, if they had succeeded in
their attempt, to change one thing for another. Such a change could not be ef-   480
fected except by either tyranny or a general council, or at least by unanimous
accord among princes and bishops. To wish for a tyrannical remedy does
not become those who profess the gospel. It is a mark of piety to turn to the
profit of religion the calamities that have been inflicted on us from elsewhere.
'It was expedient that the temple at Jerusalem be destroyed,' you write. Yes,   485
but that was done by the Romans, not by Christians.[110] Nonetheless, your
method could have succeeded a little better if it had been conducted by men
against whose fortunes and life the people had no reason to make accusations. You would say that they could be fabricated. True, but made-up stories
soon vanish. So Luther, at the beginning, was said to be of a Jewish father and   490
a Bohemian mother. It was circulated that he was a heavy drinker, a shameless womanizer, a demoniac, and what else? But these stories disappeared of
themselves. However, by changing his garb and taking as his wife an ex-nun,
with whom it is said he had relations many years before that, he diminished
his authority.[111] I am not examining here whether these accusations are true;   495
I am speaking about the judgment of the masses. An inadequacy in family
background should not constitute a source of disgrace for anyone, but the
populace, nevertheless, evaluate men more from their fortune than from the
good or bad qualities of their soul. There are at present a great number in
your fraternity who abandoned the priesthood and the monastery, who took   500
wives in opposition to conventional opinion, who are handicapped by their
family origins, and finally whose life not only in the past but at present is, on
real or plausible grounds, the subject of reproach.[112] I think you have heard
about Wolfgang.[113] Christ abrogated the law of Moses so that he could pre-

* * * * *

110 The destruction of the second temple by the Romans in 70 AD
111 In June 1525, Luther, having long since abandoned his monk's cowl ('changed
his garb'), married Katharine von Bora, one of a group of Cistercian nuns who
had left their cloister and turned up in Wittenberg, and for whom husbands
consequently had to be found. Traditionalists reacted to the news of a renegade
monk marrying a runaway nun with a combination of indignation and hostile
merriment. See, for example, Ep 2247 introduction and n11.
112 This language perfectly describes Bucer himself: a former Dominican who had
married a nun, whose father was a cooper, and whose duplicity in translating
Luther and Bugenhagen (see n56 above) had earned him public reproach.
113 Allen interpreted this as a reference to Wolfgang Capito's impending marriage
(11 April 1532) to the widow of Johannes Oecolampadius (see Ep 2613 n19),
but this seems unlikely. If Erasmus had advance knowledge of the marriage,
he would have known that Bucer had not only 'heard about it' but was actively

serve it in the meantime and not seem to be pleading his own cause.[114] Care   505
should have been taken that those who joined your sect should so order their
lives that everyone could ascertain that they were made better as well as
more in accord with customary practice. It would have been better not to undermine any of the things that were right but rather to leave alone things that
were not too harmful to piety, such as the use of images and the invocation of   510
the saints. In other matters, whatever had the stamp of superstition should
have been corrected gradually and by persuasion rather than by force. Now
things have come to such a pass that there is nothing left to do but to implore
God to turn this ill counsel of men to a good end. As far as I am concerned, I
will not be led by any fear or any hope to profess concerning religion things   515
of which I am not convinced. If I were convinced, I would pass of my own
will into your camp. From those for whom I fight such ingratitude is given
in return that not only shall I not write anything anymore, but, if you will
permit me, I regret having written even a single word. With what virulence
Béda raged against me, and that not only once, and then Cousturier and   520
Pio![115] Then the incredibly stupid censures of the Sorbonne appeared.[116] After
that came a book with a false title bursting from all sides with such frenzied
invectives and the most shameless lies[117] that Orestes could not say anything
more insane or a clown anything more clownish.[118] Since the book is manifestly defamatory, the theologians pretend not to take notice, but the name   525
of the bailiff of Paris is appended, whom they call a criminal lieutenant. He
excuses himself to me, but insincerely.[119] I know the style of the author as

* * * * *

involved in arranging it. It also seems unlikely that Erasmus would suddenly
use 'Wolfgang' for someone to whom he otherwise always (as in this letter)
referred as 'Capito.' That said, the identity of Wolfgang remains a mystery.
There was a pastor in one of Strasbourg's suburban parishes named Wolfgang
Schultheiss; and in Basel Wolfgang Wissenburg was the pastor at St Theodor,
the parish to which Bonifacius Amerbach belonged. But nothing that is known
about either man explains why Erasmus would mention him here.

114 Cf Matt 5:17–20.
115 See Epp 2486 n11 (Béda), 1804 n65 (Cousturier), 2486 n10 (Pio).
116 The *Determinatio* of the Paris theologians (Ep 2552 n10)
117 *Julii Caesaris Scaligeri Oratio pro M. Tullio Cicerone contra Des. Erasmum Roteroda-*
     mum; see Ep 2565 n12. The falseness in the title was, according to Erasmus, the
     naming of Julius Caesar Scaliger as the author; see n120 below.
118 See Ep 2581:1–13.
119 Jean Morin; see Ep 2577.

well as I know his face.[120] Such are the apostles Rome is sending us now. I bear no public hatred for you unless you continue to twist what I say against unprincipled men to include everyone. I have put aside my suspicion of you, certainly as far as the *Chronica* is concerned. All the same, I do not have such a high opinion of your integrity or Capito's that I would entrust this little soul into your protection. I see that you need wise and salutary advice, and I pray that Christ will deign to inspire all of you. I have poured out my whole heart into your bosom. It is up to your goodness of heart to take my frankness in good part. Farewell.

2 March [1532].[121]

2616 / To Caspar Hedio   Freiburg, 3 March 1532

This letter was first published in Salomon Hess *Erasmus von Rotterdam, nach seinem Leben und Schriften* 2 vols (Zürich 1790) II 604–5. The autograph is in the municipal archives at Strasbourg (MS Epist eccl ii no 207). For Caspar Hedio see Ep 1477B introduction. Apart from that letter, only this one and Ep 3020 survive from the correspondence between him and Erasmus.

Greetings. I am grateful, my excellent friend, for your letter,[1] which though it had nothing new to report, was most welcome because it came from a most loyal friend. Just as you, as you write, never depart from your habitual loyalty, so I have never nurtured the slightest bitter feelings towards you.[2] If you are guilty of some fault, it was a fault of loyalty. You have always looked after one who was in danger; often, however, taking thought for the wicked

* * * * *

120 For Erasmus' conviction that Scaliger was a pseudonym for Aleandro, see Ep 2565 n12.
121 Allen includes the year-date as though it were in the manuscript. The MBB editors, on the other hand, found no date, but they state that 1532 is amply confirmed by the contents of the letter.

2616
1 Not extant
2 Relations between Erasmus and Hedio had become strained after the latter adhered to the Reformation, but, as here, communication between them always remained civil, in contrast to that between Erasmus and some other reformers, like Zwingli, Capito, and Bucer. Cf Ep 1477B.

is harmful to the good.[3] I approve your diligence in translating the sacred
authors, [4] although, as I judge from your letters, you seem suited for a higher
calling, whether in translating Greek authors into Latin or, if perhaps you
do not know Greek, in explaining in a commentary the obscurities of the   10
Scriptures. But it may be that in your wisdom you see that the Scriptures are
more obscured than clarified in the multitude of translations. Who has not
written on the Psalms? Recently a Carthusian has published a huge volume
in Cologne.[5] Sadoleto, bishop of Carpentras, is in the process of writing on
the epistles of Paul.[6]   15

I would like to know what the reverend Father Paul Volz is doing,
whether he continues to be his former self after changing camp. For previously I found him to be a man of such morals that you could not wish
anyone more holy and more pure. Please give him my greetings.[7] I pray that
Christ will deign to inspire in princes and cities peaceful and salutary ac-   20
tions. Farewell.

Freiburg, 3 March 1532
Erasmus of Rotterdam in his own hand, in haste
To the most learned Master Caspar Hedio, preacher. In Strasbourg

* * * * *

3 Possibly a reference to the brief residence of Sebastian Franck in Strasbourg
  (1529–31), or to Hedio's failure to support Erasmus' demand (Ep 1477A) for
  the punishment of the publisher Johann Schott for publishing works against
  Erasmus (Ep 1477B)
4 Hedio devoted much effort to translating works of church Fathers and other
  ancient authors, including Eusebius and Josephus, into German.
5 *D. Dionysii a Rickel Carthusiani insigne commentariorum opus in Psalmos omnes
  Davidicos* (Cologne: P. Quentel 1531). Erasmus does not seem to have recognized the name of Denis the Carthusian (Denis van Leeuwen of Rijkel), 1402 /
  3–1471, the most prolific scholastic theologian of the fifteenth century, whose
  works were published at Cologne in the period 1521–38. Cf Ep 1332 n4.
6 For Jacopo Sadoleto see Ep 2611. His *In Pauli epistolam ad Romanos commentariorum libri tres* was published at Lyon in 1535 by Sebastian Gryphius. Erasmus'
  frank criticisms during the years of its preparation caused him some anxiety
  concerning his friendship with Sadoleto; see Allen Ep 2816 introduction.
7 Paul Volz (Ep 368) was the Benedictine abbot to whom Erasmus addressed
  Ep 858, the important introductory letter to the new edition of the *Enchiridion
  militis christiani* in 1518. From 1521 onwards Volz went through a gradual process of conversion to the Reformation. By 1526, the year of his formal conversion, he was in Strasbourg as preacher and chaplain to the nuns in the cloister
  of St Nicolaus in undis. Despite this, the friendship between Erasmus and Volz
  continued without interruption or strain, and Erasmus bequeathed one hundred gold pieces to him.

2617 / To Johann Koler   Freiburg, [March] 1532

This is the preface to *Duae homiliae divi Basilii de laudibus ieiunii* (Freiburg: Johannes Faber Emmeus 1532. Both book and preface lack a month-date, but the preface (Ep 2618) to the *Precatio pro pace ecclesiae*, which follows in the same volume, is dated 5 March 1532. For Johann Koler, see Ep 2505.

DESIDERIUS ERASMUS OF ROTTERDAM TO THE MOST HONOURABLE
GENTLEMAN MASTER JOHANN KOLER, PROVOST OF CHUR, GREETING
So that you will not always receive sterile letters that bear no gifts, I send you two *Homilies on the Merits of Fasting*, which, as we now see and regret, has been removed for the most part from the life of Christians. You will say 5
that these homilies have been translated before; I admit it, presumably by Raphael Volaterranus.[1] But I have taken on this task specifically to show how dangerous it is to trust any translation at all, and how much better it is to draw from the sources themselves. I am certain that you yourself will be astonished if you compare each of our translations with the Greek. To make it 10
easy for everyone to do this, the Greek text of Basil has been made available.[2] The second homily does not seem to be by Basil but by some scholar who wished to emulate the first homily.[3]

I will certainly not put up a fight if someone thinks otherwise. I believe however, that learned men will subscribe to my opinion. I approve of the 15
genre of *declamatio*,[4] but I do not approve of the pretence of those who thrust their bastard and degenerate productions upon the world under the title of great men. We find this kind of imposture in the writings of Athanasius and all the most eloquent authors. At least the divine quality of Basil the Great should have deterred them from this audacity. But they made fewer errors in 20

* * * * *

2617
1 A substantial portion of the preface to the Froben edition of Basil in Greek (Ep 2611:118–70) consists of a catalogue of the mistakes of Raffaele Maffei of Volterra (known as Volaterranus) in his translation of Basil's *De laudibus ieiunii*.
2 See Ep 2611.
3 Modern scholars uphold Basil's authorship.
4 Erasmus here uses the word *exercitatio* to refer to the rhetorical exercise, inherited from Cicero and the schools of rhetoric of the first century AD, known as *declamatio*. The humanists favoured the type of declamation called *suasoria*, a deliberative speech counselling a course of action. Training in this kind of rhetoric formed part of the arts curriculum from the fourteenth through the sixteenth centuries. Examples of the genre are Erasmus' *Declamation in Praise of Matrimony* and Cornelius Agrippa's *Declamation on the Nobility and Pre-eminence of the Female Sex.*

this author. I have added also the *Hiero* of Xenophon, to which I have given some second thoughts.[5] Farewell.

Given at Freiburg im Breisgau, 1532

2618 / To Johann Rinck   Freiburg, 5 March 1532

This is the preface to the *Precatio ad Dominum Iesum pro pace ecclesiae*, first published with the *Duae homiliae divi Basilii de laudibus ieiunii* (Ep 2617 introduction). For Johann Rinck, jurist of Cologne, see Ep 2285 introduction.

DESIDERIUS ERASMUS OF ROTTERDAM TO THE MOST ILLUSTRIOUS
DOCTOR IN CANON AND CIVIL LAW JOHANN RINCK, GREETING
Your letter, most honourable sir, in which, as befits your sagacity, you per-
ceptively foresee the disasters threatening Germany, and at the same time piously try to avert them by prayer,[1] profoundly moved my spirit to compose,   5
to the omnipotent peacemaker and, as Paul calls him, mediator,[2] a prayer by
which all of us together can call upon the Lord, who is certainly angered, as
it seems, but not inexorable. You lovingly and faithfully, but too late, remind
me about not moving Camarina,[3] but it is what the foolish audacity of certain
people deserved, and friends were not lacking who encouraged me by letter   10
in my intent. Farewell, most loyal of friends.

Freiburg, 5 March 1532

2619 / To Ambrosius von Gumppenberg   Freiburg, 5 March 1532

This letter was first published in the *Epistolae palaeonaeoi*. It is the first of the six
surviving letters in the correspondence between Gumppenberg and Erasmus.
The others are Epp 2926, 2929, 3015, 3023, 3047.

Born into a noble family of Bavaria, Ambrosius Freiherr von Gumppenberg
(d 1574) studied at Tübingen and Ingolstadt. By 1519 he was already a canon
at Regensburg and well launched into the career of an influential churchman.
From 1525 he was in Rome, where he acted as agent for numerous German
princes and bishops. At the same time, he entered the service of Cardinal

* * * * *

5 See Ep 2273 introduction.

2618
1 The letter is not extant.
2 1 Tim 2:5
3 Ie not stirring up unnecessary trouble; see *Adagia* IV vi 65.

Ambrosius von Gumppenberg

Cajetanus and served Pope Clement VII as an able diplomat. During the sack
of Rome in 1527 he took refuge with Clement in the Castel Sant' Angelo,
where he used his knowledge of German to mediate between the pope and
the German *Landsknechte*. He accompanied Cardinal Cajetanus to the Diet of
Augsburg in 1530. Back in Rome, he won the favour of Pope Paul III and his
family (the Farnese), and lived the life of a wealthy, influential prelate and
patron of the arts. Although the two never met, Gumppenberg gladly facili-
tated Erasmus' contacts with Cardinal Cajetanus and other important figures
in Rome, and their friendly correspondence lasted until Erasmus' death. In
1545 Gumppenberg returned to Germany in the service of Cardinal Alessandro
Farnese, and in 1546–7 accompanied the papal troops under the command of
Ottavio Farnese that participated in the emperor's war against the League of
Schmalkalden. From this point on Gumppenberg resided in Germany, chiefly
in Eichstätt and Augsburg, though he held canonries in seven other places as
well. He proved himself to be an energetic and capable servant of the Catholic
church and an implacable foe of all religious innovations, but his hopes for
a bishopric were never realized. See Ferdinand Gregorovius 'Gumppenberg,
Ambrosius Freiherr von' *Allgemeine Deutsche Biographie* 10 (Leipzig 1879) 122–3.

ERASMUS OF ROTTERDAM TO AMBROSIUS VON GUMPPENBERG,
PRONOTARY, GREETING

I am truly ashamed, my excellent friend Ambrosius. I suspect that your letter was delivered to me, together with many others, when I was exhausted
by the labours of study and the reading of letters.[1] It sometimes happens   5
that among many letters, one may be overlooked and escape attention, either
because it was not read or because it was glanced at only casually. At the
present moment, as I was sifting through piles of letters with the intention of
answering them, I came upon yours.[2]

I learned from it that you had sent a letter of the reverend Cardinal   10
Cajetanus to me.[3] Be assured that nothing has come to me from him except
books on the Eucharist, confession, and the invocation of the saints, in which
I was immensely pleased by both his learned brevity and the soberness of the

* * * * *

2619
1 The letter is not extant.
2 For Erasmus' complaints of the burden of his correspondence, cf Ep 2451:11–13.
3 The letter is not extant. For Tommaso de Vio, better known as Cardinal
   Cajetanus, see Ep 891:26n. Gumppenberg seems to have been mistaken in believing that he had forwarded a letter from Cajetanus to Erasmus; see Allen Ep
   2690:4–5. But Cajetanus did eventually write a letter, to which Erasmus replied
   with Ep 2690.

discussion, since questions are now debated with such great commotion that
from the greatest confusion comes even greater confusion.[4] I read them with   15
great pleasure and shared them with learned friends, and finally entrusted
them to the printers.[5] If in addition to this the letter of the reverend Cardinal
Cajetanus had arrived, I would truly have exulted. I did not want you to be
unaware of this, and I pray you to pardon this misfortune and to excuse me
to your patron, to whose eminent self I wish to be commended.   20

Farewell

Freiburg im Breisgau, 5 March 1532

2620 / To Erasmus Schets   Freiburg, 7 March 1532

The autograph of this letter, which was first published by Allen, is in the British
Library (MS Add 38512 folio 68). Allen calls it Erasmus' reply to Ep 2593. That
may well be so: there is much in the letter (eg the references to the Courtrai
pension in lines 5–10, to the transfer of funds via Hieronymus Froben in lines
17–20, and to Erasmus' *Declarationes* in lines 31–2) that can be seen as a response
to Ep 2593. At the same time, however, it is noteworthy that there are a number
of passages (eg the references to the possibility of a council in lines 2–3, and to
the bishop of Rochester and Baron Mountjoy in lines 12–13, 22–3) that appear
to be direct responses to matters not mentioned in Ep 2593. One suspects that
Erasmus had in front of him another letter from Schets that has not survived.

Greetings. The emperor is in Germany, but there is a strange silence about
what he is doing.[1] I suspect there will not be a council. The pope doesn't like

* * * * *

4 Erasmus had evidently received copies of two short books by Cajetanus: *De sacrificio missae adversus Luteranos iuxta scripturas tractatus* (Rome: Gerardo Blado
   1531) and *De communione, de confessione, de satisfactione, de invocatione sanctorum
   adversus Luteranos tractatus* (Rome: Antonio Blado 1531).
5 It seems that the books were accompanied by the request that Erasmus arrange for their publication in Germany. But to which printers did he send
   them? There is no record of an edition at either Freiburg or Basel. It was Peter
   Quentel in Cologne, with whom Erasmus is not otherwise known to have had
   any dealings, who published the works in one volume under the title *Adversus
   Lutheranos iuxta scripturam tractatus: De sacrificio missae; De communione; De confessione; De satisfactione; De invocatione sanctorum.* The year-date 1531 appears on
   the title-page, but the colophon gives the date 1532.

2620

1 On 28 February Charles V had arrived in Regensburg to attend the diet that
   would open on 17 April; see Ep 2593 n7.

councils;[2] the situation will be decided by the sword, if I am not mistaken.
May the Lord grant a happy outcome.

About the sum that Pieter Gillis was holding, it may be that my mem- 5
ory fails me, but as far as I can remember, his letter and his receipt estimated
it at 117 florins and some stuivers.[3] It is possible also that in the exchange of
money they decreased by two florins. But I am used to these losses.

I cannot cease to wonder about Pierre Barbier, the theologian; nor do I
understand his letters, which speak so ambiguously.[4]   10

Luis de Castro does not know where he should pursue his investiga-
tions.[5] The bishop of Rochester does not owe me anything nor has he promised anything.[6] The archbishop had promised that he would give the money
within seven days.[7] And perhaps the money is in the hands of his agents,
but they are holding on to it, expecting the death of their master.[8] They are 15
harpies, or something more rapacious than harpies, if such a thing exists.[9]

I have authorized Hieronymus Froben to receive the money that will be
paid in Frankfurt.[10] I know that it is annoying for you, used to larger sums
of money, to deal with small sums. But according to Paul, charity suffers all
things.[11]   20

I will await the return of Froben from the fair. If nothing has been sent
either by the archbishop or by Mountjoy, who in his letters promised a specific sum, I will send another of my servants to England, so that I will finally
be delivered from it.[12]

* * * * *

2 See Ep 2516 n11.
3 The precise sum was 115 Carolus florins, 18 stuivers; see Epp 2511, 2530, 2552,
   2558, 2578 and 2593.
4 See Ep 2613:18–21 with n4.
5 Luis de Castro was Schets' agent in London.
6 John Fisher (Ep 229)
7 Archbishop William Warham, who paid Erasmus' English pension; cf Ep
   2512:2–4.
8 Warham was in poor health and would die on 22 August 1532.
9 Cf Ep 2496:12–14 with n2.
10 During the spring book fair
11 1 Cor 13:7
12 Erasmus had been making efforts to redeem his pension for a fixed sum over
   three years; see Ep 2487:23–5 with n9. William Blount, Baron Mountjoy, was
   not involved with the pension from Warham but independently sent Erasmus
   sums of money that were also collected and transmitted by Luis de Castro; see
   Epp 2530:9–11, 2576:22.

I have been called back to Brabant,[13] but I fear three things: first, that   25
this frail little body will no longer support the cold and windy weather there;
then, that the favour of Queen Mary will not be able to fend off the furies of
the monks; and last, that the court will be my undoing, since I can hardly
sustain my life here hidden in my bedroom.[14]

The theologians whose cause I upheld show such gratitude that I regret   30
having written a single word against the Lutherans. I answered their criticisms, but with great moderation, and not without deliberation.[15] I have no
intention of responding to the more than defamatory and utterly insane book
that was published right after the censures with a false title.[16] Such are the
legates the pope sends us.[17]   35

Farewell, dearest Schets.

Freiburg, 7 March 1532

Your Erasmus of Rotterdam, in his own hand

To the honourable Master Erasmus Schets, merchant. In Antwerp

2621 / To Johann (ii) Paumgartner   [Freiburg], 7 March 1532

First published in the *Epistolae palaeonaeoi*, this is a letter of thanks for a gift of
pure gold (see lines 3–5, 13–14 below). For Johann (ii) Paumgartner see Ep 2603
introduction.

ERASMUS OF ROTTERDAM TO THE MOST ILLUSTRIOUS GENTLEMAN
JOHANN PAUMGARTNER, GREETING

Would that I could extract from the vein of my character a gift worthy of our
friendship, illustrious sir, as easily as you can extract it from the veins of the
earth. When you were still unknown to me, it was Zasius, to whom in vir-   5
tue of his innumerable services to me I am not permitted to refuse anything

* * * * *

13 Most recently by Nicolas Olahus in Ep 2607, but by other friends as well; see
    Ep 2511:34–47 with n17.
14 See Ep 2613, and cf Ep 2582 n9.
15 In the *Declarationes*, his response to the *Determinatio* of the Paris theologians; see
    Ep 2552 n10.
16 Ie *Julii Caesaris Scaligeri Oratio … contra … Erasmum*, which Erasmus insisted
    had been written by Girolamo Aleandro; see Ep 2565 n12.
17 Aleandro (see preceding note) had recently arrived in Brussels as papal legate
    to the imperial court; see Ep 2565 n4.

whatsoever, who by his vigourous exhortations instructed me to write to
you.[1] I have long been beholden to him on this account, and now even more
so because he has augmented the list of my friends by the addition of a most
loyal gentleman. You would find few sincere friends these days. But the sur-   10
est proof of genuine benevolence is the desire to have your own friends in
common with a friend.

So then, although I am exceedingly pleased that you have sent me natural, unwrought gold, symbol of a soul free of all pretence, it nevertheless
seems to me that I have become more rich in gaining you as a friend than in   15
receiving a present, which, however, your modesty does not wish to be so
called, but prefers that it be called an earnest.[2] I have not hitherto rendered
you any service, and I do not at all see what I could do, but if there is anything I can bestow upon you, I shall bestow it on one who well deserves it.[3] I
repeat what I said in my previous letter, if I am not mistaken, that by as many   20
tokens as Zasius is obligated to you, by that same number is Erasmus also
obligated to you.[4] It remains for me to give thanks, both to Zasius, the mediator, and to you, my dear friend, ready to return the favour if either you or
Zasius should indicate some way in which I can oblige you. If it please you,
make trial of whether I say this sincerely or not. I wish you and your dear   25
ones the best of health.

7 March 1532

2622 / From Bernhard von Cles   Regensburg, 7 [March] 1532

For Bernhard von Cles, bishop of Trent and chancellor to King Ferdinand, see
Ep 2504. The letter was first published by Allen. For the manuscript, an autograph rough draft, see Ep 2515 introduction. The month-date was determined
by the place of the letter in a packet containing correspondence from 29 January
to April 1532.

* * * * *

2621
1 In Ep 2602
2 Erasmus uses the word *arr[h]a*, which in contract law means a nominal sum
   ('earnest money') given to confirm a contract, and more generally signifies a
   pledge or token of something to follow.
3 For the ways in which Erasmus kept this pledge, see Ep 2603 introduction.
4 Ep 2603:13–17

TO ERASMUS

By Pollux![1] the author of the *Chronica* has received a fitting recompense for
his exploits,[2] concerning which we were informed by your letter of the eighth
of last month.[3] Since his writings are now known to all and have been deservedly condemned by learned men, we believe they can henceforth be consid-　5
ered of little importance, and that it need not be feared that our princes will
be hostile to you,[4] since from another letter of mine you can be certain that
they think well of you; under their protection you will be free of calumny
and be at peace for the rest of your life, which we hope will be long, and from
the bottom of our heart we wish that it will be so.　10

We gave the booklet that was sent to us to the reverend bishop of Vienna
for him to read,[5] together with a letter from the city council of Strasbourg,
which we send you.[6]

The emperor and the king, who are our masters, have come here to
do something good for the common welfare, certainly something which the　15
present state of affairs requires.[7] There is nothing else worthy of being committed to a letter. In the meantime we wish you good health.

Given at Regensburg, on the seventh day

2623 / To Bernhard von Cles　　　　　　　　　　　　　　[Freiburg, March 1532]

This letter was first published by Allen, on the basis of the autograph rough
draft in the Royal Library at Copenhagen (MS G K S Fol, folio 240). The manuscript has no heading or address, but Cles' reply to it, Ep 2634, makes clear that
he is the person addressed. The approximate date is based on the reference in
lines 9–11 to the *Precatio pro pace ecclesiae*, the preface to which (Ep 2618) is dated
5 March 1532.

* * * * *

2622

1　*Edepol!* (Cles spells it *Aedepol!*), a Roman interjection meaning 'indeed!' or
　　'truly!'
2　Sebastian Franck; see Ep 2615 introduction.
3　Not extant
4　For Erasmus' fear that the references to him in Franck's book would discredit
　　him in the eyes of princes, see Ep 2615:53–81.
5　Franck's *Chronica* was a folio of eight books, so the booklet must have been
　　some other work. The bishop of Vienna was Johannes Fabri (Ep 2503).
6　Not extant
7　Emperor Charles and King Ferdinand were in Regensburg to attend the impe-
　　rial diet that would convene on 17 April; see Ep 2511 n20.

Cordial greetings, most reverend prelate. That your letters always bring me cheer and comfort is proof of your sincere benevolence towards me. They have a certain good spirit that brings not terror but joy to those to whom they are sent.

All those who still possess some good sense pray with you that the Lord will give his aid to the very devout initiative of the princes.[1] The situation has progressed to the point that even those who staged this play to the great applause of many people are weary of it. Since many others, according to their letters, pray for the same things as your most reverend Lordship, I decided to write a prayer formula that would permit all of us who love the dignity of the house of God to pray together. I send you the little book.[2]

I do not know whether I divined correctly the enigma of the lion and the dragon; I think you mean the violence of Turks and the venom of heretics.[3] The dragons are now a bit more subdued; would that they would all turn into lambs. I beseech your Highness to remember what I indicated to you some time ago,[4] that more account be taken of the work I contributed to the church in these tumults than of certain people who calumniate me, motivated by human passion. Not to mention other things, by means of two books that I published last year I impeded certain people's incredible machinations that cannot prudently be mentioned in a letter.[5] And once again I have made enemies of several of my sworn friends.[6] It is for the Lord that we

* * * * *

2623
1 At the Diet of Regensburg; cf Ep 2622:14–16 with n7.
2 See Ep 2618.
3 In Ep 2634:11–12 Cles acknowledges that Erasmus had solved the riddle correctly.
4 Not in any surviving letter
5 The first book was presumably the *Apologia adversus rhapsodias Alberti Pii*, which Erasmus wrote in the belief that Alberto Pio's two books against him had been written in collusion with (among others) Girolamo Aleandro and with the encouragement of Noël Béda; see Ep 2486:33–9 with nn9–11. The second book would have been the *Declarationes*, Erasmus' reply to the *Determinatio* of the Paris theologians (Ep 2552 n10), which had been written by the end of 1531 and appeared in print early in the new year. Erasmus was convinced that both Aleandro and Johann Eck had been at Paris and encouraged the theologians to publish their condemnation; see Ep 2565:4–8 with nn3–4. It was Aleandro in particular whose machinations Erasmus regarded as too dangerous to mention in letters, in general referring to him by name only in letters that he withheld from publication.
6 This may be a reference to Erasmus' success in persuading the magistrates of Strasbourg to ban the sale Sebastian Franck's *Chronica*, the publication of which he had blamed on Martin Bucer and Wolfgang Capito (Ep 2615 introduction), both of them former friends whom he had already denounced in the *Epistola ad fratres Inferioris Germaniae* (Ep 2312 nn2–3).

are fighting; he, whose judgment never fails and who does not delude those who have earned merit, will pay our wages.

I hope that he will assist the spirit of princes so that the tumult that has now become intolerable will be settled with the least possible shedding of 25 human blood, and that the victory will result not to the profit of men but to the good of the church and the glory of Christ.

2624 / From Hector van Hoxwier   Franeker, 16 March 1532

First published as Ep 169 in Förstemann / Günther, this is Hoxwier's answer to Ep 2586. The autograph was in the Burscher Collection of the University Library at Leipzig (Ep 1254 introduction).

Nothing will ever happen to me more pleasing or more delightful than your letter, dear Erasmus, incomparable ornament of our age; it not only abundantly satisfied my wishes and expectations but also surpassed my hopes and anticipation. But what delighted me most was your singular honesty and humanity and that pure simplicity that despises conceit. For although 5 no one could have more or greater reason for arrogance than you alone, you so cast yourself down and so despise yourself, I dare to say, that you do not at all seem to take it ill to be numbered in our company and fellowship. Who would not be astonished and elated, who would not love to see among your splendid and magnificent gifts, whose brilliance has for so long illuminated 10 all of Europe, these little pearls, as it were, of modesty and gentleness? Your gifts, to be sure, make of you a figure to be admired and respected, but these humble qualities temper and moderate the grandeur of your accomplishments in such a way that because of your affability you are as much loved by good men as you are revered by the learned for your outstanding merits. 15 And yet this same modesty, it seems to me, has a bad effect daily on your enemies and detractors. Those who are convinced that it is within their power to attain to this themselves never cease jumping up to latch on to the fringes of your garment and rip and tear away pieces to delay you in your efforts to promote the study of good letters or, what they consider a master stroke, to 20 make you look backwards. Since they understand that you do not despise anyone and that by your writings you have made many known to the public who would otherwise have remained unknown in the perpetual darkness of ignorance, there is no one who does not seize this opportunity of acquiring name and fame for themselves. But while they wrong-headedly pursue this 25 aim by heaping opprobrium on the head of Erasmus and busy themselves in casting aspersions on your reputation, they seem to accomplish nothing but to spit against the sky, and their spit falls back in their face, and they befoul

themselves with their own filth. If you had treated them as they deserved
from the beginning and did not consider them worthy of anything more than   30
what their perversity merited, your venerable old age would long ago have
been rid of these monsters, who deserve to be eliminated. But such is their
impudence and obstinacy that this could not be hoped for from those whose
sole end in life is their gullet, their ambition, and popular favour, to which
all their desires and thoughts are directed. If one would wish to torment and   35
punish them, it would perhaps most easily be accomplished by silence and
contempt; that would deprive them of any reason in the future of slandering
great and honourable names.

I do not say these things in order to seem to be your counsellor or guide,
or because you yourself do not have a method for subduing this hydra –   40
what could be more foolish or arrogant? – but because I am distressed that
you, a seasoned veteran, or rather such a great leader and general of letters,
are spat upon by camp followers and stable boys, who, taking advantage of
your goodness, devise new stratagems of calumny against you, so that in the
end they can enjoy some little glory, as impudent as it is stupid – these are   45
things I can in no way abide. But even admitting that it is your fate that neither your integrity of life, nor sublimity of intellect, nor power of eloquence
nor, finally, the favour of princes can preserve you from these cancers or provide security, nevertheless, they will never succeed in winning the approval
of good and discerning spectators for the play they have performed to the   50
applause of their minions. In contrast, the excellent virtues of your mind and
spirit, together with the amiable gentleness of your life, will consecrate you
to the everlasting memory of men, so that for all ages the name of Erasmus
will win favor and applause. Although I am aware that you have often exercised your generosity in honouring and recommending your friends, so that   55
it is not something new to me, nevertheless, it has procured me much joy that
that same generosity judges me worthy of your letter, especially written in
your hand, which awards singular praise to our friend Viglius.[1] If I did not
recognize what an honour that is for me, then I would merit what was said of
a stupid man by the comic writer: 'blockhead, cretin, ass, moron.'[2] But your   60
honorific reference to Viglius because of his love for me, which he often manifested in his letters to me and reciprocally because of my affection for him,
could not but have been most pleasing to me, for besides his rare native intelligence and the indubitable hopes of his advanced learning there are many

* * * * *

2624
1 See Ep 2586:28–40.
2 Terence *The Self-Tormentor* 877

reasons for my being much indebted to him. By exhibiting every friendly of- 65
fice to my brother,[3] whom he left in Bourges, in spurring him on and encouraging him and, as it were, lending him a hand in his more precise exploration
of the knowledge of civil law, he has bound me to him by his extraordinary
service. In this matter I am no less indebted also to Karel Sucket, who is very
dear to you, I know. Fortune will never be lacking to Viglius, I hope, which he 70
will attain through his intelligence and industry, with which he will be able to
shape his own fortune, but your recommendations as well will be of help, of
which every word, as Cicero said, constitutes a singular affidavit.[4]

The counsellor Haio has been absent now for three months on the other
side of the Ems;[5] they say that he is quite dangerously ill, but I know nothing 75
for certain. Cammingha is in good health, but he is completely occupied in
making up for his delay and the time lost.[6] As far as correspondence is concerned, I know that up to now he was very busy, protesting that he was writing
to Erasmus, and for that reason I was astonished that you wrote that nothing
had been brought to you from him.[7] This led me, as soon as your letter reached 80
me, to transmit to him the portion that makes allusion to him, knowing how
much you esteem him and how much he is indebted to you.[8] He has not yet
committed himself to employment but is still weighing whether he should
take the halter, as you say,[9] or return to you, or depart for France.

For the rest, my father-in-law Gerard van Herema wished that I express 85
the greatest thanks to you in his name for your having deigned to honour

* * * * *

3 Ausonius van Hoxwier (documented 1528–42), who from c 1528 studied with
  Conradus Goclenius at Louvain and subsequently encountered Viglius in
  Bourges. He moved back to Friesland, married in 1535, and seems to have had
  some involvement in Frisian politics.
4 *Ad familiares* 16.8.2
5 Cf Ep 2586:40–3. Franeker, the town from which this letter is written, and
  Emden, Haio Herman's hometown, are on opposite sides of the river Ems, the
  boundary between West and East Friesland (on the present-day boundary between the Netherlands and Germany).
6 For Haio Cammingha, see n8 below. The reference here may be to the wanderings to Italy and back again that caused Cammingha to be so tardy in the delivery of letters entrusted to him; see lines 92–4 below.
7 In the surviving text of Ep 2586 (cf following note) Erasmus notes only (lines
  40–2) that he has not heard from Haio Herman.
8 The complimentary passage about Cammingha is not found in the surviving
  text of Ep 2586. It was in the original letter, but by the time of the publication
  of it in the *Epistolae palaeonaeoi* (September 1532) Erasmus was so annoyed with
  Cammingha for non-payment of a debt and for other reasons as well (see Ep
  2587:47–51) that he excised the passage (see Allen 2810:26–34).
9 Ie get married; cf Juvenal *Satires* 6.43

him with your letter,[10] that is, that you presented him with something sought
by the most exalted princes. That you sowed that very letter in the garden of
your *Epistolae floridae,* by which he sees that he has attained immortality, he
thinks that he cannot possibly requite his debt by any rendering of thanks;   90
nonetheless he desires nothing so much as to be given the opportunity to
demonstrate his intention in very fact. But your letter was not delivered until
almost two years later, for after he left you Cammingha took it with him to
Italy, then to Louvain, and finally to Friesland.[11] I have added this detail so
that you would not believe that we are the same as the Trojans and their city,   95
in that we give thanks too late.[12] May what I promised you long ago please
you as much as it will certainly last forever. If you would deign on occasion
to inform me about literary matters, your health, and conditions in Germany,
provided it is of that kind that can be safely committed to a letter, and if
it is no trouble, you would do something most agreeable to me and very   100
much in keeping with your recent good will towards me. Witness my fidelity.
Farewell, and love in return one who is most devoted to you.

From Franeker, 16 March 1532

Hector van Hoxwier, at your service if he can be of help

To Desiderus Erasmus of Rotterdam, theologian, by far the most emi-   105
nent and illustrious scholar in every kind of learning. In Freiburg im Breisgau

2625 / From Erasmus Schets   Antwerp, 16 March 1532

This letter was first published by Allen. The autograph is in the Öffentliche
Bibliothek of the University of Basel (MS Scheti epistolae 29).

†

Greetings. I wrote to you in the month of January,[1] my dear master Erasmus,
but I have had no letter from you since then.

* * * * *

10 Ep 2262
11 See Ep 2262 introduction.
12 Cf *Adagia* I i 28, 'The Phrygians learn wisdom too late.' As an example of those
   who repent of their stupidities too late and suffer disasters, Erasmus cites the
   Trojans, who only began to think of giving Helen back to King Menelaus ten
   years after he had asked for her, thus inviting the countless calamities of the
   Trojan war.

2625
1 Ep 2593

I have given orders to my agents in Frankfurt to pay Hieronymus Froben in your name, at the spring fair,[2] 203 gold florins and 18 shillings, and to obtain a receipt from him. I think he is so faithful to you that I have no 5 doubts about his paying you back. And so that you may see the calculation of the above-mentioned money, I go back to my letter,[3] which I sent to you last 18 October, in which I informed you that I had had 245 florins and 18 stuivers in our coinage of your money. Since that time I have received what Castro remitted to me by a bill of exchange, 39 florins and 11 stuivers for the 5 pounds 10 sterling received from a certain Zacharias in England.[4] The sum of your money that I now have in my possession amounts to 285 florins and 9 stuivers, which, converted into gold florins for their full value, are equivalent to the above-mentioned 203 gold florins and 18 shillings,[5] which, as mentioned above, I have ordered to be paid to Hieronymus Froben in Frankfurt. Thus, 15 as I am currently not holding any of your money, I shall await a new receipt of funds. Castro complains to me day after day that despite his frequent polite exhortations, which are free of importunity, he cannot collect anything.

Rumour has it that you are going to move from where you are and come here.[6] When you are more close by, there will be better chances of your being 20 paid your money than there are now. At present, people think that even if you are alive, you may at any moment set out for the heavens and they will be liberated from their payments. You were invited, I hear, by Queen Mary, who is most devoted to you.[7] If you refuse her now and reject us and your native land, believe me, many who have long nurtured the hope of your return 25 here will abandon it in despair.

I send you together with this a bundle of letters transmitted to me by Goclenius, and a few days ago I put together several other bundles of letters

* * * * *

2 Ie at the Frankfurt book fair
3 Ep 2558
4 For Zacharius Deiotarus see Ep 2496. Luis de Castro was Schets' agent in London for the collection of monies owed to Erasmus.
5 That is, Rhenish florins. Schets explains that it represents 285 florins, 9 stuivers 'in our coinage,' by which he means Carolus florins (see Ep 2558 n8); and this, in turn, was the sum of 245 florins, 18 stuivers Schets was holding for Erasmus plus the equivalent of five pounds sterling (39 florins, 11 stuivers) remitted by bill from England. The total was equivalent to £49 19s 0d groot Flemish or almost six years' wages of an Antwerp master mason/carpenter (CWE 12 650 Table 3, 691 Table 13).
6 See Ep 2511 n17.
7 See Ep 2583 introduction.

sent to you from all over to be transmitted to you. I directed everything to my
agents in Frankfurt so that they may be entrusted to Hieronymus Froben.[8]   30

The current state of affairs has not produced anything worth writing
about. The Diet of Regensburg will yield something that will either give
wings to the disorders of this age or disperse them.[9] If only the party I fear
the most would not succeed!

Keep well, my dearest Master Erasmus, and if you do not come your-   35
self, write back concerning the money to be received by Froben.

From Antwerp, 16 March 1532

Your most sincere friend, Erasmus Schets

To the most beloved Master Erasmus of Rotterdam. In Freiburg im
Breisgau   40

2626 / From Henricus Cornelius Agrippa   Cologne, 17 March 1532

This letter was first published in *Agrippae Opera* II 1003. The autograph is in
the Rehdiger Collection of the University Library at Wrocław (MS Rehd 254 4).

Greetings. I recently responded, most venerable Erasmus, to your most
kind letter,[1] which the priest Andreas brought to me, and arranged that it
be delivered to you by Maximilianus Transsilvanus.[2] I do not know whether
you received it, but I think you did, although I have not received a further
letter from you. As a matter of fact, I was absent from Brabant for several   5
days, guest of the most reverend and illustrious prince-elector, archbishop
of Cologne, who loves and venerates you with singular devotion.[3] Very often our conversation turns to your blameless, irrefutable teaching. There are
many in his service who extol your name, among whom Tielmannus Gravius
is the most zealous of all.[4] When he mentioned that he had a messenger avail-   10
able who was heading in your direction, I thought it was not right that he
should go without a letter from me, even if I have nothing to write to you at
present except that I am ever devoted and obliged to you, who deigned to
shed lustre on an unknown man of modest literary culture by initiating the

* * * * *

8 It seems that none of these letters has survived.
9 The diet would formally convene on 17 April 1532; see Ep 2511 n20.

2626
1 Ep 2544, to which Agrippa's response was Ep 2589
2 See Epp 2544 n3 (Andreas), 1553 introduction (Maximilianus Transsilvanus).
3 Hermann von Wied (Ep 1976)
4 Ep 1829

correspondence between us. Since your generosity is such that you, a man of   15
great brilliance, do not disdain the letter of an obscure correspondent, pardon
my audacity if I ask that you write back to me sometime, at your leisure. I
hope that there will be occasion to write back and forth to each other on important questions. Wishing you the best of health.

From Cologne, 17 March 1532   20
I will remain here for another month and then will return to Brabant.
Most devoted to your Excellency, Henricus Cornelius Agrippa, in his
own hand
To Erasmus of Rotterdam, blameless in doctrine, life and morals, object
of my sincere admiration. In Freiburg im Breisgau   25

2627 / From Johann Koler   Augsburg, 17 March 1532

First published as Ep 170 in Förstemann / Günther, this is the surviving
fragment of an original autograph letter. The fragment was in the Burscher
Collection of the University Library at Leipzig (Ep 1254 introduction).

Cordial greetings. For a long time I have not been able to write you any
news ...[1]
The two Rems, father and son,[2] send their sincere regards; the son was
going to write to you save that he was already setting out for the diet.[3] I wish,
dear Erasmus, that you continue to be in good health in Christ.   5
Given at Augsburg, 17 March 1532
Your friend, Johann Koler
I have remunerated the bearer of this letter; you owe him nothing.

* * * * *

2627
1 Allen took this first sentence, which did not survive in the fragment, from Johann
   Friedrich Burscher *Index et argumentum epistolarum ad D. Erasmum Roterodamum
   autographarum* ... (Leipzig: G.G. Sommer 1784) 47 no 5. Burscher, who evidently owned the original letter, supplied the following summary of the topics covered: 'Concerning reasons for the long silence. A sincere opinion about
   a letter of Erasmus [not extant] to a Spaniard, in which he praises [Johann (II)]
   Paumgartner; concerning this opinion, examined by himself; the advice of Koler
   himself. A harsh judgment and advice concerning a letter of Luther; a provocation
   of Erasmus against Luther, including the opinions of others. On disturbances in
   Germany, adding his own opinion. Concerning [Ambrosius von] Gumppenberg,
   who sent an Anticicero [more likely an Anticiceronianus] from Rome. Again concerning Luther; on the state of religion in Augsburg and an opinion of the bishop.
   On private matters. A very lengthy letter, but worth reading.'
2 See Ep 2419 introduction.
3 The Diet of Regensburg; see Ep 2511 n20.

To the most illustrious and learned Master Erasmus of Rotterdam, theologian. In Freiburg 10

2628 / To Jean de Pins Freiburg, 20 March 1532

This letter was first printed by Preserved Smith in Appendix II of *Erasmus: A
Study of His Life, Ideals and Place in History* (New York 1923; repr New York
1962) 448. The surviving manuscript is a seventeenth-century copy in the
Bibliothèque Municipale at Nîmes (MS 215 folio 168 verso). For Jean de Pins
and the circumstances of the writing of this letter, see Ep 2569 introduction.

ERASMUS OF ROTTERDAM TO THE MOST ILLUSTRIOUS MASTER
JEAN DE PINS, BISHOP OF RIEUX IN FRANCE, GREETING
For my part, at least, it was not an unfortunate error that revived the memory
of our very pleasant acquaintance, which took place in Bologna some time
ago, during our studies of good letters.[1] I was convinced that the most rever- 5
end bishop of Rodez possessed a copy of Josephus in Greek. He wrote to me
that it belonged to you and that it had gone back to you by right of recovery.
Your generosity, which I observed and experienced at first hand in the past,
gives me the firm hope that you will make a copy of the volume available to
Hieronymus Froben for a few months. After consulting with various schol- 10
ars, he has decided to restore from the authenticity of the Greek manuscript
this historian, preeminently famous but pitifully corrupted and contaminat-
ed by the ignorance of translators and scribes. This enterprise will not only
be of no little value to general studies but will also bring great praise to your
name. Hieronymus is a man of proven trustworthiness, but if you have any 15
doubts, take me as a surety, for in this case I have no fear of that oracle 'ruin
is at hand.'[2]
　　I would like to know what our friend Bombace is doing; for many years
I had no news of him.[3] In his last letter he told me that he was heading for
Bologna with his cardinal, who died recently,[4] and that he was going to pay 20
3,000 ducats for the villa that he had bought.[5]

* * * * *

2628
1 Ep 928:43n
2 *Adagia* I vi 97
3 Erasmus' last contact with his old friend Paolo Bombace (Ep 210 introduction)
　had been in 1525 (Ep 1631). Bombace perished in the sack of Rome on 6 May
　1527.
4 Lorenzo Pucci (Ep 1000), who died in September 1531
5 The letter is not extant.

In other respects, if there is anything at all in which your humble little
friend of times past, now your humble servant, can be of service to you, you
will find him readily disposed to execute your commands. Farewell.

Given at Freiburg im Breisgau, 20 March 1532   25
Erasmus of Rotterdam in my own hand, in haste

2629 / From Jan van Campen   Frankfurt, 21 March 1532

The autograph of this letter is in the Rehdiger Collection of the University
Library at Wrocław (MS Rehd 254 44). It was first published by Dr Franz
Wachter in *Zeitschrift des bergischen Geschichtsvereins* 30 (1894) 205–6. The body
of the letter is dated from Courange, where the bishop of Liège had a palace;
the number in the month-date is not easily decipherable: 9[?] March 1532. The
postscript is dated from Frankfurt on 21 March.

For Jan van Campen, who had recently entered the service of Johannes
Dantiscus, Polish ambassador to the imperial court, see Ep 2570:83–107.

The day before yesterday, as my master Dantiscus, bishop of Kulm, and I
were reading some books for relaxation in the castle to which the most reverend cardinal of Liège, who had been treating him with great kindness for
several days, had generously invited him, the most reverend himself suddenly entered my master's bedroom.[1] He brought with him your letter to the   5
most reverend cardinal dated 12 December and gave it to me to read aloud.[2]
After I had read it from beginning to end, he stated not once or twice but
many times that it had given him such pleasure that he could barely put it
down after having read it more than ten times. He said, however, that there
was something in it that caused him considerable distress, for it seems that   10
you have conceived an adverse opinion of the most reverend cardinal because certain individuals have written to you comments more offensive than
the situation warranted.[3]

Therefore, since the most reverend cardinal wishes that you be dis-
abused of this suspicion, he ordered me to write to you in his name, and to   15
do this in the presence of my most reverend master, whom he wished to be
present as witness, that he has never wished you anything but the greatest
good, and that in serious conversation he has never spoken of you except as

* * * * *

2629
1 The cardinal was Erard de la Marck (Ep 2054).
2 The letter is not extant.
3 For recent reports from Maarten Lips and Jakob Spiegel concerning the cardinal's attitude towards Erasmus, see Ep 2566:126–9, 2590:16–20.

of one most dear to him, and that not even in jest has he ever said anything
that he himself could have believed would damage either your reputation or 20
your person. He added that he had so disapproved the action of Eustachius
van der Rivieren that he, who as a general rule would give several gold coins
to one who was begging for a mendicant order, would refuse to give anything
to this man, angered that he wrote against you and did not scruple to dedicate
his repulsive inanities to him.[4] In this way the gaping crow, cleverly tricked 25
by you, went away.[5] He added besides that he was truly so well disposed
towards you that if he had only one loaf of bread left he would gladly give
half of it to you, if it were necessary, and he asserted that you would find this
to be true in very fact if you ever asked of him anything in which he could
be of assistance. I write this all the more willingly at the bidding of the most 30
reverend cardinal because I believe you will find it most gratifying. Farewell.

Courange, 9[?] March 1532

In the meantime you may believe as much as you wish.[6] It seemed to
me and to master Dantiscus that he was speaking seriously. Again farewell.

Frankfurt, 21 March 35

Your friend in every regard, Jan van Campen

To Master Erasmus of Rotterdam, his master. In Freiburg

2630 / From Bonifacius Amerbach [Basel, c 22 March 1532]

This letter (= AK Ep 1612) was first published as Ep 86 in Burckhardt. The manuscript, a much corrected autograph rough draft, is in the Öffentliche Bibliothek
of the University of Basel (MS C VIa 73 22). Erasmus' reply is Ep 2631. For the
background of the letter, namely, Bonifacius' difficulties with the magistrates
of Basel because of his refusal to participate in the reformed celebration of the
Eucharist, see Ep 2519 introduction.

Concerning the Eucharist, most illustrious Erasmus, I was and am of the opinion that a spiritual eating is enacted solely through faith in Christ, by which
we believe that he died for us and made satisfaction for our sins. Moreover, I
believe that the sacrament of the supper is not only the mark and sign of our

* * * * *

4 Eustachius van der Rivieren (Ep 2264 introduction) had dedicated his *Apologia
   pro pietate in Erasmi Roterod. Enchiridion canonem quintum* (Ep 2522 n8) to Erard
   de la Marck; cf Epp 2500:20–6, 2522:83–95, 2566:185–8.
5 To 'trick the gaping crow' is to outwit someone on the lookout for a reward in
   the way that a crow is always on the lookout for carrion; see *Adagia* I vii 15.
6 Erasmus in fact refused to take the cardinal's protestations of good will seriously; see Ep 2590 n6.

belief, but that it was left to us to increase and enliven our faith. There are two   5
things, if I am not mistaken, that must be considered of particular importance
in it; first, that we show gratitude in memory of the Lord for the ineffable favour he has bestowed upon us; second, that we have confidence in his words.
Since he is all-powerful, we can hardly be uncertain that he can do greater
things than what his words promise, not to speak of the unanimous inter-   10
pretation of these words that has been accepted for so many centuries. Since
the words are 'This is my body, this is my blood,' I am induced to believe, or
rather, I am compelled to believe, that the body and blood of Christ are truly
present there and are distributed in the supper; how that happens, as it is
inaccessible to human reason, I affirm is known by faith in the word of God.[1]   15
    Since our preachers have a completely different view of the matter, I
have so far remained a nonparticipant, even though I have been vexed by
summonses to take part. But I don't know how long they will leave me alone,
for the period of truce that was accorded me when I pleaded my cause before
the city council has almost run out.[2] What they will do then is uncertain. I   20
do not doubt that the preachers will allow me to maintain my opinion as
long as I receive communion. That is where I stand at the moment, between
the shrine and the stone.[3] For if I am summoned again, the fact that I disagree with them would seem to discourage me from complying. On the other
hand, since priests or preachers have no jurisdiction over this sacrament and   25
do not have the power to add to or subtract anything from it, given that it
depends on the words of Christ and still more on its institution, I feel that I
can approach the sacred table with more confidence and with an unshaken
conscience. And so, while I was in a state of mental uncertainty, not knowing
what I should say if I am summoned, I decided to pour out all the anxieties   30
of my mind into the bosom of the best of all patrons, whose sole judgment is
of such value to me that whatever you advise constitutes a settled judgment,
or rather removes all doubts about what is right for me to do.
    Therefore, in virtue of this predisposition of yours towards me, with
which you have honoured me beyond my merits, but also in the name of   35
Christ, our Saviour, I ask and beseech you to free me of this scruple and
not refuse to communicate your opinion to me. If by chance you do not sufficiently understand me (because of limitations of time I did not have the

* * * * *

2630
1 This statement, like that in Ep 2519:14–27, is remarkably consonant with
  Lutheran teaching.
2 The deadline was Easter 1532 (31 March).
3 Ie between the hammer and the anvil; see *Adagia* I i 15.

opportunity of writing more at greater length on the subject) I will willingly
explain it to you in person.   40

I have no doubt that Sadoleto has your letter by now. I sent it through
someone who has discharged his obligation faithfully in transporting letters
back and forth.[4] I have been invited to Dole to teach civil law publicly.[5] I will
need your counsel in this matter also. If I often take advantage of it without
due consideration for your dignity, you will take it in good part, in your   45
kindness, which allows me complete freedom in my correspondence with
you. Farewell.

2631 / To Bonifacius Amerbach   Freiburg, 25 March [1532]

> First published by Allen, this letter (= AK Ep 1614) is Erasmus' reply to Ep 2630.
> The autograph is in the Öffentliche Bibliothek of the University of Basel (MS AN
> III 15 26).

Cordial greetings. Most honourable Bonifacius, this will now be a case of
what is called the sow teaching Minerva,[1] since it is you (to whom it is not
possible for me to refuse anything) who ask it of me. There can be no doubt
about the reality of the body of the Lord. About the manner of the presence
one can have doubts to a certain degree, since it is more accurate to say that   5
the church discusses it rather than pronounces on it, or at least in general to
believe what the church believes, especially for a layman.

But keeping in mind your opinion, which differs from theirs, I would
in no way advise you to take articles of faith from them. For even if dis-
simulation is free of vice, two great disadvantages result from it: first, by   10
your example you will both confirm a great number of people in their error,
and perhaps you will drag not a few into error, regarded as you are by all
as a man of great learning and integrity. Then, once you join the faction by
receiving communion, there will be no possibility of repudiating it in the future, and you will be compelled to embrace at the same time everything that   15
they have taught or will teach – for they are still nurturing I know not what

* * * * *

4 See Ep 2612 n3.
5 In early March 1532 Bonifacius received a message aimed at securing him for a
professorship at Dole (AK Ep 1611), and a month later he received a formal invitation from the rector of the university (AK Ep 1617). Sometime before 15 May,
Bonifacius declined the offer (AK Ep 1640).

2631
1 *Adagia* I i 40

monstrosities. And my intuition forebodes that these sacramentarians will have a wretched end.[2] We have seen the beginnings.[3]

Imagine for a moment what is far from the truth, namely, that the substance of the body of the Lord is not present in the Eucharist, but that God will not be able to impute this error to anyone. When we adore in the Eucharist, the silent reservation is always present: 'if he is really there.' For it is not known to us whether the priest has consecrated with the proper rites. But in the case of someone who follows those people, some of them capricious, some infamous, what excuse will he allege?

Perhaps they will not press you, now that they have become more subdued, as I hear.[4] But if they do exert pressure on you, you will be able to object that their first dogma was that no one should be forced to receive the Eucharist.[5] Therefore it is absurd that they themselves do what they reproached in the pope as tyrannical. I would answer that my conscience is not yet peaceful in this regard and that he who acts against his conscience, even when he performs a pious action, sins. But if they deny you further time to deliberate, I would indicate that I would accept any inconvenience rather than suffer the loss of good intention. When they perceive this, perhaps they will give in rather than lose such a citizen. In this, however, they must not be irritated by harsh words.

Concerning your statement that priests cannot change anything in the Eucharist, they only have the power, that if the will to consecrate is not present, at least according to the intention of the universal church, there is nothing but bread and wine.

And if only priests can consecrate, where will they get priests, when those they now use are dead? Is the situation not tending towards paganism?

If it torments your spirit that for some years you have lived without taking part in the rite, necessity has no law, and there is a remedy ready at hand. You can communicate secretly either here or at the home of your father-in-law. If it is discovered, the fine is light.[6]

Nor am I unaware that there are many things that hold you back: your native land, your relatives, your relations by marriage, your wife, your home,

* * * * *

2 On Erasmus' use of the word 'sacramentarian' cf Ep 2579 n1.
3 Ie the deaths of Zwingli and Oecolampadius in October and November1531
4 Following the death of Oecolampadius
5 Bonifacius had in fact already used this argument; see Ep 2519:5–7 with n1.
6 When (October 1532) the bookbinder Niklaus Kantus was fined for not taking communion, the fine was 'ein pfund' (AGBR IV 168), presumably a Basel pound, which was worth slightly less than a Rhenish florin (51.3d groot Flemish; see Ep 2598 n3) and equivalent to six days' wages of an Antwerp master mason/carpenter (CWE 12 650 Table 3, 691 Table 13). Whether the fine was 'light'

your family, your possessions. But perhaps greater evils would hang over one who has made open profession. The emperor is at hand.[7] And it is well known how Ares favours those people.[8]   50

I have read carefully what Oecolampadius has written against Melanchthon;[9] he has not convinced me.

I have pointed out what I would do according to my conscience. Now consult yours and decide what is best under the inspiration of Christ's spirit.

Concerning the terms offered by Dole, you will make that decision   55 more easily yourself.[10] The university has few students, the city is rather cold, the people, as I hear, are perverse and seditious.[11] Moving is both bothersome and expensive, especially for one who is married. I do not know anything about the remuneration.[12] Nevertheless, I am happy that this has happened, for thanks to it, they will be less willing to dismiss you.[13]   60

I have carefully written my opinion of the matter; I do not know whether I understood your intention sufficiently. God himself will give you auspicious counsel.

Alciati is again in Bourges, so writes Viglius,[14] a young man of high hopes, who will also write to you.[15] On his trip to Italy Sucket was detained   65 at Turin, with a salary of a hundred crowns.[16]

* * * * *

would, obviously, depend on class position: for a wealthy law professor, such as Amerbach, it would have been light; for a worker it would have been much more burdensome.

7 He was in Germany on his way to Regensburg to preside over the imperial diet; see Ep 2593 n7.

8 Ares was the Greek god of war; the Romans knew him as Mars.

9 In August 1530 Bonifacius had sent Erasmus a copy of Oecolampadius' just published *Quid de Eucharistia veteres ... senserint, dialogus in quo epistolae Philippi Melanchthonis et Ioannis Oeclampadii insertae*; see Ep 2372:16–18 with n7.

10 See Ep 2630 n5.

11 Erasmus' source of information may have been his famulus Gilbert Cousin, who studied at Dole; see Ep 2381 n1.

12 The university offered 300 francs per annum, but were prepared to double the offer; see AK Ep 1617.

13 'They' were the magistrates of Basel.

14 See Ep 2594:26–30.

15 Two letters from Viglius to Bonifacius survive for the year 1532: AK Epp 1616 (29 March) and 1655 (3 June).

16 In Ep 2594:47–8 Viglius Zuichemus reports that Karel Sucket's journey to Padua had been interrupted at Turin, but he does not say why. Erasmus' knowledge that Sucket had been appointed to a lectureship in law at a specific salary must derive from another source.

Lee, in England, was consecrated as archbishop of York instead of being named cardinal.[17] Vulturius has found great favour in Augsburg.[18] Capito
is preaching there, which does not surprise me.[19] The preachers are going
about their business; unless they lost several cities, they themselves were   70
lost.[20] Capito is more calm now; he teaches that papists are not to be harmed
or constrained, but that one must pray that God will touch their hearts.[21]
But it was the disaster that taught them this mildness.[22] Oecolampadius was
singing a very different song.[23] The bishop of Augsburg is on his way to the
diet,[24] although he had said that he would not go. He is a more lenient papist   75
than certain people would want.[25]

Negotiations are proceeding with the city of Schweinfurt to determine whether it wishes to obey the emperor. They will also purge other cities that have not yet openly admitted sects.[26] They are now threatening my

* * * * *

17 Erasmus' old antagonist Edward Lee (Ep 765) was anointed archbishop of York
    on 10 December 1531.
18 Vulturius was Gerard Geldenhouwer (Ep 2238 n1). At some point in the year
    1531 the city council of Augsburg appointed Geldenhouwer first rector of the
    new school that had been established in the abandoned Carmelite monastery of
    St Anne.
19 The Strasbourg reformer Wolfgang Capito (Ep 459) was in Augsburg from
    mid-February until c 5 March 1532; see *The Correspondence of Wolfgang Capito* ed
    and trans Erika Rummel and Milton Kooistra 3 vols to date (Toronto 2005–   )
    Epp 466–8.
20 This seems to be a comment on the disastrous outcome of the Second Kappel
    War for Zürich and its allies (see n22 below). In order to preserve what they
    had, the evangelical city-states (cantons) of Switzerland were obliged to aban-
    don their aggressive campaign, eagerly promoted by Zwingli, to extend the
    Reformation to other areas of the Confederation and indeed to retreat from
    some areas already occupied; cf Ep 2173 n10.
21 Cf lines 91–2 below.
22 Ie the overwhelming defeat of the Protestant cantons, including Basel, at the
    battle of Kappel on 11 October 1531, during which Zwingli was killed. Oecolam-
    padius' death followed on 21 November.
23 A reference to Oecolampadius' strenuous efforts to enforce the mandate requir-
    ing participation in the reformed Eucharist; see Ep 2519 introduction.
24 At Regensburg; see Ep 2511 n20. The bishop was Christoph von Stadion
    (Ep 2029).
25 As, for example, in his favourable response to the Lutheran Augsburg Confes-
    sion; see Ep 2384:5–9 with n2.
26 Schweinfurt am Main was one of the free imperial cities that had joined in
    the 'protestation' against the recess of the Diet of Speyer (1529), which called
    for strict enforcement of the Edict of Worms (1521) against Luther and his

theologian,[27] making many charges against him, but two in particular, that he   80
has a shaved head instead of a tonsure, and also that he sometimes received
the Eucharist among lay people. But these are theological matters. I am waiting to see what will be my fate.[28] The emperor is most obedient,[29] Ferdinand
is not altogether averse to religion. Aleandro has various talents.[30] You know
about Eck and Fabri.[31]   85

I will not do anything more about the house; I would, however, have
wished for more convenient conditions than the ones I proposed.[32]

If you come here at your convenience, no guest could be more welcome.[33] Then I will reveal everything. I am awaiting Anselmus also, but I am
afraid it is too late.[34]   90

That Capito says that people are not to be forced into a sect I learned in
a letter from the bishop of Augsburg.[35] This argument will be of use to you
before the magistrate.[36] It is reasonable to think that they do what he teaches,
since they pay him such regard.

* * * * *

followers. As a result, they had been threatened with the displeasure of the emperor. The language here indicates that Schweinfurt and other imperial cities
that were sympathetic to the Reformation but had not yet formally established
an evangelical church order were under continuing pressure to conform to the
emperor's wishes regarding religion or risk his disfavour.

27 Ludwig Baer: see Ep 2550 n2. 'They' were evidently Catholic conservatives in
Freiburg, perhaps fellow members of the exiled cathedral chapter of Basel.

28 Presumably wondering if he will be able to remain in Freiburg or be compelled
by disorders arising from the religious conflict to move away.

29 Probably a reiteration of Erasmus' belief that the emperor was too inclined to
do as the pope says; see; see Epp 2472:33–5 and n9, 2479:41–2.

30 Girolamo Aleandro, the papal legate at the imperial court (Ep 2565 n2)

31 For the attempts of Johann Fabri to restrain Johann Eck's machinations against
Erasmus, see Ep 2503:7–18.

32 This appears to be an expression of regret that he had not secured better terms,
ie a less 'iniquitous' price, when purchasing his recently occupied house, which
had needed extensive renovation to make it suitable for occupation; see Epp
2506 n1, 2517 n11.

33 The visit took place in April; see AK Ep 1621:4–5.

34 Erasmus had invited Anselmus Ephorinus to live on the ground floor of his
new house; see Ep 2554: 25–8, and cf Ep 2535.

35 Cf lines 71–2 above. The letter was clearly not Ep 2592, in which there is no
mention of Capito.

36 Cf n5 above.

In Augsburg those who were removed from the city council have been   95
reinstated.[37] They must do one of two things: either avoid this storm by con-
trolling things, or prepare themselves for violence with all their strength.[38]
But the first solution seems more advisable. Farewell.

Freiburg, 25 March

You will recognize your devoted friend.   100

To the most illustrious Master Bonifacius Amerbach. In Basel

2632 / From Viglius Zuichemus   Padua, 28 March 1532

This letter, Viglius' answer to Ep 2604, was first published as Ep 25 in vze.
Erasmus would in due course respond to this letter as well as to Ep 2657 in
Ep 2682.

The Frenchman with the auspicious name, most learned Erasmus, having
changed his plans to go to Rome, stopped off here. When I questioned him
he answered that he had delivered all the letters.[1] I arrived here by ship on

* * * * *

37 Among those removed but quickly restored was Johann Rehlinger, the father-
   in-law of Anton Fugger; see Ep 2480 n5.
38 At this stage, the chief obstacle to the formal adoption of evangelical reform in
   Augsburg, where evangelical sentiment was already deeply entrenched, was
   the city council's fear of intervention by the city's powerful Catholic neigh-
   bours: a Hapsburg territory (Burgau) to the west, Bavaria to the east, and the
   domain of the prince-bishop of Augsburg to the south. Any one of them could
   endanger the city by cutting off supplies. Moreover, the Hapsburgs, who had
   close dealings with the great Augsburg banking houses, protected Augsburg's
   trade monopolies, and ruled in areas crucial to European and transatlantic
   trade, were in a position to do the city serious economic harm. Only in 1534 did
   the city fathers set aside such political and economic considerations and take
   the first steps in the long process (1534-7) of dismantling Catholicism in the
   city and replacing it with a reformed church order that endured until the rein-
   troduction of Catholicism following the emperor's victory over the League of
   Schmalkalden in 1547. In 1555 the Peace of Augsburg made Augsburg one of a
   handful of imperial cities in which Catholicism and Lutheranism were required
   to coexist.

2632
1 The Frenchman was Pierre Mondoré. Erasmus had suspected that the letters
  had not been delivered; see Ep 2604:3-7.

the eve of the feast of St Martin and received your second letter,[2] which gave me great delight, not only because you continue in the habit of writing to me   5 (and I also enjoy your pleasantries against the opinion of all the Ciceronians here, into whose number you wish to force me), but also because I think you have given me licence to blurt out some jokes to you in return.

You ask me in what matters I agree with the Ciceronians and in what matters I contend with them. If I want to explain this, you will have to bear   10 with my ineptitudes for a while. As far as the theories of those who have written on imitation is concerned, since that question is too vast and too difficult for my comprehension, I prefer, like one of the crowd, simply to follow the other side rather than to discuss more precisely why I do it. I have always agreed more with the opinion which seems to have been that of all learned   15 men after Cicero, namely, that students should imitate him especially, but not exclusively; that they should not imitate him so superstitiously that they never depart from his footprints, but should try to emend an otherwise free style, not bound by any constraint, in imitation of the brilliant facility and elegance of Marcus Tullius. For he who thinks that he should seek everything from the   20 same writer and never depart from him does not, in my opinion, clearly conceive how wise and infinite, so to speak, are the boundaries of writing and speaking. And in Cicero that part of the function of the orator from which eloquence itself has taken its name was always admired. But even admitting that he excels most in it, he is not the only one to be embraced. Language   25 was invented in order to explain things. For this reason, what praise, I ask you, can those who do not learn things themselves merit from their empty jangling of words? Or what can they produce that is worthy of posterity? The poets call Ulysses wise 'because he saw the customs and cities of many men.'[3] Shall we not believe in the same way that learning is not acquired by the   30 imitation of one person, but by the reading of many authors?

Who will give the name of learned to someone who has neither touched theology nor applied himself to jurisprudence or medicine or philosophy, and has spent his whole life reproducing Cicero? someone who thinks he has

* * * * *

2 The feast of St Martin of Tours is 11 November. Erasmus' first letter addressed
   to Viglius in Italy is not extant; it was answered by Ep 2594. His second letter
   to Viglius was Ep 2604, the answer to Ep 2568. This is Viglius' reply to that
   second letter.
3 Horace *Epistles* 1.2.19–20

achieved his goal of being like Cicero if you just look at the surface and the   35
skin and the outer coloring? But in the composition of the clauses, in the meat
and the juice, which is the real substance of an oration, he will be altogether
different. Perhaps I would not be wrong in comparing him to these Italian
women who have the habit of painting themselves every day, but if you were
to see them after they have removed their makeup, you would, not without   40
good reason, laugh at their wrinkled and deformed faces. I hope you will
pardon me for these trivialities. Why should I not call by that name things
that I write to Erasmus about a subject not sufficiently known to me?

But nevertheless, trusting in your kindness, I shall come to the point.
Jokingly you put me in the ranks of the Ciceronians, against their opinion   45
and mine. I solemnly swear to you that I have never devoted my attention to
imitation, not even to the kind of imitation that you do not seem to condemn.
My age, which still remains within the years when the praetor accorded full
restitution, will attest to it.[4] And it is now the seventh year, having discon-
tinued the study of good literature, that I have devoted all my attention to   50
the discipline of civil law, not confined to a course in law but examining the
commentaries of the usual interpreters. Even if they are written in a barbarous language, they contribute much to the knowledge and explanation
of subjects that are treated in law.[5] Therefore, neither my age nor even my
studies permitted such imitation, which was completely foreign to them, or   55
rather contrary and opposed to them. You would surely concede it as true if
you knew how much the Ciceronians avoid the schools of the jurisconsults
here. Before I had applied my mind to this discipline, the opinion that had
risen up concerning Cicero did not yet exist here. And at that time my age,
lacking judgment, did not yet permit me to distinguish what to choose or   60

* * * * *

4 This was Viglius' clever law student's way of saying that he had not yet turned
  twenty-five (his twenty-fifth birthday, 17 October 1532, was still almost seven
  months away). In Roman law a male was a minor until he reached the age of
  twenty-five. During his years of minority the law protected him against economic exploitation, and a magistrate (praetor) could award him the full restitution of property taken from him fraudulently (*Digest* iv.4.1).
5 The study of law in which Viglius was engaged included texts and intepretations
  of the glossators of the *Corpus iuris civilis* active in Bologna at the end of the elev-
  enth century and the beginning of the twelfth, as well as those of the postglos-
  sators of the fourteenth century. They used a highly technical, legal Latin, much
  like that of the scholastic theologians, that was often ridiculed by the humanists.

what to imitate or how I should go about it. But since Cicero is usually read
in the schools, it happened that I profited from this author more by learning
than by imitating. Already when as a boy I eagerly read Lorenzo Valla, I confess that I drew great pleasure from reading Cicero because of the frequent
examples he takes from him.[6] That was before the turning-point of my stud-   65
ies. When I began to turn my attention to the learning of law, since I retained
only what I had learned in the schools and realized that I did not have much
time for the literature to which I was previously dedicated, I did not have the
leisure, as I had before, to read Cicero and many other authors, but I browsed
through all the approved and ancient authors, one after another. Why then   70
should I not be astonished that you attributed to me that which most people,
devoting all their energies to the imitation of Cicero, consider themselves
happy to have achieved, even fainting away with the necessary unremitting
toil? Therefore I candidly confess that I have never imitated Cicero, but perhaps I learned something from him at one time, which of itself, without any   75
intention of imitation, improved my style somewhat.[7]

But when I had learned the rudiments of law as best I could, and little
by little became familiar with the commentaries, not a little offended by the
unpolished and barbarous style of those whom I nevertheless saw could not
altogether be disregarded because of the subject matter, it occurred to me   80
by chance that I might institute a new kind of imitation. Since the prolixity of the interpreters provoked my disgust, and observing the marvellous
brevity and simple elegance of Latin in the jurisconsults from whose books
the *Pandects* were put together,[8] as well as in the constitutions of the ancient
emperors, contemporaries of the jurisconsults, who adapted their style in the   85
formulation of laws, I decided to transfer into my daily commentaries the
style I heard in the schools or read in Bartolo especially,[9] the Coryphaeus of

* * * * *

6 The reference is to Lorenzo Valla's *Elegantiae linguae Latinae* (1441), the hugely
   influential manual of correct classical Latin.
7 Viglius in fact writes excellent Latin, with clear similarities to the style of Cicero.
8 The *Pandects*, also known as the *Digest*, is the compendium of Roman law
   compiled by order of Emperor Justinian I in the sixth century. It is one part of
   the *Corpus iuris civilis* issued under Justinian. Another was the *Institutes*; see
   n11 below.
9 Ep 2604 n8

our interpreters.[10] I was further motivated to pursue this practice because I
perceived that the jurisconsults had done the same thing, because there was
such uniformity in their responses that they seemed to have been formed in   90
the same school, or that, if the names of the authors were removed, all the
Pandects could be thought to have been written by the same person. This
graceful brevity of style, and though not excessive, nonetheless full, clear,
proper, and pure, seemed perfectly suited to the interpretation of laws. All
that is required in it is to demonstrate by reason or some authority of the   95
law what is just, fair, and good, and what is the opposite. I made use of this
method for a considerable time, so that even when I was giving private les-
sons on Justinian's *Institutes*,[11] I attempted for the sake of practice to express
more briefly and clearly the annotations made by various interpreters, and to
alter them to conform to the style of the jurisconsults.   100

This work certainly profited me, because in the daily commentary I both
emended and rectified the style to some degree. Thus, most learned Erasmus,
you can observe how I did not affect Ciceronian style, and whence came this
stylistic ability, whatever its worth. I abandoned that first effort at imitation
some time ago, when I saw that I was wasting so much time that I could more   105
properly devote to reading the interpreters, whose number is almost infinite,
and also when I recognized that a jurisconsult must use the language of the
courts that long ago banished the pure style of the ancient writers. Yet I do not
regret my work, since I gained much profit from it, to the extent that, whatever progress I made, I seemed to you a candidate for Ciceronian eloquence   110
– unless you were entirely joking with me. But I prefer to interpret what you
write in this way, and in the meantime enjoy the benefit of your opinion.

Listen now, I pray you, to the reasons for the controversies in which I
am engaged here with the aforesaid Ciceronians. When I arrived in Padua, I
frequented at the beginning certain compatriots of mine, as custom demand-   115
ed, and I was introduced through them to some Italians of this sect; I heard
Lazzaro lecture and paid my respects to him.[12] He was teaching Cicero's *De
oratore*, which did not attract me very much. There was something else that

* * * * *

10 The *coryphaeus* was the leader of the chorus in attic drama, hence the use of the
    word to describe the leader of any company or movement.
11 Whereas the *Pandects* (n8 above) were intended for use by advanced law stu-
    dents, the *Institutes*, also part of the *Corpus iuris civilis* of Justinian, was a text-
    book for beginners.
12 Lazzaro Bonamico (Ep 2568 n6)

drew me away from hearing him, namely that a jurisconsult of great renown
was lecturing shortly before him, and since the other lecture was of no great   120
interest to me, and I did not relish the discussions that customarily took place
after the lecture, in which permission is given to the hearers to argue against
the opinions of the master in the circle of students. When I left Lazzaro's lecture they immediately resented it, as if I despised a man endowed with such
outstanding learning and Ciceronian eloquence.   125

I immediately heard the reproach that they consider to be terrible, that
I was not a Ciceronian and therefore was an Erasmian. I had a good laugh at
that, and indeed I gloried in it and answered that not only was I an Erasmian
but would always be one. After this initial encounter, they praised Lazzaro
to me on any occasion whatever, extolled Bembo,[13] whose praises I did not   130
wish to question, then denigrated Erasmus, had no use for learned men across
the Alps, and denied them all judgment, learning, and humanity.[14] I could not
swallow this, and I did not lack arguments for refuting their cavils. But it was a
certain odious captiousness that enflamed the contention. If by chance a word
was uttered that they did not remember having found in Cicero, they became   135
agitated, as if some heinous crime had been committed. In fact one of them
boasted that he had thrown a stool at Haio of Friesland's head because he
defended too vigorously a word that was not Ciceronian.[15] Who would tolerate that everyday speech, which should be relaxed and free, be constrained by
such superstition? It is too puerile and pedantic in the middle of a conversation   140
on other subjects to burst out in vituperation over a single little word.

So when I perceived their obstinacy and saw that I had either to break
off the familiarity that I had established with them or adopt their views, I
asked that they allow me to play the soloist and they be the comic actors. I
said that my profession conflicted with their studied eloquence and I asked   145
that they allow me to be what I am, that is, that they consider me as a jurisconsult of the school of Bartolo, since I had never aspired after a place among
the disciples of Crassus or Scaevola.[16] They seemed to be satisfied with this

* * * * *

13 Ep 2594 n15
14 Erasmus and Bonamico did not themselves feel the animosity towards one
    another that animated some of their followers.
15 For Haio Herman of Friesland, see Ep 2568 n7.
16 Lucius Licinius Crassus (140 BC–91 BC) was considered the greatest orator of
    his day. He is the chief speaker in Cicero's De oratore. Quintus Mucius Scaevola
    Pontifex (d 82 BC) was the leading lawyer and orator of the later Roman republic.

response, for now they allow me to speak even in the vernacular whereas previously they would not even allow me to speak in Latin unless it was   150 Ciceronian. They think it absurd that anyone who professes to teach good letters should depart even a hair's breadth from the best author.

You see what my relations are with them; now I shall briefly explain what triumphs they are preparing. When I set out for Venice in the festive days that precede Lent, I had the impression that the Ciceronians were   155 whispering something about a certain Giulio Camillo.[17] A friend revealed this mystery to me later: Camillo had written an *Apology* against your *Ciceronianus*, which most people told me they had read. But I have not yet been able, though I tried hard, to obtain this famous book, in which the initiates secretly delight.[18] They say also that this same man has constructed an   160 amphitheatre, a work of admirable ingenuity. Anyone who is admitted to see it will be able to speak on any subject no less eloquently than Cicero himself. At first I thought it was a fable until, after a conversation with Giambattista Egnazio,[19] I understood the whole thing more clearly. They say that this architect has reduced into certain topics whatever Cicero has said on any sub-   165 ject. He has also searched out all the words he used and how many times, and in what sense. Then he has arranged certain patterns and gradations of figures of style and has annotated with astonishing industry and a certain divine subtlety many other things never before noticed in Cicero. They say that he has transcribed all these things onto pieces of paper that can be folded   170 and unfolded, which when they are hung on the walls of the amphitheatre

* * * * *

17 Giulio Camillo Delminio of Friuli (c 1480–1544), an extreme Ciceronian whom Erasmus had met and heard preach during his visit to Italy in 1506–9, and who is mentioned briefly in the *Ciceronianus* (CWE 28 384–5)

18 Published in incomplete form only after Camillo's death, in a volume entitled *Due trattati* (Venice: Farri 1544), his *Trattato della imitatione* was in fact a polite criticism of Erasmus' *Ciceronianus*. Meanwhile, Erasmus jumped to the conclusion that the work was in fact Scaliger's *Oratio*, the authorship of which he attributed to Aleandro (Ep 2565 n12); see Allen Ep 2682:21–48. Even after he had been informed by Viglius that Camillo had written the work as a gift for the king of France and did not intend to publish it, Erasmus continued to suspect that Camillo had contributed to the *Oratio*; see Allen Ep 2736:1–5.

19 For Egnazio see Ep 2568:7–10.

can immediately supply the information one is seeking.[20] What more can I say? He and your Nosoponus are in total agreement.[21]

Camillo has given the opportunity of examining his amazing invention to anyone at random. He destines it for the king of France, to whom he 175 recently gave a foretaste in France, naming it for him and receiving five hundred gold ducats in payment. So the prodigious Daedalus is totally taken up with his apparatus.[22] I have heard that he will come here; he is not in Venice. If that happens I will observe the man very carefully to see whether the contemplation of that theatre will be able to reconcile me with the Ciceronians. 180 If I am inspired by some divinity, and if I discern something that I think you should know, I will be most happy to write to you, as long as you grant me pardon for writing you so much nonsense. What Pietro Bembo's opinion of this sort of thing is, I cannot determine. He is worshipped more than anyone

* * * * *

20 Camillo's mysterious project of a 'theatre of memory' has been described as follows: '[The] wooden memory palace was shaped like a Roman amphitheater, but instead of the spectator sitting in the seats looking down on the stage, he stood in the center and looked up at a round, seven-tiered edifice. All around the theater were paintings of Kabbalistic and mythological figures as well as endless rows of drawers and boxes filled with cards, on which were printed everything that was known, and – it was claimed – everything that was knowable, including quotations from all the great authors, categorized according to subject. All you had to do was meditate on an emblematic image and the entirety of knowledge stored in that section of the theater would be called immediately to mind, allowing you to "be able to discourse on any subject no less fluently than Cicero." Camillo promised that "by means of the doctrine of loci and images, we can hold in the mind and master all human concepts and all the things that are in the entire world"'; Joshua Foer *Moonwalking with Einstein: The Art and Science of Remembering Everything* (New York 2011) 149–50. For a full account of Camillo and his theatre, see Frances Yates *The Art of Memory* (Chicago 1966) chapters 6 and 7. The project elicited the interest, at least for a time, of Francis I of France, who invested in it (see lines 175–7 below); and others too thought well of it. But it is easy to understand why Viglius, who subsequently saw the model of the theatre at Venice, and Erasmus, to whom Viglius reported his impressions, regarded the entire business as quackery; see Allen Epp 2657:30–60, 2682:19–21.
21 Nosoponus, one of the interlocutors in the *Ciceronianus*, represented Italian Ciceronianism at its most uncompromising. Some Italians supposed him to be a caricature of Bembo, others of Longueil (n23 below).
22 The sculptor Daedalus was so renowned for statues that seemed to live and move that 'works of Daedalus' came to mean 'creations of any novel technical skill which compels our admiration' (*Adagia* II iii 62).

else by all the Ciceronians, and it was he who encouraged Longueil in that   185
strange emulation,[23] as he stated openly in a letter to Gianfrancesco Pico.[24]
   Farewell.
   Padua, 28 March 1532

2633 / From Gerard Morrhy   Paris, 30 March 1532

   This letter, minus lines 1–15, was first published in LB III / 2 1751C-1752D
   Appendix epistolarum no 366. The autograph, address-sheet missing, is in the
   Rehdiger Collection of the University Library at Wrocław (MS Rehd 254 111).
   For Gerard Morrhy of Kampen, at this time still a book publisher in Paris, see
   Ep 2311. As Allen observes, the hesitant tone of the opening paragraph indi-
   cates that Morrhy had perhaps not received an answer to Ep 2311.

Greetings. I had decided on my own never to write to you again, most learned
friend, because I was always afraid that I might be a hindrance to your truly
pious occupations in the republic of letters. But I was driven to it in part by
our common native land, in part by the stimulus of a grateful spirit, and finally by the instigation of Jacobus Omphalius, a most loyal man,[1] with whom   5
every time I go for a walk to relax my mind, good God! with what words
he extols the sincere and benevolent sentiments of Erasmus towards lovers
of literature. You see, dearest Erasmus, what motivated me to cast off my
feeling of shame, taking no account of your dignity and learning. Together
with myriads of scholars, I feel grateful to you for your more than Herculean   10
labours expended with such great readiness in enhancing and promoting
literature, and I am ready on every occasion to be vigilant lest I seem to be

* * * * *

23 For Christophe de Longueil, the immediate target of Erasmus' *Ciceronianus*,
   and his connection with Bembo, see Epp 1948 introduction and 2059 n7.
24 There is no mention of Christophe de Longueil (Ep 1948 introduction) in
   Bembo's letter of 1 January 1513 to Gianfrancesco Pico della Mirandola; see *Le
   epistole 'De imitatione' di Gianfrancesco Pico della Mirandola e di Pietro Bembo* ed
   Giorgio Santangelo (Florence 1954) 39–61. As a skilled Ciceronian, however,
   Longueil enjoyed the favour of Jacopo Sadoleto and Pietro Bembo, with both of
   whom he had an extensive correspondence that was published in 1524 (see Ep
   2059 n7). Viglius may be mistakenly attributing something he had read in that
   correspondence to the letter of Bembo to Pico.

2633
1 See Ep 2311 n14.

the bad or, to speak more truthfully, the ungrateful student of a good teacher;
if you wish to make trial of it, place a burden upon my shoulders that I can
support and you will find that what I say is true.   15

You have in the Collège de Sorbonne friends who wish you well with
all their heart, but they are forced to whisper their feelings rather than express them; that is the extent of the tyranny of certain men. It is now the
third year that I have frequent contact with the theologians, seeing that I
live in their quarters. Those who are your supporters rejoice greatly that you   20
responded with such moderation to the *Determinationes* printed by Bade,[2]
for they were afraid that you would brand the whole faculty with a mark
of infamy in the eyes of posterity, which you could have done with every
right. I would write at greater length on this subject but you would judge me
indiscreet, I know, if I were to confide to a letter what could weigh heavily   25
on both me and them.

I have often been distressed at seeing that you are so often distracted
from serious studies by the calumnies of sycophants. The poets exalt the constant diligence of Hercules and Theseus in taming so few monsters, but what
would they have said of you, who subdue at the same time so many monsters   30
advancing on you from every side to destroy you, while we read that they
never took on two at a time?[3] But 'God will put an end to these trials also.'[4]

That you decided not to give any answer to the calumnies of Scaliger
(whom Jacques Colin, abbot of St Ambroise and *lecteur* of the king, is accustomed to calling Sacrilege, using the figure of metathesis) has received the   35
approval of all good men, and they applaud you heartily, as I have ascertained.[5] Whoever he was, he is nothing but a fool and ridiculous exaggerator
of old women's delusions. There are some here who find the author lacking
even in common sense.

I believe you heard about the comedy publicly performed here recently,   40
the subject of which was: the University of Paris is founded on a monster.

* * * * *

2 See Ep 2552 n10.
3 See *Adagia* I v 39: 'Not even Hercules can take on two.'
4 Virgil *Aeneid* 1.199
5 For Scaliger and his *Oratio* see Ep 2564. Jacques Colin of Auxerre (d 1547) enjoyed the patronage of Francis I, whom he served (1523–36) as *valet du chambre*,
diplomat, *lecteur*, and grand almoner, receiving as his reward a number of ecclesiastical preferments, including the abbacy of St Ambroise, Bourges. He was
also principal of the Collège des Bons-Enfants, a correspondent of Guillaume
Budé, and the translator of (among other things) portions of Homer into French.

Noel Béda,[6] thinking that this was directed at him, has made preparations
for a convocation of the whole University in the house of the Mathurins,[7] so
that the faculty may decide what penalty to inflict on the author. The affair
has been brought to the inquisitors of the faith, but so far nothing more has 45
been done.

Our friend Omphalius must be warned not to provoke the anger of the
theologians against him by this kind of wit,[8] for once they are irritated he will
barely be able to appease them with great effort, as I nearly learned several
years ago to my own misfortune, when it was forbidden that your *Colloquies* 50
be taught to young boys in the schools.[9] For when the question came to a vote
in our German nation, I was of the opinion that they should be taught until
the theologians fashioned better ones, and the great majority of those who
voted in the German nation agreed with my opinion, although some candi-
dates in theology complained because they feared, I think, that they would 55
have the last place in the order of promotion, as they call it. Wrongs of this
sort are customarily avenged at that time.

Farewell, dear Erasmus, and make use of me, if you wish, as your most
devoted servant in all things.

Paris, from the Sorbonne quarter, 30 March 1532 60

Master Gerard Suckeraet, canon of Utrecht and doctor of medicine, a
man assuredly most devoted to you, sends sincere greetings.[10]

Gerard Morrhy of Kampen, your servant in all things

2634 / From Bernhard von Cles   Regensburg, [c 30] March 1532

This is Cles' answer to Ep 2623. For the manuscript, an autograph rough draft,
see Ep 2515 introduction. This letter is in the same packet as Ep 2622.

* * * * *

6 Ep 2486 n11
7 Ie in the monastery of the Mathurins, also known as the Trinitarians. Allen incorrectly read this passage as a reference to Maturin Cordier (d 1564), who had
   studied theology and taught rhetoric at Paris, but by 1528 had embarked on a
   career as a teacher in various other locations in France.
8 This seems to indicate that Omphalius was the author of the comedy in question.
9 See Epp 2033 n15, 2037 introduction.
10 Gerard Suckeraet of Deventer (d 1533), licensed in canon law (but, apparently,
   not medicine, as indicated here), was canon and vicar-general of the Utrecht
   chapter. There is no other evidence of any contact between him and Erasmus.

TO ERASMUS

I have heard with pleasure that my letters have always been welcome to you, although that should be attributed more to your kindness than to anything in them that could deservedly please you. The only consolation that remains to me is that although my letters are such that they cannot bring you any 5 pleasure, at least they are of a kind that do not weary you.

I have read and reread the prayer that you composed, and I think it is very appropriate for the present time; and please God that we can find many of this conviction, who would only do or wish what is fitting for us and the house of God. 10

You have interpreted the enigma of the lion and the dragon correctly, and according to my way of thinking.[1]

As to your imploring me to be mindful of what you told me some time ago, I do not wish to conceal from you that before the reception of your letter, in the presence of his royal Majesty,[2] when the conversation turned to your 15 person, as often happens, his Majesty expressed such a good opinion of you that you would not have been able to obtain any greater testimony of his benevolent feelings towards you. And if you let me know your intentions more specifically, I will leave nothing undone at the court of their Majesties and among all others to oblige you in any way I can; for which functions you 20 will find me always at your disposal.

Given at Regensburg, March 1532

* * * * *

2634
1 Cf Ep 2623:12–14.
2 King Ferdinand

JOHANNES DANTISCUS TO ERASMUS

Johannes Dantiscus to Erasmus   [Brussels, end of October 1531]

This is the previously unpublished Latin text of the letter to Erasmus, unknown to Allen, that appears in this volume as Ep 2563A. The manuscript, a copy in a secretary's hand, undated and signed only 'J,' is in the Czartoryski Museum at Cracow (DE 230: CCM 1615, 13015). On the attribution of the letter to Dantiscus and the assignment of the approximate date, see the introduction to Ep 2563A. The transcription and notes are by Charles Fantazzi.

Salutem plurimam. Tametsi nullam unquam operam libentius aut maiori cum voluptate impendam quam legendis tuis literis aut scribendis ad te meis, ad eas tamen quas xvi Cal. Augusti ad me dedisti propterea distuli respondere quo Caesaris literas ad senatum et clerum Bisontinum (quas petieras) meis adiungerem, ne ulla ex parte meus erga te animus vel negligentiae nomine 5 tibi suspectus esse videretur. Nunc demum et rescribo et literas Caesaris mitto quibus pro temporis ac rerum necessitate utaris, eas tibi Caesar facile et praeter multorum spem atque opinionem concessit. Nam vix credas, mi Erasme, quam hic quoque sint perversa hominum iudicia, quam prava et ad malum semper procliviora ingenia, quam inscitiae plena omnia, quam pro 10 ludo habeant linguis veneno tinctis in hominum quantumvis benemeritorum famam invehi omnesque bonarum literarum amatores haereticos aut saltem haereticorum fautores proclamare. Te autem tanquam huius Germaniae dissidii autorem, Deum immortalem, quibus non telis confodiunt, idque non in domorum saeptis tantum sed in frequentissimis hominum coetibus, neque 15 apud sui similes blatterones, sed ipso nonnunquam Caesare praesente. Ad haec omnia vincit singularis Caesaris in te benevolentia quam in ipso literarum exemplo facile perspicies, si ex Gallico in Latinum sermonem verti curabis. Nolui enim eas Latine sed Gallice, hoc est peculiari Caesaris idiomate, scriptas, ne quae iudicio tibi in his Caesar tribuit, meo erga te affec- 20 tui tribuantur, et quae ille de tuis virtutibus honorificentissime praedicat, a me (quod et amem) composita esse videantur. Quo fit ut eas ipsas Caesaris literas quasi simbolum constantissimae eius erga te voluntatis et de virtute atque eruditione tua iudicii servare debeas. Haec ideo a me dicta sunto, non quod meum studium tibi probem (scio tibi satis exploratum esse hunc homi- 25 nem totum, quantus est, tuum esse), sed quo Caesaris in te favorem diu tibi quam multis argumentis perspectum magis atque magis agnoscas.

Ad tuas literas venio, in quibus domum te Friburgi emisse et in his caminum Italicum extruere et nidum hybernum apparare scribis. Quid ego audio? Erasmus philosophus et prope septuagenarius emit domum? Atqui 30 dolio contentus erat Diogenes et fortassis plus molestiarum tu cum tua domo hauries quam ille cum suo dolio passus fuerit. Sed existimo te caminum tibi

extruxisse, domum autem haeredibus emisse. Sed quibus, obsecro, haeredibus, aut qui fieri potuit ut una domus inter tot haeredes dividatur? Ego
Erasmi haeredes voco non qui tibi sanguine coniunctiores sint, sed quos ipse   35
Christo genuisti, quos virtutibus ornasti et ditasti; nunc tu vide an tuae aedes
tot haeredibus suffecturae sint. Sed extra iocum, quis genius tibi persuasit
ut domum emeres, et in Germania, dissidiorum plena; nonne vides in quae
tempora inciderimus? Non venit in mentem quantum malorum emolumenta
omnia nobis portendunt? Quid minentur duae cometae? Quid Iris in caelo   40
hora secunda post occasum et xliii [...]¹ post plenilunium visa? Auditae vo-
ces lugubres in Vaticano. Tres soles Troiae Apulae civitate. Tres lunae Leodii,
sanguinis fontes, panis pluvia, gemelli qui simul ac nati sunt, alter dixisse
fertur 'Ubinam tantum tritici reponemus?'Alter: 'At ubi condemus tot ca-
davera?' Tria diademata ignea super Hierosolymam per totos novem dies   45
visa quae magno impetu irruerunt et eam templi partem quae ad orientem
spectat diruerunt. Quod si de aliis portentis libeat scribere quae passim con-
spiciuntur et quae a nobis (ne crabrones irritemus) omittuntur. Cui non ea
maximum terrorem incuterent et tum cui duodecima iam diei hora adest,
ut apud Plutarchum Deiotaro regi Crassum dixisse legi? Emis domum et in   50
Germania? An non et hoc portento simile est? Illud quoque haud multum
dissimile quod Academia Parisiensis scribit in Erasmum? An non et hoc omnium maximum portentum est, eam Academiam ad quam omnes tanquam
ad Apollinis oraculum confugiebant, stultum adeo specimen de se dedisse?
Mihi crede, ut ingenue fatear, Academiae Parisiensis adversus Erasmum   55
censura prima fronte maximum terrorem movit, non quod vererer ne quid
parum Christianum in libris tuis deprehendisset, sed quod dolerem monachos celeberrimae Academiae auctoritate triumphum adornaturos, at ubi
rem introspexi, vix (ita me Deus amet) a risu temperare potui cum viderem
viros tantos tantum inscitiae, tantum naeniarum, calumniarum et sycophan-   60
tiarum collegisse, ut dum te haereticum efficere conantur, suam ipsorum
prodant malitiam atque ignorantiam, tuamque doctrinam eruditis omnibus
ac bonis magis commendent! Memini me tibi multoties suasisse ut eos qui
in te scribunt suo morbo relinqueres et tua responsione indignos iudicares;
nunc autem cum Rabinis istis Parisiensibus aliter tibi agendum censeo, ut   65
videlicet rem prius mature consideres et si quae non intempestive annotata
deprendes, pro officio illis gratiam habeas eaque in lucubrationibus tuis ipse
corrigas, licet tibi ea correctione non admodum opus esse videatur. Nullum

* * * * *

1   A word or phrase is evidently missing here.

est enim telum quo acrius et ad internicionem[2] usque eos confodias, quam si
in aliquibus etiam leviusculis illi concedas, ne te pertinaciae nomine accusare   70
possint. Quod ubi feceris, commodum licebit tibi in caeteris omnibus eos
tuo more tractare, omittere posthac Stunicas, Leos, Bedas, Quercus, Sutores,
Egmondas, Caravajallos, et si quae sunt alia huiusmodi animantium genera
quae in te nunquam non debacchantur, et cum Rabinis istis conflictari, homi-
nes ita uti meriti sunt tractare et ostendere quis sit Erasmus, quem artificem   75
provocaverint, ad quem lapidem impegerint, et quod alias saepe praestitisti
in rebus multo levioribus, nunc qui vir sies[3] declarare. Illustrabunt (mihi
crede) tuam dignitatem horum protervitas et iniuriae, sed ne ego impudens
sim[4] qui haec ad te scribam, qui ea longe melius et consultius aut praestitisti
aut praestaturus es quam ego excogitare, nedum scripto monere sciam.   80

Sed tu audaciam meam boni consules, vellem mihi nuntiares quo pacto
res tuae se habeant post ortum inter Helvetios tumultum an apud vos tran-
quilla sient[5] omnia. Vereor enim ne tibi alio immigrandum sit etiam, hyberno
nido derelicto. Sperabamus Caesarem Imperii comitia Spirae habiturum et te
ad nos aut nos ad te venturos, ut quae amicitia per literas inita est mutuo col-   85
loquio datisque dextris firmaretur. Sed, ut vides, ea nobis negata est occasio:
indictus est enim Conventus Ratisbonae, quod si tibi molestum non est, fac te
videamus Spirae. Equidem quod ad me attinet, mallem Friburgum ad te veni-
re quam ut tu nostra causa tantum laboris et incommodi susciperes. Attamen
haud scio an per publica negocia id mihi praestare fas erit. Sunt praeterea   90
quam multi ex nostris videndi tui percupidi. Patriarcha Indiarum bonorum
omnium fautor, summus praeceptor equestris ordinis Calatraveri magnae
probitatis et apud Caesarem auctoritatis, tum Archidiaconus Toletanus, iuvenis tui studiosus, ingeniique et eruditionis longe quam pro aetate maioris, in
quem hinc Fortuna, inde Gratiae omnes sua munera abundantissime contu-   95
lerunt. Expectamus praeterea Archiepiscopum Toletanum, cuius in te animus
tibi notior est quam ut meo testimonio sit opus. Sunt et multi alii nobiles qui
inviti e Germania te insalutato discederent. Tu si nos Spirae conveneris rem
nobis gratam et tibi neque inutilem neque iniucundam feceris quod ut (citra
tamen valetudinis tuae dispendium) facias, te etiam atque etiam rogo. Vale. J.   100

* * * * *

2 *internitionem* in the manuscript
3 Archaic form of *sis*
4 *sum* in the manuscript
5 Archaic form of *sint*

TABLE OF CORRESPONDENTS

WORKS FREQUENTLY CITED

SHORT-TITLE FORMS
FOR ERASMUS' WORKS

INDEX

TABLE OF CORRESPONDENTS

WORKS FREQUENTLY CITED

AGBR   *Aktensammlung zur Geschichte der Basler Reformation in den Jahren 1519 bis Anfang 1534* ed Emil Dürr and Paul Roth, 6 vols (Basel 1921–50)

Agrippae Opera   *Agrippae ab Nettesheim … Opera …* (Lyon: Beringer Brothers [c 1580–1600]) 2 vols

AK   *Die Amerbach Korrespondenz* ed Alfred Hartmann and B.R. Jenny (Basel 1942–   )

Allen   *Opus epistolarum Des. Erasmi Roterodami* ed P.S. Allen, H.M. Allen, and H.W. Garrod (Oxford 1906–58) 11 vols and index

ASD   *Opera omnia Desiderii Erasmi Roterodami* (Amsterdam 1969–   )

BAO   *Briefe und Akten zum Leben Oekolampads* ed Ernst Staehelin, Quellen und Forschungen zur Reformationsgeschichte 10 and 19 (Leipzig 1927–34; repr New York / London 1971) 2 vols

BOL I   C. Augustijn, P. Fraenkel, and M. Lienhard *Martini Buceri Opera Latina* I Studies in Medieval and Reformation Thought 30 (Leiden 1982)

Bataillon   Marcel Bataillon *Érasme et l'Espagne: Nouvelle édition en trois volumes* ed Daniel Devoto and Charles Amiel (Geneva 1991)

BRE   *Briefwechsel des Beatus Rhenanus* ed Adalbert Horawitz and Karl Hartfelder (Leipzig 1886; repr Hildesheim 1966)

Burckhardt   Theophilus Burckhardt-Biedermann *Bonifacius Amerbach und die Reformation* (Basel 1894)

CEBR   *Contemporaries of Erasmus: A Biographical Register of the Renaissance and Reformation* ed Peter G. Bietenholz and Thomas B. Deutscher (Toronto 1985–7) 3 vols

CWE   *Collected Works of Erasmus* (Toronto 1974–   )

Enthoven   *Briefe an Desiderius Erasmus von Rotterdam* ed L.K. Enthoven (Strasbourg 1906)

Epistolae familiares   *Des. Erasmi Roterodami Ad Bonif. Amerbachium: cum nonnullis aliis ad Erasmum spectantibus* (Basel 1779)

Epistolae floridae   *Des. Erasmi Roterodami epistolarum floridarum liber unus antehac nunquam excusus* (Basel: J. Herwagen, September 1531)

Epistolae palaeonaeoi	*Desiderii Erasmi Roterodami Epistolae palaeonaeoi* (Freiburg: J. Emmeus, September 1532)
Förstemann / Günther	*Briefe an Desiderius Erasmus von Rotterdam* ed. J. Förstemann and O. Günther xxvii. Beiheft zum *Zentralblatt für Bibliothekwesen* (Leipzig 1904)
Gerlo	*La correspondance d'Érasme traduite et annotée d'après l'Opus epistolarum de P.S. Allen, H.M. Allen, and H.W. Garrod* ed and trans Aloïs Gerlo and Paul Foriers (Brussels 1967–84) 12 vols
Horawitz	Horawitz *Erasmiana* ed Adalbert Horawitz, Sitzungsberichte der phil.-hist Classe der kaiserlichen Akademie der Wissenschaften (Vienna 1878, 1880, 1883, 1885) 4 vols
Ipolyi	*Oláh Miklós Levelezése* ed Arnold Ipolyi, Monumenta Hungariae historica: Diplomataria xxv (Budapest 1875)
Knecht	R.J. Knecht, *Francis I* (Cambridge 1982)
Lasciana	Dalton, Hermann *Lasciana [Denkschriften und Briefe], nebst den ältesten evangelischen Synodalprotokollen Polens, 1555–1561* (Berlin 1898; repr Nieuwkoop 1973)
LB	*Desiderii Erasmi opera omnia* ed J. Leclerc (Leiden 1703–6; repr 1961–2) 10 vols
LP	*Letters and Papers, Foreign and Domestic, of the Reign of Henry VIII* ed J.S. Brewer, J. Gardiner, and R.H. Brodie (London 1862–1932) 36 vols
Major	Emil Major *Erasmus von Rotterdam* no 1 in the series *Virorum illustrium reliquiae* (Basel 1927)
Marichal	*Catalogue des actes de François Ier* ed Paul Marichal (Paris: Imprimerie Nationale 1887–1908) 10 vols
MBB	Martin Bucer *Briefwechsel / Correspondance* ed Berndt Hamm et al (Leiden 1979–) 8 vols to date. Because line numbers are not continuous, citations include page numbers where such precision is required.
MBW	*Melanchthons Briefwechsel, kritische und kommentierte Gesamtausgabe* ed Heinz Scheible et al (Stuttgart-Bad Canstatt 1977–) 27 vols to date. The edition is published in two series: *Regesten* (vols 1–12 in print); and *Texte* (vols T1–T15 in print). The letter numbers are the same in both series. In both series, the letters have identical sub-sections marked by numbers in brackets.

Miaskowski	Casimir von Miaskowski 'Erasmiana. Beiträge zur Korrespondenz des Erasmus von Rotterdam mit Polen. Teil II' *Jahrbuch für Philosophie und spekulative Theologie* xv (1901) 195–226, 307–60
Opuscula	*Erasmi opuscula: A Supplement to the Opera Omnia* ed Wallace K. Ferguson (The Hague 1933)
Opus epistolarum	*Opus epistolarum Des. Erasmi Roterodami per autorem diligenter recognitum et adjectis innumeris novis fere ad trientem auctum* (Basel: Froben, Herwagen, and Episcopius 1529)
Pastor	Ludwig von Pastor *The History of the Popes from the Close of the Middle Ages* ed and trans R.F. Kerr et al, 6th ed (London 1938–53) 40 vols
PG	*Patrologiae cursus completes … series Graeca* ed J.-P. Migne (Paris 1857–66; repr Turnhout) 161 vols. Indexes F. Cavallera (Paris 1912); T. Hopfner (Paris 1928–36) 2 vols
PL	*Patrologiae cursus completus … series Latina* ed J.-P. Migne, 1st ed (Paris 1844–55, 1862–5; repr Turnhout) 217 vols plus 4 vols indexes. In the notes, references to volumes of PL in which column numbers in the first edition are different from those in later editions or reprints include the date of the edition cited.
Potter	G.R. Potter *Zwingli* (Cambridge 1976)
Roth	Paul Roth *Durchbruch und Festsetzung der Reformation in Basel* (Basel 1942)
Sieber	Ludwig Sieber *Das Mobiliar des Erasmus: Verzeichnis vom 10. April 1534* (Basel 1891)
Staehelin	Ernst Staehelin *Das Theologische Lebenswerk Johannes Oekolampads* (Leipzig 1939; repr New York 1971)
Stuttgart *Vulgata*	*Biblia Sacra iuxta Vulgatam versionem* ed Robert Weber et al, 3rd edition (Stuttgart 1983)
Vita Erasmi	Paul Merula *Vita Desiderii Erasmi … Additi sunt Epistolarum ipsius Libri duo …* (Leiden 1607)
de Vocht CTL	Henry de Vocht *History of the Foundation and the Rise of the Collegium Trilingue Lovaniense, 1517–1530* (Louvain 1951–5) 4 vols

VZE

Viglii ab Aytta Zuichemi Epistolae selectae = vol 2/1 of C.P. Hoynck van Papendrecht *Analecta Belgica* (The Hague 1743) 3 vols in 6

WA

D. Martin Luthers Werke, Kritische Gesamtausgabe (Weimar 1883–1980) 60 vols

Wierzbowski

Teodor Wierzbowski, *Materyały do dziejów piśmiennictwa polskiego i biografii pisarzów polskich* (Warsaw 1900) 2 vols

Titles following colons are longer versions of the same, or are alternative titles. Items entirely enclosed in square brackets are of doubtful authorship. For abbreviations, see Works Frequently Cited.

Acta: Academiae Lovaniensis contra Lutherum *Opuscula* / CWE 71

Adagia: Adagiorum chiliades 1508, etc (Adagiorum collectanea for the primitive form, when required) LB II / ASD II-1–9 / CWE 30–6

Admonitio adversus mendacium: Admonitio adversus mendacium et obtrectationem LB X / CWE 78

Annotationes in Novum Testamentum LB VI / ASD VI-5–10 / CWE 51–60

Antibarbari LB X / ASD I-1 / CWE 23

Apologia ad annotationes Stunicae: Apologia respondens ad ea quae Iacobus Lopis Stunica taxaverat in prima duntaxat Novi Testamenti aeditione LB IX / ASD IX-2

Apologia ad Caranzam: Apologia ad Sanctium Caranzam, or Apologia de tribus locis, or Responsio ad annotationem Stunicae … a Sanctio Caranza defensam LB IX / ASD IX-8

Apologia ad Fabrum: Apologia ad Iacobum Fabrum Stapulensem LB IX / ASD IX-3 / CWE 83

Apologia ad prodromon Stunicae LB IX / ASD IX-8

Apologia ad Stunicae conclusiones LB IX / ASD IX-8

Apologia adversus monachos: apologia adversus monachos quosdam Hispanos LB IX

Apologia adversus Petrum Sutorem: Apologia adversus debacchationes Petri Sutoris LB IX

Apologia adversus rhapsodias Alberti Pii: Apologia ad viginti et quattuor libros A. Pii LB IX / ASD IX-6 / CWE 84

Apologia adversus Stunicae Blasphemiae: Apologia adversus libellum Stunicae cui titulum fecit Blasphemiae et impietates Erasmi LB IX / ASD IX-8

Apologia contra Latomi dialogum: Apologia contra Iacobi Latomi dialogum de tribus linguis LB IX / CWE 71

Apologia de 'In principio erat sermo': Apologia palam refellens quorundam seditiosos clamores apud populum ac magnates quo in evangelio Ioannis verterit 'In principio erat sermo' (1520a); Apologia de 'In principio erat sermo' (1520b) LB IX / CWE 73

Apologia de laude matrimonii: Apologia pro declamatione de laude matrimonii LB IX / CWE 71

Apologia de loco 'Omnes quidem': Apologia de loco taxato in publica professione per Nicolaum Ecmondanum theologum et Carmelitanum Lovanii 'Omnes quidem resurgemus' LB IX / CWE 73

Apologia qua respondet invectivis Lei: Apologia qua respondet duabus invectivis Eduardi Lei *Opuscula* / ASD IX-4 / CWE 72

Apophthegmata LB IV / ASD IV-4 / CWE 37–8

Appendix de scriptis Clichtovei LB IX / CWE 83

Appendix respondens ad Sutorem: Appendix respondens ad quaedam Antapologiae Petri Sutoris LB IX

Argumenta: Argumenta in omnes epistolas apostolicas nova (with Paraphrases)
Axiomata pro causa Lutheri: Axiomata pro causa Martini Lutheri *Opuscula* /
   CWE 71

Brevissima scholia: In Elenchum Alberti Pii brevissima scholia per eundem
   Erasmum Roterodamum ASD IX-6 / CWE 84

Carmina LB I, IV, V, VIII / ASD I-7 / CWE 85–6
Catalogus lucubrationum LB I / CWE 9 (Ep 1341A)
Christiani hominis institutum, carmen LB V / ASD I-7 / CWE 85–6
Ciceronianus: Dialogus Ciceronianus LB I / ASD I-2 / CWE 28
Colloquia LB I / ASD I-3 / CWE 39–40
Compendium vitae Allen I / CWE 4
Conflictus: Conflictus Thaliae et Barbariei LB I / ASD I-8
[Consilium: Consilium cuiusdam ex animo cupientis esse consultum]
   Opuscula / CWE 71

De bello Turcico: Utilissima consultatio de bello Turcis inferendo, et obiter enarratus
   psalmus 28 LB V / ASD V-3 / CWE 64
De civilitate: De civilitate morum puerilium LB I / ASD I-8 / CWE 25
Declamatio de morte LB IV / ASD I-2 / CWE 25
Declamatiuncula LB IV / ASD IV-7
Declarationes ad censuras Lutetiae vulgatas: Declarationes ad censuras Lutetiae
   vulgatas sub nomine facultatis theologiae Parisiensis LB IX / ASD IX-7 / CWE 82
De concordia: De sarcienda ecclesiae concordia, or De amabili ecclesiae concordia
   [on Psalm 83] LB V / ASD V-3 / CWE 65
De conscribendis epistolis LB I / ASD I-2 / CWE 25
De constructione: De constructione octo partium orationis, or Syntaxis LB I / ASD I-4
De contemptu mundi: Epistola de contemptu mundi LB V / ASD V-1 / CWE 66
De copia: De duplici copia verborum ac rerum LB I / ASD I-6 / CWE 24
De delectu ciborum scholia ASD IX-1 / CWE 73
De esu carnium: Epistola apologetica ad Christophorum episcopum Basiliensem
   de interdicto esu carnium (published with scholia in a 1532 edition but not in
   the 1540 Opera) LB IX / ASD IX-1 / CWE 73
De immensa Dei misericordia: Concio de immensa Dei misericordia LB V / ASD V-7 /
   CWE 70
De libero arbitrio: De libero arbitrio diatribe LB IX / CWE 76
De philosophia evangelica LB VI
De praeparatione: De praeparatione ad mortem LB V / ASD V-1 / CWE 70
De pueris instituendis: De pueris statim ac liberaliter instituendis LB I / ASD I-2 / CWE 26
De puero Iesu: Concio de puero Iesu LB V / ASD V-7 / CWE 29
De puritate tabernaculi: Enarratio psalmi 14 qui est de puritate tabernaculi sive
   ecclesiae christianae LB V / ASD V-2 / CWE 65
De ratione studii LB I / ASD I-2 / CWE 24
De recta pronuntiatione: De recta latini graecique sermonis pronuntiatione LB I /
   ASD I-4 / CWE 26
De taedio Iesu: Disputatiuncula de taedio, pavore, tristicia Iesu LB V / ASD V-7 /
   CWE 70

Detectio praestigiarum: Detectio praestigiarum cuiusdam libelli Germanice scripti
LB X / ASD IX-1 / CWE 78
De vidua christiana LB V / ASD V-6 / CWE 66
De virtute amplectenda: Oratio de virtute amplectenda LB V / CWE 29
[Dialogus bilinguium ac trilinguium: Chonradi Nastadiensis dialogus bilinguium
ac trilinguium] *Opuscula* / CWE 7
Dilutio: Dilutio eorum quae Iodocus Clichtoveus scripsit adversus declamationem
suasoriam matrimonii *Dilutio eorum quae Iodocus Clichtoveus scripsit* ed Émile V.
Telle (Paris 1968) / CWE 83
Divinationes ad notata Bedae: Divinationes ad notata per Bedam de Paraphrasi
Erasmi in Matthaeum, et primo de duabus praemissis epistolis LB IX / ASD IX-5

Ecclesiastes: Ecclesiastes sive de ratione concionandi LB V / ASD V-4–5 / CWE 67–8
Elenchus in censuras Bedae: In N. Bedae censuras erroneas elenchus LB IX / ASD IX-5
Enchiridion: Enchiridion militis christiani LB V / ASD V-8 / CWE 66
Encomium matrimonii (in De conscribendis epistolis)
Encomium medicinae: Declamatio in laudem artis medicae LB I / ASD I-4 / CWE 29
Epistola ad Dorpium LB IX / CWE 3 (Ep 337) / CWE 71
Epistola ad fratres Inferioris Germaniae: Responsio ad fratres Germaniae Inferioris
ad epistolam apologeticam incerto autore proditam LB X / ASD IX-1 / CWE 78
Epistola ad gracculos: Epistola ad quosdam imprudentissimos gracculos LB X /
CWE 16 (Ep 2275)
Epistola apologetica adversus Stunicam LB IX / ASD IX-8 / CWE 15 (Ep 2172)
Epistola apologetica de Termino LB X / CWE 14 (Ep 2018)
Epistola consolatoria: Epistola consolatoria virginibus sacris, or Epistola
consolatoria in adversis LB V / ASD IV-7 / CWE 69
Epistola contra pseudevangelicos: Epistola contra quosdam qui se falso iactant
evangelicos LB X / ASD IX-1 / CWE 78
Euripidis Hecuba LB I / ASD I-1
Euripidis Iphigenia in Aulide LB I / ASD I-1
Exomologesis: Exomologesis sive modus confitendi LB V / ASD V-8 / CWE 67
Explanatio symboli: Explanatio symboli apostolorum sive catechismus LB V /
ASD V-1 / CWE 70
Ex Plutarcho versa LB IV / ASD IV-2

Formula: Conficiendarum epistolarum formula (see De conscribendis epistolis)

Hyperaspistes LB X / CWE 76–7

In Nucem Ovidii commentarius LB I / ASD I-1 / CWE 29
In Prudentium: Commentarius in duos hymnos Prudentii LB V / ASD V-7 / CWE 29
In psalmum 1: Enarratio primi psalmi, 'Beatus vir,' iuxta tropologiam potissimum
LB V / ASD V-2 / CWE 63
In psalmum 2: Commentarius in psalmum 2, 'Quare fremuerunt gentes?' LB V /
ASD V-2 / CWE 63
In psalmum 3: Paraphrasis in tertium psalmum, 'Domine quid multiplicate'
LB V / ASD V-2 / CWE 63
In psalmum 4: In psalmum quartum concio LB V / ASD V-2 / CWE 63

In psalmum 22: In psalmum 22 enarratio triplex LB V / ASD V-2 / CWE 64
In psalmum 33: Enarratio psalmi 33 LB V / ASD V-3 / CWE 64
In psalmum 38: Enarratio psalmi 38 LB V / ASD V-3 / CWE 65
In psalmum 85: Concionalis interpretatio, plena pietatis, in psalmum 85 LB V /
    ASD V-3 / CWE 64
Institutio christiani matrimonii LB V / ASD V-6 / CWE 69
Institutio principis christiani LB IV / ASD IV-1 / CWE 27

Julius exclusus: Dialogus Julius exclusus e coelis *Opuscula* / ASD I-8 / CWE 27

Lingua LB IV / ASD IV-1a / CWE 29
Liturgia Virginis Matris: Virginis Matris apud Lauretum cultae liturgia LB V /
    ASD V-1 / CWE 69
Loca quaedam emendata: Loca quaedam in aliquot Erasmi lucubrationibus per
    ipsum emendata LB IX
Luciani dialogi LB I / ASD I-1

Manifesta mendacia ASD IX-4 / CWE 71
Methodus (see Ratio)
Modus orandi Deum LB V / ASD V-1 / CWE 70
Moria: Moriae encomium LB IV / ASD IV-3 / CWE 27

Notatiunculae: Notatiunculae quaedam extemporales ad naenias Bedaicas,
    or Responsio ad notulas Bedaicas LB IX / ASD IX-5
Novum Testamentum: Novum Testamentum 1519 and later (Novum instrumentum
    for the first edition, 1516, when required) LB VI / ASD VI-2, 3, 4

Obsecratio ad Virginem Mariam: Obsecratio sive oratio ad Virginem Mariam in
    rebus adversis, or Obsecratio ad Virginem Matrem Mariam in rebus adversis
    LB V / CWE 69
Oratio de pace: Oratio de pace et discordia LB VIII / ASD IV-7
Oratio funebris: Oratio funebris in funere Bertae de Heyen LB VIII / ASD IV-7 / CWE 29

Paean Virgini Matri: Paean Virgini Matri dicendus LB V / CWE 69
Panegyricus: Panegyricus ad Philippum Austriae ducem LB IV / ASD IV-1 / CWE 27
Parabolae: Parabolae sive similia LB I / ASD I-5 / CWE 23
Paraclesis LB V, VI / ASD V-7
Paraphrasis in Elegantias Vallae: Paraphrasis in Elegantias Laurentii Vallae LB I /
    ASD I-4
Paraphrasis in Matthaeum, etc LB VII / ASD VII-6 / CWE 42–50
Peregrinatio apostolorum: Peregrinatio apostolorum Petri et Pauli LB VI, VII
Precatio ad Virginis filium Iesum LB V / CWE 69
Precatio dominica LB V / CWE 69
Precationes: Precationes aliquot novae LB V / CWE 69
Precatio pro pace ecclesiae: Precatio ad Dominum Iesum pro pace ecclesiae
    LB IV, V / CWE 69
Prologus supputationis: Prologus in supputationem calumniarum Natalis Bedae
    (1526), or Prologus supputationis errorum in censuris Bedae (1527) LB IX / ASD IX-5

Purgatio adversus epistolam Lutheri: Purgatio adversus epistolam non sobriam
  Lutheri LB X / ASD IX-1 / CWE 78

Querela pacis LB IV / ASD IV-2 / CWE 27

Ratio: Ratio seu Methodus compendio perveniendi ad veram theologiam (Methodus
  for the shorter version originally published in the Novum instrumentum of 1516)
  LB V, VI
Responsio ad annotationes Lei: Responsio ad annotationes Eduardi Lei LB IX /
  ASD IX-4 / CWE 72
Responsio ad Collationes: Responsio ad Collationes cuiusdam iuvenis
  gerontodidascali LB IX / CWE 73
Responsio ad disputationem de divortio: Responsio ad disputationem cuiusdam
  Phimostomi de divortio LB IX / ASD IX-4 / CWE 83
Responsio ad epistolam Alberti Pii: Responsio ad epistolam paraeneticam Alberti
  Pii, or Responsio ad exhortationem Pii LB IX / ASD IX-6 / CWE 84
Responsio ad notulas Bedaicas (see Notatiunculae)
Responsio ad Petri Cursii defensionem: Epistola de apologia Cursii LB X / Ep 3032
Responsio adversus febricitantis cuiusdam libellum LB X

Spongia: Spongia adversus aspergines Hutteni LB X / ASD IX-1 / CWE 78
Supputatio: Supputatio errorum in censuris Bedae LB IX
Supputationes: Supputationes errorum in censuris Natalis Bedae: contains
  Supputatio and reprints of Prologus supputationis; Divinationes ad notata Bedae;
  Elenchus in censuras Bedae; Appendix respondens ad Sutorem; Appendix de
  scriptis Clithovei LB IX / ASD IX-5

Tyrannicida: Tyrannicida, declamatio Lucianicae respondens LB I / ASD I-1 / CWE 29

Virginis et martyris comparatio LB V / ASD V-7 / CWE 69
Vita Hieronymi: Vita divi Hieronymi Stridonensis Opuscula / CWE 61

Index